TH … OF

THE TEXT AND ITS HISTORY

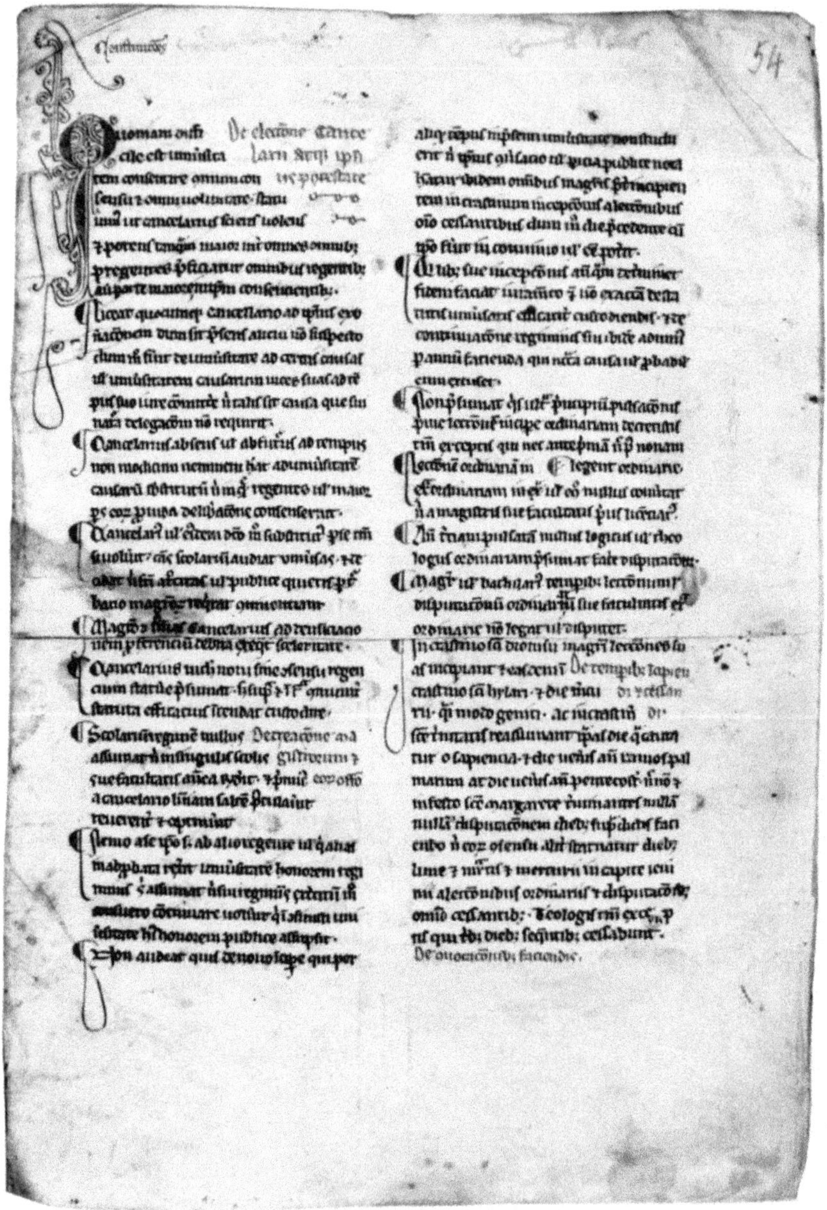

Angelica MS 401, fo. 54r, the first folio of the Cambridge statutes. The photograph was made before the MS was repaired and rebound in 1962 and shows clearly the crease across the centre and some letters which are now partly obliterated. The original is almost twice the size of this reproduction.

THE ORIGINAL STATUTES OF CAMBRIDGE UNIVERSITY

THE TEXT AND ITS HISTORY

by M. B. HACKETT, O.S.A., PH.D.

CAMBRIDGE
AT THE UNIVERSITY PRESS
1970

CAMBRIDGE UNIVERSITY PRESS
Cambridge, New York, Melbourne, Madrid, Cape Town, Singapore, São Paulo, Delhi

Cambridge University Press
The Edinburgh Building, Cambridge CB2 8RU, UK

Published in the United States of America by Cambridge University Press, New York

www.cambridge.org
Information on this title: www.cambridge.org/9780521070768

First published 1970
This digitally printed version 2008

A catalogue record for this publication is available from the British Library

Library of Congress Catalogue Card Number: 69–10217

ISBN 978-0-521-07076-8 hardback
ISBN 978-0-521-08519-9 paperback

TO MY MOTHER

CONTENTS

Contents

FOREWORD

The document that forms the kernel of this book caught the eye of Dr Benedict Hackett when he was leafing through a catalogue of a Roman library. It proved to be a set of statutes of the infant university of Cambridge which antedated by far not only all extant constitutions of Cambridge, but all formal codes of statutes known to exist of any European university. Rarely does a scholar make such a find, though this, and its only comparable rival in recent years, the discovery of the *Book* of Margery Kempe, show what treasures may still lurk in unlikely places.

Some years later, indeed, Dr Hackett learnt that a Norwegian scholar had noted the manuscript several decades earlier, but had failed to exploit his discovery, which a compatriot had published after an interval in an academic journal at Oslo. The text printed below, therefore, is not technically speaking an *editio princeps*, but it is the first wholly accurate text accompanied by adequate notes, and full credit must be given to the present editor for realizing at once the full significance of his discovery.

When Dr Hackett brought his photostats to Cambridge and expressed his willingness to edit the text, the Syndics of the Press at once accepted his projected work for publication. This was some ten years ago, and it was then thought that a small book, consisting of text, translation and a few notes, would soon be ready. When, however, Dr Hackett began work he saw that the text demanded for its understanding to be set in the academical context of the mid-thirteenth century, and that it was valuable not only as the acorn from which all later constitutional documents at Cambridge grew, but as a fixed point to which the early organization of Oxford as well as that of Cambridge could be referred. His work thus expanded in scope, and this, together with hindrances from other duties, delayed its publication. As it now stands, it is a study of the history of the original text of the Cambridge constitution down to Tudor times, with a detailed examination of the resemblances and differences between Oxford and Cambridge in the thirteenth century. When read in conjunction with the forthcoming work of Dr A. B. Cobban on the King's Hall, which is largely concerned with the fourteenth century, it undoubtedly shows the university of

Cambridge, in its two first centuries of existence, to have taken a more significant place in the academic and national life of the country than historians in the past have supposed.

In addition, Dr Hackett *chemin faisant* has caught in his headlights several lesser points of interest. In particular, he has gone far to solve the problem that has long exercised those who, with Hastings Rashdall, have failed to discover a motive that could have led migrants from Oxford 'to that distant marsh town'[1] in 1209. Most readers will feel that Dr Hackett's suggestion, though made almost with nonchalance, is the true answer.[2] But beyond this and other *obiter dicta* of interest, this book will supply for all future historians of Cambridge a firm picture of the early framework of the university and its gradual development. Dr Hackett, though not himself a Cambridge man, has deserved well of all those to whom any addition to the knowledge of their university's history is precious.

DAVID KNOWLES

[1] *The Universities of Europe in the Middle Ages* (ed. Powicke and Emden), I, 34.
[2] Below, p. 46.

ACKNOWLEDGEMENTS

I am most profoundly grateful to Professor Knowles, who first publicized my 'discovery' of the earliest Cambridge statutes and personally sponsored the work from the start. Over the years he has given me every help and encouragement. His continuous prodding kept me going and ensured that the book finally reached the printers. He saw to its acceptance for publication by the University Press; he was good enough to read the study in draft and again the final typescript. He also read the proofs and as a crowning act of kindness wrote the foreword. *Quid amplius!* My indebtedness to many others is very great. In the course of the volume I have acknowledged the help I have received from scholars, keepers of manuscripts and muniments and librarians. I should like to make special mention here of a few.

Dr Emden supplied me with proofs of his register as it went through the press, and in addition loaned me his copy of the 1852 edition of the Cambridge statutes. He untiringly answered queries and brought valuable information to my notice. I am also most grateful to him for reading the proofs. The main centre of my research at Cambridge has been the University Archives. No words of mine can adequately express my sense of gratitude to the Keeper, Miss H. E. Peek, who deserves to be congratulated on the admirable state of the archives entrusted to her care, despite the restricted space in which she has had to work. Her kindness, hospitality and unlimited patience with my often importunate requests to see registers and documents deserve my best thanks, and in this connection I must also mention her assistant, Miss M. E. Raven. At the University Library I received much practical help from Mr E. Ansell before his retirement as Deputy Librarian. Without the consent of the Director of the Angelica Library, Dottore A. M. Giorgetti Vichi, it would not have been possible to publish the text of the statutes at all. I thank her most cordially for granting me the necessary permission and for leave to reproduce fo. 54 of the manuscript as the frontispiece, and I am also grateful to her for assisting me with inquiries. I have likewise been able to print the earliest dated official act of the university through the courtesy of the Master and Fellows of St John's College. On the technical side my deepest gratitude goes to Professor Ludwig Bieler of University College, Dublin. With characteristic generosity and patience he assisted in deciphering some very uncertain readings in the early part of the Angelica manuscript. I am particularly grateful to him and to Dr R. W. Hunt, Keeper of western manuscripts at the Bodleian Library, for checking part II of the book. I must also record here my thanks to Professor Stephan Kuttner of Yale, Professor Walter Ullmann, Professor Bruce Dickins and Mr Philip Grierson, Fellow and Librarian of Gonville and Caius College, who in season and out of season gave me every facility for consulting the important collection of thirteenth-century manuscripts of Cambridge provenance in the College Library.

Within my own order I owe most to Fr N. P. Duffner, who at a critical stage helped with the typing, corrections and preparation of my MS. The Very Rev. Fr J. A. Meagher likewise came to my aid when I was very hard pressed for time. A special word of thanks is also due to Fr Edmund Colledge for making a draft translation of the text of the statutes.

I cannot conclude without expressing my gratitude to the Syndics and staff of the University Press for the expert handling of a somewhat difficult typescript.

M. B. HACKETT, O.S.A.

Clare Priory
Suffolk

INTRODUCTION

The past ten years have witnessed a welcome revival of studies in the medieval history of the university of Cambridge. In 1959 the long-awaited volume of the Victoria County History appeared under the general editorship of Dr J. P. C. Roach, who in fact contributed the central article on the university. Though his survey and the articles of his collaborators carry the story down to modern times, they have much that is of particular interest for the medievalist. A timely and very useful historical introduction to the archives of the university was provided in 1962 by the Keeper, Miss Heather Peek, and Mrs Catherine Hall. It was followed in 1963 by Professor A. C. Chibnall's slender but revealing book on an aspect of the administration of the university in the early fourteenth century. The same year saw the publication of Dr Emden's biographical register of scholars and members of the university who flourished during the first three centuries or so of its existence. The volume is a mine of information derived from vast and accurate research, especially in original unpublished records, and is easily the most valuable contribution yet made to the study of the medieval university. In addition, the years have seen editions of original documents, beginning with Professor Ullmann's critical text in 1958 of an important thirteenth-century statute, and latterly Mrs Hall's edition of the oldest inventory of the medieval muniments of the university.[1] There have been other publications as well, including one to which we shall return in a moment.

The only historian who has attempted to write a full-length history of the university from the time of its inception is Mullinger. It is significant that the first volume of his study, which appeared in 1873, was largely made up of padding; indeed the section on the early medieval period is little more than a restatement in Cambridge terms of Oxford history. Any serious scholar who might have thought of investigating the organization of the university in the thirteenth century must have experienced a chilling sense of insecurity. The earliest complete collection of the statutes known to exist dated from only *c.* 1500. With the rediscovery of the original constitution of the university the position has dramatically changed,

[1] Now add: A. B. Cobban, *The King's Hall within the University of Cambridge* (Cambridge Studies in Medieval Life and Thought, 3rd series, 1 [Cambridge, 1969]).

and at long last there is a firm foundation for a study of the medieval history of Cambridge.

When I identified the manuscript of the earliest statutes of the university in the Angelica Library, Rome, the news was hailed as a gift from the gods. It has since transpired that unknown to everybody a Norwegian scholar repeated history by getting to the pole first. The late Professor Oluf Kolsrud, it seems, noted the manuscript when working in Rome some thirty years earlier and submitted a short report on the text at a meeting of the Norske Videnskaps-Akademi in Oslo on 3 April 1925.[1] Neither the late Sir Maurice Powicke nor his colleague, Dr Emden, was aware of Kolsrud's discovery either before or after they published their edition of Rashdall in 1936. Even such a distinguished authority as Professor Sven Stelling-Michaud knew nothing of the Norwegian's report when he read a masterly, up-to-date and bibliographically complete paper on the medieval universities at the International Congress of Historical Sciences held at Stockholm in 1960. Kolsrud never publicized his research. Apart from the brief note which appeared in the year-book of the Videnskaps-Akademi for 1925, not another trace of Professor Kolsrud's study has come to light. His report was never printed; whatever notes he made from the manuscript have disappeared; and if he made a transcript of the text it is now lost.[2] As a matter of fact the records of the Angelica Library suggest that he never handled the manuscript; his name is not entered in the list of readers of this particular codex.[3] It may well be that the *elenco* was not kept at the time Kolsrud studied in Rome, and although he cannot be officially credited with the resurrection of the manuscript one does not wish to deprive him of his due, now that he is no longer with us to vindicate his claim.

Some years after my projected edition of the statutes was announced, Dr Vegard Skånland, a compatriot of Kolsrud's, stumbled on the text. It is strange, to say the least, that he proceeded forthwith to edit the statutes. The register at the Angelica Library clearly states that my edition was in progress; an entry to this effect

[1] Cf. *Det Norske Videnskaps-Akademi i Oslo årbok 1925* (Oslo, 1926), p. 14: 'Kolsrud gav en meddelelse: *Nyfunne universitetskonstitusjoner fra det 13de århundre.*'

[2] Professor Kolsrud's papers are deposited in the Norsk Historisk Kjeldeskrift-Institutt, Oslo. I am much obliged to the secretary, Dr J. Jansen, for instituting a search for the missing report and other relevant materials. The results of the search were entirely negative.

[3] The first name to appear in the register for Angelica MS 401 is in fact my own.

occurs only four lines above the space where he signed for the manuscript on 28 December 1963. While any contribution to the medieval history of Cambridge is more than gratifying, Dr Skånland's edition, it must be said, is unsatisfactory both in text and notes. The reader will therefore understand why I make no further reference to it.[1]

It has been tempting to call the present book the 'foundation statutes of the university of Cambridge'. But such a title implies that the university started with a prepared set of statutes and was founded about 1250, the approximate terminal date of the text. Neither of these implications is admissible. What can be said is that the Angelica manuscript is a copy of the first constitution of the university, and from the manuscript we are able to reconstruct the original text itself. All the medieval recensions of the Cambridge statutes derive from a lost exemplar of which Angelica is the only surviving witness. Its preservation makes a full critical edition of the statutes now possible. It is clear that the collection on which Rashdall and other scholars based their conclusions presents a misleading picture of the medieval constitution of the university. The analogy so often made between Oxford and Cambridge is seen to be only partly true, granted that comparison is difficult, since the earliest register of the Oxford statutes is almost a century later than the Cambridge text. The Angelica manuscript reveals for the first time how the university of Cambridge was organized and governed in the early thirteenth century, from its beginnings in fact. And we can also trace the evolution of its constitution down to the close of the middle ages. It will doubtless prove a disappointment that the text is not more detailed and that it says nothing about the curriculum. This is indeed regrettable but hardly surprising. It would be anachronistic to expect of the constitution, given its exceptionally early date, a syllabus of textbooks and studies. By 1250 university courses and requirements for admission to degrees were regulated generally

[1] Cf. V. Skånland, 'The earliest statutes of the university of Cambridge', *Symbolae Osloenses*, fasc. xi (1965), 83–98. Dr Skånland, who only learned of Kolsrud's report after he completed his article, gives the impression that Dott. L. Morrica, a former assistant at the Angelica Library, traced the MS of the statutes back to the library of Cardinal Cervini, afterwards Pope Marcellus II (1555). This is not so. Morrica's knowledge of the history of the MS was derived from a note communicated by me to the Director of the Angelica Library. The contents of the note were entered by the assistant in the library copy of Narducci's catalogue of the MSS.

by unwritten custom. The earliest Parisian statute containing a relatively detailed programme for the B.A. dates from 1252; the corresponding Oxford statute is later still. The fact that neither of these statutes was entered in an official register and consequently never became part of the written constitutions of their respective universities may also help to explain the absence from the Cambridge constitution of a curriculum.

Ever since Father Heinrich Denifle published his celebrated if controversial work on the medieval universities in 1885 doubts have been entertained about the status of Cambridge as a university or *studium generale* before the fourteenth century. Rashdall ventured to modify the contention of the great Dominican scholar, but as he was unable to adduce a thirteenth-century constitution of the university he was at a grave disadvantage. The question might never have arisen had the existence of the Angelica text been known. The document does not furnish the complete answer to Denifle's theory, but it alone provides an essential basis for resolving the problem. There can be no doubt now that Cambridge was a properly constituted university in the thirteenth century, even by 1250, though the faculties of civil law and medicine were not established at this time.

The Angelica text has a wider significance. As a contemporary guide to the university system of the early thirteenth century it is unique. Even if the text only confirmed what we already know from later records it would still be valuable: there is more to it than that. Actually, it calls for a revision or reappraisal of some accepted ideas about the original constitution of Oxford, from which Cambridge was founded, but the text also merits the attention of the student of Paris and other medieval universities, not excluding Bologna. One must not exaggerate the importance of the Angelica text. It is short and often tantalizingly vague. Yet, when seen in its historical context and studied closely, it acquires a significance which is by no means confined to the medieval history of Cambridge.

ABBREVIATIONS

Add.	Additional.
Angelica	Biblioteca Angelica, Rome, MS 401.
B.A.	Bachelor of arts.
Bibl. Nat.	Bibliothèque Nationale, Paris.
B.M.	British Museum, London.
Bodl.	Bodleian Library, Oxford.
BRUC	A. B. Emden, *A biographical register of the university of Cambridge.*
BRUO	A. B. Emden, *A biographical register of the university of Oxford.*
B.Th.	Bachelor of theology.
c.	chapter.
c.	*circa.*
Caius	Gonville and Caius College, Cambridge, MS 706, part II.
Cal. papal letters	*Calendar of entries in the papal registers... papal letters.*
Cal. pat. rolls	*Calendar of the patent rolls.*
CAS	Cambridge Antiquarian Society.
CASP	*Cambridge Antiquarian Society Proceedings.*
Chart. Univ. Paris.	*Chartularium universitatis Parisiensis*, edd. H. Denifle, O.P. and É. Chatelain.
Close rolls	*Close rolls of the reign of Henry III.*
Cons. Univ. Canteb.	*Constituciones universitatis Cantebrigiensis.*
Cooper, *Annals*	C. H. Cooper, *Annals of Cambridge.*
CUA	Cambridge University Archives.
CUL	Cambridge University Library.
D.C.L.	Doctor of civil law.
D.Cn.L.	Doctor of canon law.
Docs	*Documents relating to the university and colleges of Cambridge.*
D.Th.	Doctor of theology.
E.H.R.	*English Historical Review.*
Ely Dioc. Rec.	Ely Diocesan Records.
fo., fos.	folio, folios.
Hare MSS	R. Hare, 'Priuilegia et alia rescripta vniuersitatem Cantebrigie concernentia' (CUA, parchment copy).
Harl.	Harleian.

Junior Proctor	Junior Proctor's Book (CUA).
Liber mem. ecc. de Bernewelle	*Liber memorandorum ecclesie de Bernewelle*, ed. J. W. Clark.
M.A.	Master of arts.
mag.	magister.
Markaunt	Thomas Markaunt's Book (CUA).
M.D.	Doctor of medicine.
M.Gram.	Master of grammar.
n.s.	new series.
OHS	Oxford Historical Society.
Old Proctor	Old Proctor's Book (CUA).
Peek and Hall, *Archives*	H. E. Peek and C. P. Hall, *The archives of the university of Cambridge.*
PL	*Patrologia Latina*, ed. J. P. Migne.
P.R.O.	Public Record Office, London.
Rashdall, *Universities*	H. Rashdall, *The universities of Europe in the middle ages*, edd. F. M. Powicke and A. B. Emden.
Rymer, *Foedera*	T. Rymer, *Foedera, conventiones...acta publica* (ed. 1816–69).
SA	*Statutum Antiquum.*
s.a.	*sub anno.*
saec.	saeculum.
SAUO	*Statuta antiqua universitatis Oxoniensis*, ed. S. Gibson.
SC	F. Madan and others, *Summary cat. western MSS Bodl.*
Senior Proctor	Senior Proctor's Book (CUA).
Soc.	Society.
Vat.	Biblioteca Apostolica Vaticana, Vatican City.
V.C.H.	*Victoria County History.*
Vet. Lib. Archid. Elien.	*Vetus liber archidiaconi Eliensis*, edd. C. L. Feltoe and E. H. Minns.

CITATION OF CAMBRIDGE DOCUMENTS AND STATUTES

Original, unclassified documents in the archives of the university are cited as 'CUA, doc. no. 1' (etc.). The numbers correspond with those in H. R. Luard, 'List of the documents in the university registry', *CASP*, iii (1879), 385–403.

Statutes in Angelica are cited as '*Cons. Univ. Canteb.* I. i' (etc.). The upper-case and lower-case roman numerals indicate chapter and paragraph; added within brackets are page and line references to the edition printed on pp. 197–217. All quotations are from this critical text and not from the manuscript itself, unless otherwise stated.

Statutes in Markaunt are cited as 'Markaunt 1' (etc.), followed by page and line references to the text in Appendix 1.

The citation of statutes in the other codices should present no difficulty. It should be noted that the statutes in Caius are not numbered in the manuscript; they have been numbered here in order to facilitate reference. On the other hand, the statutes in Junior and Senior Proctor are cited by the folio only. In both manuscripts numbers were later assigned to the statutes by different hands, but these tend to give a misleading impression of the chronological order in which the statutes were actually entered; moreover, the numbers in Junior Proctor bear little relation to the sequence of the majority of the statutes.

In quoting original documents and manuscript material I have tried to reproduce as faithfully as possible the source, which accounts for the presence of unusual capitals, spelling, punctuation and other peculiarities.

PART I

ORIGIN AND NATURE OF THE TEXT

Chapter 1

ANGELICA MS 401

MISCONCEPTIONS

In his classic study of the medieval universities Rashdall offered the following excuses for his inability to describe the development of the constitution of Cambridge: 'There are scarcely any statutes which can be with any confidence referred to a period before 1381: the great majority of them belong to the fifteenth century: the earliest extant fragment of a statute-book dates from *circa* 1398, the earliest proctor's book from 1417.'[1] It would be difficult to find elsewhere in Rashdall's *Universities* four such misleading statements in a row.

There is, one feels, behind his first statement an assumption, which he was neither the first nor the last to entertain, that the revolt of the citizens of Cambridge against the privileged position of the university in 1381 resulted in the complete destruction of the existing statute-books. Indeed, the university itself claimed as much and more in its petition to parliament for redress. It stated that the townspeople under the captaincy of James de Grantchester and aided by crowds of outsiders broke open the common chest of the university at St Mary's on Saturday 15 June and consigned to the flames royal grants of privilege, charters, papal bulls and other documents. It was also alleged that over the week-end a bonfire was made in the market-place of the statutes, ordinances and a quantity of archival material, and that an old lady named Margaret Sterre took particular pleasure in casting to the winds the incinerated documents, crying: 'Away with clerical learning, away with it!'[2] Nor did the ex-mayor of Cambridge, Edmund Lister, who held office at the time of the riots, when summoned by parliament to respond to the charges, deny their truth.

The story, which Rashdall appears to have accepted as factual, of

[1] Rashdall, *Universities*, iii. 286.

[2] The outrages and their aftermath are described very fully in Cooper, *Annals*, i. 120–5. The primary sources are the parliamentary process printed in *Rotuli parliamentorum*, iii (London, 1783), 106–9, and *Nicholai Cantalupi historiola de antiquitate et origine universitatis Cantabrigiensis*, ed. T. Hearne in *Thomae Sprotti chronica* (Oxford, 1719), pp. 258–61. Nicholas Cantelow, O.Carm., the author of the *historiola*, died 27 Sept. 1441 (*BRUC*, p. 120).

the wholesale destruction of the university muniments is a gross exaggeration.[1] If even a fraction of what the university alleged was true, it is certainly a mystery how the originals of some forty royal charters dating from before 1381 happened to be extant in the university archives, the common chest, in the fifteenth century. One has only to compare the list of the contents of the chest drawn up in 1363 with the inventory compiled by William Rysley in 1420 to see at a glance how limited in fact the extent of the disaster of 1381 was.[2] The register of the university containing the statutes was not kept in the chest and hence is less likely to have fallen into the hands of the mob. Though the accounts of the riot mention the destruction of the statutes and ordinances, it is not stated that the statute-book as such was burned. On the other hand, there is no denying that the *Registrum Cancellarii et procuratorum* which was extant by 1374 has disappeared.[3] It is more than tempting to link its disappearance with the depredations committed by the townspeople and their adherents in 1381. The events of the summer of that year would provide a ready-made explanation for the loss of the university register, but it is not so easy to see how the earliest surviving register, the *Liber procuratoris antiquus*, or, to give it its more homely title, the 'Old Proctor's Book', could have been compiled in that event. The original part of this composite and rather mutilated manuscript contains the earliest known calendar and official codex of the statutes of the university. It dates from *c.* 1385–98, and was clearly derived from an official source.[4] Obviously some university statute-book, as distinct from a private collection of the statutes, must have escaped destruction in 1381. If one or more of the earlier registers cannot now be traced, their loss need not and indeed should not be attributed to the violent deeds perpetrated by the populace between 15 and 17 June of that year, notwithstanding the protestations made by the university at the time.[5]

[1] Peek and Hall, *Archives*, pp. 3, 24–5, and Emden in *BRUC*, p. xiii, have rightly queried the accuracy of the traditional view.

[2] The proctors' account, dated 11 Oct. 1363, is printed in *Grace Book Γ*, ed. W. G. Searle (Cambridge, 1908), pp. x–xi. There is a facsimile of the document in Peek and Hall, *Archives*, p. 64, plate 9. Rysley's inventory has now been edited by Mrs C. P. Hall, 'William Rysley's catalogue of the Cambridge University muniments, compiled in 1420', *Transactions of the Cambridge Bibliographical Society*, iv (1965), 85–99.

[3] See below, p. 260.

[4] For the Old Proctor's Book, see below, pp. 261–3.

[5] Cooper, *Annals*, i. 48, states that records of the university were burned during the fracas of 1261 (*recte* 1260) between the northern and southern scholars in which

Rashdall's curt dismissal of the statute-books and the statutes themselves as fragmentary and late is fortunately unjustified. It is most inaccurate to call the text in the Old Proctor's Book a fragment; the volume lacks only nine out of a grand total of 131 statutes enacted by 1398, and those nine are missing not because the text is defective but because the folios containing them were removed and inserted in a later book of the statutes, the *Liber procuratoris junioris* or the 'Junior Proctor's Book'.[1] A slightly earlier text than that in the Old Proctor's Book is preserved in Gonville and Caius College MS 706, which although not an official text has the advantage of being complete.[2] To state, therefore, that the majority of the statutes date from the fifteenth century is very much wide of the mark; at the most fifty-five were enacted between 1400 and 1500 as against the 131 which existed by 1398.

Finally, it is erroneous to say that the earliest proctor's book dates from 1417. This is rather an early date as far as Cambridge proctors' books and indeed the corresponding Oxford registers go; would that it were correct! The earliest Cambridge proctors' books, the Grace Books, extend only from 1454. It is true of course that the Old Proctor's Book is much earlier, but Rashdall is not referring to this volume; he had in mind 'Markaunt's Book'. This register of deeds and documents of a miscellaneous character, a volume of great value, was known by 1439 as *Liber priuilegiorum et statutorum vniuersitatis Cantabriggie*. It is not an official register and thus cannot be properly classified as a proctor's book, although it was made for Thomas Markaunt who was senior proctor in 1417–18.[3] Not the

townsmen participated. This would explain the absence from the university archives of any original document earlier than 1266. But none of the sources which Cooper cites in support of this statement mentions the destruction of records. Cf. Hare MS i, fos. 16^r–19^r; *Cal. pat. rolls, 1258–66*, pp. 136, 180–2; T. Fuller, *The history of the university of Cambridge*, edd. M. Prickett and T. Wright (Cambridge–London, 1840), pp. 28–30. It does not appear that the archives of the university suffered any damage during the fire which broke out in St Mary's church on 9 July 1293. Cf. *Florentii Wigorniensis monachi chronicon*, ed. B. Thorpe, ii (English Hist. Soc., 1849), 268; *The chronicle of Bury St Edmunds 1212–1301*, ed. A. Gransden (Nelson Medieval Texts, London, 1964), p. 118. The year is wrongly given as 1290 in S. Sandars and Canon Venables, *Historical and architectural notes on Great Saint Mary's church, Cambridge* (CAS, octavo series, x [1869]), 4, citing *Liber mem. ecc. de Bernewelle*, but the year is not stated in this work. Cf. the edition by Clark, p. 230, who is also inaccurate in giving the date as 15 July and *hora nona* as 9 a.m.

1 See below, pp. 290–3.

2 The Caius MS which Rashdall overlooked is described on pp. 266–7 below.

3 The difference between the Oxford *Registrum C* which Richard Fleming, later bishop of Lincoln (1419–31), commissioned at his own expense as proctor of the

least of its most valuable texts, including a unique copy of a letter of Pope Nicholas IV concerning the university, is a copy of the statutes. Rashdall did not appreciate that the exemplar of this collection can be dated to *c.* 1304–37.[1] For some reason which is not now clear the scribe of Markaunt's text broke off the transcription after copying only thirty-eight statutes; but the exceptionally early date of the text compensates to some extent for its defectiveness. In fairness to Rashdall it must be pointed out that any scholar would have great difficulty in assigning Markaunt's text its proper place in the history of the evolution of the corpus of Cambridge statutes, unless he had before him the manuscript which the present writer re-discovered in the Angelica Library, Rome.[2] One of the baffling things about this thirteenth-century manuscript is not so much that it evaded Rashdall's notice, but that the renowned Denifle, who during his years as Vatican sub-archivist was singularly well-placed to hear of the existence of the manuscript, never came across it.

The resurrection of this manuscript, which contains easily the most important text now extant on the constitutional history of Cambridge, may be briefly related. It must be emphasized here that the text does not consist of some scattered statutes or even of a series of statutes. Individual statutes of an earlier date than the Cambridge constitution, of which the year 1231 is the *terminus a quo*, are to be found in Parisian collections and in those of Montpellier, for example, although their earliest statutes dating from 1215 and 1220 respectively were not made by the universities themselves.[3] Oxford has a collection of statutes which was put together most probably about 1275.[4] The significant point about the Cambridge statutes preserved in the Angelica manuscript is that they constitute a code, a complete code, and consequently we now have a written constitution drawn up by the university at the latest by

university in 1407, and Markaunt's Book, apart from the fact that Markaunt's register is not really a statute-book, is that Fleming made over his volume to his university whereas Markaunt did not. For Fleming's book cf. *Snappe's formulary and other records*, ed. H. E. Salter (OHS, lxxx [1924]), 95; *SAUO*, pp. xiv–xv.

[1] See below, pp. 245–8. The text of the statutes is on pp. 313–31 below.

[2] On this claim of mine see above, pp. xiv–xv.

[3] In both cases the statutes were issued by cardinal papal legates, at Paris in 1215 by Robert de Courson, at Montpellier in 1220 by Conrad. Cf. *Chart. Univ. Paris.* i. 78–9, no. 20; *Les statuts et privilèges des universités françaises*, ed. M. Fournier, ii (Paris, 1891), 4–6, no. 882.

[4] S. Gibson, 'The earliest statutes of the university of Oxford', *Bodleian Library Record*, iii (1920), 116–18.

c. 1250.[1] Oxford, the parent university, had nothing of this nature by 1253 and lagged more than a half-century behind Cambridge in codifying its statutes.[2] Neither Paris nor Bologna, the oldest and foremost of all universities, had a written constitution or a codified body of laws in the thirteenth century.[3] It goes without saying that the Cambridge constitution, enacted as it was at a remarkably early date in the history of the university, left much room for development; the task of codifying the as yet unwritten statutes on studies and on the organization of the full complement of five faculties was not undertaken until much later. The constitution, none the less, stands as a landmark in the history of the university and of the medieval universities generally.

The provenance and subsequent history of Angelica MS 401 will be described later. It must be pointed out here that the codex was listed and described by Enrico Narducci in his excellent catalogue of the western manuscripts in the Biblioteca Angelica. The catalogue was printed and published more than seventy years ago, but through some extraordinary oversight the text of the Cambridge statutes was omitted from the index to the volume.[4] The Angelica Library is hardly the first place one would think of searching for a Cambridge manuscript, and as the catalogue happens to be a formidable volume the chances of the text being noticed were slim indeed. Few catalogues of medieval manuscripts carry exhaustive and utterly reliable indexes. The Angelica Library contains a mine of Augustinian history, and the present writer while domiciled in Rome had

1 For the date of the text see below, pp. 23–40.

2 Cf. *SAUO*, pp. xlii–xliii. Gibson also in art. cit., *loc. cit.* p. 116, states that the 1275 collection of statutes marks 'the earliest phase of University legislation' at Oxford. The first attempt at codification appears in *Registrum A* which he assigns to the second quarter of saec. xiv or before 1350. It has now been proved that the original part of the register was written during the first half of 1313. Cf. G. Pollard, 'The oldest statute book of the university', *Bodl. Lib. Rec.* viii (1968), 74–6.

3 The earliest MS of the Paris statutes, Vat. Reg. lat. 406, is assigned to saec. xiv*in* by A. Wilmart, O.S.B., *Codices Reginenses latini*, ii (Vatican City, 1945), 477. Cf. Denifle in *Chart. Univ. Paris.* i, pp. xxxii–xxxiii. The oldest extant text of the statutes of Bologna university is not earlier than 1317; it is also incomplete. Cf. *Statuti delle università e dei collegi dello studio bolognese*, ed. C. Malagola (Bologna, 1888), pp. xvi, 5. Malagola was of the opinion that the law university did not put its statutes in writing until perhaps shortly before 1252, but they are not extant in a MS of that period.

4 E. Narducci, *Catalogus codicum manuscriptorum praeter graecos et orientales in Bibliotheca Angelica olim coenobii sancti Augustini de Urbe*, i (Rome, 1893). MS 401 is described on pp. 193–5 (*ibid.*). The index was added later.

particular reason for wading through Narducci's work page by page. Eventually, he came across a text entitled *Constituciones Vniuersitatis Cantebrigiensis* which was all the more interesting because the manuscript, which he had every opportunity of examining at length, was obviously written in the thirteenth century.

The Biblioteca Angelica occupies the south wing of a massive building which was at one time the head-house of the Austin Friars or the Order of St Augustine. The entrance to the library is on the small but picturesque Piazza Sant'Agostino off the Via della Scrofa in Rome. It was named the Angelica after its founder Angelo Rocca (1545–1620), the eminent Augustinian scholar and collector of manuscripts and printed books, who was papal sacristan from 1595 until his death. Like his contemporaries, Thomas Bodley and Federico Borromeo, Rocca planned to found a public library with his own valuable collection forming the nucleus.[1] The plan took shape between 1595 and 1608. The original idea was to have the collection and future acquisitions housed in the spacious monastery of St Augustine. Once Rocca decided to make his library available to the public it was obvious that some other arrangement would have to be made. He began to raise funds for the building of a separate library which was completed in 1614. On 23 October of that same year Rocca made over the day-to-day administration of the library, now familiarly known as the Angelica, to the community of St Augustine's. It remained Augustinian property until 4 December 1873 when it was formally secularized by the government of Victor Emmanuel I.[2]

THE MANUSCRIPT

Narducci on the whole described Angelica MS 401 with admirable care and at sufficient length for ordinary purposes. There is, however, a peculiar unevenness about his treatment of the contents. Some texts are very adequately listed; others, the lesser known, receive

[1] The most recent and helpful study of the origin and history of the library is by D. Gutiérrez, O.S.A., 'De antiquis ordinis eremitarum sancti Augustini bibliothecis', *Analecta Augustiniana*, xxiii (1954), 257–63.

[2] Gutiérrez, *loc. cit.* pp. 262, 363. The library was confiscated on 5 Nov. 1810 during the Napoleonic invasion of Rome, but was later restored to the Augustinians. The last prefect, Giuseppe Lanteri, the well-known Augustinian historian, in a note describing the expropriation of the library on 4 Dec. 1873, expressed the hope that history would repeat itself. That hope has not been realized; but it is only fair to point out that under state control the Angelica has rather gained than lost.

only summary attention. More than once the cataloguer failed to distinguish between the ending of one text and the beginning of another, though it must be allowed that the script in parts is very compressed and the texts are so closely aligned that the reader has difficulty in getting his bearings. Narducci was unable to identify the opening text, which begins abruptly—it is the popular *Aurea expositio hymnorum* of which several early printed editions are to be found; and he was completely foxed by the incipit of the text (fos. 34va–42ra) of Matthew of Vendôme's *Ars versificatoria*. Misreadings also occur in the printed catalogue and no light whatever is thrown on the provenance of the manuscript. Moreover, the volume has since been rebound.

Angelica MS 401 (formerly D. 3. 7) consists of fifty-five parchment folios (numbered by Narducci) measuring 285 × 215 mm; the last two folios (54–55), on which the Cambridge constitutions are written, measure 285 × 200 mm.[1] The manuscript comprises one paper flyleaf, six quires of four folded leaves, one gathering of two folded leaves, a single leaf, one folded leaf and end flyleaf (paper). At least one whole quire or eight folios is missing at the beginning. All the folios, and doubtless those which have disappeared, were ruled, the lines except on fo. 55^{v} being now somewhat faint. The texts on fos. 1^{r}–24^{v} are arranged in two columns; those on fos. 25^{r}–53^{v} in three columns; while the final text, that of the Cambridge constitutions (fos. 54^{r}–55^{v}), is set out in two columns. There are good margins throughout.[2] Three hands, all English gothic, are distinguishable. Hand *A* (fos. 1ra–52va) is small, rounded and neat; it may be assigned to the first half of the thirteenth century. The script, though probably earlier, and decoration are not unlike that of Oxford, Bodl. lat. misc. d. 80, fos. 46^{r}–51^{v} (saec. xiii*med*).[3] Hand *B* (fos. 52va–53^{vc}) is contemporary with hand *A*; it is likewise small

[1] Before the MS was rebound in 1959 it measured 292 × 218 mm.

[2] Unfortunately, some *marginalia* were cut away when the MS was being rebound.

[3] These folios contain a text of Bernardus Silvestris, *De mundi universitate*, as do fos. 42ra–49ra of the Angelica MS, but the order is slightly different. The script and decoration of Angelica fos. 1ra–52va may also be compared with that of three other but later MSS: Bodl. e mus. 96 (SC, 3582), pp. 1–480, 482–500; B.M. Harl. 4967, fos. 78^{r}–160^{v}, 169^{r}–185^{v}; and Escorial lat. I. iii. 7, fos. 89ra–109ra (the hymns). This latter MS like the Angelica was written in England and was probably sent overseas *c.* 1538–45. It contains *inter alia* a text of Grosseteste's synodal statutes and may have come from Ely Cathedral Priory. Cf. C. R. Cheney, *English synodalia of the thirteenth century* (Oxford, 1941), p. 113.

and fine but lighter and more angular.[1] Hand *C*, that of the text of the Cambridge constitutions, is clearly different from both the preceding hands. It is larger, freer and more characteristic of the second half of the thirteenth century. The script is rather impressive despite a certain unevenness and belongs to the tradition of what has been termed the *littera oxoniensis*.[2] This Oxford script is to be seen at the peak of its perfection in Vatican, Urbinate lat. 206.[3] The hand is more upright, steadier and of a much higher quality than hand *C* of the Angelica manuscript, but there is a definite, basic similarity between the two.[4] Urbinate lat. 206 was written at Oxford *c.* 1240–54 and is obviously earlier than Angelica 401, fos. 54–55, which may be safely dated to *c.* 1250–75. To endeavour to narrow down the dating is imprudent. Internal evidence shows that the text was drawn up by *c.* 1250. The possibility that fos. 54–55 of the Angelica manuscript were executed between 1250 and 1255 cannot be absolutely excluded, for the script does not appear to be very much later than that of Urbinate lat. 206. Moreover, if hand *C* of Angelica 401 is to be dated to, say, 1270 it may well be asked why anyone bothered to transcribe a code of statutes which was by then out-of-date. There is little point, however, in trying to estimate the distance in years between the Vatican and the Angelica manuscripts; it may be as great as twenty years. The enactment of new statutes and their transfer to a statute-book are two different things; there may have been an appreciable time-lag between the construction of the exemplar of the Cambridge constitutions and its transcription by the scribe of Angelica 401.[5] As matters stand, it cannot be denied that the Angelica text was written at the very latest by 1276;[6] but on a

[1] The glosses in Bodl. e mus. 96, pp. 85–96 are written in a hand of this type. Cf. also Harl. 4967, fos. 5r–75r.

[2] Cf. G. Battelli, *Lezioni di paleografia* (3rd edn, Vatican City, 1949), pp. 228, 230.

[3] Cf. C. Stornajolo, *Codices Urbinates latini*, i (Vatican City, 1902), 197–9; A. Pelzer, 'Une source inconnue de Roger Bacon—Alfred de Sareshel commentateur des météorologiques d'Aristote', *Archivum Franciscanum Historicum*, xii (1919), 46–52; Battelli, *op. cit.* p. 228. There is an excellent facsimile of fo. 75 of the MS in *Codices latini saeculi XIII* (Exempla scripturarum . . . Vaticani, fasc. i [Rome, 1929]), tab. 10; cf. also *ibid.* p. 15 for the date of the MS.

[4] I am indebted to Professor Battelli for drawing my attention to the obvious affinity between the hands. The illumination is likewise of the same genre though much more elaborate and masterly in the Vatican MS.

[5] For example, a statute enacted at Oxford by 1365 was not recorded in any of the university statute-books until 1438. Cf. *SAUO*, p. cxv, n. 2.

[6] See below, pp. 23–5.

calm, critical assessment of the palaeographical make-up of fos. 54–55 we should be content to date the script of these folios to the third quarter of the thirteenth century and suggest *c.* 1260 as a compromise.[1]

It is hardly necessary to add that the substantial resemblance between the script of Urbinate lat. 206 and hand *C* of the Angelica manuscript does not mean that the text of the Cambridge statutes was written at Oxford. The scribe may have received his training in Oxford, no doubt, but the history of Angelica 401 is, as one would expect, exclusively connected with Cambridge. It may be that the art developed and perfected at the parent university was like so many other Oxonian customs adopted at Cambridge, where it failed to reach the same high standard, if one may judge from the appearance of the two final folios of the Angelica manuscript.[2]

An examination of the gatherings reveals that fos. 1–52 originally formed one whole and that fo. 53 was added as an adjunct by the scribe of the second text on fo. 52va in order to allow space for the continuation of his transcription. The two Cambridge folios, which are conjugate, were executed separately and bound in with the main part of the volume later. There is no reason to suppose that this was not done before the end of the thirteenth century. On this question of the formation of the book it is worth noting that the decoration follows the changing pattern of the script. On fos. 1ra–52ra, which were written by the first hand, capitals are coloured alternately in blue and red; spidery artistic flourishes worked in a loop and hook design branch out from the extremities of the initials. The colour scheme of fos. 52va–53va is rather different; the lettering and the shafts are done in green with blue fillings; the tracery is also more florid. Only one capital of the Cambridge text (fos. 54–55), the initial 'Q' on fo. 54ra, is decorated. Like the hand it is quite distinctive. The circumference of the body of the letter, as well as the tail, is done in red, while the interior is made up of rather crude semicircular strokes interspersed with dots; all the fillings are worked in green as are the pendants and flourishes. A feature of the initial is

1 It is difficult to discover a difference in point of time between the script of the Angelica text and that of Vat. lat. 2412 which was executed in 1258. Cf. *Codices latini saeculi XIII*, tab. 13.

2 CUL Add. MS 3471, which is possibly of Cambridge provenance, though the hand is more regular and tasteful than that of the relevant folios of the Angelica, is not so characteristic of the script of the Vatican MS. An enlarged photograph of fo. 125ra of Add. 3471 forms the frontispiece of *BRUC*.

the absence of a naturalistic motif.[1] It is safe to regard fos. 54–55 as extraneous and this conclusion is confirmed by the presence of a crease along both folios which is not found elsewhere in the manuscript.[2]

One further observation which applies to the volume as a whole requires to be made. The parchment, particularly the front and end folios, is soiled here and there, and one meets other tell-tale signs. It would appear that the medieval covers were removed before the manuscript arrived in Rome. Some time during the late seventeenth century the volume was bound in plain, stiff, white calf. On the spine was written 'Commentaria in Hymnos et alia opuscula tum prosa tum versu', an inscription which was also made on the upper inner margin of the first folio, where it is still legible today. At the base of the spine was a shelf-mark 'R. 15', later changed to 'D. 3. 7' which was inserted inside the front cover. These useful signposts disappeared when the covers were discarded in 1959 in favour of new guards covered in dark brown calf. Fortunately, the oldest shelf-mark of all, '.$\overline{134}$.', which appears at the head of fo. 1^r, was preserved; it is this catalogue number that has enabled us to solve the riddle of how the manuscript got to Rome. All that we know of its later history points to Cambridge as its place of origin, notwithstanding the fact that the contents are dominated by works which emanated from the great French schools of Chartres, Orléans and Tours.

THE CONTENTS[3]

The first item in the volume is a text of the *Aurea expositio hymnorum* (fos. 1–4) which may have been written by a pupil of Abelard. This fairly popular commentary (it was printed at Paris in 1493) on hymns of the Roman breviary is typical of the main contents of part 1 of the manuscript. The author introduces each hymn with a short preface; he then quotes a stanza, expounds its hidden meaning,

[1] See the frontispiece. In view of the fact that there is no trace of naturalism in the design it would be unwise to date fos. 54–55 later than the third quarter of the thirteenth century. Incidentally, the form of the initial closely resembles the 'Q' on fo. 1^r (Priscian) of Gonville and Caius College MS 593, which is definitely of Cambridge provenance.

[2] See below, p. 15. The crease is plainly visible in the frontispiece.

[3] As the MS is a valuable guide to the interests of early Cambridge grammarians, it was considered worthwhile to list the incipits and explicits and provide other detailed information in an appendix. See below, pp. 340–3.

and explains difficult or unusual words and grammatical constructions. An unpretentious work, the commentary is just the type of textbook which a lecturer on grammar was likely to use as an introduction to prosody. In the manuscript the text is incomplete at the beginning and there is no title. The next treatise, *Speculum ecclesiae* (fos. 5–14), is a study of the mystical meaning of the church, the canonical hours, liturgical seasons, sacred orders, vestments, scripture and the Mass. It was at one time attributed to Hugh of St Victor, perhaps not without some justification.

The rest of the first part of Angelica 401 (fos. 14–53) is made up of short pieces and full-length writings which with one or two exceptions may be classed under the heading of grammar in the wide sense of the first of the liberal arts. On fos. 14–23 there is a collection of paradigms of proper nouns and verbs, a treatise on penance to which eleven verses are appended, and an exposition of the seven penitential psalms. Then comes a tract on syntax, followed by a group of proverbs culled from classical authors, and some artificial verses on the vices and virtues (fo. 32). These pedestrian works are succeeded by some of the best-known productions of the early twelfth-century renaissance. The *Liber lapidum* or *De gemmis* of Marbod of Rennes (*c.* 1035–1123) occurs on fos. 32–34. This metrical work by one of the most popular versifiers of the period achieved renown not merely through the author's skill with quantitative hexameters but also because of the inherent interest of the subject-matter, the properties of precious stones and their potency as amulets. On fo. 34 there is a stray copy of a letter of Innocent III to Philip Augustus, written on 17 May 1198 but wrongly dated in the manuscript. It was doubtless inserted as a formulary illustrating the style of the papal chancery. Matthew of Vendôme's *Ars versificatoria* immediately follows on fos. 34–42; in some unaccountable way the scribe introduces into the middle of the text two letters exchanged between Reginald de Bar, bishop of Chartres (1182–1217), and his former master, an archdeacon of Tours. Matthew's professor, Bernardus Silvestris, was a much more versatile author than his pupil. He is represented here on fos. 42–49 by his *magnum opus De mundi universitate*, a speculative study of cosmology and anthropology written partly in prose and partly in verse. A far more distinguished poet than either Bernard or Matthew or even Marbod was Hildebert of Lavardin (1056–1133). His celebrated metrical treatise *De concordia veteris et novi sacrificii* occupies fos.

49–51. It is followed by a set of five poems, three by Hildebert, one by an unknown author and one by Peter of Blois in praise of wine.

The last item in part I of the manuscript (fos. 52–53) is an unidentified, apparently unfinished text on the ascetical life. There is nothing original about it, apart from the author's epigrammatic sentences which are simply connecting links between quotations from classical Christian writers, notably Gregory the Great. It only remains to add that the second and final part of Angelica 401 (fos. 54–55) consists exclusively of the text of the Cambridge statutes, entitled *Constituciones Vniuersitatis Cantebrigiensis*.

It is evident that the manuscript was by and large a grammarian's book, the sort of volume which a Cambridge master of arts like Nicholas de Breckendale might be expected to possess.[1] The strong French flavour of the contents is noteworthy without being significant; the writings of Hildebert and Marbod were read in schools all over Europe as part of the Trivium.[2] It may seem strange, however, that the statutes of Cambridge University should be preserved in a volume which is mostly a collection of literary works. Actually, the oldest set of Oxford statutes is found in a manuscript which has much in common with Angelica 401.[3]

THE CAMBRIDGE FOLIOS

Folios 54^r–55^v of Angelica 401 are divided, as we have seen, into two columns. These were ruled, thirty-eight lines to each column, the text measuring 200 × 67 mm, except on fo. 55vb where there is a blank space of eleven lines at the end of the transcription. The parchment has some holes and in consequence a few letters and

[1] To the list of Breckendale's writings in *BRUC*, p. 90, should probably be added the *tractatus magistri Nicholai de gramatica et omni genere constructionum* which is extant in Douai, Bibliothèque Municipale MS 752 (saec. xiii), fos. 197–209 ('Ad lucem subsequentium diversis acceptionibus . . . construitur cum illo; non transitive'). Cf. *Catalogue général des manuscrits des bibliothèques publiques des départements*, quarto series, vi (Paris, 1878), 453–4.

[2] Cf. F. J. E. Raby, *A history of Christian-Latin poetry from the beginnings to the close of the middle ages* (2nd edn, Oxford, 1953), p. 258.

[3] MS Bodl. e mus. 96 has Huguccio, Hildebert, a treatise on versification and a tract on grammar and kindred subjects. The statutes are on pp. 480a, 481. Cf. F. Madan, H. H. E. Craster and N. Denholm-Young, *A summary catalogue of western manuscripts in the Bodleian Library at Oxford*, II. ii (Oxford, 1937), 690, no. 3582.

contraction marks have been lost.[1] It is also badly stained in places and an unfortunate crease runs across the middle of both folios from the inner margins. This disfigurement is responsible for the deterioration of the script along the crease, which must have been caused when the two folios were bound in too tightly with the rest of the manuscript.[2]

The title of the text is partly erased; all that now remains on the surface apart from the first word *Constituciones* is the outline of the initial 'V' of *Vniuersitatis* and the final 's' of *Cantebrigiensis*. There is, however, a running title on fos. 54^{v}–55^{v}. The only decorative feature is the first letter ('Q') of the incipit; but the thirteen chapters which constitute the text have rubricated titles. None of these is numbered. The rubrics with one exception are all in-cut, and paragraph marks are done by turns in green and red.[3] For some unaccountable reason the quality of the transcription falls far short of the standard of the handwriting. The scribe was a competent writer but a poor copyist. Occasionally he corrected his mistakes above the line or just stroked them through or simply marked them for deletion. On the whole his work bears evident signs of haste or carelessness.[4] He had, it would seem, a pathological weakness for confusing certain letters. Though he remains something of an enigma, we should be thankful that he made no effort to correct his exemplar, which itself was none too satisfactory. A defective exemplar will not account for all the blunders in the text, but we do know that the copyist of Angelica 401 was confronted by at least one corrupt passage. The result is that the relatively short text raises a number of critical problems which cannot be ignored though they admit of no easy solution.[5]

1 The MS was defective even before the scribe set to work. On fo. 54rb (third line from the end) he was forced to write *exce-p* for *excep*; the hole which made it necessary to separate the second *e* and *p* accounts for the gap on the verso between *cottidianum* and *pertinencia* (fo. 54va).

2 In 1959 an attempt was made to plug the holes and iron out the creases when the MS was being rebound; it cannot be said that the work was expertly done; in fact the injured script is now more difficult to read than was formerly the case.

3 The rubric *De inmunitate scolarium et pena delinquencium* of chapter XI (fo. 55ra) was overlooked by the scribe; on noticing the omission he wrote the words in the margin but placed the caret sign at the wrong point in the text.

4 To give but one example: when he retrieved the missing rubric on fo. 55ra and inserted it in the margin he wrote *inmunitat* (!) for *inmunitate* and less reprehensibly *scolarum* for *scolarium*.

5 See below, pp. 183–92.

THE HISTORY OF THE MANUSCRIPT

The removal of the original covers and binding as well as the loss of the first quire of Angelica 401 makes it difficult to determine the precise provenance of the volume, which, to add to the difficulty, is also a composite book. At the top of fo. 54ᵛ there are some scribbles and in the earlier part of the manuscript an odd marginal note occurs but nothing in the way of a clue to the medieval ownership. Both parts of the manuscript were written in England and since part II consists exclusively of the Cambridge statutes there is little or no doubt about its place of origin. The probability is that part I was also executed at Cambridge.

Our main concern here is with the ownership of the text of the statutes. The two folios could be stray leaves from a thirteenth-century register of the university;[1] but the existence of a common register before the fourteenth century is extremely doubtful. It should not be forgotten, however, that the earliest registers of the statutes of Oxford and Angers amounted to nothing more than a few quires.[2] One might argue, therefore, that fos. 54–55 of Angelica 401 constituted the *quaternus* or official register of the Cambridge constitutions. On this point the internal and external evidence is decisive: the folios were not the official record of the statutes. The quire affords no reason for thinking that it was the counterpart of the Oxford *quaterni* which the proctors kept;[3] it was not used for recording statutory additions or amendments; in other words it is a 'clean' exemplar like the late fourteenth-century manuscript of the *statuta antiqua* in Gonville and Caius College Library, whose unofficial character clearly emerges from a comparison with its contemporary, the Old Proctor's Book in the university archives. The Angelica text is rather too carelessly written for an authentic record of the constitution of the university, for it contains some very bizarre readings indeed. But apart from such considerations there is this vital fact: another manuscript, the exemplar of Angelica 401, existed by 1276 and was the official record.[4] It follows that Angelica

[1] The fragment of the statutes of Orléans University in Bibl. Nat. lat. 4223 A appears to have been torn from a *Liber rectorum* or some register of the university. Cf. Dorothy Mackay Quynn, 'Migrations of the medieval cartularies of the university of Orléans', *Humanisme et Renaissance*, vii (1940), 111, n. 5.

[2] Cf. *SAUO*, p. xiii and below, p. 65, n. 4.

[3] At Oxford the chancellor had his own register of the statutes; not so at Cambridge.

[4] A quotation from the exemplar, designated π in our *stemma codicum* (p. 306), is

was not the parent manuscript of the Cambridge constitution, but its unique value is not thereby lessened.[1]

Granted that the Rome manuscript was an unofficial copy, we can only suggest that it originated in this wise. The first part of the manuscript was evidently written for a master of arts. Universities as a rule kept their statutes under close custody. When the Dominicans at Oxford were accused early in the fourteenth century of misquoting certain statutes they pointed out the difficulty masters experienced in getting access to the register.[2] Yet the earliest collection of Oxford statutes is preserved in a manuscript which did not come from the university archives, nor can its ownership be traced to a chancellor or proctor.[3] In many ways the manuscript is remarkably similar to Angelica 401 except that the section containing the statutes is totally devoid of decoration.[4] The Angelica quire also looks more impressive and it may well be that the master who owned part 1 of the manuscript acquired fos. 54–55 on being appointed rector or proctor *c.* 1250–70 or perhaps after being elected chancellor, having graduated in one of the superior faculties. At all events the text must have been commissioned for private use or reference.

The two folios would surely have gone the way of the official Oxford *quaterni* were it not that they were bound in with the first fifty-three folios of Angelica 401. From that moment their history is that of the manuscript as a whole. The question now arises: how did the volume find its way to Rome from Cambridge? We have to rule out the likelihood of its having been sent to Avignon in 1318

embodied in a formal decree of the university, dated 17 March 1276. It consists of a paragraph which also occurs in Angelica, fo. 54vb, but the official text was not taken from this MS. See below, pp. 189–90. Needless to say, the exemplar of Angelica has not survived.

1 For the position of Angelica in relation to the parent MS of the constitution see below, p. 193.

2 The friars' riposte was: 'custodes statutorum cum difficultate permittunt Magistros uniuersitatis uidere librum in quo continentur', in Rashdall, 'The friars Preachers *v.* the university A.D. 1311–1313', *Collectanea*, ii (OHS, xvi [1890]), 235; cf. *ibid.* pp. 230, 256.

3 Bodl. e mus. 96. The owner of the MS may have been mag. Robert de la Felde, clerk, who according to two drafts of a document on p. 480^b was entitled to the payment of a debt by John de Wurthe of Witney on 19 Oct. (feast of St Frideswide) 1275. The statutes (pp. 480^a, 481) are in a different hand.

4 Bodl. and Angelica are close contemporaries. The contents (cf. above, p. 14, n. 3) are much the same; and in both cases the statutes were copied separately, but in Bodl. the folios of the statutes are an integral part of the volume.

to be studied at the papal court together with Edward II's letter of 18 March requesting John XXII to grant Cambridge apostolic confirmation of its status and existing privileges as well as new privileges.[1] There is no evidence that any text of the statutes was submitted to the Holy See, and if the university thought fit to apprise the pope of its constitution it would not stake its claim on an antiquated, rather primitive exemplar. The writing of 'Ihesus est amor meus' on fo. 55vb shows that the manuscript remained in English hands at least until the fifteenth century. There is good reason, too, for thinking that it was in the library of a religious house at Cambridge up to the time of the suppression; and in view of the Augustinian origin and history of the Angelica Library one is naturally disposed to attribute the arrival of the manuscript in Rome and its eventual acquisition by the Angelica to an Augustinian agency. The history of the convent of Sant'Agostino and the fate of Angelo Rocca's foundation are closely related. A good proportion of the Angelica manuscripts were at one time in the adjacent friary. Established in 1287, it was a *studium generale* of the order by 1358, and from then until 1882 was the official residence of the prior general and his *curia.* An inventory of the library dating from 1431–2 is extant which was superseded in all respects by a splendid catalogue in 1478.[2] The Angelica manuscript is not recorded, and the reason is not far to seek. It came to Rome after 1538 as part of the large commerce in manuscripts and printed books from the suppressed religious houses which John Bale rightly and bitterly lamented.[3] A substantial number of the manuscripts, mostly those from the dissolved Cambridge friaries, were purchased by Cardinal Marcello Cervini in 1538–45 at Rome for his library.[4] That the Angelica manuscript was among those purchased has not hitherto been recognized.

[1] See below, pp. 177–8.

[2] Both inventories have been edited by Gutiérrez, 'La biblioteca di Sant'Agostino di Roma nel secolo xv', *Anal. Aug.* xxvii (1964), 5–58; xxviii (1965), 57–153.

[3] Cf. Bale, *The laboryouse journey and serche of Johan Leylande for Englandes antiquities* (London, 1549), *Sig.* B. i; C. E. Wright, 'The dispersal of the monastic libraries and the beginnings of Anglo-Saxon studies', *Camb. Bibl. Soc. Trans.* i (1949–53), 211. See also his 'The dispersal of the libraries in the sixteenth century', *English Library before 1700*, edd. F. Wormald and C. E. Wright (London, 1958), pp. 148–75.

[4] Cf. H. M. Bannister, 'A short notice of some manuscripts of the Cambridge friars, now in the Vatican Library', *Collectanea Franciscana*, i (British Society of Franciscan Studies, v [1914]), 124–40; G. Mercati, *Codici latini Pico Grimani Pio* (Studi e Testi, 75 [1938]), pp. 124, 134, 137–42.

At the top left-hand corner of fo. 1^{r} of the manuscript a catalogue or library number '134' is boldly written. The form is peculiar: '.$\overline{134}$.'. A numeral enclosed by two full points with a horizontal stroke overhead is a typical Cervini catalogue reference.[1] His ownership of Angelica 401 is confirmed by the entry opposite '134' in the index of his manuscripts, which reads: 'Liber in quo declaratur quid sit penitentia, et qualem deceat esse confessorem. Expositio in psal. VI. et aliquos alios.'[2] This entry corresponds so closely with items 4 and 5 of Angelica 401 (fos. 17va, 18vb, 19va) that there can be no doubt as to Cervini's ownership.[3] It may be assumed that the indexer of his collection ignored the first three texts in the manuscript because they lacked a title; he picked instead the first item which had a title and cast his eye over the next two folios, fortunately noting their contents.[4] The quire which contained the incipit of the first text in the volume, the *Aurea expositio hymnorum*, was obviously missing, as it still is, when Cervini acquired the manuscript in Rome *c.* 1538–45. It is evident that the volume remained in Cambridge until that period and very probably it came from one of the houses of friars.

Though Cervini was made Cardinal Protector of the Vatican Library in 1548, a position which he filled with eminent distinction, he kept his own library separate. The manuscripts were housed partly at Montepulciano, partly in Rome, the Angelica manuscript being in the latter library. Elected pope on 9 April 1555, when he took the name of Marcellus II, Cervini died within a month and his collection of manuscripts and books passed to his family. The manuscripts comprised 160 Greek and 404 Latin codices. Twenty years later, in 1574, his library, or what remained of it, was purchased by Gregory XIII for the Vatican under pressure from and

1 Mercati, *Per la storia dei manoscritti greci* (*ibid.* 68 [1935]), pp. 189, n. 1, 198, nn. 4–7, 199; Idem, *Codici latini*, pp. 138–43, and table viii, nos. 2 and 3 (photographs of characteristic Cervini catalogue-marks).

2 Vat. lat. 8185, fo. 291^{r}; it is listed among the books in 'Cassa 9^{a}'; cf. also *ibid.* fo. 321^{r}, where it is again entered under the heading 'Libri Latini manuscripti qui sunt Romae in Bibliotheca C. [*sc.* Cervini] in membranis'. The Angelica MS is also noted in yet another catalogue of the Cardinal's library, Archivio Biblioteca Vaticana, tom. xv, fo. 92^{r}, no. 94; here '94' is a serial, not a catalogue number. Mercati, *Per la storia dei mss greci*, pp. 187–94, discusses the rather confusing indexes of Cervini's library.

3 See below, p. 341.

4 The fact that the indexer noted the text on fos. 18vb–19rb ('Qualiter debeat esse confessor') is significant. The scribe of the MS apparently thought that the text was a separate work, as did Cervini's cataloguer.

through the efforts of Cardinal Guglielmo Sirleto.[1] No one knew better than Sirleto the value of Cervini's collection. He was in his employ since 1545 and was his closest collaborator during his whole period (1548–55) as Cardinal Protector of the Vatican Library.[2] It was discovered in 1574 at the time of the sale that a number of Cervini's manuscripts were missing. His heirs may have been at fault, but it must be allowed that certain volumes were probably out on loan or pilfered during Cervini's lifetime.[3] Angelica 401 is not one of those listed as *prestati* in the catalogue of his library and it certainly does not figure in Sirleto's catalogue.[4] Evidently, the manuscript had disappeared by 1574 and was not recovered when Sirleto died in 1585. No trace of its movements appears before *c.* 1704–34; by then it had been acquired for the Angelica and was catalogued by the deputy librarian, Basile Rassegnier.[5] Almost as a matter of course one veers to the conclusion that Angelo Rocca himself secured possession of the manuscript and made it over to the Angelica. From *c.* 1565 he was keenly interested in adding to his collection, the bulk of which he had put together by 1608.[6] He was probably instrumental in getting hold of at least four manuscripts formerly in Sirleto's keeping, including possibly another

1 The story of Cervini's MSS and the sale of 1574 have been put in their true light by Mercati, *Per la storia dei mss greci*, pp. 181–202. One MS is now in Munich (*ibid.* p. 198, n. 2).

2 Cf. R. de Maio, 'La biblioteca apostolica Vaticana sotto Paolo IV e Pio IV (1555–65)', *Collectanea Vaticana in honorem Anselmi M. Card. Albareda* (Studi e Testi, 219 [1962]), 265, n. 1 for a bibliography. It is just possible that Angelica 401 was bought for Cervini by Sirleto in one of the bookshops he frequented on the Campo dei Fiori or the Via del Pellegrino. Cf. L. Dorez, 'Le registre des dépenses de la Bibliothèque Vaticane de 1548 à 1555', *Fasciculus Ioanni Willis Clark dicatus* (Cambridge, 1909), p. 161).

3 Cervini was Cardinal Protector of the Augustinians in 1551. Cf. 'Testimonium Card. Marcelli Cervini protectoris ordinis', *Anal. Aug.* ii (1907–8), 11–13. If the Angelica MS were of special interest to the Order Cervini might have parted with it and more than likely it would have come to the Angelica; but the MS is non-Augustinian.

4 The Latin 'libri prestati' are listed in Cervini's catalogue, Vat. lat. 8185, fos. 313^r–315^r. The catalogue of Sirleto's library is Vat. lat. 6163; the Latin MSS are entered on fos. 257^r–340^r.

5 In his 'Index Manuscriptorum Bibliothecae Angelicae auctorum et materiarum ordine alphabetico dispositus' the MS is entered as 'in Hymnos Commentaria &. fol. R-15' (Angelica 1078, p. 56).

6 Cf. *Bibliotheca Angelica litteratorum, litterarumque amatorum commoditati dicata Romae in aedibus Augustinianis* (Rome, 1608). On p. 90 Rocca refers to two elaborate catalogues which he compiled for the benefit of those using his library; the one was an author-index arranged alphabetically, the other a subject-index. Both unfortunately are missing.

Cervini.[1] Few of his contemporaries knew better than Rocca the wanderings of Sirleto's library after his death in 1585.[2] It is questionable, however, if Rocca acquired Angelica 401, since no mention is made of it in a catalogue drawn up apparently *c.* 1665. Both the date and completeness of this particular guide are open to doubt, and its omission of Angelica 401 need not mean that the manuscript did not come to the library through Rocca.[3] If it was not acquired by him, it is difficult to know how or when it came to the Angelica. It did not form part of the collection bequeathed by Luke Holsten in 1661, nor was it among the books of Cardinal Enrico Noris which were incorporated in the library in 1704.[4] The great library of the adjoining convent and *Curia Generalizia* of the Augustinian Order, Sant'Agostino, was amalgamated with the Angelica possibly in 1670 or more likely in 1786, a fusion which incomparably augmented the manuscript section of Rocca's foundation; but it is unlikely that Angelica 401 was acquired in this way.[5] The manuscript was not among the rich *fonds* of Cardinal Domenico Passionei's manuscripts and books purchased by the Order at a very high price (30,000

1 The MSS are Angelica 70, 116, 162, 1084. This last is a magnificent volume, profusely illustrated and written in England; it may be dated as saec. xiii*ex*–xiv*in*. On fo. 1^r a catalogue reference 'no 19' has been deleted and '61' substituted. In Cervini's catalogue no. 61 is given as 'S. Augustini libri de Trinitate' (Vat. lat. 8185, fo. 290^r). The Angelica MS, fos. 1ra–12va, has a summary of Augustine, *De trinitate*, and the text proper begins on fo. 20ra. I hope to show elsewhere that the MS is a companion volume of Vat. Ottob. lat. 200, 202, 211, 229, 342, which were owned by Fr. John de Clare, who must be identified with the Austin friar who incepted in theology as master, the first of his Order to do so, at Cambridge in 1304. Cf. J. R. H. Moorman, *The Grey Friars in Cambridge 1225–1538* (Cambridge, 1952), pp. 36, 231; *BRUC*, pp. 136–7.

2 Cf. Dorez, 'Recherches et documents sur la bibliothèque du Cardinal Sirleto', *Mélanges d'Archéologie et d'Histoire*, xi (1891), 490.

3 The catalogue, Angelica 481, fos. 206^r–216^v, comprises only the MSS which were in the upper part of the library. The system of press-marks which it employs is later than that in vogue *c.* 1704–34 and closely resembles the classification which appears in Marcolini's index of 1788. Cf. F. Blume, *Bibliotheca librorum manuscriptorum italica* (Göttingen, 1834), pp. 135–48, where only selections are printed. Marcolini's catalogue is not now extant. In the catalogue compiled by Guglielmo Bartolomei in 1847 Angelica 401 is entered under 'D 3 7' (Angelica 2393, fo. 41^v). It was given this press-mark most probably *c.* 1766–88, and retained it until Narducci devised the present system of serial numbers.

4 An inventory of Holsten's library is extant in MS 1059 of the Bibliothèque Municipale, Nancy. The keeper of the MSS, M. Vicuet, informs me that Angelica 401 is not listed. Indeed all Holsten's books appear to have been printed volumes. The list of Cardinal Noris's books is in Angelica 195, fos. 275^r–288^v.

5 It was almost certainly in the Angelica before the two libraries were made into one.

scudi) in 1762;[1] and it was on the shelves of the library for a century or more when the last important accession of Latin manuscripts took place in 1849 with the transfer of the collection at S. Maria del Popolo, the oldest Augustinian house in Rome, to the Angelica.[2] Unless the manuscript was acquired by individual gift or through the less likely medium of purchase by 1704–34,[3] we may ascribe its possession by the Angelica Library to the founder, Angelo Rocca, and assign the date of its acquisition to *c.* 1608–20. The Angelica is perhaps the last place one would expect to find a thirteenth-century manuscript of the constitution of Cambridge University, but the migrations of medieval university cartularies and records of statutes suggest that Rome is the first place one should search for missing collections.[4]

1 Cf. E. Celani, 'La Biblioteca Angelica', *Bibliofilia*, xiii (1911–12), 49; Gutiérrez, 'De antiquis O.E.S.A. bibliothecis', *loc. cit.* pp. 160–1, 350–5. Celani is in error when he writes that no catalogue of Passionei's library is extant. There is a catalogue in Vat. Ottob. lat. 3195–6. I have searched these two volumes with negative results.

2 Gutiérrez, *loc. cit.* pp. 264–88, prints an inventory of the S. Maria MSS which dates from 1480–2. If the majority of the MSS listed survived by 1849 the accession was clearly a most valuable one.

3 MSS acquired by gift or purchase from private sources usually carry details of the acquisition. Cf. the inscriptions in Narducci, *Catalogus*, pp. 68, 124. There is a useful though imperfect handlist of former owners, entitled 'Elenco per ordine numerico dei possessori dei manoscritti' (1881), in the library.

4 The story of Angelica 401 is almost exactly paralleled by that recounted by Quynn, *loc. cit.* pp. 102–22, concerning the cartularies of Orléans University. They were dispersed not long after the Cambridge MS. One is Vat. Ottob. lat. 3083. If Cervini's library had remained intact, Angelica 401 would in all probability be now among the Ottoboni MSS, too, with most of the English MSS which ultimately owe their place in the Vatican Library to the cardinal.

Chapter 2

THE DATE OF THE TEXT

(*c.* 1236–54)

The dating of statutes of the medieval universities poses special problems. Even when they carry a date there are pitfalls.[1] Where there is question of undated statutes something can be learned from the script and composition of the manuscripts; but palaeographical criteria are seldom wholly satisfactory and leave room for uncertainty or dissent; on this basis alone it is wellnigh impossible to obtain anything like precision.[2] The Angelica text of the Cambridge statutes is undated. Most probably the manuscript was executed *c.* 1250–70, and it is reassuring to find that this calculation, which is based on the script and general appearance of the manuscript, is more than justified by the internal evidence of the text itself. At the outset it can be shown that the text cannot possibly be later than 1276.

In that year the chancellor of the university found himself at loggerheads with the archdeacon of Ely and the rector of the local grammar schools over the question of jurisdiction. The dispute was referred to the bishop, Hugh Balsham, who on 6 October issued a decree from his manor at Downham. Three statutes of the university are recited in this document. The first relates to the bedells, the second to the *matricula* which each master was bound to keep; the third guaranteed for the *familia* of scholars, scribes and other servants, the same immunity and liberty which the scholars themselves enjoyed.[3] In the Angelica text the first two of these statutes are found under

1 Gibson in his admirable edition of the Oxford statutes has drawn attention to the difficulties set by the re-enactment or reshaping of statutes. Cf. *SAUO*, pp. xvii–xviii.

2 The principle adopted by Gibson, namely 'the approximate date of the handwriting... as a *terminus ad quem*' (*ibid.* p. xvii), is liable to yield varying results. A group of Oxford statutes which he assigned on this principle to *c.* 1415–30 was subsequently redated by him '1445', apparently on the same tenuous evidence.

3 The original of the decree consigned to the chancellor and an exactly contemporary working-copy are in CUA, doc. no. 5. A full text derived from the archdeacon's copy is printed in *Vet. Lib. Archid. Elien.* pp. 20–3. A Latin–English version will be found in A. F. Leach, *Educational charters and documents 598 to 1909* (Cambridge, 1911), pp. 202–9.

chapters VIII and XI.[1] Neither the third statute nor the bishop's authoritative interpretation of its terms appears. This statute was obviously enacted some time after the constitution of the university was hammered out and codified. If the Angelica text were an inchoate, loose collection of statutes the absence of one or more statutes might not necessarily imply that the text was put together before their enactment. But the constitution in the Angelica manuscript is whole and entire, arranged chapter by chapter in due order. The fact that it lacks the statute cited by Hugh Balsham can only mean that the text was finalized before this particular statute was made. It is certainly not later than 6 October 1276. Not only did Cambridge possess a constitution in the proper sense of the term by this date, but apparently the Angelica text was revised and republished in a new recension before, perhaps well before, the bishop inspected the statutes.[2]

There is reason for thinking that the text underwent certain alterations as early as *c.* 1255–68.[3] An earlier document than Balsham's ordinance confirms the view that the Angelica text cannot be later than 1276. On 17 March the university, treading on very slippery constitutional ground, enacted a statute giving unusual powers to the two rectors. In the decree promulgating this new enactment part of an earlier statute on the office of the rectors is recited.[4] The original statute is found complete in the Angelica manuscript, which, however, exhibits no trace whatever of the new enactment.[5] Yet this enactment appears in all the later statute-

[1] *Cons. Univ. Canteb.* VIII. iii (see below, p. 207, lines 18–21), XI. i (see below, p. 211, lines 4–10).

[2] Commenting on the statute concerning the *familia* of scholars, the bishop says: 'Et quia in statutis vniuersitatis eiusdem inter alia continetur...' (CUA, doc. no. 5; *Vet. Lib. Archid. Elien.* p. 21). This statute slightly altered, doubtless as a result of the decree of 6 Oct. 1276, is Markaunt 26 (see below, p. 325, lines 5–7). Cf. *SA* 33 (*Docs*, i. 328).

[3] See below, pp. 221–5.

[4] The decree of 17 March 1276 promulgating the new statute has been critically edited from the original text in CUA, doc. no. 4 by W. Ullmann, 'The decline of the chancellor's authority in medieval Cambridge: a rediscovered statute', *Historical Journal*, i (1958), 181–2. The text is dated 'die sancte Wydburge, anno Domini millesimo ducentesimo septuagesimo quinto', which the editor wrongly gives as 17 March 1275; it should be of course 17 March 1276. There were two feasts of St Withburga; the first, the actual feast-day, was celebrated on 17 March; the second, the feast of her translation, was observed on 8 July. Cf. Calendar in *Vet. Lib. Archid. Elien.* pp. 153, 157.

[5] Cf. *Cons. Univ. Canteb.* VII. iv (see below, p. 205, line 22 to p. 207, line 2).

books.[1] The omission, therefore, of the statute on servants, scribes and others in the employment of scholars, a statute which is definitely earlier than the date of Balsham's ordinance, and the absence of the 1276 enactment prove conclusively that the Angelica text was devised at the latest during the first months of 1276. A closer examination reveals that it was put together at a much earlier date, by *c.* 1250 in fact.

The final chapter of the text contains directions for the observance of the obsequies, when they occur, of the reigning monarch and the then bishop of Ely.[2] The king is not named, but there is abundant evidence that he was none other than Henry III. Natural reason alone, declares the text, demands that remembrance should be made of those who were benefactors of the university during their lifetime, and chief among these is the present king, who endowed the university with many privileges, notably in connection with the assessment of houses, the purchase of daily foodstuffs and the treatment of criminals.[3] It was Henry III who first granted the university the legal right to fix the rents of hostels in conjunction with representatives of the town, as well as the necessary machinery for compelling the sheriff to arrest and imprison or expel from Cambridge, if the university thought fit, rebellious and troublesome scholars. Elsewhere, the constitution orders that those who fail to register under an approved master within fifteen days of their coming to the university are to be detained in accordance with the privilege received from the king.[4] This and the two foregoing privileges were granted on 3 May 1231 by writs issued at Oxford.[5] The third privilege puts beyond all doubt the identity of the king, for it was granted to the university originally by Henry III and only by him. Both he and his successors confirmed or amplified or published in more precise form the privileges relating to the renting of hostels and the ordering of undisciplined scholars. The writ of 1231 which directed the sheriff to imprison unregistered scholars, that is, those

[1] Markaunt 15 (see below, p. 318, line 27 to p. 319, line 20; Old Proctor 20 (fo. 20^{v}); Caius 20 (fos. 3vb–4ra); *SA* 57 (*Docs*, i. 342). These are revised texts, but the main revision was carried out well before the end of the fourteenth century, the date suggested by Ullmann, *loc. cit.* pp. 178–9. The Markaunt recension was executed *c.* 1304–37.

[2] *Cons. Univ. Canteb.* XIII. i (see below, p. 217, lines 8–16).

[3] *Cons. Univ. Canteb.* XIII. i (see below, p. 217, lines 9–13).

[4] Cf. *ibid.* XI. i (see below, p. 211, lines 4–10).

[5] *Close rolls, 1227–31*, pp. 586–7. The texts of the three writs with an English translation are printed in Leach, *Educational charters*, pp. 148–53.

whose names were not entered on the *matricula* of a regent master, was never reissued either by Henry himself or any later king.[1]

The reference in the Angelica text to this writ is important for another reason. It proves that the constitution of the university cannot have been arranged and promulgated before 3 May 1231, which must be considered the *terminus a quo* of the codification of the statutes. As we shall see, the statute based on this writ is an integral part of the constitution and forms the opening paragraph of chapter XI, which is followed by two more chapters; it is not therefore a later addition to the text. Since Henry III was still living when the constitution received its final form, we are now in a position to date the Angelica text within definite though admittedly wide limits, 3 May 1231–16 November 1272, this latter being the date of Henry's death. It is significant that the university placed him at the head of the list of kings of England who were its benefactors.[2]

In the chapter on the immunity of scholars the constitution forbids under pain of expulsion from the university or imprisonment any scholar from citing a clerk or layman of the town to an outside court under the clauses *quidam alii* and *rebus aliis*.[3] These general clauses were a standard formula in papal letters directed to judges delegate, and in fact formed the subject of a request addressed by the chancellor and university of Cambridge to Gregory IX. On 14 June 1233 he acceded to the request, not perhaps as fully as the university desired, and granted it an indult which in effect amounted to a grant of the *ius non trahi extra*, the earliest known concession of such a privilege to any university.[4] It was limited in its extent and dura-

[1] The oldest original of a royal charter now in the archives of the university is a writ granted by Henry III, dated 7 Feb. 1266, which ordered the rents of houses to be assessed every five years by two masters and two burgesses (CUA, doc. no. 1). The text of this and other charters of his reign is printed in W. Prynne, *The third tome of an exact chronological vindication and historical demonstration of the supreme ecclesiastical jurisdiction of our British, Roman, Saxon, Danish, Norman, English kings* (London, 1668), pp. 465–7; G. Dyer, *The privileges of the university of Cambridge* (London, 1824), i. 62–8.

[2] Cf. the roll of benefactors in 'Stokys's Book' (CUA), fo. 24^{r} (*bis*), which orders a special commemoration 'pro anima regis henrici qui sua gratia vniuersitatem istam beneficijs muniuit. et libertatibus insigniuit'. Edward I is mentioned next and then Edward II. The list ends with Henry VIII (fo. 24^{v} [*bis*]).

[3] It may be well to quote here the actual text of the constitution: 'qui clericum et laycum de uilla cantebrigie extra uillam per clausas illas quidam alii et rebus aliis conuenerint eciam nemine deferente super hoc conuicti propter quietem publicam per cancellarium et magistros ab uniuersitate sine spe restitucionis deiciantur uel in carcerem detrudantur' (*Cons. Univ. Canteb.* XI. iv [see below, p. 211, line 21 to p. 213, line 2]).

[4] See below, p. 53.

tion but was none the less an important directive. The indult prohibited anyone from summoning a member of the university to a court outside the diocese of Ely under the pretext of the general clauses *quidam alii* and *rebus aliis*, provided he was prepared to appear before the chancellor of the university or the bishop.[1] Its validity ran for three years and hence expired on 13 June 1236. The university apparently did not ask either then or later for a renewal; it may be that the indult was sought in the first place to counteract an immediate or passing problem; the desired effect having been achieved, the university probably did not consider it necessary to seek an extension of its terms for a further period. The point to be noted here, however, is that the statute of the university prohibiting citations under the clauses *quidam alii* and *rebus aliis* makes no reference to the privilege granted by Gregory IX; but unless there was papal authority or at least a precedent sanctioned by that authority the university could not, indeed would on no account dare to, write into its constitution a decree which infringed a prerogative of the Holy See and indeed the right granted by canon law to every individual and community to appeal directly to the pope to have an action heard by judges delegate.

It stands to reason, then, that the statute cannot have been devised before 14 June 1233. The university may have issued its prohibition of citations in the form of *quidam alii* and *rebus aliis* between that date and 13 June 1236, in other words, while the papal indult was still effective. When it was first framed the statute possibly carried a reference to the privilege received from Gregory IX and may well have been enacted in 1233–6. The majority of the statutes of the university set down in the Angelica text are perhaps earlier than 1233, having had the form of unwritten customs or in some cases actual enactments. Their codification and redaction as part of a written constitution of the university came later, and it is the date of this constitution that has to be determined here. If the statute pertaining to the general terms *quidam alii* and *rebus aliis* was incorporated in the constitution *c.* 1233–6 the text would almost certainly

[1] The text is printed in *Les registres de Grégoire IX*, ed. L. Auvray, i (Paris, 1896), 779–880, no. 1389; H. Denifle, *Die Entstehung der Universitäten des Mittelalters bis 1400* (Berlin, 1885), p. 370, n. 627. Cf. *Cal. papal letters*, i. 136. Neither Auvray nor Denifle prints the full text. Auvray omits the limiting clause 'Presentibus post triennium minime valituris'. Denifle for some unknown reason omits the all-important clauses *quidam alii* and *rebus aliis*. The text is in Archivio Vaticano, Reg. Vat. 17, fos. 52v–53r (ep. 175).

make mention of the papal indult. The framers of the constitution were careful to buttress other statutes with references to appropriate privileges granted by the king. In the present instance they had a much stronger reason for invoking the authority of the pope in support of a prohibition which cut across the common law of the church. As no mention whatever is made of the papal concession we have to conclude that its validity had expired. The fact that the Angelica text does not refer to the indult must mean that the constitution was drawn up some time after 13 June 1236 and if the statute in its original form did refer to the privilege granted by Gregory IX the reference was deleted at this stage.[1]

How soon the customs and statutes of the university were reduced to and embodied in codified form in a written constitution is another question. The statute under consideration is one of the few enactments which were not retained either in full or in an amended form in later recensions of the Angelica text. One may very tentatively suggest that it was deleted *c.* 1245. A petition presented on behalf of the English nation to the General Council at Lyons requested that the clause *quidam alii* be expunged from apostolic letters of delegation in which citizens of the kingdom of England were cited.[2] The pope, Innocent IV, rejected the petition; and it is possible that the university of Cambridge decided to bring its constitution into conformity with the declared will of the Holy See. If the outcome of the request made at the Council actually led the university to delete from its constitution the reference to the clauses *quidam alii* and *rebus aliis*, we should have to conclude that the text of the Angelica manuscript was put together *c.* 1236–45. And indeed there is no apparent reason for assigning the date of the constitution to *post* 1245, unless the judicial procedure briefly indicated in the text can be said to point to a somewhat later period.

In chapter X, *De ordine iudiciorum in causis scolarium custodiendo*, it is ordered that the *iuris solempnitas* is not to be observed in the university courts, and that citations (*ediciones*), contestations and the

[1] The statute makes no sense unless viewed within the context of the papal letter of 14 June 1233. There is no evidence that the Holy See granted the university a similar concession before this date. The constitution, moreover, makes provision for extraordinary lectures in canon law, which suggests that the Decretals of Gregory IX which were promulgated as an official text to be used in the schools as from 5 Sept. 1234 had been made the subject of extraordinary lectures at Cambridge by the time the constitution was drawn up.

[2] Cf. *Councils & Synods*, edd. F. M. Powicke and C. R. Cheney, II. i (Oxford, 1964), 395 and n. 1.

necessary proofs must be admitted even if not put down in writing.[1] This is clearly a departure from the directives contained in the famous decretal published by Innocent III at the Lateran Council of 1215,[2] and points to the introduction at Cambridge of the summary as opposed to the ordinary process of trial. Moreover, the constitution demands that the parties, both the plaintiff and the defendant, even if not asked to take the oath of calumny (*iuramentum calumniae*), must swear *de veritate dicenda*. The administration of this second oath, which strictly speaking was demandable only in spiritual causes, and in England not before 1237, was doubtless made statutory at Cambridge in order to speed up the hearing and termination of scholars' suits.[3] Though the form which summary trials were to take in ecclesiastical courts was not definitely settled until 1312–14 by the bull *Saepe contingit* of Clement V,[4] it is evident that the solemn procedure ordered by Innocent III and described in detail in legal manuals, notably Tancred's *Ordo iudiciarius* (*c.* 1216), began to give way in ecclesiastical courts to the less formal, summary process *c.* 1250.[5] This development which is reflected in the Cambridge constitution is not incompatible with the terminal date *c.* 1245 for the composition of the exemplar of the Angelica text, though one hesitates to believe that proceedings in the chancellor's court were conducted before *c.* 1250 according to the relatively new procedure. There is no precise evidence that the constitution of the university was or must have been finalized by 1245 or thereabouts, and it is necessary to subject the text to a closer examination.

When the constitution was drafted and definitively promulgated only three faculties existed at Cambridge, namely theology, decrees and arts; the faculties of civil law and medicine are not mentioned in the Angelica text and we have no choice but to conclude that they were established later. The medical faculty may have been founded *c.* 1270–80. In documents of this period two masters, both

1 *Cons. Univ. Canteb.* x. ii (see below, p. 209, line 17 to p. 211, line 2).

2 c. 11. x. 2. 19.

3 Cf. *Constitutiones Ottonis legati in Anglia*, c. 24 (*Councils & Synods*, ed. cit. II. i. 256).

4 The correct date of the constitution *Saepe* is 6 May 1312–21 March 1314, not 1306 as is generally stated. Cf. S. Kuttner, 'The date of the constitution "Saepe"; the Vatican manuscripts and the Roman edition of the Clementines', *Mélanges Eugène Tisserant* (Studi e Testi, 234 [1964]), p. 432.

5 Cf. S. Stelling-Michaud, *L'université de Bologne et la pénétration des droits romain et canonique en Suisse aux XIIIe et XIVe siècles* (Travaux d'Humanisme et Renaissance, xvii [Geneva, 1955]), 209. Tancred's work, as we shall see, was possibly one of the sources of c. X of the Cambridge constitution.

almost certainly Cambridge graduates, are described as *medici*. Nigel de Thornton is best known as the founder of the university chaplaincy and the owner of the site on which University Hall (the forerunner of Clare College) and the 'old' schools were afterwards erected.[1] John de Watford, who was *magister* by 1277, was appointed by Ely Cathedral Priory on 3 May 1278, to serve the monks 'in scientia medicinali'.[2] But there is no evidence that either of the two masters actually incepted in medicine and was regent master in the faculty. It can be shown indirectly, however, that medicine was established on a faculty basis by 1294.[3] This was certainly long after the publication of the first constitution of the university. The history of civil law at Cambridge is much better documented, and by concentrating on the origin of the faculty we can obtain a fairly precise *terminus ad quem* for the date of the Angelica text.

The earliest recorded professor of civil law at the university is mag. Simon de Asceles. According to the Barnwell chronicler, he studied arts at Oxford and graduated with the highest distinction as master before coming to Cambridge, where some time later he incepted as doctor of civil law.[4] This was probably in 1255, for on 22 November he was appointed collector of the tenth in Cambridgeshire and Huntingdonshire; he was then king's clerk.[5] At all events, he must have incepted as D.C.L. by 11 October 1257 when he was vested in the habit of an Augustinian canon at Barnwell, having

[1] Cf. H. P. Stokes, *The chaplains and the chapel of the university of Cambridge (1256–1568)* (CAS, octavo series, xli [1906]), 2, 5 and *passim*; Hall, 'William Rysley's catalogue', *Camb. Bibl. Soc. Trans.* iv. 97; *BRUC*, p. 585. On the location of Thornton's property cf. R. Willis and J. W. Clark, *The architectural history of the university of Cambridge* (Cambridge, 1886), i. 78, iii. 3–7.

[2] B.M. Add. MS 41612, fo. 11r; cf. *ibid.* fos. 3r, 10r; *V.C.H. Camb.* ii, 205, n. 90; *BRUC*, pp. 685–6. Watford's name is wrongly given as 'Walford' in C. H. Talbot and E. A. Hammond, *The medical practitioners in medieval England* (Wellcome Historical Medical Library, n.s. viii [1965]), 193–4.

[3] See below, p. 235, n. 1. V. L. Bullough, 'The mediaeval medical school at Cambridge', *Mediaeval Studies*, xxiv (1962), 164, thinks that the faculty was created in the late fourteenth century, but this opinion is based on a misinterpretation of the university statutes. Talbot, *Medicine in medieval England* (London, 1967), p. 69, is more discerning, for he takes into account the evidence of the college statutes, which clearly show that the faculty, as the author infers, existed by *c.* 1350. The date in fact can be pushed back by more than another fifty years.

[4] The chronicler writes of him as 'vir quidem magne eloquencie et eminentis litterature' and states: 'Dum enim erat in habitu seculari, nobiliter rexit in artibus apud Oxoniam, et processu temporis factus iuriscivilis [*sic*] professor apud Cantebrigiam . . . inter regni primates cognitus et honoratus.' (*Liber mem. ecc. de Bernewelle*, p. 73.)

[5] *Cal. pat. rolls, 1245–58*, p. 508; *BRUC*, p. 17.

decided to quit the world.[1] Every Cambridge master was strictly bound to continue as regent for at least one year after incepting unless excused for some sufficient reason. There is no hint in the *Liber memorandorum* of Barnwell that Asceles's term of necessary regency was shortened in order to facilitate his early entry into the priory, of which he became the twelfth and most illustrious superior. If he was not D.C.L. of Cambridge by 1255 he must have incepted at the very latest in 1256.[2] What is no less significant is that the chronicler in the course of his eulogy on Simon omits to say that he was in fact the father of the Cambridge faculty of civil law. If this distinction were his we need not doubt that it would have been credited to him in the *Liber memorandorum*, of which he is the unquestioned hero. The compiler was evidently an enthusiastic admirer of Asceles, whose antecedents and administration as prior of Barnwell (1267–97) he records with unconcealed affection and pride. If Simon were the first regent master in civil law at the university, such a devoted chronicler would surely have added this further title to his encomium.

The story of Simon de Asceles's vocation dates from 1254–6 when he was associated with the prior of Barnwell as collector of the crusading tenth in the diocese of Ely.[3] His expert knowledge of civil law probably won him the friendship of Jolan de Thorleye, who was actually prior of the monastery when he decided to resign his chair in 1257 after an attack of sickness and enter Barnwell.[4] As

1 The chronology of his life at Barnwell is not as confused as Clark imagined in his edition of the priory chronicle; cf. *Liber mem. ecc. de Bernewelle*, pp. xvii–xviii. Asceles's vestition took place on the feast of the translation of St Augustine of Hippo (not St Augustine of Canterbury), 11 Oct. 1257. Clark suggests that he was elected prior in 1266. This is not so. Asceles was official of Hugh Balsham before his election. He resigned the officiality on becoming prior. Hence the election cannot have taken place before 9 Sept. 1267, for by this date he was still official. Cf. the unprinted cartulary of St John's College, Cambridge (St John's College Muniments), p. 209. Asceles was actually elected on 11 Oct. 1267, the tenth anniversary of his reception of the habit, and he was inducted formally by the archdeacon of Ely, John Balsham, on the feast of St Luke (18 Oct.).

2 The date in *BRUC* (*loc. cit.*) 'before 1266' is probably a misprint for 'before 1256'. For the statute on necessary regency cf. *Cons. Univ. Canteb.* II. iv (see below, p. 199, line 18 to p. 201, line 2).

3 W. E. Lunt, *Financial relations of the papacy with England to 1327* (Studies in Anglo-Papal relations during the middle ages, i [Cambridge, Mass., 1939]), 625.

4 Jolan de Thorleye, 11th prior of Barnwell (1256–67) and Simon's immediate predecessor, is described as 'in iure ciuili peritus' (*Liber mem. ecc. de Bernewelle*, p. 71). He was justice in eyre with Nicholas de Turri for Cambridgeshire in 1262 (P.R.O. J.I. 1/1191, m. 6^{v}).

regent master at the university he occupied rooms in the great stone house in Trumpington Street owned by John le Rus which stood on the site of the Fitzwilliam Museum opposite St Edmund's chapel.[1] His *lectura* may be assigned to the years 1254–7 and it would seem that the teaching of civil law was organized on a faculty basis by *c.* 1250–5. The genesis of the faculty probably goes back to the late thirties or early forties of the century. It is to be hoped that further investigation will help to clear up the uncertainty and provide a reasonably satisfactory explanation for the reluctance or inability of the university to erect the faculty when or shortly after canon law was given this status.[2] The spur to make good the deficiency may have been supplied by the decree of the Council of Tours in 1236 which made a degree in civil law almost a *sine qua non* for the office of diocesan official.[3] It is not beyond the bounds of possibility that mag. John de Cadamo and mag. Walter de Tyrington lectured as regent masters at Cambridge after they ceased to be officials of Ely (*c.* 1225–38),[4] and that mag. John de Lindsey and Roger de Leycestria incepted in the faculty before Simon de Asceles arrived.[5] At all

[1] Cf. Stokes, *Outside the Trumpington gates before Peterhouse was founded* (CAS, octavo series, xliv [1908]), 40; Idem, *The mediaeval hostels of the university of Cambridge* (*ibid.* xlix [1924]), 100. Cf. also T. A. Walker, *Peterhouse* (Cambridge, 1935), p. 6 (facsimile facing).

[2] The ban placed on the teaching of civil law at Paris by Honorius III in 1219 cannot have affected Cambridge. For the bull *Super specula* and its significance cf. Kuttner, 'Papst Honorius III. und das Studium des Zivilrechts', *Festschrift für Martin Wolff* (Tübingen, 1952), pp. 79–101. Matthew Paris, *Chronica majora*, ed. H. E. Luard, vi (Rolls series, 1882), 293–5, reproduces the text of a spurious bull of Innocent IV under the year 1254 which purports to prohibit schools of law in various countries, including England. On this false decretal and its connection with the writ of Henry III (11 Dec. 1234) ordering the closing down of law schools in London cf. G. Digard, 'La papauté et l'étude du droit romain au XIIIe siècle à propos de la fausse bulle d'Innocent IV *Dolentes*', *Bibliothèque de l'École des Chartes*, li (1890), 381–419, especially 404–16.

[3] Cf. J. D. Mansi, *Sacrorum conciliorum nova et amplissima collectio*, xxiii (Venice, 1779), 412. Roger Bacon's caustic remark in his *Opus tertium*, c. 24, is apposite: 'plus laudatur in ecclesia Dei unus jurista civilis, licet solum sciat jus civile . . . et citius eligitur ad ecclesiasticas dignitates' (*Fr. Rogeri Bacon opera quaedam hactenus inedita*, ed. J. S. Brewer, i [Rolls series, 1859], 84).

[4] Cf. *BRUC*, pp. 116, 602–3. Both had connections with Cambridge. For Cadamo as official of Hugh of Northwold, bishop of Ely (1229–54), cf. Ely Dioc. Rec. G 3/27 (Old Coucher Book), fo. 224[ra].

[5] Lindsey was regent master (faculty not stated) in 1246 and official of Lincoln by 1263 (*BRUC*, p. 370). Roger de Leycestria preceded Simon as official of Ely; he was master by 1251 and official by 1259. Cf. P.R.O. C 85/66/7; J.I. 1/82, m. 10; and *BRUC*, p. 367. Mag. Guy of Barnard Castle who incepted by 1251 was thought to have been a lawyer by J. M. Gray, *The school of Pythagoras* (*Merton Hall*) *Cam-*

events, inceptions and ordinary lectures in civil law must have had a place in the organization of the *studium* long before the turn of the century. This was not so when the Angelica text was fashioned, and we may rightly conclude that the constitution was promulgated if not by 1245 at any rate during the following decade.

The reliability of this dating cannot be accepted until the identity of the unnamed bishop of Ely mentioned in the text is established. The 'venerable father of Ely' is said in the thirteenth and final chapter of the constitution to have honoured in various ways the scholars and especially the regents at their *principia* or inceptions. He was still alive when the text was constructed.[1] Of all the bishops of Ely the one who has the greatest claim to be remembered among the benefactors of the university is Hugh Balsham. His most enduring monument is of course Peterhouse (1280–4);[2] but well before this foundation he was associated with the university and played a decisive role in its constitutional development. On 19 December 1264 he reaffirmed a principle embodied in the constitution though not stated in so many words, namely, that the *universitas regentium* and not the chancellor was the supreme court of appeal in the university. In future, declared the bishop, no appeal from a decision of the chancellor would be entertained in the episcopal *curia* unless the appellant had first appealed from the chancellor to the university; only then might he carry his case to the bishop's court.[3] This directive was duly given statutory form; it appears in Markaunt's text of the statutes (*c.* 1304–37) and in all the later statute-books.[4] There is no trace of it in the Angelica text, needless to say, which definitely shows that the constitution was drawn up by 1264. This we already know, but it is consoling to have a firm date. The omission is important in other ways, too. It proves that the statute

bridge (CAS, quarto series, n.s. iv [1932]), 6–7. The basis of the supposition is certainly erroneous. In P.R.O. J.I. 1/95, m. 41, cited in *BRUC*, p. 39, Guy is not described as a doctor or master of civil law. He was probably never more than M.A.

1 *Cons. Univ. Canteb.* XIII. i (see below, p. 217, lines 13–16).

2 On 5 Oct. 1283 St John's Hospital agreed to transfer its patronage of St Peter's church and ownership of two nearby hostels, etc., to the scholars whom the bishop had installed as boarders in the hospital in 1280. Cf. Peterhouse Muniments, *Registrum vetus*, pp. 27–8.

3 See below, pp. 222–3.

4 The original form of the statute is preserved in Markaunt 26 (see below, p. 324, line 35 to p. 325, line 1) and in Caius 35 (fo. 6v b) and Old Proctor 35 (fo. 24v). The clause 'vel ab vniuersitate ad episcopum' was deleted from the latter after the university secured exemption from the bishop's jurisdiction in 1401. The revised form of the statute is in *SA* 33 (*Docs*, i. 327–8).

in the constitution relating to the 'taxation' or renting of houses was not based on a charter granted by the king on 7 February 1266, and likewise excludes the possibility that certain references to the sale of wine and foodstuffs echo the regulations contained in a patent letter of 1268.[1] Following a dispute between Alan, rector of St Benet's, and the university Hugh intervened and effected an agreement between the two parties on 14 March 1274;[2] and on 6 October 1276 he settled the rival claims of the archdeacon of Ely and the chancellor of the university with regard to the extent of their respective jurisdictions.[3] In more senses than one, Hugh Balsham could justifiably speak of Cambridge as 'our university'. If he was the 'venerable father of Ely' to whom the Angelica text refers, the constitution cannot be earlier than the date of his election as bishop, 14 November 1256.[4]

His foundation of Peterhouse assured Balsham a permanent place in the statutes of the university.[5] Yet, when he died on 15 June 1286 the chancellor and regents made no move to make the observance of his obit an annual duty on the university. A statute was at length promulgated at the request of the college by Geoffrey de Pakenham, the chancellor, with the consent of the regents on 26 May 1291. It ordered all the regent masters to assemble each year at St Peter's church on the vigil of SS Vitus and Modestus to recite the office for the dead and again on the morrow (15 June) for the celebration of Requiem Mass for the founder's soul. The original of the chancellor's decree stamped with the seal of the university is preserved among the muniments of Peterhouse and invites careful study.[6] The citation gives pride of place to Hugh's greatest gift to

[1] References to the texts of these writs are cited on pp. 261, n. 1, 37, n. 2.

[2] The point at issue was the ringing of the bell of the church summoning scholars to extraordinary lectures. Cf. J. Josselin, *Historiola Collegii Corporis Christi*, ed. Clark (CAS, octavo series, xvii [1880]), 56–7.

[3] See above, p. 23 and *passim*.

[4] For a correction of the generally accepted date of his election by the chapter of Ely cf. A. Maier, 'Notizie storiche del XIII e XIV secolo da codici Borghesiani', *Rivista di storia della chiesa in Italia*, iv (1950), 171–6.

[5] Cf. *SA* 180, 185 (*Docs*, i. 404–6, 413–14).

[6] The deed, written in a charter hand on parchment measuring 135 × 210 mm, is in the muniment room at Peterhouse, 'Cista Communis', document no. 4. There is a transcript in the College *Registrum vetus*, p. 27 (mod. fol.: A6r). The seal, the earliest extant of the university, is attached to the deed by a parchment slip. It is much defaced and lacks the upper and lower left sections. The legend is rather mutilated; it reads: 'SIGILLVM VNIVERSITATIS *CANTEBRIGIE*'. Cf. W. H. St John Hope, *Seals and armorial insignia of the university and colleges of Cambridge*, pt 1

Cambridge, the establishment of the college, the 'house of the scholars of the bishop of Ely', and immediately adds that he also conferred during his life as well as posthumously many benefits on all the regents and poor scholars, not to mention the privileges with which he endowed the university. It is therefore fitting, concludes the citation, that the regents should commemorate his anniversary with filial affection, mindful of one who while living made it his whole endeavour to promote manfully the good and the honour of the scholars.[1]

The tribute was richly deserved and implies that Balsham did something more for the university than the extant records would lead one to assume.[2] This may be so, but we cannot ignore the fact, presupposing that Hugh is the unnamed bishop referred to in the Angelica text, that the decree of 1291 completely ignores the earlier statute and the precise reason given there for the observance of the bishop's obit. The honour which the anonymous prelate is said to have bestowed on the regent masters at their *principia* on numerous occasions—he probably presided at their inceptions—may be covered by the terms of the 1291 citation; and if it contained an allusion, however slight, to the relevant chapter of the constitution there should be no scruple about identifying Hugh Balsham as the 'venerable father of Ely', in which case the Angelica text would have

(London, 1881), plate II, fig. 1; Idem in *Proceedings of the Society of Antiquaries of London*, 2nd series, X (1883–5), 226. Professor Knowles and Mr E. J. Kenney, the librarian, made it possible for me to examine the original deed and seal.

1 The pertinent section of the original reads: 'concessimus de communi consensu et vnanimi voluntate, ac eciam idem pro statuto irrefragabili obseruari volumus in futurum quod singulis annis... conueniant regentes in habitu magistrali pro anima bone memorie domini .H. de Balsham quondam Episcopi Elyensis qui domum scolarium predictorum fundauit vniuersos regentes et pauperes scolares non solum in vita sua set et post mortem beneficiis visitauit multipliciter et respexit, ac eciam vniuersitatem nostram priuilegiis insigniuit...qui se viuum totaliter scolaribus exhibebat, ac eorum promocioni comodo et honori caritatis oculis et animo pietatis viriliter insistebat.'

2 His bequests to Peterhouse are recorded in the *Liber* or *Historia Eliensis*, Bk III: 'Ipse insuper in extremis laborans dictis Scolaribus ad edificia de nouo construenda trescentas Marcas legauit de quibus quandam aream ex parte australi dicte ecclesie comparauerunt, et in eadem quamdam aulam perpulcram de nouo construxerunt, libros etiam plures theologie et quosdam aliarum scientiarum legauit Scolaribus' (Bodl. Laud. Misc. 647 [SC 1595], fo. 176ra). I am grateful to Dr R. W. Hunt for checking this passage for me. Cf. also J. Bentham, *The history and antiquities of the conventual & cathedral church of Ely* (2nd edn, Norwich, 1812), pp. 149–51; W. Stevenson, *A supplement to the first edition of Mr Bentham's history* (Norwich, 1817), pp. 79–80; Walker, *A biographical register of Peterhouse men* (Cambridge, 1927), pp. 1–2.

to be dated to the years 1257–64, even though this would involve stretching rather unduly the evidence with regard to the erection of the faculty of civil law. The omission from the statute promulgated by Geoffrey de Pakenham and the regent masters on 26 May 1291 of any reference to the previous statute is too striking to be ignored. It might be explained away but no more.[1] There is, however, a piece of external evidence which removes all doubt and with it Hugh Balsham's candidature for the title of the 'venerable father of Ely'.

On 5 June 1255, more than two years before the sub-prior of Ely was consecrated bishop, Henry III ordered the sheriff of Cambridge to see that effect was given to the letters patent which had been issued in favour of the university. It is galling to find that neither the original nor an enrolment nor even a copy of these letters can be traced.[2] They were apparently made out some time before the date of the writ to the sheriff and had to do principally with the assize of bread and ale, the renting of hostels and the imprisoning and delivery of scholars; they also contained 'other commodities and liberties'.[3] The interests of the university with regard to hostels and the imprisonment of scholars were safeguarded

[1] Whenever there was question of amending the constitution, as happened for example on 17 March 1276, the existing statute is usually cited. It may be suggested that the passage in the Angelica text relating to the bishop of Ely was abrogated after Balsham's death in 1286, presupposing that he was the bishop referred to; but the only reason why this might have been done was surely to make a new statute to replace the old. It would be strange indeed if the university decided to remove all mention of one whose claims for suffrages, as the 1291 decree implies, could not in justice be ignored. We can be sure that Peterhouse would not stand for it. The point of the decree is that Balsham's obit was not covered by any previous statute. His was the first to be commemorated in this way.

[2] These are not the only letters patent which were not enrolled. In a writ of 11 July 1249 reference is made to letters of the king dated 21 March 1242, but the text of the writ is known only from an inspeximus of Edward I, 28 Oct. 1294. Cf. *Close rolls, 1247–51*, p. 178; Dyer, *Privileges*, i. 62, where the writ of 1242 is dated 30 March.

[3] 'Rex vicecomiti Cantebrigie salutem. Precipimus tibi quod ordinaciones et prouisiones contentas in litteris nostris patentibus quas fieri fecimus Cancellario et vniuersitati scolarium Cantebrigie de assisa panis et ceruisie, de hospiciis taxandis, de incarceracionibus clericorum eiusdem vniuersitatis, et eorum deliberacionibus ad mandatum dicti Cancellarij faciendis, et de alijs commoditatibus et libertatibus eis per dictas litteras nostras concessis, firmiter teneri et obseruari facias secundum quod in eisdem literis continetur, ne amplius inde clamorem audiamus. Teste meipso apud Woodstok quinto die Junij anno regni nostri xxxix°.' (Hare MS i, fos. 15^{v}–16^{r}; cf. *Close rolls, 1254–6*, p. 94, where the text is printed in reported speech under the date 9 June.)

by writs issued on 3 May 1231.[1] Now the king confirms them again in the form of letters patent which in addition granted the chancellor the right to attend or be represented at the assize of bread and ale. What the other privileges were is impossible to say.[2] It is unlikely that the privilege of supervising in conjunction with the burgesses the assize of bread and ale was granted to the chancellor of Cambridge before Oxford received this privilege, for the first time in 1248.[3] Grants of this kind usually followed outbreaks of dissension between the universities and the towns. There were disturbances of the peace at Cambridge in 1249, the last that we hear of before 1260, and it may be that the letters patent referred to in the writ of 1255 were issued as early as 1250.[4] They were certainly published by 5 June 1255, which must be considered as the ultimate date of the Angelica text.

The constitution assigns to the two rectors as their primary duty the task of assessing on behalf of the university the rents of houses, and secondly of seeing that bread and wine and other supplies were sold at a just price and on the same terms to scholars as to citizens of Cambridge.[5] Elsewhere it mentions among the privileges received from the king an unspecified grant in connection with the purchase of daily supplies.[6] The assize of bread and ale is not listed as one of the privileges granted by the king, nor is any reference made to it in the Angelica text. It is mentioned in the next earliest text of the statutes which dates from *c.* 1304–37,[7] and one can only conclude that the university received the right to have observers at the making of the assize some time after the Angelica text was put together. As we have seen, this privilege was granted by 5 June 1255; it follows

1 See above, pp. 25–6, and below, pp. 72, 74.

2 An idea of their nature may perhaps be gained from a patent letter of 22 Feb. 1268. The original is extant in CUA, doc. no. 2. The text is printed from an inspeximus of Edward I, 6 Feb. 1292, in Prynne, *op. cit.* p. 465, and in Dyer, *Privileges*, i. 63–5 (from an inspeximus of Richard II where the date is wrongly given as 20 February).

3 Cf. *Mediaeval archives of the university of Oxford*, ed. Salter, i (OHS, lxx [1920]), 19. The privilege was confirmed by letters patent of 18 June 1255 (*ibid.* p. 20).

4 Cf. Matthew Paris, *Chron. Maj.* v (1880), 67–8; Cooper, *Annals*, i. 45. The writ of 1242 which ordered the sheriff to apprehend and release scholars at the direct request of the chancellor was suspended on 11 July 1249 while the commissioners of oyer and terminer whom the king appointed to investigate the disturbance were in session. Cf. *Cal. pat. rolls, 1247–58*, p. 53; *Close rolls, 1247–51*, p. 178.

5 The duties of the rectors are set out on pp. 152–8 below.

6 *Cons. Univ. Canteb.* XIII. i (see below, p. 217, lines 9–13).

7 Markaunt 12 (see below, p. 317, lines 14–16), 17 (see below, p. 320, lines 16–17). Cf. *SA* 65, 66 (*Docs*, i. 349–50).

that the text of the constitution of the university was drawn up at the very latest by that date, and may well have been given its final form by 1250.

The text of the constitution having taken shape by 1255, Hugh Balsham must drop out of the running for the title of the 'venerable father of Ely'. We are left with only two contenders, Hugh of Northwold and William of Kilkenny. If the phrase in the Angelica text, *venerabilis pater elyensis*, is to be taken at its face value, then the vote must go to Northwold. William of Kilkenny was elected to succeed him *c.* 24 September 1254 but was not consecrated bishop until 15 August 1255. He was, therefore, only bishop-elect by the time the constitution of the university was devised and hence, strictly speaking, did not merit the unqualified title of the 'venerable father of Ely'. In June 1255 when he secured the release from the king's prison at Cambridge of the eminent grammarian, Nicholas de Breckendale, he was called *venerabilis pater W. Elyensis electus*, and there is no reason to think that the framers of the Cambridge constitution would have departed from the proper way of styling him.[1] His most notable contribution to the university was the burse which he provided in his will for the support of two chaplains who had to be students in the faculty of theology, not, as one might have expected of a canonist and civilian, in the faculty of decrees or civil law.[2] As chancellor of the realm (1253–5) and in view of his brief episcopate he cannot have had much time or scope to identify himself personally with the life of the university and in particular the *principia* of the regents.[3]

[1] Breckendale was not imprisoned, when charged with homicide, in the bishop's jail, as *BRUC*, p. 90, states. Cf. *Close rolls, 1254–6*, p. 96: 'Quia venerabilis pater W. Elyensis electus regi per litteras suas patentes significavit quod Nicholaus de Brakendel', clericus, captus et in prisona nostra Cantebr' pro morte cujusdam hominis unde rettatus est detentus, legitime coram ipso electo se esse ordinatum a venerabili patre B. Cantuariensi archiepiscopo in primis ordinibus ab ipso apud Cant' celebratis, et idem electus a rege requisivit predictum Nicholaum tanquam de foro ecclesiastico existentem sibi secundum libertatem ecclesiasticam liberari, mandatum est ballivis regis Cantebr' quod eundem Nicholaum predicto electo secundum libertatem predictam et modum et consuetudinem in regno regis hactenus optentam liberent.' In a charter dated 23 June 1255 William styles himself 'Willelmus miseracione diuina Elyensis Electus' (Ely Dioc. Rec. G 3/28 [Liber M], p. 189*b*).

[2] Cf. *Liber mem. ecc. de Bernewelle*, pp. 94–6, 146–8. The legacy did not take effect until after 12 Dec. 1257, and there were difficulties as late as 1286.

[3] He was appointed envoy to King Alfonso X of Castile on 24 June 1256 and died in Spain on 21 Sept. (*BRUO*, ii. 1049).

Hugh of Northwold, on the contrary, was bishop for a quarter of a century (1229–54). Many Cambridge *magistri* were members of his *familia*, and although the university was established under a chancellor before his appointment to Ely he must have been closely associated with the affairs of the university during its constitutional development. Friend of Grosseteste, Hugh of Northwold was described by Matthew Paris as 'the flower of the black monks'.[1] It was during his episcopate that the university received from the king its first privileges. He was an essential link between the chancellor and the sheriff.[2] The earliest extant act of the university was promulgated at his request in 1246 when mag. Hugh de Hotton was chancellor.[3] In the list of bishops who were commemorated as benefactors of the university in contradistinction to those who were founders of colleges he is the first bishop of Ely recorded.[4] Of itself this is not proof that he is the anonymous bishop of whom the Angelica text speaks; but it is significant that the list begins with him and not with Eustace, who ruled the diocese when the migration from Oxford took place in 1209, or with John of Fountains or Geoffrey de Burgo, either of whom may have appointed the first chancellor.[5] Although it cannot be shown that Hugh of Northwold was a frequent visitor at inception ceremonies, the university must have had compelling reasons to be grateful to him;[6] otherwise he would not have been numbered first among the bishops who benefited the university as a whole.[7] There can be little or no doubt that he was the 'venerable father of Ely' mentioned in the constitution.[8]

1 Cf. *Roberti Grosseteste episcopi quondam Lincolniensis epistolae*, ed. Luard (Rolls series, 1861), 297–9, no. xcvi; *Chron. Maj.* v. 455.

2 He was with the king when the writs of 1231 were issued in favour of the university; as bishop of Ely he was doubtless consulted concerning the situation at Cambridge.

3 See below, pp. 55–6.

4 Cf. Stokys's Book, fo. 26^{r}. William of Louth comes next and then William of Kilkenny, thus reversing the chronological order. Was Louth considered a better benefactor than Kilkenny? Hugh Balsham is not recorded in this list of bishops (fo. 26^{r-v}). He is mentioned earlier among the founders of colleges and of course heads the group (fo. 25^{r}).

5 A chancellor of the university was appointed by 4 June 1225. See below, p. 48. John of Fountains died on 6 May and de Burgo was elected on 2 June.

6 He may have attended the inception *c.* 1245 of Edmund de Walpole, whom he later confirmed as abbot of Bury St Edmund's (Northwold's old monastery) in 1248. See below, p. 131.

7 John of Kirkby (1286–90) is not one of the bishops of Ely noted as benefactors in Stokys's Book.

8 Unfortunately, Northwold's activities in connection with the university are likely to remain even harder to assess than his career as bishop. Cf. E. Miller, *The*

Drawing the somewhat complex threads of evidence together, we may assign the composition of the Angelica text to *c.* 1236–54. The absolute *terminus ad quem* is 6 August 1254, the date of Northwold's death. If the patent letters referred to in the writ of 1255 were published in or about 1250 the text was drawn up by then; it may have been compiled *c.* 1236–45, though the judicial procedure laid down in the constitution suggests that '1250' is preferable to '1245'. The exact date must remain an open question until further evidence becomes available, but until it does we cannot do better than stand by '*c.* 1236–54' and suggest 'by *c.* 1250' as a good working date.

abbey and bishopric of Ely (Cambridge Studies in Medieval Life and Thought, i [Cambridge, 1951]), p. 279. According to Bentham, *op. cit.* p. 147, he settled scholars in the hospital of St John at Cambridge. This statement, however, is based on a misreading of Richard Parker, who simply states that Northwold introduced secular brethren (*fratres seculares*) into 'this literary hostel' *c.* 1240. Cf. R. Parker, Σκελετός *Cantabrigiensis*, ed. Hearne, *Joannis Lelandi antiquarii de rebus Britannicis collectanea*, v (2nd edn, London, 1770), 236.

Chapter 3

THE ORIGIN OF THE CAMBRIDGE STATUTES

The earliest official act of the university promulgated in the name of the chancellor and regent masters dates from 1246. It has nothing to do with the making of a statute, still less with the formation of a constitution.[1] Actual evidence of the making of a statute derives from a much later period, from 1276 to be exact. Without the aid of records such as a university register or minutes of convocation any hope of being able to trace the development of individual statutes and the evolution of the text of the university constitution by *c.* 1250 is effectively blasted. Some consolation may be drawn from the fact that it is equally impossible to follow step by step the formation of constitutions of institutions which had far deeper roots and infinitely more resources. The process whereby statutes of the realm were formulated and published cannot be perceived before 1258–9.[2] Evidently, the Angelica text was not the work of one day or one year; the selection and arrangement of the statutes, the very nature of the enactments themselves, presuppose that a period, long rather than short, of constitutional history or experiment preceded the composition of the text.[3] The obvious starting point for an investigation of the sources and formation of the constitution, in so far as these matters can be elucidated, must be the date of the foundation of the *studium* and its organization as a *universitas* or corporate body capable of making laws for its government and welfare.

The Carmelite friar, Nicholas Cantelow or Cantelupe, who was master of theology at the university before his death in 1441, was the first to attempt to give Cambridge a history.[4] The plan of his

1 The 1246 document is concerned with the exemption of two hostels from taxation. It is printed in full on p. 55 below.

2 Cf. H. G. Richardson and G. O. Sayles, 'The early statutes', *Law Quarterly Review*, l (1934), 544–7.

3 Rashdall, *Universities*, iii. 280, n. 1, divined this long ago although he had nothing to go on except the statute of 17 March 1276. His other remarks about this statute are now antiquated.

4 The *Cronica fundacionis destruccionis et renouacionis uniuersitatis* in Gonville and Caius College MS 249, fos. 191^r–193^r, is not an original work; it is in fact only a

historiola is peculiar, the centrepiece being a description of the upheaval of 1381. Three papal bulls serve as a sort of introduction, the foundation-deeds so to speak of the university in Cantelow's view; and it is not until the end of the tract that we are offered the *pièce de résistance* entitled 'De antiquitate et origine almae et immaculatae universitatis Cantebrigiae'.[1] Of the three papal documents—the letter of Boniface IX (12 January 1401) which exempted chancellors-elect from seeking confirmation in office from the bishop of Ely is not recited—only the third is genuine. This is the bull *Inter singula* granted by John XXII on 9 June 1318.[2] Cantelow's narrative of the origin and early history of the university is so fantastic that one must seriously doubt whether he himself really

transcript made by John Harryson *c.* 1464 of Cantelow's work. Harryson was the author of a chronicle covering the years 1377–1469 which occurs in the same MS, fos. 127r–134r. The university is mentioned for the first time under the year 1416 and does not figure again until the year 1457 is reached. The text has been edited by J. J. Smith, *Abbreviata cronica ab anno 1377 usque ad annum 1469* (CAS, quarto series, i, pt 2 [1840]).

1 Cf. *Nicholai Cantalupi historiola*, ed. cit. 262–80. An English version of the tract was published at London in 1721 under the title *The history and antiquities of Cambridge*; it occupies pp. 1–23. Cantelow's *historiola* is not to be confused with the *tabula de origine uniuersitatis* to which reference is made in *Grace Book* A, ed. S. M. Leathes (CAS, Luard Memorial series, i [1897]), 90. This was a tablet which hung in the Old Schools. Cf. J. Caius, *De antiquitate Cantebrigiensis academiae*, ed. E. S. Roberts, *The works of John Caius, M.D.* (Cambridge, 1912), pt 3, pp. 24–5. For MSS of Cantelow's work see *BRUC*, p. 120.

2 For a recent edition of the text see below, p. 177. The spurious character of the bulls of Honorius I (?625–38) and Sergius I (687–701) transcribed by the Carmelite was demonstrated by Dyer, *Privileges*, i. 397–410 (the bulls are printed on pp. 58–60), as long ago as 1824. There is no evidence that Cantelow invented them, and like the false Theodosian privilege of 433 which Bologna claimed to have received they may originally have served a different purpose. They were probably concocted when the university was seeking exemption from the jurisdiction of the bishop of Ely *c.* 1400. Copies certainly existed by 1420, for they are mentioned by Rysley in his inventory of the university archives; cf. Hall, *loc. cit.* pp. 94–5. These copies are still extant (CUA, doc. no. 115). The earliest precise reference to the bulls is contained in a document dated 1 June 1419, printed in Caius, *De antiq. Cant. Acad.* ed. cit. p. 56; this document was afterwards reproduced almost *verbatim* by Richard Pyghtsley, notary public, in an instrument of 9 Sept. 1429 which led to the institution of the Barnwell Process by Martin V (6 July 1430). See below, p. 287, n. 1. J. Heywood, *Early Cambridge University and College statutes* (London, 1855), i. 181–211, prints a full English version of it; there is a second-hand Latin text in J. Nichols, 'The history and antiquities of Barnwell Abbey and of Sturbridge Fair', *Bibliotheca topographica Britannica*, v. xxxviii (London, 1790), 31–44. Cf. also *Cal. papal letters*, viii. 484–5. The reasons why Popes Honorius and Sergius were chosen to carry the banner by the university and the significance of the Barnwell Process must await treatment elsewhere.

believed the rigmarole of legend and so-called history which he put out. A much more plausible theory was advanced by Peacock in 1841, who argued that the university developed as a result of the intellectual activities of the monks of Ely, Croyland and Barnwell and had its nucleus in the grammar schools at Cambridge. The motivation behind this interesting but impossible theory, which Denifle and Rashdall rejected out of hand, appears to have been the not unnatural desire on the part of a devoted son of Cambridge to minimize the debt owed to Oxford, since much is made of the influence which Paris and Orléans supposedly exerted on the growth of the university.[1] A last doomed attempt to save the idea of a spontaneous origin was made by Rouse Ball in a brilliant essay in which he sought to trace the beginnings of the university to 1189 or thereabouts, and suggested that it existed by 1209.[2] The age of special pleading has long since passed and it is now accepted that Cambridge as a university owes its origin to Oxford and Oxford alone.[3] Unlike Exeter, Lincoln or Northampton, Cambridge had no tradition as a centre of scholarship by the end of the twelfth century; apart from the grammar schools there was nothing remotely like the nucleus of a *studium* of higher learning, no schools of logic,

[1] Cf. G. Peacock, *Observations on the statutes of the university of Cambridge* (Cambridge, 1841), pp. 14–15; J. B. Mullinger, *The university of Cambridge*, i (Cambridge, 1873), 334. Creighton also favoured this theory up to a point; cf. Rashdall, *Universities*, iii. 277, nn. 1, 3, and Denifle, *Universitäten*, pp. 367–8.

[2] W. W. Rouse Ball, *Cambridge papers* (London, 1918), pp. 181–2, 186. His essay is far superior to the study of the question in E. V. Vaughn, *The origin and early development of the English universities to the close of the thirteenth century* (Univ. of Missouri Studies, Social Science ser., 2 ii [Columbia, 1908]), 108–9. The eighteenth-century German Augustinian historian, Ossinger, states that a Cardinal Thomas Ubrit (!) was the first founder of the university of Canterbury (*recte* Cambridge). Writing of his confessor Alvarus Cosme, who is said to have been a Portuguese Austin friar of the thirteenth century, Ossinger tells us that he was 'insignis theologus, acerrimus defensor fidei Catholicae in Anglia, ubi Eminentissimo Cardinali D.D. Thomae Ubrit tit.S. Croce in Jerusalem, qui primarius fundator Universitatis Cantuariensis [*sic*] exstitit, a Sacris Confessionibus fuit'; cf. J. F. Ossinger, *Bibliotheca Augustiniana* (Ingolstadt–Augsburg, 1768), p. 270. A *chronica* of Richard Wandalic is cited for the year 1257, in which reference is made, according to Ossinger, to a heresy at Cambridge. His writing of 'Cantuariensis' must be a slip for 'Cantebrigiensis'. English as well as continental writers sometimes mistook the one for the other. A heretic posing as a Carthusian was arrested at Cambridge in 1240. Cf. *Chron. Maj.* iv (1878), 32–4. Ossinger was a careful historian, but Cardinal Thomas Ubrit is unknown—the surname is surely a corruption—and Richard Wandalic and his chronicle are equally mysterious. The Augustinian scholar, it might be thought, confused him with Roger Wendover; this is not so.

[3] Cf. J. P. C. Roach in *V.C.H. Camb.* iii. 150–1.

theology and canon law, until the *suspendium clericorum* occurred at Oxford in 1209.[1] The only links with these faculties were possibly the *magistri* from Oxford whom Eustace, bishop of Ely, 1197–1215, took into his service before the secession began. They may have proved a valuable ally in winning the bishop's blessing for the dispersed scholars and smoothing over any difficulties made by the archdeacon of Ely and the master of glomery, the master in charge of the Cambridge grammar schools. But the foundation of the university was directly the result of the exodus of masters and scholars from Oxford in 1209. Granted that the university derived its origins from this migration, it may rightly be asked why the leaders decided to by-pass Northampton and settle in a place which had nothing special to offer from the intellectual point of view. The choice of Cambridge was indeed strange and ran counter to the pattern of university migrations. When the masters and scholars of Paris dispersed in 1229 some retired to Angers, Orléans and Toulouse, where there were long-established schools of standing; others came at the invitation of Henry III to Oxford and Cambridge. In 1260–1 scholars of the latter university migrated to Northampton and there was a recession from Oxford to Stamford, another prominent centre of higher education, in 1333. The 1209 dispersion was concentrated on Cambridge and Reading, the one as undistinguished as the other.[2] The group which settled at Reading doubtless wanted to remain within striking distance of Oxford, intending to return there as soon as justice or adequate satisfaction was secured. Those who took the road to Cambridge may also have had the intention of returning to Oxford and some, perhaps many, did go back after the papal legate, Nicholas, cardinal-bishop of Frascati, published his award on 25 June 1214.[3] But why did they decide in

[1] Richardson, 'The schools of Northampton in the twelfth century', *E.H.R.* lvi (1941), 602, suggests that Daniel Morley, who had connections with Cambridge, may have taught there; 'connections' is a vague term and may mean anything. The celebrated glossator, Franciscus Accursius, had connections with Oxford, but nobody holds that he organized a school in the university. Cf. G. L. Haskins, 'Three English documents relating to Francis Accursius', *Law Quarterly Review*, liv (1938), 87–94. The evidence that Grosseteste lectured at Cambridge *c.* 1199 is so flimsy and late as to be almost worthless. See D. Callus, O.P., 'Robert Grosseteste as a scholar', *Robert Grosseteste scholar and bishop*, ed. Callus (Oxford, 1955), p. 5, on the claim made by J. C. Russell, 'Richard of Bardney's account of Robert Grosseteste's early and middle life', *Medievalia et Humanistica*, ii (1943), 46, 51–2.

[2] Roger Wendover, *Flores historiarum*, ed. H. G. Hewlett, ii (Rolls series, 1887), 51; *Chron. Maj.* ii (1874), 525–6.

[3] *Med. Arch. Univ. Oxford*, i. 4–6.

the first place to part company with the Reading contingent? Why did they choose to go to Cambridge and not to Northampton or Stamford?

The answers to these questions may never be known; but Dr Emden in the introduction to his monumental register of Cambridge *alumni* provides a basis on which it is possible to construct a theory.[1] If one compares the charters granted by the bishops of Ely to the cathedral priory a marked difference will be noticed between those of William Longchamp (1189–97) and his immediate successor, Eustace, who was bishop at the time of the migration from Oxford. As a rule William's charters were witnessed by not more than two masters; their university credentials, incidentally, are open to question. Only one charter bears the signatures of three masters, the highest total.[2] Turning to the charters granted by Eustace, one is immediately struck by the number of *magistri* who attested the documents. It is rare to find a charter of his signed by less than four masters; sometimes we meet the names of six, seven, eight and even nine *magistri*.[3] The sudden appearance of a cluster of masters in Eustace's *familia* or at any rate witnessing his charters cannot be accidental. Comparable increases in the size of other bishops' staffs, excluding Ely, may not necessarily be put down to an exodus from Oxford; and it is possible that some of the *magistri* named as witnesses in Eustace's charters had joined his family before the 1209 dispersion. What cannot be denied is that, compared with the staff of his predecessor, not to mention earlier bishops of Ely, the number of *magistri* in Eustace's entourage is unprecedented. It can most easily be explained as an effect of the movement of masters from Oxford in 1209.[4]

1 See *BRUO*, p. xii. The mag. John Blund there mentioned is not the scholar listed *ibid.* p. 67.

2 Cf. Ely Dioc. Rec. G 3/28 (Liber M), pp. 160–8.

3 *Ibid.* pp. 168–7[2] (in this part of the register the pagination is duplicated).

4 None of Eustace's charters in the Ely register is dated. It can be stated that they are not earlier than 1199, since he does not, unlike Longchamp, use the title of chancellor in any of them; he was royal chancellor in May 1198–9. They may all date from 1209; in the second charter Hugh is named prior of Ely. According to *V.C.H. Camb.* ii. 209, he held office in 1200 and 1206. It may be suggested that he was still in office *c.* 1209. His successor, Roger, is stated to have died in 1210, but this is a mistake. The compiler of the list in *V.C.H.*, *loc. cit.*, wrongly assumed that Eustace died in that year; the date of his death was in fact 3 Feb. 1215. Roger, therefore, could have succeeded Hugh *c.* 1209 and died *c.* 1215. It is doubtful, however, if the charters were transcribed in chronological order. A charter of Eustace's in Cart. St John's Hosp., Camb., fo. 14^r, which lists four *magistri*, may be assigned to *c.* 1210–14 and is later than two in Ely Dioc. Rec. G 3/28, pp. 160[2]–6[2]. The second

Three of the masters were certainly at Oxford before the dispersion, and the names of some of them seem to indicate that they were natives of Cambridge, for example, mag. John and Geoffrey Grim, John Blund and John de Malketon.[1] The Grims were one of the leading families of the town in the reign of Stephen and all through the thirteenth century.[2] It was the clerk, Edward Grim of Cambridge, who stood by Thomas Becket on the fateful evening of 29 December 1170 and was himself wounded when he tried to save the archbishop. Blund or le Blund and Malketon are also Cambridge names.[3] In 1201 John Grim, then doctor of theology, was master or rector of the schools at Oxford, a position corresponding with that of head of the university or chancellor. He was still resident there *c.* 1206–9, and the signs are that he was the most likely leader or at least one of the driving forces behind the Cambridge venture.[4] His standing at Oxford coupled with his Cambridge background, assuming that he was born in the town, and the influence which his family could be depended upon to lend were possibly the decisive factors that persuaded his fellow-masters to set up business in Cambridge for the term of the *suspendium* at Oxford. If the initiative came from the masters who were natives of Cambridge and the eastern counties the fateful decision to settle for the time being by the banks of the Cam in 1209 seems rather more intelligible. All this, of course, is largely guesswork and rests on a very narrow basis indeed. Yet as a theory it has much to commend itself and provides at least a working hypothesis.

In addition to the Grims, Blund and Malketon, the following

of these was attested by mag. John Grim, the only one which he witnessed. He almost certainly arrived with the dispersed masters in 1209 and as the charter was also witnessed by Richard Barre, archdeacon of Ely, it is probably not later than *c.* 1210. Stephen de Ridale was archdeacon *c.* 1210–14. Cf. J. le Neve, *Fasti Ecclesiae Anglicanae*, ed. T. D. Hardy (Oxford, 1854), i. 350.

1 For these scholars cf. *BRUC*, pp. 67, 272, 386. Not all the *magistri* mentioned in charters of Eustace are listed.

2 Ely Dioc. Rec. G 3/28, p. 213; *Pleas before the king or his justices 1198–1202*, ed. D. M. Stenton, i (Selden Soc. lxvii [1953]), 290, no. 3067; *Great roll of the pipe... Michaelmas 1205*, ed. S. Smith (Pipe Roll Soc. lvii, n.s. xix [1941]), 86; A. Gray, *The priory of Saint Radegund* (CAS, octavo series, xxxi [1898]), 75, no. 3*a*, 92, no. 81, 93, no. 93, 95, no. 100*a*, 100, nos. 130, 132; 135, no. 320, 136, no. 332. A John Grim (not the master) was bailiff in 1278 and William Grim, chaplain, was at Cambridge by 1279. Cf. Stokes, *Outside the Trumpington gates*, p. 11; *Rotuli hundredorum*, ii (London, 1818), 382*a*.

3 Cf. Gray, *op. cit.* 92, no. 86, 93, no. 93; Stokes, *op. cit.* p. 12.

4 See *BRUC*, p. xii.

magistri, mostly members of Eustace's staff, probably lectured at Cambridge in 1209–15: Nicholas de Derlega, Thomas de Driffeld, John de Foxton, Adam de Horningsea, Richard de Kirkeham, Stephen de Maunecestre, John de Storteford, Adam of Tilney, Thomas de Whattele and Robert of York.[1] Of these the last two were like John Grim definitely Oxford graduates. Since John Grim attested only one of the bishop's charters it may be that he together with Horningsea, Maunecestre, Whattele and other masters who were not members of the episcopal family did most to organize the *studium*. The majority of the dispersed masters and scholars doubtless went back to Oxford when the ban was lifted in 1214.[2] But the continuity of schools at Cambridge after 1214 shows that there was no question of a mass movement back to the old university. The six years which elapsed between the dispersion in 1209 and the reopening of Oxford were sufficiently long to allow schools to be firmly established at Cambridge. How rapidly a faculty of arts, the oldest and most powerful faculty all through the medieval period, developed or how soon a university in the corporate and academic sense evolved we cannot say. The addition of some old and many new masters to the staffs of Eustace's successors during the critical period, 1215–28, following the reopening of the Oxford schools is evidence of growth.[3] Horningsea and Maunecestre, possibly two of the original founders, did not sever their connection with Cambridge, and as there is no evidence that the new *magistri* who witnessed charters of Robert of York, John of Fountains and Geoffrey de Burgo, studied at Oxford one may assume that they incepted at Cambridge.[4] A most significant advance in the status and organiza-

1 *BRUC*, pp. 185, 195, 241 (cf. p. 676), 315, 338–9, 397, 560 (cf. p. 683), 588, 632, 666. It is not stated that John de Foxton witnessed charters of Eustace, but cf. Ely Dioc. Rec. G 3/28, p. 167². Adam of Tilney was appointed archdeacon of Ely in 1214 and Robert of York was elected to succeed Eustace as bishop in 1215.

2 Mag. Henry de Welles appears to have hesitated about returning, that is, if he can be identified with the scholar who was at Oxford in 1228. Cf. *BRUC*, p. 625, where 'Eustace—1215' should read 'Robert of York, bishop-elect of Ely, between 1215 and 1219'.

3 The sheriff of Cambridge was ordered by the king on 18 Feb. 1218 to take steps to expel clerks who supported Louis of France. It has been assumed that these were probably students at Cambridge, but it is more likely that they were French clerks who accompanied Louis to England. Cf. *Rotuli litterarum clausarum*, i (1833), 377; Rymer, *Foedera*, I. i. 143, 150.

4 The *magistri* include William de Argentein, William de Bankes, Roger of Durham, John de Escalariis, Stephen de Hedon, Adam de Horningsea, Richard de

tion of the *studium* is evident by 4 June 1225, when the existence of a chancellor is recorded, apparently, for the first time.[1] Developments at the parent university must have been closely watched, for the institution of this office was inspired by the action of the bishop of Lincoln, Hugh of Wells, who appointed Grosseteste chancellor by 1221.[2] The bishop of Ely lost little time in following suit; and it is a tribute indeed to the progress of Cambridge that within four years of the first mention of a chancellor at Oxford it, too, had a head. The chancellor's name is not disclosed. As a rule chancellors were masters of either theology or canon law or civil law. Since the official mentioned in 1225 appears in the capacity of a judge at an ecclesiastical court outside the university,[3] it may be assumed that he was a doctor of canon law[4] and could well be mag. Richard de Leycestria or Wethringsette, the author of the very popular manual for parish priests and confessors, the *Summa* 'Qui bene presunt presbiteri'.[5] He probably held office by *c.* 1222 and was still chancellor

Kenilleworthe, Stephen de Maunecestre, William de Rising, Richard of Stow, Ernulph de Straham, William de Westhale. Cf. Ely Dioc. Rec. G 3/28, pp. 167[2]–76; *BRUC*, pp. 16, 35, 202, 214, 297, 315, 336, 397, 482, 561, 630. The names of certain of these masters, viz. Bankes, Horningsea, Stow, Straham and Westhale, suggest that they were natives of Cambridgeshire and adjacent parts. Roger of Durham was not a member of the staff of Eustace; the statement in *BRUC*, p. 202, is inaccurate. He witnessed a charter of Robert of York (Ely Dioc. Rec. G 3/28, p. 167[2]).

1 *Curia regis rolls, 9–10 Henry III*, xii (1957), 129–30, no. 646; *Bracton's notebook*, ed. F. W. Maitland, ii (London, 1887), 553, no. 722. These references were overlooked in *V.C.H. Camb.* iii. 7, n. 97, 151. Hitherto, the earliest mention of a chancellor was noted by Salter, 'The beginning of Cambridge University', *E.H.R.* xxxvi (1921), 420, in a document of 1226. A correction of his source-reference will be found in *V.C.H. Camb.* iii. 151, n. 16. Rouse Ball, *Camb. papers*, p. 182, had some inkling of the 1225 reference, but he cited no source.

2 There was no chancellor by 25 July 1214. Cf. *Snappe's formulary*, p. 319, where Grosseteste's claim to be considered the first chancellor of Oxford is considered. The letter of Honorius III, 30 March 1221, the earliest reference to a chancellor of Oxford, is printed in *Med. Arch. Univ. Oxford*, i. 10.

3 The entry in the *Curia regis* rolls, *locc. citt.*, has to do with a suit brought by Adam of Lynn against Charles of Yarmouth and his wife, Alice. They had sued him in an ecclesiastical court over a lay fee before the archdeacon of Bedford, the chancellor of Cambridge and the precentor of Barnwell. The sheriff of Cambridge testified to the king by 4 June 1225 that the justices were clerks. A mandate was accordingly sent to the bishop of Norwich to distrain the archdeacon and the chancellor, presumably because both were of the diocese; and Geoffrey, then bishop-elect of Ely (2–28 June 1225), was ordered to distrain the precentor of Barnwell.

4 There was no faculty of civil law at this time.

5 Cf. *BRUC*, pp. 367, 679, and A. L. Kellogg, 'St Augustine and the Parson's Tale', *Traditio*, viii (1952), 425.

perhaps *c.* 1232–46.[1] If he was not the first he is certainly the earliest known chancellor of Cambridge before Hugh de Hotton (1246).[2]

The institution of the office by 1225 at the latest is important. It means among other things that the masters and scholars were treated by the bishop as a distinct canonical society within the diocese and were exempt from the jurisdiction of the archdeacon of Ely and the dean of Cambridge. It may be that the body which migrated from Oxford in 1209 were at no time subject to the control of the archdeacon. By 1225 at all events the position is clear. Jurisdiction and direction of the *studium* were vested in the chancellor, whose immediate superior was the ordinary of the diocese. The holder of the office was in the first instance the delegate of the bishop, from whom he received his canonical powers. These were chiefly judicial but in virtue of his office the chancellor was capable of granting a scholar the licence to proceed to the *magisterium*. The first chancellor was doubtless appointed directly by the bishop, on whose will depended the length of the term of office. No doubt he acted on the advice of the regents, who we may presume were allowed to have some voice in determining the duration of the commission. Under the first constitution of the university no limit is placed on the number of years a master might continue as chancellor; custom no doubt was the guiding rule. By *c.* 1250 the days of direct appointment by the bishop had passed and the right to elect chancellors was reserved exclusively to the regent masters. This is good evidence indeed that the *studium* enjoyed the status of a *universitas*, for the right to elect officers, particularly a head whom all recognized as the *maior inter omnes*, was one of the most important privileges of a university according to the romano-canonical concept of a corporate body whether academic, capitular, conventual or civil. Other characteristics of a *universitas* were the right to hold property in common with its attendant obligations, to sue or be sued in the law-courts as a 'person', and the power to make written constitutions or statutes binding under oath or pledge of faith on all

1 If Richard wrote his *Summa* as chancellor, which is quite possible, his appointment may date from 1215–22. He would appear to have been chancellor at least by *c.* 1232, for he attested a charter of Maurice Ruffus or le Rus, a prominent Cambridge citizen, who was dead about that time. Cf. Cart. St John's Hosp. fo. 19r; Stokes, *Outside the Trumpington gates*, pp. 38–9; *Pedes finium: or fines relating to the county of Cambridge*, ed. W. Rye (CAS, octavo series, xxvi [1891]), 16, no. 31.

2 Stokes, 'Early university property', *CASP*, xiii, n.s. vii (1908–9), 168, 177, suggests that a certain John Michael was an early chancellor. This is not so.

members of the society, and likewise authority to punish or expel those who refused to obey the elected officials of the community.[1] The clearest sign that the *studium* at Cambridge ceased to be a free association of persons engaged in teaching and studies at an advanced level and had become a statute-making body is its acquisition of the status of a *universitas*.

To fix the year of transition from what we may call the primitive state to that of a properly constituted university is extremely difficult even in the case of the great universities of Bologna, Paris and Oxford, or indeed any university of the early thirteenth century.[2] At Paris the masters, that is the regent masters, for they were the 'university', seem to have taken the first steps towards forming a *universitas* about 1209. Though the earliest positive proof of its status appears in 1221, there is good reason for thinking that the masters constituted a legal corporation or 'university' by 1215.[3] The evidence for Oxford and Cambridge is less satisfactory. Oxford admittedly was an important centre of study before 1165 and rose to a position of eminence during the following twenty or thirty years; but it is virtually impossible to determine when the masters formed themselves into a university.[4] The legatine ordinance of 1214 is extremely vague. The *studium* is not called *universitas*; indeed it seems to have been only loosely organized, since the papal legate left it to the bishop to decide whether the scholars should be placed under the authority of the archdeacon or his official, or under

1 The views of Savigny, Gierke, Maitland, Denifle and Rashdall on the idea of a *universitas* or the 'fiction' theory of a corporation are well known. The best study of the Parisian type of university, the model of Oxford and Cambridge, is by G. Post, 'Parisian masters as a corporation, 1200–1246', *Speculum*, ix (1934), 421–45, reprinted in the same author's *Studies in medieval legal thought* (Princeton, 1964), pp. 27–60. References here are to the article in *Speculum*. Cf. also P. Michaud-Quantin, 'Collectivités médiévales et institutions antiques', *Antike und Orient im Mittelalter* (Miscellanea mediaevalia, i [Berlin, 1962]), 239–52, and the admirable critique of the nature of a corporation in H. Lubasz, 'The corporate borough in the common law of the late year-book period', *Law Quarterly Review*, lxxx (1964), 228–43.

2 Cf. Rashdall, *Universities*, ii. 65–8, on the foundation of the 'university' of Palencia in 1208–9.

3 Post, *Speculum*, ix (1934), 444–5. For a balanced appraisal of conflicting opinions on this question cf. Stelling-Michaud, 'L'histoire des universités au moyen âge et à la renaissance au cours des vingt-cinq dernières années', *XIe congrès international des sciences historiques, rapports* (Göteborg–Stockholm–Uppsala, 1960), i. 111.

4 Salter, 'The medieval university of Oxford', *History*, xiv (1929–30), 57–61. Richardson, *loc. cit.* p. 604, tends to minimize unduly the importance of Oxford by saec. xii*ex.*

a chancellor.[1] This was done by 1221 when, as we have seen, the pope was aware of the existence of a chancellor of Oxford.[2] The king's writ of 3 May 1231 refers to the 'university'.[3] It may come as a surprise then to find Innocent IV writing in 1246 of the *studium* and not the university of Oxford,[4] especially since Gregory IX in 1233 addressed himself to the 'chancellor and university of scholars' at Cambridge. The non-use of the term *universitas* in papal documents should not be interpreted as evidence that the Holy See did not recognize the masters and scholars of Oxford, for example, as a corporate body;[5] the terms *studium* and *universitas* by this time were not mutually exclusive, and in any case Pope Innocent was not concerned with the juridical status of the university of Oxford but its organization precisely as a *studium* or what we may call an academic centre.[6] Allowance, too, must be made for the vagaries of the papal chancery, where there seems to have existed some doubt as late as 1247 concerning the actual location of the university.[7] The first grant of a charter on the part of the crown dates from the following year,[8] and in a letter of 6 October 1254 addressed to the 'university of masters and scholars' Innocent IV confirmed *en bloc* the immunities, liberties, ancient and reasonable customs, 'necnon constitutiones approbatas et honestas' of the university.[9] What precise constitutions Oxford possessed at this date apart from two statutes enacted in 1252–3 is uncertain. There is reason to believe that certain constitutions were in vogue from a much earlier period, though not before 1214.[10] A statute compelling each master to enter the names of his scholars on a roll is stated to have been drawn up and registered 'ab

1 Cf. *Med. Arch. Univ. Oxford*, i. 3: 'uel archidiaconi loci seu eius officialis aut cancellarii quem episcopus Lincolniensis ibidem scolaribus preficiet.' To be precise the function of the bishop's delegate, as Salter (*ibid.* p. 8) points out, was to rule not the schools but the scholars.

2 Grosseteste held the office at the time, although the bishop, Hugh of Wells, forbade him to call himself 'chancellor'. Cf. *Snappe's formulary*, p. 319.

3 *Close rolls, 1227–31*, pp. 586–7. The writ, which was also made out in favour of Cambridge, does not explicitly speak of the 'university of Oxford'.

4 *Les registres d'Innocent IV*, ed. É. Berger, i (Paris, 1884), 277, no. 1859.

5 The term 'university' was applied to Paris in a papal letter for the first time only in 1245. Cf. Post, *loc. cit.* p. 425.

6 Cf. Denifle, *Universitäten*, pp. 5–11; Rashdall, *Universities*, i. 5–6.

7 *Reg. Innocent IV*, i. 488, no. 3243.

8 *Med. Arch. Univ. Oxford*, i. 18–19.

9 *Munimenta academica*, ed. H. Anstey, i (Rolls series, 1868), 26. Cf. *ibid.* p. 27; *Reg. Innocent IV*, iii. 519, nos. 8081–2; *Cal. papal letters*, i. 306.

10 The statute or ordinance of 1252 on preserving the peace refers to existing 'antiqua statuta' (*SAUO*, 85, 24).

antiquo', but it is unlikely to have been made until *c.* 1231.[1] The wording of the controversial statute *De theologis licenciandis ad incipiendum*, which was finally enacted after much difficulty on 12 March 1253, definitely implies that Oxford had no register of its constitutions by the middle of the thirteenth century.[2]

The presence of a chancellor in Cambridge by 1225 suggests that he and the masters and scholars under his jurisdiction formed a distinct ecclesiastical corporation within the organization of the diocese of Ely. Whether the first chancellor was appointed by Eustace, Robert of York, John of Fountains or Geoffrey de Burgo, the corporation, we may take it, derived its juridical constitution from the fiat of one of these bishops. That is to say, the *studium*, although founded by the masters who led the secession to Cambridge in 1209, received its title and its capacity to act as a *universitas* from one of the bishops who ruled the see of Ely between 1209 and 1225. The earliest instance of the actual title of 'university' being applied to Oxford and Cambridge occurs, as we have seen, in one of the writs issued by Henry III on 3 May 1231. It must be admitted, however, that the phrase 'consuetudo universitatis' is open to question. In none of the four writs do we find specific mention of 'the university of Oxford' or 'the university of Cambridge'.[3] On the other hand, the context of these writs leaves little doubt that the king was not referring to the custom of universities everywhere but in fact to the custom obtaining at both Oxford and Cambridge.[4] Moreover, although the chancellor in either case is not called 'chancellor of the university', it is evident that Henry III assumed that the chancellor and masters would act or were in the habit of acting as a corporate entity, even though the terms of the writs seem to imply that the chancellor required the authorization of the masters or at least their concurrence before taking action against rebellious clerks.[5] Needless to say, this cannot be interpreted as

[1] Gibson, *ibid.* 82, 13, dates this statute 'Before 1231'. The reference to 'quod ab antiquo fuerit ordinatum et registratum, scilicet "quod quilibet magister habeat nomina scolarium suorum et cetera"' (*ibid.* 61–6–8) seems to indicate a different statute.

[2] Cf. *ibid.* 49, 15–16.

[3] In later charters the word 'university' is almost invariably followed by the place-name 'Oxonie' or as the case may be 'Cantebrigie'; if the place-name has been mentioned earlier in a document the phrase usually reads 'universitatis predicte'.

[4] It is significant that the Cambridge constitution on this matter, i.e. the renting of hostels, makes no reference to the relevant writ. See below, p. 77.

[5] 'providimus quod quotiens predicti cancellarius et magistri perpenderint...et secundum quod predictus episcopus tibi significabit et predicti cancellarii [*sic*] et

meaning that the chancellor was not in law the recognized head of the masters. Expressions like the 'dean and chapter' or 'mayor and bailiffs', and hence 'chancellor and masters', must be taken as denoting a body corporate, which is not to say that a dean, chancellor or mayor even as heads of their respective corporations could not act on their own authority in matters which did not affect the common good of their communities. But if the writs of 1231 are ambiguous, and hence the status of both Oxford and Cambridge, the existence of the 'university' of Cambridge was recognized by the Holy See by 14 June 1233. A letter of Gregory IX of that date was addressed to the 'chancellor and university of scholars at Cambridge'.[1] As in other papal documents, 'scholars' here is a generic term covering both masters and students. It is possible that the pope assumed that the students composed, as at Bologna, the *universitas*, but the term *scolares* was used even by popes who studied at Paris and were well aware that the masters constituted the 'essential university' or the corporation as such.[2] The crucial point about Gregory IX's letter is that it explicitly accords the title as well as the status of *universitas* to the schools at Cambridge, and, what is not less significant, the *ius non trahi extra*. Rashdall calls this—he is referring to Paris—'*the* characteristic university privilege', but he failed to notice that Cambridge was the first university to obtain the coveted *ius*, which was not granted to Paris until 1245 nor to Oxford before 1254.[3] Though the papal indults directed to Paris and Oxford differ from the Cambridge concession to the extent that scholars could not be summoned beyond Paris or Oxford whereas the indult granted to Cambridge made the diocese of Ely the boundary and not the town of Cambridge, it was essentially the same privilege. Indeed in some respects Cambridge secured better terms than did the university of Paris.[4] The indult of 14 June 1233

magistri tibi dicent...et...secundum consilium predictorum cancellarii et magistrorum...' (*Close rolls, 1227–31*, p. 586).

1 'Cancellario et universitati scolarium Cantebrig. Eliensis diocesis' (*Reg. Grégoire IX*, i. 779, no. 1389; Denifle, *Universitäten*, p. 370, n. 627). In the body of the letter the pope refers to 'quenquam de universitate vestra'.

2 Cf. Post, *loc. cit.* p. 434.

3 *Chart. Univ. Paris.* i. 181, no. 142; cf. *ibid.* p. 235, no. 207; p. 400, no. 351; and Rashdall, *Universities*, i. 342, 418 and n. 5. For the indult to Oxford cf. *Cal. papal letters*, i. 306; Rashdall, *op. cit.* iii. 55.

4 The privilege was limited to causes (contracts are specified in the Oxford indult) which occurred within the city of Paris and did not empower the rector of the university to adjudicate. It is not surprising that neither the chancellor nor the

vests in the chancellor of Cambridge a judicial power which the bishop was incapable of granting him, a power which no archdeacon possessed *ex officio*, and in effect placed the chancellor's court on the same footing as that of the bishop with regard to suits which would otherwise have been reserved to judges delegate of the pope. From the point of view of jurisdiction the bishop was not more privileged than the chancellor of the university; their competence to hear and decide cases delegated by the Holy See was derived equally and independently from the same source. As judge delegate of the pope the bishop could not withdraw into his own court the kind of suit envisaged in the papal letter of 14 June 1233 unless a scholar-defendant preferred not to appear before the chancellor.[1]

The indult of Gregory IX puts beyond a shadow of doubt the status of the *studium* as a juridical entity and the office of the chancellor as head of the *universitas* of masters and scholars.[2] Though it lacked one of the properties of a corporation, a common seal, this in no way detracts from its constitution as a corporate body.[3] It had a recognized head and was regarded by both pope and king as a lawful subject of corporate privileges. By 1233 the regent masters, the governing body and legislative authority, were entitled to elect officers, make constitutions and incorporate new members either by creating masters from among the scholars or by admitting graduates of other universities to the office of regent. One may now

bishop of Paris was delegated; relations between them and the university were seldom harmonious. The pope solved the problem by appointing an extra-diocesan commission to act.

1 The pope's letter runs: 'auctoritate vobis presentium indulgemus, ne quis de cetero predictarum clausularum [sc. *quidam alii* and *rebus aliis*] pretextu quenquam de universitate vestra, filii scolares, paratum coram te, fili cancellarie, vel diocesano episcopo iustitiam de se conquerentibus exhibere, trahere possit ad iudicium extra diocesim Eliensem' (*Reg. Grégoire IX*, i. 779–80, no. 1389; Denifle, *Universitäten*, p. 370, n. 627). The indult in keeping with papal custom was limited to three years. A similar privilege granted by Alexander IV to Paris in 1259 was not effective for more than five years. Cf. *Chart. Univ. Paris.* i. 400, no. 351. The indult granted to Oxford in 1254 also retained its validity for only five years. It was renewed in 1281 for the same period.

2 It is characteristic of papal documents of this period that in a letter addressed to the bishop of Ely the day after the above concession Gregory IX speaks of the 'chancellor and scholars' and not the 'university'. Cf. *Reg. Grégoire IX*, i. 779, no. 1388; Denifle, *op. cit., loc. cit.* n. 626; *Royal and other historical letters illustrative of the reign of Henry III*, ed. W. W. Shirley, i (Rolls series, 1862), 552–3, no. 32. As Post, *loc. cit.* p. 425, points out, the absence of the term *universitas* in addresses does not imply that a legal corporation was non-existent.

3 See below, pp. 55–6.

speak with confidence of the 'university of Cambridge'; but unless a superior faculty was established by this time we must refrain from using the term 'university' in the sense of a *studium generale*.[1] Indeed the earliest definite evidence of a corporate act on the part of the chancellor and regent masters derives from the year 1246. The deed deserves to be printed exactly as promulgated, not because of its intrinsic value but rather on account of its historical significance as the first definite manifestation of concerted action by the *universitas*. It reads:

Nouerint vniuersi has literas visuri uel audituri quod Magister Hugo de hottun Cancellarius uniuersitatis Cantebrigiensis et omnes ibidem regentes ad instanciam et peticionem venerabilis Patris Hugonis dei gratia Elyensis episcopi concesserunt Magistro et fratribus hospitalis sancti Iohannis Cantebrigie ad sustentacionem infirmorum qui deferuntur ibidem tam in lectis quam in sepulturis eorum. Vt sine taxacione aliqua facienda, liceat eis duas domos distinctim habitabiles Iuxta ecclesiam beati petri extra portas de Trumpiton' [*sic*] quibuscumque et eciam qualitercumque uelint et possint libere pro eorum uoluntate locare. In cuius rei testimonium, predictus Cancellarius. et Magister Gerardus de Byngham archidiaconus Dorsett'. et magister Willelmus de Wermington. et magister Garner. et magister Iohannes de Lyndeseya. Et magister G. de Danteseya. et magister S. de Grymmesby pro se et pro omnibus aliis huic scripto sigilla sua apposuerunt. Actum anno domini. M°.cc°.xlvj.[2]

The remains of six (there were originally seven) seals are still attached to the document. Obviously, the university did not possess a common seal, which was adopted only by *c.* 1260–70.[3] The lack of a

1 See below, p. 176.

2 The original is in St John's College, Camb., Muniments, drawer 3, no. 58. The deed is written in a neat hand without embellishment on parchment from which a blank piece has been cut away. The whole measured 112 × 200 mm. I am deeply grateful to Mr F. P. White, M.A., keeper of the college records, for providing me with every facility in examining the document and also for making available to me a photostat of a transcript made by a former librarian, the late Mr Gatty.

3 The earliest pointer to the existence of a university seal occurs in a letter of Richard de Gedeneye, chancellor, and the other regent masters to Henry III (*Royal letters... Henry III*, ii [1866], 165–6, no. DXLIII). In the original, P.R.O. S.C. 1/3/2, the relevant part of the letter is defective. It reads: 'Et ut hec omnia magis in luce clarescant ⟨sigillum⟩ vniuersitatis nostr⟨e huic scripto⟩ duximus apponendum. Valeat serenitas vestra per tempora longiora.' The text is undated. It cannot be earlier than 1259 since the king is not styled duke of Normandy, a title which did not disappear from English documents until after the signing of the Treaty of Paris on 4 Dec. of that year. Cf. P. Chaplais, 'The making of the Treaty of Paris and the royal style', *E.H.R.* lxvii (1952), 250. Shirley suggests the letter dates from 1260 but cites as his reason a patent roll of 54 Henry III. This, however, has nothing to do with the contents of the letter; it concerns the fracas in which northern and southern scholars were involved in 1260; cf. *Cal. pat. rolls, 1258–66*, pp. 136

university seal does not negative the corporate nature of the act, and the practice of several regent masters appending their individual seals in the name of the university to a deed is found as late as 1221 and 1229 at Paris.[1] It will be noticed that the grant was made by the chancellor, Hugh de Hotton, and all the regent masters. This, as we shall see, is precisely what the constitution of the university requires when there is question of acts which affected the common good of the university. They as a body constituted convocation or the general congregation of the university; it was not until the opening years of the fourteenth century that the non-regent masters were co-opted as members.[2]

The name of the chancellor and those of his fellow regent masters are worth bearing in mind, since the date of the document is so close to that of the Angelica text that it may well be that the first constitution of the university was promulgated by Hugh de Hotton and the other masters who witnessed the deed. It may be taken for granted that Hotton was either doctor of theology or canon law or less likely civil law, but unfortunately the faculties in which the other *magistri* were regents cannot be named.[3] Their agreement to exempt the two hostels, which stood adjacent to each other though comprising distinct houses near the church of St Peter outside the Trumpington gates, brings us back to what was almost certainly the first written custom of the university, and provides in addition a link with the future foundation of Peterhouse.[4]

It was not until the beginning of the thirteenth century that

142, 182. The letter in question was written by the university in answer to a complaint made by the bailiffs of Cambridge that the university refused to abide by the tallage recently levied for the repair of the king's mill. The date, therefore, may be as late as 1267. Cf. *Cal. pat. rolls, 1264–8*, p. 350. But the university certainly had a common seal by April 1270. Cf. CUA, doc. no. 3 (the seal to this original indenture has been removed); Prynne, *The third tome of an exact chronological vindication*, p. 467; Dyer, *Privileges*, i. 67; Cooper, *Annals*, i. 52.

1 Cf. *Chart. Univ. Paris.* i. 100, no. 42; 118, no. 62. Oxford was probably not authorized to use a common seal before 1253. See Rashdall, *Universities*, iii. 49, n. 1. Indeed Paris did not acquire the right to have one until 1246; but the absence of a seal cannot be construed as evidence of the non-corporate nature of a university. Cf. Post, *loc. cit.* pp. 441–3.

2 See below, pp. 240–4.

3 On Hotton cf. *BRUC*, p. 316, and for Bingham, Danteseya, Garner, Grimesby, Lindsey and Wermington see *ibid.* pp. 62, 177, 251, 272, 370, 628. Lindsey was official of Lincoln in 1263, which suggests that he eventually graduated as doctor of either canon or civil law.

4 Cf. Stokes, *Outside the Trumpington gates*, pp. 16, 77.

universities began to give statutory form to their customs, which, however, continued to regulate most aspects of university life. They were never entirely displaced by statutes or written laws, for these were of their nature isolated measures and could not possibly cover every detail of the administration and general organization of a university. At Paris *c.* 1208–9 cracks began to appear in the fabric which rested on customs that for long had been sacrosanct. New masters in arts refused to be bound by certain traditional practices with regard to academic dress, the order of lectures and disputations, and funerals. To counteract this departure from custom and, we may assume, to forestall similar innovations on the part of 'progressives' the university appointed a commission of eight masters drawn from the faculties of theology, canon law and arts. Their allotted task was to reduce the unwritten customs governing the matters which had been disregarded by the younger element among the masters to formal statutes enforceable under oath. Any new inceptor who refused to subscribe to these statutes was liable to be expelled from the university, a penalty which was also imposed on those who had the temerity to violate their oaths.[1] That this idea of promulgating statutes was in itself an innovation is evident from the action of Cardinal Robert de Courson, who in 1215 set definite limits to the capacity of the university to make statutes; and in 1231 Gregory IX in his bull *Parens scientiarum*, the so-called Magna Carta of the university, only slightly enlarged the statutory powers of the masters.[2]

At no time during the formative years of the Cambridge constitutions was any bar placed by church or state on the fundamental rights of the university to regulate its internal life and take whatever steps were feasible to safeguard its wider interests. Henry III provided the necessary legal sanctions when necessary.[3] For the rest, he was content, provided the university did not encroach on rights of the crown, to treat it as any other ecclesiastical corporation and left its

[1] *Chart. Univ. Paris.* i. 67, no. 8. Cf. Denifle, *Universitäten*, pp. 107–8; Rashdall, *Universities*, i. 299–300.

[2] *Chart. Univ. Paris.* i. 79, no. 20; 137, no. 79.

[3] It will not be out of place to recall Maitland's summing-up of the relationship between a royal charter and the constitution of a corporation: 'the function of a royal charter was not that of "erecting a corporation" or regulating a corporation which already existed, but that of bestowing "liberties and franchises" upon a body which, within large limits, was free to give itself a constitution' (*The charters of the borough of Cambridge*, edd. F. W. Maitland and M. Bateson [Cambridge, 1901], p. viii).

supervision to the bishop of Ely.[1] If any opposition in the statutory field was to be encountered it was more likely to come from this quarter. The university was fortunate to have in Hugh of Northwold, who ruled the see when the constitution was taking shape, an ordinary singularly devoid of suspicion and prejudice. Later in the century, when bishops did interfere, notably Hugh Balsham and William of Louth, they respected and praised the statutory work of the university. Balsham stated in 1264 that his one aim was to uphold and extend its privileges. He was not prepared, however, to tolerate arrogance in any form. In 1276 he had occasion to remind the chancellor that he was his subject, and forbade the university under pain of excommunication to make statutes prejudicial to his jurisdiction or that of the archdeacon unless it consulted with him, the bishop, beforehand and obtained his assent.[2] Towards the end of the century the chancellor summoned a canon of Barnwell to appear in his court to answer a plea entered by a scholar of the university. For his high-handedness he received a stinging rebuke from mag. Guy de Coventre, official of Bishop Louth:

> Lord chancellor, all the jurisdiction you possess is yours by grace of my lord, the bishop, who granted you jurisdiction over the clerks. The archdeacon, however, has jurisdiction over rectors, vicars, etc. One thing only the bishop has reserved to himself, namely, jurisdiction over religious men. Do not, then, take away from my lord what is his if he pleases.[3]

[1] Edward I on 27 April 1292 ordered his justices, Elias de Buckingham and Hugh de Cressingham, to desist from proceeding with an assize of novel disseisin brought against the university by the prior of Barnwell, Simon de Asceles. The king's writ ran: 'Vobis mandamus, quod habito respectu ad Consuetudines et Statuta praedicta [*sc.* of the university], ad captionem Assisae praedictae Nobis et nostro Consilio super hoc inconsultis, nullatenus procedatis' (Prynne, *op. cit.* pp. 467–8). In the fourteenth century the friars took exception to several statutes, first in 1304–6 and again in 1364–5. In both instances they appealed to the Holy See, but only once did they succeed in having a statute quashed. This was in 1366, when parliament, following an injunction from Urban V to the archbishop of Canterbury, annulled a statute forbidding the friars to receive aspirants under the age of eighteen. Cf. *Cal. papal letters*, i. 91; *Rot. Parl.* ii (1783), 290; Gransden, 'A fourteenth-century chronicle from the Grey Friars at Lynn', *E.H.R.* lxxii (1957), 276–7. For a statute of *c.* 1386 which the prior general of the Austin Friars lamented in vain, see below, pp. 264–5.

[2] CUA, doc. no. 5; *Vet. Lib. Archid. Elien.* p. 23.

[3] *Liber mem. ecc. de Bernewelle*, p. 185; cf. Rashdall, *Universities*, iii. 280, n. 5. The official was not quite accurate in stating that rectors and vicars were subject to the archdeacon. Balsham in 1276 had made it clear that jurisdiction over these belonged to the chancellor, provided the principal cause of their coming to Cambridge was to study.

The attitude, none the less, of the bishops of Ely was markedly different from that of their colleagues at Paris and Lincoln. No sooner did the masters at Paris begin to avail themselves of the faculty granted by Courson in 1215 to initiate statutes than they were excommunicated by the bishop and a new papal legate for making constitutions binding under 'oath, faith or penalty'.[1] Nothing daunted, they proceeded despite a renewal of the sentence to enact or re-enact statutes, and in 1221 the bishop, Guillaume de Seignelay, reported to the Holy See that the 'masters and scholars have made and frequently do still make certain constitutions binding under oath which may rightly be called confederacies or even conspiracies'.[2] An echo of this charge will be found in a proclamation of Oliver Sutton, bishop of Lincoln (1280–99), concerning statutes made by the university of Oxford.[3] Before his time, Hugh of Wells and Grosseteste kept a wary eye on the pretensions of the chancellors and masters; but serious differences did not arise until the episcopates of Lexington and Sutton. Unlike Hugh Balsham, who at no time challenged the validity of the statutes enacted at Cambridge, both of these bishops took strong exception to customs and statutes of Oxford.[4] If the bishops of Paris and Lincoln took the view that the statutes made by their respective universities were in truth 'conspiracies' their attitude is understandable.[5] Both universities were essentially non-episcopal in origin and owed their growth and fame not to any exceptional largesse on the part of the bishops but to their own inherent potentialities and exertions. Cambridge, on the other hand, was very much an episcopal creation. It remained of necessity tied to the see of Ely, and in the thirteenth century because of its youth and weakness, compared with the age and strength of Paris and Oxford, it was not likely to assert its independence or cause worry in the minds of the bishops of the diocese. That the *studium* was established at all and did not become still-born in 1214 was due in large measure to the patronage of Bishop Eustace

[1] *Chart. Univ. Paris.* i. 87–90, nos. 30–1.

[2] *Ibid.* 98, no. 41.

[3] Rashdall, *Universities*, iii. 118, n. 2.

[4] The statutes are printed in *SAUO*, 96–7 (1280); 107, 16–108, 9 (1257).

[5] For a summary account of the relations between the bishops of Lincoln and the university of Oxford cf. Rashdall, *Universities*, iii. 114–21. A more benign view of Sutton's standpoint is taken by R. M. T. Hill, 'Oliver Sutton, bishop of Lincoln, and the university of Oxford', *Transactions of the Royal Historical Society*, 4th series, xxxi (1949), 1–16.

and his successors, who merited the title of founders of the university.[1] Without their blessing and active collaboration the efforts of the early *magistri* and the king would have come to nought. The first masters, as we have seen, were intimately associated with those bishops, and the see of Ely continued to be far more closely identified with the life of the university than was the case at Paris or Oxford. This meant, no doubt, that the bishops of Ely were in a better position to dominate it; but it may also mean that being surer of its dependence and allegiance they were able to trust it. Although the first constitution reads as if the bishop was non-existent, nobody could have had any illusion about his position.[2]

Edward I in 1292 was to refer to the 'statutes and customs of the same (i.e. Cambridge) university hitherto observed there from the foundation of the same without which it could not possibly exist'.[3] Customs is all that we can speak of before 1231. The dividing line between custom and statute may not always be clear-cut; but statements concerning customs dating from the beginnings of the university and references to 'most ancient statutes' cannot be accepted at their face value. There is no doubt that the customs of Oxford, at least before 1229, were all that the nascent university at Cambridge possessed in the way of constitutional directives. By 1231 the earliest datable statute had not advanced beyond the status of *consuetudo*. It is quite possible, of course, that the king's writ which refers to the

[1] In 1304 the Franciscans and Dominicans, protesting against certain statutes enacted by the university, referred to the 'loci diocesanum a quo studium Cantebrigie recepisse dicitur primarium fundamentum' (Moorman, *Grey Friars in Cambridge*, p. 228; cf. *ibid.* p. 234).

[2] Rashdall, *Universities*, iii. 280–1, attached undue weight to a remark made by mag. John de Clipston, official of Bishop Simon Montacute, in 1337 to the effect that he would not approve of any statutes made by the university without the consent of the bishop. The point at issue was the election of Richard de Harlyng as chancellor. Such remarks were common form, and the official repeated his declaration again in 1339 when the newly elected chancellor, Richard de Lyng, sought confirmation; cf. Ely Dioc. Rec. G I, [1], pt 1, fo. 9r. The official was not claiming any right to prohibit the university from making statutes unless the bishop agreed to them in advance; he simply entered a caveat against the enactment of a statute or statutes which might infringe the bishop's rights and jurisdiction, as was his duty. The episode is characteristic of the conflict which smouldered on at Oxford as late as 1369. Incidentally, Rashdall, p. 55, n. 1, was mistaken in assuming that Alexander IV did not include the university when he stated that the bishop of Lincoln had jurisdiction over the 'universitas clericorum castri Oxon.' Salter's correction of Rashdall on this point is noted *ibid.*, by Dr Emden.

[3] '...Statuta et Consuetudines ejusdem Universitatis a prima fundatione ejusdem hactenus ibidem observata, sine quibus dicta Universitas nullatenus stare posset' (Prynne, *op. cit.* p. 467).

taxing of hostels by two masters and two burgesses uses the term without excluding its being a formal statute, yet we should hesitate to describe the constitution in the Angelica text as having been enacted by the university before 1231. In documents of this period it is almost impossible to distinguish custom from statute; but if *consuetudo* meant something more than an unwritten agreement between the town and the university we should probably find the word *constitutio* or *ordinatio* used in the writ. At the same time, it cannot be without some significance that the statute in question is entered in the constitution of the university without any reference to the royal writ of 3 May 1231. Consequently, there is some ground for thinking that it was drawn up, perhaps not in exactly the same form as it appears in the Angelica text, by 1231.[1] In the next chapter the origins and dating of such statutes as lend themselves to analysis along these lines will be considered. It is not unlikely that the earliest regulations made by the university took the form of proclamations issued by the chancellor, as happened at Oxford.[2] A passage in the constitution clearly implies that the chancellor of Cambridge not only had power to issue orders or prohibitions, which is about all that the earliest Oxford statutes promulgated by or in the name of the chancellor amount to, but the right to make statutes as such. He was not on that account a law unto himself; indeed he was expressly forbidden to make any new statutes without the consent of the regent masters.[3] This restraint existed probably from the beginning of statute-making at Cambridge, and we may presume that long before the constitution was adopted every statute had to be approved by convocation, that is, by the chancellor and the regents, and carried by a majority vote. Whatever independent legislative powers a chancellor may have possessed at an earlier period were severely curtailed under the constitution. Henceforth, his proper function was to maintain the statutes enacted in common by the regents, in other words the constitution.[4]

Prior to the introduction of formal statutes the most potent weapon at the disposal of the university for enforcing the observance of its customs was the chancellor's faculty to excommunicate. The usefulness of this weapon was in practice limited; perhaps its main

1 The origin and formulation of this statute are discussed on pp. 74–7, below.

2 Gibson in art. cit. *Bodl. Library Rec.* iii (1920), 116; Idem in *V.C.H. Oxford*, iii (1954), 4; cf. *SAUO*, p. xlii.

3 *Cons. Univ. Canteb.* I. vi (see below, p. 199, lines 1–3).

4 *Ibid.*

value was connected with citations and decrees of the chancellor's court. Imprisonment or banishment from the university were effective deterrents, but their execution during the decade 1231–42 required the intervention of the bishop, without whose *significavit* the sheriff's aid could not be invoked.[1] In any case these punishments generally presupposed the commission of some serious crime; not every violation of the customs of the university could be so construed. Some time, probably during the thirties of the thirteenth century, it was discovered that the university of Paris and possibly Oxford, too, was best able to enforce order and respect for customs by drafting a formal decree or series of decrees binding not only under some penalty but better still under oath or pledge of faith. Of their nature customs did not lend themselves easily to enforcement according to these terms; they were often vague; nobody quite knew on what authority they rested or whether they were still binding; and the validity of an oath to observe something which went under the name of 'customs of the university' was itself questionable.[2] A precise, formal statute written down in black and white was a very different proposition. It allowed no escape and with the charge of perjury hanging over any would-be offender it was a most salutary instrument indeed.

To attempt to reduce all the customs of the university to statutory form, even if it were practicable, was not desirable; the effort could well defeat the peculiar sanction attaching to statutes, which in the nature of things had to be selective if they were to achieve their object. Only those matters which were regarded as particularly important or whose observance called for special measures were rescued from the shades of custom and translated into written laws. At this point it is necessary to point out that customs which never got on the statute-books did not thereby lose their force or cease to be as sacred as statutes. Tradition died hard, and well into the fourteenth and fifteenth centuries we find statutes being called customs. What a medieval university deemed worthy of being made a statute may not seem to us to be very important; but such things as

1 When the duty of imprisoning scholars convicted in the chancellor's court devolved on the burgesses, as happened before 1242, the position became still more unsatisfactory. The king on 21 March of that year allowed the chancellor to approach the sheriff directly, who had then no option but to act. Cf. Dyer, *Privileges*, i. 62; *Close rolls, 1247–51*, p. 178.

2 Bishop Montacute drew the distinction in 1342 between 'consuetudines rationabiles' and 'statuta canonica' of the university (CUA, doc. no. 32).

the habit to be worn by a master and funerals were viewed by all universities, at least in the early years of the thirteenth century, as more important from the statutory point of view than curricula and examinations. It is interesting to compare the identity of interests at Paris and Cambridge as regards what should be made a statute. The former university selected or was allowed to select *c.* 1210–31 the following matters as suitable for statutory enactment: the hours and manner of lecturing and disputing, the proper habit of a master; breaches of discipline and disregard of ones' obligations; hostels and funerals.[1] All these subjects are dealt with in the Cambridge constitution and some make up its longest chapters.[2] They were probably the first customs which the university decided to cast in the form of statutes. The overall stimulus to substitute statutory for customary law in respect of these and other matters derived basically from the need for discipline and uniformity. During the years *c.* 1225–30 and beyond the university both numerically and structurally underwent a relatively notable development; with it came the need for better organization, more efficient administration and stricter control over masters and scholars. In all this the question of hostels, the subject of the earliest statute, occupied a vital position and had a significant bearing on the internal interests of the university.[3] If the majority of the chapters of the constitution devote far more space proportionally to these rather than to relations with the external forum the reason is obvious. Unless the university could put its own house in order it stood little chance of surviving and overcoming opposition from outside. We may trace the origin of the statutes ultimately to the growth of self-consciousness among the regent masters as a corporate body and a readiness to grapple with problems which threatened its existence.

[1] Cf. *Chart. Univ. Paris.* i. 67, no. 8; 79, no. 20; 137, no. 79.

[2] These are *De creacione magistrorum et eorum officio* (II), *De inmunitate scolarium et pena delinquencium* (XI) and *De hospiciis et pensionibus domorum* (XII).

[3] On this subject see the penetrating analysis in A. B. Emden, *An Oxford hall in medieval times* (Oxford, 1927), pp. 7–10, 18–19.

Chapter 4

THE FORMATION OF THE CONSTITUTION

The competence of a university to enact statutes and give itself a constitution was explicitly recognized by the canonists. Hostiensis asks the question: 'who can make a constitution?' He answers that a pope, legate, synod and chapter may do so, and 'also a university of clerks or masters'.[1] Cambridge was the first university to arrange its statutes in the form of a constitution properly so called. It anticipated by more than sixty years the action of the law university of Bologna, which promulgated its earliest written constitution in 1317, by which time Oxford was also beginning to reduce its statutes to some kind of order. There is no preamble to the Cambridge text setting forth the reasons why it was thought necessary or advisable to draw up a constitution, and we can only suggest that the masters by *c.* 1250 were convinced that a positive, agreed and easily ascertainable body of laws, in other words, a codification of its statutes, was vitally needed. Although the *studium* had put almost a half-century of history behind it at this stage and was in a relatively advanced state of development, the threat of disintegration or dissolution still hung over it. In 1256 the bishop of Ely, William of Kilkenny, was alive to the first of these two dangers, and Henry III, as events were to show, would not hesitate to order the extinction of a university which he had earlier patronized.[2] The endemic restlessness among the masters and scholars and recurrent clashes with the town made Denifle dubious about the reality of the university as an organized institution before 1250.[3] This is a very one-sided view indeed, for it ignores the fact that Paris and Oxford

[1] 'Quis possit constitutionem facere. Et quidem Papa...capitulum...Item vniuersitas clericorum, seu magistrorum' (*Summa aurea*, Bk 1 [Basle, 1573], 17, 3–7*d*). For Hostiensis a constitution is 'Quod in scriptis redigitur' (*ibid.* 16, 1). What he says is as applicable to a code as to individual statutes.

[2] The king's preparedness to encourage the Northampton venture in 1261–5 shows that he was not averse to the dissolution of Cambridge. When he did decide to end the university at Northampton it was not the future of Cambridge that impelled him to do so but the anxieties of the bishops for Oxford. Cf. *Close rolls, 1264–8*, pp. 92–3.

[3] *Universitäten*, pp. 369–72.

had just as stormy a history if not more so than Cambridge in the thirteenth century.[1] But while those universities could weather every threat, Cambridge, lacking their durability and resourcefulness, was in no position to survive internal dissensions for long. It is not claimed of course that the adoption of a written constitution achieved wonders overnight or settled for all time the problems of the university. What may be claimed is that the enactment of a constitution at a comparatively early date contributed in no small measure to the salvation of the university. There was now an official code of laws which every master at his inception formally pledged himself to uphold, and no scholar could be unaware of the stringent coercive powers possessed by the chancellor and regent masters.

Universities generally entrusted the preparation and formulation of their statutes to a committee of masters. The first recorded Parisian statutes were devised in this way,[2] while the earliest dated Oxford statute was drafted by a body of seven.[3] When the project of codifying statutes and publishing a constitution was conceived, the head of the university or an outstanding master was commissioned to execute the work, and an advisory or consultative committee was appointed to assist him.[4] Thus the 1307 statutes of

1 Denifle, *op. cit.* p. 369, citing Henry III's writs of 1231, goes on to say: 'anderseits aber noch in ziemlicher Unordnung sich befand'; he forgets that the very same documents were directed to Oxford. Having mentioned the indults granted by Gregory IX on 14–15 June 1233 he comments: 'Zugleich aber ergibt sich aus beiden Schreiben, dass die Disciplin in Cambridge keine glänzende war' (*ibid.* p. 371). But similar indults were obtained by Paris and Oxford; and to say that 'waren die Unordnungen an der Tagesordnung' at Cambridge is to generalize recklessly. L. R. Ward, 'Notes on academic freedom in medieval schools', *Anglican Theological Review*, xlv (1963), 50–1, has completely misunderstood the point of the papal indult of 15 June 1233.

2 See above, p. 57. When Courson promulgated his statutes for the university in 1215 he stated that he made them 'de bonorum virorum consilio' (*Chart. Univ. Paris.* i. 78, no. 20). His advisers were doubtless masters of the university. See also *ibid.* 199, no. 169. Cardinal Conrad, on the other hand, appears to have consulted nobody before issuing his statutes in 1220 for Montpellier. Cf. *Statuts*, ii. 4–6, no. 882.

3 Rashdall, *Universities*, iii. 51, n. 1; *SAUO*, pp. xix–xxi.

4 The 1373 code of Angers was devised by the *scolasticus*, Pierre Bertrand, himself a doctor in canon law, with the consent of the masters. It is stated that he produced 'quemdam librum seu quaternum papyreum scriptum, in quo dicebat et asserebat contineri statuta generalia prefati studii generalis Andegavensis ab antiquis statutis ejusdem alias detracta, correctaque et emendata per ipsum' (*Statuts*, i. 282–3, no. 396). He also claimed the right to dispense with, amend, add to, correct and interpret the statutes, and with the advice and consent of the regent masters make new ones (*ibid.* pp. 284–5).

Orléans appear to have been arranged and edited by the rector with the help of the regents in canon and civil law and the proctors.[1] At Bologna the exceptionally onerous task of drawing up the constitution of the university of jurists was undertaken by Giovanni d'Andrea and a team of fourteen scholars, one being Thomas Anglicus.[2]

The Angelica manuscript of the constitution of Cambridge was probably copied at not more than two steps from the original; the text certainly shows signs of having been derived from an unpolished exemplar, if not actually from the final draft of the codified statutes. Mistakes in grammar, loosely constructed sentences, jerky turns of phrase and odd *lacunae* tend to give this impression. The style and language point to a single authorship, and since the hand of a lawyer, expert in romano-canonical procedure, is evident in more than one chapter we may conclude that the original was compiled by a doctor in decrees. At a much later period, *c.* 1350–90 perhaps, it was enacted that 'all statutes and declarations of statutes and customs of the said university' were to be registered within fifteen days of their publication or interpretation. After a statute had been discussed and approved by the congregation of regents and non-regents the university was to depute certain persons to frame the text.[3] In practice a doctor in civil law was appointed together with other masters to give the statute its final form before the proctors entered it on the register or book of the statutes.[4] We may assume that the custom of delegating a professor of law to formulate statutes goes back to the thirteenth century, and that the editor-in-chief of the constitution was a doctor in canon law, since there was no faculty of civil law at the time.[5]

1 *Statuts*, pp. 17–19.

2 *Statuti*, p. 5. Cf. Rashdall, *Universities*, i. 189.

3 *SA* 3 (*Docs*, i. 309).

4 *SA* 176 (*ibid.* 402), which was enacted on 24 May 1414, 'per doctorem iuris ciuilis vna cum alijs ad hoc specialiter electis est in formam redactum, ac per procuratores vniuersitatis vt moris est et statuta nostra iubent insertum in registro' (CUL MS Dd. 4. 35, fo. 76r; C. Hardwick, 'Articuli Universitatis Cantabrigiae: a form of petition addressed to King Henry V', *CASP*, i [1859], 90). The statute was entered in the Old Proctor's Book on fo. 10v.

5 A text entitled *Statuta vniuersitatis Cantebrigiensis* is found in a MS, CUL Mm. 4. 41, fo. 56va–vb (saec. xiv*in*), which appears to have belonged to a Cambridge canonist. He may have been appointed by the university to reduce these so-called statutes to proper form and for that purpose copied the text or had it copied into the MS, but the proposed statutes, if they were ever ratified, did not become part of the official code. See below, pp. 237–9.

To him fell the task of planning the format of the text, of selecting the material, translating unwritten customs into words and recasting the forms in which statutes were originally promulgated.[1] The responsibility for excluding, amending and adding to the customary and statutory rules of the university can scarcely have been left to the whim of one man. Convocation, which then consisted of the chancellor and regent masters only, doubtless commissioned the chancellor (unless he was the actual redactor of the text), the two rectors as representatives of the faculty of arts and one or more masters from the faculties of theology and canon law, to advise the editor and supervise the progress of the work. As no other university had yet begun to codify its laws the redactor had to chart his own course when deciding on the choice and arrangement of the subject-matter.[2]

The text comprises thirteen rubrics or chapters, the first being devoted to the chancellor, his election, powers and deputies. Next comes a chapter on the creation and office of a master, the hours of lectures and disputations, reference being made, too, to bachelors. Chapter III sets forth the divisions of the academic year. It is followed by the shortest chapter of the whole text, a paragraph in fact, on the habit of the masters. Chapter V deals with convocations, and then comes a section on the court of the masters, the only institution for which there was no Oxford precedent. Having devoted almost half of the text to the regents, the redactor only now introduces us to the two rectors, the most important officials of the university after the chancellor. Their duties and authority are duly described, and in a separate chapter the office of the bedells. Chapters IX and X lay down the rules concerning litigation and procedure in the university courts. Two of the longest sections of the constitution

1 The earliest dated statute of the university, Markaunt 15 (see below, pp. 225–6, 256–7) = *SA* 57 (*Docs*, i. 342), was promulgated on 17 March 1276. The changes which the original text underwent when it was transferred to the statute-books can be seen in Ullmann's edition, *Historical Journal*, i. 181–2.

2 Despite Gibson's great work there is still room for a study of the earliest Oxford attempt at codification, namely the oldest part of *Reg. A*; cf. *SAUO*, pp. x–xiii and above, p. 7, n. 2. It cannot be said that the redactor was particularly careful; several duplicated entries reappear, e.g. *SAUO*, 37, 26–8 = 53, 19–21; 54, 5–7 = 54, 23–4; 58, 24–5 = 67, 27–68, 2; 81, 4–6 = 90, 26–91, 2. Moreover, 70, 7–13 is out of place. It is also evident that an earlier, possibly better, arrangement of the statutes existed. There is a reference in 41, 23–4 to 'priori statuto' which must be 42, 6–22. Likewise, the statutes on theology originally preceded those on civil and canon law; cf. 44, 24–5; 47, 12–13 and 50, 5–6.

follow, the one relating to scholars and discipline, the other to lodgings and schools. The thirteenth and final chapter, *De exequiis defunctorum*, appropriately provides for the observance of the obsequies of the king and the bishop of Ely, the patrons of the university, the regent masters, scholars, non-regents and the bedells.

The plan adopted by the editor is straightforward and with one notable omission comprehensive enough. It might have been better had the chapters on the rectors and bedells been inserted immediately after the chapter on the chancellor and his deputies, as was done when the earliest extant recension of the text was made. The compiler of the Angelica text, however, may have been guided by the position which the rectors occupied by *c.* 1250 in the constitutional organization of the university; the new status which they acquired in virtue of the statute of 17 March 1276, a statute that invested them with authority to supersede the chancellor or vice-chancellor in certain circumstances, is reflected in the revised text, but the author of the constitution could not be expected to foresee this development. Once the decision was taken to shift forward the chapter on the rectors, the obvious thing was to group the various officials together, including the bedells. The weakest section of the constitution, chapter II, was considerably augmented in the late thirteenth and early fourteenth centuries and formed the penultimate part of the *c.* 1385 recension.[1] Apart from these changes the original plan was broadly adhered to; indeed later recensions cannot be said to have improved to any considerable extent on the original model, and needless confusion marks the arrangement of the statutes in the Junior and Senior Proctors' Books, which date from *c.* 1494–1502.

The greatest defect in the constitution is on the side of studies. Apart from some general rules about requirements for admission to the *magisterium* it says absolutely nothing on the organization of lectures and disputations in any faculty, textbooks, curricula or the various stages through which every scholar had to advance before responding for the degree of master. This whole department of the life, the heart, of the university was regulated no doubt by unwritten customs, a practice which obtained at all universities with the possible exception of Paris in the early thirteenth century.[2] The

[1] See below, pp. 273–6.

[2] The earliest Parisian statutes on studies were promulgated in 1215; they relate only to the faculties of arts and theology and are by no means as complete as Rashdall, *Universities*, i. 439, would lead one to believe, even for arts.

oldest surviving Oxford statute to throw even a glimmer of light on the question of studies in any faculty dates only from 1253 and the next earliest from 1268.[1] Compared with the Montpellier statutes of 1220–42 the Cambridge constitution is far more revealing, and no matter how much one regrets the author's failure to outline the curricula of the three faculties, arts, canon law and theology, then in existence, what he put down in writing is invaluable. The Angelica text remains a unique historical document as far as university records go. The gaps in the constitution may very well indicate that the materials at the disposal of the editor were none too full or concrete. On the other hand, it is evident that he did not purport to present a complete picture of the organization of the university; custom continued to regulate many aspects which were not considered to require statutory definition or declaration.[2] That the editor achieved a laudable measure of success is shown by the fact that the forms in which he clothed the statutes were preserved with remarkable fidelity down to 1549, when the *statuta antiqua* were superseded, though even then not entirely, by the Edwardian code.

To identify the sources of the constitution and analyse how they were utilized is extremely difficult. Only once does the author refer to an established custom of the university,[3] and at no point do we find references to earlier statutes. And yet there can be no doubt that the bulk of his materials were the lawful customs and statutes which the university possessed by the time the constitution was drawn up.[4] It may be profitable, however, to examine the text

1 Cf. *SAUO*, 25, 17–27, 9 (1268); 49, 15–27 (1253).

2 The late Father Pelster's comments on the Oxford statutes are apposite: 'As with other universities in the thirteenth and beginning of the fourteenth centuries, the earliest statutes of Oxford are very defective and sparse. Especially we fail to find adequate data about the customs relating to lectures and disputations in the daily life of the university. To some extent inferences can be drawn from later statutes.' In A. G. Little and F. Pelster, S.J., *Oxford theology and theologians c. A.D. 1282–1302* (OHS, xcvi [1934]), 25.

3 The bedell of the faculties of canon law and theology is ordered to ring the bells 'horis debitis et consuetis' (*Cons. Univ. Canteb.* VIII. ii [see below, p. 207, lines 14–15]).

4 It is possible that the redactor had at his disposal a collection of customs and statutes of the type found in CUL Mm. 4. 41 (see above, p. 66, n. 5). In this connection the formation of the Oxford code offers a more fruitful subject for study. Gibson, unfortunately, never seriously considered the relationship between the Oxford collections in MS Bodl. e mus. 96, B.M. Royal MS 12 D. xi, and *Reg. A.* With one major exception (*SAUO*, 60, 18–61, 3), and allowing for certain omissions, the sequence of the statutes in Bodl. is the same as that adopted by the

in the light of the customs and statutes of Oxford. The university at Cambridge was organized, like any daughter-foundation, on the parent model. The original connection between the two was also maintained over the years during which the Cambridge constitution took shape. In 1240 a second migration from Oxford took place,[1] and individual masters such as Simon de Asceles and scholars like Walter Giffard passed from the one university to the other *c.* 1250–5, not to mention the friars.[2] Moreover, the interrelationship between the two universities is explicitly recognized in the Cambridge constitution.[3] There is direct evidence, too, that at a later period Oxford customs and statutes were observed at Cambridge and continued to influence the formation of its statutes.[4] If this is true of the period *c.* 1250–1337, *a fortiori* it applies to the formative years of the first Cambridge statutes.

A problem immediately presents itself. The Oxford constitution did not become fixed until about the beginning of the fourteenth century.[5] Only four statutes in the earliest surviving register can be assigned definitely to the years *c.* 1231–53. The first was made independently and probably contemporaneously at Cambridge;[6] two are of purely local significance for Oxford;[7] the fourth, the

original author of *Reg. A*; this is only partly true of the collection in the Royal MS, which appears to have been derived from an earlier though closely related exemplar of Bodl. The relevant statutes entered by the earliest hand in *Reg. A* were not copied, apparently, from either source.

1 Matthew Paris, *Chron. Maj.* iv (1887), 7–8.

2 For Simon de Asceles see above, pp. 30–2. Giffard studied arts at Cambridge before proceeding to Oxford, where he incepted as master in 1251 (*BRUC*, p. 257).

3 Oxford is the only university, apart of course from Cambridge itself, mentioned by name. Cf. *Cons. Univ. Canteb.* XI. iii (see below, p. 211, lines 16–18).

4 Little and Pelster, *Oxford theology*, pp. 53, 180, but see below, p. 125, n. 1, for a criticism of Pelster's methodology. The opening section and at least twelve of the thirty-eight statutes of Markaunt's text reveal traces of Oxford influence. In some cases, however, it is evident that the parallel passages derive from common or independent sources. Thus Markaunt 22 ('statuimus quod principales persone factum ipsum per se proponant', see below, p. 322 lines 34–5) was directly borrowed from the Decretals of Gregory IX ('principales personae non per advocatos, sed per se ipsas factum proponant', c. 14. X. 2. 1). Cf. *SAUO*, 89, 21–90, 3.

5 This was the considered opinion of no less an authority than Strickland Gibson. See his article in *V.C.H. Oxford*, iii (1954), 9.

6 See below, pp. 72–4.

7 The earlier of the two—if we can call it a statute of the university—is an ordinance made by Grosseteste on 11 March 1240 regarding the administration of the St Frideswide chest (*SAUO*, 74, 17–76, 16). On an unspecified date in 1252 (?1253) the university drew up regulations for the preservation of peace between the northern and southern scholars (*ibid.* 84, 15–87, 16). The terms of this concord are of

earliest statute of the university bearing a precise date (12 March 1253), was probably enacted after the Cambridge constitution was promulgated.[1] How many of the undated statutes in the original hand of the oldest register go back to the first half of the thirteenth century is an open question.[2] It might be assumed that those at any rate that appear to have influenced the composition of the Angelica text were drawn up by *c.* 1250; but the history of the statutes of the two universities should make one cautious about following this approach.[3] On the other hand, since a number of the Cambridge statutes preserved in Markaunt's Book and in subsequent recensions are not later than 1254, the same may be postulated of perhaps the bulk of the statutes entered in the earliest part of the Oxford *Registrum A* without a date. If exact parallels are difficult to find this may be due to alterations made at Cambridge in texts copied from Oxford, and it is equally possible that the Cambridge statutes approximate more closely to the forms in which Oxford statutes were clothed when transcribed into lost sources such as the *quaterni* of the chancellor and proctors, the Red Book and the register which

immediate interest here. There, as we have already noted, is an allusion to 'antiqua statuta' of the university (85, 24). Gibson did not try to identify these statutes; they may be the five (81, 13–82, 12) which are also found with variations in 108, 12–28; 642, 1–26; 643, 8–13. The form of the oath prescribed in the ordinance (86, 6–16) appears separately in 19, 13–21; this latter statute should, therefore, be dated '1252–3'. The same form of oath was introduced at Cambridge after the enactment of the constitution, which may help to fix its terminal dating more exactly. See pp. 224–5 below. It is noteworthy that the 1252 ordinance was copied into the Oxford *Reg. A*, whereas the later concord of 29 Nov. 1267, bearing on the same subject, though entered 'in registro', does not appear in the statute-book. Cf. *Med. Arch. Univ. Oxford*, i. 28.

1 The statute, *SAUO*, 49, 15–27, whether earlier or later than the Cambridge text, was definitely not one of its sources. The crucial provision of the statute, namely, that no scholar unless he had been regent in arts could incept as D.Th. without a grace, was made the law at Cambridge, too, but not before 1254. See below, p. 222.

2 Pollard, 'The university and the book trade in mediaeval Oxford', *Beiträge zum Berufsbewusstsein des mittelalterlichen Menschen* (Misc. Med. iii [1964]), 336, rightly remarks that a number of the statutes can now be dated more closely than Gibson found possible; this, we may add, applies especially to those which he was content to give as 'Before 1350'.

3 There is evidence that certain statutes were enacted at Cambridge before they were introduced at Oxford, e.g. *SA* 3 (*Docs*, i. 309), which is not later than 1390, was adopted by Oxford in 1412; cf. *SAUO*, pp. xix–xx, 211, 27–212, 11. The feasts of St Benedict and the translation of St Augustine of Hippo were made *dies non legibiles* at Cambridge also by 1390; cf. *SA* 173 (*Docs*, i. 400). At Oxford the same rule was made obligatory *c.* 1400 (*SAUO*, 189, 5–9).

was extant by 1267.[1] Having made these observations, we may now proceed to evaluate the dependence of the Cambridge constitution on the customary and written laws of Oxford.

The earliest statute, although it was issued in the name of the chancellor and not by the university, which has left its mark on the Cambridge text is one which has been dated as pre-1231. This is the decree ordering every scholar to enrol under a specific regent master, whose school he was to frequent for at least one ordinary lecture each day. Henry III in the second of the writs which he issued on 3 May 1231 in favour of both Oxford and Cambridge refers to this matter; it is worth comparing the writ with the relevant statutes of the two universities:

Oxford

Item, mandat Cancellarius, quod quilibet scolaris habeat magistrum proprium actu regentem, in cuius rotulo scribatur nomen eius, et de quo audiat saltem vnam lectionem ordinariam singulis diebus, nisi fuerit bachillarius nouiter incepturus; alioquin non gaudebit priuilegio scolarium. (*SAUO*, 82, 13–18.)[2]

Henry III

precipimus...quod nullus clericus moretur in villa illa qui non sit sub disciplina vel tuitione alicujus magistri scolarum; et si aliqui tales fuerint in villa illa, eam exeant infra xv dies postquam hoc clamatum fuerit, et si ultra terminum illum inventi fuerint in eadem villa hujusmodi clerici capientur et in prisona nostra mittentur. (*Close rolls, 1227–31*, p. 586.)

Cambridge

Indignum esse iudicamus ut quis scolarem tueatur qui certum magistrum infra quindecim dies post ingressum uniuersitatis non habuerit aut nomen suum infra tempus prelibatum in matricula sui magistri redigi non curauerit...Immo si quis talis sub nomine scolaris latitans inueniatur retineatur iuxta domini regis libertatem. Hii soli scolares gaudeant inmunitate qui saltem per tres dies in septimana scolas magistri sui ingrediantur tres lecciones ad minus audituri. (*Cons. Univ. Canteb.* XI. i–ii [see below, p. 211, lines 4–13].)

The basic difference between the Oxford and Cambridge statutes is that the Oxford decree makes no reference to the king's writ and

[1] See above, p. 71, n. 1, and *SAUO*, p. xiii.

[2] This appears to be the original form of the statute. Other versions are found *ibid.* 60, 18–61, 12; 107, 1–13; 641, 30–642, 7, 24–9. There is no certain proof that the statute was enacted before 1231. Gibson, *ibid.* p. xxi, states that it may be earlier than 1231 (he is referring to 107, 1–13, which he prints under the caption 'Before 1231').

does not allow scholars fifteen days' grace to enrol under a particular master. We may conclude that the statute was enacted before 3 May 1231.[1] The Cambridge statute, on the contrary, definitely appears to have been inspired to some extent by the writ. In keeping with its terms scholars are granted fifteen days' freedom to choose a master and enlist under his protection,[2] and there can be no doubt that the royal privilege cited in the statute is the right accorded to the chancellor and masters in virtue of this writ to have unofficial scholars arrested and imprisoned by the sheriff. Nevertheless, the rule about formal enrolment under a specific master was almost certainly derived from Oxford. It is not laid down in the king's writ, which, moreover, does not make attendance at lectures a condition for the enjoyment of the privilege of scholarity.

The custom of affiliating scholars to a master instead of to the university as such did not originate at Oxford. It received official sanction at Paris in 1215 in the form of a statute which made it compulsory for a scholar if he wished to retain his status to have a definite master.[3] Gregory IX confirmed this ruling in 1231, adding that those who failed to attend the schools or had no master came under the heading of fictitious scholars and consequently were not entitled to privilege.[4] In neither statute is it stated that each master must keep a roll of his students or that scholars are bound to have their names entered in the *matricula* of their master. Indeed, masters were not ordered to write down the names of their scholars until 1289.[5] We may conclude, therefore, that the Cambridge enactment basically had its origin in the Oxford decree; but when it goes on to say that scholars who frequent the school of their master three days in the week are covered by privilege a departure from the Oxford rule is immediately apparent. At Oxford one had to attend every day. Perhaps too much should not be made of this divergence.

1 Emden, *An Oxford hall*, p. 18, suggests that the statute was made *c.* 1231 as part of a drive by the university to extend its authority and that the aid of the secular arm was invoked for this purpose. Though the statute was re-enacted without reference to the royal writ this cannot be said to negative the significance of the omission. Statutes were often copied and recopied as originally promulgated irrespective of subsequent developments. Cf. *SAUO*, pp. xvii–xviii, and below, p. 77, n. 2.

2 At Bologna scholars were also granted fifteen days in which to select a master. Cf. *Statuti*, p. 248, rubr. xxxvj; Rashdall, *Universities*, iii. 355, n. 1. This statute may not be earlier than 1405 and applied only to students of arts and medicine.

3 See below, p. 210 *app. crit.* ad 4–6.

4 See below, p. 167, n. 5.

5 *Chart. Univ. Paris.* ii. 36, no. 561.

At the same time it is interesting to find that the less stringent Cambridge statute is more in harmony with the practice of Paris, Bologna and other continental universities.[1] Whether or not the Oxford regulation originally obtained at Cambridge and was relaxed as a result of the advent of Parisian masters and scholars in 1229, it is evident that the university made its own rules independently of Oxford and in framing a derivative statute had recourse to other sources, in the present instance the king's writ of 1231.

One of the earliest statutes made at Cambridge forms the first paragraph of chapter VII of the constitution, which treats of the office of the rectors. It was enacted apparently before the date of the king's writs of 1231 and concerns the 'taxation' of houses or hostels. Here if anywhere the influence of Oxford customs on the development of Cambridge legislation is most likely to be found. The question of rents of houses provoked the last of the writs issued by Henry III on 3 May 1231 and it is necessary as a preliminary to see the statutes of the two universities in relation to the actual terms of this writ:

Oxford	*Henry III*	*Cambridge*
Item, quatuor taxatores in prima congregacione post festum sancti Michaelis a procuratoribus eligantur...Item, statutum est quod taxatores deferant in ultima congregacione singulorum terminorum, in cedulis scriptas, taxaciones omnium domorum uel scolarum, quas illo termino taxauerint ...Et similiter faciat Cancellarius, si que per ipsum et maiorem fuerint taxate. (*SAUO*, 71, 9–18.)	mandamus firmiter injungentes quatinus, super predictis hospitiis locandis vos [*sc.* maior et ballivi] mensurantes secundum consuetudinem universitatis, per duos magistros et duos probos et legales homines de villa vestra ad hoc assignandos hospitia predicta taxari, et secundum eorum taxationem ea locari permittatis. (*Close rolls, 1227–31*, p. 587.)	Duo rectores per cancelarium et magistros deputati una cum duobus burgensibus iuramento astricti congruam domorum faciant taxacionem in publicam scripturam redigendam per eosdem. (*Cons. Univ. Canteb.* VII. i [see below, p. 205, lines 2–5].)

[1] *Chart. Univ. Paris.* i. 223, no. 197 (1251): 'bis ad minus in septimana'; cf. ii. 503, no. 1040: 'ad minus bis vel ter in septimana.' For Bologna see Rashdall, *Universities*, i. 196. One of the 1307 statutes of Orléans is closer still to the Cambridge regulation: 'Nullus reputetur scolaris nisi doctorem proprium habeat a quo audiat ordinarie, cujus scolas qualibet septimana ter ad minus intret' (*Statuts*, i. 22, no. 24, § 19).

The textual gap between the Oxford and Cambridge statutes is so obvious that there can be no question of direct borrowing: the Cambridge enactment was definitely not modelled on the Oxford text. Yet the royal writ makes no distinction between the custom of the two universities. By 1231, evidently, the rents of houses or hostels at Oxford and Cambridge were assessed by two masters and two burgesses.[1] Though the Oxford statutes do not state that the taxors, like their Cambridge counterparts, were bound by oath, this may be presumed.[2] Both universities insisted on having the assessments put down in writing and made available for public inspection. Hence, despite the textual dissimilarities of the Oxford and Cambridge statutes the practice at both universities was basically the same. One striking difference cannot be glossed over. At Oxford the university taxors were elected by the proctors; under the Cambridge constitution the two rectors or proctors were themselves the taxors. Indeed, it appears that this was the primary reason for their institution in the first place. This identification between the offices of taxor and rector suggests very strongly that the Oxford proctors were originally the taxors and that the office of proctor was created precisely for the purpose of securing a fair assessment of the rents which tenant scholars were obliged to pay for lodgings. A relic of the ancient connection between the two offices may be discerned in the Oxford statute which reserves to the proctors the exclusive right of electing the taxors.

The textual differences between the Oxford and Cambridge statutes represent simply different stages in their transmission. None

1 The system which operated at Oxford before 1209 is uncertain; the rents were fixed 'communi consilio clericorum & burgensium' (*Med. Arch. Univ. Oxford*, i. 3). In 1214 the papal legate decreed that in future four masters and four burgesses were to assess the rents (*ibid.* 2–3). Emden, *An Oxford hall*, pp. 12, 14, holds that this arrangement obtained before the *suspendium* (1209–14) and that the legatine decree simply revived it. But if, as the distinguished author suggests very rightly, Oxford followed the practice of Paris, then we must conclude that by 1209 the taxors comprised only two masters and two representatives of the town, and that the legate's ruling was an extraordinary measure aimed at lessening the tension which this matter provoked at Oxford. For the Parisian custom see below, p. 76, n. 4. The commune of Bologna sanctioned the practice *c.* 1274 which was written into the statutes of the university. Cf. A. Gaudenzi (ed.), 'Gli antichi statuti del comune di Bologna intorno allo studio', *Bullettino dell'istituto storico italiano*, 6 (1888), 126, no. VIII; *Statuti*, p. 121, rubr. lxiij. The rectors of the university appointed two scholars (not two masters) to act as taxors.

2 The reference to four taxors is to be understood as comprising the two masters deputed *ex parte universitatis* and the two burgesses nominated by the town corporation. Cf. Rashdall, *Universities*, iii. 56, n. 1.

of the Oxford enactments is probably as early as the text of the Cambridge constitution.[1] They offer no explanation for the appointment of taxors; the officials are not even called taxors of houses, though the context makes this plain. So much is taken for granted that it was not considered necessary to add that they had to be two masters of the university and two burgesses.[2] The title itself of taxor is more in keeping with the usage of the second rather than the first half of the thirteenth century.[3] It is difficult to believe that these Oxford statutes were formulated before the *suspendium* of 1209–14 or even by the time the Cambridge statute or the Angelica text was devised.

The Cambridge statute presents a very different picture. It is typical of an early enactment and compares so closely with a Parisian statute promulgated on 14 April 1231 that the two may be regarded as contemporary.[4] In all probability the Cambridge statute is the earlier; it certainly antedates the royal writs of 3 May 1231. As we have seen, the editor of the constitution cites one of these writs with reference to the enrolment of scholars; he refers to it also in chapters IX and XI when describing the penalty which those who are guilty of misdemeanours or who flout the jurisdiction of the university incur.[5] Yet although there was as much if not greater reason for citing the writ on the renting and letting of houses as part of the statute, no mention is made of the royal privilege. Furthermore, and this is decisive, in the last chapter of the constitution readers are

[1] The detail about the time of the election of the taxors in the Oxford statute bears comparison with the recension of the Angelica text in Markaunt's Book; cf. Markaunt 11 (see below, p. 316, line 15), 12 (see below, p. 317, line 13). Such details are not characteristic of early university statutes.

[2] In contrast with the specific terms of the legate's award of 1214 the royal charter of 1256 is surprisingly vague. It states that houses are to be taxed 'secundum arbitrium clericorum & laicorum ex utraque parte iuratorum' (*Med. Arch. Univ. Oxford*, i. 21). This mode of expression is more reminiscent of the custom observed by 1209.

[3] The term 'taxor' is not found in the Parisian statute of 1231. It appears to have come into use late in the century and was applied to masters appointed to price books or *peciae* as well as to those charged with assessing the rents of houses. Cf. *Chart. Univ. Paris.* i. 597, no. 511; ii. 12, no. 28, 98, no. 628, 191, no. 733. Taxors are not mentioned as such in the Cambridge constitution. They were instituted *c.* 1255–68 to relieve the rectors of the duties of fixing rents and supervising the assize of bread and ale. See p. 221.

[4] The Parisian statute reads: 'Hospitiorum quoque taxationem per duos magistros et duos burgenses ad hoc de consensu magistrorum electos juramento prestito fideliter faciendam' (*Chart. Univ. Paris.* i. 141, no. 82). In promulgating this statute Gregory IX made it clear that he was simply ratifying existing custom. For the text of the Cambridge statute see above, p. 74.

[5] *Cons. Univ. Canteb.* IX (see below, p. 209, lines 11–12); XI. iv (see below, p. 213, lines 2–3).

reminded of the many liberties which the university owed to the king's generosity, first as regards the taxation of houses.[1] The only convincing explanation why this privilege was not referred to in the relevant statute is that the text was drawn up before the issue of the writ and was copied into the constitution in the form in which it was originally enacted. Though the precise date of the statute cannot be determined there is good reason for holding that it is earlier than 3 May 1231.[2] It is doubtful if any of the extant parallel Oxford statutes are of comparable antiquity.[3]

What all this leads to is that the Cambridge constitution has preserved the otherwise unknown fact that the rectors were the original taxors *ex parte universitatis* and were really instituted for this purpose. Had the Angelica manuscript not survived we would naturally assume that the task of assessing rents was entrusted from the beginning of the university to two masters, not specifically to the rectors. Hence the Oxford proctors must have been originally constituted to act as taxors, since the office of the rectors at Cambridge was modelled on the custom of the parent university. Far from disproving Oxford influence, the Cambridge constitution reveals, as does nothing else, the origin of the rectorship or proctorship at both universities, and we are entitled to claim that Oxford custom formed the basis of the oldest Cambridge statute.[4]

Chapter XII, the penultimate chapter, of the Angelica text is

[1] Cf. *Cons. Univ. Canteb.* XIII. i (see below, p. 217, lines 9–13) and the corresponding statute, *ibid.* VII. i (see below, p. 205, lines 2–5).

[2] The medieval reverence for the *littera scripta* may explain why a reference to the writ or to the charter of 7 February 1266 which modified its terms was not added to later editions of the statute. When the text was amended and transposed to form a new chapter, *De officio taxatorum*, following the transfer of the duty of assessing rents to taxors, the necessary alterations were executed with the utmost economy. See below, pp. 220–1.

[3] The use of the term *consuetudo* in the writ instead of *statutum* is immaterial. These terms were employed in royal and episcopal and other official documents in the thirteenth century and later without distinction. Thus in the writ of prohibition issued by Edward I on 27 April 1292 the offering of a caution or security for rent is described as having been made 'juxta consuetudinem Universitatis' (Prynne, *The third tome of an exact chronological vindication*, p. 467). This custom received statutory recognition in the constitution and it would have been more accurate if *statutum* had been used in the writ in place of *consuetudinem*. For an analysis of the statute see below, p. 172.

[4] Edward I's reference in 1292 to the statutes and customs observed at Cambridge since the foundation of the university may in this instance be accepted as an approximate statement of fact. He was referring to the taxation and letting of hostels. See below, p. 173, n. 1.

devoted to the question of the hiring of houses and schools, rents and tenancies. The approach to these matters is markedly different from that of the Oxford statutes. Local conditions doubtless account for this. Yet there is not much to choose between the regulations of the two universities, and one particular Oxford custom again provided Cambridge with the heads of its statute on the right of a principal or head-tenant to continue as occupant of a house from year to year:

Oxford	*Cambridge*
Consuetudo est etiam quod nullus principalis a domo sua uel scolis suis possit expelli, si ante hore prime pulsationem in crastino natiuitatis beate Virginis hospiti domus, uel in defectum eius, Cancellario uel eius vicegerenti prestiterit cautionem. (*SAUO*, 80, 1–5.)[1]	Qui domum principaliter conduxerit ius inhabitandi in anno sequenti solus habebit. dummodo hospiti uel cancelario si hospes non inueniatur de sequentis anni pensione ante natiuitatem beate uirginis satisfaccionem obtulerit cum effectu. (*Cons. Univ. Canteb.* XII. v [see below, p. 215, lines 10–13].)

Apart from one or two slight divergencies and the mode of expression the Cambridge statute corresponds so closely with the Oxford custom that it is unnecessary to seek another source.[2] The Oxford text, however, goes on to declare that a landlord may resume possession provided he warns the principal tenant before the feast of St John the Baptist (24 June) of the current year that he requires the house for himself and his family.[3] The absence of this clause from the Cambridge constitution and the fact that a similar concession was inserted at the end of the chapter in the next earliest recension suggests that the plea was not recognized by *c.* 1250.[4] Presumably, the same holds for Oxford.

The statutes on the taxation of houses and matriculation were most probably the first written laws enacted at Cambridge. Their Oxford

[1] It may be significant that this statute or custom was transcribed by Robert Hare when he compiled his collections of records of the university of Cambridge; but he did not copy it from any Oxford statute-book; his source was 'antiquum Registrum manu scriptum magistri Ricardi Hant, fo. 82' (Hare MS i, fo. 47^{v} *s.a.* 1298–1300). Neither Hant nor his register has been identified.

[2] There is no Parisian or Bolognese statute on the leasing of houses or schools which can be adduced as a more likely source than the Oxford custom. At the same time it cannot be denied that much the same customs and statutes concerning this matter obtained at universities generally. As at Oxford and Cambridge the feast of the Nativity of Our Lady was the terminal date for renewing leases at Bologna. Cf. *Statuti*, p. 123, rubr. lxv.

[3] *SAUO*, 80, 5–9.

[4] Cf. Markaunt 32 (see below, p. 328, lines 8–13). The Oxford statute also authorizes a landlord to terminate a lease if he has to farm out his property for ten years. This exception is not mentioned either in the Angelica text or the recension in Markaunt's Book.

origin can hardly be disputed. It might also be assumed that the Cambridge statute on the mode of electing the chancellor would have been shaped in the same way as the corresponding Oxford statute, since the office itself was directly copied by Cambridge from the parent university. Indeed, at first sight the statutes look very much alike:

Oxford	*Cambridge*
prouisum est et constitutum communiter quod...ille [*sc.* regens] in quem maior pars [*sc.* regentium] consentit ad predictum officium [*sc.* cancellarii] admittatur. (*SAUO*, 64, 5–15.)	statuimus ut cancelarius...per regentes preficiatur omnibus regentibus aut parte maiore in ipsum consencientibus. (*Cons. Univ. Canteb.* I. i [see below, p. 197, lines 3–6].)

The phrase 'parte maiore in ipsum consencientibus' of the Cambridge text looks a good imitation of the Oxford 'in quem maior pars consentit'; and the preference for 'maior pars' in both statutes instead of the celebrated canonical expression 'maior et sanior pars' is also arresting. But appearances tend to be deceptive. If the full text of the Oxford statute had been quoted we should see that the election of the chancellor was based on an indirect system of voting. At Cambridge he was elected by direct vote of all the regents. Consequently, since the statutes differ on such a vital issue there can be no question of borrowing on the part of Cambridge.[1] In this connection it may be pointed out that there is no early Oxford statute on the office of the chancellor as such. Thus, chapter I of the Cambridge constitution must be regarded as wholly original, and the same is true of the format of the chapters on the rectors and bedells. It is curious that the Cambridge legislators having adopted these offices from Oxford should have framed the relevant statutes quite independently of their basic source.

The most striking example of the influence of Oxford on the composition of a Cambridge statute and how the editor of the constitution worked over his source is to be seen in chapter V, *De habitu magistrorum*. The parallel texts are:

Oxford	*Cambridge*
nullus regens in artibus, uel decretis, uel theologia, in capa manicata lectiones legat ordinarias, set in pallio uel capa clausa. (*SAUO*, 56, 28–30.)	In theologia decretis et artibus regentes capis clausis uel palliis in leccionibus et disputacionibus ordinariis utantur. in eodem habitu ad incepciones et exequias decenter incedentes. (*Cons. Univ. Canteb.* V [see below, p. 203, lines 14–16].)

[1] The texts derive ultimately from a common source, a decree of the Fourth Lateran Council. See below, p. 107.

The wearing of the *cappa clausa* (closed cope) was prescribed by the provincial council held at Oxford in 1222 for church dignitaries and priests. The canon makes no rule as regards schoolmen or the use of the *pallium* as an alternative clerical costume.[1] Even so, it need not be doubted that the decree of the council, granted that the statutes of Oxford and Cambridge were not immediately influenced by it, led to a tightening-up of the rules pertaining to dress and to the introduction of the *cappa clausa* as the statutory habit of regent masters, though not to the exclusion of the *pallium*.

This latter form of the magisterial habit may have been recognized before 1222 in accord with the Parisian custom which was ratified in 1215 by Courson. His statute has left more than one mark on the regulations made by Oxford.[2] The long-term effect of the canon of the council of 1222 is no less evident. Courson's statute refers only to masters in arts and obliges them to wear the *cappa rotunda*. The Oxford statute prescribes the *cappa clausa*, and this departure from the rule at Paris is in line with the tenor of the decree of the council.

The striking verbal agreement between the Oxford and Cambridge statutes must mean one of two things: either both were derived from a common source or Cambridge borrowed directly from Oxford. There is no evidence that Courson's statute was ever received at Cambridge, and furthermore it makes no order concerning the habit to be worn by regents at inceptions and obsequies. Oxford had directives on these matters which correspond with the rule laid down in the Cambridge statute.[3] Indeed, its

[1] The relevant part of c. 33 reads: 'decrevimus ut tam archidiaconi quam decani et omnes alii in personatibus sive dingnitatibus constituti, item omnes decani rurales et presbiteri, decenter incedant in habitu clericali et capis clausis utantur' (*Councils & Synods*, II. i. 116). Evidently, the decree was not aimed directly at scholars, but they were in any case bound to wear the clerical habit and some because of their ecclesiastical office would belong to the classes specified. There is a reference to *cappae* and *pallia* in the legate's award to Oxford in 1214, following the *suspendium* of 1209. Those who had an active part in causing the dispersal were ordered to do penance 'sine capis & palliis' (*Med. Arch. Univ. Oxford*, i. 4).

[2] 'Nullus magistrorum legentium in artibus habeat capam nisi rotundam, nigram et talarem, saltem dum nova est. Pallio autem bene potest uti. Sotulares non habeat sub capa rotunda laqueatos, nunquam liripipiatos' (*Chart. Univ. Paris.* i. 79, no. 20; cf. also 586, no. 501). The colour of the artists' *cappa* at Oxford was also black (cf. *SAUO*, 56, 31); and it was also laid down that 'nullus cuiuscumque facultatis magister sotularibus liripipiatis...calciatus lectiones legat ordinarias' (*ibid.* 57, 2–4). These Oxford statutes, occurring one after the other, appear to have been directly inspired by the Parisian statute.

[3] Newly created masters in arts and medicine at Oxford had to wear the *pallium* at their first disputation. Other masters in these faculties wore the *chimera*, a garment

wording clearly implies that the redactor did have a copy of the Oxford statute before him.[1] But it is also clear that when framing his statute he was not content to reproduce his source *verbatim*, and it is not unlikely that he had access to a copy of the canon of the 1222 council and adopted some of its phrasing.[2]

One will not find in the whole of the Cambridge constitution another statute which is so obviously based on an Oxford source. This and the custom safeguarding the right of a principal to continue as tenant of a hostel, as well as the statute ordering scholars to register under specific masters, are the clearest instances of the adoption by Cambridge of Oxford customs or statutes. In all other cases where the rules of the two universities are fundamentally the same, even to the point of being formulated in identical or almost identical language, the Cambridge approach or the context or emphasis of its statutes is usually different.[3] It is also necessary to enter a caveat

which resembled the *cappa clausa*; a later amendment states that they should appear in 'capis suis nigris', i.e. the *cappa clausa* worn by the artists. Cf. *SAUO*, 39, 17–23 and *apparatus criticus ad* 23. Masters at inceptions as distinct from the inceptors doubtless attended in the habit (*cappa clausa* or *pallium* for seculars) which they wore at ordinary lectures; cf. *ibid.* 38, 24–30; 57, 5–7. At funerals they came 'in habitu quo legunt' (*ibid.* 59, 5–7).

1 The Cambridge enactment must have been made by *c.* 1240–50, since it includes regent masters in theology. See below, p. 132. The fact that it makes no reference to regents in civil law and medicine is noteworthy. No doubt, they are not mentioned in the Oxford statute either. It may be that these two faculties were not fully organized at the time or what is more probable the masters were allowed to wear the *cappa manicata* and hence did not come under the prohibition. The Cambridge statute, on the contrary, would also have carried a reference to this form of the *cappa* if the faculties of medicine and civil law had been established when the constitution was promulgated. Under a later statute expanding the terms of the original decree regents in these two faculties were obliged to wear the *cappa manicata*. Cf. *SA* 147 (*Docs*, i. 388). The provisions of this statute have been misread by W. H. Hargreaves-Mawdsley, *A history of academical dress in Europe until the end of the eighteenth century* (Oxford, 1963), p. 116, who is also gravely mistaken in stating more than once that Hugh Balsham in 1276 gave a body of statutes, including *SA* 147, to Cambridge. See below, p. 230.

2 Cf. c. 33 '...decenter incedant in habitu clericali et capis clausis utantur' (*loc. cit.*) and the Cambridge constitution '...capis clausis...utantur. in eodem habitu... decenter incedentes' (*Cons. Univ. Canteb. loc. cit.*). The decree of the 1222 council was reaffirmed in 1237 by c. 14 of the constitutions of Otto, but the Cambridge statute is textually closer to the earlier canon. Otto's constitution reads: 'capis clausis utantur in sacris ordinibus constituti, maxime in ecclesia et coram prelatis suis et in conventibus clericorum' (*Synods & Councils*, II. i. 251–2).

3 An Oxford statute which orders regents to answer the summons of the chancellor reads: 'Item, ad uocationem Cancellarii pro negociis vniuersitatis tractandis... tenentur venire' (*SAUO*, 57, 18–22). The chapter of the Cambridge constitution

with regard to parallel passages. An Oxford statute which appears to be the source of a Cambridge regulation may in fact have been enacted after the constitution was adopted. A turn of phrase does not of itself constitute evidence of direct borrowing. By way of illustration we may compare the Oxford statute prohibiting the carrying of arms with the corresponding texts of the Cambridge constitution and its later recension:

Oxford	*Cambridge* (A)	*Cambridge* (B)
Item, prohibet Cancellarius sub pena excommunicationis ne aliquis ferat arma de die uel de nocte causa mali perpetrandi, et si quis super hoc conuictus fuerit in carcerem detrudetur. (*SAUO*, 81, 20–3.)	...arma ad nocendum uel ad uindictam precipue de nocte defferentes ...super hoc conuicti... in carcerem detrudantur iuxta formam supradictam. (*Cons. Univ. Canteb.* XI. iv [see below, p. 221, line 20 to p. 213, line 3].)	...arma deferentes seu deferri facientes...causa mali perpetrandi...de die vel de nocte...in carcerem detrudantur. (Markaunt 37 [see below, p. 331, lines 13–17].)

Apart from the penalty of excommunication which the Oxford statute carries, there is little to choose between these three passages. It will be noticed, however, that the revised form (*B*) of the Cambridge enactment introduces a phrase, 'causa mali perpetrandi...de die vel de nocte', which looks as if it was taken straight from the Oxford text and substituted for the reading of the original Cambridge constitution: 'ad nocendum uel ad uindictam precipue de nocte'. That the redactor of Markaunt had access to a copy of the Oxford statute when engaged on recasting the Angelica text is highly probable.[1] This is more than can be said of the first editor of the constitution; had he used the Oxford source his phrasing would doubtless have anticipated the reading found in Markaunt. Consequently, the phrase 'super hoc conuictus [-i] in carcerem detrudetur [-antur]', which occurs both in the Oxford statute and the Angelica text, may not imply more than the use

on convocations of the regents begins: 'Vniuersi regentes ad uocacionem cancelarii omnibus intersint incepcionibus...conueniant de communi utilitate et publica quiete communiter tractaturi' (*Cons. Univ. Canteb.* IV [see below, p. 203, lines 7–10]).

[1] The influence of Oxford is much more apparent in the Markaunt recension than in the Angelica text. See above, pp. 70, n. 4, 78, n. 4. Cf. also Markaunt 18 (see below, p. 320, lines 21–8) and *SAUO*, 69, 28–70, 6; Markaunt 34 (see below, p. 329, lines 29–32) and *SAUO*, 83, 9–15.

of common forms.[1] At every step this possibility must be taken into account.

The question of terminology presents rather a different problem. Certain expressions occur in the Cambridge text which are not the standard terms used in the earliest recorded Oxford statutes; for example, *regimen* instead of *regentia*, 'rector' instead of 'proctor', *principium* in contradistinction to *inceptio*, 'bedell' for 'servant', *generalis congregatio* for *congregatio regentium*. It would be unwise to attach much weight to such divergencies or to interpret them as evidence that Cambridge in some matters adhered to the usage of Paris or Bologna rather than to that of Oxford. All through the medieval period a certain fluidity is discernible in the statutes of Cambridge and Oxford, as indeed in those of Paris, with regard to titles and forms. In effect, any comparison between the language of the Cambridge constitution and the expressions most commonly found in the extant statute-books of Oxford, even in the oldest register, is bound to prove indecisive. For one thing, the Cambridge text exemplifies the usage of the early thirteenth century, and we have no guarantee that the Oxford statutes reproduce the forms which were customary at the university *c.* 1200–50. Some support for this suggestion may be found in the occasional appearance of the above-mentioned Cambridge terms in the statutes of Oxford.[2] There are, however, two exceptions. The title of rector is one. Its equivalent, 'proctor', invariably occurs in the statutes of Oxford and is found as early as 1252.[3] Whether the term was by then long established is open to doubt, for in a letter of the following year written by Adam Marsh hot from Oxford the proctors are called 'rectors'.[4] The original title may well have been 'rector', and its appearance in the Cambridge constitution cannot be regarded as evidence that the university derived some of its terminology from Paris or Bologna rather than from Oxford.[5]

1 The omission of 'super hoc conuicti' by the redactor of Markaunt may have been deliberate or just an oversight. At this point he resumed the Angelica text, which he had abandoned earlier.

2 Cf. *SAUO*, 73, 20; 178, 13 (*regimen*); 39, 3 (*principium*); 68, 19; 70, 3; 112, 18 ('bedell'); 118, 1–2 (*congregatio generalis*).

3 *SAUO*, 86, 19. In a royal charter of 1248 reference is made to the proctors. Cf. *Med. Arch. Univ. Oxford*, i. 18–19; *Close rolls, 1247–51*, p. 114.

4 *Epistolae fratris Adae de Marisco*, ed. Brewer, *Monumenta Franciscana*, i (Rolls series, 1858), 347, no. CXCII.

5 By 1231 'rector' and 'proctor' were synonymous at Paris. Cf. *Chart. Univ. Paris.* i. 147, no. 95. See also Rashdall, *Universities*, i. 311–14.

Generally speaking, Cambridge was slower to discard ancient forms, and although at length it conformed to Oxford usage by adopting 'proctor' the title of rector never quite disappeared from the statutes.[1] On the other hand, it did not hesitate to invent new titles. 'Vice-chancellor' is a Cambridge creation. It was introduced some time after the enactment of the constitution, which vaguely describes the chancellor's *locum tenens* as his 'substitute', a term which is also applied in the statutes of Bologna to the deputy whom the rector may have when absent.[2] By 1276 Cambridge abandoned this makeshift title and replaced it with the more distinguished appellation, vice-chancellor.[3] Oxford declined to adopt this nomenclature before 1450.[4] The earlier, and during the whole medieval period the much commoner, title was 'commissary'. It, too, appears in the Cambridge statutes, though not in the constitution, and may possibly have been copied from Oxford, but this is unlikely, since the Oxford commissary filled the role of the Cambridge vice-chancellor. At Oxford the duties of the Cambridge commissary—he was really judge delegate of the chancellor—were entrusted to *hebdomadarii*.[5]

Another term which was also used differently at Cambridge, at any rate in the early thirteenth century, is *generalis congregatio*. In the Oxford statutes it signifies a congregation of the regent and non-regent masters or convocation; as employed in the Cambridge constitution it denotes a meeting of the entire body of regents, which was the meaning it originally had at Paris.[6] Was this also true of Oxford? If the general pattern of the development of Cambridge terminology is any guide, it would seem that the more comprehensive use of the term came into vogue at Oxford only when the non-regent masters were permanently accorded co-legislative rights with the regents.[7] Earlier, the non-regents were convened on special occasions and asked to give their assent to certain statutes, and these extraordinary joint sessions doubtless led to the extension of the term *generalis congregatio*. In this context it should be noted

[1] Cf. Rashdall, *Universities*, iii. 58–9, and below, pp. 255–6, 272.

[2] *Statuti*, p. 15, rubr. xij.

[3] See p. 113. Montpellier had a vice-chancellor in 1281 (*Statuts*, ii. 15, no. 898).

[4] Cf. *SAUO*, p. lxxiv.

[5] See below, p. 112.

[6] Cf. *Chart. Univ. Paris*. i. 182, no. 144; 399, no. 350; 575, no. 490.

[7] There is a reference under the year 1314 to 'congregacione generali omnium magistrorum actu regentium' (*SAUO*, 118, 1–2). By 1344 the phrase reads: 'generali congregacione regencium et non regencium' (*ibid.* 143, 22).

that the title of non-regent master does not once appear in the Cambridge constitution. The nearest we get to it is in the last chapter of the text, where provision is made for attendance at 'exequias scolarium non regencium et bedellorum'.[1] It is difficult to decide whether *scolarium* goes with *non regencium* or not. The terms are not mutually exclusive; any master who completed the statutory year of regency and proceeded to study in a higher faculty ranked as a non-regent scholar or non-regent bachelor, as the case may be. By *c.* 1385–95, if not at a much earlier date, the ambiguity of the passage in the constitution was recognized; the statute was accordingly amended and it is evident that 'scholars' and 'non-regents' were meant to be taken disjunctively.[2] Scholars comprise ordinary students or undergraduates, to use an anachronism, bachelors and non-regent masters reading for a doctorate; the non-regents are those masters who had ceased lecturing and retired from the university. It is a revealing commentary on their status that they are placed between scholars in general and the bedells. One may justifiably ask if their position was any different at Oxford before 1250. The question again arises: are its *statuta antiqua* an accurate guide to the organization of the university during the first half of the thirteenth century? Paradoxical as it may seem the Cambridge constitution is on the whole perhaps an even better guide.

'Bedell' is one of those terms which illustrate the fluctuations which university nomenclature underwent at Oxford and Cambridge and also Paris. The title of bedell, long since adorned with the style of 'esquire', is not as ancient as one might think. At Paris the bedells were originally and quite properly called 'public servants' of the university. The same custom obtained at Oxford, and although the title of bedell crept into the statutes the correct designation of the officers was 'servants'.[3] Whatever the early usage at Cambridge, by *c.* 1250 they were officially known as the 'bedells', and it is interesting to discover that contemporaneously this title was gaining ground at Paris.[4] There is no reason to think that the

1 *Cons. Univ. Canteb.* XIII. iii (see below, p. 217, line 21).

2 Cf. below, p. 281.

3 Cf. *SAUO*, 61, 19, 24; 62. 5 and the statutes *De electione seruientum* and *De officio seruientum*, *ibid.* 68, 9–69, 23. The Parisian expression, 'public servants', occurs in the concord of 1252 (*ibid.* 85, 14).

4 A statute of 1251 mentions 'bedelli tam communes quam speciales cujuscunque fuerint facultatis' and in 1254 the university refers to 'publicos servientes nostros, quos bedellos nominamus' (*Chart. Univ. Paris.* i. 223, no. 197; 256, no. 230).

terminology of the Cambridge constitution in this matter was influenced in the slightest degree by the Parisian development. What is certain is that Cambridge did not automatically imitate every custom of Oxford.[1] It borrowed institutions from the university but not always the titles.

More often than the facts warrant it has been assumed that Parisian customs or usage lingered on at Cambridge after disappearing at Oxford, for example, the custom of referring to places of residence as 'hostels'.[2] How misleading this assumption is may be seen from a reading of the Cambridge constitution. The word occurs just once and then only as part of a rubric or chapter-heading.[3] Throughout the text, as in the earliest Oxford statutes, scholars' lodgings are called *domus* or houses.[4] Moreover, the concession granted by the university in 1246 to St John's hospital with regard to the letting of its property outside the Trumpington gates shows that 'houses', not 'hostels', were taxed.[5] The later appropriation of the term *domus* to collegiate foundations such as Peterhouse and Michaelhouse has obscured its original meaning as a generic word for designating places where individual scholars or groups resided. As a matter of fact it was also used at Paris in this sense;[6] and even though Cambridge and Oxford came to describe the private residences of scholars differently, in the early thirteenth century it was customary at both universities to call places of residence 'houses'.[7]

The distinctive features of the language of the Cambridge constitution are few indeed, and there is no solid basis for the opinion that Cambridge preferred to follow Parisian rather than Oxford usage. If written statutes of an earlier or comparable date were available for Oxford the divergencies which do appear would very probably seem less striking. None the less, it must be admitted

[1] In Cambridge deeds of *c.* 1270 Walter de Oxonia, one of the university bedells, is described as *serviens*; cf. Stokes, *The esquire bedells of the university of Cambridge* (CAS, octavo series xlv [1911]), 129–31. The appellation 'common servant' is found in *SA* 167 (1304) and in some fifteenth-century statutes.

[2] Rashdall, *Universities*, iii. 293. Cf. Emden, *An Oxford hall*, p. 44.

[3] *Cons. Univ. Canteb.* XII (see below, p. 213, line 10).

[4] There is one reference to *hospicia* in the lengthy constitution *De domibus et scolis*; cf. *SAUO*, 79, 25.

[5] See above, p. 55. In the rent rolls of the hospital *hospitium* does not occur until the early fourteenth century and then only intermittently; cf. the cartulary (St John's College, Muniments), fos. 8^r–9^v, 81^v–86^r.

[6] Cf. *Chart. Univ. Paris.* i. 177–8, no. 136; 563, no. 478.

[7] See Emden, *op. cit.* pp. 43–5, for the whole question of nomenclature.

that by *c.* 1250 the Cambridge rectors were officially known at Oxford as proctors and the bedells as servants. A change or difference of title is not in itself of great significance, as long as the constitutional aspect of the office remains unaffected; but the refusal on the part of Cambridge to bring its terminology into line with that of Oxford is indicative of a wider and deeper cleavage.

There is no denying that the university at Cambridge was organized on the model of Oxford and that the constitution ultimately owes much to Oxford traditions and laws. The precise extent of this dependence is, however, questionable, for unlike the statutes of universities which were founded or influenced through migrations from Paris and Bologna, the Cambridge constitution is anything but a *réchauffé* of Oxford ingredients. Definite traces of these can be discerned and it is obvious that the chapter on academic dress is the Oxford statute, *De habitu magistrorum*, only slightly reshaped and augmented. This one instance apart, there is little textual evidence of the use of Oxford sources.

In Mullinger's history of the university one meets the staggering statement that its statutes 'had originally been little more than a transcript of those of Paris'.[1] How he arrived at this conclusion is a mystery. He had no knowledge of the existence of the Angelica manuscript, and the first volume of the *Chartularium universitatis Parisiensis*, which covers the period 1200–86, was not published until sixteen years after he went to press. Even if he did no more than compare the printed *statuta antiqua* of Cambridge with the Parisian texts published by de Boulay he could not possibly have made the above assertion. One is led to conclude that it was inspired by a misguided interest in eliminating any question of direct Oxford influence on the origin and development of the constitution of Cambridge. The author's most unhistorical acknowledgement to Paris in the cause of Cambridge is now best forgotten.[2]

The *a priori* possibility that the Cambridge constitution was moulded to some extent by Parisian customs and legislation cannot be dismissed. From the very beginnings of the *studium* at Cambridge there were contacts with Paris. Eustace, who was bishop of Ely when the migration from Oxford took place in 1209 and who fathered the new foundation, had been himself to Paris, where he was

[1] *University of Cambridge*, i. 343. He brackets Oxford with Cambridge.

[2] Mullinger appears to have accepted at its face value the thesis propounded by Peacock, *Observations*, p. 15n.

remembered as a master of great personal and scholarly distinction.[1] Some of the *magistri* who opened the first schools at Cambridge may have studied at Paris, and it is possible that there were Parisian scholars among the clerical adherents of Louis of France who were ordered out of the country by Henry III in 1218.[2] What is much more to the point is that the earliest evidence of statute-making at Cambridge derives from the years immediately following the general cessation of lectures at Paris in 1229. That an appreciable number of the dispersed masters and scholars availed of the open invitation of Henry and settled in Cambridge is implicitly confirmed by his reference to the 'multitude' of native and overseas scholars who had converged on the town by 1231.[3] One of these was in all probability Alan de Beccles, whom Matthew Paris places first among the famous English masters who returned home.[4] With the advent of the Friars Minor and Preacher *c.* 1225–38 the way was opened up for a fairly steady flow of ideas and writings and exchanges of personnel between Paris and Cambridge.

Notwithstanding the fact that Cambridge was directly exposed to Parisian influence, the editor of the constitution cannot be said to have utilized any written customs or statutes of the university. There are parallels in the text with enactments made at or for Paris; some of these we have already seen; but textual similarities are not enough. The catalogue of malefactors which forms part of chapter XI of the Angelica text runs somewhat like a section of the oath prescribed for regents in arts at Paris in 1251. If the Cambridge list was compiled from this source it would probably be indistinguishable from the version which appears among the 1307 statutes of Orléans; a comparison shows immediately which was derived from Paris and which was not:

[1] His obit was observed at the abbey of St Victor on 4 Feb. (he died on 3 Feb. 1215). The eulogy in the *necrologium* of the abbey speaks of him as 'magistri Eustachii Elyensis episcopi, qui vita celebris et scientia...' (*Chart. Univ. Paris.* i. 15, no. 17, n. 2).

[2] See above, p. 47, n. 3.

[3] 'Rex majori et ballivis Cantebrigie salutem. Satis constat vobis quod apud villam nostram Cantebrigie studenti [*sic*] causa e diversis partibus, tam cismarinis quam transmarinis, scolarium confluit multitudo' (*Close rolls, 1227–31*, p. 586).

[4] *Chron. Maj.* iii. 168. Alan was master by 1201 and hence could not possibly have incepted at Cambridge as suggested in *BRUC*, p. 49, where the reference 'EDRO, Liber B, p. 184' under the year 1226 is misleading. 'Liber B' should read 'Liber M' or more correctly 'G 3/28'. The date of the document cited, a charter of Hugh of Northwold which Alan de Beccles witnessed as archdeacon of Sudbury, is *c.* 1233–43, not 1226. Fuller details of this scholar will be found in *BRUO*, i. 145.

Paris	*Orléans*	*Cambridge*
nullum diffamatum de melleia frequenti, raptorem mulierum, fractorem hospiciorum, de nocte errabundum... petet [*sc.* regens] tamquam scolarem liberari. (*Chart. Univ. Paris.* i. 223, no. 197.)	nullum diffamatum de mesleya frequenti de nocte errabundum raptorem mulierum, fractorem hospitiorum... deffendet Universitas vel juvabit. (*Statuts*, i. 22, no. 24, § 21.)	Effractores domorum raptores mulierum Insidiatores uiarum. arma ad nocendum uel ad uindictam precipue de nocte defferentes...ab uniuersitate sine spe restitucionis deiciantur uel in carcerem detrudantur. (*Cons. Univ. Canteb.* xi. iv [see below, p. 211, line 19 to p. 213, line 2].)

This example should put us on our guard when tempted to see in other parallels between the Cambridge constitution and statutes of Paris evidence of borrowing. It is seldom that comparisons between the statutes of Cambridge and those of other universities which were influenced by Paris are possible, but when the opportunity does arise, as in this instance, the apparent connection between the Cambridge text and the corresponding Parisian statute or statutes is seen to be an illusion.

The degree to which the groundwork or actual formation of the Cambridge constitution was influenced by the diaspora of 1229 may best be judged by setting the text against the statutes of Angers, Orléans and Toulouse. Should anyone be tempted to doubt the known historical fact that these three universities benefited most from the Parisian exodus, a perusal of their statutes will quickly dispel any misgivings.[1] The stamp of Paris is plainly impressed on them. A very different image is presented by the Cambridge text. Whatever effect the influx of masters and scholars from Paris may have had on the intellectual life of the university it failed to make any real impact on its statutory development. Such vestiges or apparent vestiges of Parisian customs and legislation as meet the eye are inconclusive, and it must first be proved beyond a shadow of doubt that these were not legacies from Oxford.

The one institution that Cambridge may have adopted from Paris is the *curia magistrorum*, of which there is no trace in the statutes

[1] The earliest statutes of the three universities are conveniently assembled in *Statuts*, i. 15–23 (Orléans, 1307); 281–91, 320–35 (Angers, 1373, 1398–1410); 458–61, 467–95 (Toulouse, ?1280–1320, 1311–14).

of Oxford. Each regent master at Cambridge was empowered by the constitution to hold court and give judgement in all causes in which his scholars were defendants, other than suits of rents, gross offences and the peace.[1] A scholar was not obliged to stand trial before his master; he was entitled if he wished to have the case tried in the chancellor's court. There is nothing specifically Parisian about the jurisdiction vested in individual regent masters, and it would be difficult to prove that the relevant chapter of the constitution is only an elaboration of the statute promulgated by Courson at Paris in 1215: 'Quilibet magister forum sui scolaris habeat.'[2] The privilege ultimately derives from the Authentic *Habita* of Frederick I, and it became customary in England as elsewhere for bishops, chapters and abbots to delegate the masters of their schools with jurisdiction to hear and decide the causes of their scholars.[3] At Cambridge prior to the establishment of the office of chancellor a regent master in virtue of this custom probably had cognizance of suits of his scholars; the principle was doubtless too strongly entrenched for the chancellor to succeed in gaining exclusive control over the administration of justice in the university. At no time did his judicial powers *vis-à-vis* the regents become as absolute as those of the chancellor of Oxford.[4] The retention, therefore, of the *curia magistrorum* in the constitution, and the rules made for its functioning, need not be connected in any way with Courson's statute of 1215, which continued to be the sole statutory pronouncement during the century on the courts of the masters at the university of Paris.[5]

In the absence of apodictic proof of direct Parisian influence on the formation of the Cambridge constitution it is not to be expected that the statutes of Angers, Orléans or Toulouse have anything new to offer in the way of source material.[6] The statutes of Mont-

[1] *Cons. Univ. Canteb.* VI (see below, p. 203, lines 18–23).

[2] *Chart. Univ. Paris.* i. 79, no. 20.

[3] See below, pp. 149–50.

[4] Had the jurisdiction of the master of glomery or superintendent of the local grammar schools at Cambridge been absorbed by the chancellor, just as the office of *magister scolarum* was amalgamated with that of the chancellor at Oxford, the courts of the masters would probably have disappeared with the centralization of justice, irrespective of whether the scholars were members of the university or only grammarians.

[5] Cf. *Chart. Univ. Paris.* i. 622, no. 515 (1284).

[6] Peacock, *Observations*, p. 15n., thought that Orléans may have served as a model for Cambridge. His only justification for this unlikely suggestion is a reference to glomerels or grammar boys at Orléans. There was a master of glomery at Cambridge and mention is made of glomery schools (*scole glomerie*); but there was nothing significant about these terms. Cf. A. F. Leach, *The schools of medieval*

pellier deserve closer attention, although these, too, derive in part from Paris, granted that the law school was modelled on the pattern of Bologna, which thereby influenced the constitution of the university as a whole. None the less, more than one historian has commented upon the similarity between the organization of Montpellier, Oxford and Cambridge.[1] What is still more relevant to our present inquiry is that the statutes of the French university are earlier than the Cambridge constitution.

The Montpellier statutes are in no sense an organic body of laws devised for the government of the university. On 17 August 1220 Cardinal Conrad, the papal legate, made and published a batch of regulations for the faculty of medicine. Two further sets were issued in 1240, and on 27 March 1242 the bishop of Maguelone promulgated directives for the faculty of arts; his regulations are little more than a reissue of the 1220 constitutions.[2] In all three collections the figure of the bishop looms large.[3] The very first statute enacted in 1220 states that no one unless he has been regent in the university may lecture publicly until the bishop and some regent masters have examined and approved of him.[4] Another statute declares that the bishop and three masters, one of whom must be the senior, are to elect the chancellor, whose function will be to hear civil causes of scholars and administer justice.[5]

Though Hugh of Northwold as bishop of Ely attended the inauguration of new masters at Cambridge the constitution did not accord him any say in the approving or rejecting of candidates for the *magisterium*. The form of examination envisaged in the Montpellier statute may represent an adaptation of the custom in the faculty of theology at Paris; it never became part of the Cambridge system.[6] At Montpellier the bishop, not the chancellor, granted or

England (London, 1915), pp. 171–2; Rashdall, *Universities*, iii. 288, nn. 2–3. One has only to look at the 1307 statutes of Orléans, the earliest extant for the university, to realize how far removed they are from those of Cambridge.

[1] Rashdall, *Universities*, ii. 123–5; C. Thouzellier, 'La papauté et les universités provinciales en France dans la première moitié du XIIIe siècle', *Études médiévales offertes à M. le doyen Augustin Fliche* (Montpellier, 1952), pp. 194–5.

[2] *Statuts*, ii. 4–10, nos. 882, 885–6.

[3] Cf. in general Rashdall, *Universities*, ii. 123–4.

[4] *Statuts*, 4, no. 882; cf. 8, no. 885 (1240).

[5] *Ibid.* 5, no. 882.

[6] The old name for the actual ceremony of inception in theology at Paris was *aula*, so called because it took place in the bishop's palace. Cf. *I più antichi statuti della facoltà teologica dell'università di Bologna*, ed. F. Ehrle S.J. (Universitatis Bononiensis Monumenta, i [Bologna, 1932]), p. cxcvi, 1–2, 42; Pelster in *Oxford theology* pp. 45–7; Rashdall, *op. cit.* i. 484–6.

refused the licence to incept.[1] Under the Cambridge constitution this privilege was vested solely in the chancellor. Moreover, he was elected not by the bishop and a select body of masters but by the university of regents. In so far as the Cambridge chancellor was *par excellence* the university judge one may concede that his office resembled that of the chancellor of Montpellier. There, however, the parallel ends. The chancellor of Cambridge was both by institution and in virtue of the constitution head of the university; not so the chancellor of Montpellier. At Cambridge every member of the university was bound to obey the chancellor; he summoned and presided over convocations; and his jurisdiction was not constitutionally limited to the civil forum. Unlike the Montpellier chancellor he could delegate his judicial powers whether absent or not from the university, and he also possessed the faculty of excommunication. At Montpellier the chancellor was beholden to the bishop to back up his decrees with ecclesiastical censure, and there was no intermediate court.[2] The Cambridge constitution, on the contrary, recognizes the university of regents as a higher court than the chancellor's in certain matters. Clearly, the basis and direction of the constitutional organization of Cambridge differed from that of Montpellier.

There were, admittedly, some common features. The judicial character of the chancellor's office is one. Both universities insisted that bachelors must respond in all or most of the schools of their faculty (medicine at Montpellier) in order to qualify for the *magisterium*, but this was prescribed at every university.[3] The crucial point is that Cambridge did not require inceptors to undergo a formal examination, and certainly not before the bishop, as a prerequisite for obtaining the licence. In this whole matter it harnessed its practice to the Oxford system.[4] Montpellier scholars were obliged to incept under their actual masters.[5] This may well have been customary, too, at Cambridge by *c.* 1250 and it does seem that the master holding or presiding at the inception had to be a regent; but the constitution suggests that the inceptor had freedom of choice. At both universities inceptors were not admitted to the

[1] *Statuts*, ii. 9, no. 886. So jealously did the bishop covet this privilege that when absent he delegated his official, not the chancellor, to confer the licence. Cf. Rashdall, *op. cit.* ii. 124.

[2] Cf. *Statuts*, ii. 5, no. 882.

[3] For the Montpellier statute of 1240 cf. *ibid.* 7, no. 885.

[4] See below, pp. 119–22.

[5] Cf. *Statuts*, ii. 5, no. 882.

society of masters unless they swore to uphold the statutes. A corporal oath was demanded at Montpellier, whereas Cambridge, doubtless adhering to the Oxford custom, did not impose on all inceptors the duty of taking a formal oath; a pledge of faith might be accepted as an alternative.[1]

We also find in the 1220 statutes of Montpellier the regulation set down in chapter XI of the Cambridge constitution which ordered each scholar to have a definite master.[2] While it is not improbable that Cardinal Conrad in making the rule for Montpellier was influenced by the statute promulgated by his fellow-cardinal, Courson, at Paris five years earlier, there can be no doubt that the Cambridge decree was rooted in Oxford custom or law.[3]

On a wider estimate the 1220–40 statutes of the French university compare very unfavourably with those of Cambridge.[4] They shed little light on the constitution of a university whose greatest claim to fame was its school of medicine. One of the clearest proofs of the lack of communication between Montpellier and Cambridge is that the teaching of medicine is not so much as mentioned in the Angelica text. It is only too plain that the university of Montpellier exerted no influence on the constitutional and in particular the faculty organization of Cambridge; not a single statute bears the faintest resemblance to any chapter or paragraph of the text of the Cambridge constitution.

No study of university sources would be complete without taking stock of the statutes of Bologna, the archetype of most continental universities and one whose traditions profoundly affected the formation of the constitutions of medieval *studia generalia*. From a very early date England, or rather Oxford, had direct contacts with the home of jurisprudence. The connection was

1 See below, pp. 128–9. For the Montpellier statute cf. *Statuts, loc. cit.*

2 Cf. *Statuts, loc. cit.*

3 See above, pp. 72–3. Under the Montpellier statute scholars were not obliged to have their names entered in the roll of their master. Rashdall, *Universities*, ii. 124–5, suggests a relationship between the office of the proctors at Oxford and Montpellier. He also notes the use of what he calls 'the Oxford term', *cetus magistrorum*, at Montpellier. His arguments, based on Montpellier statutes of the early fourteenth century, are unconvincing. The expression *cetus magistrorum* is found in Cambridge documents before 1300.

4 The 1220 statute of Montpellier on funerals is primitive indeed when compared with chapter XIII of the Cambridge constitution. All it says is: 'Omnes tam magistri quam scolares diligenter et devote prosequantur exsequias mortuorum' (*Statuts*, ii. 5, no. 882).

maintained and deepened during the thirteenth century, though not every English scholar took law at Bologna;[1] nor did every master of Bologna come to England to lecture. Accursius, granted that he made his temporary home at or near Oxford, entered the civil service of Edward I, whose legal adviser he remained from 1273 to 1281.[2] One of the official redactors of the Bologna statutes of 1347 was the Englishman, Gilbert de Yarwell, then rector of the ultramontane nations.[3] He probably studied at Cambridge before going out to Italy and on his return may have brought back with him the copy of the *Liber Statutorum universitatis Bononiensis* which Robert Hare presented to Trinity Hall.[4] Movements of scholars or interchanges of this kind between Bologna and Cambridge cannot be traced before the end of the thirteenth century.[5] Cambridge did have a faculty of canon law at an early date, but there is no evidence of any sort which might link its establishment with the advent of a master or masters from Bologna; and the delay in erecting a faculty of civil law does not encourage one to speculate about the possibility of the constitution of Cambridge having been influenced by direct contacts with the centre of legal studies.[6] It is noteworthy that when the faculty was established its earliest known professor, Simon de Asceles, came from Oxford, not from Bologna.

1 Nicholas de Farnham, who returned from Paris with Alan de Beccles and other English masters in 1229, had previously read medicine at Bologna. He settled in Oxford. Cf. *BRUO*, ii. 669.

2 See above, p. 44, n. 1.

3 *Statuti*, p. 6. He was rector from May 1346 to May 1347. Cf. Denifle, 'Die Statuten der Juristen-Universität Bologna vom J. 1317–1347, und deren Verhältniss zu jenen Paduas, Perugias, Florenz', *Archiv für Literatur- und Kirchengeschichte*, iii (1887), 206. Yarwell was collated to the church of Blofield (not Glofeld, as stated in Denifle and Malagola) on 15 Oct. 1327. He was still rector of this church in 1347. Cf. *Statuti, loc. cit.* and *BRUC*, pp. 664, 687.

4 Cf. B.M. Harl. MS 7040 (Baker, xiii), p. 229. The copy of the statutes has long since disappeared from the library of the Hall. It is not listed in Haenel's *Catalogi librorum manuscriptorum* (Leipzig, 1830), p. 783. A MS entitled *Statuta universitatis Cantabrigiensis* is mentioned (no. 18), but it has not been traced. Cf. also M. R. James, *A descriptive catalogue of the manuscripts in the library of Trinity Hall* (Cambridge, 1907), p. viii.

5 William Comyn, brother of Earl John of Buchan, possibly incepted as master at Bologna before resuming his studies at Cambridge in 1298–9. Cf. *BRUC*, p. 153.

6 One of the sources of the constitution appears to be Tancred's *Ordo iudiciarius* (see below, pp. 98–9), but this was a standard work and there is no reason to think that it reached Cambridge through Bolognese channels. The earliest evidence of the circulation of the writings of masters of Bologna at Cambridge is apparently CUL MS Mm. 4. 41 (saec. xiii*ex*/xiv*in*); fos. 33ra–47vb contain a text of Joannes de Deo, *Summa de penitentia*.

It is against this unpromising background that one must evaluate the relationship between the customs or statutes of Bologna and the Cambridge constitution. We have seen that the vice-chancellor of Cambridge was originally known as the chancellor's 'substitute'; so, too, the official who deputized at Bologna for an absent rector. The academic year at both universities opened on 10 October (the day after the feast of St Denis), and extraordinary lectures in canon law commenced at the hour of none. The list of parallels could easily be extended and it might also be claimed that the Cambridge *curia magistrorum* is of Bolognese origin. In general it may be said that some of the parallels are purely accidental and devoid of any significance. There is no doubt, however, that certain features of the constitution of Cambridge derive from Bologna, but these were the common heritage of universities and their incorporation in the Angelica text does not point to any direct connection between Bologna and Cambridge. The constitutional relationship was a distant one and those Bolognese traditions or statutes which are reflected in the Cambridge text were transmitted indirectly through Oxford or other channels. Needless to say, there is no evidence of textual affiliations, for the Cambridge code is much earlier than Giovanni d'Andrea's digest of the statutes of Bologna.

Actually, the most tangible proof of possible Italian influence on the formation of the Cambridge statutes comes not from Bologna but from the statutes of the city of Padua. In 1260 the commune decreed that scholars must pay their rents in two instalments: the first on the feast of All Saints (1 November), the second on the feast of the Purification (2 February).[1] These were also terminal dates for the payment of rents at Cambridge; but the constitution provides for a more equitable system of payment by spreading the instalments over three instead of two terms, the third and final instalment falling due on Ascension Thursday.[2] Whether or not the commune of Padua based its system on the custom of Bologna is immaterial. Cambridge devised its own scheme of rent-payment.[3]

1 Cf. *Statuti del Comune*, ed. Denifle in *Universitäten*, pp. 801, 805. These dates also coincided with the payments of salaries to the doctors in canon and civil law.

2 *Cons. Univ. Canteb.* XII. i (see below, p. 213, lines 11–14).

3 All that the statutes of the commune of Bologna have to say is: 'pensiones hospitiorum scolarium solvantur secundum quod solvuntur per cives' (Gaudenzi, 'Antichi statuti', *loc. cit.* 126, no. VIII). The university statutes make no reference to the payment of rents on the feasts of All Saints and the Purification. The statutes of

An analysis of the statutes of other universities leads to the conclusion that of all contemporary universities Oxford has the most if not the only claim to have influenced the background and composition of the Cambridge constitution. The contribution from this source, however, was more remote than proximate; more in the nature of customs than actual statutes; indeed only one Oxford statute, that on the habit of the masters, can be identified. The Angelica text occasionally seems closer to Paris than Oxford, but it has to be remembered that the *statuta antiqua* of Oxford may not reflect more faithfully than do the 'ancient' statutes of Cambridge the usage and organization of the university during the first half of the thirteenth century. While it is true that the *curia magistrorum*, which forms the subject of chapter VI of the Cambridge constitution, was unknown at Oxford, to seek its origin in the Parisian statute of 1215 is not justified by the evidence. The common debt of both the English universities to Paris cannot be disowned, but as far as the constitution of Cambridge goes there is this difference: Oxford borrowed directly, Cambridge indirectly.

The implicit references to the writs issued by Henry III in 1231 make it necessary to extend our survey of sources. Though the king did not impose any statute on the university, cognizance was taken of his writs except in the opening paragraph of chapter VII.[1] There is also a general reference to the custom of the kingdom—it says 'region' in the manuscript—regarding feudal services chargeable on tenements.[2] Whether some of the provisions of the constitution embody directives of the bishops of Ely is impossible to say. The presumption is to the contrary, since the one chapter, that on the chancellor, where we might expect to find evidence of episcopal intervention reads as if the bishop did not matter. An indirect reference to a canon of the Council of Oxford (1222) has been noted, as well as the bearing of the papal indult of 14 June 1233 on a section of chapter XI. It is worth quoting again and rather more fully side by side with the relevant passage in the constitution to show how sources might on occasion be manipulated:

Padua University incorporate the 1260 statute of the commune, but do not state that scholars were bound to pay their rents on 1 November and 2 February. Cf. Denifle, 'Die Statuten der Juristen-Universität Padua vom Jahre 1331', *Archiv für Lit. u. Kirch. Gesch.* vi (1892), 516 (11). At all events, the statute of the Padua commune is later than the date of the Cambridge constitution.

1 See above, pp. 76–7.

2 *Cons. Univ. Canteb.* XII. viii (see below, p. 215, lines 25–6).

Gregory IX	*Cambridge constitution*
Vestra nobis sane devotio intimavit quod nonnulli clerici et alii qui simulata causa studii in villa Cantebrigie convenire ceperunt vobiscum plus seditioni quam scientie insistentes ...per litteras apostolicas super violenta iniectione manuum et rebus aliis ad judices remotos contra speciales personas et quosdam alios impetratas, pretextu illarum generalium clausularum, videlicet *quidam alii* et *rebus aliis*, eos faciunt ad iudicium malitiose vocari, non ut causam habeant contra ipsos, sed ut tuam, fili cancellarie, disciplinam eludant, et illi fatigati laboribus et expensis cogantur affecti tedio componere cum eisdem. Nos ergo... auctoritate vobis presentium indulgemus ne quis de cetero predictarum clausularum pretextu quenquam de universitate vestra...paratum coram te, fili cancellarie, vel diocesano episcopo iustitiam...exhibere trahere possit ad iudicium extra diocesim Eliensem. (*Reg. Grégoire IX*, i. 779–80, no. 1389.)[1]	...necnon et qui clericum et laycum de uilla cantebrigie extra uillam per clausas illas quidam alii et rebus aliis conuenerint eciam nemine deferente super hoc conuicti propter quietem publicam per cancellarium et magistros ab uniuersitate sine spe restitucionis deiciantur uel in carcerem detrudantur iuxta formam supradictam. (*Cons. Univ. Canteb.* XI. iv [see below, p. 211, line 21 to p. 213, line 3].)

The intent of the papal letter is clear enough. A class of unscrupulous scholars had been making a profit by procuring letters of delegation on the plea that having suffered injury at the hands of other scholars they were denied justice in the chancellor's court. It was a trick to force the defendants to compound with them for an exorbitant sum of money in order to avoid costly litigation and such incidental expenses as were connected with citations before 'faraway' judges delegate of the pope. The abuse was brought to the notice of Gregory IX by the university, at whose request he sought to prevent the misuse of papal courts by granting the cognizance of such actions to the chancellor, saving the right of the plaintiffs to plead alternatively before the bishop.

That the statute of the university was devised to curb the activities of rapacious scholars after the papal indult ceased to be effective need not be doubted; but it had also the more positive aim of blocking

[1] Collated with the text in Denifle, *Universitäten*, p. 370, n. 627. Minor changes have been made as regards punctuation and spelling.

litigious-minded scholars from circumventing the jurisdiction of the chancellor.[1] It will be noticed that it is no longer merely a question of scholar *v*. scholar; the citation of clerks and laymen of the town of Cambridge before judges delegate under the general terms *quidam alii* and *rebus aliis* is likewise probihited. Any scholar who attempted to obtain letters of delegation from the pope was to be expelled forever from the university and might even be sent to prison.[2] The statute as framed obviously exceeds the scope of the indult of 14 June 1233, and is much more restrictive than the Oxford custom which allowed, but did not compel, a scholar to sue in the chancellor's court, provided the respondent resided within the precincts of the university.[3]

Apart from the letter of Gregory IX and reminiscences of legal maxims which occur in chapters I and XII of the constitution,[4] the only remaining source that can be identified is Tancred's *Ordo iudiciarius* (1214–16).[5] The evidence, owing to the all too brief and general way in which the compiler of the Angelica text edited chapter X of the constitution, is open to criticism:

Tancred	*Cambridge constitution*
In omnibus causis hoc iuramentum [*sc.* calumniae] prestatur, exceptis spiritualibus... Sed licet in spiritualibus in principio de calumnia non iuretur, de veritate tamen dicenda iuratur in processu. (*Ordo iudiciarius*, pt iii, tit. 2, ed. F. Bergmann [Göttingen, 1842], p. 202.)	In processibus causarum tam actor quam reus sine accepcione personarum etsi non de calumpnia de ueritate tamen dicenda et falsitate subticenda iuramentum prestent corporale. (*Cons. Univ. Canteb.* x. i [see below, p. 209, lines 14–16].)

[1] There is an allusion, too, to this practice in the papal letter: 'eos faciunt ad iudicium malitiose vocari, non ut causam habeant contra ipsos, sed ut tuam, fili cancellarie, disciplinam eludant' (*loc. cit.*).

[2] They came under the category of 'malefactors' or undisciplined scholars and hence the provisions of the first of the writs issued by the king on 3 May 1231 could be invoked against them. The penalties laid down in the constitution were meant no doubt to deter scholars from declining the jurisdiction of the chancellor and presumably would not be enforced if the plaintiff withdrew his action. We find a somewhat similar rule at Bologna in the case of landlords who cited a doctor or scholar by authority of the Holy See or a papal legate or any other judge. If a landlord did not desist from the suit within eight days of being warned by the rector or rectors the penalty of banning his hostel in perpetuity was to be invoked by the university. Cf. *Statuti*, p. 125, rubr. lxviij. This statute was copied by the university of Padua exactly, like almost all its statutes, from the Bologna code. Cf. Denifle, 'Statuten der jur. Univ. Padua', *loc. cit.* 503 (19).

[3] Cf. *SAUO*, 96, 18–23.

[4] See below, pp. 196, *app. crit.* ad 2, 214 ad 21–3.

[5] The first recension of the work has been dated to these years. See B. Kurtscheid, O.F.M., and F. A. Wilches, O.F.M., *Historia iuris canonici*, i (Rome, 1943), 243, 245.

Though the Cambridge editor, unlike Tancred, makes no overt distinction between spiritual and other causes, he implies that the oath of calumny will be taken by both plaintiff and defendant in all suits, but there may be exceptions. These can only be spiritual suits. In such cases the parties must swear to tell the truth. The Cambridge text, therefore, comes to the same thing as Tancred's; the two in fact do no more than state the current canonical procedure. After all, the chancellor's court was an ecclesiastical tribunal and its proceedings were conducted according to the rules of canon law.[1] These were defined, as far as oaths are concerned, for England in one of the constitutions promulgated by Cardinal Otto at the Council of London in 1237.[2] It does not appear that this constitution had any bearing on the construction of the Cambridge enactment, and there can be little or no doubt that the actual source was the passage from Tancred's *Ordo iudiciarius*.[3] If we isolate the nuclei of this passage and the paragraph of the Cambridge constitution the relationship between the two becomes very evident indeed:

Tancred	*Cambridge constitution*
licet...de calumnia non iuretur, de veritate tamen dicenda iuratur.	etsi non de calumpnia de ueritate tamen dicenda...iuramentum prestent.

Both passages are textually so alike that one is emboldened to suggest that whoever framed the Cambridge statute had his copy of Tancred before him when drawing up the text. If so, he must have put it aside immediately afterwards, for in the very next paragraph he outlines a type of judicial procedure which fell far short of the demands of the solemn process so expertly and lucidly expounded by the great Bolognese jurist.

The foregoing survey represents a fairly exhaustive investigation into the sources of the Angelica text. Some, perhaps a number, of *fontes* have escaped detection.[4] From what we have been able to

[1] See pp. 109, 162–6.

[2] Cf. *Constitutiones Ottonis*, c. 24: 'Iusiurandum calumpnie in causis ecclesiasticis civilibus, et de veritate dicenda in spiritualibus, quo et veritas aperiatur facilius et cause celerius terminentur, statuimus prestari decetero in regno Anglie, secundum canonicas et legittimas sanctiones, obtenta in contrarium consuetudine non obstante, huic statuto utiliter adnectentes ut iudiciales inducie dentur arbitrio, iuxta legittimas et canonicas sanctiones' (*Councils & Synods*, II. i. 256).

[3] The Cambridge statute prescribes the oath *de veritate dicenda* only for the principals in a suit. It seems that witnesses were also required to take this oath according to the constitution of Otto. Cf. *ibid.* 262, n. 4, 470 (c. 8).

[4] One may detect, rightly or wrongly, in the chapter on the office of the rectors an echo of a decree made by the papal legate at Oxford in 1214 which states that the

muster it appears that no attempt was made by the editor to draw on the statutes of other universities apart from Oxford; and indeed his use of written Oxford sources was minimal. No doubt, the constitution portrays a university system of which Oxford was the prototype, and it must also be granted that Oxford customs lie at the root of many provisions of the constitution. Yet the actual text is on the whole a thoroughly original work and represents a codification of select customs which Cambridge made its own, as well as statutes framed by the university itself.

It is next to impossible to say how much of the material already existed in statutory form by 1254, the *terminus ad quem* of the composition of the Angelica text. Chapters V, VII. i and XI. i–ii are almost certainly straight transcripts of earlier statutes, and possibly chapters IV and XII. i–ii as well. The first and last chapters (I and XIII. i) are probably the most original parts of the constitution; they appear to have been specially written when the text was being prepared for publication. One can only hazard a guess about the extent to which customs entered into the making of the constitution; they may account for as much as two-thirds of the text.

From internal evidence it is possible to gain some idea of the relative dates of the various chapters. The opening chapter, *De eleccione Cancelarii atque ipsius potestate*, shows that the right of electing the chancellor had been conceded to or claimed at any rate by the university. Moreover, it contains the operative word *statuimus* and there is a cross-reference in the final paragraph to the earlier and later parts of the text, which suggests that this chapter was put together *c.* 1250, that is, when the constitution was cast in literary form. Chapter II presupposes that the university was firmly established, highly organized and conscious of its own importance. It allows for the incorporation of regents from other 'approved' and comparable universities. The faculty of theology is mentioned, which shows that the provisions of the chapter cannot be later than *c.* 1240. Chapter III, on the academic year, doubtless embodies some of the earliest customs of the university; it, too, originated

burgesses must take an oath 'quod uictualia & alia necessaria iusto & rationabili precio scolaribus uendent & ab aliis uendi fideliter procurabunt & quod in fraudem huius prouisionis graues non facient constitutiones uel onerosas per quas clericorum conditio deterioretur' (*Med. Arch. Univ. Oxford*, i. 3). Cf. *Cons. Univ. Canteb.* VII. ii–iii (see below, p. 205, lines 6–21). The significance of parallel passages of this kind must remain a matter for speculation.

by *c.* 1240, for it shows again that the theologians were an integral part of the university organization. Chapter IV (convocations) is probably one of the oldest sections of the constitution. Chapter V (academic dress) owes its inspiration to the Council of Oxford (1222); it was enacted as a formal statute by *c.* 1240, since it specifically mentions regents in theology. Chapter VI (*De curia magistrorum*) may be earlier than 1231; it refers to the rents of houses and suits concerning the peace, but it makes no reference to the king's writs of that year regarding these matters. Chapter VII (rectors) also appears to derive from the period before 1231. The first section of this chapter, as has been suggested above, appears to be earlier than 3 May of that year and was one of the first statutes, if not the very first, made by the university. Indeed the remainder of the chapter may be nothing more than a reissue of ancient customs. Chapter VIII (bedells) is certainly ancient; it relates to one of the oldest offices in the university; in its present form it is probably not later than *c.* 1240; sections i and ii contain provisions concerning the schools of theology. Chapter IX is not earlier than 1231. Chapter X (judicial procedure) is later than 1214–16 and appears to derive from *c.* 1250, since it prescribes summary trials as opposed to the elaborate procedure in vogue before the mid-thirteenth century. Chapter XI (scholarity) consists of five paragraphs, three of which date from the thirties of the century. Chapter XII (hostels) is probably pre-1231; it cannot be earlier than 1219, for it refers to houses which had been used as schools for ten years and 1209 is the date of the inauguration of lectures at Cambridge. The first paragraph of chapter XIII can be dated to *c.* 1231–54 and, as has been suggested, was written *de novo c.* 1250 by the editor of the constitution. Sections ii and iii are probably much earlier and may represent customs which go back to the origins of the university.

When the editor or committee entrusted with the task of codification produced the final draft it was doubtless discussed and possibly modified at one or more congregations of the regents before it was finally promulgated as the definitive text of the statutes in the name of the chancellor and university at a session held in St Mary's Church, the seat of convocation. Apparently, the text was not submitted to the bishop, Hugh of Northwold, for his approval. In 1276 his immediate successor but one, Hugh Balsham, had occasion to recite two of the statutes contained in the original code but made no allusion to their having been confirmed by any bishop; all he says is that the statutes were 'edited' by the chancellor and masters.[1] He was referring to the regent masters, for the constitution itself declares that the chancellor is not free to make any new statutes without the consent of the regents; rather must he see to the observance of statutes enacted in common, that is, by himself and the regent masters.[2] Not a word is said about the non-regents and we can only conclude that they had no share in the making of the constitution or in the enactment of statutes by *c.* 1250.[3]

[1] '...inter alia laudabile statutum et salubre a dictis cancellario et Magistris editum diligenter inspeximus...' (CUA, doc. no. 5; *Vet. Lib. Archid. Elien.* 22).

[2] 'Cancelarius nichil noui sine consensu regencium statuere presumat. set supra et infra communiter statuta efficacius intendat custodire' (*Cons. Univ. Canteb.* I. vi [see below, p. 199, lines 1–3]). The Orléans statutes of 1307 were also made by the head of the university, the rector, together with the doctors 'ordinarie in utroque jure regentes' and the proctors of the nations; cf. *Statuts*, i. 17–19.

[3] At Oxford the enactment of statutes was the prerogative of the 'cetus magistrorum regencium et non regencium' (*SAUO*, p. xxv), but was this true of the early thirteenth century? Does the expression 'Statuit vniuersitas Oxonie' or 'vniuersitas magistrorum' include the non-regents? These expressions are found in statutes of 1253 and 1257 and it has been assumed that the term *universitas* already comprised both regents and non-regents. The Cambridge constitution suggests that by *c.* 1250 it meant only the chancellor and regents. An examination of the statute of 1253 appears to confirm this view. It was subscribed to by the chancellor, all the regents in theology, specific mention being made of Hugh de Misterton, the regents in decrees and civil law (there is no reference to medicine, probably because there was no regent in the faculty at the time), and the two rectors or proctors representing the faculty of arts. Adam Marsh, who reported the whole incident to his provincial, was also asked to give his assent. He was then non-regent, but that was not the reason why his approval was requested. In any case the statute was passed against his wishes and indeed without the concurrence of a single non-regent. Cf. *Epp. fr. Adae de Marisco* in *Mon. Franc.* i. 346–9, no. CXCII. Yet the text of the statute begins: 'Statuit vniuersitas Oxonie' (*SAUO*, 49, 15–16). Evidently, *universitas* was synonymous with the congregation of regents, and they alone were competent to make statutes. Lest any doubt arise about Misterton's status when the statute was enacted on 12 March 1253 it should be pointed out that he was *actu regens* when he subscribed to its terms, although he resigned his chair in protest two days later or perhaps immediately after the statute was carried. Cf. Rashdall, 'The friars Preachers *v.* the university', *loc. cit.* p. 232. The fact that the non-regents both at Oxford and Cambridge were associated in 1274–6 with the promulgation of certain statutes is hardly relevant, since bachelors were likewise called upon to give their assent; the statutes were obviously exceptional measures. Cf. *Med. Arch. Univ. Oxford*, i. 33 and below, p. 226.

Chapter 5

ANALYSIS OF THE TEXT

The thirteen chapters which make up the Cambridge constitution are relatively short, and are written in a simple, straightforward style which perfectly accords with the general tone of the contents. The text envisages a university—the term *studium* is never used in this context—composed of a chancellor, masters, bachelors, scholars and common servants. The governing body consists of the chancellor, who is head of the corporation, and the regent masters. They elect two of their number as rectors, whose duties are largely administrative; they also appoint two bedells, who assist the chancellor and rectors in various capacities and are general factotums of the university. The chancellor or his deputies exercise jurisdiction and administer justice on behalf of the society, whose will both outside and inside the university they express. In addition each regent master is empowered to hold court for his own scholars, and certain directives are given about procedural matters. The admission of scholars to the degree of master and regulations concerning lectures and disputations form an important part of the constitution, so important in fact that the relevant chapter occupies a position next to that on the chancellor. The constitution also contains machinery for safeguarding the economic and social interests of the society, and provision, too, is made for the commemoration of deceased benefactors and attendance at funerals of members of the university.

Such in broadest outline is the constitution which is about to be analysed. If one turns to the text itself the picture becomes sharper and fuller, but nothing like a satisfying impression, still less a view in depth, may be expected from a perusal of the contents. The text is in fact deceptive in its simplicity; and when the scope of inquiry into the seemingly primitive statutes is widened and deepened, the brevity of the constitution appears in inverse proportion to its value. A single phrase or even a word may contain a wealth of meaning, and one is tempted to embark on an *expositio litteralis*. There are of course gaps in the constitution, the most regrettable being the absence of any precise information on the curriculum, and it is obvious that a good deal of material has been compressed into short paragraphs. The later history of the constitution goes some way towards remedying these defects, for it is only in the light of subsequent constitutional developments and enactments that much of what is hidden behind the text becomes clear.[1] To understand fully the import of the constitution we should need to see it within the wider context of the statutes of contemporary universities and most of all the medieval constitution of Cambridge as a whole.[2] Of necessity the canvas has to be severely curtailed. Fortunately, the arrangement of the text helps to facilitate a straight analysis without obscuring the total impression of the constitution.[3] We shall proceed, therefore, chapter by chapter, making such observations as the limits allow.

ANGELICA CHAPTER I: THE CHANCELLOR

A *universitas*, says the celebrated canonist, Sinibaldo de' Fieschi, who took the title of Innocent IV on his election to the papacy in 1243, is composed of two elements, the one external, the other internal: recognition by legitimate authority, and the common will of the members which gives their self-constituted society its solidarity and official form.[4] On both counts Cambridge ranked as a university by *c.* 1250. It was recognized as a public, juridical corporation by bishop, king and pope. The corporate will of its members, of which we have seen evidence in 1246, was theoretically expressed by its written constitution. In practice a society must have an acknowledged head, a centre of unity, one who signifies and declares the common if not unanimous will of the members. Indeed the Cambridge constitution suggests that the office of chancellor was not

[1] The chapters on the later recensions have therefore more than a purely textual value. It is clear that the redactors of Markaunt's text and the *statuta antiqua* were aware of the obscurities and presuppositions of the basic text.

[2] This is all the more necessary in view of Rashdall's very curt treatment of the constitution. Dr Emden's annotations and further comments atone somewhat for this deficiency; but the comments of both scholars are with one or two exceptions valid only for the period *c.* 1300–1500.

[3] Compare the plan of Gibson's admirable summary of the Oxford constitution (*SAUO*, pp. lxx–lxxxv). We cannot hope, however, to emulate his brilliant survey of the curriculum at Oxford.

[4] Cf. Michaud-Quantin, 'La conscience d'être membre d'une universitas', in *Beiträge zum Berufsbewusstsein des mittelalterlichen Menschen*, p. 11.

instituted for the purpose of conferring the *licentia docendi* or for the administration of justice but primarily because a university experiences difficulty in reaching unanimity,[1] a view which is as true today as when it was first stated by the Roman jurists, Paul and Ulpian.[2]

The framers of the Cambridge constitution imply that the office of chancellor was an autonomous creation on the part of the regent masters, in much the same way as the rectorship of Bologna University was instituted by the *universitas scholarium*.[3] It may well be that *c.* 1215 the regents elected one of their number as head of the *studium* and that the chancellorship was a natural development from this step. The evidence from Oxford on the contrary shows that the office was specially instituted by the bishop.[4] It is unhistorical to imagine that the original body of masters at Cambridge had a corporate consciousness; this was a later development. Modelled as it was on the Oxford pattern, the chancellorship combined the functions of an archdeacon with those of a chancellor of a cathedral chapter or a *magister scolarum*. The only authority competent to carve out the new office of chancellor was the bishop of the diocese.

At what date the right to elect was conceded to the regents we cannot say. One of the prerogatives of a corporation was the power to co-elect. It may be assumed that the bishop accepted or recognized this right by the time mag. Hugh de Hotton became chancellor. Hotton held office by 1246, but since the university enjoyed juridical standing as a corporate entity by 1233 there must have been at least a tacit understanding between the bishop and the regent masters before Hotton's election that the university might elect and present their candidate for confirmation in office.

The constitution views the chancellorship exclusively in terms of a corporation. There is no reference of any kind to the bishop in this connection. It is not stated that the chancellor held his commission from the bishop; that he remained only chancellor-elect until his election was confirmed by the bishop, to whom he had to make canonical submission; or that he was *ex officio* the vicegerent of the bishop, who granted him spiritual jurisdiction, which was the

[1] *Cons. Univ. Canteb.* I. i: 'Quoniam difficile est uniuersitatem consentire communi consensu et omni uoluntate' (see below, p. 197, lines 2–3).

[2] Cf. *Digesta*, 41, 2, 1, quoted *ibid.*, and Michaud-Quantin, 'Collectivités médiévales', in *Antike und Orient im Mittelalter*, p. 244.

[3] Stelling-Michaud, *Université de Bologne*, p. 27.

[4] In his award of 1214 the legate speaks of the 'cancellarii quem episcopus Lincolniensis ibidem scolaribus preficiet' (*Med. Arch. Univ. Oxford*, i. 3).

basis of his power. There was no need and perhaps no great desire on the part of the university *c.* 1250 to acknowledge all this in the constitution. Hugh of Northwold, the diocesan, must have been perfectly satisfied that his rights were fully understood and required no formal restatement. At the same time he must have agreed that the makers of the constitution were entitled to define within limits the position of the chancellor as the elected head of a corporation. Unlike the chancellor of Paris, the Cambridge official was at once both the bishop's delegate and an inner member of the university.[1]

That the constitution was an act of the university of regent masters, who formally constituted the corporation, is obvious from the use of the word *statuimus* in the very first paragraph. It is significant that the reason given for having a chancellor is not directly related either to the question of spiritual jurisdiction or the conferring of the licence. The necessity for a head is dictated by the nature of a university *qua* corporation. Unity of will and government demands that there should be someone who personifies and puts into effect that will, someone who is *maior inter omnes*. The phrase is reminiscent of communal usage and was doubtless carefully chosen, for it suggests that the chancellor is indeed the superior but not a law unto himself. The term *caput* or head, which came into vogue at a very late period and meant something very different, was not a popular expression in the university.[2] If the Oxford precedent holds good, we may assume that the chancellor in order to qualify for office had to be *actu regens* or professor in one of the superior faculties, which implies that before 1255 or thereabouts Cambridge chancellors were drawn from the faculties of canon law and theology. Actually, the only qualities expressly required by the constitution of a candidate were 'knowledge, willingness and ability'.[3] Nothing is laid down about the duration of one's tenure of office or the time of election.[4]

[1] Peacock, *Observations*, p. 19, is not quite accurate when he describes the chancellorship as a 'distinct estate' within the university.

[2] The chancellor is never described as *caput* in the constitution or even in the later statutes. The appellation was used in a sermon preached by an unnamed bishop of Ely, who in the presence of the university referred probably with some relish to 'Dominum nostrum cancellarium, caput hujus Universitatis venerabilis nostre jurisdictionis' (G. R. Owst, *Preaching in medieval England* [Cambridge, 1926], p. 263). The sermon must have been delivered before 1401.

[3] *Cons. Univ. Canteb.* I. i (see below, p. 197, lines 3–4). The usual canonical requirements were *scientia, aetas, mores*.

[4] The list of chancellors in *V.C.H. Cambs.* iii. 331–2, as Dr Emden, *BRUC*, p. xxvii, has pointed out, is unreliable. Whatever was the length of tenure in the early

According to a statement made in 1337 in reply to Bishop Montacute, who questioned the election of Richard de Harlyng, D.Cn.L., elections were carried out from time immemorial 'summarie et de plano sine scriptis'.[1] The truth of this claim is substantiated by the constitution. At Paris the rector was elected by indirect vote; so, too, the chancellor of Oxford, where the choice rested with a committee of eight chosen from the faculties. This indirect system was authorized by canon 24 of the Fourth Lateran Council as an alternative to the direct method, which was in fact the one sanctioned by the Cambridge constitution. All the regents voted as individuals and not through their faculty. They did not write down their votes but communicated them orally and in secret to three tellers who then announced the result, the candidate with a majority of the votes being declared elected.[2] The procedure differed from the decree of the council, and this happened also at Paris and Oxford, in that no record was kept of the votes and it was sufficient for the successful candidate to win the consent of the *maior pars* of the electors, not the *maior et sanior pars*, if he did not secure a unanimous vote.[3]

It was one thing to elect, perhaps 'nominate' would be a more accurate term; it was another thing to appoint. The regents at Cambridge claimed to do both: 'statuimus ut cancelarius... omnibus per regentes preficiatur'.[4] If this passage had been written two centuries later it would stand as a true statement in law. The obligation of seeking confirmation and with it the grant of ecclesi-

period, in 1283–95 the term of office varied from one to three years. For the statute on biennial elections see below, p. 247. The customary time for holding the election was around Pentecost. Cf. Ely Dioc. Rec. G I (2), fo. 76^v.

1 *Ibid.* G I (1), fo. 2^r; cf. fo. 9^r.

2 The Lateran canon states: 'statuimus ut...assumantur tres de collegio fide digni, qui secrete et sigillatim vota cunctorum diligenter exquirant et in scriptis redacta mox publicent in communi...ut is collatione habita eligatur, in quem omnes, vel maior et sanior pars consensit' (c. 42. x. 1. 6). It is possible that the two rectors and the senior religious master or doctor of theology acted as scrutators at elections *c.* 1250. Cf. the detailed procedure laid down in Markaunt 2 (see below, p. 313, line 25 to p. 314, line 17) and 11 (see below, p. 316, line 15 to p. 317, line 11); *SA* 4 (*Docs*, i. 309–10) and *SA* 53 (*ibid.* 338–9).

3 It may be that the university anticipated Gierke's view that the force of *et* in *maior et sanior pars* was not copulative but indicative, meaning *id est*. This interpretation is not borne out by the decision of the Holy See given in the interesting case which became the decretal c. 57. x. 1. 6. We shall meet the phrase again, but not in connection with the election of the chancellor.

4 *Cons. Univ. Canteb.* 1. i (see below, p. 197, lines 3–5).

astical jurisdiction from the bishop was not lifted until 1401 when Boniface IX in his bull *Dum attentae* declared that once the chancellor was elected he was deemed confirmed in office and thereby enjoyed jurisdiction.[1] Evidently, Hugh of Northwold was a much more tolerant bishop than Oliver Sutton or John Dalderby of Lincoln, neither of whom would have had the slightest hesitation about rejecting the word *preficiatur* in the Cambridge constitution.[2] This expression is all the stranger because it was used by bishops of Ely when confirming chancellors-elect; the formula varied but was generally expressed thus: 'we confirm your election and appoint (*preficimus*) you chancellor'.[3] That is precisely what the constitution says of the regents: 'the regents...shall appoint a chancellor'. The phrase may be interpreted as containing an implicit condition such as, subject to the bishop's approval, but the actual wording is surprisingly strong. At all events, after receiving his commission from the bishop the chancellor entered on office without further ceremony. He probably summoned and presided at his first congregation of the regent masters on the following day, either as a symbolic indication of his authority as head of the university or out of courtesy to his fellows; but the constitution makes no allusion to investiture with the seal of office or the key of the common chest—the chancellor's insignia.[4]

The office was a *sui generis* institution, modelled exclusively on the Oxford chancellorship. It combined the privileges, duties and powers of an archdeacon with those of the chancellor of a cathedral chapter and of the rector or head of a university. The position of the chancellor at Cambridge was very different from that of the chancellor of Paris, who was not head of the university. It differed, too, from that of the chancellor of Montpellier; he did not confer the licence; and it differed again from that of the rector or rectors

[1] Cf. *Cal. papal letters*, v. 370–1. See also below, p. 272. But it took more than this bull, as in the case of Oxford, to make the bishops finally give up their claim.

[2] Cf. *Snappe's formulary*, pp. 43–5. Sutton went so far as to deny that the university had any right to elect a chancellor.

[3] The university proctor, mag. Robert de Thurkylby, stated in 1374 that words such as 'nos confirmamus electionem tuam, et te preficimus in Cancellarium dicte vniuersitatis' were used by bishops at the confirmation in office of chancellors. Cf. Ely Dioc. Rec. G I (2), fo. 77^v.

[4] The earliest record of a seal dates from 1270. See above, p. 55, n. 3. A common chest with key was probably instituted about this time. In 1294 a statute obliging the chancellor to take an oath before the university was introduced. See below, pp. 236–7.

of Bologna, whose jurisdiction was not archidiaconal; neither did they grant the licence.

In his role of archdeacon the Cambridge chancellor ranked as *iudex ordinarius* of the bishop; as such he enjoyed and exercised ordinary jurisdiction over all who were members of the university, whether clerks, religious or lay people. He had the care and correction of morals and general discipline; he had the right to visit establishments connected with the university unless these were outside his jurisdiction; he was entitled to issue testimonial letters; admit the wills of persons who died within the university to probate; and adjudicate if needs be in matrimonial causes. His court was an ecclesiastical tribunal; its proceedings were conducted according to canonical procedure; and its decrees were enforceable under pain of excommunication, a penalty which was also imposed for contempt of the court.[1] Either the chancellor in his archidiaconal capacity or his deputy, his commissary in fact, presided.[2]

When the office of chancellor was instituted at Cambridge the bishop presumably endowed it with all the appropriate powers of an archdeacon,[3] and also attached to it the faculty of conferring the licence, one of the prerogatives of the chancellor of a cathedral chapter. Though the chancellor of Cambridge like the chancellor of Oxford makes his first appearance in written records as an ecclesiastical personage or the holder of a diocesan office,[4] he was not

1 The conduct of cases which came before the chancellor's court at Cambridge was not regulated according to the solemn process of canon law but by the simple, more expeditious form of law. See below, pp. 162–3.

2 Cf. *Registrum cancellarii Oxoniensis, 1434–1469*, ed. Salter, i (OHS, xciii [1932]), pp. xv–xvi. The introduction to this volume contains a most valuable disquisition on the chancellor's office and has particular relevance for Cambridge. The evidence, however, is drawn mainly from sources not earlier than the late thirteenth century, and it is doubtful if all the powers attributed to the chancellor were enjoyed or exercised during the first half of the century. The earliest formal statement of the chancellor's jurisdiction at Cambridge over exempt persons, wills, etc., is found in the record of the Barnwell process (1429–30). The chancellor claimed testamentary powers in the same way as did the Oxford chancellor by 1280. Cf. *SAUO*, 96, 24–30.

3 On the office of the archdeacon of Ely cf. *Vet. Lib. Archid. Elien.* pp. xiii–xviii. There is a convenient summary account of the functions and jurisdiction of a thirteenth-century archdeacon in A. Amerieu, 'Archidiacre', *Dictionnaire de droit canonique*, i (Paris, 1935), 965–78.

4 The fact that he is not called chancellor of the university in 1225–6 does not mean that the office was not instituted by this time. Honorius III in 1221 refers to the 'chancellor of Oxford', not the 'chancellor of the university of Oxford'. These references have to do with commissions which did not concern the universities. The

purely and simply the bishop's vicar general for the university. At no time was he distinct from or even superior to the university.[1] His office had no meaning apart from the university, which indeed elected him—the constitution, as we have seen, claims something more—*e gremio*, that is, from among the regent masters. As such he formed one organic body or corporation with the regents, scholars and servants. Whatever privileges the chancellor received from bishops, kings or popes were granted for the university. His position would be untenable if he lost the confidence of his fellow regents; he would have to resign.[2] It is true that his commission came from the bishop, but it appears to have been couched in very general terms.[3] The university had or secured by 1250 the right to define his exercise of that commission through the constitution, which will henceforth be the norm, too, of the powers and functions entrusted to him by the university itself.

One would imagine that the constitution after referring to the need for a chancellor as a self-evident proposition and having prescribed how he was to be elected would immediately proceed to legislate on his office. Chapter I of the Angelica text does contain some important directives on the chancellorship, but its first concern is with his deputies. This is characteristic of the text as a whole with regard to the chancellor's office. It refers, for example, only in-

'chancellor of Cambridge' is also named in two commissions of Gregory IX, the one dated 8 April 1231, the other 20 Nov. 1234; cf. *Registres de Grégoire IX*, i. 391–2, no. 612; 1211, no. 2293; *Cal. papal letters*, i. 126 (where the date of the first commission is given as 10 April 1231), 142.

[1] In 1294 this truth was brought home to the then chancellor, Henry de Boyton, who found that his commission from the bishop was not sufficient to induce the bishop's official to take his side against the regents. See below, pp. 233–4. Rashdall, *Universities*, iii. 43, tends to overstate the relationship between the chancellor of Oxford and the bishop of Lincoln *vis-à-vis* the university, doubtless because he was deeply attached to the theory of a Parisian migration and hence saw a parallel between the chancellorship of Paris and of Oxford.

[2] The constitution makes no provision for this eventuality. Rashdall, *op. cit. loc. cit.* p. 281, n. 1, misunderstood the circumstances which led Bishop Montacute to entrust the chancellor's jurisdiction to two doctors of civil law, Thomas Michell and Walter de Elveden, in 1340. We cannot go into the matter here, but it seems that on the resignation of mag. Richard de Lyng from the chancellorship an objection was raised against the assumption by the senior D.Th. John de Elm, O.Carm., of the office of acting chancellor. It was customary at Oxford for the senior theologian to hold the chancellorship during a vacancy.

[3] When confirming Richard de Aston, D.Cn.L., as chancellor in 1315 the bishop, John Ketton, went on to say: 'ad exequendum fideliter dictum officium Cancellarii tibi cum cohercione canonica committimus vices nostras' (Ely Dioc. Rec. G I [2], fo. 77v).

directly to his prerogatives of conferring the licence and summoning convocations. That he alone possessed these powers is not formally stated; neither is his position as *iudex ordinarius* explicitly acknowledged. The author of the text saw no danger of the obvious being challenged. Before we are actually told that the chancellor has power to hear and decide all causes the fact is already assumed, since the constitution declares in advance that he may delegate deputies to act for him in all causes. This was no more than an admission of the archidiaconal basis of his jurisdiction. Every ordinary was entitled to delegate; every archdeacon had the right to appoint a commissary. It was in the university's own interest that there should be an official who would relieve the chancellor of as much business as possible and so ensure speedy and efficient administration, especially of justice. It could happen that a chancellor might not be a trained lawyer, and even if he only held court twice in the week, as the rector of Bologna university was bound to do by statute,[1] he would have little time for his many other duties, for he still remained regent master. Moreover, in the external sphere he would be wise, unless he had professional qualifications, to let a commissary represent the university in legal actions. It can hardly be coincidence that the earliest known commissary, John de Bradenham, was doctor of canon law; he was the leading figure on the side of the university in a suit brought against the chancellor and mag. Henry de Wysethe by the prior and community of Barnwell in 1293.[2]

The constitution does not, nor could it, question the chancellor's right to appoint a deputy on his own authority. Nevertheless, it interposes certain conditions. The chancellor himself must be in residence;[3] the delegation of jurisdiction must be temporary; the deputy must be above suspicion—a requirement demanded by canon law of every ecclesiastical judge; and he must be a member of the university. As yet, he is not formally known by the title of commissary, but it denotes his office and by the close of the thir-

[1] *Statuti*, p. 13, rubr. x.

[2] CUA, doc. no. 9 (23 July 1293). The deed is incorrectly cited as doc. no. 6 in *BRUC*, p. 86. Bradenham appears as chancellor in 1295 (*ibid.*).

[3] In 1342 Bishop Montacute delegated Richard de Kellawe, D.Th., to absolve scholars guilty of assaulting clerks but only on condition that the chancellor was present in Cambridge. Cf. Ely Dioc. Rec. G (I), fo. 95^{r} (mod.); *BRUC*, p. 335, where the date is given as April 1341; the correct date is 6 April 1342. It is not stated in Montacute's register that Kellawe was a Franciscan.

teenth century it was officially recognized.[1] The chancellor in virtue of his enjoyment of ordinary jurisdiction was free to empower his deputy to deal with specific matters and indeed all causes pertaining to his office. The one limitation imposed by the constitution is rather obscurely described in the Angelica text as one 'which of its nature does not require delegation'.[2] Though no reference is made to the granting of the licence to incept or the calling of convocations, it must not be thought that the chancellor could assign his exercise of these prerogatives to his commissary. These were functions which did not admit of delegation as long as the chancellor was himself present in the university. In short, the commissary attended to the routine business of the chancellor's court and matters arising out of it. Commissaries served writs of excommunication, for example, but they had to be promulgated by the chancellor in the first place.[3] The Angelica text is silent on the question of appeals. One was always allowed to appeal from a decision of a commissary to the chancellor, and however tempting it may be to compare the commissary to the bishop's official, or indeed the chancellor to the diocesan official, here the parallel breaks down. The Cambridge commissary was in fact the counterpart of the Oxford *hebdomadarii*. He must be carefully distinguished from the Oxford commissary, whose office and functions devolved on another deputy at Cambridge, whose later title, 'vice-chancellor', admirably expressed his position and office.

In chapter I, paragraph iii of the Angelica text it is laid down that if the chancellor happens to be absent or is about to go away for some time, afterwards declared to be more than a fortnight,[4] he may not depute anyone *ad universitatem causarum* unless the regents

[1] Cf. *Cons. Univ. Canteb.* I. ii (see below, p. 197, lines 7–11). This paragraph was made into a separate, enlarged statute with the title *De commissario Cancellarij*. Cf. Markaunt 6 (see below, p. 315, lines 1–12). The chapter heading of *SA* 8, a conflation of Markaunt 6–7, is misleading; it gives the impression that the entire statute refers to the vice-chancellor. Cf. *Docs*, i. 311.

[2] *Cons. Univ. Canteb.* I. ii (see below, p. 197, lines 10–11). The phrase might be taken to mean duties which did not involve jurisdiction, or perhaps *extraiudicialiter* decisions. But the later recensions of the text imply that the phrase was a polite way of saying that certain matters could not be delegated, namely, atrocious crimes which merited banishment or imprisonment; suits of regents and non-regents; and rents of houses and rights of tenancy. Cf. Markaunt 6 (see below, p. 315, lines 4–8); *SA* 8 (*Docs*, i. 311).

[3] In 1295 (?) the chancellor, probably John de Bradenham, excommunicated a canon of Barnwell in this way. Cf. *Liber mem. ecc. de Bernewelle*, p. 184.

[4] Cf. Markaunt 7 (see below, p. 315, lines 15–16); *SA* 8 (*Docs, loc. cit.*).

or a majority of them formally approve of the nomination.[1] Strictly interpreted, this statute does not exclude the right of the chancellor to delegate in the circumstances his commissary for a particular case, although the previous paragraph of the text makes the appointment of a commissary conditional on the chancellor being present in Cambridge. What the constitution now forbids is the granting of a general delegation without the prior consent of the regents. It cannot be said that the office of commissary automatically lapsed when the chancellor went away for a few days or less; and on the face of it there was nothing to prevent him from delegating his commissary to take charge of one or more specific matters during his absence. But he could not delegate him for a certain category of causes or for all causes, which is what *universitas causarum* or *universitas negotiorum* means in canon law. In practice the commissary's office was suspended when the chancellor left Cambridge or was absent for a period. Having obtained the consent of the regents meeting in convocation, the chancellor delegated his jurisdiction *ad universitatem causarum* to his chosen substitute or vicar, who was officially designated vice-chancellor by 17 March 1276.[2] The office was customarily entrusted to the senior doctor of theology, though the earliest known vice-chancellor, Richard de Aston (1306), was doctor of canon law.[3] A vice-chancellor had all the powers of the chancellor; his court had the same authority as the chancellor's; he could excommunicate, confer the licence and summon and preside at convocations. His position was far superior to that of a commissary, for he ruled the university during the chancellor's absence; he may indeed have had the right to appoint a commissary or deputy of his own.[4] In all respects the office, which it goes without

[1] *Cons. Univ. Canteb.* I. iii (see below, p. 197, lines 11–15).

[2] Cf. the decree of that date, printed by Ullmann in *Historical Journal*, i. 182. The title of the office varied; 'vicegerent' (*vices gerens*) was the commonest variant of 'vice-chancellor'.

[3] *BRUC*, p. 20. Among the theologians who held office were Henry Stokton, O.S.A., D.Th. (he was not D.Cn.L., as suggested *ibid.* p. 559) and Nicholas Kenton, O.Carm., D.Th. (*ibid.* p. 336). Stokton was vice-chancellor in 1417, Kenton in 1445–6. It may be that Aston would never have been appointed if the Franciscans and Dominicans at the time had not absented themselves (they held they were excluded) from the university. This was in 1304–6; Aston was vice-chancellor by 28 May 1306. The senior theologian at this period was probably either a Dominican or Franciscan. For the controversy between the friars and the university see below, pp. 241–4.

[4] In 1524 the vice-chancellor, William Grene, D.Th., had as his 'deputy or substitute' Richard Croke, D.Th. Cf. 'Black Parchment Book' (CUA), fo. 134r (mod.: p. 316).

saying expired on the return of the chancellor, corresponded with that of the commissary at Oxford; and at both universities the vice-chancellorship became permanent in the fifteenth century.[1]

The Angelica text in its roundabout way finally introduces us to the office of the chancellor. It does not attempt to set forth more than one aspect; and what it says is equally applicable to the vice-chancellor. The chancellor, we read, may hear and decide all causes of scholars by himself if he wishes, unless it may be necessary to have a prior understanding with the masters when there is question of an atrocious offence or a breach of the public peace.[2] In that one sentence the constitution sums up the most important function of the chancellor in the eyes of the university. He is *par excellence* a judge, the chief justice of the university. This could be inferred from the two preceding paragraphs, which take for granted that he possesses ordinary jurisdiction. The reason why he is expected to consult with the masters is that the penalty for grave offences was expulsion from the university or imprisonment. While the chancellor was perfectly entitled to hear evidence in cases of this kind, only the university, that is, the chancellor together with the other regents, could actually banish a master or scholar or send a member of the university to prison.[3] Crimes punishable with degradation or deposition had to be referred to the bishop's court.[4] When the Angelica text states that the chancellor is competent to try and give judgement in all suits of scholars it must not be thought that masters were not subject to the discipline of his court. The text, it is true, generally differentiates between masters and scholars, but in this context the term 'scholars' also includes masters, and persons directly engaged in the service of the university like the bedells.[5]

The expression 'all causes of scholars' must not be misunderstood. It is simply another way of saying that the chancellor is *iudex*

[1] Cf. *Grace Book* A, p. xxxii; *Snappe's formulary*, pp. 334–5.

[2] *Cons. Univ. Canteb.* I. iv (see below, p. 197, lines 16–19).

[3] Cf. *ibid.* VI (see below, p. 203, lines 21–2); VII. iv (see below, p. 207, lines 1–2); XI. iv (see below, p. 213, lines 1–2). See also below, pp. 233–6.

[4] Cf. Dr Emden's note to Rashdall, *Universities*, iii. 115, n. 1.

[5] Chapter XIII of the Angelica text classes them with scholars and non-regents. There was never any doubt about their right to privilege, not as clerks for they were usually married but as members of the university. A statute was enacted *c.* 1255–76 which also claimed the privilege of scholars for manciples and others connected with the university. The effect of the privilege was to exempt them from the jurisdiction of the archdeacon of Ely, and Ralph de Walpole, who held office by 1276, made an issue of this. See below, p. 228.

ordinarius in the university, and that the vice-chancellor when delegated by him has the same powers. Consequently, they are the proper judges, at least in the first instance, of all suits of scholars, or members of the university. A scholar could not cite another scholar before any court except the chancellor's; and no scholar with the cure of souls in Cambridge or any religious could decline the jurisdiction of his court as long as they remained at the university. Unless this proviso obtained, rectors and vicars of Cambridge churches and members of exempt religious orders were subject to their respective ordinaries, the archdeacon of Ely or their major superiors. Having said all this, we must immediately sound a warning. The question of university jurisdiction is anything but simple. At the risk of distorting the picture we shall very briefly attempt to throw some light on it here.

Within the university regent masters were allowed under the constitution to adjudicate in cases brought against their scholars by other scholars. Chapter VI of the Angelica text legislates on this aspect of jurisdiction.[1] It suffices to add that the decisions issuing from masters' courts were amenable to the judgement of the superior court of the chancellor. The general principle governing suits between scholars is clear enough: a scholar could not cite another scholar before any court except the chancellor's. The defendant was not free to decline the jurisdiction of the chancellor, though he might claim the privilege, depending on the nature of the case, of answering the charge in the court of his master. In theory the *privilegium fori* or *privilegium scholarium* secured for the chancellor the right to hear and decide all suits, civil as well as ecclesiastical, in which one party was a scholar. More than that, his jurisdiction was extraordinary, though it is necessary to bear in mind that its peculiar range only gradually developed either from custom or as a result of outright grants of privilege from the crown, the papacy or successive bishops of Ely.

A scholar cited by a clerk or ecclesiastic who was not a member of the university was entitled to have the case heard and decided in the chancellor's court. If a scholar had a grievance against a clerk he could not cite him to appear before the chancellor unless he was under the chancellor's jurisdiction or, to use a later expression, within the liberties of the university. The same is true of laymen before 1305. On one point the university was adamant. No scholar

[1] See below, pp. 149–51.

might charge a clerk or layman of Cambridge before judges delegate of the pope under the general terms *quidam alii* and *rebus aliis*. If he had a complaint the proper place to lodge it was with the chancellor's court. In the thirteenth century generally speaking the position with regard to civil suits between scholars and laymen was not materially different from the situation where both parties were laymen.[1] Even when the university had received formal grants of civil jurisdiction from the monarchy it did not dare to claim cognizance of crown pleas or cases which pertained exclusively to the lay courts.[2] The oldest grant of criminal jurisdiction to the chancellor dates from 1268; it authorized him to claim delivery of a scholar who was imprisoned for doing serious injury to a layman of the town.[3] It might be thought, bearing in mind the special character of the chancellor's court and the nature of the university as a privileged society, that scholars enjoyed more immunity than ordinary clerks. A scholar may have been allowed by 1250 to defend himself before the chancellor on a minor criminal charge, but if he was apprehended for murder or a felony, it required the intervention of the bishop or his official to have him delivered from the common prison. Moreover, it was not his status *qua* scholar which counted. What the king required was proof of his reception of minor orders. This is very clearly shown, as far as Cambridge is concerned, by the case of Nicholas de Breckendale, which also reveals that by 1255, notwithstanding the text of the constitution, the chancellor's power to hear and decide all causes of scholars was limited.[4] At the same time the chancellor appears to have enjoyed or exercised a certain amount of civil and criminal jurisdiction well before the date of the earliest extant evidence of grants from the crown. He certainly had very wide powers in the matter of rents of houses and tenancies, an area which impinged upon the prerogative of the king as regards tenements and lay fees. The basis of the chancellor's jurisdiction,

[1] It was decreed by Edward II in parliament on 12 March 1305 that scholars were entitled to cite before the chancellor burgesses and other laypeople of the town of Cambridge in all personal causes. Cf. *Memoranda de parliamento*, ed. Maitland (Rolls series, 1893), pp. 36–7.

[2] Cf. Markaunt 26 (see below, p. 325, lines 2–5); *SA* 33 (*Docs*, i. 327–8).

[3] The writ is cited on p. 37, n. 2, above.

[4] See above, p. 38, n. 1. There is some evidence that the crown was prepared to mitigate penalties imposed by the king's bench on scholars who were found guilty of criminal conduct. In 1261 Henry III instructed his justices not to hang or mutilate scholars but to punish them in some other way on the advice of the university. Cf. Hare MS i, fos. 17^v–18^r; *Cal. pat. rolls, 1258–66*, p. 182.

which may have extended also to tradesmen who charged scholars exorbitant prices or withheld supplies from the market, can scarcely have been other than custom, reinforced by the royal writs of 1231 and the lost letters patent issued by 1255.[1] He had cognizance too of crimes committed by scholars, and which were sufficiently serious to merit expulsion from the university or imprisonment. Originally, his competence in this field must have been sanctioned by the bishop.[2] The constitution secured further recognition of these powers. Even as late as 1339 we find a scholar of the university, mag. Henry de Harowden, choosing to rest his defence before the king's justices not on any royal grant of privilege but on the statutes and approved customs of the university.[3] Edward I, it will be recalled, showed marked reluctance to allow an action of novel disseisin to proceed in 1292 because of his regard for the statutes and customs of the university. None the less, the power claimed for the chancellor in the Angelica text to hear and decide all suits of scholars would be difficult if not impossible to sustain before the common law. At no time did it extend to pleas of the crown or purely lay suits.[4]

The chancellor as well as being chief justice in the university was also its chief executive officer. He was not a law unto himself; he had

[1] See above, pp. 25–6, 36–7.

[2] The bishop of Ely, Hugh Balsham, in 1276 assumed or took for granted the chancellor's exclusive jurisdiction over questions concerning rents of houses and misdemeanours of scholars, as well as unspecified causes between scholars and laymen Cf. the ordinance of 6 Oct. of that year (CUA, doc. no. 5; *Vet. Lib. Archid. Elien.* 20–1).

[3] Harowden claimed that the chancellor's jurisdiction extended to all personal actions between clerks and laymen or laymen and clerks 'per statuta dicte vniuersitatis [Cantebrigie] per litteras apostolicas bullatas quas profert confirmata necnon per consuetudines dicte vniuersitatis approbatas' from time out of memory. Cf. *Select cases in the court of the king's bench under Edward III*, v, ed. Sayles (Selden Soc. lxxvi [1958]), 117. The only papal bull that Harowden could have produced was John XXII's *Inter singula* (9 June 1318), but it contained no confirmation of the statutes of the university. It is strange that he did not urge instead the grant made by Edward II and parliament on 12 March 1305 (see above, p. 116, n. 1), which was confirmed in 1314. Cf. *Cal. pat. rolls, 1313–17*, p. 102.

[4] For a very summary account of the growth of the chancellor's civil and criminal jurisdiction at Cambridge cf. J. F. Willard, *The royal authority and the early English universities* (Philadelphia, 1902), pp. 22–5. He assumed, wrongly, that 'statutes of Cambridge have been lost for this early period', that is before *c.* 1335 (*ibid.* p. 51)! The history of the university during the thirteenth century gives no grounds for thinking that in civil and criminal actions scholars were in practice more privileged than clerks who were not members of the university. Hence cf. F. Pollock and F. W. Maitland, *The history of English law before the time of Edward I* (2nd edn, Cambridge, 1898), i. 129–251, 440–5, 447, n. 1.

to take counsel with and win the approval of the regents when matters of serious import came before him. In his executive capacity he was bound to give effect to sentences passed by the regents in their own courts.[1] Ultimately, the chancellor had the responsibility for the actual enforcement of decrees of masters, rectors and convocations. The final paragraph of chapter I of the Angelica text contains in a nutshell the essential office of the chancellor and in the final analysis the measure of his authority. It declares that the chancellor cannot make any new statutes without the consent of the regents. His whole endeavour instead must be to maintain resolutely the constitution enacted in common by himself and the regents.[2] In view of this forthright pronouncement it seems most improbable that a chancellor was ever competent even in the earliest days of the university to hand down a statute of his own making. He was not formally forbidden under the constitution to make statutes, but since their legality was made subject to the consent of the regents any statute promulgated by him independently of them was null and void. Statutes were issued by the chancellor and *cetus magistrorum regentium* or the *universitas regentium* (until the non-regents were granted statutory powers), never by the chancellor alone.[3]

For a comprehensive view of the chancellor's powers one must go to the other chapters of the Angelica text besides the section which professedly treats of his election and office. He had the exclusive right of conferring the licence (Angelica II. i), and of holding convocations (IV). He took action when the rectors reported underhand dealings against scholars on the part of tradesmen, and punished fractious and contemptuous members of the university, especially those who continued to do business with regrators (VII. iii). He had authority to send men down from the university or to prison, and was empowered to issue prohibitions of a disciplinary nature (XI. iv–v; cf. VII. iv). He might claim certain perquisites (XI. iv), and was possessed of extraordinary powers where rents of houses and rights of tenancy were concerned (XII). In his official capacity as head of convocation he had to attend the obsequies of all deceased regents, scholars, non-regents and bedells of the university (XIII. ii–iii).

1 *Cons. Univ. Canteb.* I. v (see below, p. 197, lines 20–1).

2 *Cons. Univ. Canteb.* I. vi (see below, p. 199, lines 1–3).

3 Cf. the statutes of 26 May 1291 and 18 March 1294, pp. 34–6, 233, 240, n. 2. The earliest Oxford statutes were also issued in the name of the university. See above, p. 102, n. 3.

ANGELICA CHAPTER II: STUDIES

Under the title of the 'creation of masters and their office' the Angelica text within the compass of a single chapter covers the most obscure and intractable area of the organization of the *studium*—the system of promotion to degrees and studies. The total absence of a curriculum for any faculty has been referred to more than once; we shall have to say something about it again. What the text provides in its terse and rather disjointed fashion is nevertheless of the greatest value. If the eight paragraphs which form chapter II raise more questions than they answer, their importance, given the date of the text, far exceeds the confines of Cambridge; but we must sternly resist the temptation to exploit the statutes for the later history of the university or draw out their implications for the organization of graduation and studies at contemporary universities.

The first three paragraphs of chapter II are entirely devoted to the question of regency and inception. No doubt, the sequence of the eight paragraphs could be bettered, but the Cambridge legislators had perhaps more reason than we think for putting the requirements for admission to the *magisterium* or master's degree in the forefront. In 1246, just when the constitution was probably in the process of formation, Innocent IV sent a mandate to Oxford. Grosseteste had complained that scholars were setting themselves up as masters without undergoing proper examination. The pope thereupon ordered that no one was to teach in any faculty unless he was examined and approved according to the custom of Paris.[1] At Cambridge unauthorized, self-appointed masters are likely to have posed a greater problem than at Oxford, and we may see in the sequence of the paragraphs of Angelica II evidence of the university's determination to crush illegal practitioners. Paragraph i states that nobody may assume the rule (*regimen*) of scholars who has not previously responded in all the schools of his faculty and obtained the chancellor's licence.[2] To rule meant to act as regent master.[3] The

[1] *Registres d'Innocent IV*, i. 277, no. 1859. None the less, there is no evidence that formal examinations in the Parisian sense were prescribed for the degree of master either by Oxford or Cambridge. Cf. Rashdall, *Universities*, iii. 141–3.

[2] *Cons. Univ. Canteb.* II. i (see below, p. 199, lines 5–7).

[3] The term *regimen* in scholastic usage was synonymous with teaching and particularly the mastership of a recognized school. In university circles it had the same meaning as regency; the time which a master spent in lecturing was called *regimen*

test of one's intellectual ability was reducible to one's performance as respondent at ordinary disputations of the masters; it was the basic requirement for admission to the *magisterium* and at Oxford and Cambridge it took the place of the Parisian examination, though there, too, responsions were essential.[1] The number of times a candidate for the licence had to respond is not laid down. It would depend on the ratio of regents during the year or period of final preparation (*tempus profectionis ad cathedram*) for the degree; one responsion under each master of the faculty was doubtless sufficient.[2]

It may be opportune at this point to comment upon the non-use of the term 'bachelor' in the Angelica text with reference to the candidate for the licence. The baccalaureate at this time (*c.* 1250) was a recognized degree, a vital prerequisite for promotion to the office of master. Originally it signified a status rather than a degree; indeed the title itself only came into vogue *c.* 1215–40 at Paris.[3] By 1245 bachelors formed a distinct class of students; they were advanced scholars, accredited assistant lecturers to the masters, and well on the way to becoming regents themselves. It does not follow that admission to the baccalaureate was accompanied by any formal conferring of a licence or degree. At Montpellier in 1240 it was the student's master, not the chancellor, who licensed him to read as bachelor in medicine, a custom which derived from Bologna and possibly from Paris as well. The Cambridge constitution in a later section of chapter II shows that bachelors had an official status above the ordinary run of scholars; their functions cor-

at Paris. Cf. *Chart. Univ. Paris.* ii. 509, n. 2, no. 1045. See also *ibid.* i. 87, no. 29; 137, no. 79; 165, no. 120. On 3 March 1256 Alexander IV wrote to the chancellor congratulating him for licensing St Thomas even before the arrival of the pope's mandate, and ordered him: 'cito facias regiminis habere principium' (*ibid.* i. 307, no. 270).

1 For the meaning of ordinary disputations and responsions see below, pp. 139–41. When a pope requested a university to admit a scholar by way of exception to D.Th., he would dispense from the normal requirements but not from the obligation of responding.

2 The earliest extant Cambridge statute on M.A. prescribes only three responsions. See below, p. 277. This was a departure from the early constitution of the university. When separate statutes were devised for each faculty, a development which took place almost certainly before 1300, Angelica II. i ceased to retain its identity as a statute; its provisions were incorporated in the statutes governing admission to the *magisterium* in arts, medicine, civil and canon law and theology.

3 Montpellier furnishes the earliest use of the title. Cf. *Statuts*, ii. 7, no. 885. Courson's statutes of 1215 for Paris eschew this term. Cf. *Chart. Univ. Paris.* i. 78–9, no. 20, and Rashdall, *Universities*, i. 451, n. 1.

responded with those of the Parisian bachelors, whom we meet for the first time in 1245.[1] Yet the constitution makes no regulations for the acquisition of the degree and almost pointedly refrains from calling the candidate for the licence 'bachelor'.[2] Its reticence does not mean, however, that scholars were not licensed by the chancellor to read or dispute by *c.* 1250.[3]

It would appear that the granting of the licence to incept as master was accompanied with some ceremony. The bachelor, as we may now refer to the candidate, supplicated the chancellor *reuerenter* (i.e. kneeling) to bestow the licence.[4] He was presented no doubt by his own master in much the same way as an archdeacon presented a candidate for holy orders.[5] An interval must have elapsed between the reception of the supplicat and the conferring of the licence, since the chancellor could not act until the masters of the faculty had made their depositions. By 1300 depositions were certainly *de rigueur.* A master deponed either from personal knowledge (*ex scientia*) or from belief (*ex credulitate*) concerning the moral and intellectual fitness of a candidate:[6] in the superior faculties all the masters were bound to testify orally under oath *ex scientia*;[7] in the faculty of arts

1 *Chart. Univ. Paris.* i. 178–9, no. 137.

2 The Angelica text still uses the term 'scholars' where one would expect to find some distinction between bachelors and students, namely, in the list of university men whose funerals the chancellor and regents were bound to attend. Cf. *Cons. Univ. Canteb.* XIII. iii (see below, p. 217, lines 21–2). The same generic reference to scholars occurs in a statute of Paris enacted in 1251. Cf. *Chart. Univ. Paris.* i. 223, no. 197.

3 Yet at no time, apparently, did the chancellor licence scholars to read as bachelors in arts. Cf. *SA* 140–1 (*Docs*, i. 384–5). The earlier form of *SA* 140 is printed below, pp. 300–1.

4 The Angelica text, whether on purpose or not, has '*saltem* postulauerit reuerenter' (italics mine). Was the bachelor expected to do something more than merely supplicate? Canon law forbade the chancellor to demand a fee for the licence; it was probably the established custom then as later for a candidate to make an offering in kind.

5 Cf. the formula prescribed by *SA* 126 (*Docs*, i. 378) for a master when presenting a bachelor. Virtually the same form was used at Oxford. Cf. *SAUO*, 29, 16–20.

6 Cf. *Cons. Univ. Canteb.* II. iii: 'Non audeat quis de nouo incipere...nisi ipsius conuersacio uel [=et] pericia publice nota habeatur ibidem' (see below, p. 199, lines 12–14).

7 By 1365 a master when deponing in the faculty of theology said in effect: 'scio talem sufficientem esse et aptum ad incipiendum in sacra theologia' (Archivio Vaticano, *Reg. Vat.* 254, fo. 136v). In the seventeenth century a master testified by striking out 'scio', 'credo' or 'nescio', as the case may be, which were written opposite the candidate's name on a sheet of paper prepared by the bedell of the faculty. Cf. 'Buck's Book' (*c.* 1665), ed. in part by Peacock, *Observations*, App. B, pp. lxxiii–lxxvi.

the rule was less stringent.[1] Once the depositions had been collated there would be little delay on the chancellor's part in granting a bachelor the licence, provided the votes were favourable.[2] Formulae seldom changed from century to century, and since the same formula or almost the same was used at Oxford and Cambridge at the presentation of bachelors, we may conclude that the chancellor at Cambridge adhered to the form prescribed by statute for Oxford for the conferring of the licence.[3] The chancellor in his own name and in the name of the university authorized the bachelor to incept, read, dispute and perform all the acts of a master in his faculty, provided he went through an inception ceremony, for unless he did he remained simply an inceptor as in the case of William of Ockham. It was the chancellor's prerogative as delegate of the bishop to grant the licence; the actual creation of a new master belonged from the very nature of a *universitas* to the university, since it was a question of incorporation into the brotherhood of the masters. The very next paragraph of the Angelica text makes it abundantly clear that at Cambridge the creation of a master was reserved to a regent.

'Regency is an honour which no one may take to himself; he must receive it from another regent or from someone who has ruled at one time in an approved university.'[4] If this passage means anything, it is surely aimed against self-constituted masters. It seems to imply, however, that a non-regent master from another university, such as Oxford, could admit a bachelor to regency. If the constitution does not recognize as competent Cambridge masters who are not regents, *a fortiori* it cannot be said to authorize masters who graduated elsewhere but were now scholars in a higher faculty, or who for one reason or another did not resume their lectures after coming to Cambridge. A distinguished visitor might be invited to

[1] Twelve masters deponed, five *ex scientia*, seven either *ex credulitate* or *ex scientia*. See p. 277. The statute there printed was enacted by 1390. The text suggests that the method of deponing represents a revision of an older ruling; it is not unlikely that in the thirteenth century all the masters in arts had to testify like the regents in the superior faculties.

[2] A candidate in the higher faculties had to secure, apparently, the approval of each and every master of his faculty. This was the position in the faculty of theology by 1330. It was modified by statute on 4 July 1359 which declared that a candidate was not to be rejected if only one or two masters voted against him. Cf. *Jean XXII (1316–1334) — lettres communes*, ed. G. Mollat, ix (Paris, 1928), 260–1, no. 49041; *Cal. papal letters*, ii. 495; *SA* 163 (*Docs*, i. 396).

[3] Cf. *SAUO*, 36, 12–18.

[4] *Cons. Univ. Canteb.* II. ii (see below, p. 199, lines 8–9).

preside at an inception ceremony; the Angelica text expressly states that the bishop of Ely (Hugh of Northwold) honoured regents at their *principia* (the older term for inceptions);[1] but apart from exceptions of this kind the rule that every bachelor had to incept under a regent master held good.[2] Whether the master himself had incepted at Cambridge or no, he had to be *actu regens*.[3] He might be allowed to resume as regent for the occasion if he was not actually regent at the time; but unless he was very keen indeed to hold an inception it is unlikely that he would bind himself to continue as regent for one whole year.[4] The phrase 'someone who has ruled at one time in an approved university' must be understood of a master who incepted at Oxford or Paris, for instance, and resumed at Cambridge.[5] He was not obliged to incept again or undergo any test; he was admitted *ad eundem* once he took the oath to observe the statutes and act as regent for not less than one year, as prescribed in Angelica II, paragraph iv. If, on the other hand, he had not incepted publicly, that is, at a proper inception ceremony in a university of equal standing, he would have to incept in the normal way. One cannot help feeling that the expression 'of equal standing' carries a concealed note of self-consciousness on the part of the framers of the constitution that their university merited something far more than provincial or national fame. Its degrees were certainly recognized at Oxford, and there is no evidence that Paris made any difficulties. A very much stiffer line was taken at all three universities towards the close of the century, though if Paris is to be believed it was the two English universities which first insisted on a preliminary examination, called 'determination' or 'repetition' at Cambridge, before they would allow Parisian masters to resume.[6]

The third paragraph of Angelica II contains all that the constitu-

1 *Cons. Univ. Canteb.* XIII. i (see below, p. 217, lines 13–15).

2 Cf. *SA* 143 (*Docs*, i. 385).

3 The Parisian definition of *actu regens* was a master who read on every legible day in the schools in his proper habit and at the proper hour. Cf. *Chart. Univ. Paris.* i. 531, no. 461.

4 *SA* 131 (*Docs*, i. 380) certainly implies that a non-regent could resume even on the very day of the inception or rather on the preceding day when the first part of the ceremony, the vespers or *vesperiae*, took place.

5 Cf. the revised text of Angelica II. ii in *SA* 144: 'Non incipiat hic aliquis nec solenniter resumat, nisi sub magistro, qui hic inceperit vel solenniter resumpserit' (*ibid.* 386). At Oxford one could incept under a non-regent. Cambridge only allowed this when there was no regent available in a faculty, usually medicine but also canon and civil law. Cf. *SA* 131 (*loc. cit.*).

6 See below, p. 177, n. 4.

tion has to say about the curriculum. It is most uncommunicative. Anyone incepting for the first time must have spent a period as student in the university, and if a scholar's good character and learning are common knowledge in Cambridge he need not have studied there at all![1] There is more to this than meets the eye. First, a scholar who came to Cambridge with an outstanding reputation must have earned it after a long period of studies in another university. Secondly, provided he complied with certain exercises a bachelor who had determined in arts at Oxford or Paris would not have to repeat the course at Cambridge in order to qualify for M.A. The vague term 'a period' in the constitution was afterwards defined as one year.[2] No scholar, not even a qualified bachelor, would be admitted to the *magisterium* unless he spent some time at the university, and one year would be sufficient to enable the masters of a faculty to assess his competence as respondent during that time. The normal run of students, however, were Cambridge undergraduates; the position in their case was very different. The Angelica text maintains an impenetrable silence as regards the curriculum. We are not going to lift the curtain here, tempting as it may be. One or two general remarks will not be out of place, although to generalize at all on the question of Cambridge studies at any period during the middle ages is liable to be misleading.[3]

There is no knowing how long a student starting at the foot of the ladder had to spend in the faculties of arts, canon law or theology by 1250 before he could respond for the licence. After a prolonged and rather searching study of a wide range of evidence, one is led to conclude that the curriculum, at any rate in arts and theology, was substantially the same in the thirteenth century as it was a

[1] *Cons. Univ. Canteb.* II. iii (see below, p. 199, lines 12–14). The text in point of fact has 'conuersacio uel pericia'. This is one case where *uel* has the force of *et*. Cf. Pollock and Maitland, *History of English law*, i. 173, n. 3. In the revised version of the statute *et* replaces *uel*. Cf. *SA* 144 (*loc. cit.*).

[2] *Ibid.*

[3] Cf. Rashdall's remarks concerning the Oxford curriculum in *Universities*, iii. 140. For a conspectus of the Cambridge courses cf. Mullinger, *University of Cambridge*, i. 341–65 (based on Peacock, *Observations*) and Leathes's introduction to *Grace Book* A, pp. xxiii–xxix. Their summaries are derived from the very late edition of the statutes in *Docs*, i, and have little value. Two articles on the Oxford curriculum in the fourteenth century point the way for similar studies of the Cambridge curriculum. Cf. L. Boyle, O.P., 'The curriculum of the faculty of canon law at Oxford in the first half of the fourteenth century', *Oxford studies presented to Daniel Callus* (OHS, n.s. xvi [1964]), 135–62; J. A. Weisheipl, O.P., 'Curriculum of the faculty of arts at Oxford in the early fourteenth century', *Mediaeval Studies*, xxvi (1964), 143–85.

century later, if allowance is made for some modifications, especially in the theological course in or shortly after 1365. It appears to be generally true that it took a student as long to graduate as master by *c.* 1250 as it did by *c.* 1385. Ralph de Walpole was a brilliant scholar. In all probability he was M.A. by 1268, when he became archdeacon of Ely. At least eleven years elapsed before he incepted as master of theology *c.* 1280. Had he taken the degree of D.Th. *c.* 1380 his studies after he completed his year of regency in the faculty of arts and enrolled in the higher faculty would have lasted just as long. If the theology course comprised eleven years by *c.* 1280 we may assume that the arts course was spread over seven years as in the fourteenth century. Altogether, Walpole was a student, teacher and student for almost twenty years before he qualified for the supreme award in the university, the *magisterium* in theology.[1] Though the Angelica text lists no prescribed textbooks—there may not have been any such books—and we have no very early evidence of lectures at Cambridge, some extant manuscripts suggest that the course in logic, at all events, covered the same books which were ordered to be read and heard in the faculty of arts by *c.* 1385.[2] With these few observations, from which it would be fatal to generalize, we must leave the question of Cambridge studies for the present.

Each new master was expected to feast his seniors after his inception.[3] It was a cherished and universal custom at universities. In

1 The above reconstruction of Walpole's scholastic career differs in point of dating from Dr Emden's account in *BRUC*, p. 612. Walpole must have incepted as D.Th. *c.* 1280. Mag. John de Trussebut, O.P., who himself incepted about that time, was his master. Pelster in *Oxford theology*, p. 53, misunderstood the meaning of 'determinavit archidiaconus Elyensis' in Assisi MS 158 (cf. *ibid.* p. 114). Walpole was not *magister resumens*, as Pelster believed. He was incepting for the first time in the faculty of theology, and hence it was his duty and privilege to determine the question under Trussebut, his master. It should be noted that Pelster was using Cambridge evidence to establish what was the custom at Oxford. Incidentally, the *questiones* in the Assisi MS are the earliest written records of disputations at Cambridge. They are earlier than the Oxford *questiones* in the same MS and prove how advanced was the teaching of theology at Cambridge by *c.* 1280.

2 The texts exhibited by two Cambridge MSS, Gonville and Caius College 465 and 466, both saec. xiii*ex*, are precisely those prescribed by the earliest extant statutes on B.A. and M.A. which we have resurrected. They are printed on pp. 277, 298–9, 300–1, below.

3 It must have been quite an occasion at Cambridge when Robert Bruce, king of Scots, gave a banquet *c.* 1301–2 after his brother's inception. Robert Mannyng de Brunne, author of the celebrated *Handlyng Synne*, was present. Cf. *BRUC*, pp. 99–100, 388.

return all the masters had to abstain from lecturing on the morrow. The day after the inception was reserved for the new master's inaugural lecture, which would occupy most of the day, as the exercise included his determination or magisterial solution to the problem disputed at his inception. The Angelica text reminds the inceptor in a sort of oblique way that if he fails to invite all the masters to dinner on the day of his inception any master not invited will lecture on the following day and thus steal some of his thunder as *magister principians*.[1]

One of the essential marks of a properly organized, approved university was its right and practice of holding inceptions. If the procedure failed to conform with the established ritual of 'vespers' and *principium*, which was observed at the great universities, the newly created master did not incept publicly, and consequently his status would not be recognized. The earliest proof that the traditional, acceptable form of inception was observed at Cambridge is provided solely by the Angelica text, which is also the earliest statutory evidence that vespers and *principium* were the constituent parts of an inception ceremony at the two English universities.

It is a peculiar phenomenon that some of the most celebrated ceremonies derive their name from an incidental word or phrase in the ritual, as, for example, 'Mass' (*missa*). 'Inception' or its more modern equivalent 'Commencement' is of course a translation of *principium*, but the actual word 'inception' was directly derived from the opening words spoken by the rector or proctor at the second part of the ceremony, when he invited the presiding master to open the proceedings by saying 'incipiatis' or 'Domine doctor incipiatis'.[2] 'Vespers' obviously comes from the fact that the ceremony began on the eve of the *principium* or inception properly so called.[3] The basic element of the two parts was a solemn disputation. On receiving his licence the inceptor informed the chancellor of the date on which he proposed to have his inception. A graduation ceremony could be held at any time during the academic year except in vacation,

[1] Cf. *Cons. Univ. Canteb.* II. iii (see below, p. 199, lines 14–17).

[2] By 1496 the inception banquet (*commensatio*) also appears to have influenced the adoption of the term 'commencement'! Cf. *SA* 51 (*Docs*, i. 337–8); *ibid.* 419 (3 July 1505).

[3] The statutes of the faculty of theology of Bologna, which date from 1364, state: 'Vesperie dicte sunt propter horam quasi vesperarum, scilicet decimam nonam' (*I più antichi statuti*, ed. Ehrle, 40, 16–17).

provided the licenciate chose a *dies legibilis* (a day of ordinary lectures) for his vespers and a *dies disputabilis* (a day set aside for ordinary disputations) for the inception proper.[1] The chancellor duly confirmed the date of the inception and summoned the regents to attend; the making of a new master was the primary reason for holding convocations. The vespers took place in the schools, if at all possible in the school of the inceptor's master, and began in the evening except during Lent. It consisted almost wholly of a highly technical, solemn disputation conducted according to a most intricate pattern of principal and secondary arguments, propositions, suppositions, responsions, oppositions, replications and conclusions.[2] At the close of the disputation the senior rector invited the presiding master, who was normally the licentiate's master, to begin his commendation or speech in praise of the inceptor, who meanwhile sat with bowed head over which his hood was drawn, a picture of abject humility and utter embarrassment. By *c.* 1250 this marked the end of the vespers, though it is possible that the bedell of the faculty formally asked the moderator to announce the question or questions to be disputed at the *principium* or commencement and state when and where it was being held.[3] At a later period, perhaps in 1291, the inceptor was required to take an oath after the commendation that he would not appeal against the statutes of the university nor countenance such an appeal on the part of anybody else.[4] The commencement ceremony originally took place on the next day after Mass in St Mary's church. Each regent wearing *cappa clausa* or *pallium* was in his place. When the stage was set the rector

1 Cf. *SA* 127, 129 (*Docs*, i. 378–9). The first Tuesday of July was designated Commencement Day for all faculties by the Edwardine statutes of 1549, a ruling which was afterwards embodied in the Elizabethan statutes of 1559 and 1570. Cf. J. Lamb, *A collection of letters, statutes, and other documents* (London, 1838), pp. 124, 280, 317 (c. II); *Docs*, i. 456. The day was also known as *Dies comitiorum* or *Magna comitia* or simply *Comitia*.

2 An idea of the complexity of a vesperial disputation may be obtained from the summaries printed by Gibson in *SAUO*, 644–5. Cf. also Little and Pelster, *Oxford theology*, pp. 45–52, 273–5.

3 Cf. Stokys's Book, ed. Peacock, *Observations*, App. A, pp. xxiii–xxiv.

4 Cf. Markaunt's text (see below, p. 313, lines 7–11). The oath was replaced by another, the former being taken at the licensing ceremony, which bound the inceptor not to resume the status of bachelor in the same faculty. Cf. *SA* 130 (*Docs*, i. 380); Stokys's Book, *loc. cit.* A corresponding Oxford statute concerning bachelors in arts is assigned to 1264 in *SAUO*, 36, 24–5. The basis of this dating is open to question. Cf. R. L. Poole, 'Henry Symeonis', *E.H.R.* xxvii (1912), 516. We may assume at all events that the statute was not made obligatory at Cambridge until the fourteenth century.

said to the presiding master 'incipiatis', thereby inviting him to proceed with the creation of the new master. The ceremonial differed somewhat in the faculties of arts, canon law and theology; basically it consisted of the inceptor's investiture with a square cap (biretta) for a master in arts and the *pileum* or round cap in the higher faculties, followed by the induction of the new master into the *cathedra magistralis* (master's chair). The inceptor, for he was not yet entitled to the title and status of master, then read a text from which he elicited a question. A disputation immediately followed. It is at this point that the Angelica text enters the picture. Chapter II, paragraph iv, decrees that each master at his inception before he determines the question, that is at the close of the disputation, must pledge faith, although not necessarily in the form of an oath, that he will observe the statutes of the university and continue as regent for one year at least unless excused.[1]

An inception ceremony marked the entry of a scholar into the brotherhood of the regents; he contracted to obey and uphold its statutes and perform the duties of regency. The contract was enforceable by his pledge of faith or by oath;[2] in either case he incurred the stigma and penalty of perjury if he violated his contract.[3] Apparently, many Cambridge masters did commit perjury by claiming privilege for scholars who were not enrolled in the *matricula* of a master.[4] This was directly forbidden by one of the statutes which each regent had to subscribe to at his inception. The pledge of faith was given by the inceptor as he placed his right hand in his master's immediately after the disputation. At Oxford inceptors in theology were required to swear on the bible (a corporal oath), and it is possible that masters in the faculty at Cambridge

[1] *Cons. Univ. Canteb.* II. iv (see below, p. 198, line 18 to p. 201, line 2).

[2] Salter, *Med. Arch. Univ. Oxford*, ii. 275, was mistaken about this. He held that a Cambridge graduate was fined or rather forfeited his caution if he failed to carry out the duties attached to his degree. The position with regard to masters at Cambridge was the same as at Oxford; a regent was bound by oath or pledge of faith to perform the duties of regency. Fines were levied on licentiates who failed to incept within a year and on bachelors, but this was a later development.

[3] Cf. Pollock and Maitland, *History of English law*, i. 108–9.

[4] Hugh Balsham in his award of 1276 states: 'Et licet quilibet Magister antequam ad regimen admittatur statutum huiusmodi fide prestita firmare teneatur, intelleximus tamen quod plures Magistri periurii reatus sepius incurrentes contra eiusdem statuti tenorem aliquos ut scolares defendendo fidem suam nequiter uiolarunt' (CUA, doc. no. 5; *Vet. Lib. Archid. Elien.* 22). The statute in question is *Cons. Univ. Canteb.* XI. i (see below, p. 227).

were the exception mentioned in Angelica II. iv, where the possibility of a formal oath being demanded from inceptors is not excluded.[1] By *c.* 1390 the pledge of faith was abolished and a corporal oath was made binding on all inceptors.[2]

After formally pledging himself to keep the statutes and perform his duty as regent, the new master was requested by the rector to determine the question sitting down. He was now about to exercise his first magisterial act. A determination by a master took the form of an exhaustive analysis of the question and indeed of the entire disputation. The determiner, as it were, replayed the debate. He resumed the conclusions, oppositions and replications of the contestants; he dissected the arguments that contradicted his own thesis; he distinguished the premises of syllogisms and denied the conclusions drawn by his opponents. He met and answered in the course of his exposition any inherent objections in his argumentation. Finally, he stated his definitive solution of the question; in other words, he determined it.[3] Some of the most valuable contributions of medieval schoolmen to human thought have come down to us in the form of determinations. The exercise might take several hours and as the inception ceremony itself occupied most of the morning, and longer if there happened to be more than one inceptor, the detailed determination was held over until the following day. Hence the newly created master just briefly recapitulated the principal arguments advanced during the disputation, and simply determined the question by using a set formula: 'Ad hec et ad alia sufficiunt magistrorum responsa.'[4] Then and only then, as Markaunt's text quaintly but significantly puts it, was the new master 'first

1 'Quilibet...fidem faciat iuramento eciam non exactam' (*ibid.* II. iv [see below, p. 199, lines 18–19]). Cf. *SAUO*, 19, 3–7 (*app. crit.* ad 3). As the friars more or less dominated the faculty of theology and remained to some extent outside the university (they were not M.A.s), they may have been compelled to take a corporal oath at their inceptions.

2 Cf. *SA* 134 (*Docs*, i. 381). Earlier, a pledge of faith continued to be sufficient for the observance of the statutes, but an inceptor had to promise under oath to fulfil his year of regency (afterwards known as necessary regency). *SA* 134 abolished the pledge of faith and prescribed a corporal oath under both headings.

3 One of the major defects of Rashdall's *magnum opus*, as Powicke pointed out in *Universities*, i. 492, is the very inadequate treatment of disputations. This applies especially to masters' determinations. Rashdall, *ibid.* pp. 450–6, has a good deal to say about B.A. determination, but there was no parity between the two types of determination.

4 Markaunt (see below, p. 313, line 4). The phrase was conventional, though it varied slightly at Oxford. Cf. *SAUO*, 38, 22–3.

made a brother of the masters'.[1] His career as regent began on the next day, when he delivered his *lectio solemnis* or inaugural lecture in his own school, which he hired at the beginning of term.[2] The lecture was little more than an introduction to his determination of the question that he dismissed so abruptly at his inception.

To read and dispute was the essence of a master's office. With perfect logic the Angelica text treats of lectures and disputations immediately after its ruling on inception. This it does with the utmost economy of detail. Beyond stating some general rules concerning the hours and mode of lecturing and disputing, the text tells us very little. What it has to say is rather interesting and in some ways important; for all its vagueness it is much more revealing than the early Oxford statutes as regards the horarium.[3] Only three faculties are named: arts, decrees or canon law and theology. The absence of civil law is noteworthy. That jurisprudence was taught at Cambridge before the middle of the thirteenth century is unquestionable, but it was not organized as a separate faculty and the doctorate was not conferred. Lectures were given *extraordinarie* as part of the course in canon law, for which they served as an essential preparation. Shortly after the constitution was promulgated civil law became one of the constituent faculties of the university, and inceptions were certainly held by 1256.[4] Evidence of the institution of a faculty of medicine is difficult to come by. It was probably erected in the early years of the reign of Edward I; as at Oxford the faculty remained rather weak all through the medieval period.[5] There was no faculty of grammar in the thirteenth century and although the degree of master was conferred *c.* 1385 grammarians never enjoyed more than quasi-faculty status and were not members of the congregation of regents.[6] By *c.* 1250, therefore, the university

[1] Markaunt (see below, p. 313, line 5). The outline given above of an inception ceremony at Cambridge is based mainly on Markaunt's fragmentary text and on the account preserved in Stokys's Book, ed. cit. pp. xx–lii, which represents the custom of the late fifteenth century. Due allowance has been made for this fact.

[2] See below, p. 171, n. 2. For references to the *lectio solemnis* cf. *Grace Book* A, pp. 51, 184.

[3] Cf. Gibson's remark in *SAUO*, p. lxxxi.

[4] See above, p. 31.

[5] See above, pp. 29–30. The Oxford statutes allow for the possibility that there may be only one regent in medicine in the university. Cf. *SAUO*, 41, 18. Rashdall overlooked this point when he drew attention to the Cambridge statute, *SA* 103 (*Docs*, i. 366–7). Cf. Rashdall, *Universities*, iii. 285, n. 2; the actual passage there cited is a very late addition to the statutes.

[6] The first Cambridge scholar to graduate as M.Gram. appears to be Robert Laverok. It may be taken as certain that he incepted in grammar by *c.* 1385. See below,

comprised not more than three faculties. The faculty of arts existed from the very beginnings of the *studium* and always contained the greatest number of students and masters. One is less certain about the genesis of the faculty of canon law. It may well have been founded during the chancellorship of Richard de Leycestria (*c.* 1222–32), who was himself a canonist. Among the masters who incepted before 1250 should be numbered Edmund de Walpole, who was 'doctor in decretis' before he became a monk at Bury St Edmunds in 1246.[1] Though there is no record that he took his degree at Cambridge, his vocation to this East Anglian abbey is very suggestive, particularly as he is not known to have graduated at Oxford or any European university.[2]

The most significant of the three faculties mentioned in the Angelica text is the faculty of theology. Whatever fame Cambridge achieved in the middle ages was due to its theological school. The highest distinction in the academic world, the *magisterium* in theology, was obtainable only at Paris, Oxford and Cambridge in the thirteenth century and during the greater part of the fourteenth century, if we exclude the *studium generale* founded at the papal court in 1245.[3] So great was the theological standing of the three universities that the foundation statutes of the faculty erected at Bologna in 1364 forbade admission *ad eundem* to bachelors, however famous, of another university unless they happened to be graduates of Paris, Oxford or Cambridge.[4] The sole credit for establishing and developing the faculty of theology at Cambridge was claimed by the Dominicans and Franciscans in 1304.[5] While no one can dispute

p. 265, n. 5. There is an excellent study of Oxford grammarians by R. W. Hunt, 'Oxford grammar masters in the middle ages', in *Oxford studies pres. to D. Callus*, pp. 163–93.

1 He was elected abbot in 1248. Cf. *Cronica Buriensis*: 'Anno Domini M°CC°XLVIII° magister Edmundus de Walpol, monachus Sancti Edmundi et doctor in decretis, electus est in abbatem nonis Julii, et confirmatus ab Hugone episcopo Eliensi v^to^ kal. Octobris.' (*Memorials of St Edmund's abbey*, ed. T. Arnold, iii [Rolls series, 1896], 29.) It is strange that he is not accorded the title of D.Cn.L. in the chronicle edited by Mrs Gransden. Cf. *Chronicle of Bury St Edmunds*, pp. 15, 21.

2 At a later date Bury certainly had links with the faculty of canon law at Cambridge. The first Benedictine to study there and incept as D.Cn.L. was, apparently, Simon, monk of Walden; he incepted in 1297. Cf. *ibid.* p. 140. See also *BRUC*, p. 685, s.v. Waldene (he was D.Cn.L., not D.C.L.), and below, p. 244.

3 Cf R. Creytens, O.P., 'Le "Studium Romanae Curiae" et le maître du Sacré Palais', *Archivum Fratrum Praedicatorum*, xii (1942), 5–83.

4 *I più antichi statuti*, 32, 15–33, 2; cf. *ibid.* pp. cciii–cciv.

5 The closure of their schools they declared was to the detriment of the *studium* 'et precipue theologice facultatis que a fratribus ibidem initium sumpsit pariter et

that they dominated the faculty in the second half of the thirteenth century, the faculty itself was probably founded before they opened schools at the university. Vincent de Coventre, the Franciscan, was the first friar to hold a chair of theology at Cambridge. He did not incept at either Oxford or Paris. The only other university at which he could have taken his degree was Cambridge. Hence he must have incepted under a secular master, most likely *c.* 1240.[1] It must not be forgotten that the founding fathers of the university, John Grim, John Blund and Robert of York, all probably taught theology. Grim was certainly D.Th. when he took up residence in Cambridge in 1209. Blund was also master of theology. For all we know, Alan de Beccles and other Parisian masters who migrated there in 1229–31 may have been professors of theology and helped to organize the faculty on a solid basis. Unless it existed by *c.* 1240 Coventre could not have incepted at the university.[2] The important thing is that the faculty was fully organized by *c.* 1250, which is all that concerns us here. We may now proceed to examine what the Angelica text has to say about lectures and disputations.

incrementum' (quoted in Moorman, *Grey Friars in Cambridge*, p. 235). For the controversy with the university which caused the friars to cease lecturing see pp. 240–4, below.

1 Scholars differ about the date of Coventre's *lectura*. In *BRUC*, p. 164, he is stated to have been master by 1225 and lector after 1236. Moorman, *op. cit.* pp. 116, 143, suggests he was lector in 1230–5, while the date 'by 1252' is advanced by Russell, *Dictionary of writers of thirteenth-century England* (*Bulletin of the Institute of Historical Research*, special supplement, 3 [London, 1936]), p. 206.

2 The late A. G. Little, who pioneered research into the origins of the theological faculty of Cambridge, would not agree that Coventre incepted there; but *salva reverentia* I cannot see what other meaning one can deduce from the remarks of Eccleston, the primary source. Moreover, he says explicitly that Coventre did not read at Oxford. Cf. *Fratris Thomae vulgo dicti de Eccleston tractatus de adventu fratrum minorum in Angliam*, ed. Little and revised by Moorman (Manchester, 1951), p. 57. For some reason which is not apparent, Little in *Oxford theology*, p. 94, adopted a different attitude towards Eccleston's lists from the interpretation which he put forward in his edition of the *tractatus* or in his admirable article 'The friars and the foundation of the faculty of theology in the university of Cambridge', *Franciscan papers, lists, and documents* (Manchester, 1943), pp. 122–43. In *Oxford theology*, *loc. cit.*, Little states that Roger de Marston, O.F.M., must have incepted at Cambridge, since his name appears in Eccleston's list of Cambridge *magistri*, even though the list explicitly states that he incepted at Oxford. It would seem incontestable, then, that Vincent de Coventre, William of Poitiers, John de Weston, William de Milton (not to be confused with his namesake who incepted at Paris by 1248) and Humphrey de Hautboys, who were masters at Cambridge *c.* 1240–59, actually incepted there. If they had incepted at Oxford Eccleston would have said so; he does in fact state that Eustace de Normanville and Thomas de York, the third and sixth masters in his list, took their degree at Oxford.

The Cambridge constitution recognizes two classes of lectures and disputations, ordinary and extraordinary.[1] This division has the great merit of simplifying a most involved subject. It also preserves the original classification of lectures, which we owe to Bologna. There was a third class called 'cursory'. They were Paris's contribution to the medieval curriculum, and it is very surprising that the Angelica text makes no mention of them. The later statutes are replete with references to all three classes, which makes the omission all the more curious. We cannot go into the question here in any detail; though numerous scholars have tried to explain the triple classification and have succeeded with varying success in disentangling ordinary, extraordinary and cursory lectures, the distinction between the three has not yet been satisfactorily explained. To read *cursorie* was the proper function of a bachelor, so much so that admission to the status or degree was synonymous with authority to read a text or book cursorily. Masters might also read *cursorie*, but their proper function was to read *ordinarie*. Both masters and bachelors could lecture *extraordinarie*. It is these two classes of lectures that the Angelica text invites us to consider.

At the risk of indulging in over-simplification we may say that the statutory, formal, morning lectures of regent masters were the ordinary.[2] The reading of ordinary lectures was reserved to masters; these lectures constituted the most important part of their weekly programme. Ordinary lectures could be given only on legible days; if a master read on days classified as non-legible or disputable or non-disputable days he did so *extraordinarie* or *festinanter* or *cursorie*. At Cambridge a master was not obliged by statute to lecture ordinarily on every legible day. He was expected to read on at least three days if the week had as many legible days. Normally, a conscientious regent would read on the average roughly 140 ordinary lectures during the academic year or not less than 100 or so if he held an ordinary disputation every week.[3] It would be

1 *Cons. Univ. Canteb.* II. v–viii (see below, p. 201, lines 3–12).

2 In the faculty of canon law bachelors were permitted and indeed encouraged *c.* 1330 to read *ordinarie* in the morning. As at Oxford this was a special form of lectureship introduced in order to relieve the congestion of lectures which the new collections of decretals created. Oxford with perhaps a finer sense of tradition referred to these morning lectures as *quasi ordinarie*. Cf. Boyle, art. cit. pp. 146–51. The relevant Cambridge statute is *SA* 104 (*Docs*, i. 367–9).

3 This piece of arithmetic, interspersed with not a little guess-work, was arrived at from a study of the earliest surviving university calendar, which is preserved in the Old Proctor's Book, fos. 11^r–16^v. The much later calendar in the Senior Proctor's

difficult in view of the arrangement of the horarium of arts and theology for a master in these faculties to deliver more than one or two ordinary lectures the same day. Two at any rate was the maximum allowed at Paris, and the same rule doubtless applied at Cambridge.

Everything connected with the formal lectures of a regent master went by the name of ordinary. The time assigned to these lectures was known as the *hora ordinaria*, the best hours of the day. Masters at ordinary lectures had to wear their proper habit, the *habitus ordinarius*. The lectures were confined to the recognized, public schools of the university; their official character was sufficiently attested by the attendance of the bedells of the respective faculties. The books which formed the basis of the *lectura ordinaria* were the 'ordinary' books. In this context the term is ambivalent. Bachelors as well as masters might read the same texts. The fundamental difference, that which made the one 'ordinary' and the other 'cursory', was of course the relative status of the lecturers but still more the method of lecturing.[1] When all is said and done it was the mode of exposition which distinguished an ordinary lecture from every other sort of lecture. An ordinary lecture consisted of a diffuse, authoritative, *questiones* commentary based on an exact and profound understanding of the text. It differed from the textual, *expositio litteralis* reading of a bachelor. This does not mean that a cursory lecture was superficial or hastily delivered. Its object was to enable a student to familiarize himself with the content of a text and understand its literal meaning. In other words the bachelor had to read the text with its glosses, explain the terminology and elucidate the sense. It was a sort of running commentary, though in the hands of an experienced bachelor a *lectio textualis* or *expositio litteralis* might not fall far short of the type of commentary given by a newly created master who graduated directly, say, from arts to theology.[2]

At first sight the distinction between an ordinary and an extra-

Book is printed in C. Wordsworth, *The ancient kalendar of the university of Oxford* (OHS, xlv [1904]), 216–27.

[1] It may be disconcerting to find Parisian statutes of theology applying the term *ordinarie* to lectures on the Bible given by the lower ranks of lecturers. In this connection it is to be understood as meaning *cursorie* or, to be more exact, *biblice*.

[2] It is easy to see how the friars were able to dominate the faculty of theology. When they arrived at the universities they had already been blooded as lectors in their own *studia* and had lectured on the Bible and Sentences, which were the subject-matter of their *lectura* as bachelors.

ordinary lecture is clear and decisive. The one is or should be the direct antithesis of the other. Unlike the ordinary, extraordinary lectures were not the preserve of masters. All bachelors reading for the *magisterium* or *pro forma* had to read *extraordinarie*, a term which we shall have to look at again when we come to relate what is said here about the two classes of lectures to the provisions of the Angelica text. Masters could deliver extraordinary lectures anywhere and were not obliged to wear their ordinary habit. Neither were they restricted when reading *extraordinarie* to legible days. Extraordinary lectures were given on days specifically designated as *le. fes.*, as well as on days which were non-legible or non-disputable.[1] The traditional designation of certain books as 'extraordinary' is not a good yardstick, as we have remarked already, for distinguishing between ordinary and extraordinary lectures. It is useful in the field of law, but even there the distinction is not water-tight.[2] What can be said is that masters were free to read unprescribed books or at all events books which were not part of the ordinary course.[3] The association of ordinary lectures with the morning and extraordinary with the afternoon would be more meaningful if it were put this way: extraordinary lectures could not be given during the hours of ordinary lectures. In the final analysis, it was the mode of lecturing which really marked off an extraordinary from an ordinary lecture. The one was less formal, less exhaustive, less penetrating than the other, though the distinction could be very fine. A lot would depend on the nature of the text and on the master's approach.

The Angelica text, for all its vagueness, is a little more informative about the Cambridge horarium than are the pre-1350 statutes of Oxford about the horarium there. At Cambridge by *c.* 1250 ordinary lectures in arts and theology commenced before the hour of prime and could not be prolonged beyond the first stroke of the bell. The hours of the day were not regulated by the clock but by the times of the liturgical offices. Prime, the first hour, might be as early as 4 a.m. and as late as 7 a.m. It varied according

1 The term *le. fes.* (*legibilis festinanter*) does not mean that one had to read quickly, though one might do so. It signified cursory reading, and meant that the lecture must not be prolonged beyond a certain hour. This was the decisive meaning of the term.

2 Cf. Rashdall, *Universities*, i. 206–7 and n. 1; 433, n. 1; Boyle, art. cit. p. 148.

3 Mag. Nicholas de Breckendale's *lectura* on the *Exoticon* of Alexander of Hales, which he completed at Cambridge on 17 Nov. 1261, must have been given *extraordinarie*. Cf. *BRUC*, p. 90, and above, pp. 14, 38.

to custom and with the seasons. Generally, we may say that the hour of prime corresponded with 6 a.m. The actual times at which lectures had to begin were fixed by the rectors, who were also empowered to change them. Ordinary lectures in arts and theology ran concurrently, the masters and scholars being summoned to the schools by the ringing of the bell of St Mary's.[1] An ordinary lecture probably lasted at least one whole hour; if a master in arts or theology read only one ordinary lecture in the day (it was forbidden at Paris to read more than two in arts) he would have to commence lecturing by 5 a.m. It is quite possible that lectures were held at a much earlier hour. At all events, regents in arts and theology had to finish their *lectura* at prime, after which the canonists began their ordinary lectures.[2] The same horarium was observed at Oxford.[3] Though the Angelica text openly implies that canonists could read *ordinarie* until the hour of none (about 3 p.m.), we may assume that if they commenced their lectures immediately after prime they would not continue beyond the hour of terce (about 9 a.m.), which was the rule at Bologna.[4] The phrase 'nec post nonam legent ordinarie' is another way of saying that extraordinary lectures in the faculty begin after none, the *hora extraordinaria* at Bologna, and that these will be given by the masters.[5]

The phrasing of this passage seems to suggest that afternoon lectures were confined to the faculty of canon law; in other words, that masters read *extraordinarie* after none but not in the faculties of arts and theology. The bell of St Benet's church was rung to summon scholars to extraordinary lectures. A row flared up in 1274 over the ringing of the bell; apparently it was not unconnected

[1] Rashdall, *Universities*, i. 433–4, states that masters in theology at Paris lectured after terce (about 9 a.m.), which gave masters in arts, who had by then finished their lectures, an opportunity of hearing ordinary lectures in theology. In this he was mistaken, following Ch. Thurot, *De l'organisation de l'enseignement dans l'université de Paris au moyen-âge* (Paris, 1850). Regents in theology read at prime, bachelors at terce. Cf. *Chart. Univ. Paris.* i. 79, no. 20; ii. 692, no. 1188 (5).

[2] *Cons. Univ. Canteb.* II. v (see below, p. 201, lines 3–5).

[3] Cf. *SAUO*, 175, 19–21. An earlier statute which says that masters of arts must not read after prime on funeral days does not mean that they could lecture after prime on legible days; cf. *ibid.* 59, 5–9.

[4] When the faculty of civil law was established at Cambridge doctors could read at prime, following the custom of Oxford. But the Cambridge statute shows that the canonists retained their right of lecturing at this hour if they wished. Cf. *SA* 121 (*Docs*, i. 376); *SAUO*, 44, 3–4. For the Bologna statute cf. *Statuti*, p. 42, rubr. xliiij.

[5] We may take it that Cambridge professors lectured *extraordinarie* on the decretals of Gregory IX by *c.* 1250.

with the fee payable to the bellringer by lecturers in law, and the university, after peace was restored through the good offices of Hugh Balsham, enacted a statute ordering each reader in canon and civil law to swear on oath at the time of his admission that he would pay his *pro rata* share of the stipend payable to the clerk for ringing the bell for lectures after dinner.[1] By 1274, therefore, one may presume that extraordinary lectures after none were officially associated with the faculty of law. This does not mean that extraordinary lectures in the other faculties could not be held in the afternoon on legible days, but the arrangement of the horarium left the entire morning after prime free for extraordinary lectures in arts and theology, and it may be assumed that the hours between 6 a.m. and 3 p.m., or at least up to dinner-time, were availed of for this purpose. Some precision is called for as regards the use of the term 'extraordinary' of these morning lectures; but first let us see what the Angelica text itself has to say about extraordinary lectures.

Chapter II, paragraph vi, reads very like a Parisian statute of 1255 which states that regents in arts must not make their ordinary lectures extraordinary.[2] The Angelica text is a little more explicit. It lays down that no one, that is, no master, may change an ordinary into an extraordinary lecture or *vice versa*, unless the other masters of his faculty give permission.[3] This is one of the very few parts of the text to be discarded in the later recensions. As we shall see, another statute was substituted in its place, prohibiting masters and scholars who were not M.A.s of Cambridge from reading extraordinary lectures in law between prime and none. The original statute, namely the Angelica text, had a wider application. The purpose of the enactment was to prevent masters of any faculty from reading *extraordinarie* when they should be reading *ordinarie*; from using an extraordinary book at their ordinary lectures; and from interchanging the hours of ordinary and extraordinary lectures. The constitution does allow exceptions,[4] and it is interesting that the granting of a dispensation is vested in the masters of the faculty, not in the rectors, which would seem to indicate that by *c.* 1250 at

1 Cf. *SA* 106 (*Docs*, i. 369). See also p. 34, above.

2 Cf. *Chart. Univ. Paris.* i. 278, no. 246, quoted on p. 200, *app. crit.* ad 6–7.

3 *Cons. Univ. Canteb.* II. vi (see below, p. 201, lines 6–7).

4 At Bologna it was permissible for the extraordinary hour to be changed from none to terce for a just cause. Cf. *Statuti*, p. 40, rubr. xliij.

Cambridge the word 'faculty' had acquired the technical meaning of a consortium of masters engaged in teaching the same subject.[1]

Analogous to this statute is another paragraph of the Angelica text, which decrees that no master or bachelor may read *extraordinarie* during the hours of ordinary lectures.[2] A master of arts might finish his ordinary lecture an hour before prime, but he could not use the remaining time for an extraordinary lecture; if he wished to read up to prime he would have to read *ordinarie*. Likewise, a bachelor in theology could not lecture until after prime; and no master or bachelor of canon law was permitted to read *extraordinarie* before none. This particular statute was relaxed by *c.* 1390 in favour of scholars who had ruled in arts at Cambridge, and in 1505 it was allowed to all bachelors in canon and civil law to read after mid-day.[3] The most peculiar feature of the early thirteenth-century statute is its use of the term *extraordinarie* of bachelors as well as masters. What the statute really excludes is the reading of cursory lectures during the hours assigned for ordinary lectures. In the faculty of law masters read either *ordinarie* or *extraordinarie*; the same would also appear to be true of regents in the other two faculties. Bachelors always read *cursorie*, though in the faculty of law they might also lecture *extraordinarie* but not in their official role as bachelors (*cursorie legentes*) but as substitutes (*extraordinarii*) of the masters. The author of the Angelica text may very well have had history on his side in using *extraordinarie* as a blanket-term. It was the reverse at Paris, where *cursorie* was the term. By 1255 the distinction between lectures given by masters and lectures given by bachelors was established: masters read ordinary and extraordinary lectures, bachelors read cursory lectures.[4] It is impossible to say when Cambridge adopted this classification, but it was certainly some time after *c.* 1250.

If a regent's primary office was to read, his secondary office was to dispute. The Cambridge constitution reduces all disputations to two classes: ordinary and extraordinary. This represents possibly

[1] The expression 'faculty' in this sense occurs for the first time at Paris in a statute of 19 March 1255 (*Chart. Univ. Paris.* i. 278, no. 246).

[2] *Cons. Univ. Canteb.* II. viii (see below, p. 201, lines 10–11). This is the earliest reference in the text to bachelors.

[3] Cf. *SA* 85 (*Docs*, i. 360), 151 (*ibid.* 389).

[4] *Chart. Univ. Paris.* i. 278–9, no. 246. This at any rate seems to be the implication of the statute. Thurot, *op. cit.* pp. 76–8, whom Rashdall again follows (*Universities*, i. 433), writes 'extraordinary' when the statutes say 'cursory'.

the earliest classification of disputations and has much to commend it. Somehow it never gained currency.[1] One would expect that the old division of lectures into ordinary and extraordinary would be reflected in the field of disputations, since there was originally a close link between the *lectio* and the *disputatio*, or rather between the *questio* which was disputed and the *lectio* which provoked it.[2]

The Angelica text does not elaborate on the distinction between the two categories of disputations, but the little it has to say is none the less interesting. No master of arts (*logicus*) or theology (*theologus*), we read, may hold an ordinary disputation before the hour of terce.[3] The implication is that in both faculties such exercises commenced at or shortly after 9 a.m. That ordinary disputations were held in the mornings of disputable days is only what one would expect. It has been suggested, however, that these disputations took place at Oxford in the faculty of theology in the afternoon.[4] One need not have the slightest doubt that the Cambridge constitution mirrors the customs of the parent university; and consequently we may conclude that ordinary disputations at both universities in theology as well as arts were held in the morning at the hour of terce during the thirteenth century. Chapter II of the Angelica text makes no mention of disputations in canon law. That these exercises took place in the faculty by *c.* 1250 is certain, and they were proclaimed with the same solemnity as theological disputations.[5] In view of the regulation concerning the commencement of the exercises in arts and theology it seems that the canonists disputed at the hour of prime (6 a.m.), a deduction which the later statutes confirm.[6] We may assume, however, that Cambridge doctors like their Oxford colleagues did not dispute very regularly. Where disputations counted most was in the faculties of arts and theology. The Angelica text when it states that no logician or theologian may dispute before

[1] Little in *Oxford theology*, p. 247, scented something when he wrote apropos of *questiones* in Worcester MS Q. 99: 'What "ordinarie" means does not appear; there is no reference to questions disputed "extraordinarie".'

[2] See M.-D. Chenu, O.P., *Introduction à l'étude de Saint Thomas d'Aquin* (Univ. de Montréal—Institut d'Études Médiévales, xi [1950]), 66–81.

[3] *Cons. Univ. Canteb.* II. vii (see below, p. 201, lines 8–9). The text of *SA* 151 in *Docs*, i. 390, line 4, should read: 'vel theologus ordinariam...' See below, p. 276, n. 4.

[4] Little, *op. cit.* p. 230. He was misled by a late statute of 1456.

[5] In both faculties the bells summoning the disputants were rung by the bedell. See below, p. 161.

[6] Markaunt 19 (see below, p. 321, lines 9–11); *SA* 72 (*Docs, loc. cit.* 354). Cf. also *SA* 121 (*ibid.* 376).

terce gives the impression that their ordinary disputations took place at the same hours.[1] The horarium was in fact the reverse of the horarium of ordinary lectures, except that no disputations began before prime. Just as ordinary lectures could be given only on legible days, so, too, ordinary disputations were held only on disputable days. All lectures were suspended on the day of an ordinary disputation. The ideal, if not the rule, was that there should be disputations in each faculty every week, at least once. On the whole, this cannot have been too difficult to observe; a certain week, owing to the onset of feast-days, might not yield three legible days, and as lectures took precedence over disputations, no ordinary disputation would be possible that week; but the chancellor together with the rectors could designate a day in exceptional circumstances.[2]

An ordinary disputation was public and magisterial. It took place in one of the schools of a regent master; the regents had to wear their ordinary habit; the hours were 'ordinary'; and no one was allowed to dispute *extraordinarie* during those hours.[3] The formal character of the disputations is also underlined by a regulation in the constitution which orders the bedells to visit the schools not only during the hours of ordinary lectures but in addition when ordinary disputations were being held. Moreover, the bedell of canon law and theology had the duty of ringing the bell for the first disputations in the two faculties.[4] More than one question might be debated at a disputation, and evidently two disputations, time permitting, could be held in the same faculty on the one day but not simultaneously.[5] At each disputation a master presided and no other master was permitted to dispute elsewhere *ordinarie* while the disputation lasted. All the bachelors and scholars of the faculty had to attend, and provided the respondent and opponents. It was at

[1] At Oxford disputations in arts and theology were interconnected. Cf. Little, *op. cit. loc. cit.*

[2] But the consent of the masters of the faculty would be necessary. See below, p. 143.

[3] *Cons. Univ. Canteb.* II. viii (see below, p. 141, n. 3).

[4] See below, p. 161, n. 3.

[5] Concursory disputations were permitted in the faculty of theology at Oxford and very probably at Cambridge as well because of the great number of inceptors. Cf. *SAUO*, 51, 22–4; 179, 12–15; 226, 1–6. Pelster in *Oxford theology*, p. 38, surmises with good reason that these disputations were not authorized before 1314, but he mistook the meaning of concursory. Though Oxford forbade by statute of 1456 more than one master in theology to dispute on a given day, at Cambridge two disputations were allowed by the late fifteenth century. Cf. Stokys's Book, ed. cit. p. xlix.

these disputations that candidates for the licence did their responsions. Masters might also participate in the disputation, and at the close the master in charge of the exercise determined the question or announced that he would give his determination on another day.

Though the classification of disputations as extraordinary is most uncommon, their nature is clear enough.[1] Any disputation which falls short of the requirements of an ordinary disputation may very properly be called 'extraordinary'. By stating the distinction in this way we avoid confusion with a third category known as 'solemn'. To this class belonged the disputations held at the vespers and *principium* of an inception ceremony, and likewise quodlibetical disputations.[2] Masters or bachelors could hold extraordinary disputations on any disputable day after the ordinary disputations in the faculty finished.[3] The purpose of these exercises was to supplement the teaching in the schools and most of all to equip scholars and bachelors for the rigorous test which they would have to undergo as opponents or respondents at public or ordinary disputations. Repetitions, collations and convent (and later college) disputations also ranked as extraordinary.[4] There was one species which the term covered and it was perhaps the most distinctive genre. These were the disputations of 'determiners in Lent'.[5] Scholars who had responded to the question and received the licence to read *cursorie* in arts had to dispute in public under a master and determine the question or questions before they could actually lecture as bachelors. The disputations were held after dinner in the afternoon and were

1 There are references to extraordinary disputations, for example, in the statutes (1460–1505) of the faculty of arts of Freiburg (see the edition cited on p. 278, n. 3, below). But these statutes throw as little light as does the Angelica text on the disputations.

2 Mag. Roger de Marston, the Franciscan, may have been the first to dispute *de quolibet* at Cambridge during his term as regent in theology (*c.* 1269–71 or *c.* 1275). Cf. *BRUC*, p. 393. Little in *Oxford theology*, pp. 94–5, assigns the *quodlibeta* to Marston's term at Oxford (*c.* 1280–4). This genre of disputations was certainly unknown at Cambridge by the time the Angelica text was executed.

3 'Magister uel bachilarius temporibus...disputacionum ordinariarum sue facultatis extraordinarie non...disputet' (*Cons. Univ. Canteb.* II. viii [see below, p. 201, lines 10–12]).

4 For the meaning of *collationes* (collations) cf. Pelster in *Oxford theology*, pp. 53–6. On conventual disputations see E. Ypma, O.S.A., 'Le "Mare magnum" — un code médiéval du couvent augustinien de Paris', *Augustiniana*, vi (1956), 309–12. The code dates from *c.* 1351–4 and its provisions for private disputations are very similar to those of the Sorbonne.

5 The earliest surviving part of the Cambridge statute on determination is printed on pp. 300–1 below. Cf. also Stokys's Book, ed. cit. pp. iv–xv.

obviously extraordinary, though they were required *pro forma.* It may be assumed that they constituted the most important class of disputations at which bachelors were permitted by the constitution to dispute *extraordinarie.*

ANGELICA CHAPTER III: THE ACADEMIC YEAR

There were three terms.[1] The winter term started on 10 October (the day after St Denis) and ended on 16 December (O *sapientia*), a day earlier than at Oxford.[2] The Lent or second term began on 14 January (the day after St Hilary) and finished on the Friday before Palm Sunday, again a day earlier than at Oxford. The summer term, the longest by far of the three, was divided into two parts. The Easter part, as we may call it, consisted of thirty-eight days. On the Wednesday after Quasimodo Sunday (the first Sunday after Easter) the masters resumed their lectures, as did their Oxford colleagues, and continued lecturing until the Friday before Whit Sunday. Following a break of ten days (it was longer at Oxford), lectures recommenced on the Monday after Trinity Sunday, term ending on 20 July, the feast of St Margaret of Antioch. Both parts were reckoned as one, full term.[3] It totalled ninety-seven days and made the winter term (sixty-eight days) and the Lent term (sixty-four days) look short by comparison.[4] By 1309 the last day of the academic year was changed from 20 July to 6 July, the vigil of the translation of St Thomas of Canterbury, which also became the final day of term at Oxford.[5] The number of legible, disputable and

[1] *Cons. Univ. Canteb.* III (see below, p. 201, line 14 to p. 203, line 1).

[2] In the fifteenth century winter term was also known as michaelmas term.

[3] Cambridge and Oxford statutes sometimes give the impression that full term was the sum total of the three terms. Cf. Statutes of King's College, Cambridge, c. xxxi (*Docs,* ii. 552), *SAUO,* 133, 22–4; 236, 30–2. Markaunt 7 (see below, p. 315, lines 14–15) is the counterpart of the Oxford statute (*SAUO,* 133, 22–4) and shows that full term is to be understood as one term. *SA* 8 (*Docs,* i. 311) omits the all-important phrase 'in vno termino' of Markaunt.

[4] In the fourteenth century lectures on the decretals and in civil law continued until 1 Aug. or 15 Aug. Cf. *SA* 104 (*Docs,* i. 368), 152 (*ibid.* 390). Cf. also *SAUO,* p. lxxxi. The period between the end or cessation of lectures in July and the start of the new academic year in October was called the autumn term. Cf. *Grace Book* A, pp. xxx–xxxi.

[5] Cf. *SA* 150 (*Docs,* i. 389); *SAUO, loc. cit.* For the agreement between the Cambridge burgess, Nicholas le Barber, and the university, dated 23 July 1309, which shows that the change of date from 20 to 6 July took place by 1309, see below, p. 171.

other academic days varied from term to term. The oldest available university calendar was executed *c.* 1390–5.[1] On the basis of such a late compilation it is extremely imprudent to calculate the number of legible and disputable days each of the three terms contained *c.* 1250; but taking everything into consideration and allowing for a margin of error, we can say with perhaps more confidence than is justified that the winter term—the safest to assess—comprised some thirty-eight legible and ten disputable days, one in fact for each week of the term.[2]

The Angelica text, unlike the revised version of the statute, suggests that neither the beginning nor the close of the academic year was marked by the celebration of solemn Mass.[3] It is much more concerned to state that no disputations must be held on the days that the masters resume and finish their lectures; and there can be no departure from this rule without their consent.[4] On Shrove Monday and Tuesday and on Ash Wednesday, that is, *Carnevale* and the beginning of Lent, ordinary lectures and disputations were suspended except in the faculty of theology. The theologians had their recompense on the three following days, a privilege which they retained when free days were abolished in the other faculties on Shrove Monday and Tuesday.[5]

ANGELICA CHAPTER IV: CONVOCATION

The Angelica text confirms the correctness of Rashdall's view that convocations were originally and principally associated with inceptions and funerals.[6] The primary reason given in the constitution for calling the regents together is inceptions; funerals are not mentioned under the heading *De conuocacionibus faciendis*, but it is

1 Old Proctor's Book, fos. 11r–16v. See below, pp. 261–5.

2 An Oxford statute of 1431 states that a term in arts must contain at least thirty legible days. Cf. *SAUO*, 234, 18–19.

3 *SA* 150 (*loc. cit.*).

4 The word *statuatur* in this context ('nisi eorum consensu aliter statuatur') may have the force of 'enacted', but it is more correct to translate it as 'decreed' or 'ordained'. There can only be question of an *ad hoc* ordinance by the rectors.

5 It will be noticed that the Angelica text says nothing about the traditional Ash Wednesday sermon preached in the Dominican and Franciscan churches which sparked off the dispute that proved so bitter between the friars and the university in 1303–6. See below, pp. 241–2.

6 Rashdall, *Universities*, i. 292–3; iii. 54, n. 2.

obvious from other references in the text that the obsequies of members of the university were occasions for convocation.[1] It is not stated that the convoking of the regents was the chancellor's prerogative; indeed the text is as unexplicit on this point as is the corresponding statute of Oxford.[2] The Oxford proctors, however, from an early or comparatively early date, certainly by 1257, had authority to order congregations of the regents.[3] The chancellor also had this right, though he only used it, or was empowered to use it, when the proctors refused to act. The situation at Cambridge was quite the opposite. Convocations were summoned by the chancellor, never by the rectors or proctors. A statute was enacted on 17 March 1276 authorizing them to convoke the regents on a particular occasion even without approaching the chancellor, if he declined to take action.[4] This enactment should not be interpreted as an extension of the jurisdiction of the university at the expense of the chancellor's spiritual jurisdiction or as a sharing of his prerogative with the rectors.[5] It must be clear by now that the chancellor was not the highest authority in the university; he was the principal executive, the chief justice; yet there was a higher court, the *universitas regentium*, over which he presided, but which he was not at liberty to set aside. It was the supreme tribunal and court of appeal in the university. The right to convoke the regents was not connected with the chancellor's spiritual jurisdiction. Inceptions, the basic purpose of convocations, had nothing to do with his ecclesiastical office. The granting of the licence was distinct from, though a necessary prerequisite for, the creation of a new master, a matter which pertained exclusively and collectively to the corporation of regent masters. Yet there is no denying that the chancellor was alone competent to summon convocations. The statute of 1276 did not diminish or curtail his prerogative or its exercise. It recognizes his right by providing a remedy against its abuse. Moreover, the revised text of Angelica chapter IV shows that by *c.* 1304–37

[1] *Cons. Univ. Canteb.* IV (see below, p. 203, lines 7–12). Cf. *ibid.* V (see below, p. 203, lines 14–16); XIII. ii–iii (see p. 217, lines 17–23).

[2] Cf. *SAUO*, 57, 18–24.

[3] *Ibid.* 108, 6. Ullmann, *Historical Journal*, i. 178, n. 8, cites a statute of 1322 as the earliest evidence of the proctors' right to summon the regents.

[4] Ullmann, *ibid.* p. 181.

[5] The bedells were authorized to convoke the regents when the two proctors were unable to agree. Cf. *Docs*, i. 418–19. This statute may not be earlier than 1535. Cf. *ibid.* 418, n. 1.

the chancellor's prerogative had been strengthened by statutory action on the part of the university.[1]

Under the constitution the term 'convocation' has the meaning which a general congregation of the regent masters had at Paris and possibly at Oxford, too, by 1259. This expression, 'generalis congregacio', actually occurs at the end of the chapter of the Angelica text on convocations. Both terms are correlative and signify a meeting of all the regent masters.[2] After 1304 when the non-regents were admitted on a permanent basis to convocation these terms took on a different meaning, and with one exception corresponded with Oxford usage.[3] The exception is 'Great Congregation' (*Congregatio magna*). It was instituted at Cambridge in 1270 and was the name given to the annual ceremony at which among other things ten burgesses representative of the town and thirteen scholars drawn from the four 'nations' (England, Scotland, Ireland and Wales—in that order) in the presence of the university of regents pledged themselves by oath to keep the peace.[4] At Oxford *Congregatio magna* denoted the combined houses of regents and non-regents.

The fact that the Angelica text uses the term 'general congregation' does not mean that the faculties, or at least the masters of arts, formed particular congregations. Faculties probably met to consider the applications of masters who wished to avail of the concession provided for in the constitution, chapter II, paragraph vi, for instance, and to propose or discuss new statutes.[5] There is no evidence of the existence of a congregation of the artists, unless we include under this heading the annual elections of the rectors and taxors; but originally they were elected by the whole body of regents.

The regular place of convocation was St Mary's church. With

[1] The significant passage 'Ad vocacionem–expediens' in Markaunt 9 (see below, p. 315, lines 26–8) is an addition to Angelica IV.

[2] Alexander IV in 1259 specifically mentions with reference to general congregations at Paris 'omnes magistri Parisius actu regentes' (*Chart. Univ. Paris.* i. 399, no. 350).

[3] Cf. *SAUO*, pp. xxi–xxxi.

[4] This ceremony, which became most humiliating for the town after 1382, was familiarly known as the 'Black Assembly'. Cf. *Cambridge borough documents*, ed. W. M. Palmer, i (Cambridge, 1931), pp. xlv, 160; Peek and Hall, *Archives*, p. 54.

[5] The university was always somewhat suspicious about private conferences among members of the institution, but masters were allowed to discuss in groups matters affecting the common good, in other words, the agenda for convocations. Cf. Markaunt 33 (see below, p. 328, lines 28–33); *SA* 41 (*Docs*, i. 331).

regard to inceptions, the constitution expressly lays down that all the regents must answer the chancellor's summons and not depart from the ceremony, unless granted permission, until the inceptor has determined. Their presence up to and including this part of the proceedings was required because even though the disputation might have little interest for the faculties not concerned they had to witness the incorporation of the new member into their fraternity and especially his pledge of faith or oath to uphold the statutes. To leave before he determined the question, the climax of the ceremony, would have been rank discourtesy, for the determination, granted that it was only a matter of form, was the new master's first magisterial act.

The other purposes of convocation are classified under the general headings of *communis utilitas* and *publica quies*.[1] Common utility or interest might embrace a very wide range of business: relations with the crown, the diocese, the town and even the papacy; the election of the chancellor and other officers; the introduction and approval or rejection of legislation; the exemption of houses from 'taxation';[2] and other matters. Public order had to do with breaches of the peace, atrocities and violations of the statutes. As these and other offences specified in chapter XI of the constitution merited expulsion from the university or imprisonment the intervention of convocation was necessary before the chancellor passed definitive sentence, and when he did he acted as chief justice of the court of convocation. In a word, the university of regents was the supreme governing body. No master could absent himself from its meetings without reasonable cause, and when convocation met disputations of the regents were suspended for the day.

ANGELICA CHAPTER V: ACADEMIC DRESS

The background to the formulation of this chapter has been traced above.[3] It is a short but interesting enactment, which imposes on regents in theology, canon law and arts the obligation of wearing

[1] The phrasing of the Angelica text at this point is very reminiscent of a letter sent to Paris by Innocent IV in 1245. See p. 202, *app. crit.* ad 10.

[2] Hugh of Northwold's request in 1246 to allow two houses outside the Trumpington gates to be leased without having the rent fixed was considered at a convocation of the regents. See above, pp. 55–6.

[3] See above, pp. 79–81.

the *cappa clausa* or closed cope, or the *pallium*, at ordinary lectures and disputations, inceptions and funerals.[1] The *cappa clausa* was worn over the clerical dress and, as the name suggests, resembled the liturgical cope. It was a sleeveless, ample garment, reaching down from the shoulders to the ankles and covering them. Unlike the ceremonial cope, it was sewn down the front, where there was an opening in the centre for the hands. The *pallium* must be distinguished from the stole worn by metropolitans. It was in all respects identical with the *cappa clausa* except that it had two slits, one at either side, instead of a single opening in front.[2] The colour of both the habits was black, but secular doctors in canon law, as at Paris, wore a red *cappa*.[3]

The earliest representation of Cambridge academic costume is probably the historiated initial of the manuscript of Richard de Leycestria's *Summa* in the university library.[4] The miniature is reproduced, much enlarged, in Dr Emden's biographical register.[5] It shows two full figures, the one—a master—seated on a faldstool, the other, a scholar genuflecting before him. The master, holding an open book in his left hand, has his right hand raised in blessing. Here we have a vignette of an inception ceremony with the presiding master giving the open book—one of the insignia of a doctor's office—to the inceptor.[6] There are, however, some very peculiar features. The master does not wear the *pileus*, the round, peaked cap of a master in a superior faculty, but what is still more remarkable is the dress. Neither the master nor the inceptor is dressed in the *cappa* or *pallium*. The master's garb is classical, not the habit prescribed in the Angelica text but rather the dress of a pro-

1 *Cons. Univ. Canteb.* v (see below, p. 203, lines 14–16).

2 It is difficult to discover from the writings of authorities on medieval academic costume the precise difference between *cappa clausa* and *pallium*. The distinction adopted here is derived from M. G. Houston, *Medieval costume in England and France* (London, 1939), p. 155. Cf. E. C. Clark, 'English academical costume (mediaeval)', *Archaeological Journal*, l (1893), 102–3 (Cambridge), 137; Hargreaves-Mawdsley, *History of academical dress*, pp. 107–37 (Cambridge), 190–3. Both scholars misdate the Cambridge statutes.

3 Cf. *SA* 147 (*Docs*, i. 387). This part of the statute concerning the red *cappa* cannot be earlier than 1304.

4 CUL, Add. MS 3471 (saec. xiii*med*/*ex*), fos. 125ra–169vb.

5 *BRUC*, frontispiece.

6 Dr Emden states that the master is Richard de Leycestria and is shown lecturing. With all due respect I must dissent. At inceptions in the superior faculties the master handed a book to the inceptor with a blessing. Scholars did not kneel at lectures.

fessor of rhetoric in antiquity.[1] A closer model of the *cappa* is shown on the oldest surviving seal of the university, which dates from 1291. The chancellor is clothed in the *cappa clausa* and wears the *pileus*. Two scholars stand at his side, and we should have no hesitation in identifying them as the rectors only that their dress is not in keeping with the status of regents in arts.[2] Easily the best illustration of the bald reference in the Cambridge constitution to academic dress is the initial 'E' of the charter which Edward I granted to the university on 6 February 1292. Two kneeling figures wearing black *cappae clausae* with the opening in front for the hands and hoods represent the two rectors or proctors, as they may have been familiarly known by then. A doctor stands behind them, dressed in the *pallium* with two slits. He is presumably a doctor of canon law; and by his side stands another doctor.[3]

Chapter V of the Angelica text makes no allusion to regents in civil law and medicine. In itself the omission is not particularly significant, but when viewed in the light of other evidence provided by the constitution it becomes very plain indeed that the reason why no ruling is made about the habit to be worn by regents in these two faculties is that there were no regents in civil law or medicine when the text was drawn up. The historical development of chapter V confirms this conclusion.[4] Hardly less significant than the absence of all reference to regents in civil law and medicine is the explicit mention of regents in theology. No distinction is made between them and regents in canon law and arts; they are equally bound to wear the *cappa clausa* or *pallium* when lecturing or disputing *ordinarie*

[1] Cf. the portrait of Augustine of Hippo as a scholar, reproduced from the sixth-century fresco in the Lateran Museum, by J. Wilpert, 'Il più antico ritratto di S. Agostino', *Miscellanea Agostiniana*, ii (Rome, 1931), 1–3, with plate.

[2] The seal is still extant in Peterhouse (see above, p. 34, n. 6). St John Hope, *Soc. Antiq. Lond. Proc.*, cit., *ibid.*, states that the chancellor's cap is round; W. de G. Birch, *Catalogue of seals in the department of manuscripts in the British Museum*, ii (1892), 30, says it is flat; while Hargreaves-Mawdsley, *op. cit.* p. 107, describes it as 'stiff and apexed'! Unfortunately, the part of the seal containing the chancellor's head is now missing.

[3] Cf. the excellent and splendidly chosen plate (no. 12) in Peek and Hall, *Archives*. The two scholars kneeling in front cannot be masters of theology; they are not *pileati*. But the second doctor is doubtless D.C.L., as stated *ibid.* He is wearing the *cappa manicata* or sleeved cope. The remains of the seals attached to the deed of 1246 (see above, pp. 55–6) have no academic connections.

[4] Regulations on the dress of regents in the two faculties were made the subject of a separate statute probably by 1292 if the illuminated initial 'E' of the charter of Edward I mentioned in the above note depicts Cambridge masters.

and attending university functions. This injunction must refer to secular masters of theology. Members of religious orders at universities wore their own habit; as regents they did not wear the *cappa clausa* or *pallium*, which in any case were the dress of secular clerks, and religious were forbidden by canon law and their constitutions to wear it. There can be no doubt that the Angelica text legislates for secular masters or doctors in theology, and in its oblique way undermines the accepted notion that by *c.* 1250 the friars or to be more precise the Franciscans and Dominicans monopolized the chairs of theology in the university. The statute may go back to a more or less earlier date, but it is obvious that a new approach to the foundation and growth of the faculty is now necessary.

ANGELICA CHAPTER VI: THE MASTER'S COURT

The Cambridge constitution recognizes three distinct courts: the court of a regent master, the chancellor's court and convocation.[1] The origin of the first of these courts is to be sought not in any direct influence of Parisian custom but in the prehistory of the university of Cambridge itself. Its *curia magistrorum* was a natural projection of the court of the masters of grammar schools all over England and right on its doorstep at Cambridge. The Authentic *Habita* (1158) has been called the source of all academic liberties. This is a sweeping claim indeed. The *Habita* was issued by Frederick I for the benefit of lay scholars and that is how it was regarded by canonists.[2] Yet it did probably contribute to the definition of the proper forum of clerical as well as secular scholars. In canon law a defendant was entitled to respond to legal charges in *his* court. What was not so clear was the court which a clerical scholar could claim as his forum. He was subject to the jurisdiction of his bishop and more immediately to that of the archdeacon of the place where he was domiciled. One may suggest that the *Habita* helped to crystallize the principle accepted implicitly by Alexander III in 1170–2 that all scholars, clerical as well as lay, must be cited before their masters if they choose to stand trial before them. The master of a grammar school on being collated to the headmastership was granted exercise of the

1 'Chancellor's court' includes the commissary's and the vice-chancellor's.

2 Cf. Ullmann, 'The medieval interpretation of Frederick I's Authentic "Habita"', *L'Europa e il diritto romano—Studi in memoria di Paolo Koschaker* (Milan, 1954), i. 104–11, 131 and *passim*.

necessary jurisdiction.[1] Cambridge regent masters received their jurisdiction as part of the *regimen scolarium* which was contained radically in their licence and which became operative when they actually incepted.[2]

The constitution declares that every regent shall have the right to hear and decide all causes of their scholars who are cited as defendants.[3] The use of this privilege is made subject to certain conditions and limitations. A scholar in order to secure its application in his favour had to have his name registered with a particular master, whose schools he was obliged to attend at least three days in the week.[4] Before the master could adjudicate he was bound to signify to the chancellor his intention of taking the case, but he could not refuse if the scholar made the request. The scholar of course was free to renounce the forum of his master and plead directly before the chancellor or his commissary. Plaintiffs were not so anxious to bring actions in the court of the defendant's master, feeling no doubt that the judge would be prejudiced in favour of his scholar. After the constitution became effective some litigants at any rate tried to by-pass the master's court by alleging that his scholar had caused them grievous injury, whereas the crime, if any, did not come under the category of atrocities. This ruse was scotched, largely, it seems, because masters complained that since such cases had to go to a higher court they were being deprived of whatever emoluments accrued to them from their office as justice.[5] It is important to note that although plaintiffs were generally scholars, a defendant if charged by a layman was still entitled to have the case heard in the court of his master.[6] No records of these inferior courts have survived, but that they functioned in the late thirteenth and early fourteenth centuries is certain. The proceedings were

1 Cf. Leach, *Schools of medieval England*, pp. 45–6, 170–2, 187–8, and *passim*. Hugh Balsham in his award of 1276 makes it quite clear that the master of glomery—the headmaster of the grammar schools at Cambridge—was entitled to hear and give judgement in all causes of grammar boys *ex parte rea*. Cf. CUA, doc. no. 5; *Vet. Lib. Archid. Elien.* 20, 289.

2 This aspect of the *regimen scolarium* was not recognized at Oxford. See above, pp. 89–90.

3 *Cons. Univ. Canteb.* VI (see below, p. 203, lines 18–19).

4 See below, pp. 166–7.

5 Cf. Markaunt 6 (see below, p. 315, lines 8–12); *SA* 8 (*Docs*, i. 311).

6 This can be deduced from the terms of Balsham's decree of 1276, which states that the chancellor must not interfere in causes between grammar students and laymen, unless the rents of houses or gross offences give rise to litigation. When cited under these headings a grammarian was obliged to appear before the chancellor.

conducted in summary fashion according to the rules of judicial procedure laid down in chapters IX and X of the constitution; and sentences were transmitted to the chancellor for execution in accordance with chapter I, paragraph v.

The master's court was a tribunal of first instance. Both plaintiff and defendant had the right to appeal from its decision to the chancellor.[1] The court was not competent to entertain actions relating to rents of houses and lettings, nor could it hear criminal charges or causes in which regent masters were plaintiffs or defendants. The hearing and deciding of these cases was reserved to the higher tribunal, the chancellor's court, the ordinary court for all matters of litigation.[2] Its powers, however, were limited. If the gravity of an offence required sentence of banishment from the university or imprisonment the chancellor or his commissary held a court of evidence, but the court was not empowered to make an order in respect of these penalties. This was a matter for the supreme court of the university, the *universitas regentium* or convocation, at whose sessions the chancellor sat with the masters. The evidence on charges of atrocity or breaches of the public peace was reviewed by this court, which might either confirm or reject the findings of the chancellor's court. If satisfied that the charge was proved the regents imposed sentence and the chancellor saw to its execution.[3] The *cetus magistrorum regentium* retained its exclusive power as the highest tribunal in the university, even after the non-regent masters were admitted to convocation, and the right to judge appeals from the court of the chancellor.[4]

1 Balsham's decree reads: 'Si vero magister glomerie cognoscat inter scolarem actorem et glomerellum reum...volumus et ordinamus quod ad Cancellarium appelletur qui in ipsa causa appellacionis procedat secundum ordinem obseruatum cum ab alio magistro regente...ab alterutra parcium ad Cancellarium appellatur' (CUA, doc. no. 5; *Vet. Lib. Archid. Elien.* 20–1).

2 The Angelica text does not state that regents had to plead in the chancellor's court, but this was an unquestioned principle. It was made explicit in the later statutes. Cf. Markaunt 6 (see below, p. 315, lines 6–8); *SA* 8 (*loc. cit.*).

3 In Angelica VI the phrase 'cancelarii uel magistrorum requirat audienciam' refers in the first place to the rents of houses; cases of this kind could be heard by the chancellor without the intervention of the regents; in the second place it refers to heinous deeds and disturbances of the peace; these cases had to be referred ultimately by the chancellor to the house of regents.

4 At Oxford there was no appeal from the chancellor's sentence if one was convicted of causing a breach of the peace. Cf. *SAUO*, 84, 6–13.

ANGELICA CHAPTER VII: THE RECTORS OR PROCTORS

The origin of the office of proctor at Oxford was the subject of much excogitation on the part of Dean Rashdall.[1] He convinced himself that this office, the second most important function in the university, was copied directly from Paris, but that it evolved along different lines at the English university, whose constitution he described as 'an arrested development' of the Parisian model. He was right for the wrong reason, his pet theory being that the organization of Oxford (and hence its institutions) was determined in a striking way through a migration from Paris which he vainly thought occurred *c.* 1167. The fallacy of a supposed migration notwithstanding, it must be admitted that there is a clear parallel between the officers of the 'four nations' at Paris and the officers of the 'two nations' at Oxford. The very title of rector or proctor, though not the offices, developed in much the same way at the two universities. The older title of rector became gradually appropriated at Paris to the dean of the faculty of arts and later in effect to the head of the university. Meanwhile the officers of the four nations were almost invariably designated the 'proctors'. At no time were the Oxford proctors either singly or jointly heads of the university, but their original title was almost certainly 'rector', a usage which was preserved at Cambridge as late as the close of the fourteenth century. Its Parisian origin can hardly be disputed, and in furtherance of his view that the Oxford proctorship was modelled on the office at Paris Rashdall could claim that at both universities the officers were elected by and from among the regents in arts grouped into nations. The northern scholars at Oxford elected one of their number as their representative and likewise the southern bloc. It was part of a wider system which the university adopted in the hopes that nationalistic feelings, a source of endemic strife, would be satisfied through granting proportional representation for all offices other than those of chancellor, bedell and one or two more.[2]

If the Oxford constitution represents an accommodated version of that of Paris, the same may be said of Cambridge in relation to Oxford. The opening paragraph of chapter VII of the Angelica

[1] *Universities*, iii. 53–9.

[2] Cf. Emden, 'Northerners and southerners in the organization of the university to 1509', *Oxford studies pres. to D. Callus*, p. 3.

text illustrates one facet of this and at the same time leads to the discovery of the original function of the Oxford proctors. Rashdall in pursuance of his inquiry into the genesis of their office suggested that the first officials elected by the nascent university at Oxford were very likely the taxors, and he actually went close to committing himself to the view that they were identical with the proctors.[1] Had he known of the Angelica text and its significance as a guide to early Oxford practice there can be little doubt that he would not have stopped short of making the identification. The Cambridge constitution plainly reveals that the two offices—if we can speak of two—of taxor and rector or proctor were combined by *c.* 1250, so much so that one is forced to conclude that the *raison d'être* or the original purpose of having proctors was to bring the rents of lodgings under control.[2] That this was the origin of the office at Oxford can scarcely be disputed. At what period the proctors ceased to be taxors is an open question, but the fact that Cambridge appears to have separated their functions *c.* 1255–68 suggests that the division took place much earlier at Oxford.[3] It is worthy of note that when the area of their responsibilities was narrowed at Cambridge the university, following no doubt Oxford precedent, called the new class of officials 'taxors', yet maintained the traditional title of rectors for their predecessors. This reluctance to conform wholly and at a single step with moves made by Oxford runs right through the constitutional history of Cambridge.

The first point of contrast between the Oxford and the Cambridge constitution on the rectors—the title given to the proctors—is the mode of election. At Cambridge the chancellor and the masters appointed them.[4] Throughout the Angelica text 'chancellor and

[1] *Universities*, iii. 47, 56, n. 1. Unfortunately, Rashdall was mesmerized by his theory of a Parisian migration and toyed with the idea that there were four proctors *c.* 1228. As Dr Emden pointed out (*ibid.*), there is no evidence for this assumption. Rashdall was probably more attracted than he admits to the mystic number because of the legatine ordinance of 1214, which decreed that four masters were to act as taxors on behalf of the university. It is very doubtful if at any time more than two masters were taxors. See above, p. 75, n. 1. Emden, cited *ibid.*, was of the opinion that from the beginning there were four university taxors and that the number was reduced when the university was divided into two nations. The earliest evidence of the existence of a northern and southern bloc dates from 1252, which must be regarded as the *terminus a quo* of the allocation of offices on a 'national' basis. This was long after the custom of having two masters as taxors was established.

[2] Cf. *Cons. Univ. Canteb.* VII. i (see below, p. 205, lines 2–5).

[3] See below, pp. 221–2. [4] *Cons. Univ. Canteb.* VII. i (see below, p. 205, line 2).

masters' has only one meaning: convocation or *cetus magistrorum regentium*. The chancellor and the regent masters of theology and canon law as well as arts elected the two rectors. They were, therefore, not the representatives of the faculty of arts or of any nation but of the entire university.[1] That the two rectors were masters in arts is certain; that the one represented a northern bloc and the other a southern bloc is far from certain; indeed the contrary is the case. At no time in its history did Cambridge countenance a constitutional distinction between *boreales* (northerners) and *australes* (southerners). Yet the law and reality do not always coincide. 'National' antipathies did raise their head at Cambridge as at Oxford and provoked a violent clash in 1260 which almost wrecked the university, the northern masters and scholars withdrawing to Northampton. Mag. John de Huntingfeld and mag. William de Chelviston are possibly the two earliest known rectors of Cambridge; they were bearers of a letter from the university to Edward I in 1292–3, a commission entrusted always to the proctors.[2] Huntingfeld or Huntingfield is a Suffolk place-name; any man from the county of Suffolk was classed as a southerner at the university. Chelviston is in Northamptonshire, which was definitely within the 'northern' hemisphere. Most probably the two masters John de Huntingfeld and William de Chelviston were the senior and junior rectors in 1292–3 and it looks as if they were elected to represent the south and the north, even though this territorial division was never recognized officially at Cambridge.[3] The Angelica text simply says that the rectors were deputed or appointed by the chancellor and masters. It makes no reference to annual election or the duration of

[1] By *c.* 1304–37 the position had changed. The regents in arts and they alone elected the rectors and taxors. Cf. Markaunt 11 (see below, p. 316, lines 15–19); *SA* 53 (*Docs*, i. 338–9); Markaunt 12 (see below, p. 317, lines 13–16); *SA* 65 (*loc. cit.* 349). There was a reversion, probably temporary, by 1500 to the thirteenth-century custom of election. Cf. *SA* 69 (*loc. cit.* 352–3).

[2] Little, 'An unknown chancellor of the university of Cambridge at the end of the thirteenth century', *Cambridge Review*, liv (1933), 412. The letter was sent in the name of 'Gilbertus de Segrave vniuersitatis Cantib' Cancellarius ac magistrorum ibidem regencium cetus vnanimis'. For Segrave cf. *BRUC*, p. 516.

[3] It would be interesting to trace the provenances of Cambridge rectors, as Dr Emden has done for Oxford in his article 'Northerners and southerners' (cit.), and see if they were elected on a north–south basis. Chelviston was made rector of Rattlesden, Suffolk, in 1305, but this would not affect his Northamptonshire origins. Cf. *BRUC*, p. 134, and p. 322 for Huntingfeld. Hitherto, the earliest known rector or proctor of the university was Hugh de Leveryngton (1314–15) (*ibid.* p. 365).

the office. The later statute *De electione rectorum seu procuratorum*, which does not appear to be earlier than 1304, states that the proctors are to be elected each year on 10 October.[1] The regent who secures the highest number of votes shall be known as the senior proctor; presumably the runner-up received the title of junior proctor.[2] No one could hold office for more than two consecutive years, but it may be doubted if many sought re-election after their first term in office.[3]

The majority of scholars were poor and if landlords were free to charge them excessive rents for lodgings the university would soon be empty. On the other hand, lectures and other academic exercises would be brought to a standstill if masters were unable to hire schools except at exorbitant prices. Accommodation was essential, and it was the first duty of the two rectors and the original reason for the institution of their office to see that houses and schools were made available on reasonable terms. They and two burgesses appointed by the corporation were sworn in annually before the chancellor and the mayor as taxors or rent-assessors of all dwellings in the town.[4] The four taxors promised to carry out a fair assessment of the rents and enter them in a schedule which had to be produced for public inspection on request.[5] This system of joint-taxation was

[1] Markaunt 11 (see below, p. 315, line 15); *SA* 53 (*Docs*, i. 338–9).

[2] Possibly a proctor served his first year in office as junior proctor and his second as senior. Emden, art. cit., *loc. cit.* p. 18, holds that the distinction between senior and junior proctor was based on the relative academic status of the officials. The master who incepted first probably received the majority of the votes.

[3] Mag. Thomas Stoyle was an exception. He was J.P. in 1441–2 and S.P. in 1443–5. Cf. *BRUC*, p. 561.

[4] The constitution omits details of the oath-taking ceremony, but we can presume that it was held each year, almost certainly at the beginning of the winter term. In 1266 the king ordered the taxation of houses to be made every five years. This does not mean that the annual appointment of taxors was abolished. New houses might be built from year to year or a house might be vacated by the owner. All these would have to be taxed as soon as they became available. The 1266 writ envisages a general review of all rents every five years. The original letters patent in CUA and references to printed texts are cited on p. 26, n. 1 above. See also p. 76, n. 2 above for a similar charter granted to Oxford in 1256.

[5] No schedules have survived. There is a misleading entry in Gonville and Caius College MS 170 (saec. xvi), fo. 211^r, which purports to contain a list of the rents of houses made in the reign of Henry V, *recte* Henry III. The document is nothing more than a copy of the suit brought by the prior of Barnwell against mag. Ralph de Leycestria in 1290–2 over the house owned by the priory in the parish of Holy Sepulchre. See below, pp. 172–3, 232. The rent-rolls of houses owned by St John's Hospital, which date from the late thirteenth century, are not of course the schedules compiled by the four taxors, though they doubtless correspond with the rents fixed by them. Cf. Cart. St John's Hosp., cited on p. 86, n. 5 above.

nothing new, and the constitution merely gives statutory effect to the custom observed by 1231.

If living-quarters and schools were required for the proper functioning of the university, food and drink were only one degree less necessary. Hence, the second duty of the rectors was to safeguard the economic needs of both masters and scholars. Shortly after the enactment of the constitution the university transferred the obligation of taxing houses and attending the twice-yearly assize of bread and ale to a new body of officials, two in number, who were henceforth known as the 'taxors'.[1] The rectors, however, continued to hold a watching brief with regard to the marketing and sale of bread and wine and foodstuffs generally. Masters and scholars were at the mercy of producers and tradesmen, who could hardly be expected to forgo the opportunity of raising their profits by cashing in on their necessities.[2] Consequently, the university detailed the rectors to see that scholars were not charged unjust prices or treated more unfairly than people of the town. They were particularly enjoined to investigate monopolies. Regrators or retailers made their living by buying up all kinds of supplies when the market opened and reselling them at a profit later, for the market was held only twice in the week and if one ran short of food or drink on other days one would have to buy from the shopkeepers. The Angelica text suggests that these businessmen were not above forming rings by mutually agreeing to withdraw stocks and keep up prices so that scholars had to pay more for a commodity than the retail price, which was of course higher than the market price. The worst offenders in the eyes of the university were the bailiffs and their wives; the constitution singles them out for special attention.[3]

[1] See below, pp. 221–2.

[2] Salter, in his edition of *Munimenta civitatis Oxonie* (OHS, lxxi [1920]), xvi–xxvi, gives an excellent account of the position of a university like Oxford or Cambridge in relation to the town. In royal charters the terms 'regrator' and 'forestaller' frequently occur. Salter aptly points out that a regrator or retailer was not a forestaller, that is, a person who intercepted goods on the way to the market and bought them up, so as to resell them at an exorbitant price. A rapacious retailer would doubtless indulge in forestalling, but it was a risky business and was strictly prohibited by the law of the land.

[3] Cf. *Cons. Univ. Canteb.* VII. iii (see below, p. 205, lines 13–14). The members of the town corporation were all tradesmen; cf. Salter, *op. cit. loc. cit.* p. xv. The papal legate ordered the burgesses at Oxford in 1214 to take an oath 'quod uictualia & alia necessaria iusto & rationabili precio scolaribus uendent & ab aliis uendi fideliter procurabunt' (*Med. Arch. Univ. Oxford*, i. 3). 'Burgesses' here means the town bailiffs or rather, as Salter (*ibid.* 9) held, the sub-bailiffs, who were permanent

Should the rectors succeed in uncovering sharp dealings at the expense of scholars they were to report the offenders' names to the chancellor. He had power, apparently, to confiscate the supplies of food and drink sold by tradesmen and publicans who victimized members of the university;[1] but the more usual punishment was the penalty of discommoning.[2]

The rectors were the principal administrative officers of the university and were responsible for the maintenance of discipline. They had their agents or 'bull-dogs' to assist them in tracking down masters and scholars who were guilty of criminal conduct, and also those who broke the rules, especially hardened offenders.[3] Their names, too, were to be delated to the chancellor. But the most important and exclusive concern of the rectors was the academic management of the university. They arranged the hours of lectures and disputations according to seasonal changes; and as circumstances required they determined the form of these exercises. They had particular responsibility of course for the faculty of arts; they could intervene at disputations and regulate the procedure; if a master or some disputant wandered off the point or rambled on for too long they cut him off. They made arrangements about funerals and detailed regents to read the lessons and chant the responses at the office and Mass of the dead. They drew up the programme for inceptions, acted as masters of ceremonies, administered the pledge of faith or the oath to the inceptor and invited him to make his formal determination at the close of the function. One of their distinctive duties was to see that masters, bachelors and scholars observed holy days and other feast-days.[4] They were empowered to

officials; they were deputed by the bailiffs elected each year to keep the assize of the town. The Cambridge constitution, however, has the *prepositi* or annual bailiffs in mind; at least this seems to be the proper interpretation of the text. The bailiffs' wives were probably to be seen as often as their husbands behind the counter at Cambridge; they do not appear to have been any whit less grasping than their spouses.

1 The Angelica text is corrupt at this point.

2 Discommoning was a form of boycott. The university blacklisted tradesmen convicted of discriminating against scholars and declared their premises or stalls out of bounds. This form of punishment was invoked at Oxford only at a much later date. Cf. Salter, *Medieval Oxford* (OHS, c [1936]), 57, n. 5.

3 *Cons. Univ. Canteb.* vii. iii (see below, p. 205, lines 17–21).

4 *Cons. Univ. Canteb.* vii. iv (see below, p. 205, lines 22–3). The expression *feriarum obseruancie* is wider than 'holy days of obligation' which is the usual translation of *dies feriatae* or *festa ferianda*. Cf. Ullmann, art. cit., in *L'Europa e il diritto romano*, i. 118; Cheney, 'Rules for the observance of feast-days in medieval England',

punish anyone, including the bedells, who disobeyed their orders concerning these particular matters, which specially pertained to their office. The Angelica text does not say that they had *ex officio* authority to suspend masters and bachelors from lecturing and scholars from entering the schools, but this is implicit in the phrase 'cohercione concessa eisdem'.[1] They certainly had the power of suspension by 1276.[2]

The Angelica text fails to convey the multiplicity of duties which the office of rector in practice entailed, though it must be said that chapter VII is much more enlightening than the basic Oxford statute *De officio procuratorum*.[3] The rectors or proctors were the heart of the university.[4] Though the institution of the separate office of taxors brought them some relief, their range of business went on increasing as the university grew in stature and became more and more powerful. The surprising thing is that any regent in arts ever sought a second, not to mention a third, term of office.[5]

Inst. Hist. Research Bull. xxxiv (1961), 117. At Bologna *dies feriatae* included both holy days of obligation and certain saints' feast-days. Cf. *Statuti di Bologna*, ed. L. Frati, i (Bologna, 1869), 400–2. Bachelors at Cambridge usually read on feast-days and of course *festinanter*. Cf. *SA* 137 (*Docs*, i. 383).

1 The Cambridge rectors or proctors had the power of direct suspension; the Oxford proctors were only entitled to declare someone suspended. Cf. *SA* 64, 84, 91, 151 (*ibid.* 348–9, 360, 363, 389–90); *SAUO*, 67, 10–13; 107, 16–108, 9. Rashdall, *Universities*, iii. 54, n. 2, commenting on this last statute, enacted on 2 June 1257, says that the chancellor's assent was necessary because the statute concerned the suspension of a master's licence. This is a forced interpretation of the matter. In any case, the chancellor was always associated with the enactment of statutes.

2 Cf. the decree of 17 March: 'liceat rectoribus suspendere tantum transgressores statuti ad eorum officium spectantis' (Ullmann, *loc. cit.* 181). The decree goes on to quote the statute, *Cons. Univ. Canteb.* VII. iv (p. 226, n. 3, below).

3 *SAUO*, 66, 22–67, 2. I take this part to be the original form of the statute. It appears to have been enacted after 1254. What follows, 'Casus–etc.' (*ibid.* 67, 3–13), refers to the statute on suspension and hence cannot be earlier than 2 June 1257 (*ibid.* 107, 16–108, 9). An older statute on suspension is lost; there is a reference to it *ibid.* 107, 21–2.

4 When the university treasury or chest was founded they were put in charge of it. There is an entry in a rent-roll of St John's Hospital which reads: 'De rectoribus vniuersitatis pro tenemento quod quondam dominus Robertus capellanus vniuersitatis tenuit .ij. solidi '(Cart. St John's Hosp. fo. 9r). This rent-roll dates from *c.* 1290. Stokes, *Outside the Trumpington gates*, p. 12, n. 2, misjudged the date of the later rolls in the cartulary. They are not earlier than the fourteenth century.

5 For a conspectus of the duties of the proctors by the fifteenth century cf. Mullinger, *University of Cambridge*, i. 144; *Grace Book* A, pp. xxxiv–xxxv.

ANGELICA CHAPTER VIII: THE BEDELLS

Every university had its bedells, and their functions were much the same whether they were attached to Bologna, Paris, Oxford or Cambridge. The office was as ancient as any university post and may well have preceded the institution of the chancellorship and perhaps the rectorship of Cambridge. The bedells were formally invested with their office when they were sworn in, a precaution which the university insisted upon, not so much as a guarantee that the bedells would carry out their duties faithfully, but in order to bind them to secrecy.

Cambridge had never more than two official bedells.[1] Normally there would be three: one for the faculty of arts, one for the faculty of law and one for the faculty of theology. As the same bedell was assigned to the faculties of canon law and theology, this would seem to confirm our supposition that the university of Cambridge began with only two faculties, arts and canon law. Each had a bedell, one for the inferior faculty and one for the superior faculty. When the second superior faculty, theology, was added the bedell of canon law was accredited to it. The same arrangement was made when the other higher faculties, civil law and medicine, were set up. The fact that a bedell of either of these faculties is never mentioned in the statutes suggests that they were established well after the erection of the first two major faculties, canon law and theology, and furthermore that the time-lag between the foundation of these two faculties may not have been very great.

All that the constitution has to say about the bedells was probably best appreciated by Ralph Piroun and Robert Gosnel, who were in office *c.* 1250.[2] Since Piroun precedes Gosnel in the roll of honour, we may presume that he was the bedell of theology and canon law, while Gosnel looked after the faculty of arts. The two bedells,

[1] *Cons. Univ. Canteb.* VIII. i (see below, p. 207, lines 4–5, 10). M. Bateson, *Grace Book* B ii (CAS, Luard Memorial series, ii [1905]), p. xxii, states that the bedell of arts replaced the bedell of canon law when this faculty was suppressed in 1535. This is inaccurate. As we shall now see, the functions of the bedell of canon law and theology were exercised by one and the same person. When the teaching of canon law was resumed under Queen Mary there was no need to appoint a bedell for the faculty. The bedell of theology simply resumed his ancient charge of both faculties.

[2] Cf. Stokes, *Esquire bedells*, pp. 49–50. It should be noted that his source, Stokys's Book, fo. 28^r, has Pironis (Pironi dative) for Piroun, and Gosnol for Gosnel.

however, were officially the bedells of the university. Their immediate superiors were the rectors, and their major superior was the chancellor, though they had a special relationship with the masters of their respective faculties. They were forbidden to have a companion or an assistant except by special permission of the chancellor.[1] Again it was a question of safeguarding the secrets of the university and a means of impressing on the bedells that they were expected to carry out their duties personally.[2]

The primary duty of the two bedells was to look after the schools of their faculties and everything connected with them. The provision of seating is mentioned in particular. They were, we might say, the clerks of the schools.[3] No doubt, they would be responsible like their Paduan counterparts for spreading sufficient straw or rushes on the floors in winter time and covering the unglazed windows with linen cloths to keep out the damp, cold air and the fogs that collected over the marshes which encircled Cambridge. In summer they had to keep the schools aired and clean.[4] Being not merely the servants of their faculties but more important still the servants of the university, they had all sorts of court duties to perform on behalf of the chancellor and the masters.[5] They gave notice of sittings; served summonses and citations; and saw to the execution of the decrees. A bedell was strictly forbidden to take advantage of poor scholars by making his services dependent on the payment of a fee. If the university made an order for someone to be sent to prison, the bedells took the condemned person in hand and brought him to the town gaol. In 1287 Thomas de Sutton was imprisoned by

[1] The text actually mentions 'substitutum comitem uel eciam pedagogum' (*Cons. Univ. Canteb.* VIII. i [see below, p. 207, lines 11–12]). 'Pedagogue' cannot bear its accepted meaning here; indeed the opposite if anything is meant, viz. assistant. Cf. *ibid.*, *loc. cit. app. crit.* ad 11. A distinction was introduced in the fifteenth century between the two official or principal bedells and a third or secondary bedell. We also hear of three bedells. See below, pp. 283–5.

[2] This was also laid down by the university of Bologna. Cf. *Statuti*, p. 26, rubr. xxvij.

[3] The bedell of theology and canon law must have been hard-pressed by *c.* 1304–37, for in addition to these schools he had to attend also to the needs of the schools of lecturers on the decretals. Cf. Markaunt 19 (see below, p. 320, lines 32–3); *SA* 72 (*Docs*, i. 354). There is no reference to the schools of civil law and medicine; but the specific mention of *scolarum decretalium* shows how important the decretals had become as part of the canon law curriculum. Evidently, Cambridge was keeping pace with Oxford. Cf. Boyle, art. cit. p. 124, n. 3, above.

[4] Cf. the Paduan statutes, ed. Denifle, *Archiv für Lit. u. Kirch. Gesch.* vi. 451 (13).

[5] *Cons. Univ. Canteb.* VIII. i (see below, p. 207, lines 7–9).

William Russel and Robert le Bedel, who when cited on a charge of wrongful imprisonment pleaded that they had only carried out the duty incumbent on their office.[1]

On days of ordinary lectures and disputations they had to make a round of their schools during the hours of lectures.[2] The bedell of the canonists and theologians was specifically ordered to ring the bells for their disputations 'at the proper and customary hours' with strict impartiality, not favouring one person or discriminating against another.[3] They were present at all university functions and it was on these occasions that they really gloried in their office. Wearing full dress, they carried their staves at inception ceremonies, including both the vespers and *principium*, convocations, funerals and all other assemblies.[4] No one else was permitted to carry a staff, for this was the symbol of the bedell's office, and the official servants of the university were deeply conscious of their dignity.[5]

The office was considered lucrative. In addition to adventitious gifts of one kind or another and the dues known as 'visitation' money, the bedells took up a collection, the *communis collecta*, in the schools.[6] If the custom of other universities obtained at Cambridge two collections were made during the year, one before Christmas and one before or after Easter. The proceeds at all events

1 Cf. Hare MS i, fo. 46ᵛ. Sutton was a scholar, but he is not listed as such in *BRUC*, though he is referred to on pp. 299, 483, 497.

2 The same rule obtained at Paris *c.* 1251–60: 'Item debet quilibet bedellus summo mane die qualibet circuire scolas.' The statute has many points in common with the Cambridge constitution. Cf. *Chart. Univ. Paris.* i. 418, no. 369.

3 The text reads: 'bedello decretistarum et theologorum horis debitis et consuetis primam ad eorum disputacionem pulsaturo' (*Cons. Univ. Canteb.* VIII. ii [see below, p. 207, lines 14–15]). I have translated 'primam ad eorum disputacionem' as 'for their first disputation'. See p. 206, *app. crit.* ad 15. The text in Markaunt and the *statuta antiqua* is a revision, but it is not a happy one; it reads as if disputations in theology were held at prime. Cf. Markaunt 19 (see below, p. 320, lines 9–11); *SA* 72 (*Docs*, i. 354). Theologians were expressly forbidden to dispute before terce; it was the canonists who disputed at prime. The redactor of Markaunt would have done better had he retained the order of the two faculties as set down in the Angelica text.

4 Stokes, *Esquire bedells*, reproduces the seal of Walter de Oxonia, who was bedell *c.* 1270–1. He is shown wearing a round cap with tuft and is dressed in a tabard caught at the waist by a girdle. In his left hand he holds a long, plain staff. Cf. Stokes, *op. cit.* plate facing p. 82.

5 The bedell of the master of glomery was forbidden by Bishop Balsham in 1276 to carry his staff in the presence of the chancellor and masters. Cf. CUA, doc. no. 5; *Vet. Lib. Archid. Elien.* 21.

6 On the fees payable to the bedells cf. Stokes, *op. cit.* pp. 23–33, but his account is derived mostly from fifteenth-century evidence and from Stokys's Book.

were divided evenly between the bedells, an arrangement that satisfied both officials until a third party, the 'secondary' bedell, began to claim a share; but this was long after the date of the Angelica text.[1] If the bedells did not perform their duties satisfactorily they were deprived of the common collection; and if they disobeyed the orders of the rectors or revealed a secret they could be suspended or dismissed from the service of the university. The same penalties might also be imposed for crass negligence.[2]

The Angelica text leaves many questions unanswered such as the election or appointment of the bedells. It would take more than one chapter to cover their multifarious activities, which included the office of stationer to the university, though it is doubtful if this important post came within their terms of reference by *c.* 1250.[3] Yet chapter VIII of the constitution proved its adequacy as the basic statutory ruling on the bedells' office throughout the first three centuries of the university's existence and remained almost unaltered until replaced under the Edwardine code of 1549.

ANGELICA CHAPTERS IX–X: JUDICIAL PROCEDURE

In chapters IX and X of the Angelica text certain general principles are set forth concerning litigation and court procedure. These rules were formulated for the chancellor's court, which being an ecclesiastical tribunal was subject to the prescriptions of canon law. It has been pointed out earlier that the Cambridge constitution departs from the *solemnitas* or *rigor iuris* laid down by Innocent III and worked out in great detail by the canonists. Though the non-compliance with the solemnities of judicial procedure negatived a process and consequently the sentence of a court, by *c.* 1250 the ordinary procedure, which was painfully slow and had many other disadvantages, was giving way to a summary form of trial in which the judge proceeded 'de plano et sine strepitu et figura iudicii'.[4] The aim of this mode of procedure was to accelerate the hearing of actions, thus avoiding costly litigation and making for a more rapid

[1] See below, pp. 282–5.

[2] I take these offences as coming under the heading of 'delicti qualitas uel negligentia', the reasons given in the constitution for the suspension or removal from office of the bedells.

[3] The earliest mention of stationers occurs in Balsham's decree of 1276. See below, p. 228.

[4] See above, pp. 28–9.

administration of justice. Formalities were reduced to a minimum, and it was no longer necessary to consign citations, bills, proofs and testimonies to writing as required by the solemn process.[1]

The Cambridge constitution makes use of the new dispensation. It definitely excludes formalities and gives permission for oral processes. Nevertheless, the fundamental rules of canonical procedure are not, nor could they be, set aside. The Angelica text insists on the observance of the four major steps of an ecclesiastical judicial process: citation, contest (*litis contestatio*), proof and sentence. It leaves open the question as to whether the proceedings should be recorded in writing or not.[2] The decision, evidently, was left to the discretion of the chancellor.

A plaintiff could not commence legal proceedings of any kind without first offering a bill of complaint (*libellus conventionalis*) to the judge. According to the new procedure it was sufficient to state one's case orally. If the judge was satisfied that the plaintiff had a case he then cited the defendant to appear before him.[3] It appears from the Angelica text that the normal practice of issuing citations in the form of edicts still obtained, though in urgent cases one peremptory citation was enough. If the defendant failed to appear after the issue of a third edict he was declared *contumax* and excommunicated by the chancellor. About 1295 a canon of Barnwell was cited by the chancellor to appear in court at the hour of prime—the chancellor's court usually sat in St Mary's church—to answer a charge brought by a scholar. The canon replied that he was not subject to the chancellor's jurisdiction and had no intention of complying with the citation. When he failed to appear on the appointed day the chancellor suspended him from entering the church and declared him *contumax*, and excommunicated him on the following day; but as subsequent events show, the chancellor in this case exceeded his authority and was reprimanded for his audacity by the bishop's official, mag. Guy de Coventre.[4]

1 For a convenient summary of the two types of process cf. Stelling-Michaud, *Université de Bologne*, pp. 204–9.

2 Cf. *Cons. Univ. Canteb.* x. ii (see below, p. 209, lines 17–18).

3 Tancred in his *Ordo iudiciarius*, ed. Bergmann, deals exhaustively, as do other canonists, with each of the various stages in a judicial process. The most compact and simple account is found in the work once attributed to Giovanni d'Andrea, *Summula de processu judicii*, ed. A. Wunderlich (Basle, 1840). It is now established that the *Summula* was written in Germany *c.* 1215–54.

4 The chancellor, who was John de Bradenham if Clark's dating of the case in *Liber mem. ecc. de Bernewelle*, p. xlii, is correct, appears to have lost his head; in addition

When a defendant answered a citation the judge gave him an opportunity of studying the charge. If he admitted it, all that remained to be done was for the judge to impose sentence; if on the other hand the accused decided to contest the issue, then the stage was set for the trial to proceed. Such in brief is the background to chapter IX of the Angelica text, *De satisdacione litigancium et eorum iuramento*.[1] It lays down that litigants, except those in the university who own lands or tenements (immovables) and are free from suspicion, will not be allowed to prosecute or defend an action unless the plaintiff deposits a caution or pledge or offers a suitable surety that he will persevere with his action right to the end; the defendant must also give security, without further committing himself, that he will contest the charge. According to Tancred, with whose *Ordo iudiciarius* the author of the Angelica text appears to have been familiar, the plaintiff had to find someone to go surety for him before he actually offered his bill of complaint to the judge, whereas the defendant produced his surety after considering the plaintiff's statement and deciding to defend the suit.[2] This was certainly the logical course of events and we need not doubt that it was observed at Cambridge. The author of the Cambridge constitution, however, does not quite agree with Tancred as regards what is to be done if sureties cannot be found. At Cambridge if the parties find it impossible to obtain sureties their oaths are accepted instead.[3] It meant, needless to say, that should either party decline to commit itself under oath to proceed with the suit there would be no trial: if the plaintiff refused, the case was dismissed and he might find himself charged in turn with malicious prosecution; if the defendant refused, this was tantamount to a confession of guilt. When the accusation was one of serious crime the procedure was much simpler: the defendant was lodged in prison to await trial or was put under close guard.[4]

to excommunicating the canon he proceeded to excommunicate also his prior, Simon de Asceles; cf. *ibid.* pp. 184–5. The admonition addressed to the chancellor by Coventre is quoted above, p. 58.

[1] *Cons. Univ. Canteb.* IX (see below, p. 209, lines 5–12).

[2] Cf. Tancred, *Ordo iudiciarius*, pt ii, tit. 14–15, ed. Bergmann, pp. 174–5.

[3] Tancred says that if the plaintiff swears he cannot produce a surety (*fideiussor*) he must give a 'juratory' caution, i.e. take an oath that he will pay whatever fine the court imposes should he fail to persevere with the suit until sentence is given. The defendant's position was less happy. In his case a juratory caution, provided he owned real estate, might be accepted or it might not.

[4] *Cons. Univ. Canteb.* IX (see below, p. 209, lines 11–12). The text refers to the king's writ of 1231 on imprisonment.

Once the preliminaries were completed and the accused decided to fight the charge, the issue was joined; this was known as *litis contestatio*.[1] The case now entered the instance or proof phase of the trial. At the outset the judge administered to the parties the oath of calumny or malice, or the oath to tell the truth and not to conceal falsehood, or both oaths. It was one way of speeding up the trial. The oath of calumny was demandable in ecclesiastical and civil suits; in spiritual cases the oath *de veritate dicenda* had to be taken but not the oath of calumny, at any rate before the promulgation of the Sext (1298). The Cambridge constitution does not conflict with the procedure laid down by Eugenius III and reimposed by Cardinal Otto at the Council of London in 1237.[2] The paragraph of the Angelica text (X. i) might have been formulated with better effect, but the meaning is clear enough: the oath to tell the truth must be taken at all trials whether or not the oath of malice is administered. The only occasions on which this latter oath will not be demanded of the parties is when the suit is a purely spiritual one. On taking the oath of calumny the plaintiff swore that he was acting in good faith and without malice; the defendant swore that he would answer the charge in like manner. The oath to tell the truth and expose falsehood bound the parties to speak the truth when questioned by the judge; to refrain from giving proof which they knew to be false; and not to seek an adjournment with the intention of absconding.[3]

Immediately after the administration of the oath or oaths the trial entered the probative stage. The *debite probaciones* are not defined in the constitution. There were various kinds.[4] After the witnesses, if any, were examined by the judge and the barristers had made their submissions the case concluded. The judge either then or later pronounced sentence. It was definitive at this stage and at Cambridge the chancellor enforced it under pain of excommunication, and anyone who frustrated its enforcement was likewise excommunicated for impeding his jurisdiction. There was no

1 In chapter X. ii of the Angelica text there is a reference to *contestationes*.

2 See above, pp. 98–9, where Tancred is shown to be the source of Angelica X. i. Stelling-Michaud, *op. cit.* p. 208, inverts the proper order of the oaths or rather their application.

3 Cf. Tancred, *op. cit.* pt iii, tit. 2, pp. 201–5; Hostiensis, *Summa aurea*, Bk II, ed. cit. 398, 1*b*–2*e*; *Summula de processu judicii*, c. vi, pp. 28–30.

4 The following are listed *ibid.* c. vii, pp. 38–41: *evidentia facti, aspectus corporis, fama, juramenti delatio, testes, instrumenta, presumptio.*

appeal from the sentence of a diocesan official to the bishop, but in the university one was entitled to appeal from the Chancellor to the *universitas regentium* and, before 1401 at any rate, from this court to the bishop.

ANGELICA CHAPTER XI: DISCIPLINE

The title to this chapter in the Angelica text is misleading: *De inmunitate scolarium et pena delinquencium.*[1] The privilege of immunity of scholars is treated in a very negative way and the chapter is little more than a descriptive catalogue of scholars, mostly unsavoury types, who either fail to qualify for the privilege of immunity or forfeit it through their misdemeanours. The privilege was but one of the privileges of scholars and is used here as a generic term. All scholars of the university were clerks, but not every clerk in Cambridge was a scholar.[2] This probably explains why the constitution refers throughout to scholars and only once refers to clerks though, significantly, they are called clerks of the town, not clerks of the university.[3] If a scholar lost or was deprived of the privilege of immunity he did not automatically lose the *privilegium clericorum*, of which personal inviolability was the first division.

The status of scholar was accorded only to one who within fifteen days of his arrival in Cambridge or entry into the university had secured a master and had his name entered in his *matricula* or roll. If the student through culpable negligence failed to comply with these prescriptions and continued to pose as a scholar he faced imprisonment.[4] Each regent master was bound to keep a roll of his

[1] *Cons. Univ. Canteb.* XI. i–v (see below, p. 211, line 3 to p. 213, line 9). The title of this chapter is misplaced in the MS.

[2] The distinction is stated very clearly in *SA* 49 (*Docs*, i. 336). The statute embraces 'tam clericos scholares quam clericos non scholares infra jurisdictionem cancellarii seu universitatis'. There is a general reference to the limits or liberties of the university in two fourteenth-century statutes, *SA* 91, 156 (*ibid.* 362, 391). According to a document which was copied in the eighteenth century the precincts of the university extended for a mile, an English mile, around the town, measured 'ab extremis Aedificiis'; cf. Gonville and Caius College MS 604, fo. 194^{r}.

[3] When the bishop's official, Guy de Coventre, stated in 1295 (?) that the bishop had given the chancellor jurisdiction over clerks he was referring to clerks in the university and probably, too, to clerks who resided or were found within its liberties. See above, p. 58.

[4] *Cons. Univ. Canteb.* XI. i (see below, p. 211, lines 4–10). Cf. also Markaunt 36 (see below, p. 330, line 25 to p. 331, line 2); *SA* 43 (*Docs*, i. 333). The statute in its present form was enacted after 3 May 1231. See above, pp. 73–4.

scholars, but we must not think that this meant writing their names into a special book or on a quire of parchment or on membranes like the public rolls. Among the manuscripts of Gonville and Caius College is preserved probably the earliest surviving roll of a Cambridge master, a regent in arts. The volume dates from the second half of the thirteenth century and consists of texts of the Old Logic. On the margins of seven folios are written the names of sixty scholars, and opposite most of the names we find the figures '2', '3', '4' and in one case '6', which probably represent the second, third, fourth and sixth year students.[1] Only one is known to have become master, Thomas of St Edmunds, who incepted by 1268. As he was still a scholar when his name was entered in the roll, the *matricula* cannot be later than that year.[2]

The minimum age for entry into the university is not stated; it was probably fourteen years,[3] and doubtless a student once he was accepted by a master had to pay fees.[4] But matriculation was not sufficient to secure the privilege of immunity. Scholars were obliged to attend the schools of their masters at least three days every week and hear not less than three ordinary lectures.[5] The master, however, had to give these lectures himself; if he failed to do so, presumably he was not entitled to collect fees. A scholar could be excused on occasions from attending lectures, provided the master approved or there was some sufficient reason.

Not every scholar who presented himself at Cambridge was accepted, but the only individuals who were expressly excluded were scholars who had been expelled from Oxford. Relations

[1] Gonville and Caius College MS 465, fos. 43^{v}, 44^{v}, 45^{v}, 47^{r}, 48^{v}, 49^{v}–50^{v}. The names are written in pencil and are very difficult to decipher. Twenty-nine are printed in James, *A descriptive catalogue of the manuscripts in the library of Gonville and Caius College, Cambridge*, ii (Cambridge, 1908), 539–40. I hope to publish the complete roll. Shorter lists are in MSS 385, 593.

[2] His name occurs on fo. 44^{v} of the roll, where the figure '3' is placed opposite it. Cf. also *BRUC*, p. 502.

[3] The evidence is very late. Cf. *SA* 50 (*Docs*, i. 337). But fourteen was the minimum age for entry into Paris in the thirteenth century, and so the same regulation was probably in force at Cambridge by *c.* 1250. Cf. Rashdall, *Universities*, iii. 352.

[4] There are numerous references to lecture fees in the later statutes. Post, 'Masters' salaries and student-fees in the mediaeval universities', *Speculum*, vii (1932), 181–98, omits all mention of Cambridge.

[5] Attendance at the schools was made an explicit condition for the enjoyment of immunity at Paris by Gregory IX in 1231: 'illi, qui simulant se scolares, nec tamen scolas frequentant nec magistrum aliquem profitentur, nequaquam scolarium gaudeant libertate' (*Chart. Univ. Paris.* i. 137, no. 79). See also above, p. 74, n. 1.

between the two universities must have been friendly at this period, and the secession from Cambridge to Northampton in 1260 served to draw them yet closer.[1] The Angelica text refers to the reception of letters from the chancellor of Oxford, naming malefactors. Apart from the notorious Henry Symeon, the most famous of these was undoubtedly mag. William de Barneby, the instigator of the Stamford schism during the Michaelmas term of 1333.[2] He was denounced by the chancellor, Robert de Stratford, as a perjurer and founder of the *studium adulterinum*—crimes which made him a malefactor twice over. In 1337 word reached Oxford that he was thinking of going to Cambridge to incept as doctor of canon law, and Stratford wrote to the university, urgently requesting it not to admit Barneby. In his letter he mentioned the good relations which hitherto existed between the two universities.[3] On occasion, too, Cambridge asked Oxford to help in tracing wanted scholars.[4]

Five proscribed classes of scholars are listed in chapter XI, paragraph iv, of the constitution.[5] Housebreakers, assaulters of women, footpads and scholars who arm themselves in order to do violence were formally outlawed by most universities.[6] Cambridge had a category all its own, namely, scholars who cite a clerk or layman of the town of Cambridge under the general clauses *quidam alii* and *rebus aliis* by obtaining papal letters of delegation. The background to and the formation of the statute have been discussed elsewhere in this study.[7] Apparently, the indult granted by Gregory IX in 1233 concerning citations before judges delegate of the Holy See proved effective in restraining scholars from citing other scholars under the general clauses; it must have greatly helped to establish the principle that in all actions between scholars the chancellor has

1 See below, pp. 224–5.

2 Salter, 'The Stamford crisis', *E.H.R.* xxxvii (1922), 249.

3 'Letters relating to Oxford in the 14th century', ed. H. H. Henson, *Collectanea*, i (OHS, v [1885]), 15–16; *Formularies which bear on the history of Oxford, c. 1204–1420*, edd. H. E. Salter, W. A. Pantin and H. G. Richardson, i (OHS, n.s. iv [1942]), 94–5.

4 Cf. *ibid.* p. 131, for a copy of a citation in which the rectors of Cambridge ask the chancellor of Oxford to cite or have cited mag. J. de T., said to be living within the chancellor's jurisdiction. He had broken his pledge of faith and must present himself in the court of the chancellor of Cambridge 'et si necesse fuerit de veritate dicenda personaliter iuraturus'. The master has not been identified; the initials may be purely conventional.

5 *Cons. Univ. Canteb.* XI. iv (see below, p. 211, lines 19–22).

6 See above, pp. 82, 89. For Oxford cf. also *SAUO*, 82, 1–7; 108, 22–36; 109, 26–110, 9.

7 See above, pp. 26–8, 96–8.

jurisdiction, and that no scholar may cite another scholar outside the court of the university. The statute was a further extension of this principle. Its declared aim was to deter scholars from citing persons who were not members of the university be they clerks or laymen before judges delegate. It was one way of preventing scholars from abusing papal letters of delegation. In effect, it ensured that scholars would be unable to sue anybody, scholars, clerks or laymen, in the first instance in any court except the chancellor's.[1]

The charge of citing clerks or laymen under the general terms *quidam alii* and *rebus aliis* was serious in the extreme; no distinction was made between this offence and those committed by the nefarious characters mentioned at the beginning of the relevant paragraph of the Angelica text. All five classes of scholars were regarded as a threat to the peace. The sentence was the most severe penalty within the power of the university to impose. If convicted by the *universitas regentium* the offenders were sent down from the university or committed to prison, unless they showed signs of genuine repentance; even so, those who had planned to do violence had their weapons confiscated, the proceeds of the sale going to the poor or to the chancellor.[2] The same penalty of expulsion or imprisonment was reserved for all who conspired against his prohibition or showed themselves to be incorrigibly disobedient and contumacious.[3]

ANGELICA CHAPTER XII: HOUSES AND SCHOOLS

This chapter strikes a nice balance between the rights of property owners and the rights of scholars.[4] The first thing that one notices is the businesslike arrangement written into the constitution for the payment of rents. The annual amount levied by the taxors was

1 This part of the constitution was abrogated by *c.* 1304–37, probably because it had served its purpose.

2 The chancellor at Oxford was also entitled to monies fetched by the sale of weapons. Cf. *SAUO*, 641, 13–14 (*c.* 1275); 125, 6–24 (1322).

3 At Oxford one who disobeyed the chancellor's prohibition incurred excommunication *ipso facto* and was put in prison. Cf. *ibid.* 81, 20–3.

4 On the question of housing at Cambridge in the late thirteenth century cf. Maitland, *Township and borough* (Cambridge, 1898), pp. 52–5, 99–101, 142–9. It has been estimated that there were thirty-four 'university' hostels by 1280 (B.M. Harl. MS 4116, fos. 43^v–44^r). Stokes, *Mediaeval hostels*, is an interesting study, but the approach to the subject is more antiquarian than scholarly; moreover the plan of the work is unsatisfactory and the dating of university legislation must be treated

divided into three equal parts, payable on three fixed days. The first instalment fell due on 1 November, the second on 2 February and the third and final payment on Ascension Thursday.[1] It is tempting to assume that some of the provisions of the Cambridge constitution were based on local custom. The university, however, appears to have devised its own system as regards the payment of rents by scholars and in doing so it departed from the common practice. Tenants of properties owned by St John's Hospital paid their rents in two instalments, the terminal dates being 29 September (the feast of St Michael) and Hock Day, the second Tuesday after Easter.[2] It is disconcerting to find that some of the tenants were university masters and indeed a notable tenant was the university itself.

If a scholar was unable to pay his rent in cash he was obliged to make suitable compensation to the landord. On this question the university adopted, probably with good reason, a very firm attitude. It compelled scholars under pain of excommunication to pay their rents before leaving Cambridge and honour any debts contracted during their stay in the town. Creditors were also entitled to distrain the pledge or security offered by a third party or an expromissor on behalf of scholars. Should a scholar abscond without settling his accounts the chancellor notified his bishop that he, the defaulter, was excommunicated.[3] The censure remained in force until he discharged his debts. There is no early record of a case, though more than one master in the thirteenth century incurred arrears, as we shall see. The constitution, however, was enforced against Roger de Mouneye *alias* Huntingfield, who was excommunicated by the vice-chancellor in 1329 for failing to pay a debt owed to a creditor, but it does not appear that he was ordered to clear the debt before the censure was lifted by the pope at the request of Queen Isabella.[4]

with caution. It will not be out of place to mention that Dr Emden's excellent study *An Oxford hall* has been complemented by Dr Pantin's, 'The halls and schools of medieval Oxford: an attempt at reconstruction', *Oxford studies pres. to D. Callus*, pp. 31–100.

[1] *Cons. Univ. Canteb.* XII. i (see below, p. 213, lines 11–13). It will be noticed that the instalments were spread over the three terms of the academic year. Masters probably collected their fees at the end of each term.

[2] Cart. St John's Hosp. fo. 8r. Cf also the deed concerning the bedell, Walter de Oxonia, which was executed in 1270–1, in Stokes, *Esquire bedells*, p. 129.

[3] The chancellor was not empowered to signify excommunications directly into the king's chancery until 1383. Cf. *Cal. pat. rolls, 1381–5*, pp. 241–2. There is a file of significations covering the period 1384–1530 in P.R.O. C 85/209.

[4] *BRUC*, p. 415.

At Oxford once a house or school was rented to a scholar or master the university immediately acquired an option for all time on the letting of the property. If the owner, however, wanted to live in the building with his family he was entitled to take possession provided he informed the principal of this before 24 June. The only other way he could terminate the lease was by renting the house to somebody for ten years, in which case the university insisted that the money be paid in advance.[1] The position at Cambridge by *c.* 1250 was somewhat different. Landlords were forbidden to let a house to a layman or put it to any other use if schools were held there for ten years or more, as long as a regent or a bachelor who was due to incept required it for lectures; but if the landlord had lived in the place of necessity the premises could not be claimed, that is, provided he continued to occupy the building.[2] A prominent Cambridge citizen, Nicholas le Barber, owned a house known as the *domus scolarum* opposite St Mary's. It must have been a large building because it housed three faculties, canon and civil law and theology. Barber wished to reoccupy the house and live there with his family and indeed instal machinery. The university consented, although lectures had been held there for a long time past, probably for more than ten years, and the deed of conveyance was signed on 23 July 1309.[3] An interesting point about the settlement is that Barber agreed to allow lectures to continue in the house until 7 July 1311, by which time alternative accommodation would have been procured. The only reason why 7 July was fixed for the expiry of the lease was that by 1309 the end of the summer term and of the official academic year had been changed from 20 July, the feast of St Margaret, to the eve of the translation of St Thomas of Canterbury.

Property owners were strictly forbidden to charge a higher rent than the sum assessed by the taxors, any agreement to the contrary notwithstanding; and scholars were likewise bound not to pay anything over and above what was laid down. If a landlord was

1 Cf. *SAUO*, pp. lxxxiii–lxxxiv; 79, 11–18; 80, 1–9; Emden, *An Oxford hall*, pp. 17, 22–6, 34–5.

2 *Cons. Univ. Canteb.* XII. iii (see below, p. 215, lines 3–4). Regents were obliged to select their schools at the commencement of the academic year, bachelors at the beginning of terms. An Oxford *forma* printed in Rashdall, *Universities*, iii. 481, states than an inceptor in arts before receiving the licence had to testify under oath 'quod provisum est sibi de scholis pro anno in quo debet regere'.

3 The original deed, CUA, doc. no. 16, is printed in Stokes, 'Early university property', *CASP*, xiii, n.s. vii. 183–4.

discovered to have raised the rent the chancellor was empowered to debar scholars from lodging in his premises, and moreover the amount paid in excess of the official rate was to be handed back and given to the tenant if he asked for it. Thus a curb was placed on grasping landlords, and members of the university were restrained from outbidding one another for possession.[1]

The same premises might serve as a hostel and school, but hostels were generally places of residence only. It is with these that chapter XII of the Angelica text is mostly concerned. The person who hired a hostel and took in fellow scholars was known as the principal; he was either a master or senior scholar, in other words, a bachelor.[2] As principal he was solely responsible for the payment of the rent and the conduct of his co-tenants. Hostels were let on a yearly basis as at Oxford and Bologna and other university cities. The principal alone had the right to have the lease extended, provided he renewed his application for the tenancy each year before the feast of the Nativity of Our Lady, 8 September, the date observed at all universities. This meant offering a caution to the landlord as security for the rent. If the landlord could not be found it was sufficient to offer the pledge to the chancellor.[3] The constitution, however, did not expressly authorize him to grant or confirm a tenancy should the landlord perhaps refuse to accept the caution. In 1290 Simon de Asceles, prior of Barnwell, declined to take the pledge offered by mag. Ralph de Leycestria, who wished to continue as tenant of a stone house owned by the priory in the parish of St Sepulchre. Thereupon the regent master went with his caution to the chancellor, Geoffrey de Pakenham, who accepted it and installed him as tenant. The prior then brought a suit of novel disseisin, but on 27 April 1292 the chancellor obtained a writ of prohibition from the king, who ordered his justices not to proceed with the action without consulting him and his council. In the end the bishop's official, mag. Guy de Coventre, arbitrated and Leycestria agreed to vacate the premises.[4] The interesting point is that the university claimed the right by custom of granting tenancy to a scholar whose caution was rejected

1 *Cons. Univ. Canteb.* xii. iv (see below, p. 215, lines 5–9).

2 Cf. Emden, *An Oxford hall*, pp. 23–4. Dr Emden has recently published the earliest extant accounts (*c.* 1244×9?) of an Oxford hostel. Cf. his article 'Accounts relating to an early Oxford house of scholars', *Oxoniensia*, xxxi (1966), 77–81.

3 Cf. *Cons. Univ. Canteb.* xii. v (see below, p. 215, lines 10–13). There were two kinds of cautions. See below, p. 238, n. 4.

4 For the terms of the settlement see below, p. 232.

by the landlord. It was stated that this custom existed from the very foundation of the university. That may be so, but it was not given statutory recognition or force when the constitution was drawn up, though Pakenham could justify his action by appealing to the relevant statute, which empowered him to accept a caution when the landlord was not available. It was a short step from this to claim the right of granting a tenancy even if the landlord rejected a scholar's application.[1]

In the king's courts a plea based on custom might possibly have succeeded; in the diocesan court nothing less than a statute carried weight. Thus the prior of Barnwell was again successful in vindicating the rights of the priory as landlord on 23 July 1293, this time against mag. Henry de Wysethe, who had rented one of its houses in the vicinity of St John's Hospital. Once again the priory instituted a suit of novel disseisin. The action was withdrawn when the official of the bishop intervened. Wysethe was allowed to remain in occupation until 8 September, the terminal date of the annual lease. On the appointed day, or earlier if he wished, he was to surrender possession and refrain from offering a caution.[2]

Both Leycestria and Wysethe were more than willing to guarantee in advance the payment of the rent of the house or school owned by Barnwell. But if a principal failed to deposit a caution before the feast of the Nativity of Our Lady the lease which he had of a building automatically lapsed, and the landlord was free to instal somebody

[1] Leycestria pleaded in 1290 'quod ipse nichil clamat in libero tenemento predicti mesuagij nisi hospicium suum tantum secundum statuta vniuersitatis Cantebrigie' (*Liber mem. ecc. de Bernewelle*, p. 183; Hare MS i, fo. 37^{v}). The point at issue was not covered by any statute of the university, and Leycestria was not entitled to rest his case on anything more than custom. It is worth quoting the appropriate part of the king's writ of 1292, which embodies the claim made by the university: 'secundum Statuta et Consuetudines ejusdem Universitatis a prima fundatione ejusdem hactenus ibidem observata, sine quibus dicta Universitas nullatenus stare posset, Scolares hujusmodi Domos conducere volentes, in defectu hospitum quorum Domus illae fuerint, si hospites illi inventi non fuerint, vel malitiose se absentaverint, vel si forte inventi Domos suas Scholaribus locare noluerint, et sufficientem cautionem de dicta pensione pro Domibus illis solvenda a dictis Scholaribus admittere recusaverint, Cancellarium Universitatis praedictae adeant, qui recepta a dictis Scholaribus cautione sufficiente, domos illas eis, sicut moris est, in eadem Universitate liberari faciat inhabitandas; ac praedictus Cancellarius [Pakenham]...per bonam cautionem juxta consuetudinem Universitatis praedictae [domum] inhabitandam liberavit' (Prynne, *The third tome of an exact chronological vindication*, p. 467). The custom is mentioned in the so-called 'statutes' of the university in CUL MS Mm. 4. 41. See below, p. 239, n. 3.

[2] CUA, doc. no. 9.

else as tenant, in which case any arrangement which the outgoing tenant made with another person as regards transfer of lease became null and void.[1] The constitution, it must be admitted, goes more than half-way to meet the legitimate demands of landlords. It decrees that should a tenant stay on in a house after 8 September he is held to have rehired it tacitly and unless the landlord allows him free lodging he is liable for the rent of the whole of the following year.[2] Moreover, the Angelica text lays down that the principal shall be personally responsible for payment of the entire rent for the year, and he must answer for any culpable damage done to the property either by himself or his companions.[3]

Finally, the constitution recognizes the customary right of overlords to distrain their fees for perpetual services but not for rent owed to the immediate landlord by a master or scholar. In other words, the overlord could seize their chattels if they failed to pay their share of the feudal dues owed to the lord from property held in fee. Originally, these dues took the form of a service, but by this time they were generally commuted to a money payment. In technical language the payment was known as a rent charge, while the rent due from the tenant to his landlord was called rent service.[4] The Cambridge constitution leaves no doubt that an overlord was entitled to take a distress even if the tenants were members of the university, but he could distrain only for the recovery of the rent charge, not for rent service. In such a contingency the chancellor was empowered to reduce the 'agreed temporary rent' in proportion to the length of time a master had used the building for schools or a scholar had lived in the place. The difference between the agreed or, we might say, taxed rent and the new assessment was to be paid back to the master or scholar as the case might be.

[1] According to the later version of the statute cautions had to be deposited between the feast of St Barnabas (11 June) and the feast of Our Lady's Nativity (8 Sept.). Cf. Markaunt 32 (see below, p. 327, lines 25–7); *SA* 67 (*Docs*, i. 351). See also below, p. 239, n. 2.

[2] This was a principle of roman law. Cf. *Dig.* 19, 2, 13, 11 quoted on p. 214, *app. crit.* ad 21–3.

[3] For the sake of cohesion I have reversed the order here of paragraphs vi and vii of Angelica XII.

[4] Cf. Pollock and Maitland, *History of English law*, i. 232–8; ii. 129. See also the interesting case in *Liber mem. ecc. de Bernewelle*, pp. 312–17.

ANGELICA CHAPTER XIII: FUNERALS

This, the final chapter of the Angelica text, need not detain us long. The first paragraph makes provision for the celebration of the obsequies of the king, Henry III, and the bishop of Ely, Hugh of Northwold. The former died on 16 November 1272, the latter on 6 August 1254.[1] References of this kind prove beyond any doubt that the text was put together as an organic whole and at a date in Cambridge history which was not later than 1254. Henry III is praised for his great generosity towards the university, on which he conferred many privileges concerning the taxation of houses, the purchase of daily food supplies and the correction of malicious and undisciplined scholars. Hugh of Northwold also favoured the university and it held in grateful memory the marks of honour which he showed to scholars and especially the regents, whose inceptions he attended many times. No doubt, when Henry and Hugh died, the entire university carried out the duty laid down in the constitution of chanting the vespers for the dead and the office and Mass for the bishop in 1254 and for the king in 1272.

The remainder of the chapter is devoted to the obsequies of deceased regents, scholars, non-regents and bedells with a passing reference to grammar masters.[2] From the moment when news of the death of a regent arrived, all lectures and disputations were to be suspended until after the burial. The chancellor and regents assembled together in convocation and kept vigil throughout the night as they recited their psalters. This was not obligatory in the case of a deceased non-regent, scholar or bedell. The chancellor and regents were to assemble for their obsequies and attend the burial, but some lectures, apparently, could be given that day. Disputations, however, were strictly forbidden. There was no obligation on the chancellor or regents to attend the funerals of teachers of grammar. They might do so for religious reasons, provided this did not interfere with lectures or disputations. The text, incidentally, makes no distinction between the head of the local grammar schools, the master of glomery, and his assistants. Presumably,

1 The text does not mention either the king or the bishop by name, but there can be no reasonable doubt about their identity. See above, pp. 25–6, 38–9.

2 *Cons. Univ. Canteb.* XIII. ii–iii (see below, p. 217, lines 17–25).

all were included in the phrase 'those who teach nothing but grammar'.[1]

When studied at close range, using external evidence and the comparative method, it is remarkable how revealing the Angelica text proves to be. Its greatest significance lies in the unique picture which it presents of the actual internal organization of the university by the middle of the thirteenth century. Far from being an amorphous collection of schools with masters and scholars grouped in an indeterminate number of faculties of uncertain standard, Cambridge at a relatively early date in its history possessed the corporate and academic structure of an authentic university or *studium generale*.

Few historical concepts are harder to define than this vague, ambivalent term. It was only towards the end of the thirteenth century that it acquired the classic meaning of a seat of higher learning which conferred degrees of universal validity and whose right to do so was authorized or confirmed by a general power, the pope or emperor. Earlier in the century and indeed long afterwards superior schools were classified as particular or general. A *studium particulare* catered only for the 'primitive' sciences, grammar and philosophy.[2] There is no danger of confusing it with a *studium generale*, which was essentially a university and which conferred the degree of master 'publicly' not only in arts but, what was infinitely more important, in medicine or law or theology as well.[3] In other words, it contained one or more of the higher faculties. On the evidence provided by its constitution Cambridge by *c.* 1250 was certainly a *studium generale*. Even such an exacting critic as Denifle, although he had no knowledge of the Angelica text, conceded as much.[4] His interpretation of the bull *Inter singula* (9 June 1318),

[1] *Cons. Univ. Canteb.* XIII. iii (see below, p. 217, line 24). The degree of M.Gram. was not instituted until very late in the fourteenth century. See below, p. 265, n. 5.

[2] Cf. *Chart. Univ. Paris.* ii. 448, no. 992, 504, no. 1040. See also Rashdall, *Universities*, i. 6, n. 2; ii. 78.

[3] A master incepted publicly at a university and by going through the twofold ceremony of *vesperiae* and *principium*. The evidence for the existence of these exercises at Cambridge in the faculty of theology provided by the Angelica text is as early as the evidence for Oxford. Cf. Pelster in *Oxford theology*, p. 45.

[4] Rashdall, *op. cit.* iii. 282–4, gives the impression that Denifle refused to accord Cambridge the status of a *studium generale* before 1318. Referring to Toulouse and Montpellier Denifle speaks of Cambridge, 'dessen Generalstudium scheinbar erst am 9. Juni 1318 von Johann XXII. errichtet wurde, während es doch als solches bereits seit der 1. Hälfte des 13. Jhs. existiert hat' (*Universitäten*, p. 353).

however, suffered in consequence. There is no substitute for an actual text of the constitution of the university. Denifle was too good a historian to take the bull of John XXII literally. It reads as if the pope were creating something which in fact already existed, namely, a *studium generale* at Cambridge.[1] For Denifle the real significance of *Inter singula* was that it helped to renew the *studium* by placing its faculties on a proper footing and secure its future by granting the university public recognition.[2] We now know that Cambridge had two fully established superior faculties, canon law and theology, by *c.* 1250 with a third, civil law, soon to follow, while later in the century a faculty of medicine was erected. The fact is that it was the only university apart from Oxford which had the full complement of four higher faculties before 1300. The danger of extinction was purely hypothetical, but circumstances made the acquisition of a papal bull most desirable.

During the second half of the thirteenth century it became the common teaching of the jurists that only a *potestas generalis* could found a *studium generale* or grant a university the right to confer the *ius ubique docendi*. The more prominent of the long-established universities which lacked a papal deed of foundation set about securing *de jure* recognition or confirmation of their titles from the Holy See.[3] Montpellier was the first to make a move and was quickly followed by Bologna and Paris, which obtained bulls in 1291–2. Oxford made application to Boniface VIII on 3 September 1296 through the bishop of Carlisle, John de Halton. Had the request proved successful Cambridge would doubtless have also pressed its claim without much delay. Halton's letter was ignored. Two further attempts were made by Oxford, the one by Edward I in 1303–4, the other by Edward II on 26 December 1317, but nothing resulted.[4]

1 The original of the bull, which was at one time in the university archives, has not survived. It was probably surrendered with other papal briefs in 1535 and destroyed. The best edition is in A. B. Cobban, 'Edward II, Pope John XXII and the university of Cambridge', *Bulletin of the John Rylands Library*, 47 (1964–5), 77–8, where the text in Archivio Vaticano, *Reg. Vat.* 68, fo. 66^{r}, is reproduced. Instead of giving variant readings from the printed texts in Fuller and Dyer, the editor would have placed us much more in his debt had he collated the text in *Reg. Vat.* with the draft in *Reg. Aven.* 9, fos. 217^{v}–218^{r}, and the copy in Markaunt's Book, B fo. 9^{v}, which was directly derived from the original.

2 Cf. *Universitäten*, pp. 352–3, 375.

3 Haskins, 'The university of Oxford and the "ius ubique docendi"', *E.H.R.* lvi (1941), 282–3.

4 It is generally held, indeed the Oxford statutes imply, that Paris on receiving its bull in 1292 set itself against recognizing Oxford degrees. Halton's letter of 1296

Cambridge was now forced to look after its own interests, and on 18 March 1318 the king wrote on its behalf to John XXII asking him to confirm its privileges and grant it new ones.[1] The letter was not more specific. What Cambridge really wanted was a formal grant of the *ius ubique docendi*, or better still a declaration from the pope that it already enjoyed the privilege. The vaguely worded petition was interpreted, however, at Avignon as a request to have the university raised to the status of a *studium generale*. When the bull *Inter singula* was issued on 9 June 1318 it decreed that there should be henceforth a *studium generale* in each faculty at Cambridge and that the college of masters and scholars be reputed as a university and enjoy all the rights of a legitimately constituted university. The form in which the bull was made out probably caused disappointment in Cambridge; but although it contained no overt reference to the *ius ubique docendi* the privilege was implicit in the grant of a *studium generale* 'in qualibet facultate'.

Actually, the significance of the bull was more decorative than substantial, since Pope John's predecessor, Nicholas IV, had already recognized that Cambridge was a *studium generale*. Both Denifle and Rashdall overlooked a letter of 9 June 1290 in which Pope Nicholas expressly stated that Cambridge was a *studium generale*.[2] The state-

suggests on the contrary that it was Oxford which threw down the gauntlet, possibly because of wounded pride. Halton clearly hinted in his letter to Pope Boniface that there would be trouble unless Oxford was granted the same terms as Paris. Cf. *The register of John de Halton, bishop of Carlisle, A.D. 1292–1314*, ed. W. N. Thompson, i (Canterbury & York Soc., xii [1913]), 77–8. It was Paris in fact which first complained that its masters were not being admitted *ad eundem* in England; the complaint was lodged in 1296–1316. Cf. *Chart. Univ. Paris.* ii. 182, no. 728; cf. *ibid.* 184, no. 728a. As it refers to England and not specifically to Oxford, we must conclude that Cambridge also declined to accept Parisian degrees. Given the reciprocal relations which existed between the two English universities, Cambridge had no choice.

1 Rymer, *Foedera*, II. i. 357. Cobban, art. cit. *loc. cit.* pp. 66–8, argues for a connection between the mission sent by Edward to Avignon in December 1316 concerning the foundation of King's Hall and his petition on behalf of the university. The argument is based on the assumption that the mission was still at Avignon when Edward's letter arrived. But the letter was not sent before 18 March 1318 (it is wrongly dated '1317' in the article), by which time the royal emissaries had long since returned to England.

2 'Canthebrigia, Eliensis diocesis, ubi generale viget studium' (*Registres de Nicolas IV*, ed. E. Langlois, i [Paris, 1886–91], 455, no. 2731). The letter has to do with the request of the Gilbertine canons attending the university for permission to occupy the house of the Friars of the Sack when it became vacant. The crucial clause 'ubi generale viget studium' is omitted in *Cal. papal letters*, i. 514, which doubtless explains how it has escaped the notice of historians.

ment is highly significant; it means that the university was competent in the eyes of the Holy See to confer the *ius ubique docendi*. It was the same pope who granted Montpellier its bull the year before and who confirmed the privileges of Bologna and Paris within a year or two of his reference to Cambridge. In a papal document of this period the term *studium generale* is synonymous with the *ius ubique docendi*. The declaration of Nicholas IV concerning the status of Cambridge puts in its proper perspective the bull which John XXII issued exactly twenty-eight years later. All that *Inter singula* meant for the university was *de jure* recognition or formal confirmation of the rank which Cambridge enjoyed in the fullest sense by 1290 and, as the Angelica text suggests, even by *c*. 1250.[1]

1 The theory that a *studium generale* was a university of more than local or national repute is verified to some extent by the provision of the constitution which states that masters who graduated at a university of similar standing may be admitted *ad eundem*. Cf. *Cons. Univ. Canteb.* II. ii (see below, p. 199, lines 8–11). Cambridge certainly attracted scholars not only from Oxford but from Paris during the first half of the thirteenth century, as the 1229–31 migration shows. It was the friars, however, who forged the closest links between Cambridge and the continental universities.

PART II

THE TEXT

Chapter 6

PROLEGOMENA

Angelica 401, fos. $54^{r\,a}$–$55^{v\,b}$, is strictly speaking a *codex unicus*. The text should be printed exactly as it stands unless obviously corrupt or erroneous. It is well to remember that the parchment is rather stained and was perforated in places both before and after the date of transcription. The holes have now been repaired, but the long creases which marred the appearance of fos. 54–5 have remained obstinate.[1] Unfortunately, the repair work is of an inferior quality and in consequence some letters, already partly defaced, are no longer legible. I had the good fortune to see and examine the manuscript before it was sent to be repaired. The photograph reproduced as the frontispiece to this book gives an impression of what the text looked like then. The important thing is that none of the script was lost when this transcript was made. Hence any corruptions or errors in the text are due to either the exemplar or the scribe.

Short as it is the text presents a number of difficult problems. In attempting to arrive at the true reading of the exemplar or discover what the scribe intended to write but did not, it is very tempting to restore the text from the later manuscripts of the statutes. No fault whatever could be found with this approach if it were a question of reconstructing an archetype; it would be the bounden duty of the editor to collate all the sub-archetypal witnesses and on the basis of the manuscript tradition make his decision. But Angelica 401 antedates the archetype of the *statuta antiqua*. Help from any quarter, particularly statute-books, is to be welcomed. Markaunt and the proctors' books, as well as the Caius manuscript, derive, however deviously, from the original, and since style is a vital guide in textual reconstruction we can learn a lot from these fourteenth- and fifteenth-century codices.[2] Yet the history of the statutes shows

[1] Minor blemishes are not noted in the *apparatus*, nor will attention be drawn to the creases and holes now put right, except where there is question of damage to a reading. The manuscript is described in detail on pp. 8–15 above. I must express again my heartfelt gratitude to Professor Bieler and Dr Hunt for subjecting this part of my work to a critical examination. Unfortunately, it has not been possible to incorporate more than a few of their suggestions.

[2] We must not forget, however, that the rules which apply to textual criticism of the classics have only limited application in this context. Statutes, no doubt, were

what scant respect might be paid to earlier recensions when new editions were being put together. The wonder is that so much of the Angelica text survived despite the almost continuous re-editing, recasting and other vicissitudes which it sustained. It would be a simple matter to correct the faults of Angelica by adopting the readings of Markaunt and the other manuscripts, but in fact their variants have no more value *per se* than emendations proposed by a corrector today. Even quotations must be treated with circumspection, that is, quotations from the original.[1] The earliest of these date from 1276. By then a partial revision of the exemplar of Angelica 401 had been carried out, a factor that must be taken into account when judging its faithfulness or not to the parent. Moreover, Angelica represents a much older and purer tradition than do Markaunt and the later manuscripts, which underlines the need for discretion in reconstructing the original text or the exemplar of Angelica on the basis of readings, superior as they may be, presented by the recensions.

The critical problem is not one of editing a corrected version of the Angelica text—a comparatively straightforward exercise; the problem lies in the reconstruction of the exemplar, which in effect means the original. The basic instrument is of course our manuscript. From it we must try to form a mental picture of what the exemplar looked like as a palaeographical production. Moreover, it must not be assumed that the author of the parent text or the writer of the exemplar was incapable of making an error; indeed the author wrote some inferior Latin even by medieval standards. Basically, the problem is reducible to the question of the relationship between Angelica 401 and its exemplar. Either or both may have been incorrectly executed, and generally it is impossible to distinguish between the one and the other when endeavouring to identify the precise source of some blunder. Still, a close study of the manuscript inevitably forces one to conclude that generally the scribe rather than the maker of the exemplar is the more likely to have blundered.

'Assimilation of terminations and accommodation to neighbouring

framed in a somewhat traditional style, but the texts were not the work of a single author. The Angelica text, or rather the original, is of course different. Here it is a question of a single authorship; unfortunately we have no means of testing peculiar readings against another work by the same author.

[1] It is not a question of comparing quotations which the author himself introduced. There are echoes of quotations in the text, but there are no explicit citations.

constructions'[1] explains many of the blatant errors which occur in the Angelica manuscript. The copyist allowed his eye to read ahead and there is no doubt that in the course of his work he was influenced by auditory-visual impressions of what he had just written. Thus we get *cessantibus* for *cessantes* (III), *cessionem* for *cessione* (XII. v) and so forth. Mechanical blunders abound. Again and again the scribe dropped contraction marks and it is evident that a number of mistakes could have been avoided if he had studied his exemplar with more care. Now and then he corrected himself by placing a dot under a letter to be deleted or by simply crossing it out; twice he indicates an accidental omission by the use of an asterisk as a caret mark, the missing letter or letters being written in either on the line itself or overhead.[2] A peculiar feature of the transcription was his inability to distinguish between *o* and *i*, *iu* and *uo*; *excepto* (X. ii) is written as *excepti*, and *quamdiu* or *quam diu* (XII. iii) as *quam duo*.[3] Perhaps the most glaring example of carelessness is the rendering of *circa* as *cerca* (VII. iv). To his credit it must be said that the one mistake he did not make was to tamper with or correct his exemplar.[4]

There is no difficulty in, nor can there be any hesitation about, rectifying misreadings which are clearly scribal blunders. We do meet from time to time some problematical passages that cannot be so easily dismissed. It is sound methodology not to reject any reading in a manuscript as long as it is not patently erroneous or can possibly make sense. This rule I have followed, hard as it has been at times to obey.[5] In a dozen instances or so the problem is rather different and requires closer study.

1 F. W. Hall, *A companion to classical texts* (Oxford, 1913), p. 153.

2 It is difficult occasionally to decide whether the scribe intended to delete a letter or not. There is a dot, for example, under the third stroke of *m* in *enormitas* (VI), but as the word was written correctly in the first place we may regard the dot as an inkstain. The same applies to *solempnitas* (X. ii) which has a mark under the initial *s*. On the other hand, twice in the same column of text a dot occurs under the second *l* of *cancellario* (*-ii*); since it was the scribe's normal practice to spell *cancellarius* with only one *l*, it may be assumed that he corrected (!) himself in both instances.

3 It is possible that the exemplar was hard to decipher, but how the scribe could write *uideamus* or *iudeamus* for *iudicamus* (XI. i) is a mystery.

4 He might have been tempted to substitute *unanimi uoluntate* for *omni uoluntate* (I. i) or omit *omni* altogether, as did the redactor of Markaunt. Cf. Markaunt 2 (see below p. 313, line 26).

5 It has been tempting to supply *fuerit* before *licenciatus* in II. vi. A more felicitous rendering of 'die mercurii quasimodo geniti' (III) would be 'die mercurii post quasimodo geniti', which is the reading in *SA* 150 (*Docs*, i. 388), or better still 'die mercurii post dominicam qua cantatur quasimodo geniti'; cf. *SAUO*, 5,

I. ii: 'Liceat quocumque cancellario.' This is the reading of the manuscript. It goes without saying that *quocumque* is a blunder, but it is not the sort of mistake the scribe usually makes. Markaunt and the later codices have *quoque*, which at first sight is an attractive emendation. There are two reasons why it will not do. It does not fit the context; and the scribe is far more likely to have shortened rather than expanded the reading in his exemplar. Had he in fact written *quoque* we should have queried if perchance he had not dropped a contraction mark, as he was prone to do. This is one case where it must be seriously questioned whether the author of the original text did not himself lapse into bad grammar.[1] The correct reading is of course *cuicumque*.[2] It is unlikely that the writer of the exemplar of Angelica 401 corrupted this into *quocumque*.[3] The scribe of our manuscript was quite capable of writing *uo* for *ui*, but there is not a single instance in the whole text of the use of *q* for *c*, which is not too uncommon in medieval texts. The simple explanation, however reluctantly we may assent to it, is probably the true one: the error was present in the parent manuscript of the text and passed uncorrected until replaced inadvisedly by *quoque* at a much later stage.

II. iv: 'Quilibet sue incepcionis antequam determinet.' Here some word like *hora* or *die* or *tempore* has been overlooked. *SA* 134 reads: 'Quilibet tempore inceptionis, antequam suam determinet quaestionem' (*Docs*, i. 381). The text is a revised one, but *tempore* may be admitted, although the passage offers no clue as to thc rcason for the omission. We can only suggest that the scribe was guilty of an oversight.

At the end of the same paragraph we encounter one of the most puzzling anomalies of the Angelica text: 'ad minus per annum facienda qui necessaria causa uel probabilis eum excuset.' The difficulty is *qui*. In the manuscripts of the *statuta antiqua* the word is *nisi*, an obvious solution; yet, erratic as the scribe of Angelica was,

14–15; 55, 17. But the phrase in Angelica 401 is not without parallels in the Cambridge statute-books. Cf. Senior Proctor: 'die veneris aduentus domini' (fo. O^v).

[1] Cf. Strickland Gibson's comment on the Oxford registers: 'The drafters of the statutes were often very careless...the most obvious blunders not only being left uncorrected but copied and recopied' (*SAUO*, p. ix).

[2] Cf. *ibid.* 245, 29–30: 'Cancellarius quiscumque futurus.'

[3] If *cuicumque* had been corrupted into *quocumque* in Angelica 401, then we should have some reason for thinking that the parent of Markaunt and the archetype of the *statuta antiqua* were descended from the MS, but the history of the text rules this out.

he cannot have confused *qui* and *nisi*. It may be taken for granted that he missed *nisi*, but *qui* must represent some corresponding word in his exemplar. The possibility that *qui* is a misreading of *quin* can be rejected; apart from grammatical reasons, this construction never occurs in the text. Almost invariably a negative conditional clause is introduced by *nisi* which is usually followed by a genitive. The scribe could have wrongly deciphered *quod* as *qui*, since the letter 'q' with a diagonal or horizontal stroke through the shaft is an abbreviation of *qui*, *que*, *quia* or *quod*. The writer of Angelica 401 made worse mistakes than to read *qui* for *quod*. As a tentative solution to the problem one might suggest that the exemplar had *nisi quod*. This combination is admittedly foreign to the text—the nearest parallel is *excepto quod* (X. ii)[1]—but there seems to be no other way out of the difficulty.[2] The emendation *nisi quod* need not be rejected because the manuscripts of thc *statuta antiqua* omit *quod*; a redactor might well feel justified in simply writing *nisi*.

IV: 'nec simul omnes conueniant.' There is something wrong here, as the context—the duty of regents to attend convocations—means the very opposite. If we retain *nec*, as we must, and suppose that the scribe overlooked *non* (a case of mistaken identity?),[3] the original can be restored with the utmost economy to read 'necnon simul omnes conueniant', which neatly gives the sense. In Markaunt and the other codices the passage, indeed the entire paragraph, is much revised and no conclusions can be profitably drawn from these witnesses about the true reading of the exemplar.

VII. iii: 'ipsis potibus et cibariis cum ipsis transgressoribus communionem habere uel mercimonium omnino inhibendis.' There is a lacuna here between *cibariis* and *cum* which was probably caused through homoioteleuton (*cum* or *con*...*cum*). It is possible to restore the text by conjecture but not by adopting the device employed by the redactor of Markaunt, who came across a convenient passage elsewhere in the text (XI. iv) and utilized it here.[4] The very fact that he was obliged to alter the defective pericope ('ipsis—inhibendis') in order to accommodate the transfer strongly suggests that the

[1] The MS actually reads *excepti quod*; but in the present instance there is nothing to suggest that the scribe omitted *excepto* rather than *nisi*.

[2] Professor Bieler has drawn my attention to the possibility that the original may have read *nisi qua*. I find it more than difficult to believe that the author of the text used this classical construction (*aliqua* after *nisi*).

[3] It is possible that the exemplar was damaged at this point.

[4] See below, p. 256. Cf. *SA* 54 (*Docs*, i. 340).

lacuna in Angelica 401 derives from the exemplar or possibly from the parent manuscript itself. Markaunt's emendation assumes that food supplies withheld unjustly by retailers from scholars could be confiscated and given to the poor. Though the earliest available writ on the subject dates only from 1293,[1] we need not condemn the emendation on the grounds that it is unhistorical. Chapter XIII. i of the Angelica text implies that Henry III granted some privilege of this kind in the interests of the university, possibly by 1255.[2] Consequently, while we must reject the restoration offered by Markaunt because it does violence to the passage 'ipsis—inhibendis' the original may have read something like this: 'ipsis potibus et cibariis confiscandis et scolaribus cum ipsis transgressoribus communionem habere uel mercimonium omnino inhibendis.' I have suggested this reading in the *apparatus*, but as the original or the exemplar cannot be restored with any confidence I have printed the text in Angelica 401 without adding to it, the lacuna being indicated by a dagger (†).

Angelica VII. iv brings us to the core of the critical problem. The context refers to the office of the rectors or proctors. This is how the manuscript reads: 'Tempora et modus legendi...ad ipsos pertineant in trangressores [*sic*] cerca [*sic*] predicta ad eorum officia specialiter in bedellos. si mandatis eorum non pariunt [*sic*] cohercione concessa eisdem animaduersione grauissima per cancelarium et magistros. si opus fuerit nichilominus irroganda.' As a sample of the scribe's proneness to make mechanical blunders this extract could hardly be bettered. The crucial pericope is 'ad eorum officia specialiter in bedellos'. There is no predicate. All the recensions get around the impasse by deliberately suppressing 'ad eorum officia specialiter' and changing *circa* or *cerca* (Angelica) to *contra*, thus giving: 'contra predicta et in bedellos.' Clearly, this is a revised text, the addition of *et* being unavoidable once 'ad eorum officia specialiter' was dropped, or so one would have thought, although the fact remains that Markaunt and the other manuscripts present a truncated version of the passage.[3] The problem is to identify the missing participle, for it is this which is needed to complete the sense, and to pinpoint the lacuna.

[1] *Cal. pat. rolls, 1292–1301*, p. 18. The writ orders the forfeited foodstuffs to be distributed to the poor and the inmates of St John's Hospital.

[2] See above, pp. 36–7.

[3] Cf. below, p. 256, where Angelica and Markaunt are contrasted.

Elsewhere in the Angelica text *pertinencia* is used in a very similar construction; the chapter on the bedells has 'ad eorum officia *pertinencia*' (VIII. iii).[1] But in the passage under review *pertineant* already occurs and it is most unlikely that the author of the original would repeat the same verb, even as a participle, in the next sentence, which actually qualifies the clause containing *pertineant*. The missing participle is surely *spectancia*. This conjecture is strongly supported by the evidence of other statutes;[2] moreover, it helps to explain, as *pertinencia* will not, how the lacuna arose. The immediate succession of two words each beginning with *spec* (*specialiter spectancia* or vice versa) doubtless resulted in the loss of one through haplography. From the context it is fairly evident that the hiatus lies between *specialiter* and *in*. For reasons which will soon be appreciated the original text should be reconstructed as follows: 'ad eorum officia specialiter ⟨spectancia et⟩ in bedellos.'[3]

The presumption is that the scribe of Angelica 401 dropped *spectancia* and for good measure omitted *et* as well. It is worth remembering that the parchment was afterwards creased at this point and the possibility that the crease caused the loss of *et* cannot be excluded. Having examined the manuscript both before and after the attempt was made to remove the crease, I can definitely state that the scribe never wrote *et*. On the other hand, it is certain that he was not responsible for the omission of *spectancia*. The statute in question is recited in an official document, the decree of 1276 authorizing the rectors to summon the regents. The relevant part of the document, which is close enough in point of time to Angelica 401 and is much earlier than Markaunt, reads as follows: 'Tempora et modus legendi...ad ipsos pertineant. in trangressores [*sic*] circa predicta ad eorum officia specialiter et in bedellos.'[4] This quotation is significant in more ways than one. It would seem that

[1] Though *pertinentes* occurs in the Old Proctor–Caius redaction of Markaunt 15 (see below, p. 318, line 30), which is itself an adaptation of the decree of 17 March 1276 extending the powers of the rectors, the participle is only a variant of *spectantis*. Cf. Ullmann's edition of the decree, *Historical Journal*, i. 181, and Old Proctor 20 (fo. 20ᵛ), Caius 20 (fo. 3ᵛᵇ), *SA* 57 (*Docs*, i. 342).

[2] See the statutes quoted in the preceding note and also Markaunt 3 (see below, p. 314, line 23), 11 (see below, p. 317, line 2), *SA* 53 (*loc. cit.* 339).

[3] I am happy to find myself in agreement with Professor Ullmann, who restores the 1276 text in the same way.

[4] The full quotation as it appears in the original of the document (CUA, doc. no. 4) is printed on p. 226, n. 3 below. The scribe actually wrote *tn͡gᵉs̄sores* for *transgressores*. In Ullmann's edition the error is silently corrected and *circa* is given as *contra*.

the writer of the document had the Angelica manuscript before him, for although he avoided the mistake of rendering *circa* as *cerca* he, too, left *specialiter* hanging in mid-air and, what is still more remarkable, wrote *trangressores* for *transgressores*. It looks as if the exemplar in both cases was defective. The crucial difference between the two texts, however, is the presence of *et* before *in bedellos* in the 1276 quotation. At first sight it is a very minor divergence, but on reflection it proves that the author of the document did not work from Angelica 401. He could of course have added the particle in order to give a better reading. Yet if he was so intent on improving the text why did he not try to rectify the far more glaring defect, namely the absence of a predicate? It would be gratifying to be able to claim that he actually transcribed the passage from the Angelica manuscript, which would then rank as the official record of the statutes by 1276 and the exemplar from which all the later recensions descend, but we have to be honest. The clerk who executed the document did not use Angelica 401; it would be strange indeed if he did, because there is enough evidence from other sources to prove that the manuscript cannot be identified with the statute-book which existed by 1276.[1]

An interesting corollary follows from our analysis of the problematical passage. The scribe of Angelica was not guilty of corrupting the text, granted that he did drop the particle *et*, nor was he solely responsible for all the mechanical blunders that meet the eye. In the present instance his fault, if one can call it a fault, was a too slavish respect for his exemplar, which must have had *trangressores* for *transgressores* and also lacked *spectancia*. The manuscript from which the compiler of the 1276 document took the quotation contained precisely the same blunders.[2] The obvious inference is that Angelica 401 and the official manuscript of the statutes by 1276 go back to a common exemplar, the sub-parent manuscript of the original text.

XI. i: 'qui certum magistrum infra quindecim dies post ingressum uniuersitatis non habuerit.' Hugh Balsham cited this statute in 1276, but gave a somewhat different reading: 'qui certum Magistrum infra quindecim dies postquam vniuersitatem idem scolaris ingressus sit non habuerit'.[3] The Markaunt version is a sort of compromise

[1] See below, pp. 221–8.

[2] It may be assumed that the compiler inadvertently added the contraction mark—a horizontal stroke through the upper shafts of the *ss* in *trangressores*. Did he intend to write *trangressiones*?

[3] See below, p. 227.

between the two; it reads: 'qui certum Magistrum infra xv dies post eius ingressum in vniuersitatem non habuerit'. But the Angelica reading is supported by other statutory evidence and ought to be preferred.[1] Another passage in the same paragraph vindicates the reliability of Angelica, where *retineatur* is closer to the original than Balsham's 'uel deiciatur uel retineatur' or Markaunt's 'vel detinetur vel deiciatur'. There is reference here to the second of the writs issued by Henry III on 3 May 1231; the writ says nothing about the expulsion or banishment of scholars who omit to register with a master within fifteen days of their coming to the university. It merely decrees, as does the Angelica text, that they are to be imprisoned.[2]

XII. iii: 'a decennio et infra.' Markaunt 32 (see below, p. 327, line 11) and *SA* 67 (*Docs*, i. 350, l. 18) have *ultra* instead of *infra*. There is something to be said for the change, but it would be unwise to think that the scribe of Angelica departed from his exemplar. He could have been influenced by the memory of Matthew ii. 16: *a bimatu et infra*. It is unlikely that he was. The one mistake he did not make elsewhere was to confuse *ultra* and *infra*. Provided the meaning of *infra* in the context is grasped, the difficulty disappears. Further on in the same paragraph the writer has *eligerint* for *elegerint*. It is unnecessary to correct him here, and we may likewise allow *contingerit* (XIII. i) to stand, although it should be *contigerit*, which he correctly writes shortly afterwards. Such spellings and inconsistencies abound in medieval texts.[3]

XII. vi: 'ne plures aduersarios distringatur qui cum uno contraxit.' The subject is *hospes*. If a landlord lets a house to a principal who takes in fellow-scholars and damage is done to the property the principal is to be held personally responsible for the cost of repairs and so save the landlord the trouble of seeking compensation from the other occupants. The Latin requires some word like *contra* or *in* after *ne*. Presumably the scribe overlooked the preposition; and as the more likely victim was *in* owing to the scribe's haziness about the difference between an *e* and an *i* (cf. *circa* and *cerca* above), I have in company with Markaunt and the other codices adopted it.[4]

[1] Cf. Markaunt 22: *ingressus scole* (see below, p. 323, line 9); *SA* 30: *ab ingressu scholarum* (*Docs*, i. 326); *SA* 151: *a scholarum ingressu* (*ibid.* 389).

[2] See above, p. 72.

[3] Hence I have not standardized *in crastinum* (II. iii)...*in crastino*...*in crastinum* (III). These variations may well have been present in the exemplar.

[4] The scribe possibly had a blurred vision of *ne* as *ni* or *in* and omitted the preposition through haplography.

XII. vii: 'teneatur quasi tacite reconduxisse.' There is no verb governing the infinitive. The sense is that should a tenant remain on in a hired house after a fixed date he is assumed to have rehired it tacitly for the year ahead. It is not hard to guess the missing verb, *uideatur*, but how the scribe forgot to write it is another question. Perhaps the proximity of *teneatur* had something to do with it, the scribe's auditory-visual association of the two words causing him to commit a species of haplography.

XII. viii: 'secundum consuetudinem regionis.' Did not the Markaunt and later manuscripts contain *regni* as a variant of *regionis* one might allow the reading in Angelica 401 to pass without comment. Undoubtedly *regni* is the better word and is the almost natural complement to *consuetudo*.[1] Here it seems the *lectio difficilior* should be retained, not because it is the more plausible but because the scribe in this instance found it in his exemplar; he might have misread *regni*, not so *regionis*.

XIII. i: 'qui...fuerant largitores saltem in exitu numeracionis fiant expectatores.' The problem here is *numeracionis*. It must be a mistake, doubtless on the part of the scribe. In the exemplar the word probably consisted of five vertical strokes with a contraction mark overhead and a suspension mark after the final stroke, followed by *acionis*: *ıı̄ı̄ıı̄acionis*. The scribe took this to be *numeracionis*, whereas *memoracionis* is what he should have read. Though perhaps a little unusual, the word has the meaning of remembrance or recollection of a donor when death takes place.[2]

Ibid.: 'qui per presentem vniuersitatem...liberaliter decorauit.' Only for the presence of *per* the passage would read perfectly, *presentem* going with *vniuersitatem*; the two words, meaning the present or contemporary university, occur together also in II. iii. It is possible that the scribe elided *quippe qui*; hence we get *qui per*, the second *qui* being lost in the confusion. He was, apparently, quite oblivious of what happened; had he realized that *per* was an error he would have crossed it through as he did with *in extra* (II. vi) and *propter* (?) (XI. v). The emendation is, I must admit, somewhat contrived and must not be regarded as anything more than a conjecture; but it has some palaeographical and linguistic justification.

[1] Cf. *Med. Arch. Univ. Oxford*, i. 19. The text in Markaunt and the MSS is a revision. The redactor of recension α probably altered *regionis* to *regni*.

[2] Cf. *Novum glossarium mediae latinitatis*, fasc. 'meabilis–miles', ed. F. Blatt (Copenhagen, 1961), 355, 22–4; *Revised medieval Latin word-list*, ed. R. E. Latham (London, 1965), p. 295.

The foregoing are the most striking textual problems, some being more acute than others. From the *examinatio* the scribe emerges as the main culprit. The few corrections which he made on noticing his errors do not compensate for the many foolish mistakes which escaped his attention. Yet the most serious faults in the text appear to have had their origin elsewhere, either in the exemplar of Angelica 401 or in the parent manuscript. If more evidence like the decree of 1276 were available as a control, it is possible that the scribe would have to be acquitted of introducing many of the mechanical blunders which characterize the transcription.

Having studied the critical problem, we are now in a position to reconstruct the place of the Angelica manuscript in the *stemma codicum*. One thing is certain: Angelica 401 in contradistinction to the text does not come in the direct line of descent from the original.[1] In one way this is regrettable but not if one is more interested in the text than in the manuscript, granted that both are intimately related. From the point of view of the original text there are only three manuscripts to be considered. Their relationship need not detain us long. Angelica 401—to proceed from the known to the unknown—is not the parent manuscript of the Cambridge constitution. This much is evident from our examination of the textual problem, not to mention the fact that the original text was consigned to writing by *c.* 1250, which is certainly earlier than the date of our manuscript. It is also clear that Angelica was not derived immediately from the parent, but there is no valid reason for doubting that it was copied from an exemplar which was directly descended from the original. The relationship is therefore a very simple one:

Parent
|
exemplar
|
Angelica

As Angelica 401 was not written at more than one remove from the parent manuscript of the first constitution of the university, it is only a short step towards reconstructing the original text.

In editing the text the aim has been to reproduce as closely as possible the peculiar features of the manuscript, particularly since it is a *codex unicus*. Thus the scribe's use or neglect of capitals, his spelling (unless absolutely wrong) and his system of punctuation have been rigidly followed. Expansions are not indicated, apart

[1] See the *stemma codicum* on p. 306 below.

from the word *econuerso* (II. vi), which as written in the manuscript might be expanded with some justification as *econtro*. Manifest errors are relegated to the *apparatus*. Angular brackets are used to signify a conjectured restoration or correction, while a dagger indicates the existence of a hiatus or corruption which we would do well not to attempt to remedy. Chapter headings are printed in italics; they are rubricated in the manuscript. For the convenience of the reader and in order to make reference easier the chapters and paragraphs have been numbered in the margin. Upper-case roman numerals represent chapters, lower-case numerals paragraphs.

In the *apparatus* references to and readings from Markaunt and the *statuta antiqua* have been deliberately kept to a minimum. Apart altogether from reasons of economy it would be disastrous if these witnesses were seen to get between, as it were, the Angelica text and its parent. Their position in the edition itself is purely adventitious and any emendations, however useful, they exhibit must be regarded as nothing more than conjectural. Where these later texts enter the picture is in relation not to the original but to the subsequent history of Angelica and the various recensions it went through *c.* 1300–1500. Far from taking us closer to the original they in fact lead us further away.[1] Markaunt occupies a place apart and it has been touch and go whether to print its parallel statutes in the *apparatus*. The effect would be to distend grossly this part of the edition even if I confined myself to listing individual variants. In certain instances these are noted, but it is much better to have the full text. This I have given in an accompanying appendix and it is the first time that Markaunt has been printed *in extenso*. To facilitate comparison precise cross-references are added in the *apparatus* both to Angelica and Markaunt.[2] As regards the *statuta antiqua* the most that is required, pending the publication of a critical edition, are page and line references to the relevant statutes in the 1852 reprint.

The English translation does not purport to be a literal rendering of Angelica; one such version was prepared but was rejected as being too stilted. The lower margins of the English text have been utilized to supplement the *apparatus* to the Latin. There will be found general references to Markaunt and the *statuta antiqua* as well

[1] For example, they have *conuenienciam* for *conniuenciam* in I. iv, and *precipue* for *principiis* in VIII. iii. Both emendations are erroneous.

[2] The reader is reminded that chapter 9 of the present work is devoted to a comparative study within the limits available of Angelica and Markaunt. In chapter 10 the examination is extended to the archetype of the *statuta antiqua*.

as other information pertaining to the text. Some technical terms are very briefly explained, the reader being referred to the relevant pages, where these matters are discussed in some detail.

EDITORIAL NOTE

The roman numerals in bold type beginning the upper tier of footnotes on the Latin page refer to the chapter and paragraph numbers above. Both sets of bold arabic numerals in the footnotes refer to the line numbering on the Latin page. (See above, p. 194, for a fuller explanation of the critical *apparatus*.)

Chapter 7

THE CONSTITUTIONS OF THE UNIVERSITY OF CAMBRIDGE

I *The election of the chancellor and his powers*

i Since it is difficult for a university to agree by common consent and unanimous will, we enact that all the regents or a majority of them shall appoint a chancellor of their own choosing who has the knowledge, will and power to be as it were the superior of all.

ii Any chancellor, whilst he is in residence, may lighten his burden by commissioning on his own authority someone of good standing, provided he is a member of the university, to act for him temporarily in certain matters or all matters, unless the case be such that no delegation is required.

iii If the chancellor is absent or intends to be away for more than a short period, he may only appoint as his deputy for all matters someone approved by the regents or a majority of them after careful deliberation.

iv The chancellor or his deputy so appointed shall alone hear and decide, if he wishes, all suits of scholars, unless the atrocity of the offence or the disturbance of the public peace requires the concurrence of the masters.

v The chancellor must promptly execute the masters' sentences when they bring them to his notice.

---

2 *Quoniam...consentire:* cf. Paul: 'quia universi consentire non possunt' (*Dig.* 41, 2, 1 [*ad finem*]), and Michaud-Quantin's art. cited on p. 105, n. 2 above.

2–3 *communi...uoluntate*: this phrase is repeated in a slightly different form in a decree of the university dated 26 May 1291: 'concessimus de communi consensu et vnanimi voluntate' (above, p. 35, n. 1).

3–6 *statuimus...consencientibus*: cf. the text of the Oxford statute and the decree of the Fourth Lateran Council on elections, above, pp. 79, 107, n. 2.

3–4 *sciens uolens et potens*: this is probably a legal dictum.

4 *maior inter omnes*: cf. 'the mayor of a corporation'.

9 *uniuersitatem causarum*: another legal term identical in meaning with *universitas negotiorum*; see above, p. 113.

19 *conniuenciam*. Cf. Innocent IV (1253): 'sine conniventia sedis apostolice' (*Chart. Univ. Paris.* i. 247, no. 222); Alexander IV (1255): 'absque conniventia nostra' (*ibid.* 327, no. 284), etc. Both Markaunt 8 and *SA* 9 have *convenientiam*, which is an unfortunate correction; Angelica 401 has preserved the true reading.

20–1 Cf. VI (see below, p. 203, lines 18–23).

Chapter 7

CONSTITUCIONES VNIUERSITATIS CANTEBRIGIENSIS

[Biblioteca Angelica, Roma, MS 401, fos. $54^{r\,a}$–$55^{v\,b}$]

I *De eleccione Cancelarii atque ipsius potestate*

i Quoniam difficile est uniuersitatem consentire communi consensu et omni uoluntate, statuimus ut cancelarius sciens uolens et potens tanquam maior inter omnes omnibus per regentes preficiatur omnibus regentibus aut parte maiore in ipsum consencientibus.

ii Liceat ⟨cui⟩cumque cancellario ad ipsius exoneracionem dum sit presens alicui non suspecto dummodo fuerit de uniuersitate ad certas causas uel uniuersitatem causarum uices suas ad tempus suo iure committere nisi talis sit causa que sui natura delegacionem non requirit.

iii Cancelarius absens uel abfuturus ad tempus non modicum neminem habeat ad uniuersitatem causarum substitutum nisi in quem regentes uel maior pars eorum prouida deliberacione consenserint.

iv Cancelarius uel eiusdem dicto modo substitutus per se tantum si uoluerit, causas scolarium audiat vniuersas. et decidat nisi facti atrocitas uel publice quietis perturbacio magistrorum requirat conniuenciam.

v Magistrorum sentencias Cancelarius ad denunciacionem profe-rencium debita exequatur sceleritate.

I. i Cf. Markaunt 2 (see below, p. 313, lines 25–31); *SA* 4 (*Docs*, i. 309).
ii Markaunt 6, *De commissario Cancellarij* (see below, p. 315, lines 2–5); *SA* 8 (*loc. cit.* 311).
iii Markaunt 7, *De Vicecancellario* (see below, p. 315, lines 15–18); *SA* 8 (cit.).
iv Markaunt 8 (see below, p. 315, lines 20–3); *SA* 9 (*Docs*, i. 312).
v Cf. *SA* 13 (*loc. cit.* 314).

Tit. in rub. Vniuersitatis Cantebrigiensis *del., sed adhuc legi possunt* V...s (*ult.*); *totus titulus apparet sub luce speciali. Cf. etiam folia sequentia, ubi ad caput scribitur eadem manu qua textus* Constituciones Vniuersitatis Cantebrigiensis (54^{v}, 55^{r}) *vel* Constituciones Vniuersitatis cantebregiensis (55^{v}).
7 cuicumque: quocumque MS. *Vide supra, p.* 186.
17–20 si...Can- *macula.*
20 sentencias: -e(*pr.*)- *pergamena perforata est super lineam.*

vi The chancellor may not presume to make any new statutes without the consent of the regents: his aim must be to safeguard with all his powers the statutes enacted in common and set forth above and below.

II *The creation of masters and their office*

i No one may presume to act as regent unless he has already responded in all the schools of his faculty, and has first formally approached the chancellor with due respect and obtained his licence.

ii Regency is an honour which no one may take to himself; he must receive it from another regent or from someone who has ruled at one time in an approved university, unless he has already publicly received the honour in a university of equal standing and wishes to continue as regent in the customary way.

iii Let no one dare to incept for the first time who has not studied in this university for a period, unless his good character and learning are already well known here. On the day following the inception all the masters except the inceptor himself are to abstain altogether from lecturing, provided that they were at his banquet the previous day or could have been.

iv Each one at the time of his inception before he determines shall pledge faith, even if not required to do so under oath, that he will effectively maintain the statutes of the university and continue as

---

5 *Scolarium regimen* has the general meaning of 'teaching'. It is used here in the technical sense of lecturing and disputing at a university as regent master. Honorius III, writing to Paris in 1219, uses the phrase *regendi regimine* (*Chart. Univ. Paris.* i. 87, no. 29). See also above, p. 119, n. 3.

8–9 *Nemo...honorem regiminis sibi assumat.* Cf. Hebr. v. 4: *nec quisquam sumit sibi honorem.*

9 *rexerit*, i.e. has ruled or acted as regent.

12 *incipere*: to incept means to become master. The ceremony known as 'commencement' derives its name from the word *inceptio*, though there is a suggestion in the statutes that it may also derive from *commensatio* (cf. above, p. 126, n. 2), that is, the banquet to which reference is made in line 17. The older and more precise term *principium* occurs below in VIII. iii and XIII. i.

14 *uel* must here mean *et* (and), a meaning which it often has. See above, p. 124, n. 1.

18–20 *Quilibet...custodiendis*: Hugh Balsham in 1276 mentions that many masters, so he understands, commit perjury by violating one of the statutes (XI. i) to which each master 'antequam ad regimen admittatur...fide prestita firmare teneatur'. See above, p. 128, where it is pointed out that theologians were obliged to take a formal oath at Oxford and doubtless at Cambridge, too.

18 *determinet*: the new master 'determined' the question, that is gave his solution to the problem debated at his inception. It followed his taking of the oath (later oaths) and was the climax of the ceremony; cf. IV. See also Markaunt's text below, p. 313, lines 3–4, and above, pp. 129–30.

vi Cancelarius nichil noui sine consensu regencium statuere presumat. set supra et infra communiter statuta efficacius intendat custodire.

II *De creacione Magistrorum et eorum officio*

i Scolarium regimen nullus assumat nisi in singulis scolis sue facultatis antea responderit. et primitus a cancelario licenciam saltem postulauerit reuerenter et optinuerit.

ii Nemo a seipso set ab alio regente uel qui alias in abprobata rexerit uniuersitate honorem regiminis sibi assumat nisi sui regiminis excercicium modo consueto continuare uoluerit qui in consimili uniuersitate huiusmodi honorem publice assumpsit.

iii Non audeat quis de nouo incipere qui per [fo. $54^{r\,b}$] aliquod tempus in presenti uniuersitate non studuerit nisi ipsius conuersacio uel pericia publice nota habeatur ibidem omnibus magistris preter incipientem in crastinum incepcionis a leccionibus omnino cessantibus dummodo die precedente cum ipso fuerint in conuiuio uel esse poterint.

iv Quilibet ⟨tempore⟩ sue incepcionis antequam determinet fidem faciat iuramento eciam non exactam de statutis uniuersitatis efficaciter custodiendis. et de continuacione regiminis sui

---

vi Markaunt 4 (see below, p. 314, lines 28–30); *SA* 6 (*loc. cit.* 311).
II. ii Cf. *SA* 144 (*Docs*, i. 386 *ad fin.*).
iii *Ibid.*
iv Cf. *SA* 134 (*loc. cit.* 381).

---

10 excercicium: exercitum MS.
11 assumpsit: assupsit MS.
16 fuerint: fuerit MS. *Cf. SA* 144 (*Docs*, i. 386, *l. ult.*).
17 poterint: poterit MS.
18 tempore *supplevi. Cf. SA* 134 (*loc. cit.* 381, *l.* 9) *et supra p.* 186.
19 uniuersitatis: uniuersatis MS.
20 efficaciter: -ffi- *macula.*

regent here for at least one year, unless a necessary or reasonable cause excuses him.

v No one may presume to begin an ordinary lecture after the bell begins to ring the hour of prime, the canonists alone excepted, who shall not read *ordinarie* either before prime or after none.

vi No one may change an ordinary into an extraordinary lecture or vice versa, unless first permitted by the masters of his faculty.

vii Before terce has been rung, no logician or theologian may presume to dispute *ordinarie*.

viii No master or bachelor may read or dispute *extraordinarie* during the hours of ordinary lectures and disputations in his faculty.

III *The beginning and end of terms*

The masters shall begin their lectures on the day after St Denis (9 October) and resume them on the day after St Hilary (13 January), on the Wednesday [after] *Quasimodo geniti* and on the day after Trinity Sunday. They are to finish lectures on the day on which *O Sapientia* is sung (16 December), on the Friday before Palm Sunday, on the Friday before Whit Sunday, and also on the feast of St Margaret (20 July). On these stated days no disputation is to be

---

2 *causa...probabilis*: defined by *SA* 17 as a reason which a majority of the regents regard as 'causa justa et sufficienti absentiae proponentis' (*Docs*, i. 315).

3–8 *prime...nonam...terciam*: these hours of the day varied with the seasons and also locally. Speaking very generally, and excluding winter and Lent particularly, we may say that prime (the first hour) was 6 a.m., terce (the third hour) was 9 a.m. and none (the ninth hour) was 3 p.m. The rectors had the duty of regulating, as it were, the clock. Cf. VII. iv.

4–11 *ordinariam...ordinarie...extraordinariam...extraordinarie*: the meaning of these terms whether applied to lectures or disputations is much too complicated to be explained here. It is sufficient to note that ordinary lectures and *mutatis mutandis* disputations were formal exercises reserved to regent masters and were held in the morning; extraordinary lectures and disputations were, one might say, the opposite of ordinary; bachelors were qualified to lecture and dispute *extraordinarie*. But see above, pp. 133–5.

6–7 *Leccionem...conuertat*: cf. a Parisian decree of 1255: 'nulli liceat legere lectiones ordinarias plures duabus, nec eas extraordinarias facere' (*Chart. Univ. Paris.* i. 278, no. 246).

15 *hylarii*: the feast is now celebrated in the Roman rite on 14 January. In the oldest extant calendar of the university the day is 13 January. Cf. Old Proctor's Book, fo. 11r.

15–16 *quasimodo geniti*: the opening words of the introit of the Mass for the first Sunday after Easter Day.

17 *o sapiencia*: the first of the great O antiphons at vespers during the week before Christmas. In the Old Proctor calendar the day is 16 December (17 December in the Roman breviary) and opposite is written 'Hic cessabunt'.

18 *Margarete:* St Margaret of Antioch, virgin and martyr; not to be confused with St Margaret of Scotland, whose feast-day (8 July) is not marked in the university calendar.

ibidem ad minus per annum facienda ⟨nisi⟩ qu⟨od⟩ necessaria causa uel probabilis eum excuset.

v Non presumat quis ultra principium pulsacionis prime leccionem incipere ordinariam decretistis tantum exceptis qui nec ante primam nec post nonam legent ordinarie.

vi Leccionem ordinariam in extraordinariam uel econ*uer*so nullus conuertat nisi a magistris sue facultatis prius licenciatus.

vii Ante terciam pulsatam nullus logicus uel theologus ordinariam presumat facere disputacionem.

viii Magister uel bachilarius temporibus leccionum uel disputacionum ordinariarum sue facultatis extraordinarie non legat uel disputet.

III *De temporibus incipiendi et cessandi*

In crastino sancti dionisii magistri lecciones suas incipiant et easdem in crastino sancti hylarii. et die mercurii. quasimodo geniti. ac in crastinum sancte trinitatis reassumant ipsas die qua cantatur o sapiencia. et die ueneris ante ramos palmarum ac die ueneris ante pentecosten. necnon et in festo sancte Margarete

---

v–viii Cf. *SA* 151 (*Docs*, i. 389–90), where vi is replaced by what amounts to virtually a new statute.

III Cf. *SA* 150 (*ibid.* 388–9).

---

1 nisi *supplevi ex SA* 134 (*loc. cit. l.* 4). *Vide supra, pp.* 186–7.
quod: qui MS. *Cf. supra loc. cit.*
6 extraordinariam: in extra *add. sed del.* MS.
11 ordinariarum: -ar(*pr.*)- *suprascript.*
15 hylarii: hylari MS.
15–16 die...geniti: *cf. supra, p.* 185, *n.* 5.

held unless otherwise decreed with the masters' consent. They are not to give ordinary lectures or hold disputations on any account on the first Monday, Tuesday and Wednesday of Lent, the theologians alone excepted, who will not lecture or dispute *ordinarie* on the three following days.

IV *The holding of convocations*

All the regents when summoned by the chancellor must be present at every inception, and they are not to leave without permission until the inceptor has determined. Likewise, they are to assemble together, unless reasonably excused, to discuss in common matters affecting the general good of the university and public order. They are not to dispute on days when a general congregation is held.

V *The masters' dress*

Regents in theology, canon law and arts are to wear the *cappa clausa* or the *pallium* at ordinary lectures and disputations; and they are to go, properly dressed in this fashion, to inceptions and funerals.

VI *The court of the masters*

The regents are to hear all actions brought against their scholars and give judgement, on condition that they have asked for this or the defendants have alleged it, unless the rents of houses are concerned, or unless the enormity of the delict or the common peace requires the case to be heard by the chancellor or the masters, or unless the persons cited have expressly or tacitly declined the court of their master.

7–10 *Vniuersi...tractaturi*: cf. the corresponding Oxford statute quoted on p. 81, n. 3 above.

10 *communi utilitate*: cf. Innocent IV to Paris (1245): 'universitatem vestram monemus...quatinus ad generales congregationes, quas pro communi utilitate studii fieri contigerit, nisi legitimo fueritis impedimento detenti, accedere nullatenus omittatis' (*Chart. Univ. Paris.* i. 182, no. 144).

14–16 *In...incedentes*: this statute appears to be a conflation of two sources, *SAUO*, 56, 28–30, and canon 33 of the Council of Oxford (1222), quoted above, p. 80, n. 1.

14 *capis clausis uel palliis*: the *cappa clausa* (closed cope) was a flowing, sleeveless garment, reaching from the shoulders down to and covering the feet, with a small opening in front through which the hands could be pushed. The *pallium* (cloak) was identical, except that it had two slits, one for each hand. See also pp. 146–8.

21–2 *enormitas...audienciam*: cited almost *verbatim* in Markaunt 21 (see below, p. 322, lines 22–3); *SA* 29 (*Docs*, i. 325). Cf. also I. iv.

terminantes nullam disputacionem diebus supradictis faciendo nisi eorum consensu aliter statuatur diebus lune et martis et mercurii in capite ieiunii a leccionibus ordinariis et disputacionibus omnino cessantes, Theologis tantum exceptis qui tribus diebus sequentibus cessabunt.

IV *De conuocacionibus faciendis*

[fo. 54v a] Vniuersi regentes ad uocacionem cancelarii omnibus intersint incepcionibus non nisi licenciati inde recessuri quousque incipiens determinauerit nec⟨non⟩ simul omnes conueniant de communi utilitate et publica quiete communiter tractaturi quos absencia racionabilis non excusat diebus in quibus generalis fit congregacio non disputaturi.

V *De habitu Magistrorum*

In theologia decretis et artibus regentes capis clausis uel palliis in leccionibus et disputacionibus ordinariis utantur. in eodem habitu ad incepciones et exequias decenter incedentes.

VI *De curia magistrorum*

Regentes causas scolarium suorum ex parte rea existencium audiant et decidant vniuersas dummodo hoc postulauerint uel conuenti hoc idem allegauerint nisi de pensione domorum uel nisi enormitas delicti uel quies communis cancelarii uel magistrorum requirat audienciam uel conuenti expresse uel tacite foro magistri sui renunciauerint.

IV Cf. Markaunt 9 (see below, p. 315, line 25 to p. 316, line 3); *SA* 11 (*Docs*, i. 313).
V Cf. *SA* 147 (*Docs*, i. 387–8).
VI Cf. Markaunt 29 (see below, p. 325, lines 19–24); *SA* 36 (*loc. cit.* 328–9).

---

1 nullam: nullam nullam *ex ditto.* MS.
4 cessantes: cessantibus MS.
Theologis: Teologis MS.
exceptis: *spatium inter* -e(*alt.*)- *et* -p-; *perg. antea perforata erat.*
9 non *supplevi; cf. supra, p.* 187.
13 De: -e *macula.*
14 theologia: -og- *macula.*
18 causas: causis MS.

VII *The office of the rectors*

i Two rectors appointed by the chancellor and masters, and two burgesses, bound by oath, are to make an equitable assessment of houses, which is to be entered by them in a document of a public nature.

ii They must take great care that bread and wine and other things necessary for daily sustenance are sold at a fair price, according to seasonal changes and the qualities of the commodities, to scholars as to laypeople; and in all business transactions scholars and their servants are to be given preference over all other buyers.

iii They must keep careful watch on monopolists, that is, tradesmen who make private agreements or conspire to act together in withholding food and drink so that these are not generally sold to scholars below a certain price; and especially on bailiffs and their wives who trade in daily supplies of victuals during their term of office, most of all by holding back food and drink from the open market. The rectors must also be diligent in seeking out by themselves or through others those in the university who are evildoers, disobedient and contumacious. They are to send their names to the chancellor for severe punishment. The drink and victuals [are to be confiscated and scholars] forbidden to associate or do business with the offenders.

iv To them is entrusted the ordering of the times and manner of lecturing and disputing, services for the dead, inceptions and the observance of holy days. They enjoy coercive powers against those who transgress in these matters which specially pertain to their

---

1 *rectorum* (rectors): the earlier term for 'proctors'.

2–5 *Duo...eosdem*: cf. the parallel Parisian statute of 1231, p. 76, n. 4 above.

6–8 *alia...uendantur*: cf. the legatine ordinance of Cardinal Nicholas at Oxford in 1214, cited above, p. 156, n. 3.

11 *Monopolios*: the text suggests that these were 'regrators' rather than 'forestallers', though the terms are not mutually exclusive. See p. 156, n. 2.

13 *balliuos*: at Oxford these were the sub-bailiffs, who were permanent officials. The Angelica text (*durante officio*) seems to refer to the bailiffs properly so called, who were elected annually; they would, like the mayors and aldermen, be tradesmen by profession. See above, p. 156, n. 3.

14–20 *eorum...communionem*: an Oxford statute enacted by 1380 absolutely forbade any scholar 'cum eis [*sc.* laicis] aut eorum vxoribus aut seruientibus emendo vel vendendo quocumque colore communicare' (*SAUO*, 181, 9–11).

17–18 *contumaces*: a term which frequently occurs in the text. Technically it means those who refused to appear in court after repeated citations. Here it probably has the more generic meaning of incorrigible offenders.

22–(p. 207) 2 *Tempora...irroganda*: cf. the decree of 17 March 1276 cited from the original on p. 226, n. 3.

22 *Tempora...disputandi*: cf. Gregory IX to Paris (1231): '...de modo et hora legendi et disputandi' (*Chart. Univ. Paris.* i. 137, no. 79); see also *ibid.* 597, no. 501.

VII *De officio rectorum.*

i Duo rectores per cancelarium et magistros deputati una cum duobus burgensibus iuramento astricti congruam domorum faciant taxacionem in publicam scripturam redigendam per eosdem.

ii Diligenter curent ut panis et uinum et alia uictui cotidiano necessaria secundum uarietates temporum et rerum qualitates iusto precio non secus scolaribus quam laicis uendantur scolaribus et eorum seruientibus omnibus aliis negociacionis causa emptoribus semper preferendis.

iii Monopolios id est uenditores inter se pasciscentes uel ad inuicem colludentes de esu et potu non nisi certo precio ut scolaribus uendantur communiter detrahendis et precipue balliuos et eorum uxores et huiusmodi mercimonia ad uictum cottidianum pertinencia durante officio excercentes et maxime cibum et potum contra communem prouisionem detrahentes necnon et in vniuersitate male[fo. 54$^{v\,b}$]factores inobedientes et contumaces per se et per alios diligenter inuestigent ut eorum nomina referant cancelario grauiter puniendorum ipsis potibus et cibariis † cum ipsis transgressoribus communionem habere uel mercimonium omnino inhibendis.

iv Tempora et modus legendi et disputandi et exequias celebrandi et incipiendi et feriarum obseruancie ad ipsos pertineant in transgressores circa predicta ad eorum officia specialiter ⟨spectancia et⟩ in bedellos. si mandatis eorum non paruerint coher-

VII. i Cf. Markaunt 17 (see below, p. 320, lines 13–15); *SA* 66 (*loc. cit.* 349).
ii–iii Cf. Markaunt 13 (see below, p. 317, line 36 to p. 318 line 13); *SA* 54 (*Docs*, i. 340).
iv Cf. Markaunt 13 (see below, p. 317, lines 27–31); *SA* 54 (*Docs*, i. 340).

14 cottidianum: *spatium ante* pertinencia; *perg. perforata est infra lineam.*
19 referant *corr. ex* referent MS.
cancelario *corr. ex* cancellario MS.
20 *Fortasse leg.* cibariis ⟨confiscandis et scolaribus⟩ cum ipsis *e.q.s.; cf. supra, pp.* 187–8.
21 inhibendis *corr. ex* inihibendis MS.
24 transgressores: trangressores MS.
circa: cerca MS.
24–5 spectancia et *supplevi. Vide pp.* 188–9.
25 paruerint: pariunt MS.

office and against the bedells if they disobey their orders. Nevertheless, it is for the chancellor and masters to inflict the direst punishment should this be necessary.

VIII *The offices and privileges of the bedells and apparitors*

i There shall be only two bedells or apparitors, bound by oath, of whom one shall be responsible for seating and everything else in the schools of theology and canon law, the other in all the other schools. They must be always ready to carry out the chancellor's orders. When the chancellor and masters hear legal actions they must at their command announce the sittings, serve citations and execute the decrees. They are to receive nothing from poor scholars by way of bargain in return for such services. Neither of them may have a substitute or a companion or even a pedagogue, except by special permission of the chancellor.

ii Each day they must go into every school at a time when lectures and disputations are in progress. The bedell of the canonists and theologians will ring the bell at the proper and customary hours for their first disputation. On no account is he to ring too soon or too late to oblige one person or to do a disservice to another.

iii They must also be present, carrying their staffs, at all vespers, *principia*, assemblies, funerals and all other convocations. They are not on any account to leave before the departure of the masters. No one else is to carry a staff to their prejudice. If, however, they are discovered to be negligent or remiss in these and other matters

---

1–2 *animaduersione...irroganda*: the gravest penalties—expulsion or imprisonment—could be imposed only by convocation, i.e. the chancellor acting in concert with the regent masters.

6 *omnium aliarum* [sc. *scholarum*]: these were the arts schools; the faculties of medicine and civil law had not yet been established.

9–10: *citaciones...recepturi*: cf. *SAUO*, 69, 16–17: 'citaciones pro quolibet scolare liberaliter faciant [bedelli], nichil exigentes ab eo.'

11 *pedagogum*: a peculiar word in the context, which does not suit 'teacher', 'instructor' or 'guide'. Some word like attendant, servant or usher must be understood: is *pedagogus* a mistake for *pedisequus*? At Oxford the bedells were allowed to have assistants if the university considered them necessary. Cf. *SAUO*, 68, 12–13.

15 *primam...disputacionem*: the phrase is not free from ambiguity. It probably refers to the first disputation held by a newly created master after his inception; or it may mean that the bedell was to ring the bell for the first disputation when two disputations took place one after the other.

18–21 *Intersint...delaturo*: this statute is quoted in Bishop Balsham's ordinance of 1276. See below, p. 227.

18 *uesperis et principiis*: the two component parts of an inception ceremony; the former took place on the eve of the commencement, while *principium* was the original name of the actual ceremony of inception.

cione concessa eisdem animaduersione grauissima per cancelarium et magistros. si opus fuerit nichilominus irroganda.

VIII *De officiis bedellorum et apparitorum et eorum honoribus*

i Duo tantum bedelli seu apparitores iuramento astricti habeantur quorum alter scolarum theologie et decretorum alter autem omnium aliarum onera circa sedes et alia subeat vniuersa semper parati mandata cancelarii adimplere. De precepto cancelarii et magistrorum de causis cognoscencium conuocaciones citaciones et execuciones faciant vniuersas nichil inde a pauperibus conuencione recepturi. Neuter eorum habeat substitutum comitem uel eciam pedagogum nisi de licencia cancelarii speciali.

ii Ingrediantur singulis diebus scolas singulas aliqua hora leccionum et disputacionum bedello decretistarum et theologorum horis debitis et consuetis primam ad eorum disputacionem pulsaturo. tempora in vnius fauorem uel alterius preiudicium nullatenus anticipando uel eciam prorogando.

iii Intersint eciam uirgam deferentes omnibus uesperis et principiis conuentibus defunctorum exequiis et omnibus aliis conuocacionibus ante recessum magistrorum nullatenus recessuri nullo alio in eorum preiudicium uirgam delaturo si uero negligentes uel remissi circa premissa et alia ad eorum officia pertinencia

---

VIII. i Markaunt 19 (see below, p. 320, line 32 to p. 321, line 6); *SA* 72 (*loc. cit.* 353–4).
ii–iii Markaunt 19 (see below, p. 321, lines 8–22); *SA* 72 (*loc. cit.* 354).

---

4 Duo: D- *macula.*
8 cancelarii *corr. ex* cancellarii MS.
9 citaciones: -a- *perforatio infra lineam.*
10 conuencione: couencione MS.
recepturi: -u- *perforatio super lineam.*
15 pulsaturo: pulsaturis MS.
20 nullatenus: ullatenus MS.

pertaining to their office, the common collection in the schools must be absolutely denied to them; and they are to be removed from office, either permanently or temporarily, and replaced by others who are suitable, should the character of the offence or their negligence require their removal.

IX *Litigants' sureties, and their oath*

Litigants, apart from those in the university who own real estate and have not been under suspicion before, will not be heard unless first the plaintiff gives security either in the form of a pledge or by a suitable surety that he will proceed with his action to the end, and the defendant gives surety simply that he will offer legal defence. Should sureties be impossible to obtain, then their oath will be accepted, unless the enormity of the deed calls for imprisonment or other physical custody, according to the king's privilege.

X *The order to be observed at scholars' suits*

i At judicial processes both the plaintiff and the defendant, without respect of persons, even if not asked to take the oath of calumny, must none the less personally take a corporal oath to tell the truth and not to conceal falsehood.

ii The formalities of law are on no account to be observed at the hearing of actions, but edicts, pleas and essential proofs, without

---

1–4 *communis...postulauerit*: cf. Markaunt 18 (see below, p. 320, lines 28–30); *SA* 71 (*Docs*, i. 353).

6–12 *Litigatores...libertatem*: this statute is not found in Markaunt nor among the *statuta antiqua*.

6–7 *inmobilium*: i.e. lands or tenements.

7–9 *pignore...satisdederit*: cf. Tancred, cited above, p. 164, n. 3.

12 *regis libertatem*: the privilege of having clerks detained in the king's prison at the discretion of the university was conceded by the first of four writs dated 3 May 1231. Cf. *Close rolls, 1227–31*, p. 586.

14–15 *sine...personarum*: 1 Pet. i. 17 *sine acceptione personarum.*

14–16 *In...corporale*: cf. Tancred, quoted on p. 98, above.

15–16 *calumpnia...corporale*: in taking the oath of calumny or malice the plaintiff swore that he was acting in good faith and without deceit; the defendant swore he would respond or answer the charge in like manner. The oath of truth and *de falsitate subticenda* were taken together, both parties swearing that they would answer the judge truthfully and not give false evidence or proof, and would not seek an adjournment in order to escape.

16 *iuramentum...corporale*: a corporal oath was one taken on the gospels.

17–(p. 211) 2 *In...recipiantur*: Markaunt 27 and *SA* 34 present a much revised version of this statute.

17 *solempnitas*, sc. *iuris.*

18 *ediciones*: the edicts had to do with citations. *contestaciones*: the entering by the defendant of a plea of guilty or not guilty was known as *litis contestatio.*

deprehendantur [fo. 55ra] communis collecta omnino in scolis denegetur eisdem. uel ab officio perpetuo uel ad tempus ammoueantur. et alii ydonei in locum ipsorum substituantur. si delicti qualitas uel negligencia remocionem postulauerit.

IX *De satisdacione litigancium et eorum iuramento*

Litigatores non audiantur exceptis in uniuersitate rerum inmobilium possessoribus et alias non suspectis nisi prius pignore dato uel fideiussore ydoneo actor de iure suo prosequendo usque in finem. et reus simpliciter iure sistendo satisdederit nisi sibi inpossibilis fuerit satisdacio. tunc enim eorum iuramento credatur nisi facti atrocitas incarceracionem uel aliam corporum custodiam postulauerit iuxta regis libertatem.

X *De ordine iudiciorum in causis scolarium custodiendo*

i In processibus causarum tam actor quam reus sine accepcione personarum etsi non de calumpnia de ueritate tamen dicenda et falsitate subticenda iuramentum prestent corporale.

ii In examinacione causarum solempnitas nequaquam obseruetur excepto quod eciam sine scriptis ediciones contestaciones et

---

X. i Cf. Markaunt 28 (see below, p. 325, lines 15–17); *SA* 35 (*Docs*, i. 328).
ii Cf. Markaunt 27 (see below, p. 325, lines 10 to 13); *SA* 34 (*Docs*, i. 328).

---

6 Litigatores *corr. ex* Litaigatores MS.
11 aliam: -a(*alt.*)- *denuo suprascript. quia atramentum fluxit.*
13 *scolarium*: constit' *add. sed del.* MS.
16 subticenda: substicenda MS.
17 In *in marg. librarius tit. cap. prox. errore scripsit.*
nequaquam: -q(*pr.*)- *perg. super lineam perfor., ideoque* -a(*pr.*)- *suprascript. evanuit.*
18 excepto: excepti MS.
ediciones *corr. ex* edicionis MS; *hic etiam perg. def.*

which no sentence can be reached, must definitely be admitted, even if not in writing.

XI *The immunity of scholars and the penalty for delinquents*

i We judge it unworthy for anyone to defend a scholar who a fortnight after his entry into the university still has no particular master, or who has not troubled to have his name entered on his master's roll within the stated time, unless this has been prevented by the master's absence or a genuine engagement. Indeed if anyone is found passing himself off as a scholar in this way, he is to be detained in accordance with the king's privilege.

ii Only those scholars enjoy immunity who attend the schools of their master at least three days in the week and hear not less than three lectures, provided that the master himself lectures on three days of the week, unless they have their master's permission or a reasonable cause for absence.

iii A scholar coming here who is known by letters of the chancellor of Oxford or in any other legitimate way to have been expelled from the university of Oxford as an evildoer is never to be admitted.

iv Burglars, assaulters of women, footpads, those carrying weapons, especially at night, to injure others or take revenge, and also those who have cited a clerk or layman of the town of Cambridge to a court outside the town, under the clauses *quidam alii* and *rebus aliis*, and are convicted of this, even if no one has lodged a complaint,

---

4–6 *Indignum...habuerit*: cf. Courson's statute for Paris (1215): 'Nullus sit scolaris Parisius qui certum magistrum non habeat' (*Chart. Univ. Paris.* i. 79, no. 20).

4–10 *Indignum...libertatem*: Hugh Balsham quotes this paragraph in his decree of 1276. See below, p. 227.

4–13 *Indignum...audituri*: for parallel passages in the statutes of Paris and Orléans, see above, pp. 74, n. 1, 167, n. 5.

10 *regis libertatem*: cf. the writ of 3 May 1231, quoted above, p. 72.

11–12 *Hii...ingrediantur*: cf. the Orléans statute quoted on p. 74, n. 1 above. At this point Markaunt 35 and *SA* 42 introduce a large accretion.

11 *inmunitate*: the privilege of immunity or exemption from military service and other civic duties, as well as from charges or taxes levied on citizens. But see p. 166 above.

19–21 *Effractores...defferentes*: cf. parallel texts from the statutes of Paris and Orléans, printed on p. 89 above.

20–(p. 213) 2 *arma...detrudantur*: cf. *SAUO*, 81, 20–3, quoted on p. 82 above.

21 *clericum et*: here *et* must mean *vel* (or).

22 *quidam alii et rebus aliis*: the general terms under which papal letters of delegation were issued. See above, pp. 26–8, 96–8.

debite probaciones sine quibus ad sentenciam non peruenitur omnino recipiantur

XI *De inmunitate scolarium et pena delinquencium*

i Indignum esse iudicamus ut quis scolarem tueatur qui certum magistrum infra quindecim dies post ingressum uniuersitatis non habuerit aut nomen suum infra tempus prelibatum in matricula sui magistri redigi non curauerit nisi magistri absencia uel iusta occupacio illud impediat. Immo si quis talis sub nomine scolaris latitans inueniatur retineatur iuxta domini regis libertatem.

ii Hii soli scolares gaudeant inmunitate qui saltem per tres dies in septimana scolas magistri sui ingrediantur tres lecciones ad minus audituri dummodo per tres dies in septimana magister per se legerit. nisi magistri sui licencia [fo. 55$^{r\,b}$] uel causa racionabilis ipsorum abscnciam cxcusaucrit.

iii Aduenticius malefactor nunquam recipiatur quem per litteras cancelarii oxonie uel alio legitimo modo ab uniuersitate oxonie constiterit fuisse eiectum.

iv Effractores domorum raptores mulierum Insidiatores uiarum. arma ad nocendum uel ad uindictam precipue de nocte deffe-rentes. necnon et qui clericum et laycum de uilla cantebrigie extra uillam per clausas illas quidam alii et rebus aliis conuenerint eciam nemine deferente super hoc conuicti propter quietem

---

XI. i–ii Markaunt 35 (see below, p. 330, lines 2–8, 16–20); *SA* 42 (*Docs*, i. 332–5).
iii–iv Cf. Markaunt 37 (see below, p. 331, lines 9–18); *SA* 45 (*Docs*, i. 334–5).

---

1 sentenciam: -e(*pr.*)- *quasi oblit., necnon memb. partim dep.*
3 *inmunitate*: *inmunitat* MS.
scolarium: *scolarum* MS.
4 iudicamus: uideamus (*vel fortasse* iudeamus) MS.
5 post ingressum uniuersitatis: *vide supra, pp.* 190–1.
7 absencia *corr. ex.* absenlcia MS.
9 latitans: latitante MS; sic latitare (compertus fuerit) *Markaunt* 35 (*vide infra, p.* 330, *ll.* 6–7), *SA* 42 (*loc. cit. ll.* 6–7). *Vide etiam infra, p.* 227.
inueniatur: inueneniatur MS; compertus fuerit *Markaunt et SA* (*locc. citt.*).
16 Aduenticius (-tic- *quasi oblit.*): et *add.* MS.

shall be sent down by the chancellor and the masters from the university without hope of readmittance, for the sake of the public peace, or they may be imprisoned under the terms of the abovementioned writ. Persistent offenders are to be more severely punished, unless they show repentance which justifies different treatment. Confiscated weapons are to be sold without question for the good of the poor or of the chancellor.

v Those who conspire against the chancellor's prohibition, and those who are otherwise disobedient to him or contumacious, are to be similarly punished, without respect of persons, if this is merited by the insolence of those who scorn lawful authority.

XII *Hostels and rents of houses*

i On three fixed dates, namely, All Saints Day (1 November), the Purification of the Blessed Virgin Mary (2 February) and Ascension Day, one third of the rents of houses is to be paid absolutely or the landlords are to be suitably compensated.

ii No one, under pain of excommunication, is to leave the town, whether he has finished his studies or not, without first making proper payment of his rent and other debts contracted there. If he has not done this his caution may be lawfully distrained on the agreed date by his creditors, and the one who stood security or promised payment for him may be required to make good the guarantee there and then, or at the discretion of the creditors. Anyone so absconding is to be denounced to his diocesan bishop by the chancellor as excommunicated, until the creditors have been fully reimbursed. If necessary, the time for making payment can be extended by the chancellor in cases where the creditors show impatience.

iii No one may rent houses as living-quarters or put them to any other use, if they have been used as schools for ten years or more, as long

---

3 *formam supradictam*: i.e. the writ of 1231, referred to in XI, i.

5–6 *in...conuertendis*: cf. p. 256. In Markaunt 37 and *SA* 45 it is replaced by another passage ('Liceat...dispensare').

8 *sine...personarum*: 1 Pet. i. 17 (cf. p. 209, lines 13–14).

11–14 *Tribus...eisdem*: for a somewhat similar statute of Padua, see above, p. 95.

18 *pignus*: the pledge, as the text clearly implies, might be either a *cautio pignoraticia* (a book or some valuable) or a *cautio fideiussoria* (a surety; two were required at Cambridge according to CUL, MS Mm. 4. 41; cf. below, p. 238, n. 4).

19 *expromissor*: there is probably a distinction here between the one who goes surety for the rent (*fideiussor*) and the one (it might of course be the same person) who makes himself legally responsible for other debts (*expromissor*).

23 *inprobitatem*, literally 'badness'.

25 *infra*, i.e. not less (than ten years back) (Professor Bieler's communication).

publicam per cancellarium et magistros ab uniuersitate sine spe restitucionis deiciantur uel in carcerem detrudantur iuxta formam supradictam grauius cohercendi si hoc meruerit pertinacia delinquencium nisi eorum penitencia aliud persuadeat armis ipsis in utilitatem pauperum uel cancelarii omnino conuertendis.

v Contra prohibicionem cancellarii colluctantes et alias sibi inobedientes et contumaces sine differencia personarum simili pena coherceantur si hoc meruerit proteruitas contumacium.

XII *De hospiciis et pensionibus domorum.*

i Tribus terminis id est diebus omnium sanctorum. purificacionis beate marie uirginis. et ascensionis domini, pensiones domorum in tres partes equaliter diuidende omnino exsoluantur uel congrua hospitibus satisfactio prestetur de eisdem.

ii Sub pena excommunicacionis tempore studii completo. uel eciam antea uillam nullus egrediatur nisi prius de pensione domorum et aliis debitis ibidem contractis congrue satisfecerit. et si contra fiat pignus datum pro eodem a creditoribus tempore conuento licite distrahatur et fideiussor seu expromissor absque ulla dilacione uel arbitrio creditorum exigatur sic recedens per cancelarium suo deocesano excommunicatus denuncietur donec plenarie creditoribus fuerit satisfactum tempore solucionis faciende propter inprobitatem creditorum per cancellarium si opus fuerit moderando.

[fo. 55[v a]]

iii Domos in quibus scole esse consueuerunt a decennio et infra nullus ad inhabitandum conducat seu ad alium usum conuertat

---

v Cf. Markaunt 25 (see below, p. 324, lines 22–5); *SA* 10 (*Docs*, i. 313).

XII. i–viii Cf. Markaunt 32 (see below, p. 326, line 28 to p. 328, line 8); *SA* 67 (*loc. cit.* 350–1).

---

7 alias: alios MS.

9 meruerit: propter (?) *add. sed del.* MS.

19 expromissor: expremissor MS.

25 infra: *vide supra, p.* 191.

as the regents, according to their number at the beginning of the year, or those at the start of any term who are about to incept have chosen them for schools, unless the owners themselves have been living there through genuine necessity.

iv The owners of buildings may receive nothing more, even by agreement, than the rent fixed under oath, nor must the tenants pay anything in excess of this. Should the chancellor so decide, the premises may be prohibited as places of residence for scholars, and the extra rent received is to be handed back to the tenant if he so desires.

v He who rents a house as principal shall have the sole right of living there during the following year, provided that he has actually guaranteed in advance the year's rent before the Nativity of the Blessed Virgin (8 September) to the landlord or to the chancellor if the landlord cannot be found. Otherwise, the landlord is free to dispose of his house after this date; and any transfer of tenancy promised by the principal to another wholly lapses.

vi Item, only the principal shall pay the entire annual rent to the landlord and be solely responsible for damages which may happen through his fault or that of his fellows, so that the landlord, having made a contract with one man, has not to take action against a number of adversaries.

vii Anyone who has stayed on in a rented house after the Nativity of the Blessed Virgin shall be bound to pay the rent for the whole of the following year, as he would seem to have tacitly rehired it, unless the landlord has clearly granted him free lodging.

viii Feudal lords may lawfully distrain their fees according to the custom

---

2 *incepturi...eligerint*: it has been difficult to render this passage without giving the impression that inceptions took place at the beginning of terms. There was nothing laid down about this. See above, p. 126. What the text means is that a scholar due to incept as master in a given term had to choose or hire a school at the beginning of that term, so that he would be in a position to commence lecturing immediately after graduation.

5 *pensionem...taxatam*: i.e. the rent fixed by the two rectors (later the taxors) and two burgesses, as in VII. i.

10 *principaliter*: a master or bachelor who rented a house and shared it with other scholars was known as the principal; as such he was answerable to the university for their conduct, and was responsible for damages caused to the property by himself or his fellow-tenants, as the text goes on to state.

10–13 *ius...effectu*: cf. the very similar custom at Oxford quoted on p. 78 above.

15–16 *cessione...cessante*: for a sidelight on this practice see below, p. 239, n. 3.

21–3 *Qui...uideatur*; cf. Ulpian: 'Qui impleto tempore conductionis remansit in conductione, non solum reconduxisse videbitur, sed etiam pignora videntur durare obligata...taciturnitate utriusque partis colonum reconduxisse videri' (*Dig.* 19, 2, 13, 11).

15–(p. 217) 1: *Liceat...perpetuis*: lands or tenements held in fee were subject to feudal

quamdiu regentes iuxta numerum eorundem in principio anni uel incepturi in iniciis terminorum scolas sibi eligerint in eisdem nisi domini earundem de necessario sine fraude personaliter ibidem inhabitauerint.

iv Edifficiorum proprietarii ultra pensionem iuramento taxatam eciam ex conuencione nichil recipiant nec eciam inquilini ultra eandem aliquid exsoluant edifficiis ipsis arbitrio cancelarii a scolarium inhabitacione suspendendis ac recepcione eius quod excedit soluenti nichilominus concessa si uoluerit.

v Qui domum principaliter conduxerit ius inhabitandi in anno sequenti solus habebit. dummodo hospiti uel cancelario si hospes non inueniatur de sequentis anni pensione ante natiuitatem beate uirginis satisfaccionem obtulerit cum effectu. alias autem hospes de sua domo libere disponat ultra terminum prelibatum cessione ab ipso principali alteri facienda omnino cessante.

vi Item principalis de pensione tocius anni hospiti solus satisfaciat et de dampnis culpa sui et suorum sociorum contingentibus solus respondeat ne ⟨in⟩ plures aduersarios distringatur qui cum uno contraxit.

vii Qui ultra natiuitatem beate uirginis in domo remansit conducta ad pensionem tocius anni sequentis teneatur quasi tacite reconduxisse ⟨uideatur⟩ nisi dominus palam gratuitam sibi concesserit inhabitacionem.

viii Liceat quoque dominis feodorum feoda eorum distringere secundum consuetudinem regionis non pro pensione conuenta

---

1 quamdiu: quam duo MS.
2 uel: uel' MS.
3 earundem: eorundem MS.
6 ex conuencione: -x c(*pr.*)- *macula atque perforatio; hodie reparatione codicis peracta litt.* x, c *vix legi possunt.*
8 scolarium: scolar īū MS.
12 inueniatur *corr. ex* inuenniatur MS.
15 cessione: cessionem MS.
19 solus respondeat: -u-, r—p *partim oblit. in plicatura praeterita.*
in *supplevi ex Markaunt* 32 (*vide infra, p.* 327, *l.* 39); *cf. SA* 67 (*Docs,* i. 351, *l.* 24). *Vide supra, p.* 191.
23 uideatur *suppl. ex Markaunt* 32 (*vide infra, p.* 328, *l.* 2); *cf. SA* 67 (*loc. cit. l.* 28). *Vide supra p.* 192.
26 regionis MS: regni Markaunt 32 (*vide infra, p.* 328, *l.* 4), *SA* 67 (*loc. cit. l.* 30) (*in utroque* regni *ante* consuetudinem). *Vide iterum supra, p.* 192.

of the country, not for an agreed temporary rent but for perpetual services, even if a master has lectured there or a scholar has been occupant. In this case the chancellor may at his discretion reduce the rent payable to the landlord, in proportion to the length of time, and even grant the tenants the difference.

XIII *The exequies of the dead*

i Since it is congruent with natural reason that those who whilst they lived were in actual fact most generous in granting privileges should at least expect a thought at death, when the illustrious king of England comes to die, inasmuch as he liberally endowed the present university with privileges concerning the assessment of houses, the purchase of daily food supplies, the imprisonment or direction of criminals and the undisciplined, and also with regard to many other things, or if the venerable father in God, the bishop of Ely, who in various ways honoured the scholars and especially the regents at their *principia*, happens to die, all the scholars shall assemble both in the evening and in the morning to perform his obsequies with proper reverence.

ii The chancellor shall assemble with the regents for all obsequies of deceased regents, and they are to recite their psalters throughout the night. Lectures and disputations are to be entirely suspended from the time of death until the body is given ecclesiastical burial.

iii The chancellor and regents shall attend the funerals of scholars, non-regent masters and bedells. On no account are they to leave before the interment has taken place. Disputations are to be entirely omitted on the day of burial, except only in the case of those who teach nothing but grammar, whose obsequies the persons mentioned above need not attend except out of piety.

---

charges payable to the original owner or overlord. He was entitled to recover these dues by distraining the tenant's chattels if he failed to pay the charges, which were known as 'rent charges'. This terminology can be confusing because the 'temporary' rent (the rent charge was perpetual) which the tenant paid to his landlord was known as 'rent service'.

3–4 *interesse...prestando*: the text does not make clear to whom the difference was to be paid. Markaunt 32 and *SA* 67 explicitly state that the tenant, i.e. master or scholar, was to be refunded, which is what one would expect.

9 *rege anglie*: Henry III (1216–72).

9–13 *qui...decorauit*: cf. above, pp. 25–6, 36–7.

13–14 *patre...elyensi*: Hugh of Northwold (1229–54).

14 *principiis*: see p. 206, ad 18.

21 *scolarium non regencium*: 'scolarium' and 'non regencium' are to be taken separately; cf. below, p. 281.

24 *qui...gramaticam*: i.e. the teachers at the local grammar schools, whose head was familiarly known as the master of glomery.

temporali set pro seruiciis perpetuis eciam si magister ibidem legerit uel scolaris inhabitauerit pensione arbitrio cancelarii propter hoc pro rata temporis diminuenda et interesse sibi nichilominus prestando.

XIII *De exequiis defunctorum*

i Quoniam naturali congruit racioni ut qui superstites liberalitatum eciam actualiter [fo. $55^{v\,b}$] fuerant largitores saltem in exitu memoracionis fiant expectatores cum aliquid humanitus de illustri rege anglie contingerit qui⟨p⟩pe ⟨qui⟩ presentem vniuersitatem circa taxacionem domorum uictus cotidiani comparacionem malefactorum et inobediencium incarceracionem seu direccionem et eciam circa alia multa libertatibus liberaliter decorauit seu eciam de uenerabili patre contigerit elyensi qui scolares et precipue regentes in eorum principiis multipliciter honorauit tam in sero quam in mane scolares conueniant vniuersi ipsius exequias congrua celebraturi deuocione.

ii Ad exequias regencium decedencium vniuersas cancelarius conueniat cum regentibus psalteria sua per totam noctem dicturis leccionibus et disputacionibus a tempore mortis donec corpus ecclesiastice traditum fuerit sepulture omnino cessantibus.

iii Ad exequias scolarium non regencium et bedellorum cancelarius ueniat et rege[n]tes ante corporum sepulturam nullatenus recessuri d[ie] sepulture disputacionibus omnino caritura illis t[antummodo] exceptis qui artem solam docent gramaticam ad quorum exequias nisi ex deuocione non conueniant supradicti.

XIII. ii–iii Cf. *SA* 178 (*Docs*, i. 403–4).

---

8 memoracionis: numeracionis MS; *vide supra, p.* 192.

9 quippe qui: qui per MS; *vide supra loc. cit.*

11 inobediencium: -nc- *macula.*

14 precipue: -ip- *perforatio; atramentum quasi def.*

15 multipliciter: *atra. paene def.*

22–4 (u)eniat...ar(tem) *macula; textus est graviter mutilatus ob veterem plicaturam et perforationes; quaedam litterae iamdudum quasi deperditae penitus evanuerunt cum codex instauraretur.*

22 regentes: -n- *litt. amissa in perforatione.*

23 die: -ie *atramentum evanuit.*

sepulture: se- *quasi oblit.*

disputacionibus: -pu- *perforatio super lineam.*

24 (t)antummodo: *antea mutil. ex perfor. et nunc omnino deperd.*

docent: -c- *atramentum def.*

gramaticam: g—m (*pr.*) *partim deformat.*

25 *Post* supradicti *add. manu crassiore saec. xv* Ihesus est amor meus.

PART III

HISTORY OF THE TEXT

Chapter 8

THE GROWTH OF THE TEXT

(*c.* 1250–1300)

It will not be out of place to remind ourselves that the Angelica manuscript, invaluable as it is, does not occupy a key role in the history of the transmission of the Cambridge statutes after the middle of the thirteenth century. It was a private copy, an unofficial record; as such it had no successor. Hence when we speak of the Angelica text it must always be understood, unless reference is made to the actual manuscript, that the critically restored text or the original constitution of the university is meant.

When Angelica 401 was executed certain developments were taking place—indeed one had taken place—which affected the organization of the university. These changes are not shown in the manuscript for the very good reason that it was copied from an unrevised exemplar of the parent manuscript. Thus the establishment of the faculty of civil law is not reflected in Angelica 401. One would naturally expect that such a major development would have entailed some rewriting of the constitution, but not every change was immediately incorporated in university statutes.[1] It is more likely that the first revision of the original text was carried out rather later, *c.* 1255–68, following successive grants of privilege to the university as regards the assize of bread and ale—a coveted concession.[2] In the normal course of events the rectors or proctors

[1] The traditional respect for the *littera scripta* possibly explains why the text of Angelica V was never altered. The statute (see above, p. 203, lines 14–16) caters for the regents of only three faculties, theology, decrees and arts. When the faculties of civil law and medicine were added, no change was made in the text, even by 1500. Instead, a separate statute was devised for the regents of these two faculties, but the original text was left untouched. Cf. *SA* 147 (*Docs*, i. 387–8).

[2] It is certain that the university was granted some control over the conduct of the assize by 5 June 1255; cf. the royal writ printed on p. 36, n. 3 above. The precise nature of the privilege is not known, but a charter of 1268 suggests that it was similar to the concession granted to Oxford in 1248 and confirmed in 1255. The Cambridge charter of 1268 reads: 'Temptacio panis fiat bis in anno. videlicet in quindena post festum sancti Michaelis, et ⟨c⟩irca festum sancte Marie in Marcio. Et assisa Cerui⟨s⟩ie fiat eisdem terminis secundum valorem bladi et braesij [*sic*]. Et quocienscumque debeat fieri temptacio panis et ceruisie, Intersit cancellarius predicte vniuer⟨sitatis vel⟩ aliqui ex parte sua ad hoc deputati, si super hoc requisiti

would have been deputed to attend the inspection of weights and measures and the fixing of the prices of foodstuffs and drink. The university, one may surmise, decided to entrust the protection of its economic interests to two officials, called 'taxors', elected from among the regents in arts.[1] The two masters apart from attending the twice-yearly assize were likewise deputed to carry out the original function of the rectors, namely, the assessing of the rents of lodgings. A statute authorizing the institution of the new office was neatly devised by the simple process of decapitating chapter VII (*De officio rectorum*) of the Angelica text and making the severed opening paragraph into a separate chapter entitled *De officio taxatorum*. All that remained to be done then was to substitute 'taxors' for 'rectors' and add a reference to the assize of bread and ale. Apart from these changes the original text was scarcely tampered with.[2]

The Oxford statute of 1253 which required masters in theology to have ruled in arts before incepting in the higher faculty was probably adopted at Cambridge without much delay. In a statute dated 17 April 1304 the university describes its regulation as 'ancient'.[3] This may mean that it was enacted as early as 1254, but a more prudent guess is that the statute, *SA* 124, was promulgated *c.* 1255–65. It is very doubtful, however, if all the stringent conditions laid down for admission to the *magisterium* in theology were introduced at this stage.[4]

In 1264 steps were taken to remedy a flaw in the constitution of the university. The Angelica text contains no ruling on appeals from the chancellor's court. There may have been an unwritten law

interesse ⟨vol⟩uerint. quod si non intersint nec super hoc requisiti fuerint nichil ⟨va⟩leat temptacio predicta' (original in CUA, doc. no. 2; references to printed texts are cited on p. 37, n. 2 above). The parallel passages in the Oxford charters of 1248–55 are printed in *Med. Arch. Univ. Oxford*, i. 19–20.

[1] The Oxford charter of 1248 authorized the chancellor and proctors or 'aliquos ad hoc deputatos per ipsos' to attend the assize; cf. *ibid.* 19. It was customary probably by 1255 to delegate two masters to act as *supervisores*, for the charter states that in addition to the chancellor and proctors the assize may be witnessed by 'alios electos, vel per aliquos ad hoc deputatos' (*ibid.* 20).

[2] Cf. *Cons. Univ. Canteb.* vii. i (see above, p. 205, lines 2–5); Markaunt 17 (see below, p. 320, lines 13–17); *SA* 66 (*Docs*, i. 349–50). This latter contains an addition ('Si quis...incurrat') to the earlier editions of the statute. Another statute providing for the election of the taxors was drawn up by *c.* 1304–37. Cf. Markaunt 12 (see below, p. 317, lines 13–25); *SA* 65 (*Docs*, i. 349).

[3] *SA* 167 (*ibid.* 397–8). For this statute see below, pp. 242–3.

[4] Cf. *SA* 124 (*Docs*, i. 377).

that an appellant before seeking redress from the diocesan court, as he was perfectly entitled to do, had first to submit his case to the judgement of the supreme court of the university, the *cetus magistrorum regentium.* Owing to the absence of a positive law scholars were not slow to take advantage of the loophole in the constitution, and the university sought to have the matter put right by enlisting the help of the bishop, Hugh Balsham, who was personally involved. From his manor at Downham he dictated a letter on 19 December 1264 which he addressed to 'our chancellor and university of Cambridge'. It marks the earliest recorded grant of episcopal privilege.[1] At the outset the bishop takes pains to explain that if he has had occasion to write to the university in connection with appeals his motives must not be misunderstood. Far from wishing to take from its privileges he desires rather to preserve and augment them. Henceforth, it is decreed that an appellant must proceed *gradatim*, from the chancellor to the university and only then to the bishop.[2] Having won their point, the chancellor and regents, we may be sure, wasted no time in having the bishop's ruling written into the constitution.[3] Following the gradual extension by the crown of the

[1] The original of the letter is missing from the university archives. There is a transcript in B.M. Add. MS 9822 (saec. xiv–xv). Hare used this MS, which is an Ely priory register. The history of the MS, which Bentham calls MS A, is briefly told in S. J. A. Evans, *Ely chapter ordinances and visitation records 1241–1515, Camden miscellany*, xvii, pt 1 (Camden Soc., 3rd series, lxiv [1940]), pp. xvii–xix. At the top of fo. 91^{r} (medieval foliation: 104^{r}) is the heading: 'Hic scribuntur priuilegia Episcopalia. priuilegium super non gradatim appellantibus.' The text of Balsham's letter follows immediately. Though the bishop's name is left blank in the MS, Hare was right in ascribing the letter to the time of Balsham's episcopate (Hare MS i, fos. 32^{v}–33^{r}). In the Add. MS the text precedes Balsham's ordinance of 1276 on the respective limits of the jurisdiction of the archdeacon of Ely and the chancellor of Cambridge. Both documents were issued from the manor at Downham, and the style of the letter is typical of Balsham's instruments.

[2] 'Et quia frequenter accidit vniuersitatem nostram perturbari pro eo quod aliqui per insolenciam vel importunitatem a Cancellario vestro omissa vniuersitate ad nos immediate aliquando duxerant appellandum volumus et concedimus quod a Cancellario vestro ad nos de cetero appellantes in Curia nostra non audiantur nisi prius ab eo. ad vniuersitatem appellauerint et vniuersitas eis in causis appellacionum denegauerit exhibere iusticie complementum. Datum apud Dounham die veneris proximo post festum sancte lucie virginis pontificatus nostri Anno octauo' (B.M. Add. 9822, fo. 91^{r} [med.: 104^{r}]; cf. Hare MS i, fo. 32^{v}). Mullinger, *University of Cambridge*, i. 225, wrongly dates this letter to 1275 and completely misunderstood its import.

[3] The relevant statutes are cited on p. 33, n. 4 above. It may be noted here that the following grade of appeals was prescribed until 1401: first, from the commissary to the chancellor; next, from the chancellor to the university; and finally, from the university to the bishop. It is clear that the ordinary business of the chancellor's

civil jurisdiction of the university, the question came up again in the fourteenth century. Judgement was given by Simon Montacute, bishop of Ely (1337–45), in a decree dated 17 March 1342. Basing his decision on the privileges and statutes of the university, he upheld the competence of the chancellor's court in the purely civil sphere.[1] He also laid down that appeals in other cases would not be allowed by him or his official unless the appellant or his proctor swore on oath that there were genuine grounds for an appeal; that they had proceeded *gradatim* (as decreed by Hugh Balsham); and that the caution or security required by university statute was tendered.[2]

An infinitely more critical problem called for statutory action about this time. Midway through the Michaelmas term in 1260 some twenty-eight southerners from the counties of Norfolk, Suffolk and Cambridge, led by mag. John de Depedale and mag. Hugh de Thorneham, violently attacked men from the north, who in protest began a secession to Northampton, probably under the leadership of mag. Robert de Dryfeld or Driffeld.[3] A similar outbreak had occurred at Oxford in 1252 and when the parties agreed to bury the hatchet an oath to keep the peace, demandable of every incepting master, was drawn up and imposed by statute.[4] Having experienced its first taste of nationalistic feeling, Cambridge determined to

court was handled by his deputy, the commissary. The statutes say nothing about appeals from the court of an individual regent master; they were heard in fact by the chancellor. Cf. Balsham's award of 1276 (CUA, doc. no. 5; *Vet. Lib. Archid. Elien.* 21).

1 CUA, doc. no. 32. There are two exemplars of the decree in the university archives; one is the original (the seal is missing), the other a working-copy. Montacute's award was confirmed by his successor, Thomas de Lisle, on 2 August 1347 (*ibid.* doc. no. 36). It is strange that no copies of the documents are found in their registers, Ely Dioc. Rec. G I (1).

2 The statute in question is Markaunt 30 (see below, p. 325, line 26 to p. 326, line 9) = *SA* 37 (*Docs*, i. 329). It cannot, therefore, be later than 1342. In fact, it must have been enacted by 1337 since it forms part of Markaunt's text.

3 The names of the southern group pardoned by the king early in 1261 are printed in *Cal. pat. rolls, 1258–66*, p. 146. Emden, *BRUC*, p. 195, suggests that Dryfeld or Driffeld was chancellor when the disturbance broke out at Cambridge in Nov. 1260. The entry in the patent roll which is cited for this supposition does not state that he was chancellor; all it says is that mag. Robert de Dryfeld and some of his companions reported to the king on the attack on their hospice and the injuries which they suffered. Cf. *Cal. pat. rolls*, cit. pp. 180–1; Hare MS i, fo. 16^r. Dryfeld was certainly a northerner, probably from Yorkshire, but that he was ever chancellor of Cambridge is most unlikely.

4 Cf. *SAUO*, 19, 13–21 (this statute should be assigned to 1252); 86, 6–21.

prevent as far as possible another outbreak and could think of no better measure than to adopt the Oxford oath of 1252 and make it statutory for all inceptors.[1] The Northampton venture was brought to an abrupt end in 1265 under pressure from Oxford, which was as violently opposed as was Cambridge to the setting up of a third university in the country. Both universities took common action and imposed an agreed form of oath on future inceptors. Every new master had to swear that he would not incept in another faculty or resume his lectures elsewhere in England except at Oxford or Cambridge, and would not recognize as master anyone who incepted at any other English *studium*.[2] It is highly probable that the two Cambridge statutes were inserted at the end of chapter II of the Angelica text *c.* 1265.[3]

One of the most significant additions made to the Cambridge code in the late thirteenth century is the statute *De potestate rectorum in defectu cancellarii*.[4] It would be a mistake to regard the making of this statute as illustrating the standard procedure before 1300. The earliest constitutions make no explicit provision for the enactment of new statutes, except that the chancellor was forbidden to make laws without the consent of the regents. They were in fact the legislative body. New statutes or amendments of the existing constitutions were a matter for convocation, that is the chancellor acting in

1 Cf. Markaunt (see below, p. 312, lines 6–11). The statute occurs in the latter part of *SA* 134 ('Jurent etiam tactis sacrosanctis...exerceri' [*Docs*, i. 381]). Cf. also *SA* 114 (*ibid.* 373).

2 Cf. *SAUO*, 19, 23–7 and Markaunt (see below, p. 312, lines 11–14). In *SA* 134 'Juret etiam...habeatur' (*Docs*, i. 382) the passage is truncated.

3 *Cons. Univ. Canteb.* II. iv (see above, p. 199, line 18 to p. 200, line 2). Cf. *SA* 134 (the passage 'exceptis diebus...observabunt' [*Docs*, i. 381] is a saec. xiv accretion). There are two early statutes concerning disturbers of the peace: Markaunt 33 (see below, p. 328, line 15 to p. 329, line 20), *SA* 41 (*Docs*, i. 330–2); and Markaunt 36 (see below, p. 330, line 25 to p. 331, line 7), *SA* 43 (*loc. cit.* 333); but there is no reason to think that these were promulgated as early as *c.* 1261–5. Indeed Markaunt 33 is strikingly reminiscent of an Oxford statute of 1327; cf. *SAUO*, 128, 27–131, 14. Markaunt 36 is directed against false scholars and those guilty of immorality. It is stated in *Docs*, i. 334, n. 1, that *SA* 44 has to do with clashes between northern and southern scholars. The statute, on the contrary, makes no reference to nations; it prohibits in fact faculty groupings and mock ceremonies on Ash Wednesday which led to disturbances in the students' quarters. *SA* 172 (*ibid.* 399) is directed against 'national' gatherings on patronal feasts in public places. The statute existed by 1390, but it was possibly enacted much earlier. A similar statute was enacted at Oxford before 1350; cf. *SAUO*, 82, 26–83, 9.

4 Markaunt 15 (see below, p. 318, line 28 to p. 319, line 20); *SA* 57 (*Docs*, i. 342). Professor Ullmann, it will be remembered, has edited the decree of the university embodying this statute in *Historical Journal*, i. 181–2.

concert with the regent masters. The new statute extending the powers of the rectors, on the other hand, was put through at an extraordinary meeting of the university held at St Mary's on 17 March 1276. The chancellor, John Hooke, and all the regent masters were present, also the non-regents and the senior bachelors. The association of these latter with the enactment shows clearly that the session was anything but normal.[1] The only reason why they and the non-regents were invited to attend was doubtless the fact that the motion itself was extraordinary; it struck at what was hitherto a prerogative of the chancellor, the right to summon convocations of the regents. Moreover, his disciplinary and jurisdictional rights were also affected. The immediate interest of the new statute is that it cites the relevant section of the constitution on the office of the rectors.[2] The passage in the Angelica manuscript is certainly corrupt, but its authenticity is guaranteed by the quotation in the decree of 1276.[3] Some time between 1276 and *c.* 1304–37 the text of the statute was altered to give a better reading.[4] It is one of the anomalies of the textual history of the statutes that the more glaring hiatus in the passage formulated by *c.* 1250 was retained in the statute *De potestate rectorum in defectu cancellarii* until replaced by a cross-reference to the original chapter on the rectors.[5] The new statute is nothing more than a straight transcript of the decree of 17 March 1276 stripped of its introduction and conclusion.

[1] The senior bachelors were summoned on another occasion to join the regent masters in making a decree against dances in public places. Cf. Markaunt 34 (see below, p. 329, lines 22–4). Ullmann, *loc. cit.* 178, following Rashdall, *Universities*, iii. 389, equates *maiores bachilarii* with bachelors of the higher faculties. This interpretation is not supported by other references in the statutes. Cf. Markaunt 35 (see below, p. 330, lines 20–3); *SA* 42 (*Docs*, i. 333). Here it is quite certain that senior bachelors were those who were next in line for promotion to the *magisterium*. They were generally known as bachelors *noviter incepturi*. The Cambridge statutes also make a distinction between senior and junior masters of a faculty. Cf. *SA* 53, 154 (*Docs*, i. 339, 391).

[2] *Cons. Univ. Canteb.* VII. iv (see above, p. 205, line 22 to p. 207, line 2).

[3] The quotation reads: 'Tempora et modus legendi et disputandi et exequias celebrandi et incipiendi et feriarum obseruancie ad ipsos pertineant: in trangressores [*sic*] circa predicta ad eorum officia specialiter et in bedellos si mandatis eorum non paruerint cohercione concessa eisdem animaduersio⟨n⟩e ⟨g⟩rauissima per cancellarium et magistros si opus ⟨f⟩uerit ⟨nich⟩ilominus irroganda' (CUA, doc. no. 4; cf. Ullmann's edition, *loc. cit.* 181).

[4] For Markaunt's amended text see below, p. 256.

[5] Cf. Markaunt 15 (*loc. cit.*), which is the earliest extant text of the actual statute. In the Old, Junior and Senior Proctor's Books the opening part of this statute is amended and only the first four words of c. VII. iv of the Angelica text are quoted. See below, p. 257, n. 2.

On 6 October of the same year Hugh Balsham arbitrated in a dispute between the archdeacon of Ely and the chancellor of the university. Before settling the points at issue or the areas of their jurisdictions, the bishop made a close study of the constitution of the university. He singled out three of the statutes, two of which form part of the Angelica text, and commented upon them. It is interesting to compare Hugh's quotations with the statutes as set down in the Angelica text:

Hugh Balsham

Et quia in statuto vniuersitatis uidimus contineri quod duo Bedelli vniuersitatis intersint virgam deferentes omnibus vesperis. principiis. conuentibus. defunctorum exequiis et omnibus aliis conuocacionibus nullo alio in preiudicium eorum virgam delaturo. (CUA, doc. no. 5; *Vet. Lib. Archid. Elien.* 21.)[1]

inter alia laudabile statutum et salubre a dictis cancellario et Magistris editum diligenter inspeximus ne quis aliquem pro scolare tueatur qui certum Magistrum infra quindecim dies postquam vniuersitatem idem scolaris ingressus sit non habuerit. aut nomen suum infra tempus prelibatum in Matricula sui Magistri redigi non curauerit. nisi Magistri absencia uel iusta *rerum* occupacio illud impediat. Immo si quis talis sub nomine scolaris latitare inueniatur *uel deiciatur. uel* retineatur iuxta regis libertatem. (CUA, doc. no. 5; *Vet. Lib. Archid. Elien.* 22.)

Angelica text

Duo tantum bedelli...Intersint eciam uirgam deferentes omnibus uesperis et principiis conuentibus defunctorum exequiis et omnibus aliis conuocacionibus ante recessum magistrorum nullatenus recessuri nullo alio in eorum preiudicium uirgam delaturo. (*Cons. Univ. Canteb.* VIII. i, iii [see above, p. 207, line 4; p. 207, lines 18–21].)

Indignum esse iudicamus ut quis scolarem tueatur qui certum magistrum infra quindecim dies post ingressum uniuersitatis non habuerit aut nomen suum infra tempus prelibatum in matricula sui magistri redigi non curauerit nisi magistri absencia uel iusta occupacio illud impediat. Immo si quis talis sub nomine scolaris latitans inueniatur retineatur iuxta domini regis libertatem. (*Cons. Univ. Canteb.* XI. i [see above, p. 211, lines 4–10].)

The bishop evidently allowed himself some freedom when quoting; his omission of 'ante...recessuri' in the first extract is a case in point and likewise his handling of the beginning of the second statute. What is equally clear is that Balsham's exemplar was closely related to the Angelica manuscript. His retention of *vesperis* and *principiis*

[1] There are two duplicates of the original extant in the university archives which are listed as doc. no. 5. Both have been damaged by damp, but it is possible to reconstruct the original by comparing the one with the other. There are numerous transcripts of the decree, the earliest being Markaunt's Book, fo. 42^{r-v} (E 4^{r-v}), B.M. Add. MS 9822, fos. 91^{r}–92^{v} (med.: 104^{r}–105^{v}) and *Vet. Lib. Archid. Elien.* 20–3.

in the first statute is noteworthy; in the later statute-books we find *vesperiis* and *precipuis*, this latter a blunder.[1] None the less, Balsham's quotation points the way to changes which make their appearance in Markaunt and the official registers of the fourteenth and fifteenth centuries. The words we have italicized in the second extract are accretions to the Angelica text and show that it had been worked over by 1276.[2]

The bishop cites a third statute which deserves attention; not only is it an addition to the primitive code, but it provides our earliest evidence of the growth of the commercial side of university life, which further complicated the question of jurisdiction:

Et quia in statutis vniuersitatis eiusdem inter alia continetur quod familia scolarium scriptores et alii officia ad usum scolarium tantum deputata exercentes, eadem immunitate et libertate gaudeant qua et scolares ut coram archidiacono non respondeant sicuti nec scolares qui sunt eorum domini. hoc ita tenore presencium declaramus. quod in hoc casu nomine familie solummodo volumus contineri, Mancipia scolarium in domibus cum eis commorancia dum personaliter deseruiunt scolaribus antedictis. Item nomine scriptorum et aliorum officia ad usum scolarium tantum deputata exercencium uolumus intelligi de scriptoribus. Illuminatoribus et stacionariis qui tantum deseruiunt scolaribus quod sub Cancellario respondeant. (CUA, doc. no. 5; *Vet. Lib. Archid. Elien.* 21.)

The statute 'familia...domini' must have been enacted some time between *c.* 1250 and 1276. No trace of it appears in the Angelica manuscript. It occurs for the first time in Markaunt's collection. Moreover, the enactment is not found, as one might expect, tacked on to the statute on the immunity of scholars which Balsham was to quote later in his award. On the contrary, it appears as a pendant to the statute incorporating his decree of 1264 concerning the order in which appeals were to proceed.[3] It may well be that the statute covering manciples, scribes, illuminators and stationers was introduced *c.* 1264–76 and is earlier than the statute of 17 March 1276 extending the powers of the rectors.

Bishop Balsham's reference to those engaged in the book-trade

[1] Markaunt 19 (see below, p. 321, line 15); *SA* 72 (*Docs*, i. 354). *Vesperiae* and *principia*, as we have seen, are correlatives and represent the two parts of an inception ceremony; the bedells attended at both functions. It is possible to make sense out of *precipuis conuentibus*, but this is to lose sight of the true meaning of the text.

[2] The text used by Balsham was itself remodelled more than once in the fourteenth century. Cf. Markaunt 35 (see below, p. 330, lines 2–8); *SA* 42 (*Docs*, i. 332).

[3] Cf. Markaunt 26 (see below, p. 325, lines 5–7); *SA* 33 (*Docs*, i. 328). The part of the statute referring to the *familia* of scholars was revised apparently after 1276; it is not the same as the version quoted by Balsham.

is a reminder that the subject still awaits patient investigation. There are no statutes as early as those made for the stationers at Bologna about this period;[1] but sources are not entirely lacking.[2] The bishop of Ely, at all events, was not prepared to allow the wives of stationers and their suppliers to shelter under the wing of the chancellor,[3] which may or may not have been a disappointment for John the *scriptor* whose son, Walter, was a student at the university and graduated as master by *c.* 1272.[4]

The eighties of the century saw a lull in the flow of statutory developments; at least no enactments have come to light for the years *c.* 1280–90. At this point, therefore, it will be convenient to take a backward glance at the growth of the Angelica text by 1276. Five new statutes were definitely promulgated after *c.* 1250 and very probably two more as well. It is certain that the Angelica text itself was revised to some extent, and the paragraph ordering the performance of liturgical offices on the death of Henry III may have been deleted after 16 November 1272.[5] The possibility that a fresh code was prepared by 1276, making provision for the orderly insertion of the new statutes, cannot be overlooked. The third statute quoted by Hugh Balsham in his ordinance of 6 October of that year comes between his quotations from chapters VIII and XI of the first constitution of the university. This could be significant, especially since the statute continued to hold more or less the same position in Markaunt's text. If a new code was actually made, the work was carried out presumably between 1264 and 1276. It must be allowed, however, that Balsham may not have cited the statutes according to the order in which they appeared in the statute-book but rather in

1 M. Boháček, 'Zur Geschichte der Stationarii von Bologna', *Symbolae Raphaeli Taubenschlag dedicatae*, ii (*Eos*, 48 [Warsaw, 1957]), 247–95.

2 Valuable indications are to be found in Little and Pelster, *Oxford theology*, pp. 56–64. There was a parchment-maker (*pergamentarius*) named William at Cambridge *c.* 1258, cf. Gray, *Priory of St Radegund*, p. 119, no. 231*a*; but the earliest known stationer is apparently William de Nessfylde (*c.* 1309–10). See C. H. Talbot, 'The universities and the mediaeval library', *The English library before 1700*, p. 73.

3 The restrictive meaning which Balsham placed on the statute was not publicized by the university in subsequent editions of the text.

4 Stokes, *Outside the Trumpington gates*, pp. 12, 30, 66.

5 The statute made no provision for the observance of the anniversary of Henry and once the funeral obsequies had been performed it was no longer relevant. The second part of this statute was already obsolete after 6 August 1254, following the burial of Hugh of Northwold. Cf. *Cons. Univ. Canteb.* XIII. i (see above, p. 217, lines 8–16).

relation to the questions submitted to him for an authoritative declaration.

A recent writer on the history of academic costume has stated that Bishop Balsham issued statutes for the university in 1276 and in addition a draft of rules pertaining to 'the halls of Cambridge'.[1] The evidence adduced in support of these contentions turns out to be very late copies of the *statuta antiqua* contained in the Junior and Senior Proctors' Books. On closer examination we find that everything rests on just one statute, *SA* 147.[2] The first part of this statute is chapter V of the Angelica text and was enacted at the latest by *c.* 1250;[3] the remainder of the statute cannot be precisely dated, but as written it cannot be earlier than 1304.[4] The entire statute deals solely with the matter of academic dress and has nothing to do with halls of the university; in any case 'halls' did not exist by 1276. In short, the notion that Hugh Balsham drew up statutes for the university is an illusion.

On the surface the decade 1280–90 was a barren period in the constitutional history of Cambridge. Yet these years could well have seen the formation of the very important group of statutes bearing on studies and admissions to degrees in all faculties—arts, medicine, law and theology. Unfortunately, the earliest collection of such statutes dates only from the late fourteenth century, for Markaunt's transcript terminates before reaching the section on studies. Hence, although there are statutes on theology which derive from the thirteenth and early fourteenth centuries, the growth of legislation

[1] Hargreaves-Mawdsley, *History of academical dress*, pp. 116, 123.

[2] *Docs*, i. 387–8. Hargreaves-Mawdsley cites two sources, B.M. Harl. MS 7032 (= Baker, v), ¶ 146, and CUL MS Mm. 4. 47, § 147, fo. 228. The Harl. text was executed *c.* 1683–1701 and was copied from the Junior Proctor's Book (*c.* 1494–5); the transcript of the statutes occupies fos. 5ʳ–59ʳ (formerly pp. 1–109) of the MS. Hargreaves-Mawdsley's '146' is a mistake for '147', i.e. *SA* 147 (Harl. MS, fo. 44ʳ [p. 79]). The statutes are not numbered in the MS and apparently the author overlooked *SA* 125 when counting the entries. The CUL MS dates from *c.* 1758–78. According to Hargreaves-Mawdsley, *op. cit.* p. 196, the transcripts of the statutes in this volume are of 'great value'. They are in fact practically valueless. They were made from the text of the statutes in the Senior Proctor's Book (*c.* 1496–1502). This register is of course still extant in the university archives and the statutes themselves have long been available in print (1785, 1852).

[3] Cf. *Cons. Univ. Canteb.* v (see above, p. 203, lines 14–16) and *SA* 147 (*loc. cit.* 387).

[4] The text of *SA* 147 states that this part of the enactment cannot be dispensed with unless the regent and non-regent masters approve. Before 1304 authority to make statutes and consequently to dispense was vested exclusively in the regent masters. It is not evident that dispensations required the consent of the non-regents until relatively late in the century. See pp. 235–6.

dealing with lectures, disputations and requirements for degrees is all too obscure.[1]

Geoffrey de Pakenham, doctor of canon law, was chancellor in 1290–2. At least two statutes were enacted during his term of office. The first, *SA* 149, decreed that the seats for masters at convocations, inceptions and resumptions were to be allocated on a faculty basis, the higher faculties being graded above the lower.[2] Ralph de Leycestria, doctor of civil law, refused to accept the place assigned to his faculty. In retaliation, the university appears to have ostracized him, and he appealed to the Holy See; he also lodged a tuitorial appeal with the court of Canterbury and obtained an injunction from the court of Arches.[3] Meanwhile, the university made a counter-appeal to the pope, Nicholas IV, who on 1 February 1291 accordingly delegated the bishop of Norwich, Ralph de Walpole, a graduate of Cambridge and Leycestria's ordinary, to settle the dispute.[4] Somehow, both parties agreed or were prevailed upon to let the bishop of Ely, William of Louth, act as mediator. He made

[1] The process held in connection with the controversy between the friars and the university in 1303–6 (see below, pp. 240–4) contains references to earlier statutes and customs. These may be identified with *SA* 108, 112, 124, 126–7 (*Docs*, i. 370, 372, 377–8); but it must not be assumed that the statutes as set down in the registers were formulated wholly before 1300. For *SA* 124 see above, p. 222. On the other hand, a statute like *SA* 134 (*Docs*, i. 381), though obviously revised in the fourteenth century, derives substantially from the thirteenth century and was originally promulgated by *c.* 1250. See also the version of *SA* 86, rescued from the Old Proctor's Book and printed on p. 277.

[2] *Docs*, i. 388. On the disposition of faculties at Oxford congregations cf. *SAUO*, p. xxv, n. 1.

[3] Cf. CUA, doc. no. 6. This is the original of William of Louth's decree which brought the conflict to a close. In the document the christian name of Leycestria is written simply as 'R'. An endorsement on the document reads: 'quedam concordia facta de distinccione sedium inter vniuersitatem et magistrum Ric' de leicestria anno domini millesimo cc.lxxxx.' This note is not in a contemporary hand; it appears rather to be saec. xv. It is far more likely that 'R' is a contraction of 'Ralph', who was certainly involved in a row with the university *c.* 1291 and who was D.C.L. into the bargain. No one of the name of Richard de Lei(y)cestria, doctor of civil law, is known to have been at Cambridge in the late thirteenth century. A mag. Robert of Leicester 'iuris professor' occurs *c.* 1280–94. Cf. *The letter-book of William of Hoo sacrist of Bury St Edmunds 1280–94*, ed. Gransden (Suffolk Records Soc. v [1963]), 86–7, no. 166. For further details of Ralph de Leycestria cf. *BRUC*, p. 362, *s.v.* Leicester.

[4] Markaunt's Book, fo. 31^v (D 9^v). The original or a copy of the papal letter existed in the university archives in Rysley's time, where it bore the catalogue reference 'Fn'. Hall, 'William Rysley's catalogue', *Camb. Bibl. Soc. Trans.* iv. 95, prints 'En' for 'Fn'. The letter is not noticed in *Registres de Nicolas IV*, ed. Langlois, nor in *Cal. papal letters.*

a personal visit to Cambridge to see for himself the seating arrangements in St Mary's and then named three commissaries, mag. Thomas de Ludham, canon of Wells, mag. Ralph of York, chancellor of Salisbury (1288–1309), and his own official, Guy de Coventre, to hear the evidence and decide the rights and wrongs of the quarrel.[1] Leycestria climbed down and Pakenham together with the rectors and regents agreed to receive him back. The terms of the concord were approved by the bishop, who for good measure confirmed the statute in question on 19 April 1291.[2] The reconciliation was genuine and very timely. Leycestria at this time was engaged in a rather protracted legal battle with the prior of Barnwell over his tenancy of a house owned by the priory in Cambridge. The suit dragged on until 1292, complicated no doubt by the peculiar position in which Leycestria found himself; on one front he was defending university privilege; on another he was opposed to the university itself. Following his readmittance to the society of regent masters, the affair with the priory took a turn for the better as far as he was concerned owing to the success of the chancellor in having the suit withdrawn from the king's justices.[3] The case was settled out of court by the bishop's official, who prevailed on Leycestria to waive his claim. He was granted an extension of forty days as tenant of the house; on the expiry of the lease the keys were to be handed up and in addition Leycestria promised to pay forty shillings arrears of rent.[4]

The second statute issued by Pakenham during his term as chancellor had the unanimous consent of the regents. The enactment was long overdue. Hugh Balsham passed to his reward on 15 June 1286, leaving the university forever in his debt. Five years passed before any move was made to record its gratitude to the bishop who founded its first college and proved in so many ways such a notable

[1] All three *magistri* were probably Cambridge scholars. For Ralph of York cf. Le Neve, *Fasti*, ii. 649. Thomas de Ludham, canon of Wells, appears to be unknown at this time. There was a prebendary of the name in Southwell in 1259 (*ibid.* iii. 462).

[2] CUA, doc. no. 6, cit. The date of the document is not 1290, as the endorsement states. It was given at Ely 'die Cene domini videlicet. xiii°.kl.Maii Anno domini M° cc°. Nonogesimo Pontificatus nostri Anno primo [now partly effaced]'. Wm. of Louth was consecrated on 1 Oct. 1290. Holy Thursday fell on 19 April (= xiii kl. Maii) in 1291.

[3] See above, p. 172.

[4] Cf. *Liber mem. ecc. de Bernewelle*, p. 184. Clark, *ibid.* pp. 182–4, refers the dispute to the year 1295. This is inaccurate. See also Stokes, *Mediaeval hostels*, p. 34.

benefactor. On 26 May 1291 the regent masters bound themselves by statute to perform the suffrages of the dead for all time on the eve and on the day of Balsham's anniversary.[1]

Pakenham's successor, mag. Gilbert de Segrave, issued no statutes during his rather short tenure of the chancellorship (1292–3), though an echo of the clash with Barnwell may be detected in a letter which he and the *cetus magistrorum regentium* addressed to the king's chancellor, John Langton, shortly after 17 December 1292.[2] But if 1292–3 was a blank year the next twelve months brought a cluster of statutes. Eleanor of Castile, wife of Edward I, died on 28 November 1290. In her will she made provision for numerous bequests; among the beneficiaries were the friars of Cambridge, and poor scholars of the university to whom she left 100 marks. In gratitude mag. Henry de Boyton, who succeeded Segrave as chancellor, and the regent masters made a statutory order for the perpetual observance of her obit on 28–29 November. The statute was promulgated under the seal of the university on 18 March 1294.[3] Less than three weeks later the chancellor and his colleagues were at loggerheads over an issue whose outcome led to the definition of some vital constitutional principles.

Henry de Boyton was cast in a different mould from that of his predecessor, John Hooke, who made an abject surrender in 1276 of his right under the constitution to regulate the holding of convocations. But when Boyton attempted to rule the university independently of the regents, he came under heavy fire, chiefly from the faculty of theology. He was accused of interpreting and setting at nought 'that useful and praiseworthy congregation', namely, the regent masters. What provoked their ire was his sweeping interpretation of chapter XI. iv of the Angelica text, which states that the chancellor and masters may expel or send to prison anyone guilty of certain offences.[4] Boyton, as the upshot of the controversy shows, must have banished or imprisoned some master

[1] The statute, the first of its kind made by Cambridge, is embodied in *SA* 180 (*Docs*, i. 404, 406). Cf. *SA* 185 (*ibid.* 413–14) and above, pp. 34–6.

[2] Little, 'An unknown chancellor of the university of Cambridge at the end of the thirteenth century', *Cambridge Review*, liv. 412.

[3] The text of the decree is printed by Clark, *Endowments of the university of Cambridge* (Cambridge, 1904), pp. 553–4, where the date is wrongly given as 1290. Half of Queen Eleanor's bequest was paid out in 1292 (*ibid.* p. 554). The statute was ordered to be read at all inceptions, each inceptor being obliged under oath to observe the anniversary of the late queen. Cf. *SA* 180 (*Docs*, i. 405).

[4] *Cons. Univ. Canteb.* XI. iv (see above, p. 213, lines 1–2).

on his own authority, thus throwing down the gauntlet.[1] Neither he nor the regents were ready to give way and the bishop, William of Louth, deputed his official, Coventre, to adjudicate.

The suit dragged on from day to day as the chancellor, who had his adherents, and the proctor of the regents exchanged arguments. Boyton took his stand on the juridical fact—future chancellors were far from anxious to admit it—that he was the bishop's delegate in the university; the action of the regents, he argued, was an attempt to deprive him of the jurisdiction which he received from the bishop at his confirmation in office as chancellor. To question his authority was to hold up to contempt the bishop and his jurisdiction. It was a good *argumentum ad hominem* and Boyton doubtless thought that the official would side with him; but Coventre, though well known for his zeal as guardian of the rights of the bishop, scented a red herring. The fact was that the chancellor could not get around the literal meaning of the constitution, and for all his specious pleading he lost the case. Judgement in favour of the regents was given on 8 April 1294 by the court, sitting in St Michael's church. It declared that in future the statutes, customs and privileges of the university were to be taken in their grammatical sense, and ordered the chancellor to restore the *status quo* as it was at the time of his election. In the event of a dispute about the interpretation of a statute the decision of the *maior et sanior pars* of the regents must prevail. Lest this term should give rise to fresh controversy the official now proceeded to define its meaning. It denoted a majority which included three doctors, that is, regent masters, from at least two faculties, excluding arts, other than the faculty that proposed the motion.[2]

Thus was defined almost by accident a term of crucial importance for the history of statute-making at Cambridge. From 1304 onwards all statutes required the consent of the *maior et sanior pars* of both the regent and non-regent houses, and it is to be presumed that the

[1] The master against whom the chancellor proceeded was probably a regent in theology. It was this particular faculty which led the attack on Boyton.

[2] 'Et ⟨n⟩e ⟨de maiori et saniori⟩ parte in posterum vertatur in dubium ill⟨am⟩ p⟨artem⟩ saniorem reputamus et maiorem que excedit in ⟨numer⟩o ⟨re⟩gencium dum tamen ille numerus excedat per tres doctores seu m⟨agistro⟩s regentes de aliis duabus facultatibus ad minus exceptis arcistis' (CUA, doc. no. 10 [the original]). The text is defective owing to the mutilated state of the parchment. I have used the transcripts in Markaunt's Book, C fo. 10^v, and B.M. Add. 9822, fos. 92^v–93^r (med.: 105^v–106^r), in reconstructing the original.

expression continued to bear the meaning which it received in 1294, although when first propounded it applied only to statutory declarations. Hitherto, statutes as such depended for their approval on a straight vote confined to the regents; if a majority was in favour of a statute it became law. During the years 1294–1304 the power of making statutes remained the prerogative of the regents, but we may assume that any statutes enacted at that period unless carried unanimously had to be approved by the 'major and saner part' of the regents as defined by Guy de Coventre. His interpretation presupposes that if a faculty proposed a statute, declaration or amendment and put it to a vote at a full congregation of the regent masters the outcome did not depend on the number of faculties voting for or against it. Open, direct voting was still the rule; if a majority of the regents voted in favour of a statute it became law, provided the majority included three doctors, themselves regents, in at least two superior faculties.[1] There was one further proviso, namely, that if a statute was sponsored by a higher faculty, the extra votes had to come from two other higher faculties. This meant in practice that, should the faculty of theology, for example, propose to have a statute enacted it had to win a majority in the regent house, a majority which included the votes of, say, three doctors in canon law and civil law. Likewise, should the faculty of arts determine to have a statute enacted and succeeded in getting a majority of all the votes the motion was lost unless three regents in two superior faculties voted for it.[2] After 1304 the assent of the *maior et sanior pars* of the non-regents was also necessary and had to be obtained, *mutatis mutandis*, in the same way. They had no power, however, to initiate legislation and the regents continued to reserve

[1] The decree implies that the faculty of medicine was erected by 1294, since it lays down that a motion must have the support of regents in at least two faculties, excluding the faculty sponsoring the motion and the faculty of arts. It also appears that canon law and civil law voted as two distinct faculties. Rashdall, *Universities*, iii. 65, n. 2, referring to the position at Oxford, unaccountably leaves the question hanging in mid-air, although he was aware of a statute of *c.* 1480–8 which reveals that the canonists voted independently of the civilians. Cf. *SAUO*, 292, 24–6. In the new Rashdall, *loc. cit.* 77, the relevant passage is telescoped; 'the Physicians in the Chapel of S. Thomas' should read: 'the Physicians in the Chapel of S. Catherine; the Legists in the Chapel of S. Thomas.' Cf. the 1895 edition, ii. 387.

[2] It is possible that a system of direct voting also obtained at Oxford until *c.* 1303, when it was enacted that a statute became law once it had the consent of two faculties (i.e. the major part of the regents in both) and the majority of the non-regents (voting as a body). In 1314 the number of faculties was raised to three, of which arts had to be one. Cf. Rashdall, *op. cit.* 72, 77; *SAUO*, pp. xxxvi–xxxvii.

to themselves the right to interpret statutes, though by the end of the fourteenth century statutory declarations were promulgated as a rule in the name of both houses.[1]

The tussle between Henry de Boyton and the regent masters ended in triumph for the latter, who proceeded after a respectable interval to exploit their victory. At a congregation held on Thursday, 6 May 1294, the major and saner part of the regents interpreted chapter XI. iv of the constitution as meaning that the chancellor may not banish or imprison a master without the consent of the regents, who are to have audience conjointly with the chancellor of causes meriting these penalties. A new statute was approved, binding the chancellor to execute decrees of banishment or imprisonment when ordered by the university of regents, and it was also enacted that the common prison of the town was to be the place of detention. A third item on the agenda was shelved until the following Saturday, apparently to enable clerks of the bishop to attend. It is quite possible that Boyton at the Thursday session objected to the proposed decree as an unwarranted intrusion into his customary sphere of action, if not indeed contrary to the spirit of the award made by the official of the bishop. At all events, at a full congregation of the regents held on Saturday, 8 May 1294, it was declared that the chancellor or his commissary must in future forewarn the rectors when disciplinary action was being taken so that they could be present. The idea behind this ruling is clear enough. The regents through the rectors, their agents, would henceforth be in a position to control the administration of punishment and see that their decrees were executed by the chancellor or his deputy. What part the clerks of the bishop played in the debate we do not know, but they must have agreed that the regents were acting within their rights in clamping this additional rivet on the chancellor's exercise of penal jurisdiction. Either then or later it was also enacted that fines imposed in lieu of other penalties were to be received by the proctors and deposited in the common chest.[2]

This spate of statutes and declarations may not have marked the

[1] The later, revised texts of certain statutes give no indication that their declarations were made originally by the regents only. Cf. Markaunt 16 (see below, p. 319, line 22 to p. 320, line 11); *SA* 60 (*Docs*, i. 346); Markaunt 20 (see below, p. 321, line 24 to p. 322, line 8); *SA* 10 (*loc. cit.* 313); Markaunt 33 (see below, p. 328, line 15 to p. 329, line 20); *SA* 41 (*loc. cit.* 331).

[2] The earliest texts of these statutes and decrees are to be found only in Markaunt 20, which has also preserved the dates. See below, pp. 271–2.

end of Henry de Boyton's humiliation. In an Ely priory register the text of the award of 8 April 1294 is immediately followed by a piece entitled *De iuramento et obediencia Cancellarii.*[1] It is interesting to discover that this is in fact a copy of a statute of the university of which there are two versions. The older, exemplified by the Ely manuscript, states that the chancellor having been confirmed in office by the bishop must summon on his return to Cambridge a congregation of all the regents to meet at the latest on the morrow. At this assembly one of the proctors will administer an oath to the chancellor pledging him to carry out faithfully all things pertaining to his office. The proctor will then hand him the chancellor's seal together with the key of the common chest, the insignia of his office.[2] Though the statute is undated, its insertion in the Ely register as a sort of appendix to Coventre's decree of 8 April 1294 can hardly be fortuitous. The text forms a natural sequel to the defeat which the luckless chancellor, Henry Boyton, suffered at the hands of the regent masters. A statute which speaks of the 'obedience' of the chancellor to the university is more likely to have been devised in April–May 1294 than at any other period in Cambridge history, for it was then that a chancellor raised the flag of revolt for the first but not the last time.[3]

Before we pass on to consider the earliest extant recension of the Angelica text, it is necessary to take stock of a group of homogeneous statutes which remained still-born. The collection is preserved in a composite manuscript of the early fourteenth century which must have been written at Cambridge.[4] Set down at random in the middle of an anonymous *Summa aurea* ('in preceptis compre-

1 B.M. Add. MS 9822, fo. 93^{r} (med.: 106^{r}).

2 Cf. B.M. Add. MS, *loc. cit.*; Markaunt 3 (see below, p. 314, lines 19–26); Caius 5 (fo. $1^{v\,a}$); Old Proctor's Book 5 (fo. 17^{v}). The reference to the chancellor's confirmation by the bishop was deleted from the text in the Old Proctor's Book in or shortly after 1401; and it is the shortened version which *SA* 5 (*Docs*, i. 310) exhibits.

3 When the proctors sought to convoke the regents *c.* 1415 in virtue of their powers under the statute of 17 March 1276 the chancellor, Stephen Scrope, D.C.L., is said to have imprisoned them; he was not prepared to abide by this statutory encroachment on his prerogative. Cf. Hardwick, 'Articuli Universitatis Cantabrigiae', *CASP*, i. 92.

4 CUL MS Mm. 4. 41. Part II (fos. $33^{r\,a}$–$88^{v\,b}$), which includes the Cambridge text, was written in a hand which cannot be earlier than 1302. In addition to excerpts from the Sext and a copy of Boniface VIII's bull *Super cathedram* (18 Feb. 1300), this section contains the text of his decretal *Cupientes* (fo. $72^{r\,a-v\,a}$) which is dated 13 April 1302.

henditur') is a text with the title *Statuta vniuersitatis Cantebrigiensis.*[1] It consists of eleven paragraphs, clothed in racy Latin, dealing with the hiring of hostels and in particular the question of principalships. The text is a perplexing document. It was doubtless drawn up at the close of the thirteenth century; perhaps by *c.* 1300 is a more realistic date.[2] To all intents and purposes it is more of a memorandum for the guidance and benefit of principals than anything else; this is suggested by the colloquial form in which some of the items are couched.[3] The difficulty is to determine the context of the title, 'statutes of the university of Cambridge', and to relate the contents to the official statute, chapter XII of the Angelica text. In certain ways the memorandum, if we can describe it as such, supplements the information contained in the constitution of the university;[4] but the compiler seems to have been totally unaware of the existing statute, a statute which continued with very little change to be the fundamental statutory ruling on hostels throughout the medieval history of Cambridge. Moreover, there are anomalies in the memorandum compared with the Angelica text.[5] It is possible, however, that the document was drafted with a view to giving statutory force to the items listed, and this would account perhaps for their descrip-

[1] CUL MS Mm. 4. 41, fo. 56$^{v\,a-v\,b}$. The text was brought to light by Henry Bradshaw, 'An early university statute concerning hostels', *CASP*, ii (1864), 279–81, who also edited the material, *ibid.* 280–1. His edition was reproduced, not without some inaccuracies, by Mullinger, *University of Cambridge*, i. 219–20 (English version), 639–40 (Latin).

[2] Emden, *An Oxford hall*, p. 23, assigns the text to the same period as the Oxford regulations on houses and schools which he dates to saec. xiii*ex.*

[3] It was what Mullinger, *op. cit.* i. 220–1, calls the 'language', 'simplicity' and 'brevity' of the document which led him to suppose that it was compiled before *SA* 67 (*Docs*, i. 350–1). This particular statute is practically identical with the early thirteenth-century constitution *De hospiciis et pensionibus domorum*. Cf. *Cons. Univ. Canteb.* XII (see above, p. 213, line 11 to p. 217, line 4).

[4] It reveals, for instance, that the caution or security which a principal had to offer to a landlord in advance of the rent was produced in the presence of one of the bedells of the university or a notary or two witnesses. The pledge might be either a *cautio fideiussoria* or a *cautio pignoraticia*. The former consisted of two sureties; the latter took the form of a book or some valuable. Cf. Mullinger, *op. cit.* p. 639, and the references in *Cons. Univ. Canteb.* XII. ii, v (see above, p. 213, line 18 and p. 215, line 13).

[5] The so-called statutes state that a principal must give back possession of a house to the landlord and not cede it to a scholar, since this kind of transaction has proved prejudicial to landlords (Mullinger, *op. cit.*, *loc. cit.*). Not merely was it prejudicial to the owners of houses, it was explicitly ruled out by statute of the university, but the memorandum fails to mention this vital fact. Cf. *Cons. Univ. Canteb.* XII. v (see above, p. 215, lines 15–16).

tion as *statuta* in the manuscript.[1] But whether or not the text was actually placed before the regents for their approval, it failed to win formal recognition and remained outside the legal code of the university, though when chapter XII of the Angelica text came up for review some use may have been made of the still-born propositions.[2] Be that as it may, the document, problematical as it is, helps to elucidate the procedure and practice regarding the letting and hiring of hostels at Cambridge *c.* 1300 and thus makes for a fuller understanding of the implications and working of the official statute.[3]

1 It may be significant that the MS belonged to a canonist, since statutes were formulated by lawyers. See above, p. 66.

2 One of these declares that applications for principalships must be made between the feast of St Barnabas (11 June) and the Nativity of Our Lady (8 September) (Mullinger, *op. cit.* p. 639). The Angelica text simply states that cautions are to be proffered before the latter feast; cf. *Cons. Univ. Canteb.* XII. v (see above, p. 215, lines 10–13). In the amended version of this statute the period specified in the memorandum is noted. Cf. Markaunt 32 (see below, p. 327, lines 25–7); *SA* 67 (*Docs*, i. 351). These statutes add that if a landlord has of necessity to occupy the house himself he must warn the occupant before the feast of St John the Baptist (24 June). This provision, as we have seen, also formed part of the Oxford *consuetudo*. See above, p. 78. Evidently, the early Cambridge constitution was revised after the memorandum was produced. On the other hand, the document states that a principal cannot be ejected as long as he pays his rent, unless the landlord wishes to live in the house himself or has sold or alienated it; cf. Mullinger, *op. cit.* p. 640. Only the first of these contingencies is recognized in Markaunt 32 and *SA* 67, which on this point adhere faithfully to the original constitution.

3 The memorandum declares that if a landlord refuses to accept the caution offered by a prospective tenant scholar, the applicant may go to the chancellor, who will at once admit him to the tenancy (Mullinger, *op. cit.* p. 639). This was the custom by 1292. See above, p. 173, n. 1. It shows how chapter XII, par. v, of the Angelica text was interpreted in the late thirteenth century.

Chapter 9

THE MARKAUNT RECENSION

(*c.* 1304–37)

Future investigations may reveal that the statutes described in the preceding chapter represent only part of the total number of additions made to the constitution of the university before the turn of the thirteenth century. By *c.* 1304–37 at least sixteen new statutes were promulgated and it is conceivable that some, if not the majority, of these were enacted before 1300.[1] There are many more in the Old Proctor's Book (*c.* 1390–5/8) which ought, perhaps, to be assigned to the same period but cannot for lack of precise evidence.

The volume of fresh legislation during the half-century 1250–1300, which has just been surveyed, was sufficient to necessitate the production of a new and up-to-date codification of the statutes. If a compelling reason was required, the year 1304 provided it. For the first time since the establishment of the university the non-regent masters were recognized as joint partners with the regents as regards the making, repealing and amending of statutes. The supreme legislative assembly of the university was now the congregation of regents and non-regents; no statutes could be carried without the consent of both houses. How the non-regents won their new status is an interesting story. In 1276 they made their first appearance in the role of statute-makers when they participated with the regents and senior bachelors in the enactment of the statute authorizing the rectors to summon convocations of the regents in certain circumstances, should the chancellor or his *locum tenens*, the vice-chancellor, prove unwilling. The intervention of the non-regents on this occasion was beyond doubt exceptional; it cannot be put forward as proof that they, any more than the bachelors, enjoyed permanent statutory powers. Nothing is heard of the non-regents in 1290–4 when various permanent statutes were enacted.[2] It was the challenge

[1] The statutes are: Markaunt 5, 10, 14, 16, 18, 21, 22, 23, 24, 25, 30, 31, 33, 34, 36, 38.

[2] The decree of 18 March 1294 ordering the observance of the anniversary in perpetuity of Eleanor of Castile begins: 'statuit tota vniuersitas regencium' (Clark, *Endowments*, p. 553). The statute was made by the regents only. The word *statuit* in this context is of paramount importance. Cf. Rashdall, *Universities*, iii. 65, n. 1; *SAUO*, p. xxii.

to the Friars Preacher and Minor thrown down in 1303–4 by the chancellor, mag. Stephen de Haslingfeld, and the regents which elevated the non-regents to the position of co-legislators with the regent masters, thus introducing the greatest single change ever made in the constitution of the university.

On 18 March 1304 it was enacted professedly 'by authority of the whole university of Cambridge, both regent and non-regent masters' that in matters pertaining to the common utility of the university only such statutes as were made with the consent and by decree of the *maior et sanior pars* of the regent and non-regent houses were valid. A clause was inserted saving to the regents the exercise of statutes previously enacted, a proviso which further indicates that hitherto the power of making statutes was the prerogative of the regent masters.[1] What part the non-regents actually played in the enactment of this all-important statute is problematical. As will shortly appear, the non-regents did not give their assent until 2 May. It is certain, at all events, that the regents offered them the status of a co-statutory body as a *quid pro quo*. If the chancellor and the regent masters, mainly those of the faculty of arts, were to succeed in dislodging the friars from their privileged position the moral support of the non-regents was essential. The friars could rally to their aid a few non-regent masters from their own ranks but not enough to offset the number of non-regents in arts.

From the course of events outlined in the appeal which the friars through their proctors lodged with the Holy See it is evident that the statute of 18 March 1304 was proposed in order to secure the assent of the non-regents to an earlier statute which was the immediate cause of all the trouble. This statute, tabled on 22 November 1303 and purporting to be the unanimous will of the 'cetus tam

[1] Cf. Markaunt 1 (see below, p. 313, lines 20–2); *SA* 1 (*Docs*, i. 308). Both versions include a clause, a later addition, excluding the regents from using statutes specially reserved to the non-regents. The original form of the statute minus the date and place of publication is printed in Little, 'The friars *v.* the university of Cambridge', *E.H.R.* l (1935), 693. Cf. the texts in the Durham roll published by Moorman, *Grey Friars in Cambridge*, pp. 228, 235–6. This Durham roll contains virtually a complete copy of the gravamina, of which this statute was one, presented by the friars to the Holy See. Little, art. cit. *loc. cit.*, pp. 689–96, prints in full the award made by the papal delegate at Bordeaux on 17 June 1306. His source was Hare's transcript which was made from the copy in Markaunt's Book, fo. 37^{v} (D 15^{v}), stated by Little to be lost. The book is very much at home in the university archives. The original of the award was at one time in the archives, where it was listed as doc. no. 13. According to Peek and Hall, *Archives*, p. 26, it is still there complete with seal. Unfortunately, both the document and seal are missing.

magistrorum regentium quam non regentium', decreed that in future the statutory university sermons on the first Sunday of Advent, Septuagesima and Ash Wednesday were to be delivered in St Mary's church either by the chancellor or by regent masters deputed by him.[1] This was a direct affront to the Friars Preacher, who had been accustomed *ab antiquo*, as they informed the pope, to preach these sermons in their own church.[2] The offending statute was merely the thin end of the wedge. What the chancellor and his fellow regents were aiming at was to wrest control of examinatory sermons from the friars, and in effect the admission of scholars to the degree of master in theology.[3] In virtue of a third statute, also said to have been made with the unanimous consent of the regent and non-regent houses and which bears the date 17 April 1304, examinatory sermons were to be preached in the university church on a day designated by the chancellor; no incepting bachelor was bound henceforth to preach in any other church.[4]

The statute of 18 March 1304 was the crucial one. Those enacted on 22 November 1303 and 17 April 1304 depended for their validity on it. Apparently, the November statute was not formally promulgated on the said date, for in their appeal the friars stated that by 7 March, the date of their second appeal, no statutes had either been edited or published.[5] On Friday, 17 April, the third statute was due to be enacted and the friars were duly summoned

[1] The date of this statute is found only in the Durham roll (Moorman, *op. cit.* pp. 229, 236). There is a suggestion in the papal award of 1306 that the difference between the friars and the university started on 15 November 1303. Cf. Little, cit. p. 689; the text of the statute cited in the award together with its amendment is printed *ibid.* p. 693. The official statute, *SA* 168, does not include the amendment, though it adds the feast of Corpus Christi to the list of *dies predicabiles*. Cf. *Docs*, i. 398.

[2] Durham roll, cit. pp. 232, 237. Cf. Little, cit. p. 689.

[3] Hitherto, inceptors in theology were examined in preaching by the friars, who were now to be compelled to undergo examination themselves 'extra loca sua, quod nunquam fuit factum nec auditum nec Parisius nec Bononie ubi sunt sollempniora studia, nec alibi' (Durham roll, cit. pp. 232, 238).

[4] Little, cit. p. 694; Durham roll, cit. pp. 229, 237. The statute, *SA* 167 (*Docs*, i. 397–8), was amended as a result of the representations made by the friars, but the text gives no indication that 'Fratres tamen...prius' is an amendment. The friars' contention was that the chancellor might refuse to assign their bachelors a day for delivering their examinatory sermons, and hence they would be unable to incept. But even if the chancellor was co-operative, the friars argued that the rector of St Mary's might refuse them permission to preach in his church, just as certain beneficed masters had excluded them from their churches. Cf. the Durham roll, cit. pp. 232, 238.

[5] Durham roll, *loc. cit.* p. 228. The friars first appealed on 3 March.

to congregation. They had the university notified of their refusal to be present and the statute was accordingly carried without their consent.[1] The whole position is unreal. All three statutes are said to have been enacted on the aforesaid dates by the unanimous will of all the regents and non-regents. The regent friars certainly did not give their assent, and the non-regents were not asked to vote before 2 May. It was only then that they signified their approval of the statute of 18 March.[2] But even though all three statutes were ratified at a congregation of the regent and non-regent masters which lasted from 2 May to 4 May, there can be no question of unanimous consent. The friars refused outright to approve of the statutes and were expelled from the society of masters. It follows that the original wording of the three statutes is misleading unless understood in a retrospective sense, for they were not ratified unanimously by both houses of regents and non-regents until the May congregation.[3]

The effect of the statute dated 18 March 1304 was not to transfer the power of making statutes from the faculties to the regents in arts, but the definition of *maior et sanior pars* laid down in 1294 inevitably assured the artists of a preponderant voting strength in all congregations. This clause was embodied in the vital statute, and although paying lip service to the faculties it worked most to the advantage of the masters of arts. The definition was engineered in the first place largely through the efforts of the masters of theology. The leaders of the faculty were the friars; to their chagrin the principle was now turned to their undoing by their old rivals, the regents in arts.[4]

[1] *Ibid.* The friars again appealed on 25 April (*ibid.* p. 229).

[2] 'Et quidem primum statutum est...Datum M°CCCiii, xv kal. aprilis. Sed secundum veritatem ista data fuit in M°CCCiiii, secunda die maii, quo die non-regentes primo consenserunt' (*ibid.* p. 228). But some non-regents appear to have voted by 25 April 1304. Cf. *ibid.* p. 229.

[3] The friars reported that the chancellor and regents on 2 May 'assumptis secum et admissis magistris non-regentibus, ediderunt et promulgarunt talia statuta', viz. those of 18 March 1304, 22 Nov. 1303 and 17 April 1304. Cf. *ibid.* pp. 234–6. Though it was alleged by the friars that their non-regent masters were ignored and treated with contempt by the university, the fact is that the friars refused to commit themselves, adding as an extra plea that they had no authority to act while their superiors were away attending the general chapters of their orders. One suspects that if they could have mustered enough non-regent masters of their own to outnumber the non-regents in arts they would have challenged the three statutes to a vote.

[4] Little, cit. p. 687, notes how closely the events of 1303–4 at Cambridge were paralleled by contemporary developments at Oxford. It is scarcely true, however,

Two years passed before the university and the friars were reconciled. Both parties agreed to abide by the decisions of the papal delegate appointed to settle the dispute, the Dominican Cardinal Thomas Jorz, who published his award at the Franciscan convent, Bordeaux, on 17 June 1306. Two of the controversial statutes, those of 22 November 1303 and 17 April 1304, carried amendments safeguarding the privileges of the Dominicans and Franciscans. The third, the pivotal statute of 18 March 1304, was confirmed in the form in which it was approved on 2 May.[1] When the terms of the concord were ratified at Cambridge under the seal of the university, the non-regent masters were admitted as *de jure* members of its highest legislative council, and it was necessary to give statutory recognition to their right to assent to or veto future legislation. This entailed a remodelling of the constitution. It would have been a relatively simple matter to make the required adjustments without taking the existing code to pieces; as a matter of fact the insertion of references to the non-regents in the appropriate statutes presented no difficulty. It seems, however, that once the need of a revised text was admitted the opportunity was grasped of devising a new code incorporating the various enactments, amendments and decrees which had mounted up during the preceding half-century. We may assume that the work of reshaping the Angelica text, or rather the official exemplar, was undertaken by a leading canonist or doctor in civil law, assisted by a select committee of experts. There was no shortage at this period of competent men. The chancellor in 1306, mag. Stephen de Segrave, and his deputy, the vice-chancellor, mag. Richard de Aston, were both doctors in canon law, as was the monk Simon de Walden, who together with John de Ros or Ross, professor of civil law, witnessed the agreement at Bordeaux.[2]

It is not possible to date within narrow limits the redaction (α),

that the Oxford statute (*c.* 1303) on voting by faculties betokens a more developed organization of the faculty system at Oxford than at Cambridge. On the importance of the faculties as regards the initiation and enactment of statutes at Cambridge, see above, pp. 234–5. Little, it goes without saying, was gravely mistaken when he described the Cambridge statutes of 1303–4 as 'the three earliest statutes of the university which have survived' (Little, cit. p. 686).

[1] The statute was afterwards slightly amended. See above, p. 241, n. 1.

[2] Little, cit. p. 695. For Aston, Segrave and Walden cf. *BRUC*, pp. 20–1, 516, 695, and above, p. 131, n. 2. Ross is not listed by Dr Emden. He was provided to the see of Carlisle on 13 Feb. 1325 and died in 1332.

for no complete text of the new code has survived.[1] Fortunately, a partial exemplar comprising the first thirty-eight statutes is extant in Markaunt's Book. Thomas Markaunt was senior proctor of the university in 1417–18 and had the good sense to have miscellaneous documents, drawn from original sources and relating to the university, copied into a volume. The book, *Liber priuilegiorum et statutorum vniuersitatis Cantabriggie*, had a chequered history, but it is now carefully preserved in the university archives, where it is familiarly known as 'Markaunt's Book'.[2]

The significance of Markaunt's text of the statutes has never been appreciated, mainly for two reasons. The text is defective and more important still the university possessed in the Old Proctor's Book its own official register, splendidly executed and containing an almost perfect text. Consequently, Markaunt's Book was relegated to a very obscure place, meriting only perfunctory mention.[3] Yet anyone who troubled to analyse the text even cursorily would have realized that the manuscript was compiled from a much older redaction of the statutes than the exemplar of the Old Proctor's Book, granted that Markaunt's Book itself was written twenty years or more later. The form of the celebrated statute of March 1304 exhibited by Markaunt's text is obviously closer to the original than the statute entered in the Old Proctor's Book, which lacks the formal declaration that the statute was granted on 18 March 1304 in St Mary's church.[4] Not so Markaunt's text.[5] The dates of other statutes and their enactment are known only from Markaunt's text, which provides the key to the composition of *SA* 10. One would never suspect that this particular statute as recorded in the official registers is a conflation of three separate enactments.[6]

Without the aid of the Angelica manuscript the precise position of Markaunt's text of the statutes in the evolution of the Cambridge code must have given rise to much perplexity. On the basis of internal evidence one would have to conclude that Markaunt's exemplar was derived from a redaction which is earlier than the edition in the Old Proctor's Book. This is where the Angelica

1 The symbol α stands for the parent of the Markaunt recension. See the *stemma codicum*, p. 306 below. The MS is not extant.

2 A description of the book and its history is given on pp. 309–12 below.

3 Some extracts from and a few variant readings of the statutes are printed in *Docs*, i. 308–36.

4 Cf. Old Proctor 1 (fo. 17r); *SA* 1 (*Docs*, i. 308).

5 Cf. Markaunt 1 (see below, p. 313, lines 22–3).

6 See below, pp. 270–3.

manuscript assumes a new dimension in the history of the statutes. Markaunt's text taken by itself could be misleading. For example, it introduces a statute on judicial processes with an explanatory statement not found in the Angelica text nor in the later statute-books, which in this instance and to this extent only are closer to the original than is Markaunt:

Angelica X. ii	*Markaunt* 27	*SA* 34
	Vt litigantes celeri-	Item
	iorem consequantur	
	iusticiam prouisum	
	est et statutum vt	provisum
	in examinacione cau-	est ut
In examinacione causa-	sarum iuris solem-	in examinatione cau-
rum solempnitas nequa-	pnitas nullatenus	sarum juris solen-
quam obseruetur excepto	obseruetur nec super	nitas nullatenus
quod eciam sine scriptis	actibus iudicialibus	observetur, nec super
ediciones contestaciones	quibuscunque iudices	actibus judicialibus
et debite probaciones	seu partes scriptu-	quibuscunque judices
	ram edere teneantur.	seu partes scriptu-
	set omnia acta iudi-	ram edere teneantur,
	cialia sine quibus	sed omnia acta judi-
sine quibus	ad sentenciam perue-	cialia, sine quibus
ad sentenciam non	niri non poterit sine	ad sententiam perve-
peruenitur omnino	scriptura procedant.	niri non poterit, sine
recipiantur. (*Cons. Univ.*	(See below, p. 325, lines	scriptura procedant.
Canteb. p. 209, line 17 to	9–13.)	(*Docs*, i. 328.)
p. 211, lines 1–2.)		

The text of the *statutum antiquum* is identical with that of the Old Proctor's Book (fo. 24^{v}, no. 36). Though it lacks the introductory part of Markaunt, enough remains to show that the Old Proctor text, far from being derived directly from Angelica, is nothing more than a redaction of Markaunt. This does not mean that the editor of the *c.* 1385 recension worked from the exemplar of Markaunt. The penultimate paragraph of Angelica I is missing from Markaunt, but it appears in the Old Proctor's text, albeit in a somewhat different form.[1] The point, needless to say, underlines the value of the Angelica manuscript as a control in evaluating the textual tradition of the medieval statutes. Nevertheless, there can be no question that Markaunt's Book contains the earliest known redaction of the first constitution of the university, and it is important therefore to establish the date of the exemplar.

[1] See below, p. 268, n. 2.

It cannot have been made before 1304, for the statute dated 18 March of that year comes immediately after the title of the text: *Hec sunt statuta Vniuersitatis Cantabrigie primo de modo statuendi.* The statute not only heads the series; it appears in an amended form, which implies that the text was executed some time after 17 June 1306. The ultimate date for the completion of the new code must remain conjectural because in Markaunt's Book the transcription ends with statute 38. The explanation for this most disappointing fact is not far to seek. Either the scribe's exemplar was defective or, what is more likely, he realized that to continue with the remaining statutes was for practical purposes a sheer waste of time. He was copying a dead text, one which was of no interest to Markaunt, since it was now superseded by the more recent edition available in the still extant Old Proctor's Book and Caius manuscript.[1] The unfinished transcript of the earlier redaction in Markaunt's Book provides only a limited picture of the adjustments made to the early thirteenth-century text of the statutes after 1304. On the basis of thirty-eight statutes, probably but a fraction of the total, it is rash to propose a firm date for the construction of the recension. There is convincing proof, however, that it was completed before 1337. By statute dated 2 December 1322 the duration of the office of chancellor at Oxford was limited to two years.[2] A similar statute was made by Cambridge. It is not found in Markaunt, though all the later collections of the statutes have it.[3] Fortunately, the prescriptions concerning the election and office of the chancellor, proctors, taxors, and bedells are complete in Markaunt's text, where, in addition to the 1304 statute, they form the first twenty chapters or statutes. This part of the redaction is definitely complete. Since it leaves the duration of the chancellorship an open question, the exemplar, and hence the entire redaction, must have been executed before the date of the statute *De tempore quo durat officium Cancellarii.*[4] This cannot be later than 1337. At the confirmation of the newly elected chancellor, Richard de Harlyng, the proctor informed the bishop's official, John de Clipston, on 9 November

[1] For the lost MSS of the code fashioned *c.* 1385 see below, p. 261.

[2] *SAUO*, 121, 35–123, 9.

[3] *SA* 12 (*Docs*, i. 314). Cf. Old Proctor 13 (fo. 19r); Caius 13 (fo. 2va).

[4] *SA* 12 reads: 'Item statutum est quod cancellarius, qui pro tempore fuerit, ultra biennium continuum cancellarii officio non fungatur: liceat tamen majori parti regentium circa finem biennii, ut per annum unum continuum sequentem duntaxat stare valeat in dicto officio, disponere' (*Docs*, i. 314).

1337 that a new chancellor was elected every two years whether or not the man in office resigned or was relieved or gave his consent.[1] We may conclude, then, that the statutes were recodified some time between 1304 and 1337. These are the outside dates. It is unlikely that anything was done to incorporate the 1303–4 statutes in a new recension until the quarrel with the friars was patched up in 1306;[2] and a date *c.* 1314–37 for the completion and promulgation of the redaction may be suggested.[3] In any case, Markaunt's text bridges a gap of almost a century in the transmission of the Cambridge constitutions and thus assumes an importance out of all proportion to its length.

The most striking features of the recension as exemplified by the first thirty-eight statutes, and what marks it off from the early thirteenth-century code, are, first, the introduction of numbered chapters in serial order. Secondly, the division of single constitutions

1 '...post quodlibet biennium procedi potest ad electionem noui Cancellarij resignacione aut dimissione aut consensu cuiuscumque Cancellarij precedentis minime habitis aut etiam requisitis' (Ely Dioc. Rec. GI [1], pt 1, fo. 2^{v}). The same declaration was made at the confirmation of Richard de Lyng on 15 March 1340 (*ibid.* fo. 9^{r}) and John de Crakhall on 28 Oct. 1346 (*ibid.* pt 2, fo. 8^{r}). Harlyng appears to have vacated office by 24 Nov. 1339; cf. *ibid.* pt 1, fo. 9^{v}. His predecessor, Henry de Harowden, was elected *c.* Oct. 1335 and continued until 1337. A. C. Chibnall, *Richard de Badew and the university of Cambridge 1315–1340* (Cambridge, 1963), p. 35, says that he was removed from office and suggests that this was done because of his unsuitability and arrogant ways. But the university could not deprive him except by appealing to the bishop to recall his commission. There is no evidence that it did. Under the terms of *SA* 12 Harowden's term as chancellor expired automatically in 1337.

2 The first part of Markaunt 26 (see below, p. 324, lines 32–5) appears to have been constructed after 12 March 1305; the grant made by the king in parliament on that date extending the jurisdiction of the chancellor over causes involving scholars and laymen is specifically limited to the town of Cambridge. Cf. *Memoranda de parliamento*, pp. 36–7. Moreover, Markaunt 1, as we have seen, was amended most probably after 17 June 1306.

3 The 1305 concession was renewed on 7 April 1314 (*Cal. pat. rolls, 1313–17*, p. 102). The preamble to Markaunt 27 (see above, p. 246) is suggestive of the influence of Clement V's bull *Saepe*, which had for its object the acceleration of judicial processes and consequently a more rapid administration of justice in ecclesiastical courts. It is possible, therefore, that the original statute, *Cons. Univ. Canteb.* x. ii, was revised *c.* 1314. For the date of the papal constitution see Kuttner's article cited on p. 29, n. 4. One hesitates to speculate further on the question of dates; but the redaction may have been published much nearer to 1337 than to 1314. An Oxford statute of 1327 seems to have left its mark on Markaunt 33 (see below, p. 328, lines 24–8); cf. *SAUO*, 130, 28–131, 2. On 14 Dec. 1333 another statute was enacted at Oxford restricting the chancellor's leave of absence in full term to one month (*ibid.* 133, 20–8). The same provision is contained in Markaunt 7 (see below, p. 315, lines 15–16). It may well be that Cambridge copied this statute from Oxford.

into several distinct statutes. Thirdly, the redistribution of material, an arrangement that certainly made for better order and easier reference. Fourthly, the addition of completely new statutes, twenty-one out of a given total of thirty-eight. Lastly, Markaunt's relationship with the exemplar of Angelica and the Old Proctor's Book and the Caius manuscript exemplifies from a key position the transmission of the text of the Cambridge statutes during the late thirteenth and fourteenth centuries. The following plan will give some idea of the revised text of the statutes published *c.* 1304–37 and how it compares with the first code; but it must be remembered that only a fragment of the new recension survives in Markaunt:

Markaunt	*Angelica*
1 De modo statuendi	—
2 De electione Cancellarij	I. i De eleccione Cancelarii atque ipsius potestate
3 De iuramento et obediencia Cancellarij	—
4 De officio Cancellarij	I. vi De eleccione Cancelarii atque ipsius potestate
5 De modo committendi causas	—
6 De commissario Cancellarij	I. ii De eleccione Cancelarii atque ipsius potestate
7 De Vicecancellario	I. iii De eleccione Cancelarii atque ipsius potestate
8 De potestate Cancellarij	I. iv De eleccione Cancelarii atque ipsius potestate
—	I. v De eleccione Cancelarii atque ipsius potestate
—	II De creacione Magistrorum et eorum officio
—	III De temporibus incipiendi et cessandi
9 De conuocacionibus faciendis	IV De conuocacionibus faciendis
10 De officio Cancellarij resignando	—
—	V De habitu magistrorum
11 De electione rectorum seu procuratorum	cf. VII. i De officio rectorum
12 De electione taxatorum	cf. VII. i De officio rectorum
13 De officijs rectorum	VII. iv, ii, iii De officio rectorum
14 De potestate rectorum	—
15 De potestate rectorum in defectu Cancellarij	—
16 De compoto rectorum soluendo	—
17 De officio taxatorum	cf. VII. i De officio rectorum

Markaunt (cont.)	*Angelica (cont.)*
18 De consuetudine eligendi bedellos seu apparitores	—
19 De officijs bedellorum et apparitorum	VIII De officiis bedellorum et apparitorum et eorum honoribus
20 De declaracione super incarceracionibus et correctionibus	—
21 De defensoribus et procuratoribus litigancium	—
—	IX De satisdacione litigancium et eorum iuramento
22 De aduocatis	—
23 De procuratoribus admittendis	—
24 De modo veniendi ad lites seu diem amoris	—
25 De rebellantibus Cancellario	XI. v De inmunitate scolarium et pena delinquencium
26 De Iudicijs et foro scolarium competenti	—
27 De ordine iudiciorum in causis scolarium	X. ii De ordine iudiciorum in causis scolarium custodiendo
28 De iuramento litigancium	X. i De ordine iudiciorum in causis scolarium custodiendo
29 De curia Magistrorum et iurisdictione eorundem	VI De curia magistrorum
30 De penis appellancium et eorum caucione	—
31 De modo conuincendi periuros	—
32 De hospicijs et pensione domorum	XII De hospiciis et pensionibus domorum
33 De conuenticulis seu proturbacione [*sic*] pacis	—
34 De choreis et choreas ducentibus	—
35 De immunitate scolarium	XI. i–ii De inmunitate scolarium et pena delinquencium
36 De falsis scolaribus et alijs pacis perturbatoribus	—
37 De eiectis Oxonie et alijs vagabundis	XI. iii–iv De inmunitate scolarium et pena delinquencium
38 De pena eorum qui contempnunt Magistros	—
—	XIII De exequiis defunctorum

It will be observed that the 1304 statute *De modo statuendi* was logically inserted at the beginning of the revised text, and it continued to hold this position in all the later collections of statutes. It is fairly typical of the redaction that the first chapter of the Angelica text, which deals with the office and power of the chancellor, now appears as five separate statutes with appropriate titles, including those of commissary and vice-chancellor—terms not employed in the original constitution. The statute on convocations together with three new statutes brings the number of specific statutes concerning the chancellor up to ten.[1] Further evidence of the process whereby a single constitution of the Angelica text was taken to pieces and made into separate statutes is seen in Markaunt 25, 35, 37, which reverse the order of the early thirteenth-century constitution, Angelica XI. This chapter originally consisted of five paragraphs. In the Markaunt recension the final one appears first and forms the nucleus of statute 25, *De rebellantibus Cancellario*. It is printed here in bold type.[2]

Si quis de vniuersitate iurisdictionem Cancellarij contempnens propriam vel alienam iniuriam cum deliberacione vel ex intervallo vindicauerit insultum in ipsum quem deliquisse dicit aut in eius hospicium faciendo aut eundem verberando seu male tractando si monitus ad arbitrium Cancellarij vel vniuersitatis satisfacere noluerit cum effectu infra triduum ab vniuersitate expellatur ceteris penis iuxta priuilegia consuetudines et statuta malefactoribus imponendis eisdem malefactoribus nichilominus infligendis quas quidem penas. seu puniciones non tantum ad ipsos malefactores verum eciam ad eorum fautores seu defensores sine personarum accepcione volumus extendi. **Contra prohibicionem cancellarii** (cancelarij quoque prohibicionem—Markaunt) **colluctantes et alias sibi inobedientes et contumaces** cum super huiusmodi secundum modum vniuersitatis conuicti fuerint **sine differencia personarum simili pena coherceantur si hoc meruerit proteruitas contumacium** verum si magistri regentes vel non regentes vel aliquis eorum contra Cancellarium colluctans vel alias inobediens extiterit eorum causa per electas ab alijs regentibus personas tractetur et terminetur In quarum electione personarum vt omnis timor subornacionis absistat tam cancellarius quam taliter rebellantes sint absentes.

An abbreviated version of Markaunt 20 was later added to this text, which became *SA* 10.[3]

Paragraphs i and ii of Angelica XI were formed into Markaunt 35 under a shortened version of the original title of the chapter. New matter was skilfully introduced between the two paragraphs, now

[1] Angelica I. v is missing from Markaunt. On the textual significance of this omission see p. 268.

[2] *Cons. Univ. Canteb.* XI. v (see above, p. 213, lines 7–9); Markaunt 25 (see below, p. 324, lines 13–30).

[3] *Docs*, i. 312–13. See also below, pp. 270–3.

fused into one continuous statute, and a further addition was made at the end:[1]

Indignum esse iudicamus ut quis scolarem tueatur (tuetur) qui certum magistrum infra quindecim dies post [eius] ingressum uniuersitatis (in vniuersitatem) non habuerit aut nomen suum infra tempus prelibatum in matricula sui magistri (*trans.*) redigi (redigere) non curauerit nisi magistri [sui] absencia uel iusta [eorum] occupacio illud impediat. Immo si quis talis sub nomine scolaris [sic] latitans (latitare) inueniatur (compertus fuerit) retineatur (vel detinetur vel deiciatur) iuxta domini regis [super hoc concessam] libertatem. [Nullus eciam Magistrorum aliquem tanquam scolarem proprium defendat qui scolaris eius non existit cuius nomen in matricula sua non habeat insertum nisi alias quod suus sit scolaris certam de eo habuerit noticiam Caueant tamen Magistri regentes ne erga pauperes scolares suos difficiles se exhibeant set cum scolares huiusmodi suum nomen petant inseri de inopia sua facta fide Magister eos benignus admittat Prouisum est eciam et statutum vt omnes morantes in municipio nostro qui speciem gerunt scolarium sint veri scolares et lectionibus Magistrorum suorum intersint prout decet.] Hii [quoque] soli scolares (-ium) gaudeant inmunitate qui saltem per tres dies in septimana scolas magistri sui ingrediantur tres lecciones ad minus audituri dummodo per tres dies in (*om.*) septimana (*om.*) magister per se (suus) legerit. nisi magistri sui licencia uel (ex) causa racionabilis (-i) ipsorum (eorum) absenciam excusauerit (*trans.*). [Exceptis illis qui in lectura aliqua theologie Iuris canonici seu ciuilis publice fuerint occupati Exceptis eciam maioribus qui saltem bis in septimana intersint lectionibus Magistrorum suorum si commode poterint.]

In Markaunt this statute is immediately followed by another on the same subject but treating of false scholars from the point of view of morals and discipline.[2] It was doubtless the relationship between the two statutes which prompted the redactor to break the sequence of the Angelica text. Having detached paragraphs iii and iv from paragraphs i and ii of chapter XI to form a distinct statute he added a new title, *De eiectis Oxonie et alijs vagabundis*, and made it into no. 37 of the code. The thirteenth-century constitution and the early fourteenth-century recension are best compared by printing the texts in parallel columns as shown on the page opposite.[3]

There are three points to be noted about the Markaunt text. The clauses *quidam alii* and *rebus aliis* and the relevant passage have been dropped; the reviser in rephrasing the pericope on carrying weapons

[1] *Cons. Univ. Canteb.* XI. i–ii (see above, p. 211, lines 4–15); Markaunt 35 (see below, p. 330, lines 2–23); cf. *SA* 42 (*Docs*, i. 332–3). Accretions in Markaunt are printed within square brackets, variants within round brackets; only genuine variants, excluding scribal errors, are noted.

[2] Markaunt 36 (see below, p. 330, line 25 to p. 331, line 7).

[3] The corresponding *statutum antiquum* is *SA* 45 (*Docs*, i. 334–5).

Angelica XI. iii–iv

Aduenticius malefactor nunquam recipiatur quem per litteras cancelarii oxonie uel alio legitimo modo ab uniuersitate oxonie constiterit fuisse eiectum.

Effractores domorum raptores mulierum Insidiatores uiarum. arma ad nocendum uel ad vindictam precipue de nocte defferentes. necnon et qui clericum et laycum de uilla cantebrigie extra uillam per clausas illas quidam alii et rebus aliis conuenerint eciam nemine deferente super hoc conuicti propter quietem publicam per cancellarium et magistros ab uniuersitate sine spe restitucionis deiciantur uel in carcerem detrudantur iuxta formam supradictam grauius cohercendi si hoc meruerit pertinacia delinquencium nisi eorum penitencia aliud persuadeat armis ipsis in utilitatem pauperum uel cancelarii omnino conuertendis. (*Cons. Univ. Canteb.* [see above, p. 211, line 16 to p. 213, line 9].)

Markaunt 37

Aduenticius malefactor in municipio nostro nusquam recipiatur quem per literas Cancellarij Oxonie vel alio modo legitimo malefactorem esse constiterit et ab vniuersitate oxonie tanquam talem fuisse eiectum—Fractores domorum et insultores earundem raptores mulierum insidiatores viarum vagabundi cum armis vel alias arma deferentes seu deferri facientes per se vel per alios causa mali perpetrandi in villa vel iuxta villam occulte vel manifeste de die vel de nocte

per Cancellarium et vniuersitatem regencium ab vniuersitate sine spe restitucionis eiciantur vel in carcerem detrudantur. Liceat tamen Cancellario ex causa racionabili consciencie sue arbitrio relinquenda super delacione armorum ad tempus dispensare. (See below, p. 331, lines 9–18.)

seems to have drawn on an Oxford source;[1] and there is an echo of the 1294 controversy in the substitution of the phrase 'Cancellarium et vniuersitatem regencium' in place of 'cancellarium et magistros'. An independent-minded chancellor might be tempted to evade the scrutiny of the regent masters and consider himself bound to consult only the non-regents in decreeing the expulsion or imprisonment of a member of the university. This would be to put too fine an interpretation on the term *magistros*. After 1294 there was no room for doubt, and as if to make assurance doubly sure the ambiguous word was replaced by the term *universitas regentium*, which admitted of no equivocation.

The most drastic example of recasting is Markaunt 13. This is the statute on the rectors. It has been suggested in the previous chapter that the constitution was amended *c.* 1255–68, the first paragraph of Angelica VII being taken out and made the basis of a new statute on the taxors. Either then or later the remainder of the constitution

[1] See above, p. 82.

on the rectors was turned upside down, enlarged and generally rewritten. The final paragraph of Angelica VII became the first paragraph of Markaunt 13. Few chapters of the thirteenth-century text can have caused the redactor more headaches than this particular one. Angelica VII. iv, which deals with the strictly academic side of the rectors' office, was imperfect. How the editor got over the difficulty will shortly be seen, but apart from the addition of one large accretion and an amendment which appears to have been tacked on in 1294 the original statute remained almost unchanged.[1]

The sequence of Angelica VII. ii–iii was preserved by the redactor. His reworking of the text is none the less instructive. The recension compared with the original is an inferior production, vitiated mainly by the editor's penchant for repetition and especially the use of doublets. There is no difficulty in recognizing which of the following two texts is the revised version:

Angelica VII. ii–iii

Diligenter curent ut panis et uinum et alia uictui cotidiano necessaria secundum uarietates temporum et rerum qualitates iusto precio non secus scolaribus quam laicis uendantur scolaribus et eorum seruientibus omnibus aliis negociacionis causa emptoribus semper preferendis. Monopolios id est uenditores inter se pasciscentes uel ad inuicem colludentes de esu et potu non nisi certo precio ut scolaribus uendantur communiter detrahendis et precipue balliuos et eorum uxores et huiusmodi mercimonia ad uictum cottidianum pertinencia durante officio excercentes et maxime cibum et potum contra communem prouisionem detrahentes necnon et in vniuersitate malefactores inobedientes et contumaces per se et per alios diligenter inuestigent ut eorum nomina referant cancelario grauiter puniendorum ipsis potibus et cibariis †

Markaunt 13

Diligenter eciam curent vt panis et vinum et alia cotidiano victui necessaria secundum varietates temporum et rerum qualitates iusto precio non secus scolaribus quam laicis vendantur. Scolares vero et eorum seruientes omnibus alijs causa negociacionis semper preferantur. Diligenter autem investigent Monopolios id est venditores inter se paciscentes vel ad inuicem de victualibus colludentes quod nisi certo precio inter se fraudulenter taxato vt carius scolaribus vendant huiusmodi victualia distrahantur et precipue balliuos et eorum vxores huiusmodi mercimonia ad victum cotidianum pertinencia durante officio excercentes **diligenter inquirant et eorum nomine cancellario referant vt secundum priuilegia et statuta grauiter puniantur** ipsis cibarijs et potibus per eosdem **in vtilitatem**

[1] For the accretion 'Liceat eciam rectoribus...reseruata' cf. Markaunt 13 (see below, p. 317, lines 32–4). The reference in the amendment (*ibid.* lines 35–6) to the 'consensus maioris et sanioris partis regencium' suggests that it was formulated in the light of the decree of the bishop's official, Coventre. See above, p. 234.

cum ipsis transgressoribus communionem habere uel mercimonium omnino inhibendis. (*Cons. Univ. Canteb.* VII. ii–iii [see above, p. 205, lines 6–21].)

pauperum omnino conuertendis. ac eciam scolaribus cum ipsis transgressoribus comunionem habere uel mercimonium est penitus inhibendum— Idem eciam procuratores seu rectores malefactores in vniuersitate inobedientes et contumaces per se et per alios **diligenter investigent et eorum nomina cancellario referant vt per statuta et priuilegia vniuersitatis puniantur**. (See below, p. 317, line 36 to p. 318, line 16.)

It would be tedious to point out Markaunt's variants. The first and third passages printed in bold type are an obvious pair; in between is another passage which has been emphasized for a different reason; it shows that the editor was not averse to filching a phrase from a later chapter of the Angelica code in order to bridge a gap in the original.[1]

The thoroughgoing rearrangement of Angelica VII is not an isolated case by any means in the history of the recensions of the statutes. Markaunt itself suffered similar treatment when its successor was being produced. Perhaps the most striking feature from a historical point of view of Markaunt's redaction of the Angelica statute is the new emphasis placed on the strictly academic functions of the rectors. Their primary concern is no longer the taxation of houses. This matter is now the concern of the taxors. Though the division of offices was introduced probably *c.* 1255–68, the earliest statutory evidence is provided by Markaunt.

Cambridge redactors in addition to experimenting with better systems of codification and incorporating more recent statutes as well as amendments sought to iron out anomalies or correct blunders which occurred in their exemplars. In Markaunt 13 two perplexing passages in the manuscript tradition are rectified. The emendations or rather the methods adopted by the redactor are an object lesson in textual criticism, not because they reveal his genius but on the contrary the danger of assuming that a plausible emendation restores the true reading of the original. It will be helpful to see the passages side by side.

[1] See below, p. 256.

Angelica	*Markaunt*
ipsis potibus et cibariis cum ipsis transgressoribus communionem habere uel mercimonium omnino inhibendis.	ipsis cibarijs et potibus per eosdem [*sc.* rectores] in vtilitatem pauperum omnino conuertendis. ac eciam scolaribus cum ipsis transgressoribus communionem habere vel mercimonium est penitus inhibendum.

The presence of a hiatus in Angelica between *cibariis* and *cum* is certain. It was noticed either by the editor of Markaunt or perhaps by a previous redactor. At all events the omission was made good by using another passage in Angelica and inserting it with minor modifications into the gap.[1] To conclude that this was the actual reading in the original would be very unwise indeed.[2] Elsewhere in the text the reviser reveals his hand, the final clause of the entire statute 'vt per statuta et priuilegia vniuersitatis puniantur' being little more than a repetition of 'vt secundum priuilegia et statuta grauiter puniantur'.[3]

The second anomaly corrected in Markaunt 13 provides even greater food for thought:

Angelica	*Markaunt*
Tempora et modus legendi et disputandi...ad ipsos [*sc.* rectores] pertineant in transgressores circa predicta ad eorum officia specialiter et in bedellos. si mandatis eorum non paruerint...	Tempora et modus legendi et disputandi...ad ipsos procuratores seu rectores pertineant. in transgressores contra predicta et in bedellos si mandatis eorum non paruerint...

The Angelica quotation represents the official form which the statute received by 1276. It was a faulty text and in fact 'specialiter et in bedellos' should read, as perhaps it did in the parent manuscript, 'specialiter spectancia et in bedellos'.[4] When a new redaction of the statutes was being prepared by the editor of Markaunt the loss of some word was noted. No attempt was made to restore the original reading; instead the problem was quietly solved by deleting the awkward phrase 'ad eorum officia specialiter', a facile emendation but an inexcusable one. The choice of so drastic a remedy contrasts very noticeably with the same editor's approach in Markaunt 15,

[1] 'armis ipsis in utilitatem pauperum uel cancelarii omnino conuertendis' (*Cons. Univ. Canteb.* XI. iv [see above, p. 213, lines 5–6]).

[2] I have suggested a possible alternative reading on p. 188 above.

[3] See p. 254 (Markaunt), lines 20–1.

[4] This passage has been discussed in some detail on pp. 188–90 above.

where the passage is reproduced as part of the 1276 decree with the minimum of change. He retained the perplexing phrase 'ad eorum officia specialiter' and scrupulously desisted from supplying *spectancia* or *pertinencia* or some other participle as predicate.[1] Such inconsistency is characteristic of the textual history of university statutes. In due course the editor's respect for his exemplar was not appreciated; the anomaly was abruptly terminated by the removal of the quotation from the accommodated text of the decree of 1276, only the opening words 'tempora et modus legendi' being retained.[2]

One chapter of the Angelica text was suppressed either before or during the formation of the Markaunt recension. Most likely it was dropped *c.* 1304–37, for what motive we cannot say, and was never restored to the statute-books. Its title, *De satisdacione litigancium et eorum iuramento* (IX), provided the editor with an appropriate chapter heading *De iuramento litigancium* for Angelica X. i, which was made into a separate statute, Markaunt 28.[3] The original title of chapter X was reserved for the second paragraph, which for some reason which is not immediately evident was accorded priority as Markaunt 27.[4] The decision to make two distinct statutes out of chapter X may have had something to do with the elimination of chapter IX, and atoned to some extent for its exclusion.

One of the major improvements of the Markaunt recension on the thirteenth-century text was the grouping of statutes of the same genre together. A similar tendency can be discerned in the contemporary move at Oxford towards a codification of its statutes. That is the only resemblance between the two undertakings. The Cambridge editor is to be congratulated on placing the statutes relating to the officials of the university at the beginning of his text, and he was perfectly justified in transposing Angelica IV (*De conuocacionibus faciendis*) to the section on the chancellor.[5] The plan was facilitated by, if it did not inspire, the dislocation of chapters II, III and V, which pertain to the strictly academic organization of the university. These chapters fall outside the scope of the Markaunt transcript; in the actual redaction they were placed almost certainly

1 Cf. Markaunt 15 (see below, p. 318, lines 30–3). The date, 17 March 1276, is missing.

2 In Old Proctor 20 *legendi* is followed by 'et cetera. vt supra capitulo xviij°' (fo. 20v). The reference is to Markaunt's version of Angelica VII. iv ('Tempora...irroganda'); cf. Markaunt 13 (see below, p. 317, lines 27–31). See also Caius 20 (fos. 3v b–4r a); Junior Proctor (fo. 70v); Senior Proctor (fo. 15v); *SA* 57 (*Docs*, i. 342).

3 See below, p. 325, lines 15–17.

4 See below, p. 325 lines, 9–13.

5 Markaunt 9 (see below, p. 315, line 25 to p. 316, line 3.

between statute 38 and the statute corresponding to chapter XIII of the Angelica text, *De exequiis defunctorum*. Nothing pinpoints the tragedy of the incomplete Markaunt text more than the abrupt termination of the transcription at a point where the regulations of the university concerning degrees and studies commenced.[1] One chapter which held its place was Angelica VI, *De curia magistrorum*, which was assigned with some propriety to the section on discipline and litigation.[2] Here the troubled history of Cambridge is reflected in a cluster of twelve new statutes.

In terms of textual development Markaunt is more representative of the fourteenth century, as one might expect, than of the thirteenth. Yet it maintains a lingering respect for the ancient code. Typical of the transitional character of the redaction is the repeated use of the term 'proctor', which is usually preceded or qualified by the older form 'rector'. Markaunt's general position is well illustrated in the statute on the election of the chancellor:

Angelica I. i	*Markaunt* 2	*SA* 4
Quoniam difficile est	Quoniam difficile est	Item
uniuersitatem consen-	vniuersitatem in vnum	
tire communi consensu	consentire communi con-	
et omni uoluntate,	sensu et voluntate	
statuimus ut cancela-	statuimus vt Cancella-	statuimus ut Cancel-
rius sciens uolens et	rius. sciens. volens. et	larius sciens volens et
potens tanquam maior	potens. tanquam maior	potens, tanquam major
inter omnes omnibus	inter omnes. omnibus	inter omnes, omnibus
per regentes	per regentes si forte	per regentes, si forte
	xij in artibus tunc	12 in artibus tunc
	fuerint regentes.	fuerint regentes,
	Alias per regentes et	alias per regentes et
prefici-	non regentes prefici-	non-regentes praefici-
atur omnibus regenti-	atur omnibus regenti-	atur, omnibus regenti-
bus	bus si xij fuerint	bus si 12 fuerint
	vel alias omnibus	vel alias omnibus
	regentibus et non re-	regentibus et non-
aut parte ma-	gentibus aut parte ma-	regentibus aut parte ma-
iore	iori in numero de qui-	jori in numero, de qui-
	bus duo sint *pilliati*[3]	bus duo sint pileati,
in ipsum con-	omnino in ipsum con-	omnino in ipsum con-
sencientibus. (*Cons.*	sensientibus. (See below,	sentientibus. (*Docs*, i.
Univ. Canteb. [see	p. 313, lines 25–31.)	309.)
above, p. 197, lines 2–6].)		

[1] See below, p. 273.

[2] Markaunt 29 (see below, p. 325, lines 19–24).

[3] Underlined in the MS.

At this point both Markaunt and the 'ancient statute' have a long addition describing how the vote was to be taken and prescribing the words the senior rector or proctor had to use when announcing the result. A century earlier it was much simpler. The regents alone elected the chancellor by direct vote; no set words were ordained or perhaps needed for proclaiming the successful candidate.

The combination of earlier and later textual characteristics in Markaunt is also evident in the statute *De officio Cancellarij*. The word 'office', which is derived from the Angelica text, is not very appropriate here; 'power' (also found in the thirteenth-century statute) would be more correct.[1] Though Makaunt in so far as it portrays the constitutional developments of 1294–1304 approximates more closely to the text of the *statutum antiquum*, it retains an element of the ancient constitution which was omitted when the statute emerged in its final form *c.* 1385:

Angelica I. vi	*Markaunt* 4	*SA* 6
Cancelarius nichil	Cancellarius nichil	Cancellarius nihil
noui sine consensu	noui sine consensv	novi sine consensu
	maioris et sanio-	majoris et sanio-
regencium	ris partis regencium	ris partis regentium
	et sine consensv ma-	et sine consensu ma-
	ioris et sanioris	joris et sanioris
	partis non regencium	partis non regentium
statuere presumat.	statuere presumat.	statuere praesumat
set supra et infra com-	set supra et infra	sed ea que statuta sunt
muniter statuta efficacius	statuta. intendat	intendat efficaciter
intendat custodire. (*Cons.*	efficaciter custodire.	custodire. (*Docs*, i. 311.)
Univ. Canteb. [see above,	(See below, p. 314, lines	
p. 199, lines 1–3].)	28–30.)	

The amendment to the original statute, giving effect to the decrees of 1294 and 1304, involved only a minor dislocation of the text in Markaunt. The narrowing of the term 'regents' by the introduction of the qualifying phrase *maior et sanior pars* probably led to the exclusion of *communiter*; but Markaunt still kept the words 'supra et infra', which in the context are somewhat archaic. They derive from the first constitution of the university, and it is not surprising that the later statute-books omitted them altogether. The rephrasing of the final words of Angelica I in the 'ancient statute' is already apparent in Markaunt, which here as elsewhere occupies a mediate role in the history of the transmission of the Angelica text.

[1] Markaunt 8 (= Angelica I. iv) bears the title *De potestate Cancellarij*.

Chapter 10

THE OLD PROCTOR-CAIUS REDACTION (*c.* 1385)

The next major landmark in the history of the Angelica text after the production of the Markaunt recension occurs towards the close of the fourteenth century. It is certain that new statutes were enacted by *c.* 1345–59.[1] There is evidence, too, of individual statutes being codified or enlarged;[2] and at least three statutes of the faculty of theology were revised *c.* 1365–85.[3] Unfortunately, the register of the university which was extant by 1374 and was described as *Registrum Cancellarii et procuratorum* at a hearing in the Court of Arches on 17 October concerning the refusal of the chancellor, John de Donewich, to take the canonical oath of obedience to the bishop, Thomas Arundel, has not been traced.[4] References to the register of the university are found in a number of documents ranging in date from *c.* 1385 to 1475.[5] It follows that the register mentioned in 1374 escaped destruction during the June

1 *SA* 79 (*Docs*, i. 357–8) was introduced after *c.* 1304–37 but before 1345. If the statute were enacted by 1337 it would have appeared in Markaunt's text most likely after statute 19 (see below, p. 320, line 32 to p. 321, line 22), the place it occupies in Old Proctor (fo. 23^{r-v}) and Caius (fos. 5$^{v\,b}$–6$^{r\,a}$). The statute is implicitly mentioned in a decree of 25 Feb. 1345 establishing the Neel chest. Cf. Clark, 'On the charitable foundations in the university called chests', *CASP*, xi (new series, v [1907]), 84, 86. *SA* 163 (*Docs*, i. 395–6) is dated 4 July 1359.

2 *SA* 180, 'Singulis annis...devote celebraturi' (*ibid.* 404–6 [last line]) was codified in or shortly after 1355. Pollard, 'Mediaeval loan chests at Cambridge', *Inst. Hist. Research Bull.* xvii (1939–40), 122, concludes that *SA* 181 (*Docs*, i. 407–9) was codified in 1351. There is a slight misunderstanding here. The statute as printed is a chain of six statutes which were separate as late as *c.* 1385. Cf. Old Proctor 129–34 (Junior Proctor's Book, fos. 108^{v}–109^{v}); Caius 130–5 (fo. 21$^{r\,a-v\,b}$). But the statutes were certainly arranged in chronological order by *c.* 1351.

3 The statutes are *SA* 107, 108, 124 (*Docs*, i. 369–70, 377). The most problematical of these is *SA* 107; it is discussed on pp. 264–5 below.

4 During the proceedings of the court, one of the proctors of the university, mag. Robert de Thurkylby, aged twenty-eight, testified that Hugh Balsham's award of 6 Oct. 1276 was entered 'in Registro Cancellarij et procuratorum vniuersitatis Cantebrigie', but he declined to commit himself on the actual issue—was the chancellor a subject of the bishop or not? Cf. Ely Dioc. Rec. G I [2] fo. 77^{v}. Cf. also M. Aston, *Thomas Arundel—a study in church life in the reign of Richard II* (Oxford, 1967), pp. 28–33.

5 Cf. Old Proctor 3 (fo. 17^{r}); Caius 3 (fo. 1$^{r\,b}$); *SA* 3 (*Docs*, i. 309); *SA* 186 (*ibid.* 415).

riots of 1381.[1] One happy consequence of this near disaster was, apparently, the provision of a new register containing a fresh, up-to-date recension of the statutes (MS β in our *stemma*). A more serviceable volume comprising the new code and other relevant material was also commissioned for the use of the proctors.[2] In addition the university decided to make available a copy of the statutes to the heads of colleges on request, and *c.* 1390–5 a second proctor's book was provided. This would seem to be the most likely origin of Gonville and Caius College MS 706 and the Old Proctor's Book. If our reconstruction of the pedigree of the *statuta antiqua* be correct, Old Proctor and Caius (the statutes only) were copied independently from the first proctor's book (MS γ). Presumably, this earlier volume became the property of the senior proctor and Old Proctor was reserved for the junior official. The only witnesses now extant of these developments are the Old Proctor's Book and the Caius manuscript.

1 The register is cited at various intervals, *c.* 1415, 1419, 1433, 1442, 1444. The evidence suggests that it originally resembled the Oxford *Liber cancellarii* or *Registrum A*, which must be distinguished from the *Registrum universitatis* or the chancellor's register; cf. *Reg. Cancell. Oxon.* i, pp. vii–xiii. It is certain that the lost Cambridge register is neither the Old Proctor's nor the Junior or Senior Proctor's Books. It appears to have been discontinued as a statute-book by 1430. See below, pp. 286–7. But the terms 'register' and 'book of the statutes' were not clearly differentiated in the fifteenth century. Hence, allusions to the register after 1429 as likely as not refer to the statute-books. The best insight into the probable format of the pre-1430 register of the university is provided by Markaunt's Book, which, however, was not an official register; it was known as *Liber priuilegiorum et statutorum vniuersitatis Cantabriggie*, not *Registrum Cancellarii et procuratorum*. Moreover, it lacked certain items such as the bedells' fees which were noted in the common or actual register of the university. Three possible successors to the register are the Black Parchment Book (saec. xv*ex*–xvi), which was begun by mag. William Buckenham who died in 1540; the *Liber rerum memorabilium* or 'Black Paper Book' initiated in 1548 by John Mere, bedell and registrary; and Stokys's Book, a composite volume, which was put together *c.* 1574–8.

2 This book was almost contemporary with the Oxford *Registrum D*. In his addenda to *SAUO* Pollard suggests that this register should be assigned to the years 1374–85. This dating is based on the assumption that *D* contains everything which was entered before or at this time in *Registrum A*. Consequently, if a statute and its amendment which is dated 1 Feb. 1385 had been copied into *A* before *D* was executed, *D* should have these texts. As they are not found in *D*, it must be earlier than 1 Feb. 1385. This argument presumes that the amendment was copied into *A* either on or shortly after this date. That may be so, but the whole basis of the argument collapses, for there are two statutes, the one dated 1306, the other assigned by Gibson to pre-1350, both entered in *A* in the original hand, which are not found in *D*! Cf. *SAUO*, 22, 19–23, 3; 58, 21–3. But now see Pollard's article cited on p. 7, n. 2 above.

The Old Proctor's Book, alternatively called *Liber procuratoris antiquus*, is among other things an official register of the statutes and remains the earliest extant proctor's book. The original format of this untidy, rather confusing and disjointed volume is difficult to reconstruct, but the nucleus consisted of (i) extracts from the four gospels; (ii) a calendar of the university; (iii) a full and splendid text of the statutes; (iv) copies of decrees promulgating three statutes; and (v) texts of charters granted by Richard II, the latest in date being one of 12 December 1384.[1] This part, the core of the book, has survived against all the odds. Other fifteenth-century statute-books fared less successfully, and it is a miracle how the latter half of Old Proctor, if not the whole book, did not share their fate. Four folios containing fourteen statutes (123–137 [*recte* 136]) now make up fos. 107^r–110^v of the Junior Proctor's Book, while twenty-one more folios form fos. 60^r–80^v of the Senior Proctor's Book.[2] These unpardonable mutilations, which occurred in the second half of the fifteenth century, were only some of the outrages perpetrated on Old Proctor; more than one quire perhaps disappeared altogether; but sufficient remains to enable one to establish the original arrangement of the statutes.[3]

The text when first executed ran into twenty-eight folios. The leaves were foliated as a unit in the early fifteenth century and an index was added.[4] It lists 129 statutes, the last being *De cistis*, which

1 In its present form the MS consists of 48 parchment folios, measuring 284 × 190 mm, and two hard paper fly-leaves. The original binding and covers have gone, but the back cover, which is misplaced, is late fifteenth-century tooled work with five brass bosses and a staple at the top (now inverted) which held one end of the chain by which the book was carried. The remains of two clasps have also survived. The nucleus consists of fos. 9^v–40^v, but it also included 25 folios which, as we shall now see, were detached and inserted in the Junior and Senior Proctors' Books.

2 These two proctors' books also contain folios extracted from earlier fifteenth-century registers. See pp. 291, 293, n. 6.

3 Despite all its vicissitudes, the Old Proctor text escaped unscathed apart from statute 122 (fo. 40^v) or *SA* 168 (*Docs*, i. 398). The continuation of this text on fo. 41^r (now Junior Proctor's Book, fo. 107^r) was deleted and a note dated 1517 now fills the gap. The scribe of Junior Proctor probably erased the text, as he had already written the statute in full on fo. 99^v of the register. Old Proctor 11 (see below, pp. 270–3) had been rubbed out at an earlier date.

4 The statutes occupy fos. 17^r–40^v; the index is on fos. 41^r–43^r. A later hand has added additional references. The original indexer wrote the first three folio numbers in full, viz. 'primo folio' (etc.), and these and the remaining folios of the statutes were numbered in a variety of hands. Latterly, the whole volume was foliated continuously and to avoid confusion I have adhered to this modern foliation.

is a generic title for seven individual statutes.[1] As *De cistis*, using the title in its collective sense, is also the last statute entered in the contemporary Caius manuscript, there can be no doubt that the code ended at this point.[2] Another statute, dated 20 June 1398, follows after a break in Old Proctor. It was written almost certainly in the same hand as the others and numbered, wrongly, '137'.[3] Its presence has not unnaturally led to the assumption that Old Proctor was compiled *c.* 1398.[4]

Internal evidence shows that the original corpus of the statutes was in fact transcribed *c.* 1390–5; and the script, obviously that of a professional scribe whose calligraphy is a fine example of late fourteenth-century English book-hand, supports this dating. In the calendar prefixed to the statutes there is an entry under 1 March which reads: 'Exequie M. Willelmi Gotham.'[5] The entry is in the same hand as the statutes. Gotham, who held the office of chancellor more than once and who was a notable benefactor of the university, died *c.* 1385–9.[6] A closer look at the statutes, however, reveals that the text must have been executed by 1396. The later statute-books carry an amendment to Old Proctor 126 ordering a commemoration of mag. Michael de Causton 'former chancellor of this university, who enriched it and all its colleges with gifts'.[7] Causton was dead by 1396. Since the Old Proctor statute makes no mention of him, it follows that the text was written not later than that year. Putting these results together we are forced to conclude that the statutes, and thus the volume itself, were transcribed *c.* 1390–5. The actual

1 Thus the redaction comprised 135 statutes. They were numbered before the volume was broken up in the fifteenth century. The actual scribe of the statutes left it to the rubricator to add chapter numbers, for there is a reference in the body of statute 20 (fo. 20^{v}) to 'capitulo xvij^{o}' (*recte* xviij^{o}) or statute 18. Some oversights mar the numbering of the statutes. Statute 61 (fo. 29^{r}) is not marked at all, while '84' is written twice (fo. 33^{v}) opposite *SA* 119, 120. This latter should be '85'.

2 Cf. Old Proctor 135 (Junior Proctor's Book, fo. 109^{v}); Caius 136 (fo. 21$^{v\,b}$). What was originally '135' in Old Proctor ('136' in Caius) appears in the printed *statuta antiqua* as the final part of *SA* 183 ('Jurent custodes...supradictum' [*Docs*, i. 411]).

3 Now Junior Proctor's Book, fo. 110^{r-v}. The text of the redaction ended on fo. 109^{v}, leaving a blank space of about a dozen lines. The lower part of this space was afterwards used for the insertion of *SA* 170 (*Docs*, i. 399), which dates from *c.* 1423–8. The 1398 statute should have been numbered '136', not '137'.

4 *Docs*, i. 306; Rashdall, *Universities*, iii. 286. Peek and Hall, *Archives*, p. 27, give the date more correctly as *c.* 1390, but their authority for this is *Docs*, *loc. cit.*, which has *c.* 1398.

5 Old Proctor's Book, fo. 12^{r}.

6 *BRUC*, p. 266.

7 *SA* 174 (*Docs*, i. 401). For Causton (senior) cf. *BRUC*, p. 128.

redaction was made most probably *c.* 1385. Statute 14 suggests that the *terminus a quo* for the codification is 1379–80.[1] In view of the fact that Causton's death occurred not later than 1396 this must be the *terminus ad quem*. The recension can be dated still more precisely, but first it is necessary to look into a problem created by a reference in a register of the prior general of the Austin friars, Bartolomeo Veneto.

In a letter of 30 June 1386 he voiced his regret that the university had recently enacted a statute requiring students of the order to spend the whole of the year immediately preceding opponency at the university.[2] The strange thing is that a statute imposing this obligation on all students of theology was enacted as early as 1365.[3] It was vigorously contested by all four mendicant orders of friars and duly amended. Thereafter the statute applied only to English

[1] The first part of the statute declares that on no account may the chancellor hold office during his term as official of the bishop. Cf. *SA* 13 (*Docs*, i. 314). Richard Scrope was appointed official by Bishop Arundel on 16 Nov. 1375 (*BRUC*, p. 514). He was still official when confirmed as chancellor on 23 April 1378. Cf. *ibid.* p. 413; Aston, *op. cit.* pp. 31–2. He continued to hold both offices simultaneously until 20 Sept. 1379, when mag. John Neuton, D.Cn.L. (not D.C.L. as in *BRUC*, p. 421), was appointed official. Scrope retained the office of chancellor of the university; he vacated it by 28 Feb. 1380, following the election and confirmation in office of Eudo la Zouche (*ibid.* p. 358). The statute, *SA* 13, was enacted most likely *c.* 20 Sept. 1379, for it declares that no one may hold both offices together *quovis modo*. Scrope indeed ceased to preside in person at sessions of the consistory court of Ely after 8 April 1378 (Aston, *op. cit.* p. 398), but he did not relinquish the officiality until Neuton succeeded him. It should be noted that the order of the entries in the final part of the *Registrum primum causarum consistorii episcopi Eliensis* (Ely Dioc. Rec. D 2/1) is unchronological. On fo. 162^{v}, which is headed '1381', Scrope appears as official; the document, however, bears the date 22 Nov. 1377 and is preceded by one of 4 May 1382. It should be further noted that the second part of *SA* 13 was first enacted by *c.* 1250; cf. *Cons. Univ. Canteb.* I. v [see above, p. 197, lines 20–1]); *Docs, loc. cit.* The composite statute with the later part preceding the very much older enactment is found in its proper place in Old Proctor-Caius. It is difficult to believe that the redaction was made before 1380.

[2] 'Quia ex quodam statuto in universitate cantabrigiensi noviter introducto utinam non contra proximi caritatem taliter est sancitum quod ad oppositionem in dicta universitate per ordinem deputati debeant, antequam ad oppositionem procedant, in dicta universitate anno integro commorari, anno immediate sequenti ad oppositionem postmodum processuri...cui statuto, licet cum displicentia, taliter volumus adherere, ut ex eo tamen sibi (Fr. Paulo de Mediolano) nulla ulterius iniuria penitus irrogetur' (F. Roth, O.S.A., *The English Austin Friars 1249–1538*, ii [New York, 1961], 230*, no. 579).

[3] Urban V on 16 July 1365 ordered Archbishop Islip of Canterbury to investigate *inter alia* the statute 'quod nullus in dicto Cantabrigensi studio huiusmodi oppositionis actum incipere seu excercere ualeat nisi studuerit ibidem per annum proxime precedentem' (Archivio Vaticano, *Reg. Vat.* 254, fo. 136^{r}).

scholars.[1] Yet the general of the Augustinians clearly states that by 1386 European as well as native students—he mentions explicitly Fra Paolo di Milano—were obliged to spend the statutory year at the university before opposing for the degree of bachelor. Since no such ruling is found in the statute set down in the Old Proctor-Caius redaction,[2] one might be tempted to conclude that the statutes were codified not later than 30 June 1386. The inference would perhaps be justified if the text of the statute, *SA* 107, in the Junior and Senior Proctors' Books agreed with the version circulated by the Augustinian prior general. This is not the case. Both statute-books reproduce the statute exactly as it appears in Old Proctor-Caius.[3] Evidently, the new statute which Bartolomeo Veneto criticized must have been a special ruling made by the university in respect of Austin friars, and it is fairly clear from his letter that his objection to the statute rested on what he considered to be unfair discrimination against his subjects. The Augustinians more than any other order had been sending students from abroad to Oxford and Cambridge since 1355, and the years of the Great Schism saw an increasing number of continental Austin friars coming to Cambridge.[4] This no doubt led the university to take the step which the general regarded as an offence against charity. The onus placed on the foreign friars may have been merely a temporary measure of a particular character and hence did not become part of the official body of university statutes. The Old Proctor-Caius redaction, however, can be assigned to *c.* 1385 but for a different reason. Two statutes regulating inceptions in grammar were not included in the recension. Unlike the ruling binding Augustinians, these were permanent statutes applicable to all students preparing for the degree of master of grammar. They were most probably promulgated *c.* 1385, and consequently their omission from Old Proctor-Caius more than suggests that the recension was completed at this period.[5]

[1] *SA* 107 (*Docs*, i. 369).

[2] The crucial part of the statute, 'ita quod annus proximus praecedens actum opponendi in universitate ista ab indigenis impleatur' (*ibid.*), is in Old Proctor 76 (fo. 31^{v}) and Caius 76 (fo. $12^{r\,b}$).

[3] Cf. Junior Proctor's Book, fo. 83^{r-v}; Senior Proctor's Book, fo. 28^{r}.

[4] Cf. A. Gwynn, S.J., *The English Austin Friars in the time of Wyclif* (London, 1940), pp. 31–4, 96–102; Roth, *English Austin Friars*, i (1966), 418–19.

[5] The statutes are *SA* 117, 118 (*Docs*, i. 374–5). Robert Laverok, clerk of the diocese of York, was apparently the first scholar to take the degree of M.Gram. at Cambridge. He must have incepted by *c.* 1385 since he was B.A. by 1390. Cf. *BRUC*, p. 356. I have checked the Lloyd reference there mentioned against the original

Gonville and Caius College MS 706 need not detain us long. It is made up of two distinct parts dating from the late fourteenth and fifteenth centuries.[1] Part II, the earlier, consists entirely of the text of the statutes followed by a table, and has its own medieval foliation.[2] The first folio is splendidly executed and the hand throughout is rather attractive. The manuscript is slightly older than Old Proctor and may be assigned to *c.* 1385–95. It is quite possible that the two volumes came from the same scriptorium.[3] Both texts are virtually identical, but Old Proctor was not copied from Caius nor *vice versa*; they were derived separately from a common parent. The Caius transcript is an indifferent production. Though the hand is well formed and in a way rather impressive, the scribe was guilty of more than a reasonable number of blunders such as misspelling, dropped contraction marks and other oversights.[4] Yet, as with many imperfect manuscripts, these failings are offset by certain features which are of crucial importance for establishing a critical text of the statutes. On a general assessment Old Proctor is by far the better manuscript, irrespective of its intrinsic value as a university register. Even so, Caius is more faithful to the textual tradition of the statutes, strange as it may seem.[5] An exception is its division of a revised version of Angelica V into two sections; in this instance Old Proctor has rightly preserved the unity of the statute.[6]

roll, 'Colville (2)', m. 5, now restored to the university archives and listed as doc. no. 82**. The entry reads: 'Item Roberto Lauerok clerico Ebor' diocesis Magistro in Gramatica et in artibus bacallario.' This roll of petitions to the Holy See for benefices dates from 1389–90. Laverok is also listed in two of the draft Colville rolls (*ibid.*).

1 Cf. James, *Cat. MSS Gonville & Caius Coll.* ii. 682–4. Part I was compiled in 1472 and comprises a register of the college, a copy of its statutes and some documents.

2 This part, which measures 295 × 200 mm, has 24 folios. The statutes end on fo. $21^{v\,b}$. The rest of the column and fo. 22^{r} are blank. On fo. 22^{v} there is a table of the statutes in the same hand as the text and it goes on to fo. $23^{v\,b}$ with folio references in red; a later hand has also added references in the margins. The final folio is vacant, but a saec. xv*ex*–xvi*in* hand has entered the following inscription on the verso: 'Iste liber pertinet collegio de Gvnvile' (fo. 24^{v}).

3 The decoration of the Caius capitals is strikingly reminiscent of the style of Old Proctor.

4 Hence we have quoted from Old Proctor in preference to Caius except when Old Proctor is defective; in any case Old Proctor is an official register.

5 See below, p. 279.

6 The statute, *SA* 147 (*Docs*, i. 387–8), is a development of *Cons. Univ. Canteb.* V (see above, p. 203, lines 14–16). In Old Proctor it is statute 102 (fos. 36^{v}–37^{r}); in Caius it ranks as 102–3 (fo. $16^{r\,b-v\,a}$). The writer of Caius probably mistook the words 'De iuristis et eciam medicis regentibus' in his exemplar for the beginning of a separate statute. But there is no support for his partitioning of the text in the manuscript tradition of the statutes.

It is otherwise, however, with the correct order of two previous statutes of the redaction.[1] Caius also comes to the rescue with a passage which was erased beyond recall from Old Proctor;[2] more than that, it confirms that *SA* 184 (20 June 1398) is adventitious to Old Proctor and was added to the register after the statutes had been codified.[3]

In Old Proctor-Caius we have a complete constitution of the university, the earliest extant after the Angelica text. The redaction comprises six main sections: (i) statute-making (Old Proctor 1–3);[3] (ii) the chancellor and his deputies, proctors, taxors, bedells and keepers of the common chest (4–29); (iii) litigation and discipline (30–51); (iv) studies, degrees and kindred matters (52–123); (v) nations and liturgical functions (124–8); (vi) chests (129–35).[4] Even in broad outline Old Proctor-Caius represents the tremendous advance in the organization of the university that took place between *c.* 1250 and *c.* 1385. The section on the curriculum, which accounts for more than one half of the total number of statutes, is the most remarkable and provides a vivid contrast with the jejune contents of the primitive constitution. Yet the only absolutely new feature of Old Proctor-Caius are the statutes on chests, the earliest of which was founded by mag. Thomas of St Botolph by 1300, well after the date of the Angelica text.[5]

There is no need to consider the relationship between the Angelica text and Old Proctor-Caius apart from section iv and one or two other statutes. Old Proctor-Caius i–iii derive directly from the Markaunt recension, itself of course a development of the early thirteenth-century text. The Markaunt fragment does not provide an adequate basis for judging the extent to which Old Proctor-Caius adheres to or departs from the plan of the redaction made *c.* 1304–37,

1 *SA* 94–95 (*Docs*, *loc. cit.* 363–4) = Caius 63–64 (fo. 10$^{v\,b}$) = Old Proctor 64–63 (fo. 29^{r}). There is no doubt that Old Proctor wrongly inverts the order of the two statutes.

2 The code in Caius ends with *De cistis* (fo. 21$^{r\,a-v\,b}$). As in Old Proctor the statute consists of seven distinct enactments. See above, pp. 262–3. In Caius the third of these statutes has the title *De cista*, but this is not repeated in the table (fo. 23$^{v\,b}$). Because of its treatment of *SA* 147 as two statutes the MS has 136 statutes, one more than the original total in Old Proctor.

3 Because of the slight discrepancy between the number of statutes in Old Proctor and Caius, it is best to stand by the enumeration of the official codex.

4 *SA* 184 (20 June 1398) is not included here. It became the first of three statutes, a new section, in the Junior and Senior Proctors' Books. Cf. *SA* 184–6 (*Docs*, i. 411–15).

5 Cf. Pollard, 'Mediaeval loan chests', *loc. cit.* p. 119.

but the available evidence inclines one to believe that the editor of Old Proctor-Caius preserved the structure of the lost exemplar of Markaunt's text. Sections i–iii of Old Proctor-Caius are substantially the same as the arrangement of the surviving thirty-eight Markaunt statutes. Twelve new statutes complete this part of the late fourteenth-century redaction.[1] Some of the remaining eighty-five statutes, the bulk of Old Proctor-Caius, almost certainly appeared in Markaunt's exemplar, for they formed part of the Angelica text. This is not to say that the editor of Old Proctor-Caius worked from the manuscript used by the scribe of Markaunt's text. The existence of an intermediate recension between the early and late fourteenth-century redactions may be postulated; what cannot be disputed is that the Old Proctor-Caius text was not based on the actual exemplar of the thirty-eight statutes copied into Markaunt's Book. Old Proctor-Caius exhibits a wide range of variants and significantly embodies a revised paragraph of the Angelica text which is missing from Markaunt.[2] On the other hand, the redaction fails to include a passage found in Markaunt and again in the Junior and Senior Proctors' Books, whose texts ultimately derive from the *c.* 1385 recension.[3] This raises the very pertinent question of the manuscript tradition of the statutes. We shall return to this question again. These divergencies show that Old Proctor and Caius belong to a collateral branch of the family tree, whereas Senior and Junior Proctor are in the direct line of descent from the parent of the *c.* 1385 recension.

On the whole the editor of Old Proctor-Caius kept the format of the Markaunt fragment but saw fit to redistribute six of the thirty-eight statutes. Markaunt 12 (*De electione taxatorum*) was removed from its awkward position among the group of statutes on the rectors or proctors and was very properly placed immediately

[1] The new statutes are Old Proctor 2–3 (*SA* 2–3), 13–15 (*SA* 12–14), 21 (*SA* 58), 23 (*SA* 61), 29 (*SA* 79), 41 (*SA* 39), 46 (*SA* 44), 48 (*SA* 46), 51 (*SA* 49).

[2] At this point Markaunt is otherwise complete. The Angelica paragraph reads: 'Magistrorum sentencias Cancelarius ad denunciacionem proferencium debita exequatur sceleritate' (*Cons. Univ. Canteb.* I. v [see above, p. 197, lines 20–1]). Old Proctor 14 has: 'Cancellarius sentencias magistrorum cum sibi per eosdem denunciate fuerint exequi teneatur' (fo. 19ʳ). Cf. Caius 14, fo. 2ᵛᵇ; *SA* 13 (*Docs*, i. 314). This statute forms a rather incongruous pendant to the statute enacted *c.* 1379 which forbade chancellors from holding the office of diocesan official.

[3] Markaunt 11 ('Et si magister glomerie...admittatur' [see below, p. 317, lines 6–11]); Junior Proctor's Book, fo. 69ʳ⁻ᵛ; Senior Proctor's Book, fo. 14ʳ⁻ᵛ; *SA* 53 (*Docs*, i. 339). In Old Proctor-Caius the statute ends with *eligatur*. Cf. Old Proctor 17 (fo. 20ʳ); Caius 17 (fo. 3ʳ).

before the statute on the office of the taxors. Another well-judged move was to transfer Markaunt 32 (*De hospicijs et pensione domorum*) and couple it with this statute. With less justification the redactor brought forward Markaunt 25, 20 (in that order) and inserted them in the section concerning the chancellor. Nothing was gained, however, in terms of affinity or utility by making two parts out of Markaunt 23 (*De procuratoribus admittendis*) and reshuffling them. It is even more difficult to understand why Markaunt 30 (*De penis appellancium et eorum caucione*) was likewise broken up. In compensation for this unusual extravagance on the part of the Old Proctor-Caius redactor, Markaunt 6–7 were fused into a single statute, almost obliterating the distinction between the chancellor's commissary and the vice-chancellor. Lastly, Markaunt 34 (*De choreis et choreas ducentibus*) was transposed for no apparent reason and sandwiched between the revised Angelica XI. iii–iv (Markaunt 37) and the last statute of the Markaunt transcript, *De pena eorum qui contempnunt Magistros.*[1]

An important consideration with the Old Proctor-Caius redactor was the value of economy. His zeal, unfortunately, caused him to delete welcome historical clues concerning the making of certain statutes. The interesting introduction to Markaunt 34, for example, was dispensed with:

Markaunt 34	*Old Proctor* 49
Prouisum est per omnes regentes istius vniuersitatis necnon per maiores bacallarios eiusdem specialiter in plena Magistrorum congregacione ad hoc vocatos ne publice choree per plateas de cetero fiant (see below, p. 329, lines 22–4).[2]	Prouisum est ne publice choree per plateas de cetero fiant (fo. 27^{r}).[3]

If we had to depend on Old Proctor-Caius we would not know that the senior bachelors shared in the enactment of this statute. No doubt, the non-regent masters were also present, but they did not put their names to the statute. It goes without saying that some of them would be bachelors in a higher faculty and as such must

1 Thus Markaunt 12 = Old Proctor 24; Markaunt 25 = Old Proctor 10; Markaunt 20 = Old Proctor 11; Markaunt 32 = Old Proctor 26; Markaunt 23. i–ii = Old Proctor 33, 30; Markaunt 34 = Old Proctor 49.

2 This text with one very minor addition is also preserved in Stokys's Book, fo. 30^{v}. Cf. *Docs*, i. 335, n. 1.

3 Cf. *SA* 47 (*ibid.* 335).

be numbered among the makers of the statute. Strictly speaking, it was not technically a statute, which may explain why the non-regents are not formally mentioned. On the other hand, it is possible that the ban on dancing was introduced before they were accorded statutory powers. Needless to say, no hint of this appears in the Old Proctor-Caius text.

The Old Proctor-Caius redactor, beyond carrying out the duties of an editor in correcting and adding to Markaunt in the light of later developments, refrained as a rule from tampering with the texts of individual statutes. His treatment of Markaunt 33 was exceptional.[1] To illustrate how widely he transposed this statute, itself a congeries of separate enactments put together over a period, would carry us too far afield, and in any case the text was not derived from an Angelica statute. Of far more relevance is the fate of Markaunt 20 and 25.

The latter, *De rebellantibus Cancellario*, possibly because of its generic title, was inserted by the Old Proctor-Caius redactor as a corollary to Markaunt 8, *De potestate Cancellarii*. Originally, Markaunt 25 consisted of a brief paragraph from the Angelica text which had received two substantial accretions by *c.* 1304–37.[2] In Old Proctor-Caius the early thirteenth-century statute forms the centrepiece of statute 10. Having moved forward Markaunt 25, the redactor also transferred Markaunt 20. He had history on his side for aligning it with Markaunt 25, for both statutes developed out of Angelica XI. v. Had he been content to interpose the text of Markaunt 20 between Markaunt 25 and Markaunt 9 (*De conuocacionibus faciendis*) all would have been well. But he was unable to resist his penchant for pruning statutes of what he considered to be archaic or superfluous details. Eventually, Markaunt 25, 20 (Old Proctor-Caius 10–11) became *SA* 10. Before we trace the final evolution of the statute it is necessary to compare the early fourteenth-century text, Markaunt 20, with the work of the redactor of Old Proctor-Caius. As we shall see in a moment, the text in the Old Proctor's Book was very thoroughly erased in the fifteenth century and our only guide is the Caius manuscript, which escaped unscathed:

[1] Cf. Markaunt 33 (see below, p. 328, line 15 to p. 329, line 20); Old Proctor 43 (fos. 25^{v}–26^{r}); Caius 43 (fos. 7$^{v\,a}$–8$^{r\,a}$); *SA* 41 (*Docs*, i. 330–2). This statute is also found in Stokys's Book, fos. 29^{r-v}, 32^{r}, and was cited at the Barnwell Process in 1430.

[2] See above, p. 251.

Markaunt 20

De declaracione super incarceracionibus et correctionibus

Item anno domini M CC^{o} nonogesimo iiij^{to} die sancti iohannis ante portam latinam [6 May] erat statutum de incarceracionibus et bannicionibus per maiorem et saniorem partem regencium sic declaratum scilicet quod Cancellarius sine consensv Magistrorum regencium neque debet bannire neque incarcerare Magistrum aliquem qui in hac vniuersitate rexerit set cause de atrocibus delictis que requirunt penam carceris et bannicionem alicuius Magistri vt predicitur. audienciam Cancellarij requirunt simul et Magistrorum—Item ad hec adicientes statuimus quod Cancellarius qui pro tempore fuerit huiusmodi commissionem incarceracionis et bannicionis admittere teneatur cum vniuersitas regencium hoc decreuerit faciendum—Item statuimus *quod omnes qui debent incarcerari in carcere communi in villa incarcerentur*. (See below, p. 321, lines 23–35.)[1]

Caius 11

Declaracio super bannicionibus et corectionibus ac incarceracionibus faciendis

Item de incarceracionibus et bannicionibus per maiorem et saniorem partem regencium sic erat declaratum quod Cancellarius sine consensu magistrorum regencium. neque debet bannire neque incarcerare magistrum aliquem qui in hac uniuersitate rexerit set cause de atrocibus delictis que requirunt penam carceris et bannicionem alicuius vt predicitur magistri audienciam. Cancellarij requirunt simul et magistrorum. Item declaratum est quod. Cancellarius. qui pro tempore fuerit huiusmodi commissionem incaceracionis [*sic*] bannicionis admittere teneatur cum vniuersitas regencium. hoc decreuerit faciendum. Item quod omnes qui debent incarcerari in carcere domini Regis in villa incacerentur [*sic*]. (fo. 2rb.)

The continuation of the Caius statute is extant in Old Proctor, but again the redactor dispenses with Markaunt's historical introduction:

Markaunt

Item memorandum quod anno domini supradicto [1294] die sabbati proximo post festum sancti Iohannis ante portam latinam [8 May] in plena congregacione regencium eciam coram clericis domini Episcopi Eliensis erat consuetudo de correctionibus sic declarata videlicet quod in correctionibus faciendis Rectores debent assidere Cancellario vel suo commissario ita quod debeant premuniri de tempore et de loco si venire voluerint. Voluit

Old Proctor-Caius

Item declaratum est quod in corectionibus faciendis Rectores vel procuratores debent assidere Cancellario vel eius commissario, ita quod premunantur [*sic*] de

[1] The words in italics are underlined in Markaunt.

Markaunt (*cont.*)

eciam dicta vniuersitas quod ista predicta ordinacio seu disposicio super premissis vigorem habeat inconcussum—Item in correctionibus faciendis si penitenciam alicui inflictam pro commisso in penitenciam pecuniariam conuerti contingat, statuimus quod illa pecunia per procuratores vel eorum alterum recipiatur et ciste communi vniuersitatis applicetur. (See below, p. 321, line 35, to p. 322, line 8.)

Old Proctor-Caius (*cont.*)

loco et tempore si venire voluerint et ista declaracio in perpetuum maneat inconcussa.
Item in coreccionibus faciendis. si penitenciam alicui inflictam pro commisso in penam pecuniariam conuerti contingat, statuimus quod illa pecunia per procuratores vel eorum alterum recipiatur. (Old Proctor, fo. 18^{v}; Caius, fo. 2^{rb-va}.)[1]

No significance need be attached to the erasure by the redactor of Old Proctor-Caius of the passage in Markaunt which refers to the presence of clerks of the bishop of Ely at the congregation of regents, even though the omission foreshadows the bull *Dum attentae* (12 January 1401) of Boniface IX, which released chancellors-elect from the obligation of seeking confirmation in office from the diocesan.[2] The alterations carried out by the editor were purely textual and have no hidden constitutional import. That he was not an out-and-out modernist is shown by his reluctance to discard altogether the by now rather out-moded description of the proctors as the rectors.[3] What is difficult to understand is why the first part

[1] The text of Old Proctor-Caius is an edition based on both MSS with a view to reconstructing the archetype. The fact that the two MSS write *premunantur* for *premuniantur* is evidence enough, if need there be, that both descend from a common parent.

[2] The indult was probably granted all the more readily by the pope in view of the part which the university played in persuading Richard II to remain loyal to him. Cf. Ullmann, 'The university of Cambridge and the Great Schism', *Journal of Theological Studies*, ix (1958), 54–63. On receipt of the indult the university proceeded to cancel unwelcome references to the bishop in its statute-books. Old Proctor 5 reads: 'Cancellarius cum ab episcopo confirmatus fuerit et ab ipsa confirmacione ad municipium redierit ad vltimum in crastino congregacionem omnium regencium facere teneatur' (fo. 17^{v}). The passage 'ab episcopo confirmatus [fuerit]...crastino' was crudely marked *eat* in the MS. The following note may be deciphered in the outer margin: 'Nota quod quando hoc statutum fuit factum eramus sub episcopo eliensi et tunc erat ⟨o⟩rdinacio facta inter vniuersitatem et suum archidiaconum set iam sumus exempti et immediate sub papa et ideo illa [*bis*] ordinacio est nullius momenti.' For the revised version of the statute cf. *SA* 5 (*Docs*, i. 310). See also above, p. 33, n. 4.

[3] One can understand why the tail-end of Markaunt, 'et ciste communi vniuersitatis applicetur', was dropped; it was an unnecessary adjunct to the statute. The phrase 'in carcere communi in villa' in the first part of Markaunt's text, on the other hand, might well have been left to stand. At all events, the change has no historical implications. Admittedly, the castle was designated by Edward II on 3 June 1317

of Old Proctor-Caius 11 was rescinded in the fifteenth century. The text 'Item de incarceracionibus. . . faciendum' no longer appears; only the final passage 'Item. . . inca(r)cerentur' was preserved. Even this passage as well as the foregoing part was very expertly erased from the Old Proctor's Book.[1] One noteworthy fact emerges from this, namely, that the fifteenth-century redactor did not work from the official register or, to put it differently, the statute was not deleted until after the revised text was formulated; otherwise the editor could not have retained 'Item. . . incarcerentur'. The final step, therefore, in the evolution of *SA* occurred when the title and first part of Old Proctor-Caius 11 were suppressed and the remnant of the statute together with its continuation were fused with Old Proctor 10, whose title the redactor gave to the whole. Thus after surviving some two hundred years of statute-making and the attentions of various redactors the end paragraph of Angelica XI finally found its resting place in the bosom of a large, composite statute, *SA* 10.[2]

Markaunt, notwithstanding its extreme importance as the second oldest text of the Cambridge statutes, labours under the ineluctable disadvantage of being an incomplete redaction; the heart of a university constitution—a programme of studies and requirements for degrees—is missing. The copyist stopped short at this point in his transcription; it may have been a convenient place to break off, just before the commencement of a new section.[3] This is where the

as the place of imprisonment for both clerks and lay people (CUA, doc. no. 20 [original letters patent—badly damaged]; cf. *Cal. pat. rolls, 1313–17*, p. 665; Chibnall, *op. cit.* pp. 6–7). But the king's prison mentioned in the Old Proctor-Caius redaction was not the castle; it was the town prison (i.e. the tollbooth), as stated in Markaunt. The king's writ of 1317 did not prevent the chancellor from using the town prison in 1320 (Cooper, *Annals*, i. 78; cf. *ibid.* 83), though it is evident that he also utilized the castle by 1337 (*ibid.* 90). In 1383 he was allowed to use either place of detention (*ibid.* 127), and this was still the practice by 1487–8 (*Grace Book* A, p. 213). Clearly, the terms of the statute whether in Markaunt's version or the Old Proctor-Caius recension were not strictly adhered to.

1 The first letter of the title in red is all that remains in Old Proctor. Even under ultra-violet light only faint outlines of the script come up, and while it might be guessed that the lost passage was the second part of Markaunt 20 no one could tell how much was preserved or revised in Old Proctor without the aid of the Caius MS. The title of the Old Proctor statute was noted by the indexer before the text was erased (Old Proctor, fo. 41r).

2 *Docs*, i. 312–13. The passage from Angelica XI. v (see above, p. 213, lines 7–9) occurs on p. 313, ll. 2–6.

3 The last statute in Markaunt (no. 38) corresponds with Old Proctor 50; only one further statute intervenes (*SA* 49) before the section on studies in Old

value of Old Proctor-Caius really lies. The recension provides the earliest statutory evidence of the medieval curriculum at Cambridge. Three chapters of the Angelica text, it is true, are devoted to the academic organization of the university, but very little in the way of practical conclusions can be derived from their contents. Nothing is said about courses and not a single textbook is mentioned. The chapters, no doubt, represent one quarter of the entire constitution and they continued to hold a place in the later statute-books; none the less, the contrast between the meagre information they yield and the detailed prescriptions of Old Proctor-Caius could not be more complete. The difference between the three chapters of Angelica and the seventy-two chapters of the late fourteenth-century redaction is in itself a measure of the academic development of Cambridge by *c.* 1385.

In the Oxford registers the statutes on studies are grouped under faculties. The Cambridge arrangement as exemplified by Old Proctor-Caius, while maintaining the distinction between the faculties, proceeds on a different principle. The determining factor was not the relative standing of a faculty but the nature of the academic degree. At the head of the section on studies the Old Proctor-Caius redactor placed two general statutes on the observance of forms. These are followed by a group of thirty-one statutes (Old Proctor 52–82) on the degree of bachelor in arts, medicine, civil and canon law and theology.[1] The *magisterium* forms the apex of the whole section with six statutes, again set down in an ascending scale of faculties, beginning with *De inceptoribus in quacunque facultate et primo de artistis incepturis* (Old Proctor 83–8).[2] The section is rounded off with a miscellaneous collection of statutes on the licence, the ceremony of inception, solemn resumptions, the habits of the masters, the academic year, the hours of lectures, and statutes connected with regency and its duties (Old Proctor 89–123).[3] Though this tight-knit scheme inevitably contains anomalies, it was as perfect as perhaps could be devised. The tragedy is that it was not

Proctor. It is possible that the statute Old Proctor 51 (fo. 27^{v}) was in the exemplar used by the scribe of Markaunt's Book, but there is no reason to suppose that it was enacted by 1337. Hence, it is as likely as not that the copyist gave up transcribing the statutes when he came to the section on the curriculum.

[1] *SA* 137–42 (*Docs*, i. 383–5), 90–109, 111–14 (*ibid.* 362–73). For Old Proctor 54, which is not included among the *statuta antiqua*, see below, pp. 298–9.

[2] *SA* 86 (*Docs*, i. 360–1), 119–22, 124 (*ibid.* 375–7).

[3] *SA* 126–34, 143–64, 166–9 (*ibid.* 378–82, 385–98).

preserved when the Old Proctor text was dismantled and reset by *c.* 1495, throwing the statutes into a needless state of disarray.

The relevant chapters of the Angelica text, II, III and V, were not jettisoned by the Old Proctor-Caius redactor. We find them scattered through the seventy-two chapters that make up the section on studies and academic matters. It may be that the order in which they appear in the recension had become fixed in an earlier revision of the statutes; but the texts themselves show remarkably little change from the form given them by the framer of the early thirteenth-century code. The only piece that lost its original identity is the first paragraph of chapter II, *De creacione Magistrorum et eorum officio*, which declares that intending masters must respond in all the schools of their faculty and obtain the licence from the chancellor.[1] In Old Proctor-Caius the necessity of doing responsions before inception is fully reaffirmed. Unlike the Angelica text, which merely gives a general ruling, the specific Old Proctor-Caius statutes regulating inceptions in each faculty provide for the performance of responsions which are also made obligatory for the degree of bachelor. Two statutes take the place of the Angelica paragraph on the licence,[2] the granting of which is explicitly linked with the depositions of the regent masters.[3]

The remaining seven paragraphs of Angelica II can easily be identified in Old Proctor-Caius even though their sequence is disrupted and the texts are spread over a number of chapters. Paragraph iv appears first and heads a long statute on the oaths to be taken at inceptions and solemn resumptions (Old Proctor 97).[4] Paragraphs ii and iii quickly follow and bring up the rear of Old Proctor 99.[5] The continuity of Angelica II stops short at this point. Two new statutes intervene before the ancient text is resumed

1 *Cons. Univ. Canteb.* II. i (see above, p. 199, lines 5–7).

2 Old Proctor 89–90 (*SA* 126–7 [*Docs*, i. 378–9]).

3 The norm referred to in the statutes on medicine, law and theology with regard to the depositions of the regent masters is that of Old Proctor 83, which governs inceptions in arts. It is obvious that *SA* 119–20, 122, 124 should form one unit with *SA* 86. Cf. *Docs*, i. 360–1, 375–7. In the superior faculties all the masters had to depone *de scientia*; in arts five masters had to depone *de scientia* and seven either *de credulitate* or *de scientia*, unless there happened to be less than twelve regents in the faculty, in which case alternative provisions came into effect. See above, pp. 121–2, and below, p. 277.

4 Cf. *Cons. Univ. Canteb.* II. iv (see above, p. 199, line 18 to p. 201, line 2); *SA* 134 (*Docs*, i. 381).

5 Cf. *Cons. Univ. Canteb.* II. ii–iii (see above, p. 199, lines 8–17); *SA* 144 (*loc. cit.* 386).

with chapter V, *De habitu Magistrorum*, which now displays a large accretion (Old Proctor 102).[1] The next two chapters of Old Proctor-Caius consist of a cognate statute and the 1290–1 enactment on the disposition of the various faculties at inceptions and other solemn functions (Old Proctor 103–4).[2] Angelica III, *De temporibus incipiendi et cessandi*, in a somewhat altered form becomes Old Proctor 105,[3] and is immediately succeeded by the left-over paragraphs (v–viii) of chapter II (Old Proctor 106); the only loss here is the substitution of a more detailed version for paragraph vi.[4] Thus all three chapters of the early thirteenth-century constitution are accounted for. They amount to only a minimal fraction of the galaxy of statutes on lectures and other academic affairs in Old Proctor-Caius, but their survival illustrates perhaps better than anything else the durability of the Angelica text.

There is one Old Proctor-Caius statute that deserves to be reproduced in full. It is statute 83 and prescribes the course and other scholastic requirements for inception in arts; it is also the earliest statutory pronouncement on the curriculum which a bachelor had to comply with before being admitted to the degree of master in the faculty. The absence of a statute of this kind from the Angelica text underlines its glaring deficiencies when compared with the later constitution. During the early thirteenth century the course for M.A. was regulated at the most by unwritten customs; by the close of the fourteenth century detailed rules had to be complied with. The statute which is now printed for the first time as promulgated by 1390 occupies a central position in the Old Proctor-Caius text, as its very title suggests: *De inceptoribus in quacunque facultate et primo de artistis incepturis*.[5] What purports to be the same text is listed in the 1852 edition of the statutes as *SA* 86.[6] In fact we are presented with an abbreviated version dating from the late fifteenth century and shorn of the most interesting and indeed crucial part of

[1] Cf. *Cons. Univ. Canteb.* v (see above, p. 203, line 14–16); *SA* 147 (*loc. cit.* 387–8).

[2] *SA* 148–9 (*loc. cit.* 388).

[3] Cf. *Cons. Univ. Canteb.* III (see above, p. 201, line 14 to p. 203, line 5); *SA* 150 (*loc. cit.* 388–9).

[4] Cf. *Cons. Univ. Canteb.* II. v–viii (see above, p. 201, lines 3–12); *SA* 151 (*loc. cit.* 389–90). The passage 'Inhibemus...obtinere' takes the place of Angelica II. vi 'Leccionem...licenciatus'. But Old Proctor 106 drops *theologus*, as does *SA* 151, in its reproduction of paragraph vii, leaving the sense incomplete. Cf. Old Proctor's Book, fo. 37v; *Docs*, i. 390, ll. 3–4.

[5] The statute almost certainly derives from the thirteenth century.

[6] *Docs*, i. 360–1.

the Old Proctor text.[1] The earlier version, Old Proctor-Caius 83, reads:[2]

Item statuimus quod nullus admittatur ad incipiendum in artibus. nisi prius determinauerit et vltra hoc [*transp.* Old Proctor] ad minus. per triennium hic vel alibi in vniuersitate in eadem facultate continue studuerit et iterato librum posteriorum audierit vel legerit et eciam quod in vniuersitate [in eadem...vniuersitate *om. ex homoiotel.* Old Proctor] rite audierit in scolis libros aristotelis phisicorum. celi et mundi. de generacione. metheororum. de anima. de sensu et sensato. de sompno et vigilia. de memoria et reminiscencia. de morte et vita [*del.* Old Proctor] de plantis. de motu animalium metaphisicam [*del.* Old Proctor] et omnes libros ethicorum. et vna cum hoc hic vel alibi in vniuersitate audierit de geometria tres primos libros euclidis. algorismum. compotum et [*om.* Caius] tractatum de spera. ita quod libros phisicorum. celi et mundi. de generacione et corupcione. metheororum de anima et metaphisicam audiat ordinarie. et quod legerit si aularis ad minus per biennium in statu bachelarii fuerit [si...fuerit *in parenthesi* Old Proctor] per quinque terminos. videlicet per terminum / logicalia / per terminum naturalia / per terminum geometricalia / per terminum tractatum de spera. algorismum / vel compotum / per terminum moralia. et si aularis non fuerit legat logicalia ad minus per terminum / naturalia per alium / geometricalia. astrologicalia. vel moralia per terminum. legenti vero a festo translacionis sancti Thome publice vsque ad festum Natiuitatis beate marie virginis pro termino computetur. Item quod in scolis sue facultatis secundum exigenciam sui status publice opposuerit et saltim tribus magistris eiusdem facultatis in eorum disputacionibus principaliter responderit Ita quod eius noticia in statura / moribus / et sciencia apud magistros illius facultatis iure fuerit approbata. Cuius approbacionem auctoritate Cancellarii et tocius vniuersitatis sic fore intelligendam [intel- Caius] decreuimus scilicet quod quinque magistri arcium in virtute iuramenti vniuersitati prestiti [prefati Old Proctor] deponant de sciencia, et alij vij eiusdem facultatis de credulitate vel sciencia, quod fiat per scrutinium iuxta examinacionem Cancellarii et procuratorum presentante [presentat Caius], non existente in scrutinio [Scrutineo Old Proctor] et tunc demum admittatur cum formam istam [*om.* Old Proctor] se compleuisse iurauerit. numero vero regencium in artibus ad xij non extenso, vna medietas deponat de sciencia et alia medietas de credulitate si pares fuerint. et si impares excessus scientibus relinquatur. (Old Proctor, fo. 33^{r-v}; Caius, fo. 13^{rb-vb}.)

It has long been assumed that the course and the prescribed textbooks for the degree of master at Cambridge were the same as at Oxford.[3] The foregoing statute supplies a timely corrective, and is as instructive for what it includes as for what it excludes.

1 This statute was amended, and in the process drastically reduced, *c.* 1500, when provision was made for a statutory course in mathematics, for which a special lectureship was instituted under *SA* 136. See below, p. 296.

2 The punctuation is that in Old Proctor.

3 For the Oxford course cf. *SAUO*, pp. xciii–xcv; Weisheipl, 'Curriculum of the faculty of arts at Oxford', *Mediaeval Studies*, xxvi. 161–3. Rashdall, *Universities*, iii. 155–6, gives elaborate lists of textbooks, but these are based mainly on a statute of 1431.

On one major point Cambridge followed Paris rather than Oxford. Determination was essential for admission to M.A.[1] Much might be written about this Cambridge statute which presupposes a knowledge of two other statutes which we shall meet again.[2] Here we must be content to observe that although the statute on inception may represent, at least in substance, the customs of the thirteenth century, as set down in Old Proctor-Caius, it cannot be earlier than *c.* 1317–25, unless the term 'aularian' was applied to Peterhouse men and scholars of Michaelhouse before the foundation of King's Hall and University Hall, better known as Clare College. That this part of the statute was formulated after the Angelica text was recast is certain; for one thing, the end of Easter term had been moved from 20 July to 6 July, as at Oxford. Old Proctor 83 is very much a fourteenth-century statute. The revised version, on the contrary, although lacking humanist colour, exalts mathematics, a typical late fifteenth-century touch.[3]

There is a more immediate reason for reproducing here the Old Proctor-Caius text than to resurrect a forgotten piece of Cambridge legislation, illuminating as it is in its own right. Two of the variant readings confirm the surprising discovery: the Old Proctor's Book was not the basis of the fifteenth-century redactions of the

[1] The Parisian rule is contained in a statute of 1279 which shows that while determination was necessary, one was not bound to have determined at Paris; it was sufficient to have done so 'in alio studio generali, ubi sint ad minus xij magistri regentes' (*Chart. Univ. Paris.* i. 570, no. 485). Was a university not regarded as being a *studium generale* in arts unless it had twelve regent masters in the faculty? It will be remembered that this was the standard number of masters required to depone at Cambridge for inceptors. Nevertheless, if the number fell below twelve, there is no doubt that the university at any rate recognized the award of the *magisterium* even if approved only by a lesser number of masters.

[2] See below, pp. 296–302.

[3] We see a reverse trend in the contemporary statutes of the faculty of arts at Freiburg, which have now been edited by H. Ott and J. M. Fletcher, *The mediaeval statutes of the faculty of arts of the University of Freiburg im Breisgau* (Mediaeval Institute of the University of Notre Dame: Texts and Studies in the History of Mediaeval Education, x [Notre Dame, Indiana, 1964]). The importance assigned to mathematics in the 1460–3 statutes is in striking contrast with the statutes of 1490–1505, which were the very years the Cambridge Junior and Senior Proctors' Books were produced. In the second set of the Freiburg statutes all the non-Aristotelian books have vanished from the curriculum. The editors offer no explanation for this extraordinary change. It is certain that there was no swing to humanism. We have thus the strange phenomenon of the old, conservative university of Cambridge moving with the times by giving fresh impetus to mathematics and, as will be seen, to humanism, whereas the new university of Freiburg (1455–6) was going in reverse gear.

statutes. The variant *hoc vltra* as against the Caius reading, *vltra hoc*, could be dismissed as a very minor divergence. That it is not so insignificant is evident from the texts in the Junior and Senior Proctors' Books. Both agree with Caius rather than with Old Proctor, and to show that there is more in this than meets the eye, the two later redactions also retain part of the Caius text which the scribe of Old Proctor omitted by committing the mechanical fault of homoioteleuton. It is true that Junior and Senior Proctor here retain only the phrase 'in eadem facultate continue studuerit'; but this is sufficient of itself to prove the non-dependence on Old Proctor of the texts executed *c.* 1494–1502.[1] There is abundant evidence that they do not stem from Caius either. But since Old Proctor and Caius derive from a common parent (γ), this manuscript cannot be the ancestor of Junior and Senior Proctor. Old Proctor and Caius are definitely independent of each other, but as they both diverge from Junior and Senior Proctor, it follows that their immediate parent cannot have been the source of the fifteenth-century proctors' books. We have, therefore, to postulate the existence of a manuscript (β), the archetype, so to speak, of the *statuta antiqua*. It gave rise to two traditions: the one represented by the actual parent of the Old Proctor-Caius recension (γ), the other by the direct line which issued in Junior and Senior Proctor.

The thirteenth and concluding chapter of the Angelica text, which falls outside the range of the Markaunt fragment, reappears in Old Proctor-Caius, where it occupies more or less the same position which it held in the early thirteenth-century text. It is only slightly altered, at one point for the better. The first paragraph of the original statute no longer remains. It would be strange indeed, even for university statutes, if it had been allowed to stand by *c.* 1385. The paragraph (Angelica XIII. i) ceased to have any meaning once the university had celebrated the obsequies of Henry III and Hugh of Northwold, the king and bishop to whom the statute implicitly refers. Consequently, Angelica XIII is decapitated in Old Proctor-Caius:

[1] Cf. *SA* 86 (*Docs*, i. 360–1), which faithfully reproduces the text of Junior Proctor (fo. 150ʳ) and Senior Proctor (fo. 24ʳ), even though in the latter part of the statute the words 'vel de sciencia' are missing from Junior Proctor. The statute, as has been pointed out above, is a late revision of the text circulated *c.* 1385, which explains why it does not contain more of the Caius passage, omitted inadvertently by the scribe of Old Proctor.

Angelica XIII

Quoniam naturali congruit racioni ut qui superstites liberalitatum eciam actualiter fuerant largitores saltem in exitu memoracionis fiant expectatores cum aliquid humanitus de illustri rege anglie contingerit...seu eciam de uenerabili patre contigerit elyensi... conueniant vniuersi ipsius exequias congrua celebraturi deuocione.

Ad exequias regencium decedencium vniuersas cancelarius conueniat cum regentibus

psalteria sua per totam noctem dicturis leccionibus et disputacionibus a tempore mortis donec corpus ecclesiastice traditum fuerit sepulture omnino cessantibus.

Ad exequias scolarium non regencium et bedellorum cancelarius ueniat et regentes ante corporum sepulturam nullatenus recessuri die sepulture disputacionibus omnino caritura illis tantummodo exceptis qui artem solam docent gramaticam ad quorum exequias nisi ex deuocione non conueniant supradicti. (*Cons. Univ. Canteb.* [see above, p. 217, lines 6–25].)

Old Proctor 127[1]

ITem ad hospicium cuiuscumque regentis in municipio Cantebrigie discedentis conueniat Cancellarius cum omnibus regentibus[2] corpus cum processione magistrorum regencium ad aliquem locum in vniuersitate exequiis eiusdem defuncti deputatum delaturi ac exequias deuocione qua decet celebraturi necnon spalteria sua post exequias ante recessum suum complete dicturi lectionibus et disputacionibus a tempore mortis donec corpus ecclesiastice traditum fuerit sepulture omnino cessantibus Exequiis autem magistrorum non regencium omnes magistri non regentes in villa presentes vna cum regentibus interesse teneantur[3] ad exequias vero scolarium et bedellorum Cancellarius ueniat et regentes ante corporum sepulturas nullatenus recessuri, die sepulture disputacionibus omnino caritura, illis tantummodo exceptis qui artem solam docent vel audiunt gramaticam ad quorum exequias nisi ex deuocione non veniant supradicti. (Junior Proctor's Book, fo. 107^{v}.)

The only striking changes, apart from the omission of the obsolete part of the basic text, that the Old Proctor–Caius recension presents are a more precise description of the procedure to be observed at

[1] Caius 128 (fo. $20^{r\,a-r\,b}$); *SA* 178 (*Docs*, i. 403–4).

[2] Here a smaller and later hand has added 'in habitibus scolasticis' above the line. This accretion is not found in Caius (fo. $20^{r\,a}$) and was probably introduced after the enactment of *SA* 175 (*loc. cit.* 401–2), which dates from *c.* 1415–22, when mag. John Rickinghall was chancellor. Cf. *BRUC*, p. 480.

[3] The later hand has again inserted 'in habitibus scolasticis' above the line.

funerals of regents and the position now accorded to the non-regents.[1] In the thirteenth-century constitution they were classed with the general body of scholars and barely took precedence over the bedells. Their importance was bound to receive recognition with the passing of the statute of 18 March 1304, and it is more than likely that the Angelica text was amended soon after this date.[2] Old Proctor 127 incidentally clarifies the ambiguity of the phrase *scolarium non regencium* in Angelica XIII. iii: does it mean 'scholars and non-regent masters' or 'non-regent scholars'? Either interpretation could be correct, for the term 'non-regent scholar' has statutory authority.[3] Old Proctor 127 by transposing the original passage and inserting *magistrorum* before *non regencium* resolves the uncertainty; the Angelica phrase evidently is to be translated as 'scholars and non-regents'. That the author of Angelica XIII intended his wording to be understood in this sense may be judged from the fact that he wrote 'Ad exequias scolarium non regencium' and not 'Ad exequias non regencium scolarium'. Had he given this latter twist to the text we should have to translate *non regencium scolarium* as 'non-regent scholars' or 'non-regent masters'.[4]

The Old Proctor's Book contains one sidelight on the transmission of the Angelica text which reinforces the value of an official register over a private copy of the statutes. There is little to choose between Old Proctor and Caius, but the university statute-book has the singular merit of exhibiting a 'live' text, a witness to the continuous development of the statutes. The margins of the Old Proctor folios were used as convenient spaces for the insertion of new enactments, interpretations and amendments. On the outer margin of fo. 22^{v} there is a long amendment to Old Proctor 28, a statute which underwent only slight modifications since it was first formulated by *c.* 1250 as *De officiis bedellorum et apparitorum et eorum honoribus.*[5]

1 The reference to grammar students in the final part of the Old Proctor statute may foreshadow the imminent extension of quasi-faculty recognition to grammar.

2 *SA* 179 (not marked in *Docs*, i. 404), which was enacted by 1495, amends in turn the Old Proctor-Caius version. Yet another statute on funerals was issued after 1500, namely *SA* 81 (*ibid.* 358–9).

3 Cf. Old Proctor 104: 'non regens scolaris aliis scolaribus et non regens bachelarius aliis bachelariis preponatur in arguendo inceptoribus et magnatibus exceptis' (fo. 37^{r}); *SA* 149 (*Docs*, i. 388).

4 An Oxford statute confirms what the extract cited in the foregoing note plainly implies, namely, that *non regens scolaris* means the same thing as non-regent master. Cf. *SAUO*, 52, 14–17.

5 *Cons. Univ. Canteb.* VIII. (see above, p. 207, line 3 to p. 209, line 4).

The *marginale* was not incorporated in the text of the statute in the Junior or Senior Proctor's Books;[1] it must have been overlooked when Old Proctor was replaced by a fresh redaction.[2] Needless to say, the amendment is not dated, but the hand is not much later than that of Old Proctor and it is possible that the insertion was made *c.* 1400–15.[3] Granted that the amendment was ignored when the fifteenth-century statute-books took shape, we may assume that its provisions continued to have statutory force. The statute itself begins in Old Proctor as in Markaunt 19, which in turn depends on Angelica VIII:[4]

Duo tantum bedelli[5] seu apparitores iuramento astricti in ista vniuersitate habeantur [at this point there is a sign referring to the margin and indicating that the amendment is to be inserted here; it reads] scilicet principales et tercius[6] secundarius. circa quorum visitacionem formam volumus obseruari sequentem. quod videlicet vterque principalium bedellorum in facultatibus quarum specialis est bedellus integre visitetur secundum summam visitacionis hactenus vsitatam et in registro vniuersitatis expressam. Residuum vero visitacionis consuete et in dicto registro limitate. alijs duobus bedellis scilicet alteri principalium et secundario per equales porciones distribuatur. si actibus magistrorum suorum presencialiter intersint. alias non. nisi infirmitatibus sint detenti. vel circa cetera negocia ad eorum officium pertinencia racionabiliter occupati. Et hunc visitacionis modum in omnibus facultatibus volumus obseruari. secundum quod in dicto registro[7] vniuersitatis plenius declaratur Non tamen est intencionis nostre per hanc ordinacionem libertatem visitancium cohartare. quin possint summam in registro limitatam cuicunque bedellorum si[8] voluerint ad libitum augmentare. (Old Proctor, fo. 22v.)[9]

1 Cf. Junior Proctor's Book, fo. 76r–v; Senior Proctor's Book, fo. 21r–v; *SA* 72 (*Docs*, i. 353–4).

2 See below, pp. 289–90, n. 1.

3 The amendment relates precisely to the fees paid to the bedells by degree-men and newly appointed lecturers, and lays down how the money was to be allocated among the recipients. It appears to have been formulated by 24 April 1415, as it makes no allusion to the royal writ of that date on the subject of 'visiting' the bedells, which was adopted in full as *SA* 76 (*Docs*, i. 356) and led to the enactment of *SA* 73 (*ibid.* 354–5).

4 It is hardly necessary to point out again that although the Old Proctor text was based on the Markaunt recension, it was not copied from the exemplar of Markaunt's Book. In retaining *tantum*, the second word of the statute, against Markaunt Old Proctor is closer to the tradition of Angelica VIII. i. Apart from that, Old Proctor corresponds almost exactly with Markaunt 19 (see below, p. 320, line 32 to p. 321, line 22).

5 A third hand has inserted above the line the words 'scilicet prinpales' (*recte* 'principales'). These are the opening words of the amendment and have no place here.

6 'non ita principalis' *suprascript. man. rec.*

7 Written twice but corrected.

8 *suprascript.*

9 End of the *marginale*; 'quorum alter' (etc.), as in *Docs*, i. 353–4, follows.

This entry on the margin of the medieval register throws some welcome light on the distinction between the two official bedells and a third who flits in and out of the university records. From *c.* 1250 there were only two bedells, one for the faculties of theology and canon law and one for the faculty of arts; they were allowed, but only by grace of the chancellor, to have a substitute or some kind of assistant. This remained the statutory ruling down to 1549. In practice, at any rate in the fourteenth century, three bedells were not unusual. There were that many present at the confirmation of mag. John de Crakhall as chancellor on 28 October 1346.[1] Three are also listed as having held office *c.* 1350;[2] and in a petition of 1389–90 for a papal indulgence *in articulo mortis* John Wesenham, William Wykmer and William Fisshewicke are called bedells of the university.[3] The Old Proctor amendment is, however, the earliest statutory evidence of the existence of a third bedell.[4]

The purpose of the amendment was obviously not to sanction the institution of a new official but to regulate on an equitable basis the division of the fees and other perquisities to which the bedells were entitled over and above the common collection taken up by them in the schools.[5] Their 'visitation' fees, as the amendment more than once informs us, were tabled in the register of the university, which was certainly not the Old Proctor's Book.[6] The use of the titles

[1] Ely Dioc. Rec. G I (1), fo. 8v. The names of the bedells are not given, but see next note. For Crakhall cf. *BRUC*, pp. 165–6, and above, p. 248, n. 1.

[2] Stokes, *Esquire bedells*, pp. vii, 55–7. The bedells were Henry the Bedell, Adam de la More and Richard de Betellee. These may have been the unnamed officials who witnessed Crakhall's institution by Bishop de Lisle as chancellor in 1346. Betellee held office *c.* 1347–68 and de la More *c.* 1348.

[3] CUA, doc. no. 82**, Colville roll 2, m. 6. Stokes, *op. cit.* pp. 9–10, 60, citing the extract in CUL Mm. i. 53 (Baker, xlii), fo. 180r–v, was mistaken in thinking that the reference is to a lost bull of Urban VI (1386). For Fisshewicke, Wesenham and Wykmer cf. *BRUC*, pp. 231, 628, 656. Wesenham's and Wykmer's terminal dates should be 1390 (not 1396) and 1381.

[4] The 'chancellor's bedell' who makes his appearance after the university secured control of the market in 1382 was distinct from the three university bedells. His office was to collect fines imposed at the leets held in connection with offences against the assize of bread, wine and ale, and trade in general. Thomas Weryng was bedell of the chancellor *c.* 1415–20. Cf. Markaunt's Book, fo. 69r (E 30r). See also *Grace Book* A, p. 226; *Grace Book* Γ, p. 311. For the leet rolls cf. Peek and Hall, *Archives*, pp. 56, 74. Stokes, *op. cit.* pp. 122–6, identifies the bedell with the sub—or (later) inferior—bedell.

[5] Cf. Stokes, *Esquire bedells*, pp. 23–33.

[6] There is a list of fees in the Junior Proctor's Book, pp. 26–31, which was copied from a list in the Black Parchment Book, pp. 347–9. The source is the Elizabethan

'principal' and 'secondary' appears to be unique and is more in keeping with Parisian and continental usage than English.[1] This nomenclature failed to win popularity at Cambridge, possibly because the amendment was inadvertently passed over when the statutes were rearranged later in the fifteenth century.[2] By 1473 the title of esquire was assumed by John of Canterbury, then bedell;[3] strangely enough, the term 'esquire bedell' did not receive statutory recognition until 1549, when it was written into the Edwardine code.[4] It was only at a much later date that 'yeoman bedell' came into use, replacing the embarrassing title of inferior bedell granted by statute of Edward VI.[5] His office may have corresponded with that of the former sub-bedell.[6] The secondary or third bedell mentioned in the Old Proctor amendment is a hazy figure. We lose track of him before the close of the fifteenth century,[7] but his existence by 1533–4 is attested by John Mere, himself bedell of

statutes of 1570, c. XLIX; cf. *Docs*, i. 487–9. Another list of fees in the Black Parchment Book, pp. 24–6, was copied from the statutes of 1559; cf. Lamb, *Collection of letters*, pp. 296–9. It is possible that the table in Stokys's Book, fos. 52^{v}–54^{v}, 'Soluciones quedam facte officiarijs vniuersitatis de quibus nulla fit mentio in libris procuratorum', derives from the missing register of the university.

1 *Chart. Univ. Paris.* ii. 157, no. 697. Cf. a statute of Angers dating from 1398–1410 in *Statuts*, i. 335, no. 434 (CXXXVIII).

2 On the margin of Old Proctor, fo. 22^{v}, a later hand has written above the amendment 'Hoc non scribitur adhuc in nouo' [*sc.* registro *vel* libro]. There are similar entries on fos. 2^{v}, 32^{r}, 34^{r} for amendments which became *SA* 27, 110 (*Docs*, i. 324, ll. 15–20; 371) and *SA* 82 (*ibid.* 359). *SA* 110 was inserted in its proper place in the Junior and Senior Proctors' Books, but *SA* 82 almost went the same way as the amendment to Old Proctor 28; it was passed over during the transcription of Junior Proctor and was afterwards retrieved and entered on a vacant space on fo. 104^{r}. The statute was correctly placed in the Senior Proctor's Book (fo. 23^{v}), but not by the earliest hand. In both books the addition to *SA* 27 is only a *marginale*!

3 Stokes, *Esquire bedells*, p. 4. The term 'esquire bedell' or rather 'gentleman bedell' was probably used in popular parlance from a much earlier period. Cf. the reference to the will (1392) of John de Donewich in *BRUC*, p. 192; the original actually states that Donewich bequeathed 'cuilibet bedello generoso xiijs iiijd et alijs vel alteri vjs. viijd.' (Somerset House, London, Prerogative Court of Canterbury, 6 Rous [fo. 46^{v}].) It will be noticed that there is no allusion to the title of yeoman bedell.

4 'Tres erunt praecones seu viatores armigeri pari loco ac munere et unus inferioris loci bedellus' (*Statuta regis Edwardi sexti*, ed. Lamb, *op. cit.* p. 134).

5 *Ibid.* Cf. Stokes, *op. cit.* pp. 122–8.

6 John Duke was sub-bedell *c.* 1418. Cf. Markaunt's Book, fo. 66^{r} (E 27^{r}). The document is undated, but Cooper, *Annals*, i. 159, followed by Stokes, *op. cit.* p. 63, assigns it to 1418. His dating may be accepted.

7 There were only two statutory bedells in 1483–4 and by 28 June 1494. Cf. *Grace Book* A, p. 185; *Grace Book* B, i. 67; *SA* 75 (*Docs*, i. 355–6). Stokes, *op. cit.* p. viii, has three bedells for 1495, 1510, 1521.

theology;[1] and in 1549 he was placed on an equal footing with the two other bedells, all three being honoured with the title of esquire.[2] His office seems to have fallen into abeyance, or may not have materialized in 1549, for a grace was passed in 1556 authorizing the election of a third bedell.[3] The post was formally recognized in the Elizabethan statutes of 1559 and 1570, which guaranteed the holder a proportionate share of the emoluments enjoyed by his two partners.[4] Financially and otherwise, it was a more attractive proposition than the scheme outlined in the Old Proctor amendment.

1 The entry in Mere's diary is printed in *Grace Book* A, p. 227. Leathes, *ibid.* p. xxxviii, in suggesting that there may have been four bedells doubtless counted the chancellor's official as one, but we must be careful to distinguish him from the three university bedells in office by *c.* 1533–4. The duties of the third bedell with reference to academic exercises are noticed in Stokys's memorandum, which exemplifies the customs of an earlier period (saec. xv*ex*–xvi*in*) than the date of the composition of his Book (*c.* 1574–8). Cf. Peacock, *Observations*, App. A, pp. xii, xlviii.

2 Cf. *Statuta Edwardi sexti, loc. cit.*

3 *Grace Book* Δ, ed. J. Venn (Cambridge, 1910), p. 123.

4 Cf. *Statuta academiae Cantabrigiensis a visitatoribus Elizabethae reginae an. I^mo^ data*, ed. Lamb, *op. cit.* pp. 294–9; *Statuta reginae Elizabethae an. XII^mo^ edita*, cc. XXXVIII, XLIX, *ibid.* pp. 335–6, 346–8; *Docs*, i. 476–7, 487–90. The statutes of 1570 are virtually a direct transcript of those of 1559, which are little more than a copy of the Edwardine code.

Chapter 11

THE EVOLUTION OF THE EDITIO PRINCEPS

The actual history of the original text of the Cambridge constitution closed with the production of the Old Proctor-Caius recension or more precisely its parent once removed, the lost manuscript β. What follows is rather the fate of this late fourteenth-century code than the final chapter in the story of the Angelica text. One cannot fully appreciate, however, the archetypal role of the original text without some knowledge of the development of the *textus receptus* of the medieval statutes which is preserved in the Senior Proctor's Book (*c.* 1496–1502), which was privately printed as the *editio princeps* by the University Press in 1785 from a transcript made by Adam Wall (1746–98), fellow of Corpus Christi College and one-time senior proctor.[1]

Strange as it may seem, the fifteenth century is perhaps the most obscure and perplexing in the long and intricate history of the Cambridge statutes. Recension β was revised, recast and augmented more than once between 1400 and 1495. We have already mentioned the mysterious disappearance of the common register of the university.[2] What became of it or how it vanished so completely out of sight are questions that our extant records fail to answer. No doubt there are several references to a register or registers in early and late fifteenth-century records, but these only serve to complicate the matter. Many problems present themselves. Here we have to

1 The title-page of the printed volume reads: *Statuta Academiae Cantabrigiensis Cantabrigiae typis academicis excudebat J. Archdeacon* M.DCC.LXXXV. The *statuta antiqua* occupy pp. 1–94. Wall was responsible for the preparation of the entire volume for the press. The edition includes some scattered sixteenth-century statutes entitled *Statuta in ordinem non redacta* (*Docs*, i. 417–53) and the Edwardine and Elizabethan codes as well as the corresponding injunctions. Wall's MS is CUL Mm. 5. 53–4. His transcript of the medieval statutes is found in the first volume, pp. 1–132. Various notes in his hand occur in the Senior Proctor's Book and he completed the numeration of the statutes. He also worked over the Junior Proctor's folios.

2 It is not to be confused with the common register which was contrasted with the proctors' books of the statutes in 1572. Cf. Lamb, *Collection of letters*, pp. 387 (7), 398 (7). 'Register' in this context suggests the Black Parchment Book rather than *Grace Book* Δ (1542–89).

consider only one, the relationship between the missing register and the late medieval statute-books, whose origins derive ultimately, as far as present evidence goes, from the exemplar Angelica MS 401.

The institution of separate books of the statutes for the proctors *c.* 1385 foreshadowed if not the demise at any rate a change in the character of the register. Old Proctor was primarily a book of statutes; it was also a sort of register. Charters of Richard II extending the privileges of the university were copied into it contemporaneously with the statutes. By 1430 it would appear that the university register no longer constituted the official statute-book. There now existed a new book, the *liber statutorum*, which was cited at the Barnwell process on 19 October 1430.[1] It was not Old Proctor. In a way the problem would be eased if we could identify the *liber* with Old Proctor, but one would not then be able to construct a *stemma codicum* without doing violence to the textual evidence. It has been demonstrated in the previous chapter that Old Proctor cannot be the ancestor of either Junior or Senior Proctor. There must have

1 On that day the proctors of the university, John Wolpit and John Botwright, submitted in evidence an instrument drawn up by the public notary, Richard Pyghtsley, 'Copias quorundam priuilegiorum et indultorum Apostolicorum continens vna. cum alijs euidencijs munimentis et statutis. a. libro statutorum dicte vniuersitatis elicitis et extractis' (CUA, doc. no. 108 [the original transcript of the process]; cf. Nichols, *Bibl. Topo. Brit.* v. xxxviii. 38; Heywood, *Early Camb. Univ. & Coll. Stats.* p. 196). Earlier in the proceedings, on 9 Sept. 1429, another instrument also executed by Pyghtsley was presented in which he states that the proctors showed him the bulls of John XXII (1318) and Boniface IX (1401), and he adds: 'Registrumque eiusdem vniuersitatis variorum et diuersorum iurium priuilegiorum libertatum munimentorum ac Iurisdiccionis prefate vniuersitatis et ipsam vniuersitatem concernentes copias continens et inter alia duarum bullarum vnius videlicet honorij alteriusque Sergij quondam eciam Romanorum Pontificum ab archiuis eiusdem vniuersitatis extrahendo protulerunt exhibuerunt et ostenderunt... michi notario et testibus infrascriptis predictas Bullas ac eciam Registrum predictum' (CUA, doc. cit.; Nichols, *loc. cit.*; Heywood, *op. cit.* pp. 196–7). From these two documents it definitely appears that the statute-book was distinct from the register at this time. The separation may have taken place by 1417, when Markaunt's Book was in progress; indeed this was probably the reason why the scribe of Markaunt broke off his transcription of the statutes, apart from the fact that his exemplar was by then antiquated.

It should be noted that Pyghtsley's instrument of 9 Sept. 1429 was copied almost word for word from a deed written by Thomas de Ryhale, likewise a public notary, dated 1 June 1419. It states that the register of the university was produced on that occasion by the chancellor, John Rickinghall. The text is printed in Caius, *Works*, pp. 56–7. Evidently, the Barnwell process had an earlier origin than has been suspected. The full story has yet to be written; it should make interesting reading and show the unscrupulous lengths to which the university went to buttress its claim against the bishop of Ely.

existed by 1430 either the sub-archetype β or a manuscript which was directly copied from it independently of γ, the immediate parent of Old Proctor-Caius.[1] Whichever of the two, it was in all probability the *liber statutorum* mentioned in the Barnwell process. This being so, the university had three copies of the statutes in the early fifteenth century. All were official exemplars, but the authentic text, the one on which the university rested its case, was the *liber statutorum*. Whether it was β itself or δ, it need not necessarily have contained a new recension. The one or the other included *SA* 76 and *SA* 170.[2]

From now on the story can be pieced together very tentatively from the Grace Books, which begin with the year 1454. MS γ (the first senior proctor's book?) and the Old Proctor's Book had to have the chains by which they were carried repaired or renewed in 1456–8.[3] It will be recalled that there is a cryptic note at various points in Old Proctor, stating that such and such a statute or amendment was not yet inserted in the 'new book'.[4] Old Proctor likewise has a marginal entry but in a hand different from the foregoing references indicating where *SA* 55 (1490) was to be accommodated 'in nouo libro'.[5] In this particular instance we have little difficulty in identifying the new book; it was either Junior or Senior Proctor, both of which were executed after 1490.[6] But the other note, 'non

[1] The principle *entia non sunt multiplicanda* is an *a priori* argument for holding that β was the *liber statutorum*. The register could certainly have been broken up by 1430 and the part comprising the statutes formed into a distinct book. Yet we must allow for the possibility if not the probability that a new text was executed, say, *c*. 1417–30. I have recognized this in my reconstruction of the *stemma*, where the MS is denoted by the symbol δ (p. 306 below). In either case, the manuscript tradition is not affected.

[2] *Docs*, i. 356, 399. *SA* 76 (for which see p. 282, n. 3) shows that the fifteenth-century books of the statutes were not based on Old Proctor. The statute is dated 24 April, 3 Henry V (1415); it is simply a copy of a royal writ of that date. Unlike almost all the statutes enacted after 1400 it was not entered anywhere in the Old Proctor's Book, which has, however, another version of the writ bearing the date 1 March (*recte* May) 1415 on fo. 44^v. *SA* 170 dates from *c*. 1423–8 when Robert FitzHugh was chancellor.

[3] 'Item pro emendacione cathenarum libri procuratoris viijd' [1456–7]; 'Item in chatenis pro libro procuratoris iiijd' [1457–8] (*Grace Book* A, pp. 10, 13).

[4] See above, p. 284, n. 2.

[5] 'Hic interponetur stat⟨utum⟩ nouum de modo dandi voces in electione procuratorum in nouo libro' (Old Proctor, fo. 20^r). The reference in *Docs*, i. 341 to fo. 47^v under the year 1477 has to do with a different statute which for some reason or other was not included in the *statuta antiqua*.

[6] Cf. Junior Proctor, fo. 70^r; Senior Proctor, fo. 15^r.

scribitur in nouo adhuc', which occurs four times in Old Proctor, indicates that there existed an earlier 'new' book. *SA* 110, we read, was omitted from it; the statute is an integral part of the Junior and Senior Proctors' texts;[1] so we have to search back through the fifteenth century for another new book. What we find is an *embarras de choix*, the only disappointment being that nothing more than a few fragments survives.

The high mortality rate of Cambridge statute-books of the fifteenth century can be ascribed in large measure to the bad habit of taking older books apart and redistributing the folios or even whole quires when new books were being made. Thus Junior Proctor has elements from three earlier statute-books while Senior Proctor has parts of two. And yet these fragments might never have been preserved had they not been torn from their original binding and incorporated in the extant proctors' books.[2]

Apparently, a fresh book of the statutes based on the *liber statutorum* of Barnwell fame was executed *c.* 1467–8.[3] It may have been the 'new' book to which reference is made more than once in Old Proctor.[4] An equally good and probably stronger contender is the *liber senioris procuratoris* which appears in 1478–9, just after a corresponding volume was produced at Oxford.[5] At all events these were replaced by two companion volumes *c.* 1487–8.[6] What brought these into being was perhaps a complaint about statutes having been overlooked during the transcription of the 1467–8 or the 1478–9 books. In any case the time had come to provide the proctors with two parallel volumes. Hitherto, the junior official had only Old Proctor to proclaim his status, especially on formal occasions, and by now it must have looked unsightly, not to

1 Cf. Old Proctor, fo. 32^{r} (lower margin); Junior Proctor, fo. 84^{r-v}; Senior Proctor, fo. 28^{v}.

2 Fos. 6^{v}–7^{v} of Old Proctor appear to have come from a statute-book of saec. xv*ex.*

3 'Item pro Cathenis et ligacione libri ijs xd'; 'Item pro ligatione libri statutorum xiiijd' (*Grace Book* A, pp. 65–6). These two entries, as Leathes observes, *ibid.* 269, relate to the same book.

4 Unfortunately, we are unable to assign a definite date for the amendment and statutes to which the comment 'non scribitur in nouo adhuc' is added in Old Proctor, except for the latter part of *SA* 27 (fo. 2^{v}). The text is not earlier than 18 Feb. 1457, and we may conclude that the new book was executed after this date.

5 'Item pro ligacione libri senioris procuratoris et pro clauis deauratis ijs iiijd'; 'Item pro tribus catenis solutum M. tesdall pro libro senioris procuratoris iijs' (*Grace Book* A, pp. 129–30). For the Oxford book, *Reg. B*, cf. *SAUO*, p. xvi.

6 'Item cathenis pro libris statutorum xiiijd' (*Grace Book* A, p. 220).

mention its much antiquated text.[1] But the 1487–8 project was the shortest-lived of all. The recensions exhibited by the two *libri statutorum* were unsatisfactory, probably because they were constructed during a transitional period of statutory history.[2] A new book was ordered for the junior proctor *c.* 1494–6 and another was provided for the senior proctor *c.* 1496–1502.[3]

The two impressive proctors' books which safely repose on the shelves of the strong room in the university archives mark the farthest point in the growth of the Angelica text. Both Junior and Senior Proctor, or rather their texts of the ancient statutes, were copied the one after the other from their respective exemplars, the *libri statutorum* of 1487–8, both of which were defective at an identical part of the text—a sign that they were derived from a single parent, the 1478–9 senior proctor's book. The only difference between Junior and Senior Proctor and their parents was that Junior and Senior incorporated in their texts recent enactments. Here it is vital to recognize that Junior Proctor is in one respect earlier and in another much later than Senior Proctor. Junior Proctor was put together at two intervals separated by fifteen years at least. Part I, which consists of fos. 56^{r}–83^{r}, dates from *c.* 1494–6.[4] Part II, comprising fos. 83–106^{v}, was executed apparently *c.* 1510–11 but

1 The entry in *Grace Book* B, i. 10, *s.a.* 1488—'Item pro reparacione libri procuratoris ijd'—probably refers to Old Proctor.

2 See below, pp. 296–302. The 1487–8 books were repaired in 1492: 'Item pro emendacione librorum procuratorum et pro signaculo iijd' (*Grace Book* B, i. 44).

3 There should be entries in the Grace Books under these years concerning the cost of these volumes. The accounts are complete for 1494–1502 but there is no record of payment. It could be that the scribe of Junior Proctor was not paid for his work, since he failed to finish the text, as we shall shortly see. He did complete Senior Proctor by 1502; even so, he received apparently no fee. Nor do we know what the parchment and binding cost.

4 *SA* 75 (*Docs*, i. 355–6), dated 28 June 1494, is entered in its proper place (fo. 77^{r}) in the first hand. *SA* 51 (*loc. cit.* 337–8), which was enacted on 4 March 1496, is a later addition; it was transcribed on fo. 77^{v} in a saec. xvi hand. An earlier *terminus ad quem*, 21 Jan. 1495, is possible. The text of *SA* 180 (*loc. cit.* 407) was amended on or shortly after this date. It orders the observance of the anniversaries of Richard III and mag. Thomas Barowe. The original deed is extant in CUA, doc. no. 136; there is a transcript in the Black Parchment Book, pp. 145–51 (fos. 52^{v}–55^{v}), which is the 'registrum quoddam earundem exequiarum' mentioned in *SA* 180 (cit.). Unfortunately, the original text of *SA* 180 occurs in Junior Proctor on one of the folios taken from Old Proctor; it lacks of course the amendment of 21 Jan. 1495 as indeed earlier additions. Cf. Junior Proctor, fo. 108^{r}. Though there is little doubt that part I of Junior Proctor was compiled by 1495, its omission of the amendment of 21 Jan. cannot be regarded as proof of this conjecture. The scribe had broken off his transcription well before reaching *SA* 180.

was not finally completed until some time afterwards.[1] Part I, therefore, is slightly earlier than Senior Proctor, whose text can be dated to *c.* 1496–1502.[2] The same scribe wrote part I of Junior Proctor and the whole of Senior Proctor; he left it, however, to somebody else to resume the transcription of part II of Junior Proctor. What caused the original scribe of part I to cut short his work is problematical. His exemplar was obviously imperfect, and it is possible that he decided to start afresh after copying the first ninety statutes. His abortive effort is none the less a better guide than Senior Proctor to the layout of the 1487–8 recension.

The format of Junior Proctor is unusually interesting as a medieval statute-book, even if beneath its ornate, studded covers with their hooks, chain and clasps it is anything but a pleasant book to handle.[3] The heart of the volume is modelled on that of Old Proctor. It consists of (i) extracts from the four gospels taken from another statute-book, most probably one of the *libri statutorum* mentioned in 1487–8; (ii) a painting of the Crucifixion; (iii) a calendar; (iv) the text of the statutes, ten of which are written on half a quire from Old Proctor; and (v) copies of miscellaneous documents beginning with the decree of 18 March 1294 ordering the observance of the obit of Queen Eleanor and ending with the decree of the foundation of the Billingford chest, dated 27 February 1433; in between are charters of Richard II.[4] This section is also made up of folios removed from an older statute-book.[5] In order to synchronize the matter on these extraneous folios with the existing material in the volume, the

[1] In *Grace Book* B, *s.a.* 1511 there is this entry: 'Item vni scribenti statuta vniuersitatis in libro iunioris procuratoris iijs ijd' (*Grace Book* B, i. 250). Some statutes were transcribed much later.

[2] See below, p. 294.

[3] The volume is now much swollen beyond its original size through the addition of extra folios containing other and later material. At present the MS consists of vii + 225 fos. of parchment, measuring about 245 × 165 mm. The first 46 leaves are paginated (not always accurately); the rest is foliated. Wall numbered the folios of the statutes separately, which is somewhat confusing. It is best to adhere to the foliation which starts after p. 46 with fo. 47 and is continued right through to the end of the volume. The statutes are on fos. 56^{r}–110^{v} (*recte* 107^{v}), 136^{v}–137^{r}, 138^{r}–139^{r}, 150^{r-v}.

[4] The latest document in this section is dated 10 Oct. 1442; it is a copy of the decree establishing the Exeter chest (fos. 132^{v}–133^{v}).

[5] The folios are 111^{r}–130^{v}, 133^{r}–135^{v}. These are remnants of perhaps the 1467–8 or the 1478–9 codices. Junior Proctor is indeed a composite book. Pp. 32–3 (the gospels) are from a companion of the volume which contained fo. H of Senior Proctor, while fos. 107^{r}–110^{v} (*recte* 104^{r}–107^{v}) were formerly part of Old Proctor. See below, p. 294, n. 1.

compiler or rather compilers of Junior Proctor had to resort to somewhat desperate methods.[1]

Part I reads easily, although the even flow of the text, written in the hand of Senior Proctor, is occasionally broken by the rough script of later insertions. There is evidence of negligence—initials were not filled in; but in one respect Junior Proctor represents a notable advance in the technique of codification when compared with Old Proctor. Spaces were left for the addition of new statutes or amendments. In Old Proctor no such provision was made, and the serial numbering of the statutes, helpful as it is, rendered the system cast-iron.[2]

The original text of Junior Proctor comprises *SA* 1–49, 53–62, 65–9, 71–6, 79–80, 90–107. This part can be safely assigned to the period *c.* 1494–6. Compared with the Old Proctor-Caius redaction of a century earlier, Junior Proctor exhibits some marked changes, unfortunately not for the better. Old Proctor 17–29 (*SA* 53–4, 56–8, 60–1, 65–7, 71–2, 79) are thoroughly dislocated. These statutes relate to the proctors, taxors, bedells and keepers of the common chest. In Old Proctor they formed a well-defined section at the beginning of the text together with the statutes on the chancellor, vice-chancellor and commissary. This was their proper place. It is impossible to justify the order in which they appear in Junior Proctor. The disarray may stem from the exemplar, and to this source it is probably fair to ascribe the loss of *SA* 82, 83, 86, 87, 89.[3] Total confusion involving the abandonment of any pretence of

[1] The beginning of the Queen Eleanor document ('Anno domini M°CC nonagesimo tercio videlicet') is written in a hand very like Senior Proctor's in the upper margin of fo. 111^{r}. Whoever added this and the subsequent folios to Junior Proctor must have discarded the folio containing the incipit of the document. Presumably, it had other matter which was considered either irrelevant or too awkward to handle. Some folios which carried on the text on fo. 130^{v} were likewise rejected; the material was afterwards copied on fos. 131^{r}–132^{v} and 136^{r} in a sixteenth-century hand.

[2] The statutes in Junior Proctor were not numbered by the scribe or by the writers who completed the transcription. Someone began to give them numbers corresponding with those of Senior Proctor before Wall became interested in the volume. He inked over the existing numbers and completed what had been left undone.

[3] The breakdown occurred immediately before *SA* 80 (12 Oct. 1467), which was transcribed by another though contemporary hand on fo. 78^{r}. The *verso* of this folio and the *recto* of the next (fo. 79) were left blank, and the transcription was resumed on fo. 80^{r} with *SA* 90. Thus, *SA* 81–9 are missing at this point (they were entered in the sixteenth century, though not in serial order, on fos. 104^{r-v}, 106^{r-v}, 150^{r-v}). *SA* 81 and 84 may be later than 1502 (*SA* 85 is dated 3 July 1505); *SA* 86 was probably undergoing revision by 1494; and *SA* 88 may not be earlier

codification appears towards the end of the text. But long before this point of the transcription was reached the scribe had put Junior Proctor aside and applied himself to Senior Proctor. When many years later Junior Proctor was revived the continuator lightened his task by filching the four folios from Old Proctor. The folios contained ten of the last twenty statutes (*SA* 169–88) of the Senior Proctor code.[1] One, *SA* 181, itself a congeries of six distinct statutes, had long since been fused into a single entity. This did not really matter; but the next statute in Old Proctor had been transferred in or shortly after 1489 and made a pendant to *SA* 183, while yet another statute, *SA* 174, lacked an amendment dating from *c.* 1396.[2] The scribe might have fitted in this addition on the margin opposite the statute on fo. 107^{v}. There were still eight statutes outstanding. The half-quire removed from Old Proctor could not accommodate them. In the end the scribe decided to enter the first five (*SA* 171, 175–7 and 179) in his own unfinished quire together with the amendment to *SA* 174.[3] This meant wholesale dislocation, and as if thoroughly dissatisfied with the situation he gave up and left out *SA* 182, 183 and 186–8 altogether.[4] The result is that the concluding part of the text of Junior Proctor is hopelessly jumbled, and one can easily understand why the *editio princeps* was not made from this manuscript but from its companion, Senior Proctor.

The Senior Proctor's Book follows almost exactly the plan of Junior Proctor.[5] Originally it consisted of (i) a single folio comprising two extracts from the gospels (John and Luke);[6] (ii) a

than 1500. But *SA* 82, 83, 87, 89 (6 June 1466) should not have been overlooked. We can only conclude that the exemplar was defective. Cf. also below, p. 295 for the exemplar of Senior Proctor.

1 Two of these, *SA* 187–8, were added after 1502 to the text. Cf. Senior Proctor, fo. 52^{r-v}.

2 The final part of *SA* 183 ('Jurent...supradictum') [*Docs*, i. 411]) immediately follows *SA* 181 of Old Proctor (fo. 109^{v}). The amendment to *SA* 174 orders a commemoration at the three general processions of mag. Michael de Causton, chancellor. See p. 263.

3 Junior Proctor, fos. 101^{v}–104^{r}.

4 These were inserted in a later hand on fos. 136^{v}–139^{r}. The tailpiece to *SA* 183 was not added to the text, possibly because it was already written on fo. 109^{v}.

5 The volume now has xx+234 parchment folios (excluding four flyleaves of hard paper), measuring *c.* 260×165 mm. The covers with their ornaments, hooks and chain are exactly the same as those of Junior Proctor. The statutes occupy fos. 1^{r}–52^{v}, the last two, *SA* 187–8 (fo. 52^{r-v}), being later additions.

6 The folio (fo. H^{v}) should have a companion with the excerpts from the gospels of Matthew and Mark as in Junior Proctor. It is certain that the single folio of Senior Proctor came from a companion of the volume that had the two folios now in Junior Proctor. The originals were presumably the *libri statutorum* of 1487–8.

calendar; (iii) the statutes; and (iv) two and a half quires from Old Proctor on which were written deeds corresponding to those in Junior Proctor but omitting the decrees concerning the Exeter and Billingford chests.[1] The hand of the calendar and statutes is the same as that which wrote the calendar and part 1 of the statutes in Junior Proctor. It is a fine hand and, as the entire text of the statutes of Senior Proctor, apart from accretions, was written by it, the transcription is a pleasure to read, even though again the initials were not taken care of. The scribe, as in Junior Proctor, made ample allowance for future additions to the code and once more refrained from numbering the statutes.[2] He executed the text *c.* 4 March 1496–8 September 1502, having begun the work probably shortly after leaving Junior Proctor aside.[3]

[1] Fos. 60ʳ–80ᵛ. The Exeter and Billingford decrees, dated 1442 and 1433 respectively in Junior Proctor, are much later than the date of Old Proctor and hence do not appear in Senior Proctor. The modern binding of Junior and Senior Proctor prevents us from reconstructing the make-up of the final part of Old Proctor. The volume originally appears to have consisted of gatherings of eight folios. Junior and Senior Proctor have between them 25 folios of Old Proctor (fos. 107–10 in Junior Proctor, and fos. 60–80 in Senior Proctor). The Senior Proctor section should link up with that of Junior Proctor, thus making four quires totalling in all 32 folios. Somewhere along the line seven folios, possibly more, were discarded altogether. The fact that the other 25 folios are now bound in with Junior and Senior Proctor places the makers of these two books under suspicion. What happened was something like this. The author of Senior Proctor took only what he needed, i.e. fos. 60–80. He had already completed a full transcript of the statutes and hence did not require fos. 107–10. Having decided to transfer fos. 60–80 to his book, he had to make good the loss of the preamble to the Queen Eleanor document, which he did on fo. 59ᵛ (as did the scribe of Junior Proctor on fo. 111ʳ of his MS); but he omitted to complete the remainder of the text on fo. 80ᵛ. A later hand (saec. xvi) finished the transcription on fo. 81ʳ.

Once the gap was made in Old Proctor it was almost inevitable that other folios would be taken out. The problem of the unfinished text of Junior Proctor must have tempted the continuator to use fos. 107–10 so as to provide a complete copy of the statutes without further delay for the junior proctors, who had been left in a rather embarrassing and awkward position since 1496. Hence it is that one part of Old Proctor is bound in with Senior Proctor and another part with Junior Proctor. The damage done to the late fourteenth-century register was repaired in 1519–20 and cost 4*s.* 2*d.*: 'Item pro resarcione libri statutorum iiijs ijd' (*Grace Book* B, ii. 82).

[2] *SA* 1–24 (fos. 1ʳ–6ʳ) are numbered in a medieval hand in the margin but not in the hand of the text. The numbers were worked over later and continued, mostly by Adam Wall, to the end. Various attempts at numbering the statutes were made before his time and as a result the margins of the MS present a rather untidy appearance.

[3] We may take it that Senior Proctor was finished by 1500. *SA* 51 (4 March 1496) is an integral part of the text (fo. 13ʳ⁻ᵛ; cf. *Docs*, i. 337–8). On the other hand, *SA* 77

As a recension Senior Proctor does not differ materially from part I of Junior Proctor, the only section of this volume which allows for a comparison along these lines.[1] There are eight additional statutes in Senior Proctor, *SA* 50–1, 63–4, 86–9, excluding *SA* 80, which although not written in the first hand of Junior Proctor may possibly have been inserted in its text *c.* 1494–6. One of the extra statutes in Senior Proctor, *SA* 51, was enacted on 4 March 1496; its omission from Junior Proctor at this point is evidence that the text of part I was executed by that date. *SA* 50, 63–4, 88 were enacted *c.* 1496–1502. Unlike Junior Proctor, Senior Proctor has *SA* 86, 87 and 89. It would seem, therefore, that the scribe when he set about writing the new book used a better exemplar than the one he worked from *c.* 1494–6. But it was not a perfect exemplar; it lacked, as did Junior Proctor's, *SA* 81–3 if not also *SA* 84. As far as one can judge, *SA* 82–3 are late fourteenth- or early fifteenth-century statutes. There must have been a hiatus in Senior Proctor's exemplar just where the *lacuna* occurred in that of Junior Proctor, except that it was larger in the exemplar of the latter. We may conclude, then, that Senior and Junior Proctor were copied from two independent but closely related parents which were doubtless the *libri statutorum* of 1487–8.

It has been mentioned in passing that Senior Proctor was finished before Junior Proctor, the transcription of which was not taken up again until *c.* 1510–11. There is no doubt that part II of Junior Proctor (fos. 83^{v}–106^{v}) was transcribed from Senior Proctor.[2] This is evident from palaeographical and textual evidence; for example, a *marginale* to *SA* 163 in Senior Proctor is embodied in the text of Junior Proctor.[3] Other proofs could be adduced to show that this part of

(*ibid.* 357), which dates from 8 Sept. 1502, was added by another scribe on fo. 22^{v}. Moreover, Archbishop Rotherham of York, chancellor and renowned benefactor of the university, who died on 29 May 1500, is not commemorated in the calendar (fo. I^{r}), which, as we have seen, is in the same hand as the text of the statutes.

[1] The recensions were little more than straight reproductions of the texts in the 1487–8 *libri statutorum*. Neither then nor in 1494–1502 were Old Proctor and its marginal additions collated by the redactors.

[2] Fos. 107–10, which account for ten of the statutes in Junior Proctor, are, it is hardly necessary to point out again, *membra disiecta* of Old Proctor.

[3] Cf. Junior Proctor, fo. 98^{v}; Senior Proctor, fo. 41^{v}. Other marginal entries in both volumes were added subsequently, and in one case the accretion was probably written into Junior Proctor before it was inserted in Senior Proctor. Cf. Junior Proctor, fo. 95^{v}; Senior Proctor, fo. 38^{v}. The readings in *Docs* are not always correct, e.g. both Junior and Senior Proctor have *oppositurus* in their text of *SA* 110. In *Docs*, i. 371, *oppositus* is printed as the reading of Senior Proctor.

Junior Proctor was compiled after Senior Proctor was completed and that the continuator worked from the latter volume. The most striking evidence of all emerges from a textual study of *SA* 140. This statute, *De determinatoribus pro se*, has a much more significant aspect than its value as a control for determining the relative dependence of Junior and Senior Proctor.

In the fourteenth century the faculty of theology attracted the main attention of the Cambridge legislators. The pendulum swung to the other extreme—the faculty of arts—in the fifteenth century, as at Oxford. The activities of the heads of the department, the regent masters, would pass unrecognized but for the statute-books. In Senior Proctor three statutes which were entered afterwards in Junior Proctor may be briefly noticed. *SA* 87 orders the establishment of a salaried lectureship in classics, an indication, perhaps, that humanism was making its presence felt at Cambridge by 1488.[1] The second statute, *SA* 135, is not so interesting;[2] but *SA* 136, which provides for special courses in mathematics, a term embracing music, anticipates a 'devotion to the subject which has been the most characteristic feature of Cambridge studies for the last 200 years'.[3] The statute was enacted *c.* 1500.[4]

Contemporaneously with these enactments went a revision of the statute on inception.[5] The changes in the curriculum did not stop there. Old Proctor 56, which laid down the conditions for admission to the degree of bachelor, was overhauled. Ultimately, all this statutory activity was bound up with the repeal of Old Proctor 54,

[1] Cf. *Docs*, i. 361. The statute, which occurs in Senior Proctor on fo. 24^v and in Junior Proctor on fo. 104^v, also provides for similar lectureships in logic and philosophy. It may have been enacted in 1485–6; it was definitely in force by 1488. The first professor to hold the chair of humanities was Caius Auberinus, for whom see R. Weiss, *Humanism in England during the fifteenth century* (2nd ed., Oxford, 1957), p. 163; *BRUC*, p. 23. Humanism was cultivated at Cambridge before the arrival of Auberinus. Traversagni di Savona, the Franciscan, wrote part of Vat. Lat. MS 11441 there in 1478; it is strongly humanist in character and content. Cf. J. Ruysschaert, *Codices Vaticani latini codices 11414–11709* (Vatican City, 1959), pp. 41–54.

[2] It concerns the status of quaestionists. See below, p. 299.

[3] Rashdall, *Universities*, iii. 289. It is hardly necessary to remark that his study was first published in 1895. The cult of which he speaks was not too apparent in 1535–6, when the university conceded that Greek or Hebrew could be substituted in place of mathematics Cf. *Grace Book* Γ, p. 310. The concession, however, was for that particular year only.

[4] Mag. Roger Collyngwood, author of *Arithmetrica experimentalis*, was the first occupant of the new chair, which he held by 1501. Cf. *Grace Book* B, i, p. xviii; *BRUC*, p. 149.

[5] See above, pp. 276–8.

De modo audiendi textum Aristotelis. The new developments at the turn of the fifteenth century did not cause the Philosopher to topple from his pedestal. He continued to dominate the arts course but not so exclusively as heretofore. The curriculum was broadened, bringing with it a measured but definite shifting of emphasis. None of this transition is apparent from Junior Proctor, but it is clearly seen in Senior Proctor. His text is a hybrid, passing from the late fifteenth century back to the fourteenth. By the time Junior Proctor was completed the anachronism had been eliminated. The statute in question, *SA* 140, as printed in the *editio princeps* of the statutes, gives no hint that a major change had taken place in the arts course.[1] To grasp what happened, we have to see the annulled statute, Old Proctor 54, and then the unrevised text of the *De determinatoribus pro se*, *SA* 140. The one prescribes the course which an undergraduate had to follow in order to qualify for the rank of quaestionist, for only then might he proceed further in the faculty. The other, Old Proctor 56, while it covers much the same ground naturally demands something over and above, since it prescribes the actual requirements for B.A. Both statutes probably derive from the second half of the thirteenth century; they were certainly in force by *c.* 1385 and remained unchanged until late in the fifteenth century. They are full of interest apart from their importance for the textual development of the *statuta antiqua*.

The *De modo audiendi textum Aristotelis* is extant in two versions. In addition to the Old Proctor-Caius text there is a private copy written *c.* 1450 on a sheet of paper which is now a front paste-down in a manuscript of Gonville and Caius College.[2] The official version approaches the subject from the point of view of the student. There is no trace of the text of the paste-down in any of the surviving statute-books; it may be a copy of a draft of Old Proctor 54 or of an adaptation made for the guidance of regent masters in arts—a more acceptable explanation. The two versions are complementary

1 Nor does Leathes in his introduction to *Grace Book* A, p. xxi, where he states that the Cambridge curriculum was 'probably much the same' as at Oxford. We are now in a position to offer some confirmation of this assumption, but it is evident that there were marked differences.

2 MS 466 (573). The volume, which is beautifully executed and heavily glossed, is saec. xiii*ex*. Its contents consist of books of the old logic and new logic which bear comparison with the provisions of Old Proctor 54 and 56. A Cambridge scholar, John Hall, donated it to St Mary Hostel; he was M.A. by 1450 and died in 1482 (*BRUC*, p. 281). The paste-down could have been written by Hall. The paper is holed in places.

though independent, and define which books of Aristotle were to be read or heard during each term of the four years' course leading eventually to B.A.:

Old Proctor-Caius 54[1]	*Caius MS 466*[2]
De modo audiendi textum Aristotelis	hoc est statutum
Item statuimus quod scolares arcium ordinatim audiant textum aristotelis sic videlicet in primo anno veterem logicam in termino yemali librum porphirij et predicamentorum in termino vero quadragesimali libros periarmeneias sex principiorum et diuisionum In termino quippe estiuali libros topicorum aristotelis /	Sciendum est quod si aliquis magister arcium legens pro fo⟨r⟩ma sua vel pro for⟨m⟩a scolarium suorum de primo anno / tenetur legere in primo termino hoc est in termino sancti m⟨ic⟩haelis librum porphurij et librum predicamentorum / Item in secundo termino tenetur legere l⟨i⟩brum sex principiorum librum diuisio⟨n⟩um boycij cum duobus libris perarmaniarum [?]/Item i⟨n⟩ termino tercio legere tenetur libros omnes topicorum
In secundo anno nouam logicam sic videlicet in termino yemali[3] libros elenchorum in termino quadragesimali libros priorum in termino estiuali libros posteriorum /	Item statutum est quod quilibet magister arcium legens pro forma sua vel pro forma scolarium suorum de secundo anno / tenetur legere in primo termino hoc e⟨st⟩ in termino sancti mich⟨a⟩e⟨l⟩is omnes libros elencorum Item in secundo termino legere tenetur libros priorum Item in tercio termino legere debet libros posteriorum
In tercio autem anno in termino yemali et quadragesimali octo libros phisicorum /[4] In quarto anno similiter in termino yemali et quadragesimali libros phisicorum vel xii libros metaphisice audire teneantur In terminis estiualibus tercij et quarti anni libros de generacione vel libros de anima vel celi et mundi vel metheororum vel ethicorum si legantur / Nec liceat alicui scolari postquam semel audierit	Item statutum est quod si aliquis magister arcium legens pro forma sua vel pro forma scolarium suorum de tercio anno[5] vel de ⟨q⟩uarto / legere tenetur in duobus primis terminis hoc est in termino sancti m⟨i⟩chaelis et in ⟨ter⟩mino qua⟨d⟩ragesimali octo libros phisicorum In tercio autem termino tenetur legere...[6]

[1] The text in Caius (fo. 9^{va-vb}) is again carelessly written and can be disregarded.

[2] No attempt is made here to correct some peculiar spellings which occur in the text.

[3] Another hand has added *vacat* in the margin.

[4] There is a reference at this point to the margin, where another hand has written 'vel xij libros methaphisice'.

[5] One and a half lines have been erased here; the writer had probably made a mechanical blunder.

[6] The text breaks off.

ordinarie secundum formam pretactam
naturalia vel metaphisicalia[1] ad logicam
ordinarie audiendam se diuertere
transgressores vero istius statuti sicut
falsi scolares puniantur prout falsi in
statutis nostris nominantur scolares.
(Old Proctor, fo. 28^{r}.)

Without going into details we may on the basis of these two documents reduce to the following scheme the course of ordinary lectures in Aristotle which a student had to attend each term of his first four years in the faculty of arts at Cambridge, bearing in mind the fact that the rule laid down in the Angelica text requiring him to hear at least three lectures in the week still held good:[2]

First Year The Old Logic	Winter: Porphyry, *Isagoge*; Aristotle, *Praedicamenta* (*Categoriae*); Lent: Aristotle, *Perihermeneias*; Gilbert de la Porrée, *Sex principia*; Boethius, *Divisiones*; Summer: Aristotle, *Topica*.
Second Year The New Logic	Winter: *Elenchi*; Lent: *Analytica priora*; Summer: *Analytica posteriora*.
Third Year	Winter: Lent: *Physica* Summer: *De generatione* or *De anima* or *De coelo* or *Meteorica* or *Ethica*.
Fourth Year	Winter: Lent: *Physica* or *Metaphysica* Summer: as in the third year.

Such was the major part of the curriculum.[3] In the summer term of the fourth year the student could 'respond to the question' and become 'quaestionist'.[4] This rule was modified as we shall now see by another statute in Old Proctor, which decreed that responsions must be made before the feast of the Purification (2 February) in the final year;[5] but in any case one was not allowed to determine or become bachelor before Lent in one's fifth year.

[1] Written *mathaphisicalia*. [2] *Cons. Univ. Canteb.* XI. ii (see above, p. 211, lines 11–15).

[3] Cf. *SA* 139 (*Docs*, i. 384). The reading 'secundum usum scole currentis [not "terentii"] ac tractatum insolubilium' is found in Old Proctor 55 (fo. 28^{v}); cf. Caius 55 (fo. $9^{v\,b}$).

[4] *SA* 135 (*loc. cit.* 382) modifies this point; it states that he may not respond unless he has been general sophist for two years or at least one. Oxford had a very similar statute in 1409. Cf. *SAUO*, 200, 13–17.

[5] The discrepancy between these two regulations went unchecked both in Old Proctor-Caius and in the statute-books of *c.* 1494–1502.

For determination a fuller course was prescribed. In addition to hearing the foregoing lectures *ordinarie* for four years, the candidate had to make up cursory lectures, given by a bachelor, and hear Priscian, *De constructione*, once. The statute was revised almost certainly by 1488 and again during the first decade or so of the sixteenth century. If we compare the texts of Old, Senior and Junior Proctor the changing pattern of the arts curriculum is at once apparent. Priscian was dropped, his place being taken by Terence, who was accorded the honour of competing with Aristotle:[1]

De determinatoribus pro se (*SA* 140)

Old Proctor	*Senior Proctor*	*Junior Proctor*
Item statuimus quod nullus in quadragesima in artibus determinare presumat, nisi in anno precedenti citra purificationem beate marie virginis de questione responderit. Statuimus etiam ne quis de cetero citra quintum annum in artibus determinare presumat. et quod quilibet determinaturus audierit	Item statuimus quod nullus in quadragesima in artibus determinare presumat, nisi in anno precedenti citra purificationem beate marie virginis de questione responderit. Statuimus etiam ne quis de cetero citra quintum annum in artibus determinare presumat. et quod quilibet determinaturus audierit	Item statuimus quod nullus in quadragesima in artibus determinare presumat, nisi in anno precedenti citra purificationem beate marie virginis de questione responderit. Statuimus etiam ne quis de cetero citra quintum annum in artibus determinare presumat et quod quilibet determinaturus audierit

[Here Senior and Junior Proctor part company with Old Proctor]

Old Proctor	*Senior Proctor*	*Junior Proctor*
veterem logicam bis / semel ordinarie. libris boicij dumtaxat exceptis qui saltem semel cursorie vel ordinarie audiantur. Item quod audierit priscianum de construccione semel. Item quod audierit nouam logicam videlicet libros elencorum et priorum bis / et libros	in scolis ordinarie librum therencij scilicet per biennium. logicalia vero per annum. naturalia quoque seu metaphisicalia (secundum quod suo tempore ea legi contigerit) per annum, [here two lines are erased] videlicet libros elencorum et priorum bis. et libros topicorum	in scolis ordinarie librum terencij scilicet per biennium logicalia vero per annum naturalia quoque seu metafisicalia secundum quod suo tempore ea legi contigerit per annum. (Junior Proctor, fo. 92^{v}.)

[1] The *lectura* in Terence was perhaps the special lectureship in the humanities inaugurated under the terms of *SA* 87 (see above, p. 296). Bateson in her introduction to *Grace Book* B, i, p. xix, takes this view. The earliest record of payments to the lecturer dates from 1507–8, when the proctor, John Philip, received £3. 13*s.* 0*d.*, due to him 'pro lectione Terentiana' in 1505–7 (*ibid. loc. cit.* and 232).

topicorum pro maiore parte bis semel ordinarie / et librum posteriorum semel audiat. Item quod audierit librum phisicorum aristotelis semel / librum de anima et de generacione. et quod tempore sue determinacionis sit in audiendo methefisicam (*sic*) vel quod in preterito audierit. (Old Proctor, fo. 28^{v}.)

pro maiore parte bis semel ordinarie et librum posteriorum semel audiat. Item quod audierit librum phisicorum aristotelis semel librum de anima et de generacione et quod tempore sue determinacionis sit in audiendo methafisicam vel quod in preterito audierit si cursorie legantur. (Senior Proctor, fo. 35^{r-v}.)

Before we comment very briefly on the significance of these texts, it is essential to point out that the passage in Senior Proctor 'videlicet ... legantur' has diagonal lines drawn across it. Whoever was responsible for this deletion must have intended to erase the text as thoroughly as the two lines after *annum*.[1] It can be assumed that the only reason why the operation was not carried out was the waste of time and labour which the scraping off of the ink would have entailed. Though we cannot be absolutely certain, there is a striking similarity between the ink in which the second hand of Junior Proctor wrote and the ink used to indicate the deletion of 'videlicet ... legantur'. One is strongly tempted to say that Senior Proctor was disfigured when the transcription of Junior Proctor was recommenced.

The remainder of the text of *SA* 140 in the three statute-books is the same. It would be a fairly simple matter now to reconstruct the medieval curriculum in arts at Cambridge and trace its evolution by adding to the above data, including the provisions of Old Proctor 54, the earlier and later statutes on inception. From a purely textual point of view the most arresting feature of all the statutes on arts is the presence in Senior Proctor of the passage 'videlicet ... preterito audierit' in its text of *De determinatoribus pro se*. The first part of the statute clearly demonstrates that we are dealing with a transitional text. Already there is a marked departure from the tradition of Old

1 Were it not for this thorough erasure we should doubtless find that Senior Proctor also had the passage of Old Proctor which mentions Priscian. The round brackets enclosing 'secundum...contigerit' are in Senior Proctor. The eraser probably mistook his cue.

Proctor. The four years' course is divided equally between Terence and Aristotle; there is no prescribed course on Priscian. Likewise, the Aristotelian curriculum is stated in very general terms, the Metaphysics being optional. As happens so often with transitional texts the statute in Senior Proctor lays itself open to contradiction. Having departed from the form of Old Proctor's text it reverts to it again and so at the end we find, contrary to what is stated earlier, that a student must hear metaphysics even if only at the time of his determination.[1] One may reasonably assume that the patchy text of *SA* 140 was transmitted to Senior Proctor from its exemplar, which was almost certainly one of the *libri statutorum* extant in 1487–8. The same mixed text doubtless appeared in the companion volume of this recension and would have been reproduced in Junior Proctor, too, if that book had been transcribed in full from its immediate parent. The omission of the passage 'videlicet . . . audierit' from the text of Junior Proctor at any rate proves beyond a shadow of doubt that Senior Proctor was not copied from its elder brother, Junior Proctor, whose text we need not have the slightest hesitation in concluding was made up after a pause of some fifteen years from Senior Proctor and with the assistance, too, of Old Proctor.

When the syndics of the university were authorized by grace on 28 June 1783 to see to the printing of the *statuta antiqua* they decided to issue the text of Senior Proctor as the *editio princeps*.[2] Their choice was fully justified, for the book contained a smooth, straightforward and complete collection of the statutes. What can scarcely be described as other than arbitrary was the decision to limit the number of 'ancient' statutes to 188. In other words, fos. 1^r–52^v of Senior Proctor were taken as constituting the definitive canon of the *statuta antiqua*. No thought was given to chronology: these folios have statutes entered in a hand later than that of Senior Proctor; moreover the printed text excludes two if not more enactments which are actually earlier than some of the so-called ancient statutes.[3]

[1] The Metaphysics was not prescribed at Oxford for B.A. Cf. *SAUO*, p. xc.

[2] Cf. *Docs*, i. 305, where the grace is printed. Twenty-five copies were authorized: one for the vice-chancellor and proctors; one for the registrary and esquire bedells; one for the royal library (in the university library); one for the senate house; and one for each college library. Hence the 1785 printing was confined to a limited or private edition.

[3] The two statutes, dated 3 July 1505 and 1506, were indeed printed in the 1785 edition but not among the *statuta antiqua* proper; they will be found on pp. 98–9

In the 1785 edition the text is introduced as *Statuta antiqua in ordinem redacta*. This title has very little to commend it. The author of Senior Proctor certainly made no such claim.[1] If the *editio princeps* looks like a jig-saw puzzle in places the fault is not his. On closer examination it will be found that the misplaced statutes are mostly accretions which the text received after it left his hands.[2] He might, however, have summoned up enough courage to scrap the plan of his exemplar and go back to Old Proctor for his model. The re-arranging of the fifty or so statutes which had appeared since *c.* 1385 would have meant hard labour; but had he known the technique of codification and persevered to the end he would have provided Cambridge with an admirable *codex statutorum c.* 1500 and brought to a fitting climax the pioneering effort that gave us the Angelica text.

The opportunity was let go. In 1549 the Edwardine code was promulgated in the presence of the senate of the university on 6 May.[3] It did not actually displace the *statuta antiqua*, and even before the accession of Mary the university planned to review them and have a new text made.[4] On 20 August 1553 the queen ordered the ancient statutes to be restored.[5] Nothing was done, apparently, to further the work of revision until as a result of Cardinal Pole's ordinances of 18 March 1557 a commission consisting of the vice-chancellor, proctors and three regents of each faculty was appointed to examine and reform the old statutes.[6] Two widely different drafts of a new recension were, it seems, prepared;[7] but that was as far as the proposed edition had got when the first Elizabethan code was published on 22 June 1559. It was not much more than a

(*Docs*, i. 419) among the 'statuta antiqua in ordinem non redacta'. No trace has been found of a statute 'pro disputacionibus baculariorum in artibus' framed by Auberinus in 1496; cf. *Grace Book* B, i. 97. Bateson, *ibid.* p. xiv, n. 3, suggests it is *SA* 136; this is not so. Cf. *Grace Book* B, ii. 139, for a grace of 18 Jan. 1528, which refers to such disputations.

1 The title was written in much later at the top of Senior Proctor, fo. 1^{r}.

2 *SA* 70 (1 July 1506), 77 (8 Sept. 1502+), 78 (8 Aug. 1506), 85 (3 July 1505) and most probably 187–8 were enacted after the date of Senior Proctor; they are all misplaced.

3 Lamb, *Collection of letters*, pp. 109, 122 n.; Mullinger, *University of Cambridge*, ii. 109–13.

4 *Grace Book* Δ, pp. 89–90, *s.a.* 1552–3.

5 J. Strype, *The life and acts of Matthew Parker*, i (Oxford, 1821), 84–5; Lamb, *op. cit.* pp. xxx–xxxi.

6 *Grace Book* Δ, p. 123.

7 Cf. Corpus Christi College MS 118, (i) fos. 2^{r}–36^{r}; (ii) pp. 35–173. The date 26 June 1555 occurs on fo. 1^{r}; the drafts were probably made *c.* 1557–9. On p. 72 there is an interesting note: 'hic debent interponi noua statuta de electione procuratorum et ideo dimittantur tria folia.' It comes after *SA* 62.

reissue of the 1549 statutes, revised in the main by Matthew Parker.[1] The second and final Elizabethan code, fathered by Whitgift, was promulgated under the great seal on 25 September 1570. His work came in for severe criticism.[2] Even so, the code was upheld and continued to be the official constitution of the university down to 1858–82. For good measure it recognized the authority of the *statuta antiqua* as indeed that of the 1549 and 1559 editions, provided they did not contravene the authentic text of 1570.

Before a full, critical edition of the medieval statutes can be produced some minor collections will have to be taken into account. Six statutes are recited in the record of the Barnwell process (1429–30).[3] They were extracted at the time from the *liber statutorum*, now unfortunately missing, which was derived independently of Old Proctor from the parent of the recension (β) made *c.* 1385. Matthew Stokys included in his Book, compiled *c.* 1574–8, several folios taken from an earlier volume, most probably a bedell's book; these folios contain nine statutes, and two more are copied into another part of the Book.[4] The Barnwell and Stokys texts, particularly the latter, deserve close attention.[5] Finally, we should

[1] Lamb, *op. cit.* p. xxxix; Mullinger, *op. cit.* p. 175.

[2] Lamb, *op. cit.* pp. xl–xli; Mullinger, *op. cit.* pp. 222–30.

[3] The statutes are *SA* 41, 43–4, 47, 49, 172. Cf. CUA, doc. no. 108; Nichols, art. cit. in *Bibl. Topo. Brit.* v, no. xxxviii, 39–40; Heywood, *Early Camb. Univ. & Coll. Stats*, pp. 203–5.

[4] Cf. Stokys's Book, fos. 29^r–34^v (parchment), which have the nine statutes not uniformly in chronological order, as follows: *SA* 41–3, 45, 47, 44, 156, 76, 24. The two additional statutes, *SA* 73, 72, transcribed by Stokys himself, occur on fos. 56^r–57^v (paper). Stokys (*c.* 1514–91) was esquire bedell from 1557 to 1585 and registrary from 1558 until his death. His Book, a tidy volume of 172 fos., measuring 205 × 145 mm, was originally bound in black leather (long since replaced by brown leather), which has occasionally caused it to be confused with the Black Parchment Book and the Black Paper Book or *liber rerum memorabilium*. Cf. *The Cambridge portfolio*, ed. J. J. Smith, i (London, 1840), 159. The value of Stokys's Book is out of all proportion to its size. The list of university benefactors (fos. 24^r [*bis*]–28^v), which is especially of value for the names of chancellors, and the memorandum on academic exercises (fos. 13^v–24^r, 47^r–52^v), notably vespers and inceptions, are unique.

[5] The following short observations will not be out of place. Barnwell and Stokys preserve the original form of *SA* 41. The text of *SA* 43, truncated in Barnwell, is complete in Stokys, whose version is closer to Markaunt than to the proctors' books. Stokys has the original version of *SA* 44, which ends imperfectly in Barnwell; the text in the proctors' books is a revised one. Though *SA* 45 is truncated in Stokys, what remains is nearer to Markaunt than to the *textus receptus*. *SA* 47 is noteworthy. Stokys appears to be the only MS which exhibits the original text. Markaunt in so far as it preserves the preamble is close enough to Stokys, but like the MSS of the *statuta antiqua* it has a passage at the end which must be considered an accretion

mention if only as a matter of interest the existence of complete or excerpted transcripts of the *statuta antiqua*. They have no original value in themselves, for the exemplars are extant, but they range in date from *c.* 1540 to *c.* 1778 and anticipate the production of the *editio princeps* (1785).[1] It would be unwise to ignore them altogether.[2]

The story of the formation of the final text of the medieval statutes and its appearance in print enables us to present a complete *stemma codicum*. Though there remain some areas where the manuscript tradition is uncertain, this is only to be expected in view of the long and obscure history of the statute-books, many of which are only names, if even that. The preservation of the Angelica manuscript has made it possible not only to reconstruct the original constitution of the university and illustrate the evolution of the text between *c.* 1250 and 1500 but in addition to disentangle the relationship of the various manuscripts of the statutes. The history of the medieval constitution of Cambridge has yet to be written. One feels that at long last the way is open and reasonably clear.

('salva...eorundem'; cf. *Docs*, i. 335). Stokys's text belongs consequently to an earlier tradition than recension α (*c.* 1304–37). The fact that both the preamble and the tailpiece are missing in Barnwell only proves that the statute in this source was cited in a shortened form, as was the case with *SA* 44.

1 Full transcripts occur in Corpus Christi College, Cambridge, 118, (i) fos. 2r–36r, (ii) pp. 35–173 (both sets *c.* 1557–9?); CUA, 'Statuta Antiqua', pp. 1–98 (*c.* 1683–1701); B.M. Harl. 7032 (Baker, v), fos. 5r–99r (*olim* pp. 1–109) (same date as CUA); CUL Mm. 4. 46–7 (*c.* 1758–78); and Adam Wall's MS, CUL Mm. 5. 53 (*c.* 1783–5). There are excerpts in the Black Parchment Book (CUA), pp. 97–8 (*olim* fos. 28v–29r) (by 1540?); Cashel Diocesan Library (Church of Ireland) MS (*olim* K 3 24), p. 48 (from a copy by John Buck, dated 12 Dec. 1665); and Baker's voluminous transcripts (saec. xvii*ex*–xviii*in*), of which we need only note Harl. 7031, 7037 (Baker, iv, x) and CUL Mm. 1. 35 (Baker, xxiv). Many more transcripts doubtless exist. One should be warned that Matthew Wren's MS (Pembroke College Treasury, Cγ), which is cited in *Docs*, i. 307 as 'Wrenni Excerpta', does not contain excerpts of the statutes. The MS dates from *c.* 1625–34. It cannot have been of the slightest use 'for occasional emendations of the text', as claimed *ibid.*

2 The first excerpt in the Cashel MS, p. 48, begins abruptly. Like the other six excerpts in this volume it is taken from the ancient statutes, but I have been unable to locate it among the *statuta antiqua*. It concerns disputations held by masters and dates almost certainly from the fifteenth century.

Stemma[1]

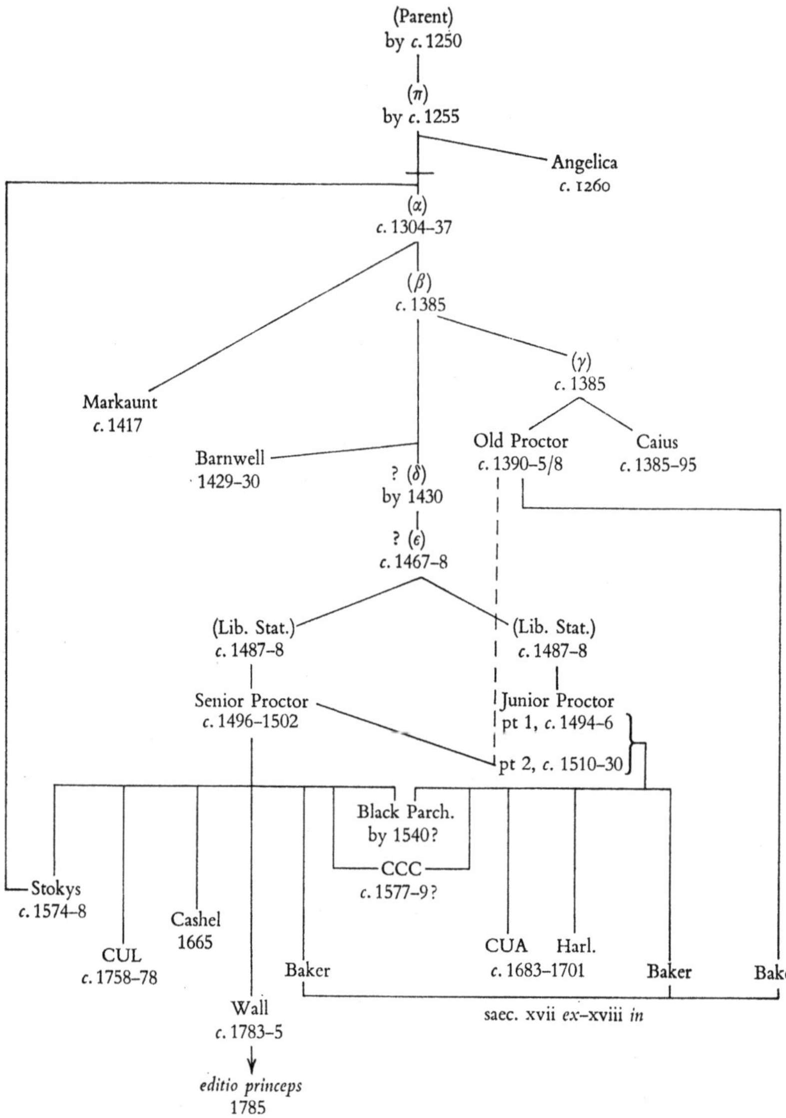

[1] MSS not now extant are shown within brackets. The slit in the line of descent between π and α indicates that room must be allowed for one recension at least between *c.* 1255 and *c.* 1300. As the historicity of δ and ε is doubtful, they are preceded by a question-mark. The broken line is a reminder that folios of the statutes in Old Proctor now form part of the text in Junior Proctor.

APPENDIXES

BIBLIOGRAPHY

INDEX

Appendix I

THE SECOND OLDEST TEXT (MARKAUNT) (*c.* 1304–37)

Thomas Markaunt (*c.* 1382–1439), M.A., B.Th. of Cambridge and Fellow of Corpus Christi College, was senior proctor of the university in 1417–18.[1] In his will, which was drawn up on 4 November 1439, he bequeathed seventy-six books to Corpus, of which only three have survived.[2] The most valuable of these is the volume once known as *Liber priuilegiorum et statutorum vniuersitatis Cantabriggie* or, to give it its modern title, 'Markaunt's Book'.[3] Robert Hare used it extensively when compiling his imposing and indeed most useful collection of materials for the history of Cambridge. Its preservation after it was removed from the chest containing Markaunt's benefaction is due in no small measure to Hare. After the manuscript was twice lost from Corpus it came into his hands and he presented it to the university in 1594.[4] Its troubles did not end there;[5] and Fuller predicted that the book, which was missing again in his time, would never be recovered.[6] Fortunately, this gloomy prophecy proved false. The *Liber priuilegiorum et statutorum* now reposes securely in the university archives.[7]

The ascription of the volume to Markaunt was challenged some years

1 Emden, *BRUC*, pp. 390–1.

2 The catalogue of Markaunt's library has been edited by M. R. James in *Sources of Archbishop Parker's collection of MSS at Corpus Christi College, Cambridge* (CAS, octavo series, xxxii [1899]), 76–82. Cf. also J. O. Halliwell, 'A catalogue of the books bequeathed to Corpus Christi College, Cambridge (A.D. 1439) by Thomas Markaunt with their prices' (CAS, quarto series, xiv: pt 1 [1847]), 15–20. Emden, *op. cit.* p. 390, incorrectly gives the date of Markaunt's will as 4 Aug. 1439.

3 Neither James nor Halliwell prints the catalogue entry as it reads: 'Liber priuilegiorum et statutorum vniuersitatis Cantabriggie qui remaneat in cista. Cuius sec*undum* fol*ium* incipit breue patens de regrat' et pen*ultimum* fol*ium* incipit cionibus amerciame*ntis*' (Corpus Christi College, MS 232, fo. 8v). The number '76' occurs in the margin. The price of the volume is given as 5 *solidi* on fo. 9r.

4 A note to this effect, written in large gothic letters, is found on the *recto* of the first of two parchment (guard?) leaves at the beginning of the volume. Cf. James, *Cat. MSS Corpus Christi Coll.* i. 532.

5 The words 'Iterum amissum restituit Matthaeus Wrenn' occur after the note referring to Hare.

6 Cf. Lamb, *Masters' history of the college of Corpus Christi* (Cambridge–London, 1831), p. 308.

7 The late A. G. Little believed it was lost. The book may possibly have been unavailable when he published his article 'The friars *v.* the university of Cambridge' in *E.H.R.* l (1935), 686–96.

ago by Professor Ullmann.[1] There is no denying that some of the documents copied into the volume are much later than Markaunt's time, and indeed the MS carries no contemporary inscription ascribing the contents to his hand or stating that the book belonged to him. Professor Ullmann, however, overlooked the all-important fact that the description of the *Liber priuilegiorum et statutorum* in the catalogue of Markaunt's library corresponds exactly with the volume preserved today in the university archives. The catalogue (Corpus Christi College MS 232, fo. 8^{v}) states that the opening words of fo. 2 were 'breue patens de regratarijs' and that the penultimate folio began with 'cionibus amerciamentis'. If we turn to the volume which since Hare's time has been known as Markaunt's Book or Register, we find that fo. 2^{r} commences with 'breue patens de regratarijs' and fo. 78^{r} with 'cionibus amerciamentis'.[2] This is proof enough that the MS is, in the words of Thomas Baker, 'none other than Markaunt's'.[3] Three documents, ranging in date from 1444 to 1460, are copied in at the back of the book. Though they were transcribed after Markaunt's death, their presence does not prove that the book was not made for him. These documents, written in different hands, are later additions.[4] Professor Ullmann's further difficulty can be easily solved. The copy of the papal letter on D, fo. 9^{v} (31^{v}) does not derive from the time of Nicholas V (1447–55), as he assumed.[5] It is, in fact, a copy of a letter of Nicholas IV, issued from Orvieto and dated 1 February of the third year of his pontificate (1291). It refers to the dispute between mag. Ralph de Leycestria and the university.[6]

Despite the haphazard and unchronological arrangement of the contents, Markaunt's Book is a most valuable and in some respects a unique record of royal and episcopal privileges, papal bulls and miscellaneous deeds.

1 'The decline of the chancellor's authority in medieval Cambridge', *Historical Journal*, i. 179, n. 12.

2 The MS originally consisted of five separate quires, A, B, C, D and E, each independently foliated, but only fos. 1–13 of C, 1–4 of D and 1–4 of E are numbered in a contemporary hand. Later, possibly in Hare's time, the MS was refoliated from fo. 13 of C onwards, yielding a total of 81 folios. In fact it should be 98 folios, excluding the two parchment folios at the beginning which contain a list of the contents. In more modern times the quires were refoliated separately, apparently by Joseph Romilly, who added a useful index or concordance and other notes. The crucial point is that fo. 78^{r} (*recte* E 39^{r}) was the penultimate folio when the book was put together, and its opening words are 'cionibus amerciamentis'.

3 Markaunt's Book, parchment folio b^{r}. This note in Baker's own hand is signed 'T.B.'

4 The documents occupy fos. 79^{v}–81^{r} (E 40^{v}–42^{r}) and are set down in this order: (i) Letter from the university to Henry VI, 8 Feb. 1444; (ii) Grant of exemption to the Provost of King's College from the jurisdiction of the university, 31 Jan. 1444; (iii) Statute of 1460 or *SA* 22 (*Docs*, i. 318–19). Markaunt's Book is the only evidence we have for the date of this statute.

5 Cf. Ullmann, *loc. cit.*

6 See above, pp. 231–2.

It also contains an otherwise untraced collection of the statutes of the university, and includes a short but very welcome account of the procedure at inceptions.[1]

Internal evidence suggests that the MS was executed during the years 1417–33.[2] Markaunt, as we know, was proctor in 1417–18 and it may well be that he had the volume compiled when he took up office, following perhaps the precedent set by Richard Fleming of Oxford in 1407.[3] The MS, which is of paper (except for the two parchment leaves containing the table of contents), has a total of 100 folios measuring generally 303 × 217 mm.[4] The original binding has gone.

In an earlier section of this work the significance of Markaunt's set of university statutes was outlined. The text, as we have seen, derives from a lost exemplar which in all probability was executed between 1304 and 1337. For some reason or other the scribe copied only thirty-eight statutes, the last being *De pena eorum qui contempnunt Magistros*,[5] although half of the folio (fo. 49^{r} [E 11^{r}]) as well as the *verso* and four additional folios could have been utilized by him. The important point is that the scribe of Markaunt's Book used a very early text (*c.* 1304–37) which throws a most welcome ray of light on the development and dating of the medieval statutes between *c.* 1250 and *c.* 1385.

The entire contents of Markaunt's Book deserve to be printed, for this register helps to supplement the losses which the invaluable collection of original documents in the University Archives have sustained over the centuries. Our concern here is with fos. 45^{r}–49^{r} (E 7^{r}–11^{r}). Some day a full critical edition of the medieval statutes of Cambridge will be undertaken; as a step in that direction, and in order to illustrate the history of the original text, which has been our primary consideration, we give a straight transcript here of Markaunt's text. It is printed exactly as it

[1] Both texts are printed here for the first time. The description of the ceremony of inception begins abruptly at the top of fo. 45^{r} (E 7^{r}) without title or introduction.

[2] A copy of a petition of 5 Dec. 1417 in French from the university is found on fo. 43^{r-v} (E 5^{r-v}). The original is in B.M. Cotton MS Faustina C III, fo. 357^{r}. On fo. 79^{r} (E 40^{r}) of Markaunt's Book is entered a copy of the bull of Pope Eugenius IV, *Dum attentae*, dated 18 Sept. 1433. This folio was the final folio of the MS in Markaunt's time. The text of the papal bull is written in a hand which is not that of the main part of the MS, and is a later addition.

[3] *Snappe's formulary*, 95; *SAUO*, pp. xiv–xv, 198–9. Compared with the Old, Junior and Senior Proctors' Books, Markaunt's cannot be properly called a proctor's book; and it is certainly not a grace book. Neither is it an official university register. Like the Oxford registers *C* and *CC* it was probably commissioned for Markaunt's personal use or interest, and to this category we may also assign the missing *Registrum Magistri Ricardi Hant* which Hare cites; cf. Hare MS i, fo. 47^{v}.

[4] The collation is: $ii + A^{4} + B^{5} + C^{11} + D^{8} + E^{21}$. This does not include two modern flyleaves and a sheet of paper entitled 'The Index' (compiled by Romilly) which is pasted in inside the front cover.

[5] See Markaunt 38 (p. 331 below, lines 20–6).

appears in the register. The spelling, punctuation and any mistakes which the scribe left uncorrected have been retained. In the apparatus the correct or more correct reading is given. Words underlined in the manuscript are printed in italics. A number of the scribe's contractions are unusual, but as his system is on the whole uniform these have been expanded silently in the normal way, though once or twice I have corrected the contraction in the apparatus. There is one peculiarity which could easily give a wrong impression. The scribe uses two downward strokes to indicate the end of a statute; he also employs the same device to signify a break in a word at the end of a line. Moreover, in critical editions of medieval texts double strokes are often used to denote a lacuna. To obviate possible misunderstanding, I have employed a hyphen instead of the scribe's double strokes. It should be noted, finally, that the statutes are numbered in the margins of the folios and the titles of the statutes are in-cut. In keeping with the tradition of the *editio princeps* of the Cambridge statutes I have placed the numbers and titles at the head of their respective statutes.

(Markaunt's Book, CUA, fos. 45^{r}–49^{r} [E 7^{r}–11^{r}])

Finita disputacione in incepcione seu solempni resumpcione dicat rector incipienti habenti manum dexteram in manu magistri sui dextera
Dabis fidem ad obseruandum statuta et priuilegia et consuetudines istius vniuersitatis approbatas
Quo facto dicat sibi rector quod apponat manum super librum dicens
Iurabis tactis sacrosanctis quod pacem istius vniuersitatis non perturbabis Nec per te nec per alium pacis perturbatoribus. fauorem. consilium vel auxilium prestabis. Insuper quod si aliquem pacis perturbatorem vel pacis perturbatores noueris eum seu eos Cancellario reuelabis Et eciam quod nec per te nec per alium impedies quominus de pacis perturbatoribus iusticia valeat excerceri Iurabis eciam quod extra istam vniuersitatem nusquam alibi in Anglia preterquam Oxonie in aliqua facultate incipies aut lectiones tuas solempniter resumes. nec consencies quod aliquis alibi in Anglia incipiens. hic pro magistro in illa facultate habeatur. Iurabis eciam quod lectiones tuas ad minus per annum continuabis. hec omnia promittis te fideliter obseruaturum sicud te deus adiuuet et sancta dei

3–4 Cf. *Cons. Univ. Canteb.* II. iv (see above, p. 199, lines 18–20); *SA* 114 (*Docs*, i. 372); 134 (*ibid.* 381); *SAUO*, 19, 5–6; Stokys's Book, ed. Peacock, *Observations*, App. A, p. xliii.

5 librum *sc.* evangeliorum.

6–14 Cf. above, pp. 244–5.

14–15 Cf. *Cons. Univ. Canteb.* II. iv (see above, p. 199, line 20 to p. 201, line 1); *SA* 134 (*loc. cit.*).

15–(p. 313) 2 Cf. *SAUO*, 20, 1–2.

Euangelia - *Quo facto dicat nouus Magister* Promitto *Et statim deosculetur librum. hijs finitis determinet questionem suam sedendo primo recitans argumenta principalia sub hijs verbis* Ad hec et ad alia sufficiunt magistrorum responsa. *Et tunc primo frater efficitur magistrorum* - Notandum quod medicus iurabit quod lectiones suas per triennium continuabit nisi infra triennium contingat alium incipere vel resumere. Notandum eciam quod in vesperijs debet rector post comendacionem a singulis bachellarijs accipere fidem sub hijs verbis. Dabis fidem quod contra statuta vniuersitatis non appellabis. nec huiusmodi appellantibus fauorem consilium vel auxilium prestabis- *Idem sacramentum quod prestitit Magister N. in persona sua tu obseruabis in persona tua sicud te deus adiuuet et sancta euangelia.* promitto

Hec sunt statuta Vniuersitatis Cantabrigie primo de modo statuendi

1. ⟨*De modo statuendi*⟩

Auctoritate tocius vniuersitatis Cantebrigie tam Magistrorum regencium quam non regencium statutum existit quod in statuendis rebus et negocijs que vtilitatem communem vniuersitatis eiusdem tangere dinoscuntur: Id tantum pro statuto habeatur, quod de consensu maioris et sanioris partis dictorum regencium et de consensu maioris et sanioris partis non regencium fuerit ordinatum et statutum per decretum. saluo regentibus excercio statutorum editorum. non regentibus non reseruatorum specialiter cum dispensacione eorundem Datum Cantebrigie in ecclesia beate Marie xv kalendis aprilis anno domini M° CCC° tercio -

2. *De electione Cancellarij*

Quoniam difficile est vniuersitatem in vnum consentire communi consensu et voluntate statuimus vt Cancellarius. sciens. volens et potens. tanquam maior inter omnes. omnibus per regentes si forte xij in artibus tunc fuerint regentes. Alias per regentes et non regentes preficiatur omnibus regentibus si xij fuerint vel alias omnibus regentibus et non regentibus aut parte maiori in numero de quibus duo sint *pilliati* omnino in ipsum consensientibus. Fiat autem eius electio per scrutinium sub hac

15 existit *recte* exstitit.
20 excercio *recte* excercicio [exercicio].

2–3 Cf. *ibid.* 38, 20–3.
4–6 Cf. *SA* 134 (*loc. cit.*); *SAUO*, 42, 20–2.
8–10 Cf. *SA* 114 (*Docs*, i. 372–3).
10–11 Cf. *SAUO*, 20, 4–6.
13–22 Cf. Markaunt's Book, fo. 37v (D 15v); *SA* 1 (*Docs*, i. 308); Little in *E.H.R.* (1935), 693; Moorman, *Grey Friars in Cambridge*, pp. 228, 235–6.
23–30 Cf. *Cons. Univ. Canteb.* I. i (see above, p. 177, lines 1–6).
23–(p. 314) 17 *SA* 4 (*Docs*, i. 309–10).

forma. duo rectores cum vno theologo seniore religioso cum per solos regentes electio celebratur. Alias cum vno non regente et theologo per non regentes electo scrutatores deputentur Qui specialiter coram congregacione iurent quod actum electionis sine fraude exequentur. Et hoc iuramentum ab alio seniore theologo vna cum iuramentis singulorum in dicta electione vota habentium exigatur. Vota eciam scrutatorum primo inter se inquirantur duobus eorum inquirentibus votum tercij quousque quilibet eorum alijs duobus duxerit votum suum. Nullus eciam Magister postquam votum suum prestiterit valeat votum suum inposterum variare: nisi ob causam necessariam scrutinium fieri oporteat iterato Scrutineo vero et collacione scrutatorum inter se priuatim secundum formam statuti factis, Alter procuratorum ipsam electionem toti congregacioni pronunciet sub hijs verbis. Ego procurator seu rector vice maioris et sanioris partis huius vniuersitatis regencium et non regencium si forte concurrant in electione eligo N. in Cancellarium vniuersitatis Cantebrigie et eius electionem vobis pronuncio secundum statuta et consuetudines huius vniuersitatis -

3. *De iuramento et obediencia Cancellarij*

Cancellarius cum ab episcopo confirmatus fuerit et ab ipsa confirmacione ad municipium redierit ad vltimum in crastino congregacionem omnium regencium facere teneatur et coram tota congregacione primo idem Cancellarius sacramentum corporale prestet quod omnia ad eius officium spectancia diligenter et fideliter exequetur. Et istud iuramentum per alterum procuratorem seu rectorem ab eodem Cancellario exigatur Et tandem habito huiusmodi iuramento Idem procurator sigillum Cancellarij vna cum claui communis ciste eidem Cancellario statim tradat -

4. *De officio Cancellarij*

Cancellarius nichil noui sine consensv maioris et sanioris partis regencium et sine consensv maioris et sanioris partis non regencium statuere presumat. set supra et infra statuta. intendat efficaciter custodire

[fo. 45^{v} (E 7^{v})] 5. *De modo committendi causas*

Statuimus quod nec cancellarius nec aliquis iudex ordinarius alicui causam aliquam committat. nisi coram Cancellario vel rectoribus statuta et consuetudines prius obseruare iurauerit in causis coram eo tractandis -

8 votum] tercij *add. et del.* MS.
11 scrutineo *rectius* scrutinio.

18–26 *SA* 5 (*Docs*, i. 310).
27–30 *Cons. Univ. Canteb.* I. vi (see above, p. 199, lines 1–3); *SA* 6 (*Docs*, i. 311).
31–4 *SA* 7 (*ibid.*).

6. *De commissario Cancellarij*

Liceat quoque Cancellario ad ipsius exoneracionem alicui non suspecto statutis consuetudinibus et priuilegijs huius vniuersitatis iurato ad certas causas vel vniuersitatem causarum vices suas ad tempus suo iure committere. nisi talis sit causa que sui natura delegacionem non requirit vt in atrocibus delictis que bannicionem vel incarceracionem requirunt. Cause autem regencium et non regencium ex parte rea vel actoris et de pencione et iure inhabitacionis domorum non committantur nec coram alio quouis modo tractentur. Et quia sub colore atrocis iniurie Magistri regentes a suis curijs defraudantur seu priuantur, statutum est quod crimina non attrocia tanquam attrocia criminaliter proponentes et in processu cause in probacione deficientes in xij denarijs communi ciste applicandis mulctentur -

7. *De Vicecancellario*

Non liceat Cancellario citra cessacionem magistrorum se ab vniuersitate absentare in vno termino vltra mensem. Cancellarius vero vltra xv dies abfuturus neminem habeat vicarium nisi in quem maior pars regencium consenserit cui virtute statuti iurisdictionem suam committere teneatur -

8. *De potestate Cancellarij*

Cancellarius vel eius vicarius dicto modo substitutus per se tantum si voluerit causas scolarium vniuersas audiat et decidat nisi facti atrocitas vel publice quietis perturbacio magistrorum requirat conuenienciam et assensum -

9. *De conuocacionibus faciendis*

Vniuersi regentes ad vocacionem cancellarij omnibus intersint incepcionibus et solempnibus resumpcionibus non nisi licenciati inde recessuri quousque incepcio vel huiusmodi resumpcio totaliter sit completa. Ad vocacionem eciam Cancellarij ob alias certas causas alijs temporibus faciendam prout eciam eidem videbitur vniuersitati expediens, conueniant omnes magistri regentes ac eciam si necesse fuerit non regentes de vtilitate communi et publica quiete seu alijs negocijs vniuersitatem contingentibus communiter tractaturi. in quo casu nullus se absentare presumat, quem

---

1–6 *Cons. Univ. Canteb.* I. ii (see above, p. 197, lines 7–11); *SA* 8 (*Docs*, i. 311).
7–16 *SA* 8 (*loc. cit.*).
16–18 *Cons. Univ. Canteb.* I. iii (see above, p. 197, lines 12–15); *SA* 8 (*loc. cit.*).
18 *SA* 8 (*ibid.*).
19–23 *Cons. Univ. Canteb.* I. iv (see above, p. 197, lines 16–19); *SA* 9 (*Docs*, i. 312).
24–(p. 316) 3 Cf. *Cons. Univ. Canteb.* IV (see above, p. 203, lines 6–12); *SA* 11 (*loc. cit.* 313–14).

absencia racionabiliter non excusat - Diebus vero in quibus fit generaliter congregacio siue regencium tantum siue regencium et non regencium, disputacio nulla fiat -

10. *De officio Cancellarij resignando*

Satutum esse noueritis quod Cancellarius cum officium suum resignare contigerit sigillum officij sui ac eciam clauem communis ciste quam penes se habuit coram tota vniuersitate regencium procuratoribus seu alteri eorum teneatur tradere. et tunc huiusmodi sigillum et clauis in presencia eiusdem vniuersitatis sigillis aliorum duorum regencium quos ad hoc per vniuersitatem deputari contigerit consignetur. Et sic in manibus alterius procuratoris remaneant consignata quousque alteri Cancellario sub forma predicta electo. ac eciam iurato coram eadem vniuersitate tradantur -

11. *De electione rectorum seu procuratorum*

Singulis annis post festum sancti Michaelis die resumpcionis Magistrorum in principio congregacionis eodem die faciende duo Magistri arcium actualiter regentes rectores seu procuratores per maiorem partem magistrorum in artibus regencium eorum iudicio in virtute iuramenti prestiti ad hoc magis idonei in diuersis scrutinijs eligantur. omnibus et singulis magistris in eadem congregacione presentibus specialiter iuratis de magis idoneo in electione preponendo ita quod ipse sic prepositus in electione, procurator senior habeatur Quod si numerus regencium in artibus ad duodecim non attigerit, non regentes arcium in eligendo procuratores regentibus sint adiuncti - Scrutatores vero deputentur magister glomerie et duo iuniores magistri in artibus actualiter regentes coram tota vniuersitate specialiter iurati quod huiusmodi scrutinium fideliter exequentur Et secundum formam in electione Cancellarij prenotatam scrutatores primo inter se dicent vota sua nec alicui magistrorum postquam votum suum duxerit nisi ex causa superius expressa liceat variare / Quod si maior pars dictorum xij regentium in artibus vt premittitur in electione procuratorum factis inter eos tribus scrutinijs nequeat concordare volumus ex tunc quod non regentes in artibus coeligendi cum eis plenariam habeant potestatem quantuscunque fuerit numerus magistrorum regencium in artibus. Scrutinio vero et collacione factis magister glomerie huiusmodi electionem toti congregacioni fideliter pronunciet in virtute iuramenti prestiti - Idem vero procuratores cum electi fuerint coram tota vniuersi-

---

1 generaliter *rectius* generalis; *sed cf. Statuts*, i. 473, *no.* xxxiv.
5 Satutum *recte* Statutum.
10 consignetur *recte* consignentur.
25 tota] congregacione *add. et del.* MS.

4–13 *SA* 15 (*Docs*, i. 315).
14–(p. 317) 11 *SA* 53 (*ibid.* 338–9).

tate corporale iuramentum prestent Cancellario illud ab eisdem exigente quod omnia et singula ad eorum officia spectancia diligenter ac fideliter exequentur. Iurent eciam quod nullius negocium procurabunt quod credent esse contra eiusdem vniuersitatis commodum vel honorem. Nullus eciam magister in procuratorem vltra secundam vicem absque alio interueniente iterum eligatur. Et si magister glomerie non sit presens aut vertatur in dubium quis sit magister glomerie tunc in loco suo si talis habeatur regens qui per biennium proximo precedens procurator fuerat subrogetur. Alioquin iunior magister [fo. 46[r] (E 8[r])] non regencium in artibus ibidem presens qui voce careat in huiusmodi electione per regentes tantummodo celebranda ad dictum scrutinium admittatur

12. *De electione taxatorum*

Item statuimus quod singulis annis post electionem procuratorum in eadem congregacione per scrutinium eligantur duo alij Magistri arcium per maiorem partem magistrorum in artibus regencium ad taxandum domos et assisas faciendas et fideliter obseruandas. Cancellario et duobus procuratoribus huiusmodi scrutinium audituris. Magistri vero taxatores sic deputati coram congregacione iurent vt officium suum diligenter et fideliter exequentur. Huic statuto adicimus quod si quis magister regencium ad officium taxatoris vt iam dicitur electus dictum officium recusauerit vel in fraudem cessauerit ex tunc per totum annum proximo sequentem in congregacione regencium vocem suam amittat nec aliquis in casu isto ad purgandum se de fraude contra ipsum presumpta, admittatur nisi ad minus suam innocenciam in hac parte proprio iuramento manifestauerit

13. *De officijs rectorum*

Tempora et modus legendi et disputandi et exequias celebrandi et incipiendi et feriarum obseruancie ad ipsos procuratores seu rectores pertineant. in transgressores contra predicta et in bedellos si mandatis eorum non paruerint cohercione concessa eisdem animaduersione grauissima per Cancellarium et magistros si opus fuerit nichilominus irroganda. Liceat eciam rectoribus per eosdem suspensos restituere exceptis regentibus et alijs casibus in quibus huiusmodi restitucio Cancellario et vniuersitati est per statuta specialiter reseruata Quod sic statuimus moderandum quod ad restitucionem huiusmodi faciendam sufficiat consensus maioris et sanioris partis regencium. Diligenter eciam curent vt panis et vinum

---

31 nichillominus MS.

12–19 *SA* 65 (*Docs*, i. 349).
19–22 Cf. *SA* 66 (*Docs*, i. 350).
26–(p. 318) 16 *SA* 54 (*Docs*, i. 340).
27–31 Cf. *Cons. Univ. Canteb.* VII. iv (see above, p. 205, line 22 to p. 207, line 2).
36–(p. 318) 16 Cf. *Cons. Univ. Canteb.* VII. ii–iii (see above, p. 205, lines 6–21).

et alia cotidiano victui necessaria secundum varietates temporum et rerum qualitates iusto precio non secus scolaribus quam laicis vendantur. Scolares vero et eorum seruientes omnibus alijs causa negociacionis semper preferantur. Diligenter autem investigent Monopolios id est venditores inter se paciscentes vel ad inuicem de victualibus colludentes quod nisi certo precio inter se fraudulenter taxato vt carius scolaribus vendant huiusmodi victualia distrahantur et precipue balliuos et eorum vxores huiusmodi mercimonia ad victum cotidianum pertinencia durante officio excercentes diligenter inquirant et eorum nomina cancellario referant vt secundum priuilegia et statuta grauiter puniantur ipsis cibarijs et potibus per eosdem in vtilitatem pauperum omnino conuertendis. ac eciam scolaribus cum ipsis transgressoribus comunionem habere vel mercimonium est penitus inhibendum - Idem eciam procuratores seu rectores malefactores in vniuersitate inobedientes et contumaces per se et per alios diligenter investigent et eorum nomina cancellario referant vt per statuta et priuilegia vniuersitatis puniantur -

14. *De potestate rectorum*

Volumus eciam quod procuratores seu rectores vniuersitatis Magistris et scolaribus beneficio carentibus de denarijs vniuersitatis sub pignore bono et valde sufficienti accomodent. nulli Magistro vltra vnam marcam nulli bachellario vltra dimidiam marcam accomodantes Magistris et bachellarijs pignora sua ad eorum mandatum redimentibus. Si autem pignora infra annum redimi non contingat. liceat procuratoribus eadem pignora premissa generali ammonicione per scolas super eorum redempcione vendicioni exponere Remaneant eciam in cista communi Centum solidi ad minus propter casus contingentes ad negocia vniuersitatis -

15. *De potestate rectorum in defectu Cancellarij*

Pro bono pacis et tranquillitate vniuersitatis vnanimi consensv est statutum quod liceat rectoribus suspendere tantum transgressores statuti ad eorum officium spectantis quod est tale tempora et modus legendi et disputandi et exequias celebrandi et incipiendi et feriarum obseruancie ad ipsos pertineant in transgressores circa predicta ad eorum officia specialiter et in bedellos si mandatis eorum non paruerint cohercione concessa eisdem animaduersione grauissima per Cancellarium et magistros si opus fuerit nichilominus irroganda. Si autem presente Cancellario in villa et ipsis rectoribus presentibus vel altero eorum a quoquam iniuria vel contumelia

---

6 nisi *recte* non nisi.

17–26 *SA* 56 (*Docs*, i. 341).
27–(p. 319) 20 *SA* 57 (*ibid.* 342). The text of the original statute has been edited by Ullmann, art. cit., *Historical Journal*, i. 181–2.
30–5 See p. 317, lines 27–31.

publice vel priuatim irrogata fuerit alicui regenti vel communitati / In quibus causis per vniuersitatem regencium extitit declaratum procuratorum vel alterius eorundem assercionem debere sufficere in hac parte. Si Cancellarius requisitus corectionem adhibere dissimulauerit neglexerit vel minus iuste distulerit procuratores vel alter eorum qui presens fuerit irrequisito Cancellario conuocet seu conuocent vniuersitatem regencium que ex tunc in illa cognoscat et sentenciet / Ad hoc statuendo discernimus quod idem procuratores vel eorum alter ob vtilitatem communem vniuersitatis predicte regentes ipsius Si Cancellarius requisitus vel eius locum tenens hoc facere dissimulauerit neglexerit vel minus iuste distulerit valeant seu valeat conuocare Et si maior pars eorundem regencium super premissis vel alicuo eorum non regentes fore vocandos decreuerit. idem procuratores vel eorum alter ipsos non regentes conuocent vel conuocet faciant seu faciat conuocari. Si vero in absencia Cancellarij presentibus rectoribus vel altero eorum aliquod tale delictum commissum fuerit rectores nullam cohercionem faciant. Set si vicecancellarius ab eis requisitus cohercionem adhibere dissimulauerit neglexerit vel minus iuste distulerit [fo. 46v (E 8v)] rectores vel alter eorum vniuersitatem conuocet sicud prius omnibus consuetudinibus imo pocius coruptelis preteritis huic statuto contrarijs hinc et in perpetuum minime valituris.

16. *De compoto rectorum soluendo*

Sngulis annis ante festum sancti Iohannis baptiste ab vniuersitate deputentur certi Magistri ad faciendum seu habendum visum compoti rectorum seu procuratorum de omnibus receptis vndecunque prouenientibus et de expensis seu misis ab eisdem factis circa negocia vniuersitatis - Magistri vero sic deputati dictos procuratores seu rectores premuniant et certum diem eis assignent citra quem cum prouida deliberacione compotum suum parare valeant. Ita quod visus dicti compoti citra communem cessacionem magistrorum habeatur. In fine vero visus dicti compoti fiat starum per modum diuidende in quo ponentur omnia remanentia in communi cista tam pignora quam pecunia ac eciam arreragia et debita ita quod omnibus constare poterit euidenter in quo statu vniuersitas fuerit quoad bona communem cistam contingencia in fine vero compotus supradicti. Statutum est insuper quod infra octo dies post festum beati dionisij tunc proximo sequens idem procuratores finale compotum soluant de omnibus a visu compoti supradicti receptis et expensis vsque ad diem quo eligi debent procuratores seu rectores de nouo post festum sancti Michaelis - Ad huiusmodi vero finalem compotum audiendum

7 illa *suppl.* causa.
12 alicuo *sic*.
22 Sngulis *recte* Singulis.
33 compotus *recte* compoti.
35 finale *recte* finalem.

21–(p. 320) 11 *SA* 60 (*Docs*, i. 345–6).

deputentur predicti Magistri vel ab vniuersitate in crastino sancti dionisij qui compotum finale audiant et starum modo supradicto faciant et demum literam acquietancie predictis rectoribus seu procuratoribus sub sigillo communi vniuersitatis faciant dum tamen vniuersitati satisfecerint in hijs que compotum predictum contingunt iusticia mediante. Volumus eciam quod in omnibus supradictum compotum tangentibus dicti Magistri deputati iuxta deliberacionem seu consensum maioris partis eorum finaliter procedant - Hoc statutum per vniuersitatem regencium extitit sic declaratum quod liceat regentibus quibuscunque in visu et finali compoto procuratorum predictorum vt premittitur faciendo interesse et persistere suo iure -

17. *De officio taxatorum*

Duo taxatores in forma statuti supradicti electi et iurati vna cum duobus burgensibus coram vniuersitate iuramento astrictis congruam domorum faciant taxacionem in publicam scripturam redigendam. per eosdem assisas eciam panis et seruicie faciant et easdem fideliter et diligenter faciant obseruari -

18. *De consuetudine eligendi bedellos seu apparitores*

In bedellorum seu apparitorum electione consuetudo talis per vniuersitatem extitit approbata videlicet quod bedelli sunt eligendi consensu seu iudicio maioris et sanioris partis regencium et non regencium Et quod singulis annis in festo sancti Michaelis quasi officium deponentes virgas officij sui in manus senioris rectoris in prima congregacione post eorundem rectorum electionem tradere debent. qui diligenter inquirat a magistris de ydoneitate bedellorum et eorundem excessu quibus virgas suas statim retradere debet nisi delicti qualitas vel eorundem negligencia circa ea que sua officia contingunt dictorum Magistrorum iudicium contrarium fieri exegerit. Communis eciam collecta in scolis per certum tempus pretextu sui delicti est deneganda vel suspencio ab officio iuxta formam statuti premissi et delicti seu negligencie qualitatem est eis infligenda -

19. *De officijs bedellorum et apparitorum*

Duo bedelli seu apparitores iuramento astricti in vniuersitate ista habeantur quorum alter scolarum theologorum et decretorum et decretalium

---

1 vel *suppl.* alij.
2 finale *recte* finalem.
16 seruicie *recte* ceruisie.
27 iudicium *rectius* iudicio.

12–17 Cf. *Cons. Univ. Canteb.* vii. i (see above, p. 205, lines 1–5); *SA* 66 (*Docs*, i. 349–50).
18–30 *SA* 71 (*ibid.* 353).
31–(p. 321) 22 *Cons. Univ. Canteb.* viii. i–iii (see above, p. 207, line 3 to p. 209, line 4); *SA* 72 (*Docs*, i. 353–4).

mane alter vero omnium aliarum scolarum. circa sedes et alia onera subeat vniuersa. semper parati mandata Cancellarij adimplere de precepto Cancellarij et Magistrorum de causis congnoscencium conuocaciones citaciones et execuciones faciant vniuersas nichil a pauperibus pro conuencione recepturi. Neuter eorum habeat substitutum comitem vel pedagogum nisi de licencia speciali Cancellarij maioris partis et sanioris regencium interueniente qui iurent coram vniuersitate ad consilia vniuersitatis celanda et eorum ministeria fideliter exequenda Ingrediantur singulis diebus scolas singulas hora aliqua lectionum ordiariarum singulis eciam disputacionibus aliqua hora intersint bedellus theologorum et decretistarum hora prima et hora disputacionis eorundem et bedellus arcistarum hora tercia qua ipsi disputare consueuerunt Campanas pulsare teneantur Tempora seu horas antedictas in vnius fauorem vel alterius preiudicium nullatenus anticipando seu prorogando / Intersint eciam virgam deferentes omnibus vesperijs precipuis conuentibus defunctorum exequijs et omnibus alijs conuocacionibus ante Magistrorum recessum nullatenus recessuri nullo alio in eorundem preiudicio virgam delaturo. Si vero negligentes vel remissi circa premissa et alia ad eorum officia pertinencia deprehendantur communis collecta in scolis omnino denegetur eisdem vel ab officio perpetuo vel ad tempus amoueantur et alij ydonei in locum ipsorum subrogentur si delicti [fo. 47^{r} (E 9^{r})] qualitas vel necligencia remocionem postulauerit -

20. *De declaracione super incarceracionibus et correctionibus*

Item anno domini M CC° nonogesimo iiij^{to} die sancti Iohannis ante portam latinam erat statutum de incarceracionibus et bannicionibus per maiorem et saniorem partem regencium sic declaratum scilicet quod Cancellarius sine consensv Magistrorum regencium neque debet bannire neque incarcerare Magistrum aliquem qui in hac vniuersitate rexerit set cause de atrocibus delictis que requirunt penam carceris et bannicionem alicuius Magistri vt predicitur. audienciam Cancellarij requirunt simul et Magistrorum - Item ad hec adicientes statuimus quod Cancellarius qui pro tempore fuerit huiusmodi commissionem incarceracionis et bannicionis admittere teneatur cum vniuersitas regencium hoc decreuerit faciendum - Item statuimus *quod omnes qui debent incarcerari in carcere communi in villa incarcerentur* Item memorandum quod anno domini supradicto die sabbati proximo post festum sancti Iohannis ante portam latinam in plena congregacione regencium eciam coram clericis domini Episcopi Eliensis erat consuetudo de correctionibus sic declarata videlicet

6 Cancellarij *suppl.* consensu *aut aliquid tale.*
9 ordiariarum *recte* ordinariarum.
17 preiudicio *recte* preiudicium. **21** necligencia *sic.*

34–5 *SA* 10 (*Docs*, i. 313).

quod in correctionibus faciendis Rectores debent assidere Cancellario vel suo commissario ita quod debeant premuniri de tempore et de loco si venire voluerint. Voluit eciam dicta vniuersitas quod ista predicta ordinacio seu disposicio super premissis vigorem habeat inconcussum - Item in correctionibus faciendis si penitenciam alicui inflictam pro commisso in penitenciam pecuniariam conuerti contingat, statuimus quod illa pecunia per procuratores vel eorum alterum recipiatur et ciste communi vniuersitatis applicetur -

21. *De defensoribus et procuratoribus litigancium*

Ordinamus et statuimus quod citatis personis in villa presentibus, nec defensores nec procuratores coram Cancellario vel eius commissario admittantur pro eisdem nisi persone citate aduersa valitudine seu alia legitima causa sint detente quominus in iudicium sui presenciam poterint exhibere de quo in principio coram Cancellario vel suis commissarijs fidem faciant iuramento quo prestito admittantur defensores seu procuratores iuxta consuetudines et statuta vniuersitatis in litem processuri et postquam semel causam peregerint, iterum tanquam procuratores seu defensores non admittantur nisi sub forma prius posita. Si vero presente actore reus fuerit abfiturus eius procurator non admittatur nisi dominus suus prius prestiterit iuramentum quod maliciose minime se absentet - Hec autem in omnibus causis artius volumus obseruari Exceptis tantum causis illis in quibus delicti enormitas seu facti ipsius attrocitas ob quietem communem Cancellarij et Magistrorum requirit audienciam in quibus causis nullatenus admittatur defensor seu procurator set contra reum siue venerit siue non venerit procedatur de die in diem a tempore notificati delicti vel denunciati Et cum conuictus fuerit ad minus infra triduum execucio fiat plenaria secundum quod statuta de malefactoribus edita plenius continent penis contra delinquentes et eorum fautores in statutis dicte vniuersitatis expressis in suo robore perpetuo duraturis -

22. *De aduocatis*

Cum prouida deliberacione sit statutum quod cause si commode possint terminentur infra triduum, nonnullis aduocatorum incertacionibus, causas vltra debitum sepius euenit prorogari quorum suspectis astucijs obuiare volentes statuimus quod principales persone factum ipsum per se proponant. Actor scilicet primo per se suam proponat actionem. reus vero

---

19 abfiturus *recte* abfuturus.
32 incertacionibus *sic*.

1–7 *SA* 10 (*Docs*, i. 313).
9–29 *SA* 29 (*ibid.* 325–6).
30–(p. 323), 17 Cf. *SA* 30 (*Docs*, i. 326).
34–5 Cf. c. 14. x. 2. 1: 'principales personae non per advocatos, sed per se ipsas factum proponant.'

per se suam afferat defensionem in ydiomate quo voluerint dum tamen intelligibili. Quod si actor contra tenorem premissorum aduocatum aliquem procurauerit pro se loqui aut ad loquendum excitauerit aut taliter verba facientem approbauerit causam suam hoc ipso amittat. Reus vero similia faciens pro conuicto habeatur Qui vero contra hoc salubre statutum pro actore seu pro reo vetitum prestiterit patrocinium, si fuerit Magister ordinarie legens vel bachellarius cursorie ex tunc a lectionibus suis per octo dies suspensus. si scolaris ingressus scole per viij dies sibi penitus sit interdictus nec pro scolari habeatur quousque communam suam vnius ebdomode communi ciste persoluerit - Si quis vero durante interdicto seu suspencione predictis ausu temerario scolas ingrediendo actibus scolasticis se ingesserit, eo ipso per annum integrum ab vniuersitate expellatur nisi vberiorem graciam ab vniuersitate meruerit obtinere Alij quidem quam Magistri vel scolares sic aduocantes seu verba facientes pro aliqua parcium predictarum si a iudice moniti non desistant tanquam pacis perturbatores puniantur. vel sicud iudicis iurisdictionem impedientes excommunicentur -

23. *De procuratoribus admittendis*

Quia ex malicia aduocatorum in fraudem statuti introductum est quod indirecte fiant aduocati per hoc quod admittuntur tanquam procuratores cum hoc directe sit illicitum malicijs eorum obuiare volentes obseruari statuimus quod de cetero nullus aduocatus procurator admittatur Per aduocatum in casu isto declaramus intelligendum quemlibet bachellarium in iure canonico seu ciuili ac omnes alios qui communiter ingerunt se ad allegandum in causis pro actore seu pro reo - Vt debitus honor vniuersitatis iudicibus Cantebrigie, deferatur ac proteruijs aduocatorum et eorum opprobrijs sufficienter obuietur. Nos Cancellarius [fo. 47^{v} (E 9^{v})] magistri regentes et non regentes dicte vniuersitatis vnanimi consensv statuimus quod nullus pro aduocato alicuius curie communiter se gerens ad postulandum in aliqua curia vniuersitatis memorate admittatur de cetero nisi iuramentum infrascriptum in congregacione regencium prius prestiterit Cancellario vel eius locum tenente hoc recipiente Ego N. ad ista sancta dei ewangelia per me corporaliter tacta iuro quod statuta priuilegia et consuetudines vniuersitatis Cantebriggie approbatas pro posse meo fideliter conseruabo. ministros dicte vniuersitatis honorifice tractabo. iurisdictionem eiusdem nullo modo impediam nec impedire volentibus seu volenti consilium vel auxilium prestabo ceteris statutis de aduocatis mencionem facientibus in suo robore duraturis -

11 predictis *recte* predicta.

22–5 *SA* 31 (*Docs*, i. 327).
29–38 *SA* 28 (*ibid.* 324–5).

24. *De modo veniendi ad lites seu diem amoris*

Statutum esse noueritis ne quis ad litem vel ad diem amoris cum honerosa multitudine venire presumat set cum Magistro suo et tribus tantum aut quatuor socijs pacificis ac modestis partibus vero taliter congregatis ad diem amoris certas hinc inde eligant personas pro consilio habendo que tamen premissum numerum non excedant. qui vero contrafecerit. actor ipso facto cadat a causa. reus vero pro conuicto habeatur. Alie eciam quecunque persone que contra huius statuti tenorem ibidem temere se ingesserint immunitate scolarium ex tunc sint priuati nisi tales sint persone et tam excellentes quibus vniuersitatis discrecio deferre duxerit in hac parte -

25. *De rebellantibus Cancellario*

Si quis de vniuersitate iurisdictionem Cancellarij contempnens propriam vel alienam iniuriam cum deliberacione vel ex interuallo vindicauerit insultum in ipsum quem deliquisse dicit aut in eius hospicium faciendo aut eundem verberando seu male tractando si monitus ad arbitrium Cancellarij vel vniuersitatis satisfacere noluerit cum effectu infra triduum ab vniuersitate expellatur ceteris penis iuxta priuilegia consuetudines et statuta malefactoribus imponendis eisdem malefactoribus nichilominus infligendis quas quidem penas. seu puniciones non tantum ad ipsos malefactores verum eciam ad eorum fautores seu defensores sine personarum accepcione volumus extendi. Contra cancellarij quoque prohibicionem colluctantes et alias sibi inobedientes et contumaces cum super huiusmodi secundum modum vniuersitatis conuicti fuerint sine differencia personarum simili pena coherceantur si hoc meruerit proteruitas contumacium verum si magistri regentes vel non regentes vel aliquis eorum contra Cancellarium colluctans vel alias inobediens extiterit eorum causa per electas ab alijs regentibus personas tractetur et terminetur In quarum electione personarum vt omnis timor subornacionis absistat tam cancellarius quam taliter rebellantes sint absentes -

26. *De Iudicijs et foro scolarium competenti*

Contra scolarem si quis causam habeat et scolaris contra aliquem dummodo sit de municipio de contractu vel quasi seu de maleficio seu quasi coram Cancellario vel eius commissario tractetur causa et debite terminetur infra triduum si comode possit quoquomodo nisi per legitimam appellacionem a comissario ad Cancellarium vel a Cancellario ad vniuersi-

35 legitimam] liām MS.

1–11 *SA* 32 (*Docs*, i. 327).
12–30 *SA* 10 (*Docs*, i. 312–13).
31–(p. 325) 7 Cf. *SA* 33 (*Docs*, i. 327–8).

tatem vel ab vniuersitate ad episcopum gradatim deferatur vel talis sit causa que pro aliqua sui parte presenciam exigat vniuersitatis illis causis dumtaxat exceptis que ad coronam regiam vel ad forum laicale vsque adeo pertinere dinoscuntur quod per nullam Cancellarij vel vniuersitatis iurisdictionem licite valeant expediri. Ceterum domesticam scolarium familiam cum scriptoribus eorundem et alijs eorum officijs in similibus deputatis simili volumus in hac parte immunitatis iure censeri -

27. *De ordine iudiciorum in causis scolarium*

Vt litigantes celeriorem consequantur iusticiam prouisum est et statutum vt in examinacione causarum iuris solempnitas nullatenus obseruetur nec super actibus iudicialibus quibuscunque iudices seu partes scripturam edere teneantur. set omnia acta iudicialia sine quibus ad sentenciam perueniri non poterit sine scriptura procedant -

28. *De iuramento litigancium*

In processibus causarum prius actor demum reus sine personarum accepcione de calumpnia et si non de veritate dicenda et falsitate subticenda iuramentum prestent corporale -

29. *De curia Magistrorum et iurisdictione eorundem*

Magistri regentes causas scolarium suorum ex parte rea existencium audiant et decidant vniuersas dummodo hoc postulauerint vel conuenti hoc idem in iudicio allegauerint nisi altera pars in vniuersitate ista rexerit vel de pensionibus domorum vel vbi delicti enormitas aut quies communis Cancellarij vel Magistrorum audienciam requirat specialem vel conuenti expresse vel tacite foro magistri sui renunciauerit -

30. *De penis appellancium et eorum caucione*

Exigit proteruitas frustratorie appellancium vt eos alicuius pene adiectione ab huiusmodi appellacionibus prout possumus arceamus hinc est quod prouida deliberacione statuimus vt quicunque a Cancellario ad vniuersitatem vel a commissario ad Cancellarium appellauerit caucionem xij. denariorum communi ciste infra octo dies applicandorum si forte eum frustratorie appellasse constiterit alteri procuratorum exponat qui statim inhibeat iudici, ne ulterius in causa procedat - Si vero super eodem articulo

24 renunciauerit *recte* renunciauerint.
28 Cancellario] a Can. *add. sed del.* MS.

8–13 Cf. *Cons. Univ. Canteb.* x. ii (see above, p. 209, line 17 to p. 211, line 2; *SA* 34 (*Docs*, i. 328).
14–17 *Cons. Univ. Canteb.* x. i (see above, p. 209, lines 14–16); *SA* 35 (*Docs*, i. 328).
18–24 *Cons. Univ. Canteb.* vi (see above, p. 203, lines 17–23); *SA* 36 (*loc. cit.* 328–9).
25–(p. 326) 6 *SA* 37 (*Docs*, i. 329).

siue a diffinitiva sentencia siue ab interlocutoria secundo appellauerit caucionem xviij denariorum secundum formam priorum exponat procuratoribus vel alteri eorum. Huic statuto statuendo adicimus quod huiusmodi caucio per appellantem [fo. 48r (E 10r)] exposita ante plenam probacionem causarum et veritatis grauaminis seu grauaminum nunquam relaxetur Statuimus quod quilibet appellans in vniuersitate ista suam appellacionem infra triduum iuridicum a tempore inhibicionis facte numerandum effectualiter prosequatur. Alioquin appellacio sua habeatur pro deserta et eo ipso comissa caucio habeatur -

31. *De modo conuincendi periuros*

Quia nonnulli proprie salutis immemores contra statutum proprium temere venientes penam periurij non verentes non solum malefactores in vniuersitate Cantebrigie contra statuta celare sed eos in sua nequicia manifeste fouere nituntur. Idcirco statutis que de malefactoribus locuntur hec adicienda decreuimus vt quicunque in aliquo articulo contra dicta statuta per duos vel tres testes de sciencia deponentes coram iudicibus ab vniuersitate deputatis de cetero venire detectus fuerit nisi notorietas aliud ostendat xl. solidos ciste communi istius vniuersitatis applicandos soluere teneatur. Si autem de dicta pecunia satisfacere detractauerit ex tunc ab omni commodo et honore vniuersitatis quousque satisfecerit ipso iure priuatus existat et sic conuictus de cetero ad congregacionem non admittatur nisi graciam vberiorem ab vniuersitate meruerit obtinere. Iudicibus procedentibus in tali causa exclusis personis que ad congnicionem cause coram congregacione non admitterentur omnibus alijs penis contra delinquentes et eorum fautores in statutis vniuersitatis expressis in suo robore duraturis -

32. *De hospicijs et pensione domorum*

Tribus terminis id est diebus omnium sanctorum. purificacionis beate virginis et ascencionis dominice pensiones domorum in tres partes equales diuidende vel diuise omnino soluantur vel congrua hospitibus satisfactio ipsis consensientibus prestetur eisdem. Statuentes eciam inhibe-

2 priorum *recte* priorem.
3 statuendo] sta^{do} MS.
11 statutum *recte* statum.
13 eos *bis*.
23 ad] congregacionem *add. et del.* MS.
31 prestetur] eidem *add. et del.* MS.

6–9 *SA* 38 (*loc. cit.*).
10–26 *SA* 40 (*Docs*, i. 330).
27–(p. 238) 13 *Cons. Univ. Canteb.* XII. i–viii (see above, p. 213, line 10 to p. 217, line 4); *SA* 67 (*Docs*, i. 350–1).

mus ne quis a municipio seu villa Cantebrigie recedat post terminum statutum de pensione soluenda nisi prius de eadem pencione congrue satisfecerit et legitime Et si contra fiat pignus datum ab eodem studij tempore in fine anni completo licite per hospitem distrahatur et si fideiussores dederit seu expromissores arbitrio hospitis conueniantur. Si vero nec pignora nec fideiussores dederit et pensione non soluta nullo modo hispiti satisfacto a villa recesserit, sic recedens ipso facto sit excommunicatus et suo diocesano excommunicatus denuncietur donec plenarie suo hospiti de pencione fuerit satisfactum tempore solucionis faciende propter hospitis improbitatem si opus fuerit per Cancellarium moderando domos in quibus scole esse consueuerant a decennio et vltra nullus ad inhabitandum conducat seu ad alium vsum conuertat quamdiu regentes iuxta numerum eorundem in principio anni vel nouiter incepturi inijcijs terminorum scolas sibi eligerint in eisdem nisi domini earundem necessitate ducti sine fraude personaliter ibidem inhabitare voluerint. Edificiorum proprietarij ultra pencionem iuramento taxatam eciam ex conuencione nichil recipiant nec eciam inquilini vltra eandem aliquid eisdem exsoluant nec quocunque titulo in huius statuti fraudem speciem vel quantitatem promittant ipsis edificijs arbitrio Cancellarij a scolarium sic delinquentium inhabitacione suspendendis. et quod vltra receptum fuerit vel promissum communi ciste ab ipso recipiente seu promittente restituatur seu applicetur. Qui domum principaliter conduxit ius inhabitandi eo anno solus habebit dummodo hospiti vel Cancellario si hospes non inveniatur vel eius procurator ad domicilium quesitus vel vbi in municipio habitare seu morari consueuerint de sequentis anni pencione tempore medio inter festum sancti barnebe iam finitum et festum natiuitatis gloriose virginis complete finiendum satisfactionem obtulerit cum effectu nuda caucione Cancellario exposita non valente. Nec dominus domus seu eius procurator huiusmodi caucionem nudam admittere teneatur nec valeat caucio ante dictum festum sancti barnebe exposita nisi pro domo tunc vacante. Si vero contra formam huius statuti caucio ab aliquo exponatur, nullum effectum inducat. imo liceat hospiti libere de domo sua disponere huiusmodi exposicione caucionis non obstante cessione ab ipso principali alteri facienda de iure inhabitandi quam habet omnino cessante quod ius inhabitandi eundem tunc demum habere volumus cum pro maiori parte anni personaliter domum ab eo conductam inhabitauerit. quod si non fecerit ipso facto vacare censeatur / Item principalis pro pensione tocius anni hospiti solus satisfaciat et de dampnis culpa sua et sociorum suorum contingentibus solus respondeat. ne in plures aduersarios distringatur qui cum vno contraxit - Qui vltra natiuitatem beate virginis in domo

7 hispiti *recte* hospiti.
13 inijcijs *sic.*
26 barnebe *sic; cf. l.* 30.

remanserit conducta ad pensionem tocius anni sequentis teneatur quasi tacite reconduxisse videatur nisi dominus palam sibi gratuitam concesserit habitacionem. Liceat quoque dominis feodorum in feodis suis pro pensione distringere secundum regni consuetudinem non pro pensione conuenta temporali set pro seruicijs perpetuis et si magister ibidem legerit vel scolares inhabitauerint pencione arbitrio Cancellarij propter hoc pro rata temporis diminuenda et interesse nichilominus conductori prestando. Volumus eciam quod hospites domos proprios inhabitare volentes ante festum Natiuitatis sancti Iohannis baptiste inhabitantes premuniant et causam necessariam [fo. 48 v (E 10 v)] personaliter inhabitandi omni fraude exclusa in die Natiuitatis gloriose virginis coram Cancellario vel eius commissario inquilino vel eius procuratore ad hoc vocato, prestito corporali sacramento legitime probet -

33. *De conuenticulis seu proturbacione pacis*

Item statuimus ne aliquis vel aliqui conuenticulam vel conuenticulas conspiracionem seu conspiraciones confederacionem vel confederaciones iudicio maioris partis vniuersitatis regencium illicitas seu inhonestas faciant aut fieri procurant aut talibus consilium auxilium vel consensum adhibeant Qui vero contrauenerit si magister fuerit ab officio regendi et magisterij ipso facto absque spe restitucionis sit suspensus Si bacallarius incepturus ad incepcionem seu honorem magistralem in dicta vniuersitate nunquam in posterum admittatur. Si vero inferioris cuiuscunque status vel qualiscunque condicionis extiterit A. collegio honore et omni beneficio dicte vniuersitatis ipso facto sit priuatus Et si beneficiatus fuerit contra ipsum super huiusmodi excessu per literas vniuersitatis sigillo communi eiusdem roboratas Episcopo suo fiat denunciacio infra mensem. saluis omnibus alijs penis que per priuilegia vniuersitatis huiusmodi delinquentibus poterunt infligi / Per maiorem et saniorem partem regencium vniuersitatis Cantebrigie hoc statutum sic extitit declaratum Magistros regentes seu non regentes coniunctim seu diuisim super negocijs vtilitatem communem vniuersitatis predicte tangentibus ad inuicem qualitercunque tractantes in presens statutum seu aliquam eius partem ex hoc incidere non debere - Hoc idem vero de fautoribus meretricum seu concubinarum vel malefactorum statuimus firmiter obseruandum

---

8 proprios *recte* proprias.
13 probet *recte* probent.
14 *proturbacione* recto *perturbacione*.
18 procurant *recte* procurent.

8–13 *SA* 67 (*loc. cit.* 351).
14–28 Cf. *SA* 41 (*Docs*, i. 330–1).
28–33 *SA* 41 (*loc. cit.* 331, ll. 19–24).
33–4 *Ibid.* ll. 17–19.

Ordinamus eciam quod istud statutum ter in anno per bedellum in scolis recitetur - Item excommunicamus et excommunicatos denunciamus omnes perturbatores pacis vniuersitatis Cantebrigie ac eciam omnes et singulos priuilegia libertates et consuetudines vniuersitatis approbatas et consuetas indebite seu maliciose inpugnantes eneruantes inpugnacioni seu eneruacioni eorundem seu alicuius earum consencientes fauentes seu consulentes seu quouis quesito colore inpugnacionem seu eneruacionem vt premittitur machinantes seu procurantes clam vel palam directe vel indirecte. omnium et singulorum in hac parte delinquencium absolucione cancellario istius vniuersitatis specialiter reseruata - Statutum.33^{m}. declaratur sic quod in notam conspiracionis et in comisso istius statuti illi intelliguntur incidere iudicio ac declaracione omnium et singulorum Magistrorum regencium qui per preces vel munera seu promissiones seu pacta quecunque ambiciosa cum aliquo vel aliquibus conspirauerint vt scolares alicuius Magistri regentis ab eo subtrahantur. si tamen per huiusmodi conspiraciones dicti scolares ab auditorio suorum Magistrorum actualiter diuertant / Item illi qui preter conscienciam Cancellarij et procuratorum ac maioris et sanioris partis regencium clanculas conspiraciones cum aliquo vel aliquibus faciunt seu pacta ambiciosa iniunt cuius pretextu gracie vniuersitatis reddantur venales -

34. *De choreis et choreas ducentibus*

Prouisum est per omnes regentes istius vniuersitatis necnon per maiores bacallarios eiusdem specialiter in plena Magistrorum congregacione ad hoc vocatos ne publice choree per plateas de cetero fiant set omnino inhibeantur et hoc non sine causa quia per certa et plurima eis apparuit indicia per huiusmodi coreas pacem vniuersitatis posse impediri et alia plurima imminere pericula statuit eciam dicta vniuersitas omnes contra dictam inhibicionem venientes ipso facto in sentenciam incidere excommunicacionis Ideo Cancellarius cum consensv et auctoritate dicte vniuersitatis huiusmodi coreas publicas sub pena de cetero inhibebat anathematis transgressores dicti statuti ipso facto anathematis inuoluendo pena nichilominus incarceracionis eisdem transgressoribus imminente salua tamen potestate Cancellario dispensandi super coreis ducendis coram incipientibus in die incepcionis eorundem -

---

6 eorundem *recte* earundem.
11 comisso *recte* commissum.
16 conspiraciones] con- *suprascr.*
19 iniunt *recte* ineunt.
31 facto *suppl.* sentencia.

1–2 *Ibid.* ll. 24–5.
2–10 *Ibid.* ll. 7–17.
10–20 *Ibid.* 332, ll. 1–11.
21–34 *SA* 47 (*Docs*, i. 335).

35. *De immunitate scolarium*

Indignum esse iudicamus vt quis scolarem tuetur qui certum Magistrum infra xv dies post eius ingressum in vniuersitatem non habuerit aut nomen suum infra tempus prelibatum in matricula Magistri sui redigere non curauerit nisi Magistri sui absencia vel iusta eorum occupacio illud impediat ymmo si quis talis sub nomine scolaris sic latitare compertus fuerit vel detinetur vel deiciatur iuxta domini regis super hoc concessam libertatem. Nullus eciam Magistrorum aliquem tanquam scolarem proprium defendat qui scolaris eius non existit cuius nomen in matricula sua non habeat insertum nisi alias quod suus sit scolaris certam de eo habuerit noticiam Caueant tamen Magistri regentes ne erga pauperes scolares suos difficiles se exhibeant set cum scolares huiusmodi suum nomen petant inseri de inopia sua facta fide Magister eos benignus admittat Prouisum est eciam et statutum vt omnes morantes in municipio nostro qui speciem gerunt scolarium sint veri scolares et lectionibus Magistrorum suorum intersint prout decet. Hij quoque soli scolarium gaudeant immunitate qui saltem per tres dies in septimana scolas Magistri sui ingrediantur tres lectiones [fo. 49ʳ (E 11ʳ)] ad minus audituri dummodo per tres dies Magister suus legerit nisi Magistri sui licencia ex causa racionabili eorum excusauerit absenciam Exceptis illis qui in lectura aliqua theologie Iuris canonici seu ciuilis publice fuerint occupati Exceptis eciam maioribus qui saltem bis in septimana intersint lectionibus Magistrorum suorum si commode poterint -

36. *De falsis scolaribus et alijs pacis perturbatoribus*

Nullus clericus de cetero moram faciat in municipio nisi sit scolaris alicuius Magistri in sua matricula positus ita quod per socios suos scolares de hoc constare poterit euidenter Statuimus eciam sub pena anathematis quod si aliqui scolares aliquem sciant sub. nomine scolaris se gerere vel in societate sua aliquem habeant qui Magistrum non habeat aut lectionibus ordinarijs Magistri sui secundum formam predictam non intersit vel qui concubinam suam manifeste tenet. vel alicuo modo per signa manifesta vel facti euidenciam male opinionis fuerit et hoc quia fur vel incon-

---

2 tuetur *recte* tueatur.
7 detinetur *recte* detineatur.
13 benignus *recte* benigne.
31 alicuo *sic*.

1–8 *Cons. Univ. Canteb.* XI. i (see above, p. 211, lines 3–10); *SA* 42 (*Docs*, i. 332).
8–16 *SA* 42 (*loc. cit.*).
16–23 *Cons. Univ. Canteb.* XI. ii (see above, p. 211, lines 11–15); *SA* 42 (*loc. cit.* 332–3).
20–3 *SA* 42 (*loc. cit.* 333).
24–(p. 331) 7 *SA* 43 (*ibid.* 333).

tinens vel pacis perturbator fuerit Magistro suo denunciet vel Cancellario vt post denunciacionem statim ab vniuersitate expelli possit - Qui vero prouisionis huius formam obseruare contempserit sine strepitu iudicij ab vniuersitate sentencialiter expellatur et Maiori et balliuis denuncietur vt talem tanquam de pacis perturbacione suspectum ammoueant a muncipio Et si beneficiatus extiterit prelato suo si fieri poterit denuncietur vt eum ad curam debitam reuocare non differat -

37. *De eiectis Oxonie et alijs vagabundis*

Aduenticius malefactor in municipio nostro nusquam recipiatur quem per literas Cancellarij Oxonie vel alio modo legitimo malefactorem esse constiterit et ab vniuersitate oxonie tanquam talem fuisse eiectum - Fractores domorum et insultores earundem raptores mulierum insidiatores viarum vagabundi cum armis vel alias arma deferentes seu deferri facientes per se vel per alios causa mali perpetrandi in villa vel iuxta villam occulte vel manifeste de die vel de nocte per Cancellarium et vniuersitatem regencium ab vniuersitate sine spe restitucionis eiciantur vel in carcerem detrudantur. Liceat tamen Cancellario ex causa racionabili consciencie sue arbitrio relinquenda super delacione armorum ad tempus dispensare -

38. *De pena eorum qui contempnunt Magistros*

Statmus quod quicunque scolaris seu seruiens scolarium in ecclesia in scolis in iudicijs vel alibi in vniuersitate in loco publico alicui Magistro regenti vel non regenti istius vniuersitatis publice aliquem contemptum contra statum sui magisterij vel officij vel aliqua verba in defamacionem seu notabilem contemptum persone ipso facto ab omnibus beneficijs ac communione vniuersitatis sit suspensus quousque leso competenter sit satisfactum -

1 denunciet *recte* denuncient.
5 muncipio *recte* municipio.
20 Statmus *recte* Statuimus.
24 persone *suppl. verbum aliquod fortasse* dixerit.

8–17 *Cons. Univ. Canteb.* XI. iii–iv (see above, p. 211, line 16 to p. 213, line 2); *SA* 45 (*Docs*, i. 334).
17–18 *SA* 45 (*loc. cit.* 334–5).
19–26 *SA* 48 (*Docs*, i. 335–6).

Appendix II

A CONCORDANCE OF THE CAMBRIDGE STATUTES WITH A CONSPECTUS OF DATES

The various redactions through which the Cambridge statutes passed before the issue of the *editio princeps* in 1785 make a concordance an essential aid for comparative purposes. Nothing illustrates so vividly as a table the growth of university legislation and the difference between the recensions. The efforts of one medieval editor after another to improve on his predecessor and the arbitrary way in which additions were made to the *textus receptus* (Senior Proctor), not to mention the fate of the code devised *c.* 1494–6 (Junior Proctor), have scarcely facilitated the construction of a concordance. The overall picture is certainly confusing, but if a similar concordance of the Oxford statutes were available, we should see that the lack of order in successive arrangements of the statutes was not confined to Cambridge.[1] Until a critical edition of the statutes is produced, the point of departure for the formation of a concordance must continue to be the 1852 edition of the *statuta antiqua*. I have, therefore, worked back from this text. The following points should be noted:

(*a*) Statutes entered in a manuscript in a hand other than that of the text are enclosed within brackets.[2]

(*b*) The statutes in Junior Proctor are numbered in the manuscript not according to the order in which they were copied but according to the arrangement of Senior Proctor, which corresponds with that of the 1785 and 1852 editions. The numbering adopted here represents, as far as part I of the manuscript is concerned, the sequence of the code fashioned *c.* 1494–6. Part II, which begins with *SA* 108, was executed at a much later date; but it may be regarded as certain that *SA* 108–68 and the statutes on the folios taken from Old Proctor (excluding *SA* 170) likewise correspond with the order established by 1495. All these are numbered consecutively. Though there is little doubt that the remainder of the pre-1495 statutes occupied the same order in the exemplar as they hold in Senior Proctor, it is best to list these and other doubtful or later entries in the order in which they actually occur in the manuscript.

[1] Brian Twyne in his projected preface to the Laudian code (1634) wrote of the Oxford statutes: 'tum vetera tum noua Academiae statuta adeo inuoluta, confusa, implicata, multiplicata etiam, aliaque aliis superaddita' (Gibson, *The keepers of the archives of the university of Oxford* [Oxford, 1928], p. 4).

[2] Only entries on the folios of the original text need be noted for Old Proctor.

(*c*) The statutes in the Angelica and Caius MSS bear no numbers; this is also true of an odd statute or two in Old Proctor. The numbers given here correspond with the sequence of the texts in these manuscripts.

The problem of dating is much more intractable, as the vast majority of the statutes seldom carry a date, and in most cases no conclusions can be drawn from internal evidence.[1] The dates provided here for undated statutes must be regarded as merely tentative. In general a statute which cannot be dated within fairly close limits is assigned a round date corresponding with that of the recension in which it first occurs. Thus a statute in the Angelica text is dated 'by 1250'; in Markaunt 'by 1330'; in Old Proctor-Caius 'by 1390'; in Junior Proctor 'by 1495' and in Senior Proctor 'by 1500'.[2] A dash (-) placed before a date denotes that the statute or amendment is not later than that date; a plus sign (+) indicates that the statute was not enacted or revised before the date which precedes the sign. The letter 'r.' means revised or amended.

ABBREVIATIONS

A = Angelica MS 401
C = Caius MS 706
M = Markaunt's Book
JP = Junior Proctor's Book
OP = Old Proctor's Book
SA = *Statutum antiquum* (*Docs*, i. 308–416)
SP = Senior Proctor's Book

Date	*SA*	SP	JP	OP	C	M	A
18 March 1304; r. by 1330; r. by 1390	1	1	1	1	1	1	—
1304+; by 1390	2	2	2	2	2	—	—
1304+; by 1390	3	3	3	3	3	—	—
by 1250; r. 1304+; r. by 1330; r. by 1390	4	4	4	4	4	2	I. i
1294+; r. 1401+	5	5	5	5	5	3	—
by 1250; r. 1304+; r. by 1390	6	6	6	6	6	4	I. vi

1 Many of the statutes were revised or amended more than once; some were constructed from separate enactments. Much as one would have liked to make the concordance as revealing as possible by quoting the relevant passages, this has not been found practicable. A large number of quotations, often lengthy, would have to be given from the MSS in addition to passages from the printed text. All that can or need be done here is to indicate that a certain statute was revised at some stage or another and to show which part is the earlier in the case of composite statutes.

2 These dates are also used where there is question of a revision or amendment which cannot be dated with some precision.

Appendix II

Date	*SA*	SP	JP	OP	C	M	A
by 1330	7	7	7	7	7	5	—
(i) by 1250; (ii) 1304+; r. by 1330; (iii) by 1250; r. by 1330	8	8	8	8	8	6–7	I. ii–iii
by 1250; r. by 1330	9	9	9	9	9	8	I. iv
by 1250; r. by 1330; r. by 1390	10	10	10	10	10	25	XI. v
6–8 May 1294; r. by 1390; r. by 1495	—	—	—	11*	11	20	—
by 1250; r. by 1330	11	11	11	12	12	9	IV
by 1337	12	12	12	13	13	—	—
(i) 1379; (ii) by 1250; r. by 1390	13	13	13	14	14	—	I. v
by 1390	14	14	14	15	15	—	—
by 1330	15	15	15	16	16	10	—
c. 1488?; by 1495	16	16	16	—	—	—	—
c. 1450?; by 1495	17	17	17	(141)	—	—	—
by 1495	18	18	18	—	—	—	—
by 1495	19	19	19	—	—	—	—
by 1495	20	20	20	—	—	—	—
28 May 1488	21	21	21	—	—	—	—
1460	22	22	22	—	—	—	—
11 July 1474 (1468?)	23	23	23	—	—	—	—
31 May 1469	24	24	24	—	—	—	—
20 Nov. 1464	25	25	25	—	—	—	—
12 May 1463+; by 1495	26	26	26	—	—	—	—
(i) *c.* 1450–67; (ii) 1457–1500	27	27	27	—	—	—	—
1304+; by 1330	28	28	28	30	30	23ii	—
by 1330	29	29	29	31	31	21	—
by 1250	—	—	—	—	—	—	IX
by 1330	30	30	30	32	32	22	—
by 1330; r. by 1390	31	31	31	33	33	23i	—
by 1330	32	32	32	34	34	24	—
(i) 1305+; by 1330; (ii) 1264+; r. 1276+; (iii) r. 1401+	33	33	33	35	35	26	—
by 1250; r. by 1330	34	34	34	36	36	27	X. ii
by 1250; r. by 1330	35	35	35	37	37	28	X. i
by 1250; r. by 1330	36	36	36	38	38	29	VI
1264–1330	37	37	37	39	39	30i	—
by 1330	38	38	38	40	40	30ii	—
by 1390	39	39	39	41	41	—	—
by 1330; r. 1500+	40	40	40	42	42	31	—

* The first part of the text has been erased from the MS.

Appendix II

Date	*SA*	SP	JP	OP	C	M	A
-1300?; by 1330; r. by 1390	41	41	41	43	43	33	—
c. 1231; by 1250; r. by 1276; r. by 1330	42	42	42	44	44	35	XI. i–ii
by 1330	43	43	43	45	45	36	—
by 1390	44	44	44	46	46	—	—
by 1250; r. ?1294+; r. by 1330; r. 1500+	45	45	45	47	47	37	XI. iii–iv
by 1390	46	46	46	48	48	—	—
by 1300; r. by 1330; r. by 1390	47	47	47	49	49	34	—
?1304+; by 1330; r. by 1390	48	48	48	50	50	38	—
by 1390	49	49	49	51	51	—	—
by 1500	50	50	(163)	—	—	—	—
4 March 1496	51	51	(165)	—	—	—	—
c. 1500–38	52	(52)	(187)	—	—	—	—
-1300?; by 1330	53	53	50	17	17	11	—
by 1250; r. 1255?; r. 1276+; r. 1294; r. by 1330	54	54	51	18	18	13	VII. ii–iv
1490	55	55	52	—	—	—	—
by 1330	56	56	53	19	19	14	—
17 March 1276; r. by 1330; r. 1390+	57	57	54	20	20	15	—
by 1390	58	58	55	21	21	—	—
22 June 1456	59	59	56	—	—	—	—
by 1330; r. by 1390	60	60	57	22	22	16	—
by 1390	61	61	58	23	23	—	—
-1460?; by 1495	62	62	59	—	—	—	—
by 1500	63	63	(167)	—	—	—	—
by 1500	64	64	(166)	—	—	—	—
-1300?; by 1330	65	65	60	24	24	12	—
c. 1231; r. *c.* 1255–68; r. by 1330	66	66	61	25	25	17	VII. i
by 1250; r. by 1330	67	67	62	26	26	32	XII
11 Oct. 1492 (1482?)	68	68	63	—	—	—	—
by 1500	69	69	(64)	—	—	—	—
1 July 1506	70	(70)	(162)*	—	—	—	—
by 1330	71	71	65	27	27	18	—
by 1250; r. by 1330; r. *c.* 1415?	72	72	66	28	28	19	VIII
1390+; r. by 1415?; r. by 1495	73	73	67	—	—	—	—
26 Oct. 1412 (1492?)	74	74	68	—	—	—	—

* The entry is duplicated in the MS.

Date	*SA*	SP	JP	OP	C	M	A
28 June 1494	75	75	69	—	—	—	—
24 April 1415	76	76	70	—	—	—	—
8 Sept. 1502+	77	(77)	(164)	—	—	—	—
8 Aug. 1506	78	(78)	(161)	—	—	—	—
by 1345	79	79	71	29	29	—	—
12 Oct. 1467	80	80	(72)	—	—	—	—
1500+	81	(81)	(178)	—	—	—	—
saec. xiv*ex*–xv*in*	82	(82)	(174)	(138)	—	—	—
1415+; by 1495	83	(83)	(180)	—	—	—	—
1500+	84	84	(179)	—	—	—	—
3 July 1505	85	(85)	(177)	—	—	—	—
-1300?; ?1304+; by 1390; r. by 1495; r. 1500+	86	86	(188)	83	83	—	—
by 1485–6? by 1488	87	87	(176)	—	—	—	—
by 1500	88	88	(175)	—	—	—	—
6 June 1466	89	89	(189)	—	—	—	—
-1300?; by 1390	90	90	73	59	59	—	—
-1300?; by 1390	91	91	74	60	60	—	—
-1300?; by 1390	92	92	75	61	61	—	—
-1300?; by 1390	93	93	76	62	62	—	—
-1300?; by 1390	94	94	77	64	63	—	—
-1300?; by 1390	95	95	78	63	64	—	—
-1300?; by 1390	96	96	79	65	65	—	—
-1300?; by 1390	97	97	80	66	66	—	—
-1300?; by 1390	98	98	81	67	67	—	—
?1335+; by 1390	99	99	82	68	68	—	—
-1300?; by 1390	100	100	83	69	69	—	—
-1300?; by 1390	101	101	84	70	70	—	—
1309+; by 1363	102	102	85	71	71	—	—
by 1390; r. 1500+	103	103	86	72	72	—	—
c. 1330–90	104	104	87	73	73	—	—
by 1390	105	105	88	74	74	—	—
1274+; by 1390	106	106	89	75	75	—	—
-1300?; r. by 1365; r. by 1390	107	107	90	76	76	—	—
-1300?; r. by 1365; r. by 1390	108	108	91	77	77	—	—
by 1390	109	109	92	78	78	—	—
by 1495	110	110	93	(142)	—	—	—
?1360+; by 1390	111	111	94	79	79	—	—
-1300?; by 1390	112	112	95	80	80	—	—
by 1390	113	113	96	81	81	—	—
(i) 1291?; (ii) *c.* 1265?; by 1390	114	114	97	82	82	—	—

Date	*SA*	SP	JP	OP	C	M	A
18 Feb. 1457+; by 1495	115	115	98	—	—	—	—
-22 June 1456?; by 1466	116	116	99	—	—	—	—
c. 1390–1400	117	117	100	—	—	—	—
c. 1390–1400	118	118	101	—	—	—	—
-1300?; by 1390	119	119	102	84	84	—	—
-1300?; by 1390	120	120	103	85	85	—	—
-1300?; by 1390	121	121	104	86	86	—	—
-1300?; by 1390	122	122	105	87	87	—	—
1467–8	123	123	106	—	—	—	—
c. 1255–65; by 1300; r. by 1365; r. by 1390	124	124	107	88	88	—	—
c. 1400?; by 1495	125	125	108*	(139)	—	—	—
-1300?; by 1390	126	126	109	89	89	—	—
by 1250; r. by 1300	—	—	—	—	—	—	II. i
(i) -1300?; by 1363; (ii) 1305–14	127	127	110	90	90	—	—
by 1390	128	128	111	91	91	—	—
-1300?; by 1390	129	129	112	92	92	—	—
-1300?; by 1330	130	130	113	93	93	—	—
by 1390	131	131	114	94	94	—	—
-1300?; by 1390	132	132	115	95	95	—	—
by 1330	133	133	116	96	96	—	—
(i) by 1250; r. by 1300?; (ii) by 1300; (iii) ?1325+; (iv) *c.* 1265?; by 1390	134	134	117	97	97	—	—
by 1495	135	135	118	—	—	—	—
c. 1500	136	136	119	—	—	—	—
by 1390	137	137	120	52	52	—	—
by 1390	138	138	121	53	53	—	—
-1300?; by 1390; abrogated by 1500	—	—	—	54	54	—	—
by 1390	139	139	122	55	55	—	—
-1300?; by 1390; r. by 1488; r. *c.* 1500–10	140	140	123	56	56	—	—
-1300?; by 1390	141	141	124	57	57	—	—
-1300?; by 1390	142	142	125	58	58	—	—
by 1390	143	143	126	98	98	—	—
(i) ?1306+; by 1330;	144	144	127	99	99	—	—
(ii) by 1250; r. by 1330	144	144	127	99	99	—	II. ii–iii
-1330?; by 1390	145	145	128	100	100	—	—
by 1365; r. by 1390?	146	146	129	101	101	—	—

* Part II of the MS begins with this statute.

Date	*SA*	SP	JP	OP	C	M	A
(i) by 1250; (ii) 1304+; (iii) by 1292; (iv) by 1390	147	147	130	102	102–3	—	V
by 1390	148	148	131	103	104	—	—
1290–1; r. by 1330	149	149	132	104	105	—	—
by 1250; r. by 1309; r. by 1390	150	150	133	105	106	—	III
by 1250; r. by 1390	151	151	134	106	107	—	II. v–viii
-1330?; by 1390	152	152	135	107	108	—	—
by 1390	153	153	136	108	109	—	—
by 1390; r. 7 May 1457; r. 1471?	154	154	137	109	110	—	—
by 1390	155	155	138	110	111	—	—
by 1390	156	156	139	111	112	—	—
by 1390	157	157	140	112	113	—	—
by 1390	158	158	141	113	114	—	—
by 1390	159	159	142	114	115	—	—
by 1390	160	160	143	115	116	—	—
by 1390	161	161	144	116	117	—	—
1304+; by 1390	162	162	145	117	118	—	—
4 July 1359; r. *c.* 1400	163	163	146	118	119	—	—
1304+; by 1365; r. 1365–90?	164	164	147	119	120	—	—
by 1495	165	165	148	—	—	—	—
by 1306	166	166	149	120	121	—	—
17 April 1304; r. 17 June 1306	167	167	150	121	122	—	—
22 Nov. 1303; r. 17 June 1306; r. *c.* 1325–90	168	168	151	122	123	—	—
?1306+; by 1390	169	169	152 =	123*	124	—	—
c. 1423–8	170	170	(181) =	(140)	—	—	—
4 Dec. 1466	171	171	(168)	—	—	—	—
by 1390	172	172	153 =	124	125	—	—
by 1390	173	173	154 =	125	126	—	—
(i) ?1290+; by 1380;	174	174	155 =	126	127	—	—
(ii) 1396+; by 1495	174	174	(173)	—	—	—	—
c. 1415–22	175	175	(169)	—	—	—	—
24 May 1414	176	176	(170)	—	—	—	—
1471–2	177	177	(171)	—	—	—	—
by 1250; r. 1272+; r. 1304+; r. 1415/22+	178	178	156 =	127	128	—	XIII. ii–iii
by 1495	179	179	(172)	—	—	—	—
(i) 1291–1355;	180	180	157 =	128	129	—	—
(ii) *c.* 1421–95	180	180	(190)	—	—	—	—

* Old Proctor 123–37 constitute 152–60 of Junior Proctor.

Appendix II

Date	*SA*	SP	JP	OP	C	M	A
c. 1300–51; r. 1489	181	181	158	= 129–34	130–5	—	—
6 Nov. 1480	182	182	(182)	—	—	—	—
(i) 2 June 1489;	183	183	(183)	—	—	—	—
(ii) 25 Feb. 1345	183	183	(183)	135	136	—	—
20 June 1398	184	184	159	= 136*	—	—	—
1398–1400	185	185	160	= (137)	—	—	—
13 May 1475	186	186	(184)	—	—	—	—
1500+	187	(187)	(185)	—	—	—	—
1500+	188	(188)	(186)	—	—	—	—

* Numbered '137' in the MS in error.

Appendix III

ANGELICA MS 401—A CAMBRIDGE GRAMMARIAN'S BOOK

The contents of this manuscript have been described in a general way on pp. 12–14 above. It is hoped that the following detailed table of incipits and explicits will lead to the identification of the anonymous treatises and pieces, some of which may well have been local in origin, and help to illustrate the interests of a Cambridge grammarian of the first half of the thirteenth century.

1 (fos. $1^{r\,a}$–$4^{v\,b}$). [*Aurea expositio hymnorum.*][1] The text begins imperfectly. *Incipit*: '[Liber iste dicitur liber hymnorum. Hymnus dicitur laus dei cum cantico]...et iam erat .xxx^ta^. annorum cum est deditus passioni. *luxtra sex* et cetera. ablatiui et accusatiui. hic possunt legi.'[2] *Explicit*: 'illi translati in requiem. gaudium eternum. Gloria et honor. deo usquequo altissimo', followed by the colophon:

> 'Laus tibi sit christe quoniam labor explicit iste
> Explicit iste liber. sit scriptor termine liber.'

2 (fos. $5^{r\,a}$–$14^{v\,b}$). [*Speculum ecclesiae.*] *In.*: [Prologue] 'De sacramentis ecclesiasticis ut tractarem.' [Text]: 'Ecclesia igitur in qua populus conuenit.' *Ex.*: 'inuenit amans quam disputas.' Printed among the works of Hugh of St Victor (*PL*, clxxvii. 335–80).[3]

3 (fos. $14^{v\,b}$–$17^{r\,b}$). Paradigms of proper nouns and verbs, taken from Lucan (9, 155) and other classical authors. *In.*: 'Amasis. Lucanus. non michi paramidum tumulis auulsus amasis.' *Ex.*: 'una tamen sumpta. ut stirps.'

[1] I have used the text printed by Antoine Caillaut at Paris and dated 8 March 1493. The B.M. copy, IA. 39485, is described in *Catalogue of books printed in the XVth century now in the British Museum*, viii (London, 1949), 51–2. The work is said to have been compiled by 'quidam vir prudens nomine hylarius'. He was possibly the disciple of Abelard. Several MSS of the exposition are extant. Cf. Dublin, Trinity College, 270 (D. 4. 9), fos. 185^r–192^r, 204^v–212^v; Escorial lat. I. iii. 7, fos. $89^{r\,a}$–$109^{r\,a}$. Both MSS end differently, in neither case as in Caillaut's edition of 1493.

[2] Cf. Caillaut's edition, *Sig.* D. $iii^{v\,b}$. I have refrained from drawing attention in this list of the contents of the MS to scribal errors, if they can be called such, just as I have also rigidly adhered to the punctuation and use or non-use of capitals in the MS. My readings, it should be noted, do not always correspond with Narducci's; his description of the contents is sometimes fuller than mine.

[3] The authorship remains doubtful, but Hugh of St Victor may have had some connection with the work. Cf. R. Baron, 'Hugues de Saint-Victor: contribution à un nouvel examen de son œuvre', *Traditio*, xv (1959), 268–9. I have not been able to see this writer's more recent study, *Études sur Hugues de Saint-Victor* (Paris, 1963).

4 (fos. $17^{v\,a}$–$19^{r\,b}$). *Quid sit penitencia et in quibus consistat. et. quis fructus eius. In.*: 'Ad maiorem ⟨euidenciam⟩ eorum que dicenda sunt.' *Ex.*: 'quod in hiis uersibus subsequentibus potes edoceri.'[1] Eleven verses follow beginning with

'Sit tibi potus aqua. cibus arridus. aspera uestis'

and ending with

'Quam te perpetuis addicat iudicis ira.'[2]

On fo. $18^{v\,b}$ 'Qualiter debeat esse confessor et quomodo suum debet excercere officium' is written and underlined in red as if introducing a separate work.

5 (fos. $19^{v\,a}$–$23^{r\,b}$). Exposition of the seven penitential psalms. *In.*: 'Domine ne in furore tuo et cetera [Ps. VI]. Istius psalmi titulus talis est.' *Ex.*: 'quam demones. perdes eandem. quia ego seruus tuus Sum.'

6 (fos. $23^{r\,b}$–$24^{v\,b}$). Treatise on syntax. *In.*: 'De Regimine partium dicturi. Videamus quid sit regimen.' *Ex.*: 'Nullum participium participaliter retentum [?] potest comparari.'

7 (fos. $25^{r\,a}$–$32^{r\,a}$). *Incipiunt prouerbia actorum. primum de claudiano magno. In.*: 'Iam non ad culmina rervm. Iniustos creuisse queror.'[3] *Ex.*: 'vt plus leteris fletus memor esse teneris.' These proverbs are derived from the classics, but Vitalis of Blois is also quoted.

8 (fo. $32^{r\,a}$). *Versus. de decem uiciis et totidem. uirtutibus. In.*: 'Dilacerare semper amantem pessima fraus.'[4] *Ex.*: 'Sepius orans. deteriores. surgere thus [?] est.'

9 (fos. $32^{r\,a}$–$34^{r\,b}$). *Incipiunt capitula numero ⟨lx⟩ de genere lapidum. Incipit liber Marbodi. In.*: 'Euax rex arabum legitur scripsisse neroni.'[5] *Ex.*: 'propter quod lapidum titulo liber iste notatur. Explicit liber iste.' The *Liber lapidum* is printed in *PL*, clxxi. 1737–70 among the works of Marbod, bishop of Rennes (1096–1123). The final three verses are omitted in the Angelica as in other manuscripts.

10 (fos. $34^{r\,b}$–$34^{v\,a}$). Letter of Innocent III to Philip Augustus. *In.*: 'Innocentius et cetera. illustrissimo Regi francorum Philippo. licet dextra domini.' *Ex.*: 'debitum exequamur. Datum Rome apud sanctum PetRum. xiij. Kl. Iunij. pontificatus anno. primo.' Listed by Potthast, *Regesta pontificum romanorum*, i (Berlin, 1873), 20, no. 199 under the date 17 May 1198.[6] The text (Ep. CLXXI) is printed in *PL*, ccxiv. 148–50.

1 There is another MS of this text in Bibl. Nat. lat. 3238F, fos. 86^{r}–87^{v} (saec. xiii), which is cited by A. Teetaert, O.F.M.Cap., 'Quelques "summae de paenitentia" anonymes dans la Bibliothèque Nationale de Paris', *Miscellanea Giovanni Mercati*, ii (Studi e Testi, 122 [1946]), 339. He misread 'de' for 'te' and 'sententia' for 'ira' in the final verse at the end of the treatise. Cf. *Bibl. Nat. Catalogue général des manuscrits latins*, iv (Paris, 1958), 412–13.

2 Cf. H. Walther, *Initia carminum ac versuum medii aevi posterioris latinorum* (Carmina medii aevi posterioris latina, i [Göttingen, 1959], no. 18341).

3 Claudian, 3, 21. Cf. Walther, *Proverbia sententiaeque latinitatis medii aevi* (Carmina, II, pt ii [*ibid.* 1964]), no. 13043.

4 *Om.* Walther, *Initia* and *Proverbia*. The first word of the incipit is smudged in the MS, but 'Dilacerare' seems to be the correct reading. Narducci, *Catalogus*, p. 194, has 'Diva certare'.

5 Walther, *Initia*, no. 5968.

6 This is the correct date.

11 (fos. $34^{v\,a}$–$42^{r\,a}$). Matthew of Vendôme, *Ars versificatoria.*[1] *In.*: [Prologue] 'Spiritus inuidie cesset non mordeat hostis.[2] Introductiuum uindocinensis opvs. ⟨N⟩e meas uiderer magnificare fimbrias.' [Text]: 'et quia ad versuum introduccionem'. *Ex.*: 'quicquid uenustum hic obrepserit. degnatus est delegare. Explicit.' The text of two letters which are not part of the treatise is inserted on fo. $38^{v\,a–v\,b}$: (i) R. bishop-elect of Chartres to his master G. Archdeacon of Tours, 'Licet cause quas';[3] (ii) G. Archdeacon of Tours to R., 'Nobis auctoritate apostolica'. Reginald de Bar was bishop of Chartres 1182–1217. His correspondent may have been Gaufridus, who was archdeacon of Tours by 1166.[4]

12 (fos. $42^{r\,a}$–$49^{r\,a}$). Bernardus Silvestris, *De mundi universitate.*[5] *In.*: [Prefatory letter to Thierry of Chartres] 'Terrico ueris sententiarum'. [Prologue or *breviarium*]: 'In huius operis primo libro qui megacosmus id est maior mundus uocatur.' [Text]: 'Congeries infomis adhuc cum silua cedet.' *Ex.*: 'ductoresque pedes omnificansque manus. Explicit philosophia benardi siluestris.' Book I occupies fos. $42^{r\,a}$–$45^{r\,a}$; Book II, fos. $45^{r\,a}$–$49^{r\,a}$.

13 (fos. $49^{r\,a}$–$51^{r\,b}$). Hildebert of Lavardin, *De concordia veteris et novi sacrificii.*[6] *Tit.*: 'Incipit tractatus hildeberti cenonensis episcopi de concordia ueteris et noui sacrificij.' *In.*: 'Scribere proposui quo mistica sacra priorum.' *Ex.*: 'Fit cibus caro panis imago manet.' Two verses follow immediately in the same hand:

'Anno milleno decento minus uno
Ierusalem capitur. iulij cum dicitur idus.'[7]

This is followed by a passage without author's name or title:

'Qualiter ordinibus ornetur curia celi...vita pudica. fides integra. sacer amor' (fo. $51^{r\,b–r\,c}$).

14 (fos. $51^{r\,c}$–$52^{v\,a}$). *Incipiunt uersus misse.* There are five pieces; the first three are by Hildebert: (i) 'Illud supplicium quod presbiter induit ante' (cf. Walther, *Initia*, no. 8736); (ii) 'Nuper eram locuplex' (*ibid.* no. 12488); (iii) 'Aduentum christi patriarchus

[1] *Ed.* E. Faral, *Les arts poétiques du XIIe et du XIIIe siècle* (Paris, 1924), pp. 109–93. There is no title in the MS but a late hand added in the margin of fo. 34^{v} 'Poetice descriptiones'.

[2] Walther, *Initia*, no. 18525.

[3] On fo. $38^{v\,a}$ 'E' is written in error for 'R'. The mistake is noted in the margin and is not repeated.

[4] Cf. J. Maan, *Sancta et metropolitana ecclesia Turonensis* (Tours, 1667), p. 258, where '1266' should read '1166'. An earlier Gaufridus was archdeacon in 1138. The printed list is obviously very incomplete, Stephanus, who held office in 1218, immediately following the later Gaufridus.

[5] *Ed.* C. S. Barach and J. Wrobel, *Bernardi Silvestris de mundi universitate libri duo sive megacosmus et microcosmus* (Bibliotheca philosophorum mediae aetatis, i [Innsbruck, 1876]).

[6] Printed in *PL*, clxxi. 1177–94. Cf. Walther, *Initia*, no. 17396. Hildebert was bishop of Le Mans 1096–1125 before his translation to Tours.

[7] Variants of the first verse—'decento' is obviously wrong (*lege* 'ducento' or 'centeno')—are noted in Walther, *Initia*, nos. 1163–4, 1182–6.

premonuisse' (*ibid.* no. 555); (iv) 'Si quis amat mundum' (*ibid.* no. 17910);[1] and lastly a piece from Peter of Blois, 'Felix ille locus' (*ibid.* no. 6332).[2]

15 (fos. $52^{v\,a}$–$53^{v\,c}$). Tract on penance, fasting, confession and perseverance. *In.*: 'Irriguum superius accipit anima.' *Ex.*: 'Nichil prodest carnis uirginitas si mente quis nupserit.' The text is little more than a farrago of excerpts from the Fathers; it probably ends imperfectly.[3]

16 (fos. $54^{r\,a}$–$55^{v\,b}$). 'Constituciones V⟨niuersitatis Cantebrigiensi⟩s.' *Rubr.*: 'De eleccione Cancelarii atque ipsius potestate.' *In.*: 'Quoniam difficile est uniuersitatem consentire.' *Ex.*: 'non conueniant supradicti'. A much larger and later English hand (saec. xv) has added 'Ihesus est amor meus'.

1 The Angelica MS is the only source cited by Walther for this piece.
2 Cf. 'Versus de commendatione vini' in *Petri Blesensis...opera omnia*, ed. J. A. Giles, iv (London, 1847), 372–3.
3 The treatise is not listed by M. W. Bloomfield, 'A preliminary list of incipits of Latin works on the virtues and vices, mainly of the thirteenth, fourteenth and fifteenth centuries', *Traditio*, xi (1955), 259–379.

BIBLIOGRAPHY

The present bibliography is strictly limited to the archival material, manuscripts, printed sources and writings cited in this book. The fact that certain standard works and studies of outstanding value are not included does not mean that they have not been consulted. Useful Cambridge bibliographies will be found in Rashdall, *Universities*, iii. 274–6, 295–323 (colleges); *BRUC*, pp. xiii–xxvi (mainly manuscript sources); Peek and Hall, *Archives*, pp. 78–86. For the medieval universities generally cf. Rashdall, *op. cit.* vols. i–iii; Stelling-Michaud (both works); and Hargreaves-Mawdsley (good for printed works; not altogether reliable as regards manuscript sources).

I. ARCHIVAL AND MANUSCRIPT SOURCES[1]

Assisi, Italy

Biblioteca Comunale MS 158, saec. xiii*ex* (*c.* 1280–90). Theological notes and *questiones* from Cambridge *c.* 1280 (fos. 1–27, 31–55, 68–83). Cf. Pelster in Little and Pelster, *Oxford theology* (*q.v.*), pp. 105–9, 112–14.

Cambridge

University Archives

(*i*) *Documents* (*originals*)

No. 1 Letters patent ordering houses to be taxed every five years by two masters and two burgesses, 7 Feb. 1266.

2 Letters patent granting the university privileges *re* the keeping of the peace, the assize of food and drink and the custody of scholars, 22 Feb. 1268.

3 Concord effected by the Lord Edward between the town and the university, 1270.

4 Decree of the university authorizing the rectors to convoke the regents in default of the chancellor or vice-chancellor, 17 March 1276. *Ed.* Ullmann in *Historical Journal*, i. 181–2.

5 Ordinance of the bishop of Ely, Hugh Balsham, concerning the respective jurisdictions of the archdeacon of Ely and the chancellor of the university, 6 Oct. 1276 (two copies).

[1] Some of the documents and MSS listed in this section have been printed. They are included here because it was found necessary to check and sometimes to quote from the originals. The descriptions have had to be kept as short as possible and are almost entirely confined to items which figure in this book.

6 Decree of William of Louth, bishop of Ely, ratifying an agreement between the university and mag. Ralph de Leycestria on a statutory ruling about precedence, 19 April 1291.

9 Agreement between the prior of Barnwell, Simon de Asceles, and the university concerning mag. Henry de Wysethe's tenancy of a house owned by the priory, 23 July 1293.

10 Decree of mag. Guy de Coventre, official of Ely diocese, terminating a dispute over constitutional issues between the chancellor, mag. Henry de Boyton, and the regents, 8 April 1294.

16 Agreement between the university and Nicholas le Barber concerning his property known as the *domus scolarum*, 23 July 1309. *Ed.* Stokes in *CASP*, xiii, n.s. vii. 183–4.

20 Letters patent on the selection of juries and the place of imprisonment in cases involving townspeople and scholars, 3 June 1317.

32 Declaration by Simon Montacute, bishop of Ely, in respect of the chancellor's jurisdiction and appeals, 17 March 1342 (two copies).

36 Confirmation of no. 32 by Thomas de Lisle, bishop of Ely, 2 August 1347.

82** Rolls (including drafts) of petitions for papal benefices on behalf of graduates, *c.* 1370–90.

108 Barnwell process, 10 Oct. 1430.

115 Bulls (spurious) of Honorius I and Sergius I, saec. xv (two copies).

136 Bequest of Dr Thomas Barowe, 21 Jan. 1495.

(*ii*) *Statute-Books*

'Junior Proctor's Book' (*Liber procuratoris junioris*), saec. xv*ex*–xvi*ex*. The text of the *statuta antiqua* (fos. 56^{r}–110^{v}, 136^{v}–137^{r}, 138^{r}–139^{r}, 150^{r-v}), with the exception of the statutes on fos. 107^{r}–110^{v}, was executed *c.* 1494–6 and *c.* 1510–30.

'Old Proctor's Book' (*Liber procuratoris antiquus*, sometimes referred to as 'Frag. Vet.' or 'Fragment. Lib. MS in Archiv. Acad.'), saec. xiv*ex*–xv*ex*. The text of the statutes (fos. 17^{r}–40^{v} (remainder in the Junior Proctor's Book, fos. 107^{r}–110^{v})) was written *c.* 1390–5/8.

Senior Proctor's Book (*Liber procuratoris senioris*), saec. xv*ex*–xvi*ex*. Contains the *textus receptus* of the *statuta antiqua*, which was the basis of the *editio princeps* (1785). The text (fos. 1^{r}–52^{v}) was executed *c.* 1496–1502 and finalized *c.* 1506. The book is a companion volume of the Junior Proctor's Book, which was completed from it.

(*iii*) *Registers*

'Black Parchment Book', saec. xv*ex*–xvi*ex*. Transcripts of charters and miscellaneous documents, including three 'ancient' statutes (pp.

97–8 = fos. 28^{v}–29^{r}). Compiled in the first place by mag. William Buckenham (died 1540).

Liber rerum memorabilium et litterarum ('Black Paper Book'), saec. xvi. The earliest extant letter book and formulary of the university. It also contains other material, viz., articles of complaint by the town against the university which date from 1532 (fos. 6^{r}–8^{v}) and graces (fo. 22^{r}). Commenced in Oct. 1548 (cf. fo. 1^{v}) by John Mere, bedell and registrary, and continued by Matthew Stokys, who wrote most of the book. The majority of the contents were printed by Lamb (*Collection of letters*, *q.v.*) from a copy in Corpus Christi College, Cambridge, MS 106.

'Markaunt's Book' (*Liber priuilegiorum et statutorum vniuersitatis Cantabriggie*), *c.* 1417–18. Not an official register, yet it is one of the most valuable sources in the archives. Executed for mag. Thomas Markaunt (*c.* 1382–1439), it contains the second oldest text of the statutes (fos. 45^{r}–49^{r} (E 7^{r}–11^{r})), which though unfinished dates from *c.* 1304–37. The book also has copies of documents (saec. xiii*ex*–xv*in*), some of which are not otherwise extant.

'Stokys's Book', saec. xvi. Put together *c.* 1574–8 by Matthew Stokys (*c.* 1514–91), bedell and registrary. It consists mainly of transcripts of charters and other records, including eleven *statuta antiqua* (fos. 29^{r}–34^{v}, 56^{r}–57^{v}). Two parts of the book are extracts from an earlier sixteenth-century (bedell's ?) book. The first is an invaluable roll of benefactors (fos. 24^{r} [*bis*]–28^{v}). The second part is an account of the procedure at university exercises (fos. 13^{v}–24^{r}, 47^{r}–52^{v}) which was printed in a rearranged form by Peacock, *Observations* (*q.v.*), from a transcript in B.M. Add. MS 5845 (Cole, 44).

(*iv*) *Manuscripts*

Robert Hare (*c.* 1515–1611), 'Priuilegia et alia rescripta vniuersitatem Cantebrigie concernentia', 2 vols (parchment), *c.* 1587. Presented by the author to the university together with a paper copy, also in 2 vols. The work is easily the most serviceable record of charters and documents, which are drawn from a variety of sources, pertaining to the history of the university.

'Statuta Antiqua', saec. xvii*ex*–xviii*in*. Transcript of the statutes (pp. 1–98) certified if not actually made by James Halman, registrary (1683–1701), and copied from the Junior Proctor's Book. The volume contains in addition a transcript of the Elizabethan statutes and some miscellaneous documents, the last being of 1725.

Bibliography

University Library

(*i*) *Manuscripts*

Add. 3471, saec. xiii*med/ex*. *Summa* 'Qui bene presunt presbiteri' (fos. 125$^{r\,a}$–169$^{v\,b}$) by mag. Richard de Leycestria *alias* Wethringsette, the first known chancellor of the university (by 1222).

Dd. 4. 35, saec. xv*in*. 'Articuli vniuersitatis Cantabrigie ad informandum dominum Regem de antiquis consuetudinibus eiusdem vniuersitatis' (fos. 74^{v}–78^{r} [*olim* 73^{v}–77^{r}]). *Ed.* Hardwick in *CASP*, i. 86–93. These articles relate to the 'vestment' controversy *c.* 1415, in which John Okham, B.C.L. was the leading figure.

Mm. 1. 35 (Baker, xxiv), saec. xvii*ex*–xviii*in*. Transcripts of statutes in the Old Proctor's Book made by Thomas Baker (1656–1740).

Mm. 4. 41, pt 2, saec. xiii*ex*–xiv*in*. *Statuta vniuersitatis Cantebrigiensis* (fo. 56$^{v\,a-v\,b}$). *Ed.* Bradshaw in *CASP*, ii. 280–1. This part of the MS has tracts by Joannes de Deo and Hugh of St Cher, and bulls of Boniface VIII.

Mm. 4. 46–7, saec. xviii*ex*. Transcript of the *statuta antiqua* from the Senior Proctor's Book made by Henry Hubbard, who was registrary in 1758–78.

Mm. 5. 53–4, *c.* 1783–5. Adam Wall's MS of the statutes, from which the *editio princeps* was directly made and printed in 1785. Vol. i comprises the *statuta antiqua* (pp. 1–132) and *statuta in ordinem non redacta* (*Docs*, i. 417–53), as well as the statutes of Edward VI, Elizabeth I (1559) and Cecil (1562). Vol. ii consists of the second Elizabethan code (1570) and college statutes. The pagination of the two volumes is continuous. Wall (1746–98) was a fellow of Christ's College and senior proctor (1778–9).

(*ii*) *Ely Diocesan Records*

D 2/1. *Registrum primum causarum consistorii episcopi Eliensis*, 1374–82.

G 1 (1), pt 1, Register of Simon Montacute, bishop of Ely, 1337–45; pt 2, Register of Thomas de Lisle, bishop, 1345–61.

G 1 (2). Register of Bishop Thomas Arundel, 1373–88.

G 2/6 ('Liber B'). Register of the cathedral priory, *c.* 1407–1515, mainly *c.* 1420–80.

G 3/27 ('Liber R'). 'Old Coucher Book', saec. xiv–xv. Survey of episcopal demesne manors, but has copies of miscellaneous documents (saec. xii–xv), including charters of Hugh of Northwold (1229–54) and Hugh Balsham (1256–86). Gonville and Caius College MS 489/485 is a companion vol.

G 3/28 ('Liber M'). Cartulary of the cathedral priory, *c.* 1290–1300. Has *inter alia* copies of charters from the time of Bishop Eustace (1197–1215) to Balsham's episcopate (pp. 160–203) which contain the names of many Cambridge *magistri*. The pagination of pp. 160–9 is duplicated.

Corpus Christi College MSS

118, saec. xvi. Transcripts of the ancient statutes: (i) fos. 2^r–36^r; (ii) pp. 35–173. The transcripts were probably made *c.* 1557–9.

232, saec. xv. Copy of Thomas Markaunt's will (4 Nov. 1439) (fos. 1^r–3^r) and list of books bequeathed by him to the college, with their prices. *Ed.* Halliwell (*q.v.*) and James, 'Catalogue of Thomas Markaunt's Library' (*q.v.*). The MS also contains a register (1439–1517) of the books borrowed by fellows of the college.

Gonville and Caius College MSS

170/91, saec. xvi. New Ely archdeacon's book. The item 'Taxatio domorum in villa Cant. pro scholar. inhabitand. per chartam d. H. Regis Quinti [del.; *recte* 'Tertii']' (fos. 211^r–214^v) is not a list of rents. It is merely a copy of documents in *Liber mem. ecc. de Bernewelle* concerning the dispute between Barnwell priory and mag. Ralph de Leycestria and the university in 1290–2.

249/277, *c.* 1464. Written by mag. John Harryson, author of a chronicle (1377–1469) on fos. 127^r–134^r which has been edited from this MS by J. J. Smith (cf. *s.v.* Harryson). The *cronica fundacionis destruccionis et renouacionis uniuersitatis* on fos. 191^r–193^r is only a copy of the *historiola* by Cantelow (*q.v.*).

385/605, saec. xiii*ex*. Writings of John of Garland, Alexander Neckam, Alexander de Villa Dei, Donatus, Remigius. The Neckam item has been printed from this MS by C. H. Haskins, 'A list of text-books from the close of the twelfth century', *Harvard studies in classical philology*, xx (1909), 75–94. The MS was used as a *matricula* or roll-book by a Cambridge regent master in arts.

465/572, saec. xiii*ex*. Works of the Old Logic. The MS, which is heavily glossed, is another example of a *matricula* but a much fuller one than MS 385.

466/573, saec. xiii*ex*. Works of the Old and New Logic. The front paste-down has the text of the statute *De modo audiendi textum Aristotelis* (saec. xv) printed above, p. 298. Formerly owned by mag. Henry de Langham, fellow of Michaelhouse (1324–32); given by mag. John Hall (died 1482) to St Mary Hostel.

593/453, saec. xiii*ex*. Priscian, Bernardus Silvestris and other grammarians. On fo. 127^v there is an apparently unpublished *questio* ascribed to mag. J. de Grimesbi (of Cambridge?), *De compositione oculi simul et de materia et de natura* ('Primo videndum est quid sit visus...

specierum ab extrinseco aduenientium'). The MS was also used as a *matricula*.

604/339, saec. xviii. Collection of Elizabethan statutes and charters made by Bartholomew Wortley (fellow, 1679–1706) in 1731 for the use of the master and scholars of the college. There is a note on fo. 194^{r} on the precincts of the university.

706/692, pt 2, saec. xiv*ex* (*c*. 1385–95). Earliest extant MS of the *statuta antiqua* (fos. $1^{r\,a}$–$21^{v\,b}$; table on fos. $22^{v\,a}$–$23^{v\,b}$). 'Iste liber pertinet collegio de Gvnvile' (fo. 24^{v}).

Pembroke College Treasury

Registrum Cγ, pt 2, *c*. 1625–34. 'Excerpta E Regist: Eliens: &C. Wrenn'. Notes made by Matthew Wren (died 1667) from Markaunt's Book (which he recovered for the university archives), John Caius's history, Ely registers and the proctor's books. On pp. 117–22 'E rotulis quibusdam e pergameno, in archivis Academiae, in capsula notata P. Sunt autem supplicationes Academiae factae D. Papae'. The originals of these rolls have now been restored to the university archives (CUA, doc. no 82** listed above). CUL MS Mm. 1. 52 (Baker, xli) was copied from this MS.

Peterhouse Muniments

'Cista Communis', doc. no. 4. Original deed of 26 May 1291 whereby the chancellor, mag. Geoffrey de Pakenham, and the regent masters made the observance of Hugh Balsham's obit binding under statute. The remains of the oldest extant seal of the university are attached.

Registrum vetus, saec. xv. Cartulary of the college. There is a list of books on pp. 1–22 and on pp. 27–8 a copy of an inspeximus of the deed, dated 5 Oct. 1283, whereby St John's Hospital assented to the impropriation of St Peter's church and the two adjacent hostels, etc., to the scholars whom Balsham had placed in the hospital in 1280.

St John's College Muniments

Drawer 3, doc. no. 58. Original (parchment) of the decree issued by the chancellor, mag. Hugh de Hotton, and regent masters in 1246 exempting the two houses or hostels owned by St John's Hospital from taxation. Oldest extant deed of the university; printed on p. 55 above.

'Cartulary of St John's Hospital', saec. xiii*ex*–xv*in*. Fos. 8^{r}–9^{v} (saec. xiii*ex*), 24^{r}, 81^{v}–88^{r} (saec. xiv*in*), are rentals. Two folios bound in at the front and back of the volume appear to contain part of a tract on memory; written in large script (saec. xiii), the folios are well glossed.

'Cartulary of St John's College', saec. xvi*in*. On pp. 205–22 are saec. xiii–xiv copies of documents pertaining to the hospital.

Cashel, Ireland

Church of Ireland Diocesan Library MS (formerly 'K 3 24'), saec. xvii*ex*. Transcripts of Cambridge statutes (1541–1629), including seven excerpts from the ancient statutes (p. 48). From a copy made by 'J.B.' (John Buck, bedell), 12 Dec. 1665. Possibly owned by Edward Jex of Norfolk, B.A. (1659–60).

Douai, France

Bibliothèque Municipale MS 752, saec. xiii. *Tractatus magistri Nicholai* [Breckendale?] *de gramatica et omni genere constructionum* ('Ad lucem subsequentium diversis acceptionibus...construitur cum illo; non transitive' (fos. 197–209).

Dublin, Ireland

Trinity College MS 270 (D. 4. 9), saec. xiii*ex*. *Aurea expositio hymnorum* (fos. 185^{r}–192^{r}, 204^{v}–212^{v}), Nicholas de Breckendale, *Deponentiale* (fos. 195^{r}–203^{v}), as well as the great medieval grammarians. An inscription 'Iste liber constat tomas (*sic*) honeton' occurs on fo. 9^{v} (fos. 1–13 are separate in an envelope).

Ely

(see *s.v.* Cambridge University Library)

El Escorial, Spain

Real Biblioteca lat. MS I. iii. 7, saec. xiii*ex*. *Aurea expositio hymnorum* (fos. $89^{r\,a}$–$109^{r\,a}$). Also has Leycestria *alias* Wethringsette, *Summa* (cf. CUL Add. 3471 *supra*), Grosseteste's statutes and a copy of a letter of presentation to a benefice from the prior and convent of N. to their bishop 'J. dei gratia Eliensis episcopi' (John of Kirkby, 1286–90?).

London

British Museum MSS

Add. 9822, saec. xiv–xv. Ely cathedral priory register (formerly 'Liber A'). Includes a section entitled 'priuilegia Episcopalia' (fos. 91^{r}–93^{r} [*olim* 104^{r}–106^{r}]). It consists of copies of Balsham's letter of 19 Dec. 1264 *re* appeals from the chancellor's court and his ordinance of

6 Oct. 1276 (cf. CUA, doc. no. 5 *supra*); the award made by Guy de Coventre, official of William of Louth, 8 April 1294 (*ibid.* doc. no. 10); and the oldest form of *SA* 5 (*Docs*, i. 310). In the earlier part of the register there is a copy of the concord effected between Archbishop Arundel and the archdeacon of Ely, John Welborne, concerning their respective rights in the Isle of Ely; it upholds the archdeacon's right to appoint the headmaster of the grammar schools in Cambridge (fos. 37^{r}–42^{v}=53^{r}–58^{v}).

Add. 41612, saec. xiii*ex*–xiv. Register of Ely cathedral priory. Has copies of charters *c.* 1273–1366 which record the names of Cambridge *magistri* and transcripts of the deeds of foundation and endowment of the saec. xiv halls and colleges except Pembroke.

Cotton Faustina C III, saec. xvi*ex*. Cambridge *collectanea* (Hare's notebook?). Bound in is an original letter, dated 5 Dec. [1417], from the university to the king's council (fo. 357^{r}).

Harl. 4116, saec. xvii*ex*. Transcripts of Cambridge documents, mostly saec. xvi*ex*–xvii*ex*, and miscellaneous notes, including formularies. There is a list of mayors and chancellors from the time of Henry VII and a list of hostels which are said to have existed by 1280 (fos. 43^{v}–44^{v} [*olim* 37^{v}–38^{v}]). The MS was purchased by Baker from the son of Alderman Samuel Newton, auditor of Trinity College (1668–1717).

Harl. 4967, pt 2, saec. xiii*ex*. Hymns, verses and grammatical works, of which the most prominent is Breckendale's *Deponentiale* (fos. 104^{r}–113^{r}; there is an incomplete text on fos. 149^{v}–150^{r}). On fos. 169^{r}–185^{v} a text of the *Centones virgiliani* occurs.

Harl. 7031 (Baker, iv), saec. xvii*ex*–xviii*in*. Copy of *SA* 23 (*Docs*, i. 319) on fo. 14^{r}.

Harl. 7032 (Baker, v), saec. xvii*ex*–xviii*in*. Transcript of the *statuta antiqua* (fos. 5^{r}–59^{r} [*olim* pp. 1–109]) made from the Junior Proctor's Book and authenticated by James Halman, registrary (1683–1701). The MS has copies also of other documents, including Montacute's statutes (1344) for Peterhouse (fos. 96^{r}–109^{v}=pp. 187–214).

Harl. 7037 (Baker, x), saec. xvii*ex*–xviii*in*. Excerpts from the ancient statutes (pp. 95–100) from a copy by John Cosin, Vice-chancellor (1639–40), and *inter alia* three lists of chancellors (pp. 131–46).

Harl. 7040 (Baker, xiii), saec. xvii*ex*–xviii*in*. Copy of Hare's *Privilegia* as far as 1535, and list of books presented by him to Trinity Hall in 1604 (pp. 227–9). One of the books was a *Liber Statutorum universitatis Bononiensis*.

Royal 12 D. xi, saec. xiv*in*. Collection of Oxford statutes and miscellaneous documents, mostly printed.

Public Record Office

(*i*) *Chancery*

C 85/66. Significations of excommunications by the bishops of Ely, 1247–85: 25 documents.

C 85/67. Significations from the same, 1287–1314: 24 documents.

C 85/209. File of significations from the university, 1384–1530.

(*ii*) *Justices Itinerant*

J.I. 1/82. Assize roll Cambridgeshire, 1260. The earliest of its kind extant for Cambs. The section containing the records of the sessions held at Cambridge has been printed by W. M. Palmer, *Assizes held at Cambridge A.D. 1260* (Linton, 1930).

J.I. 1/95. Assize roll Cambridgeshire, 1298–9.

J.I. 1/1191. Assize roll Cambridgeshire 1259–65, and other counties 1259–61.

S.C. 1/3/2. Letter from the chancellor of the university, mag. Richard de Gedeneye, and the regent masters to Henry III in reply to a report that they refused to pay tallage for the repair of the king's mill in Cambridge. The letter is undated and the seal is missing. Printed by Shirley, *Royal and other historical letters* (*q.v.*), ii. 165–6, who dates it 1260. A more probable date is 1267.

Somerset House

Prerogative Court of Canterbury. *Registrum Rous.* Wills 1384–*c.* 1454. Will of mag. John de Donewich, chancellor of the university 1371–2, 1374–5. Died 1392. Will dated 6 April; proved 27 Sept. (6 Rous).

Nancy, France

Bibliothèque Municipale MS 1059, saec. xvii*ex.* Catalogue of the library of Luke Holsten (1596–1661).

Oxford

Bodleian Library

(*i*) *University Archives*

Registrum A, saec. xiv*in.* Chancellor's register of the statutes; the oldest extant. Statutes ed. in *SAUO*.

Registrum B, *c.* 1477–8/90. Senior Proctor's Book (*Liber procuratoris senioris*). Statutes ed. *ibid.*

Registrum C, A.D. 1407. Junior Proctor's Book (*Liber procuratoris junioris*). Statutes ed. *ibid.*

Registrum D. See MS Bodl. 337.

(ii) Manuscripts

Bodl. 337 (SC 2874), by 1380. Register (*Registrum D*) of the university statutes. *Ed.* in *SAUO*.

E mus. 96 (SC 3582), saec. xiii*ex*. Huguccio; Hildebert of Lavardin; grammatical works; and earliest collection of the statutes (*c.* 1275) (pp. 480 a, 481), ed. in *SAUO*, 641–2. The MS was possibly owned by mag. Robert de la Felde (cf. p. 480 b).

lat. misc. d. 80, pt C, saec. xiii*med*. Bernardus Silvestris, *De mundi universitate* (fos. 46 r–51 v).

Laud Misc. 647 (SC 1595). *Liber* or *Historia Eliensis*. In Book III (fo. 176 r a) there is mention of Balsham's benefactions to Peterhouse. There is a transcript by Sir Simonds d'Ewes (1602–50) in B.M. Harl. 258, fo. 86 v. He refers to the Laudian MS as 'L. 58'. The reference should be 'L. 69', as Dr Hunt informs me.

Paris, France

Bibliothèque Nationale MSS

lat. 3238 F, saec. xiii*ex*. *Summa de penitencia* ('Ad maiorem evidentiam... addicat iudicis ira') (fos. 86 r–87 v).

lat. 4223 A, saec. xiv–xv*in*. Statutes of Orléans University, 1306–67. The MS (67 pp., parchment) probably formed part of a *Liber rectorum*.

Rome, Italy

Biblioteca Angelica MSS

70 (A. 7. 9), saec. xiii*ex*. Augustine. Inscription: 'Di Mons.re Ill.mo Sirleto' (Cardinal Guglielmo Sirleto, 1514–85).

116 (B. 3. 4), saec. xiii*ex*. Augustine. Old press-mark '$\overline{41}$.'. Formerly owned by Sirleto.

162 (B. 6. 15), saec. ix*ex*–x*in*. Augustine. From Sirleto's library.

195 (B. 7. 24), saec. xviii*in*. List of books received from the library of Cardinal Enrico Noris (1631–1704) in 1704 (fos. 275 r–288 v).

401 (D. 3. 7), *c.* 1250–70. *Constituciones Vniuersitatis Cantebrigiensis* (fos. 54 r a–55 v b). For a description of the MS and its history see above, pp. 8–22. The contents are listed on pp. 340–3.

1078 (S. 1. 2), saec. xviii*in*. 'Index Manuscriptorum Bibliothecae Angelicae auctorum et materiarum ordine alphabetico dispositus.' Compiled by fr. Basile Rassegnier, O.S.A., librarian *c.* 1704–34.

1084 (S. 1. 8), saec. xiii*ex*. Augustine. Written in England and almost certainly owned by fr. John de Clare, O.S.A., D.Th. Cambridge 1304. Acquired by Cardinal Marcello Cervini (Pope Marcellus II, 1555) in Rome *c.* 1538–45. Press-mark '.$\overline{61}$.' (formerly 'N° 19'). Came to the Angelica from Sirleto's library.

2393, A.D. 1847. Guglielmo Bartolomei, *Index codicum manuscriptorum Bibliothecae Angelicae*. Copy in the Augustinian General Archives, Rome, *Registrum Mm* 13.

(Not classified). 'Elenco per ordine numerico dei possessori dei manoscritti' (1881–). A handlist (not exhaustive) of former owners of MSS in the library.

Vatican City

Archivio Segreto Vaticano

Reg. Aven. 9. Register of John XXII (1316–34). On fos. 217^{v}–218^{r} is the text of the bull *Inter singula* (9 June 1318), which formally erected Cambridge as a *studium generale*.

Reg. Vat. 17. Register of Gregory IX (1227–41). On fos. 52^{v}–53^{r} (ep. 175) is the text of his letter addressed to the 'chancellor and university of scholars of Cambridge' (14 June 1233). *Ed.* Auvray, *Registres de Grégoire IX* (*q.v.*), i. 779–80, no. 1389, and by Denifle, *Universitäten*, p. 370, n. 267, but neither gives the full text.

Reg. Vat. 68. Register of John XXII, 2nd year of pontificate, pt 2. A fair copy of Reg. Aven. 9. The text of *Inter singula*, fo. 66^{r} (ep. 1230), has been edited by Cobban in *Bulletin of the John Rylands Library*, 47. 77–8.

Reg. Vat. 254. Register of Urban V (1362–70), 3rd year. Commission, dated 16 July 1365, to the archbishop of Canterbury and the bishops of Llandaff and Bangor to investigate anti-mendicant statutes recently enacted at Oxford and Cambridge (fos. 136^{r}–137^{v}).

Biblioteca Apostolica Vaticana

(*i*) *Archives*

Tom. xv, saec. xvi–xviii. Catalogue of Cervini's library (fos. 89^{r}–100^{v} [*olim* 85^{r}–96^{v}]). For the original catalogue see Vat. lat. 8185 *infra*.

(*ii*) *Manuscripts*

lat. 2412, saec. xiii (by 5 May 1258). Avicenna, *Canon*.

lat. 6163, saec. xvi*ex*. Original catalogue of Sirleto's library which was sold to Cardinal Asciano Colonna in 1588 (fos. 207^{r}–324^{v}).

lat. 8185, saec. xvi. Original catalogue of Cervini's library (fos. 258^{r}–485^{r}; the Latin MSS are listed on fos. 282^{r}–292^{v}).

lat. 11441, saec. xv*ex*. Humanistic texts written by fr. Lorenzo Guglielmo Traversagni, O.F.M., at Cambridge in 1476–82.

Ottob. lat. 200, saec. xiii*ex*–xiv*in*. Thomas Aquinas on Bk III of the Sentences. Owned by fr. John of Clare, O.S.A. Cf. Bibl. Angelica MS 1084.

Ottob. lat. 202, saec. xiii*ex*–xiv*in*. Thomas Aquinas, *Summa theologiae*, II. i, and *Quaestiones de virtutibus*. A John de Clare book.

Ottob. lat. 211, saec. xiii*ex*–xiv*in*. Thomas Aquinas, *Summa contra gentiles*. Also owned by John de Clare.

Ottob. lat. 229, saec. xiii*ex*–xiv*in*. Gregory, *Moralia*. Owned by John de Clare.

Ottob. lat. 342, saec. xiii*ex*–xiv*in*. Jerome. Also owned by John de Clare.

Ottob. lat. 3083, saec. xiv*in*. Cartulary of Orléans University.

Ottob. lat. 3195–6, saec. xviii*ex*. Catalogue of the library of Cardinal Domenico Passionei (1682–1761).

Reg. lat. 406, saec. xiv*in* (1304+). Earliest extant register of Paris University. Contents ed. in *Chart. Univ. Paris*. i–ii.

Urbinate lat. 206, *c*. 1240–50. Aristotle. The MS is a splendid example of the *littera oxoniensis*.

Worcester

Cathedral Chapter Library MS Q. 99, saec. xiv. Theological *questiones* disputed at Oxford *c*. 1300–2. Cf. Little in Little and Pelster, *Oxford theology*, pp. 319–62.

II. PRINTED SOURCES

Aurea expositio hymnorum (Paris, 1493).

Bacon, Roger. *Fr. Rogeri Bacon opera quaedam hactenus inedita*, ed. J. S. Brewer, i (Rolls series, 1859). No more published.

Bale, John. *The laboryouse journey and serche of Johan Leylande for Englandes antiquities* (London, 1549).

Blois, Peter of. *Petri Blesensis...opera omnia*, ed. J. A. Giles (4 vols. London, 1847).

Boháček, M. 'Zur Geschichte der Stationarii von Bologna' in *Symbolae Raphaeli Taubenschlag dedicatae*, ii, *Eos*, 48 (1957), 247–95. Edition of statutes *c*. 1274–6.

Bracton's notebook, ed. F. W. Maitland (3 vols. London, 1887).

Bradshaw, H. 'An early university statute concerning hostels', *CASP*, ii (1864), 279–81. Prints text in CUL MS Mm. 4. 41.

Caius, John. *The works of John Caius, M.D. second founder of Gonville and Caius College and Master of the College 1559–1573 with a memoir of his life by John Venn*, ed. E. S. Roberts (Cambridge, 1912). A reproduction of the 1574 edition by John Day. Pt 3 is *De antiquitate Cantebrigiensis academiae*.

Calendar of entries in the papal registers relating to Great Britain and Ireland: papal letters, 1198–1304 (etc.). (London, 1893–).

Calendar of the patent rolls, 1232–47 (etc.) (London, 1906–).

Cambridge borough documents, ed. W. M. Palmer, i (Cambridge, 1931). Only this one volume published.

Cambridge portfolio, The, ed. J. J. Smith (2 vols. London, 1840).
Cantelow, Nicholas. *Nicholai Cantalupi historiola de antiquitate et origine universitatis Cantabrigiensis*, ed. T. Hearne in *Thomae Sprotti chronica* (*q.v.*), pp. 221–80.
Charters of the borough of Cambridge, The, edd. F. W. Maitland and Mary Bateson (Cambridge, 1901).
Chartularium universitatis Parisiensis, edd. H. Denifle, O.P. and É. Chatelain (4 vols. Paris, 1889–97).
Chronicle of Bury St Edmunds 1212–1301, The, ed. Antonia Gransden (Nelson Medieval Texts, London, 1964).
Clark, J. W. 'On the charitable foundations in the university called chests; with a transcript and translation of the deed of foundation and statutes of the earliest of these, the Neel Chest, 1344', *CASP*, xi, n.s. v (1907), 78–101. Edition of CUA, doc. no. 35 (25 Feb. 1345), and of the oaths in the Junior Proctor's Book, fos. 114^{v}–115^{r}= 57^{v}–58^{r} (Clark).
Close rolls of the reign of Henry III, 1227–31 (etc.) (14 vols. London, 1902–38).
Codices latini saeculi XIII (Exempla scripturarum...Vaticani, fasc. i [Rome, 1929]).
Collectanea, i, ed. C. R. L. Fletcher; ii, ed. M. Burrows (OHS, v [1885], xvi [1890]).
Corpus iuris civilis, vol. i: *Institutiones*, ed. P. Krueger; *Digesta*, edd. T. Mommsen and P. Krueger (13th ed., stereotyped, Berlin, 1920).
Councils & synods with other documents relating to the English church, vol. ii (1205–1313), edd. F. M. Powicke and C. R. Cheney (Oxford, 1964). In 2 pts; pagination continuous. Vol. i not yet published.
Cronica Buriensis, ed. T. Arnold, *Memorials of St Edmund's abbey* (*q.v.*), iii. 1–73.
D'Andrea, Giovanni (pseudo-). *Joannis Andreae summula de processu judicii*, ed. A. Wunderlich (Basle, 1840).
Denifle, H., O.P. (ed.). 'Die Statuten der Juristen-Universität Bologna vom J. 1317–1347 und deren Verhältniss zu jenen Paduas, Perugias, Florenz', *Archiv für Literatur- und Kirchengeschichte des Mittelalters*, iii (1887), 196–397.
'Die Statuten der Juristen-Universität Padua vom Jahre 1331', *ibid.* vi (1892), 309–560.
Digesta, see *Corpus iuris civilis*.
Documents relating to the university and colleges of Cambridge (Royal Commission, 3 vols. London, 1852).
Dorez, L. (ed). 'Le registre des dépenses de la Bibliothèque Vaticane de 1548 à 1555', *Fasciculus Clark* (*q.v.*), pp. 142–85.

'Recherches et documents sur la bibliothèque du Cardinal Sirleto', *Mélanges d'Archéologie et d'Histoire*, xi (1891), 457–91.

Dyer, G. (ed.). *The privileges of the university of Cambridge* (2 vols. London, 1824).

Eccleston, Thomas de. *Fratris Thomae vulgo dicti de Eccleston tractatus de adventu fratrum minorum in Angliam*, ed. A. G. Little (1st English edn, Manchester, 1951; revised by J. R. H. Moorman).

Ely chapter ordinances and visitation records 1241–1515, ed. S. J. A. Evans, *Camden Miscellany*, xvii, pt 1 (Camden Soc., 3rd series, lxiv [1940]).

Endowments of the university of Cambridge, ed. J. W. Clark (Cambridge, 1904). Contains *inter alia* the text of the decree of 18 March 1294 (Queen Eleanor commemoration) from the Junior and Senior Proctors' Books.

Europa e il diritto romano — studi in memoria di Paolo Koschaker, L' (2 vols. Milan, 1964).

Formularies which bear on the history of Oxford, c. 1204–1420, edd. H. E. Salter, W. A. Pantin and H. G. Richardson (OHS, n.s. iv–v [1942]).

Gaudenzi, A. (ed.). 'Gli antichi statuti del Comune di Bologna intorno allo studio', *Bullettino dell'istituto storico italiano*, 6 (1888), 117–37.

Gibson, S. 'The earliest statutes of the university of Oxford', *Bodleian Library Record*, iii (1920), 116–18. Text of MS Bodl. e mus. 96, reprinted in *Statuta antiqua universitatis Oxoniensis* (*q.v.*).

Grace Book A *containing the proctors' accounts and other records of the university of Cambridge for the years 1454–1488*, ed. S. M. Leathes (CAS, Luard Memorial series, i [1897]).

Grace Book B *part I containing the proctors' accounts and other records of the university of Cambridge for the years 1488–1511;—part II containing the accounts of the proctors of the university of Cambridge, 1511–1544*, ed. Mary Bateson (CAS, Luard Memorial series, ii–iii [1903–5]).

Grace Book Γ *containing the records of the university of Cambridge for the years 1501–1542*, ed. W. G. Searle (Cambridge, 1908).

Grace Book Δ *containing the records of the university of Cambridge for the years 1542–1589*, ed. J. Venn (Cambridge, 1910).

Gransden, Antonia (ed.). 'A fourteenth-century chronicle from the Grey Friars at Lynn', *E.H.R.* lxxii (1957), 270–8.

Great roll of the pipe for the seventh year of the reign of King John, Michaelmas 1205, ed. S. Smith (Pipe Roll Soc. lvii, n.s. xix [1941]).

Grosseteste, Robert. *Roberti Grosseteste episcopi quondam Lincolniensis epistolae*, ed. H. R. Luard (Rolls series, 1861).

Gutiérrez, D., O.S.A. (ed.). 'De antiquis ordinis eremitarum sancti Augustini bibliothecis', *Analecta Augustiniana*, xxiii (1954), 164–372.

'La biblioteca di Sant'Agostino di Roma nel secolo xv', *ibid.* xxvii (1964), 5–58; xxviii (1965), 57–153.

Hall, Catherine P. (ed.). 'William Rysley's catalogue of the Cambridge University muniments, compiled in 1420', *Transactions of the Cambridge Bibliographical Society*, iv (1965), 85–99. From the original in CUA.

Halliwell, J. O. (ed.). 'A catalogue of the books bequeathed to Corpus Christi College, Cambridge (A.D. 1439) by Thomas Markaunt with their prices' (CAS quarto series, xiv [1847]), 15–20. See Cambridge, Corpus Christi College MS 232 (*supra*).

Hardwick, C. (ed.). 'Articuli Universitatis Cantabrigiae: a form of petition addressed to King Henry V, about the year 1415, in vindication of some ancient usages', *CASP*, i (1859), 85–93. See Cambridge, University Library MS Dd. 4. 35 (*supra*).

Harryson, John. *Abbreviata cronica ab anno 1377 usque ad annum 1469*, ed J. J. Smith (CAS, quarto series, i, pt 2 [1840]). See Gonville and Caius College MS 249.

Haskins, G. L. (ed.). 'Three English documents relating to Francis Accursius', *Law Quarterly Review*, liv (1938), 87–94.

Henson, H. H. (ed.). 'Letters relating to Oxford in the 14th century from the originals in the Public Record Office and British Museum', *Collectanea* (*q.v.*), i. 3–56.

Hoo, William of. *The letter-book of William of Hoo sacrist of Bury St Edmunds 1280–1294*, ed. Antonia Gransden (Suffolk Records Soc. v [1963]).

I più antichi statuti della facoltà teologica dell'università di Bologna, ed. F. Ehrle, S.J. (Universitatis Bononiensis Monumenta, i [Bologna, 1932]).

James, M. R. (ed.). *The sources of Archbishop Parker's collection of MSS at Corpus Christi College, Cambridge, with a reprint of the catalogue of Thomas Markaunt's library* (CAS, octavo series, xxxii [1899]). From Cambridge, Corpus Christi College MS 232 (*q.v.*)

John XXII. *Jean XXII (1316–1334) — lettres communes analysées d'après les registres dit d'Avignon et du Vatican*, ed. G. Mollat (Bibliothèque des Écoles Françaises d'Athènes et de Rome, 3rd series, 16 vols. Paris, 1904–47).

Josselin, John. *Historiola Collegii Corporis Christi*, ed. J. W. Clark (CAS, octavo series, xvii [1880]).

Lamb, J. (ed.). *A collection of letters, statutes, and other documents, from the MS. library of Corp. Christ. Coll., illustrative of the history of the university of Cambridge, during the period of the Reformation, from A.D. MD., to A.D. MDLXXII* (London, 1838).

Leach, A. F. (ed.). *Educational charters and documents 598 to 1909* (Cambridge, 1911).

Leland, John. *Joannis Lelandi antiquarii de rebus Britannicis collectanea*, ed. T. Hearne (2nd ed., 6 vols. London, 1770).

Liber memorandorum ecclesie de Bernewelle, ed. J. W. Clark (Cambridge, 1907).

Little, A. G. 'An unknown chancellor of the university of Cambridge at the end of the thirteenth century', *Cambridge Review*, liv (1933), 412. Prints original letter of mag. Gilbert de Segrave, chancellor, and the *cetus magistrorum regentium*, 1292–3, from P.R.O., S.C. 1/27/144.

'The friars *v.* the university of Cambridge', *E.H.R.* l (1935), 686–96. Prints papal award of 1306.

Mansi, J. D. (ed.). *Sacrorum conciliorum nova et amplissima collectio* (31 vols. Venice, 1759–98). Facsimile reproduction with continuation under the direction of J. B. Martin and L. Petit (Paris, 1901–).

Marsh, Adam. *Epistolae fratris Adae de Marisco de ordine minorum*, ed. J. S. Brewer, *Monumenta Franciscana*, i (Rolls series, 1858), 77–489.

Mediaeval archives of the university of Oxford, ed. H. E. Salter (OHS, lxx, lxxiii [1920, 1921]).

Memoranda de parliamento...(A.D. 1305), ed. F. W. Maitland (Rolls series, 1893).

Memorials of St Edmund's abbey, ed. T. Arnold (Rolls series, 3 vols. 1890–6).

Monumenta Franciscana, i, ed. J. S. Brewer; ii, ed. R. Howlett (Rolls series, 1858, 1882).

Munimenta academica, or documents illustrative of academical life and studies at Oxford, ed. H. Anstey (Rolls series, 2 pts, 1868). The pagination is continuous.

Munimenta civitatis Oxonie, ed. H. E. Salter (OHS, lxxi [1920]).

Ott, H., and Fletcher, J. M. (edd.). *The mediaeval statutes of the faculty of arts of the university of Freiburg im Breisgau* (Mediaeval Institute of the University of Notre Dame. Texts and Studies in the History of Mediaeval Education, no. x [Notre Dame, Indiana, 1964]).

Paris, Matthew. *Matthaei Parisiensis, monachi sancti Albani, chronica majora*, ed. H. R. Luard (Rolls series, 7 vols. 1872–83).

Patrologiae cursus completus, series prima, latina, ed. J. P. Migne (221 vols. Paris, 1844–64).

Pedes finium: or fines relating to the county of Cambridge, ed. W. Rye (CAS, octavo series, xxvi [1891]).

Pilii, Tancredi, Gratiae libri de iudiciorum ordine, ed. F. Bergmann (Göttingen, 1842).

Pleas before the king or his justices 1198–1202, ed. Doris Mary Stenton (Selden Soc. lxvii, lxviii [1953, 1952]).

Rashdall, H. (ed.). 'The friars Preachers *v.* the university A.D. 1311–1313', *Collectanea* (*q.v.*), ii. 193–273. Edition of the process between the parties.

Register of John de Halton, bishop of Carlisle, A.D. 1292–1324, The, ed. W. N. Thompson (Canterbury and York Soc. xii–xiii [1913]).

Registres de Grégoire IX, Les, ed. L. Auvray (Bibl. Écoles Franç. Athèn. Rome, 2nd series, 4 vols. Paris, 1890–1955).

Registres de Nicolas IV, Les, ed. E. Langlois (Bibl. Écoles Franç. Athèn. Rome, 2nd series, 2 vols. Paris, 1886–1905).

Registres d'Innocent IV, Les, ed. É. Berger (Bibl. Écoles Franç. Athèn. Rome, 2nd series, 4 vols. Paris, 1884–1921).

Registrum cancellarii Oxoniensis, 1439–1469, ed. H. E. Salter (OHS, xciii–xciv [1932]).

Rotuli hundredorum (Record Commission, 2 vols. London, 1812–18).

Rotuli litterarum clausarum in Turri Londinensi asservati, 1202–24 (etc.) (Record Comm. 2 vols. London, 1833–44).

Rotuli parliamentorum (6 vols. London, 1783; index [1832]).

Royal and other historical letters illustrative of the reign of Henry III, ed. W. W. Shirley (Rolls series, 2 vols. 1862–6).

Rymer, Thomas (ed.). *Foedera, conventiones, litterae et cujuscunque generis acta publica* (Rec. Comm., 4 vols. London, 1816–69; vols. i–iii each in two parts).

Select cases in the court of the king's bench under Edward I (–Edward III), ed. G. O. Sayles (Selden Soc. lv, lvii–lviii, lxxiv, lxxvi, lxxxii [1936–65]).

Silvestris, Bernardus. *Bernardi Silvestris de mundi universitate libri duo sive megacosmus et microcosmus*, edd. C. S. Barach and J. Wrobel (Bibliotheca Philosophorum Mediae Aetatis, i [Innsbruck, 1876]).

Skånland, V. (ed.). 'The earliest statutes of the university of Cambridge', *Symbolae Osloenses*, fasc. xi (1965), 83–98. From Angelica MS 401.

Snappe's formulary and other records, ed. H. E. Salter (OHS, lxxx [1924]).

Sprott, Thomas. *Thomae Sprotti chronica*, ed. T. Hearne (Oxford, 1719).

Statuta academiae Cantabrigiensis (Cambridge, 1785).

Statuta academiae Cantabrigiensis a visitatoribus Elizabethae reginae an. I^{mo} [1559] *data*, ed. Lamb, *Collection of letters* (*q.v.*), pp. 280–99.

Statuta antiqua [universitatis Cantabrigiensis] in ordinem redacta, in *Docs*, i. 308–416.

Statuta antiqua universitatis Oxoniensis, ed. S. Gibson (Oxford, 1931). Addenda and Corrigenda (1940) by the editor and Graham Pollard.

Statuta reginae Elizabethae an. XII^{mo} [1570] *edita*, in Lamb, *op. cit.* pp. 315–54; also in *Docs*, i. 454–95.

Statuta regis Edwardi sexti [1549], in Lamb, *op. cit.* pp. 122–46.

'Statutes of King's College, Cambridge', in *Docs*, ii. 481–624.

Statuti della università e dei collegi dello studio bolognese, ed. C. Malagola (Bologna, 1888).

Statuti di Bologna dall'anno 1245 all'anno 1267, ed. L. Frati (Dei Monumenti Istorici pertinenti alla Provincia della Romagna, 1st series, i–ii [Bologna, 1869]). The edition only extends to 1250.

Statuts et privilèges des universités françaises depuis leur fondation jusqu'en 1789, Les, ed. M. Fournier (3 vols. Paris, 1890–2).

Stokes, H. P. (ed.). 'Early university property', *CASP*, xiii, n.s. vii (1908–9), 164–84. Prints CUA, doc. no. 16.

Tancred, *Ordo iudiciarius*, in *Pilii, Tancredi, Gratiae libri* (*q.v.*), pp. 87–316.

'Testimonium Card. Marcelli Cervini protectoris ordinis', *Analecta Augustiniana*, ii (1907–8), 11–13.

Ullmann, W. (ed.). 'The decline of the chancellor's authority in medieval Cambridge: a rediscovered statute', *Historical Journal*, i (1958), 176–82. Critical text of CUA, doc. no. 4.

Vetus liber archidiaconi Eliensis, edd. C. L. Feltoe and E. H. Minns (CAS, octavo series, xlviii [1917]).

Wendover, Roger. *Rogeri de Wendover liber qui dicitur flores historiarum... the flowers of history*, ed. H. G. Hewlett (Rolls series, 3 vols. 1886–9).

Worcester, Florence of. *Florentii Wigorniensis monachi chronicon ex chronicis*, ed. B. Thorpe (English Historical Soc., 2 vols. 1848–9).

Wordsworth, C. H. (ed.). *The ancient kalendar of the university of Oxford* (OHS, xlv [1904]). Edits the calendar in the Cambridge Senior Proctor's Book.

Ypma, E., O.S.A. (ed.). 'Le "Mare magnum" — un code médiéval du couvent Augustinien de Paris', *Augustiniana*, vi (1956), 275–321.

III. MODERN WORKS

Amerieu, A. 'Archidiacre', *Dictionnaire de droit canonique*, i (Paris, 1935), 965–78.

Analecta Augustiniana (Rome, 1905–).

Anglican Theological Review (New York, 1918–).

Antike und Orient im Mittelalter (Miscellanea mediaevalia, i [Berlin, 1962]).

Archaeological Journal (London, 1844–).

Archiv für Lit[t]eratur- und Kirchengeschichte des Mittelalters (7 vols. Berlin–Freiburg im Breisgau, 1885–1900).

Archivum Franciscanum Historicum (Quaracchi, 1908–).

Archivum Fratrum Praedicatorum (Rome, 1931–).

Aston, Margaret. *Thomas Arundel—a study in church life in the reign of Richard II* (Oxford, 1967).

Augustiniana (Louvain, 1951–).

Ball (W. W. Rouse). *Cambridge papers* (London, 1918).

Bannister, H. M. 'A short notice of some manuscripts of the Cambridge friars, now in the Vatican Library', *Collectanea Franciscana*, i (British Society of Franciscan Studies, v [1914]), 124–40.

Baron, R. *Études sur Hugues de Saint-Victor* (Paris, 1963).

'Hugues de Saint-Victor: contribution à un nouvel examen de son œuvre', *Traditio*, xv (1959), 223–97.

Battelli, G. *Lezioni di paleografia* (3rd edn, Vatican City, 1949).

Beiträge zum Berufsbewusstsein des mittelalterlichen Menschen (Miscellanea mediaevalia, iii [1964]).

Bentham, J. *The history and antiquities of the conventual & cathedral church of Ely* (2nd ed., Norwich, 1812).

Bibliofilia, La (Florence, 1899–).

Bibliotheca topographica Britannica, ed. J. Nichols, assisted by R. Gough and others (10 vols. London, 1780–1800).

Bibliothèque de l'École des Chartes (Paris, 1839–).

Bibliothèque Nationale. Catalogue général des manuscrits latins (Paris, 1939–).

Birch, W. de Gray. *Catalogue of seals in the department of manuscripts in the British Museum* (6 vols. London, 1887–1900).

Bloomfield, M. W. 'A preliminary list of incipits of Latin works on the virtues and vices, mainly of the thirteenth, fourteenth, and fifteenth centuries', *Traditio*, xi (1955), 259–379.

Blume, F. *Bibliotheca librorum manuscriptorum italica* (Göttingen, 1834).

Bodleian Library Record (originally *Bodleian Quarterly Record* [1914–38]) (Oxford, 1938–).

Boyle, L., O.P. 'The curriculum of the faculty of canon law at Oxford in the first half of the fourteenth century', *Oxford studies* (*q.v.*), 135–62.

Bulletin of the Institute of Historical Research (London, 1923–).

Bulletin of the John Rylands Library (continuation of *Quarterly Bulletin of the John Rylands Library*) (Manchester, 1903–).

Bullettino dell'istituto storico italiano (Rome, 1886–).

Bullough, V. L. 'The mediaeval medical school at Cambridge', *Mediaeval Studies*, xxiv (1962), 160–8.

Callus, D., O.P. 'Robert Grosseteste as a scholar', *Robert Grosseteste* (*q.v.*), pp. 1–69.

Cambridge Antiquarian Society Proceedings (formerly—*Communications* [–1891]) (Cambridge, 1863–).

Cambridge Review (Cambridge, 1879–).

Catalogue général des manuscrits des bibliothèques publiques des départements [quarto series] (7 vols. Paris, 1849–85).

Catalogue of books printed in the XVth century now in the British Museum (9 pts, London, 1908–62; vol. of facsimiles, 1913).

Celani, E. 'La Biblioteca Angelica (1605–1870) — note ed appunti', *La Bibliofilia*, xiii (1911–12), 1–8, 41–58.

Chaplais, P. 'The making of the Treaty of Paris and the royal style', *E.H.R.* lxvii (1952), 235–53.

Cheney, C. R. *English synodalia of the thirteenth century* (Oxford, 1941).

'Rules for the observance of feast-days in medieval England', *Bulletin of the Institute of Historical Research*, xxxiv (1961), 117–47.

Chenu, M.-D., O.P. *Introduction à l'étude de Saint Thomas d'Aquin* (Université de Montréal—Institut d'Études Médiévales, xi [1950]).

Chibnall, A. C. *Richard de Badew and the university of Cambridge 1315–1340* (Cambridge, 1963).

Clark, E. C. 'English academical costume (mediaeval)', *Archaeological Journal*, l (1893), 73–104, 137–49, 183–209.

Cobban, A. B. 'Edward II, Pope John XXII and the university of Cambridge', *Bulletin of the John Rylands Library*, 47 (1964–5), 49–78.

Collectanea Vaticana in honorem Anselmi M. Card. Albareda a Bibliotheca Apostolica edita (Studi e Testi, 219–20 [1962]).

Cooper, C. H. *Annals of Cambridge* (5 vols. Cambridge, 1842–1908). Vol. v, ed. J. W. Cooper.

Creytens, R., O.P. 'Le "Studium Romanae Curiae" et le Maître du Sacré Palais', *Archivum Fratrum Praedicatorum*, xii (1942), 5–83.

Denifle, H., O.P. *Die Entstehung der Universitäten des Mittelalters bis 1400* (Die Universitäten des Mittelalters bis 1400, i [Berlin, 1885]). Only vol. i published.

Dictionnaire de droit canonique, ed. R. Naz and others (Paris, 1935–).

Digard, G. 'La papauté et l'étude du droit romain au XIIIe siècle à propos de la fausse bulle d'Innocent IV *Dolentes*', *Bibliothèque de l'École des Chartes*, li (1890), 381–419.

Emden, A. B. *A biographical register of the university of Cambridge to 1500* (Cambridge, 1963).

A biographical register of the university of Oxford to A.D. 1500 (3 vols. Oxford, 1957–9). Additions and corrections in *Bodl. Lib. Rec.* vi (1957–61), 668–88, vii (1962–7), 149–64.

'Accounts relating to an early Oxford house of scholars', *Oxoniensia*, xxxi (1966), 77–81.

An Oxford hall in medieval times (Oxford, 1927).

'Northerners and southerners in the organization of the university to 1509', *Oxford studies* (*q.v.*), 1–30.

English Historical Review (London, 1886–).

English Library before 1700—studies in its history, The, edd. F. Wormald and C. E. Wright (London, 1958).

Eos. Commentarii Societatis Philologae Polonorum (Lwow, 1894–1939; Warsaw, 1940–).

Études médiévales offertes à M. le Doyen Augustin Fliche de l'Institut (Université de Montpellier—Faculté des Lettres, no. 4 [Paris, 1952]).

Faral, E. *Les arts poétiques du XIIe et du XIIIe siècle* (Bibliothèque de l'École des Hautes Études, fasc. 238 [Paris, 1924]).

Fasciculus Ioanni Willis Clark dicatus (Cambridge, 1909).

Festschrift für Martin Wolff (Tübingen, 1952).

Fuller, Thomas. *The history of the university of Cambridge from the Conquest to the year 1634*, edd. M. Prickett and T. Wright (Cambridge–London, 1840).

Gibson, S. *The keepers of the archives of the university of Oxford—a lecture to be delivered in the Examination Schools on 7 March 1928* (Oxford, 1928).
Gray, A. *The priory of Saint Radegund Cambridge* (CAS, octavo series, xxxi [1898]).
Gray, J. M. *The school of Pythagoras (Merton Hall) Cambridge* (CAS, quarto series, n.s. iv [1932]).
Gwynn, A., S.J. *The English Austin Friars in the time of Wyclif* (London, 1940).
Haenel, G. *Catalogi librorum manuscriptorum qui in bibliothecis Galliae, Helvetiae, Belgii, Britanniae M., Hispaniae, Lusitaniae adservantur* (Leipzig, 1830).
Hall, F. W. *A companion to classical texts* (Oxford, 1913).
Hargreaves-Mawdsley, W. H. *A history of academical dress in Europe until the end of the eighteenth century* (Oxford, 1963).
Haskins, G. L. 'The university of Oxford and the "ius ubique docendi"', *E.H.R.* lvi (1941), 281–92.
Heywood, J. *Early Cambridge University and College statutes in the English language* (London, 1855).
Hill, Rosalind M. T. 'Oliver Sutton, bishop of Lincoln, and the university of Oxford', *Transactions of the Royal Historical Society*, 4th series, xxxi (1949), 1–16.
Historical Journal (continuation of *Cambridge Historical Journal* [1923–57], Cambridge, 1958–).
History and antiquities of the university of Cambridge in two parts, The (London, 1721). Translation of Richard Parker's Σκελετός.
History: the quarterly journal of the Historical Association (London, 1900–).
Hope, W. H. St John. *The seals and armorial insignia of the university and colleges of Cambridge* (pt 1, London, 1881). No more published.
In *Proceedings of the Society of Antiquaries of London*, 2nd series, x (1883–5), 225–52.
Houston, Mary G. *Medieval costume in England and France* (London, 1939).
Humanisme et Renaissance (7 vols. Paris, 1934–40).
Hunt, R. W. 'Oxford grammar masters in the middle ages', *Oxford studies* (*q.v.*), 163–93.
James, M. R. *A descriptive catalogue of the manuscripts in the library of Corpus Christi College Cambridge* (2 vols. Cambridge, 1912).
A descriptive catalogue of the manuscripts in the library of Gonville and Caius College (2 vols. Cambridge, 1907–8; supplement, 1914).
A descriptive catalogue of the manuscripts in the library of Trinity Hall (Cambridge, 1907).
Journal of Theological Studies (London, 1900–).
Kellogg, A. L. 'St Augustine and the Parson's Tale', *Traditio*, viii (1952), 424–30.

Kurtscheid, B., O.F.M., and Wilches, F. A., O.F.M. *Historia iuris canonici* (Rome, 1943–).
Kuttner, S. 'The date of the constitution "Saepe"; the Vatican manuscripts and the Roman edition of the Clementines', *Mélanges Tisserant* (*q.v.*), iv. 427–52.
'Papst Honorius III. und das Studium des Zivilrechts', *Festschrift Wolff*, pp. 79–101.
Lamb, J. *Masters' history of the college of Corpus Christi and the Blessed Virgin Mary in the university of Cambridge* (Cambridge–London, 1831). Continuation of Masters (*q.v.*).
Law Quarterly Review (London, 1885–).
Leach, A. F. *The schools of medieval England* (London, 1915).
Le Neve, J. *Fasti ecclesiae Anglicanae*, ed. T. D. Hardy (3 vols. Oxford, 1854).
Little, A. G. *Franciscan papers, lists, and documents* (Manchester, 1943).
'The friars and the foundation of the faculty of theology in the university of Cambridge', *ibid.* pp. 122–43.
Little, A. G., and Pelster, F., S.J. *Oxford theology and theologians c. A.D. 1282–1302* (OHS, xcvi [1934]).
Luard, H. R. 'A list of the documents in the university registry, from the year 1266 to the year 1544', *CASP*, iii (1879), 385–403.
Lubasz, H. 'The corporate borough in the common law of the late year-book period', *Law Quarterly Review*, lxxx (1964), 228–43.
Lunt, W. E. *Financial relations of the papacy with England to 1327* (Studies in Anglo-Papal relations during the middle ages, i [Cambridge, Mass., 1939]).
Maan, J. *Sancta et metropolitana ecclesia Turonensis* (Tours, 1667).
Madan, F., Craster, H. H. E., and Denholm-Young, N. *A summary catalogue of western manuscripts in the Bodleian Library at Oxford which have not hitherto been catalogued in the quarto series* (7 vols. Oxford, 1895–1953). Vol. i by R. W. Hunt; vol. ii by P. D. Record.
Maier, Anneliese. 'Notizie storiche del XIII e XIV secolo da codici borghesiani', *Rivista di storia della chiesa in Italia*, iv (1950), 171–6.
Maio, R. de. 'La Biblioteca Apostolica Vaticana sotto Paolo VI e Pio IV (1555–65)', *Collectanea Vaticana* (*q.v.*), i. 265–313.
Maitland, F. W. *Township and borough—being the Ford lectures delivered in the university of Oxford in the October term of 1897* (Cambridge, 1898).
Masters (Robert), *The history of the college of Corpus Christi and the B. Virgin Mary (commonly called Benet) in the university of Cambridge* (2 pts, Cambridge, 1753). Cf. *s.v.* Lamb.
Mediaeval Studies (Toronto, 1939–).
Medievalia et Humanistica (Boulder, 1943–).
Mélanges d'Archéologie et d'Histoire (Rome, 1881–).

Mélanges Eugène Tisserant (Studi e Testi, 231–7 [1964]).
Mercati, G. *Codici latini Pico Grimani Pio e di altra biblioteca ignota del secolo xvi esistenti nell'Ottoboniana* (Studi e Testi, 75 [1938]).
Per la storia dei manoscritti greci di Genova, di varie badie basiliane d'Italia e di Patmo (Studi e Testi, 68 [1935]).
Michaud-Quanint, P. 'Collectivités médiévales et institutions antiques', *Antike und Orient* (*q.v.*), pp. 239–52.
'La conscience d'être membre d'une universitas', *Beiträge zum Berufsbewusstsein* (*q.v.*), pp. 1–14.
Miller, E. *The abbey and bishopric of Ely—the social history of an ecclesiastical estate from the tenth to the early fourteenth century* (Cambridge Studies in Medieval Life and Thought, i [Cambridge, 1951]).
Miscellanea Agostiniana — testi e studi pubblicati a cura dell'ordine eremitano di S. Agostino nel XV centenario dalla morte del santo dottore (2 vols. Rome, 1930–1).
Miscellanea Giovanni Mercati (Studi e Testi, 121–6 [1946]).
Moorman, J. R. H. *The Grey Friars in Cambridge 1225–1538* (Cambridge, 1952).
Mullinger, J. B. *The university of Cambridge* (3 vols. Cambridge, 1873–1911).
Narducci, E. *Catalogus codicum manuscriptorum praeter graecos et orientales in Bibliotheca Angelica olim coenobii Sancti Augustini de Urbe*, i (Rome, 1893). Index, Città di Castello, 1913.
Nichols, J. 'The history and antiquities of Barnwell Abbey and of Sturbridge Fair', *Bibliotheca topographica Britannica*, v, pt xxxviii (1790).
Norske Videnskaps-Akademi i Oslo årbok 1925, Det (Oslo, 1926).
Novum glossarium mediae latinitatis ab anno DCCC usque ad annum MCC, ed. F. Blatt (Copenhagen, 1947–).
Ossinger, F., O.S.A. *Bibliotheca Augustiniana historica, critica, et chronologica* (Ingolstadt–Augsburg, 1768).
Owst, G. R. *Preaching in medieval England: an introduction to the sermon manuscripts of the period* c. *1350–1450* (Cambridge, 1926).
Oxford studies presented to Daniel Callus (OHS, n.s. xvi [1964]).
Oxoniensia (Oxford, 1936–).
Pantin, W. A. 'The halls and schools of medieval Oxford: an attempt at reconstruction', *Oxford studies* (*q.v.*), pp. 31–100.
Parker, Richard. *Richardi Parker Σκελετός Cantabrigiensis*, ed. T. Hearne, *Joannis Lelandi...collectanea* (*q.v.*), v. 187–257. For a translation see *s.v. History and antiquities.*
Peacock, G. *Observations on the statutes of the university of Cambridge* (Cambridge, 1841).
Peek, Heather E., and Hall, Catherine P. *The archives of the university of Cambridge—an historical introduction* (Cambridge, 1962).

Pelzer, A. 'Une source inconnue de Roger Bacon — Alfred de Sareshel commentateur des météorologiques d'Aristote', *Archivum Franciscanum Historicum*, xii (1919), 46–52.

Pollard, G. 'Mediaeval loan chests at Cambridge', *Bulletin of the Institute of Historical Research*, xvii (1939–40), 113–29.

'The oldest statute book of the university', *Bodleian Library Record*, viii (1968), 69–91.

'The university and the book trade in mediaeval Oxford', *Beiträge zum Berufsbewusstsein* (*q.v.*), pp. 336–44.

Pollock, F. and Maitland, F. W. *The history of English law before the time of Edward I* (2nd ed., 2 vols. Cambridge, 1898).

Poole, R. L. 'Henry Symeonis', *E.H.R.* xxvii (1912), 515–17.

Post, G. 'Masters' salaries and student-fees in the mediaeval universities', *Speculum*, vii (1932), 181–98.

'Parisian masters as a corporation, 1200–1246', *ibid.* ix (1934), 421–45.

Potthast, A. *Regesta pontificum romanorum inde ab anno post Christum natum MCXCVIII ad annum MCCCIV* (2 vols. Berlin, 1873–4).

Proceedings of the Society of Antiquaries of London (London, 1849–).

Prynne, William. *The third tome of an exact chronological vindication and historical demonstration of the supreme ecclesiastical jurisdiction of our British, Roman, Saxon, Danish, Norman, English kings* (London, 1668). The title is inverted in vols. i (1666) and ii (1665).

Quynn, Dorothy Mackay. 'Migrations of the medieval cartularies of the university of Orléans', *Humanisme et Renaissance*, vii (1940), 102–22.

Raby, F. J. E. *A history of Christian-Latin poetry from the beginnings to the close of the middle ages* (2nd edn, Oxford, 1953).

Rashdall, H. *The universities of Europe in the middle ages*, edd. F. M. Powicke and A. B. Emden (3 vols. Oxford, 1936).

Revised medieval Latin word-list, ed. R. E. Latham (British Academy, London, 1965).

Richardson, H. G. 'The schools of Northampton in the twelfth century', *E.H.R.* lvi (1941), 595–605.

Richardson, H. G., and Sayles, G. O. 'The early statutes', *Law Quarterly Review*, l (1934), 201–23, 540–71.

Rivista di storia della chiesa in Italia (Rome, 1947–).

Robert Grosseteste scholar and bishop, ed. D. A. Callus, O.P. (Oxford, 1955).

[Rocca, Angelo, O.S.A.]. *Bibliotheca Angelica litteratorum, litterarumque amatorum commoditati dicata Romae in aedibus Augustinianis* (Rome, 1608).

Roth, F., O.S.A. *The English Austin Friars 1249–1538* (Cassiciacum—Studies in St Augustine and the Augustinian Order [American series], vi–vii [New York, 1961–6]). The first volume (*History*) was published after the second (*Sources*).

Russell, J. C. *Dictionary of writers of thirteenth century England* (Bulletin of the Institute of Historical Research, special supplement, no. 3 [London, 1936]).

'Richard of Bardney's account of Robert Grosseteste's early and middle life', *Medievalia et Humanistica*, ii (1943), 45–54.

Ruysschaert, J. *Codices Vaticani latini—codices 11414–11709* (Vatican City, 1959).

Salter, H. E. *Medieval Oxford* (OHS, c [1936]).

'The beginning of Cambridge University', *E.H.R.* xxxvi (1921), 419–20.

'The medieval university of Oxford', *History*, xiv (1929–30), 57–61.

'The Stamford crisis', *E.H.R.* xxxvii (1922), 249–53.

Sandars, S., and Venables, Canon [Edmund]. *Historical and architectural notes on Great Saint Mary's church, Cambridge* (CAS, octavo series, x [1869]).

Speculum: a journal of medieval studies (Cambridge, Mass., 1926–).

Stelling-Michaud, S. 'L'histoire des universités au moyen âge et à la renaissance au cours des vingt-cinq dernières années', *XIe congrès international des sciences historiques* (*q.v.*), i. 97–143.

L'université de Bologne et la pénétration des droits romain et canonique en Suisse aux XIIIe et XIVe siècles (Travaux d'Humanisme et Renaissance, xvii [Geneva, 1955]).

Stevenson, W. *A supplement to the first edition of Mr Bentham's history* (Norwich, 1817).

Stokes, H. P. *Outside the Trumpington gates before Peterhouse was founded* (CAS, octavo series, xliv [1908]).

The chaplains and the chapel of the university of Cambridge (1256–1568) (CAS, octavo series, xli [1906]).

The esquire bedells of the university of Cambridge (CAS, octavo series, xlv [1911]).

The mediaeval hostels of the university of Cambridge from the 13th to the 20th century (CAS, octavo series, xlix [1924]).

Stornajolo, C. *Codices Urbinates latini* (3 vols. Vatican City, 1902–21).

Strype, J. *The life and acts of Matthew Parker* (3 vols. Oxford, 1821).

Symbolae Osloenses (continuation of *Symbolae Arctoae* [Christiania, 1922], Oslo, 1923–).

Talbot, C. H. *Medicine in medieval England* (London, 1967).

'The universities and the mediaeval library', *English library* (*q.v.*), pp. 66–84.

Talbot, C. H., and Hammond, E. A. *The medical practitioners in medieval England* (Wellcome Historical Medieval Library, n.s. viii [1965]).

Teetaert, A., O.F.M.Cap. 'Quelques "summae de paenitentia" anonymes dans la Bibliothèque Nationale de Paris', *Miscellanea Mercati* (*q.v.*), ii. 311–43.

Thouzellier, Christine. 'La papauté et les universités provinciales en France dans la première moitié du XIIIe siècle', *Études Fliche* (*q.v.*), pp. 187–211.

Thurot, Ch. *De l'organisation de l'enseignement dans l'université de Paris au moyen-âge* (Paris, 1850).

Traditio: studies in ancient and medieval history, thought and religion (New York, 1945–).

Transactions of the Cambridge Bibliographical Society (Cambridge, 1949–).

Transactions of the Royal Historical Society (London, 1872–).

Ullmann, W. 'The medieval interpretation of Frederick I's Authentic "Habita"', *Europa e il diritto romano* (*q.v.*), i. 101–36.

Vaughn, E. V. *The origins and early development of the English universities to the close of the thirteenth century—a study in institutional history* (University of Missouri Studies. Social Science series, 2ii [Columbia, Mo., 1908]).

Venn, J. *Biographical history of Gonville and Caius College 1349–1897* (4 vols. Cambridge, 1897–1912).

Victoria history of the county of Cambridgeshire and the Isle of Ely, The (4 vols. + index, London, 1938–59). Vol. iii (*The city and university of Cambridge*), ed. J. P. C. Roach.

Victoria history of the county of Oxford, The (8 vols. London, 1939–64). Vol. iii (*The university of Oxford*), edd. H. E. Salter and Mary Lobel.

Walker, T. A. *A biographical register of Peterhouse men and some of their neighbours from the earliest days (1284) to the commencement (1616) of the first admission book of the college* (2 pts, Cambridge, 1927–30).

Peterhouse (new ed., Cambridge, 1935).

Walther, H. *Initia carminum ac versuum medii aevi posterioris latinorum* (Carmina medii aevi posterioris latina, i [Göttingen, 1959]).

Proverbia sententiaeque latinitatis medii aevi (Carmina medii aevi posterioris latina, II. i–v [*ibid.* 1963–7]).

Ward, L. R. 'Notes on academic freedom in medieval schools', *Anglican Theological Review*, xlv (1965), 45–54.

Weisheipl, J. A., O.P. 'Curriculum of the faculty of arts at Oxford in the early fourteenth century', *Mediaeval Studies*, xxvi (1964), 143–85.

Weiss, R. *Humanism in England during the fifteenth century* (2nd edn, Oxford, 1957).

Willard, J. F. *The royal authority and the early English universities* (Philadelphia, 1902).

Willis, R., and Clark, J. W. *The architectural history of the university of Cambridge and of the colleges of Cambridge and Eton* (4 vols. Cambridge, 1886).

Wilmart, A., O.S.B. *Codices Reginenses latini* (2 vols. Vatican City, 1937–45).

Wilpert, J. 'Il più antico ritratto di S. Agostino', *Miscellanea Agostiniana* (*q.v.*), ii. 1–3.

Wright, C. E. 'The dispersal of the monastic libraries and the beginnings of Anglo-Saxon studies', *Transactions of the Cambridge Bibliographical Society*, i (1949–53), 208–37.

'The dispersal of the libraries in the sixteenth century', *English Library* (*q.v.*), pp. 148–75.

XIe congrès international des sciences historiques, Stockholm 21–28 août, 1960 — rapports (6 vols. in 1, Göteborg–Stockholm–Uppsala, 1960).

INDEX

I PERSONS AND PLACES

The main entries are printed in **heavy type**

II SUBJECTS

Main entries are again printed in **heavy type** *and generally at the beginning. Items are occasionally listed in their logical rather than in their alphabetical order. Unless otherwise specified, the university referred to is Cambridge. For the assistance of the reader, references to Markaunt's text of the statutes are followed by the letter 'M' and the number of the statute in brackets*

Index

Milton Keynes UK
Ingram Content Group UK Ltd.
UKHW010853110324
439075UK00008B/67

9 780521 085199